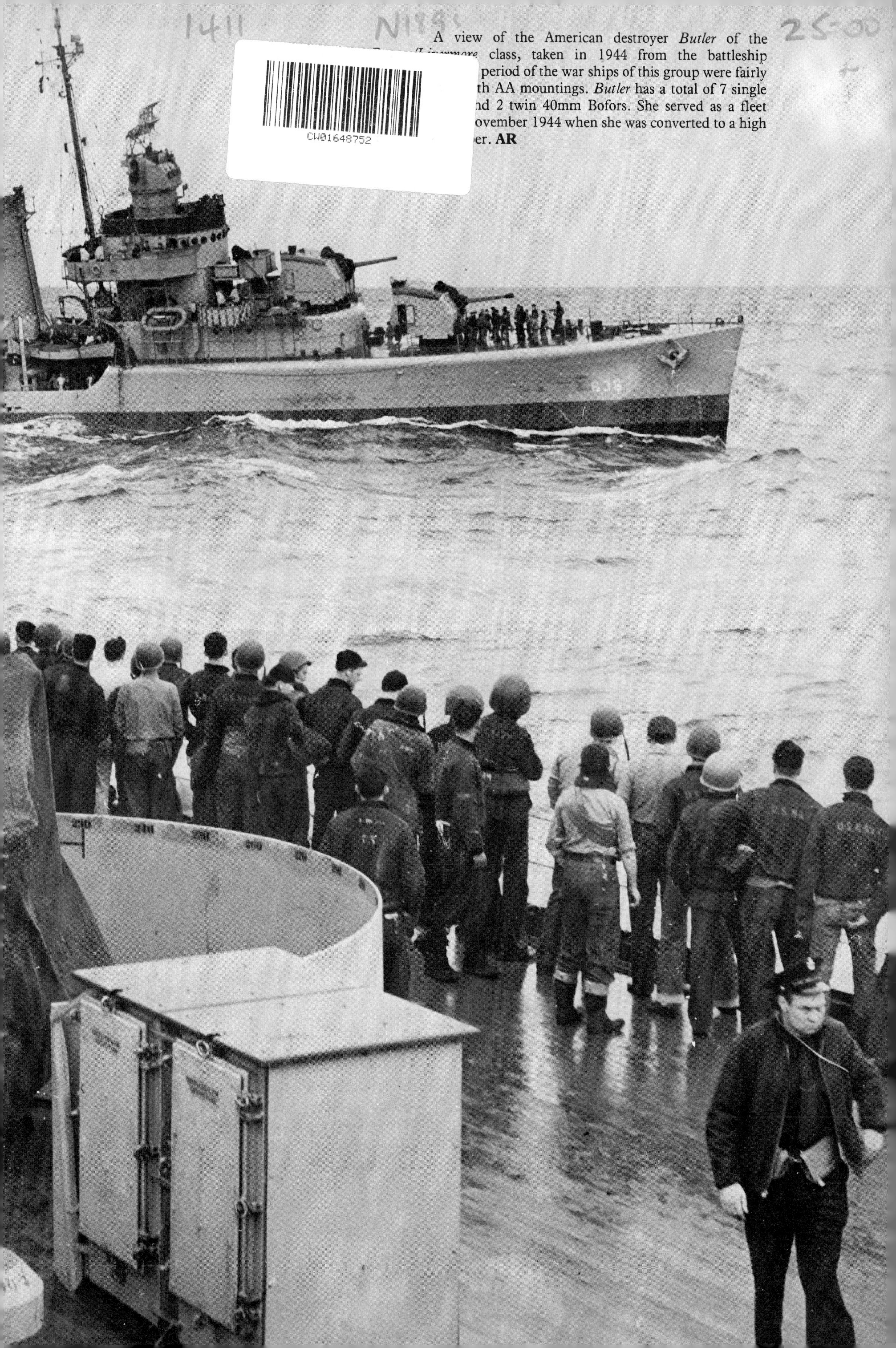

A view of the American destroyer *Butler* of the … /*Livermore* class, taken in 1944 from the battleship … period of the war ships of this group were fairly … th AA mountings. *Butler* has a total of 7 single … nd 2 twin 40mm Bofors. She served as a fleet … ovember 1944 when she was converted to a high … per. **AR**

CAMERA AT SEA
1939-45

Illustrious, a *C* class AA cruiser and *Valiant* steam at about 20 knots through the calmer waters of the Western Mediterranean after leaving Gibraltar on 30 August 1940. The type 79 radar with which these ships were equipped required two masts for the separate transmitting and receiving antennae and a mast has been added on the flight deck inboard of the after end of *Illustrious'* island to carry the transmitting antenna. Three Fairey Fulmar fighters of 806 Squadron are ranged on deck, their wings folded. **DB**
CPL

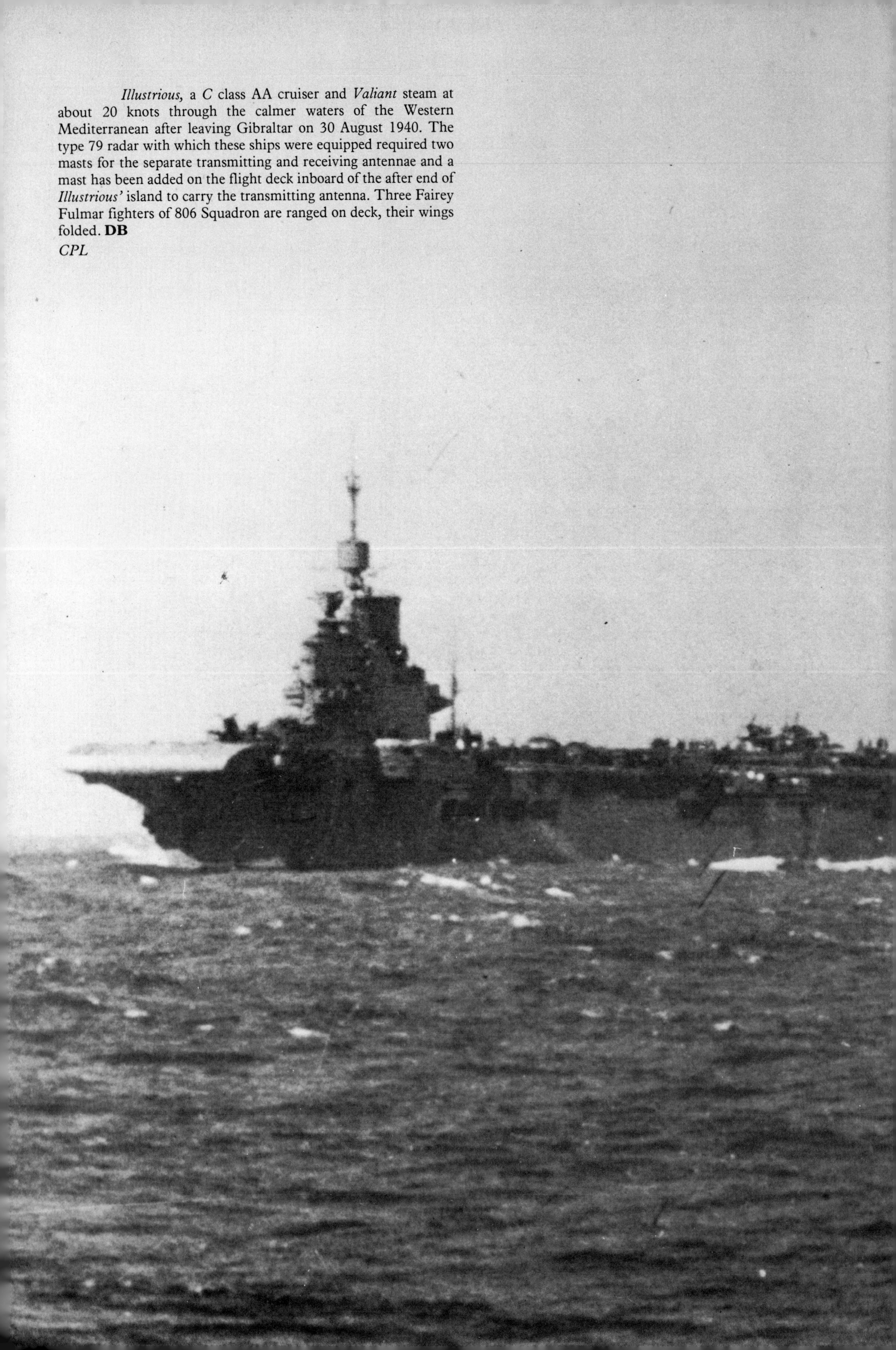

CAMERA AT SEA 1939-45

Edited and produced by the staff of WARSHIP

Managing Editor Robert Gardiner
Editor Antony Preston
Art Editor Geoff Hunt

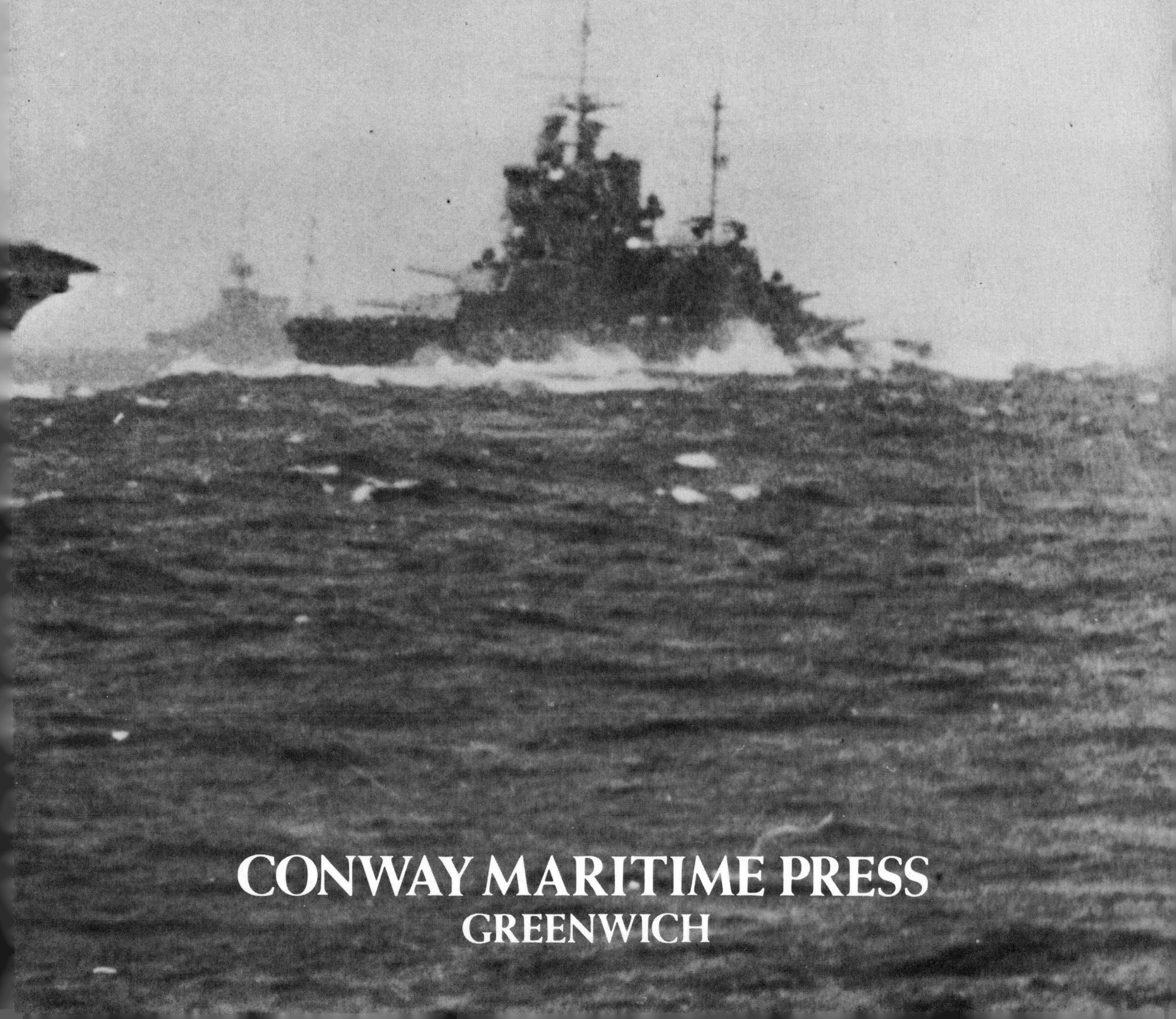

CONWAY MARITIME PRESS
GREENWICH

FRONT JACKET PHOTO
The forecastle of the German heavy cruiser *Prinz Eugen* in heavy weather, with the turrets turned to starboard to protect the guns: the Baltic, October 1940.
Ferdinand Urbahns

BACK JACKET PHOTO
Taken only moments before photo 5.21 (see page 94) *Indomitable* prepares to fly off four Hellcats and two Avengers, January 1945.
CPL

First published in 1978 by
Conway Maritime Press Ltd
2 Nelson Road
Greenwich
London SE10 9JB

ISBN 0 85177 124 6

Designed by Geoff Hunt
Typesetting and artwork from Letterspace, Barnet
Printed in the UK by Page Bros (Norwich) Ltd

Foreword

During the course of the Second World War at sea, hundreds of thousands of photographs were taken by private individuals, the Press, and official organisations, yet today the same few shots are used time and time again in books and magazines.

There is a huge store of unpublished or rarely seen photographs, and *Camera at Sea 1939-45* was born out of the desire to unearth and present some of these forgotten pictorial gems. Consequently this book was never intended to be an illustrated history, but instead it concentrates on the most graphic and telling photography from all the major participating nations. In passing it touches on almost every aspect of the war, and gives a better impression of what naval combat was really like than any number of written accounts.

Wartime photography was done for a variety of reasons, ranging from photo-journalism to the official recording of alterations to ships, as was the standard practice in the US Navy. We have included examples of most of these uses, and although we have preferred the little-known to the hackneyed view, some photographs will be familiar because they are the best, or even the only illustration available. For example, the *Graf Spee* was the first big news story of the naval war and had to be included for that reason, but although there are many photos of the ship at Montevideo only the few much-syndicated views taken by the crew of the *Graf Spee* covered the pocket battleship's cruise.

Finally, it must be said that this book would have been impossible without the *Warship* journal; the massive pictorial archives of our associate company, Popperfoto, provided the majority of the photographs; a distinguished list of contributors to the journal wrote the captions; and the book was edited, designed and produced by the staff of *Warship*.

Robert Gardiner

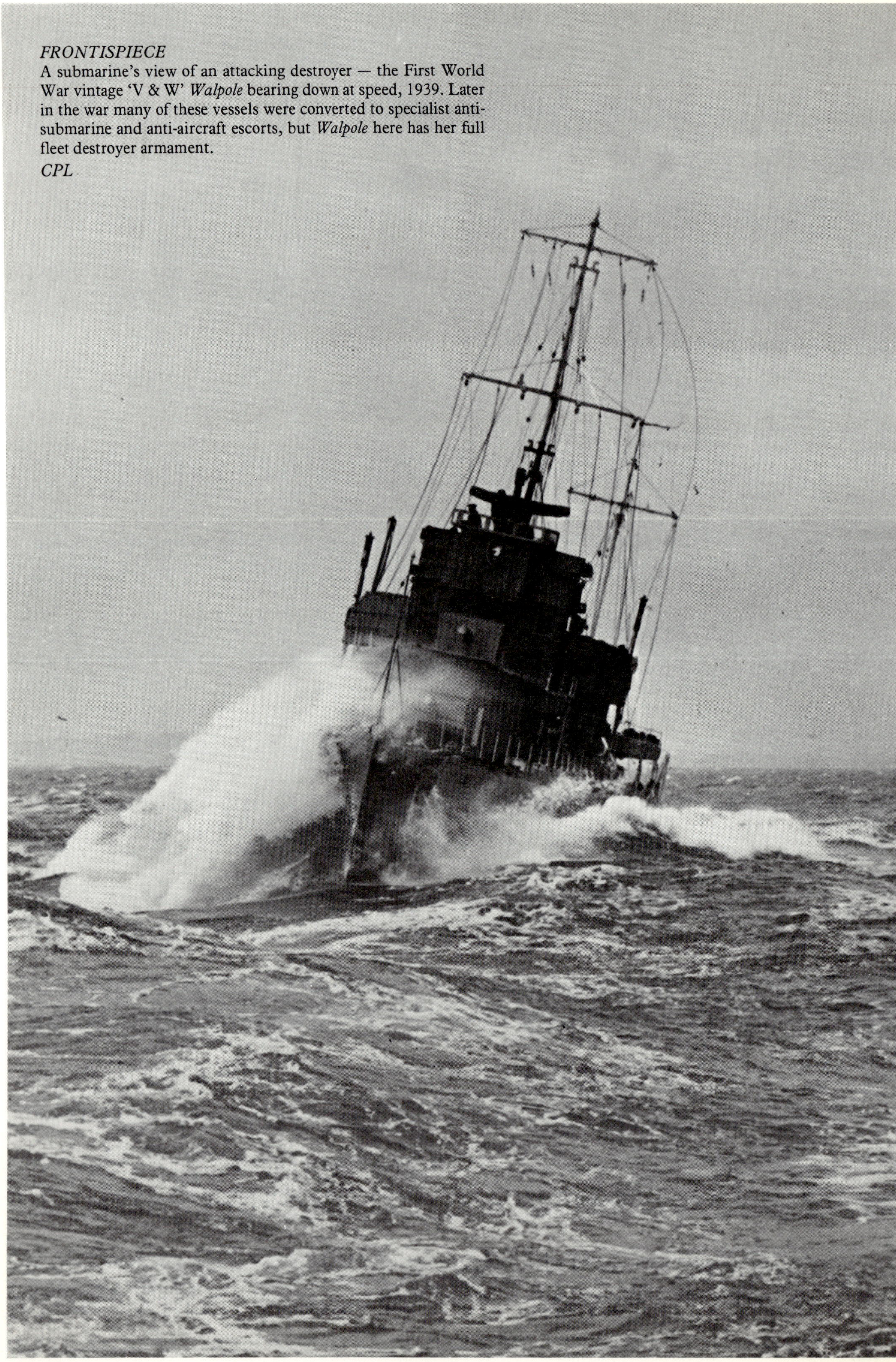

FRONTISPIECE
A submarine's view of an attacking destroyer — the First World War vintage 'V & W' *Walpole* bearing down at speed, 1939. Later in the war many of these vessels were converted to specialist anti-submarine and anti-aircraft escorts, but *Walpole* here has her full fleet destroyer armament.
CPL

Contents

A view looking aft down the port side on an ex-US 'four-stacker' showing the 4inch mounting and a US 0.5inch machine gun. These latter were introduced into the USN during the late 1920s to deal with close range attack by aircraft. The guns were water cooled, the water being circulated through the pipes, visible at the front of the mounting, to the jacket around the barrel. The magazine, an oblong box with a curved top, was mounted on the left of the gun. In this photograph it is not in position, but can be seen on the deck about 6 ft behind the man operating the gun. **JR** *CPL*

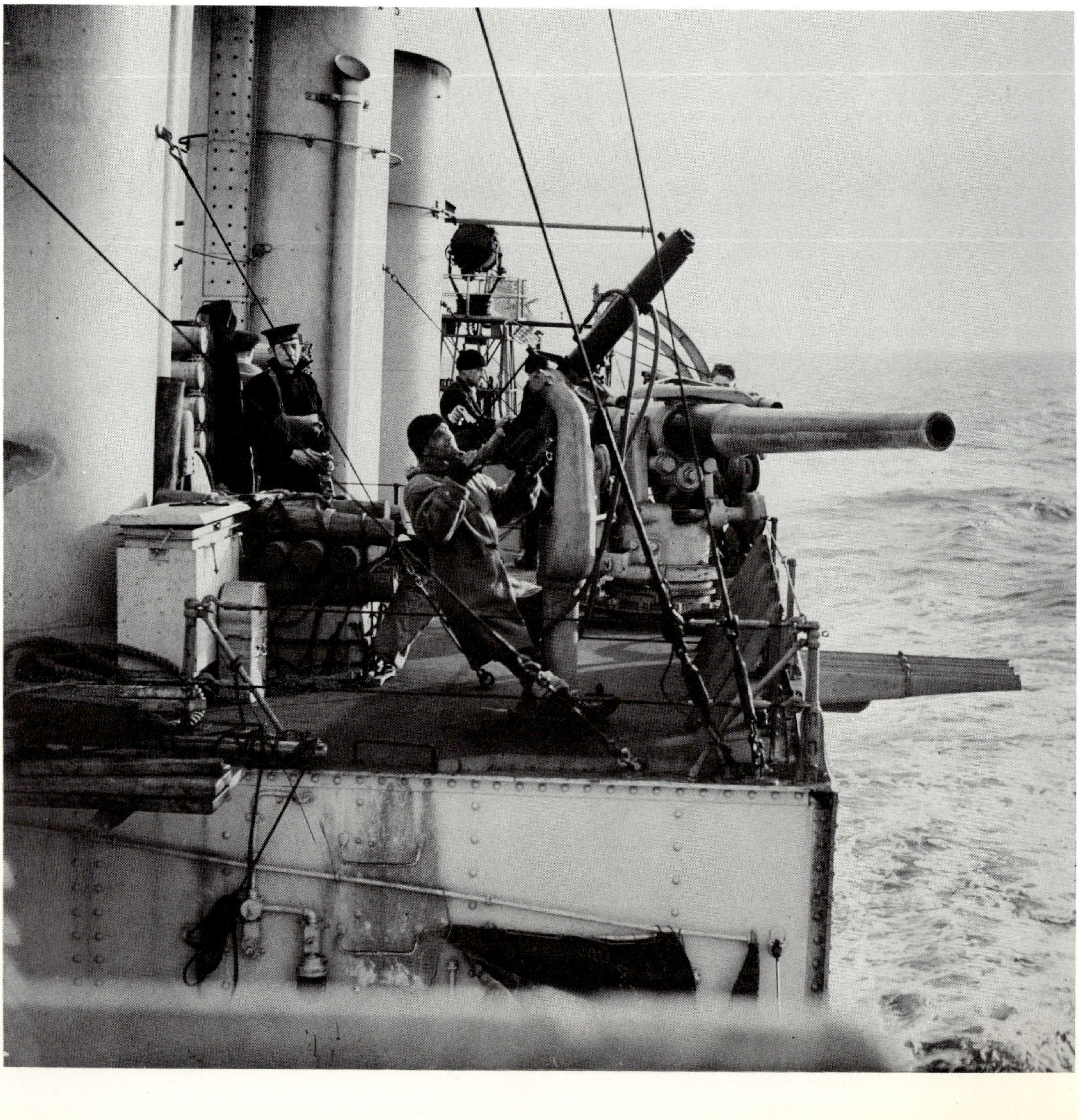

The Photographs

The largest single collection of photographs in this book is drawn from the Conway Picture Library, credited *CPL* in italics below each caption. These photos were taken for the defunct *Illustrated* magazine and few have been seen before — or at least, not since the wartime issues in which they made their only appearance. However, Conway Picture Library itself is now part of Popperfoto — possibly Europe's largest commercial picture agency — and more photos were drawn from this source. These have been credited *CPL* also, to save confusion.

The second major source was the outstanding personal collection of Commander Aldo Fraccaroli, a retired naval officer and well-known authority on the Italian Navy. From over 10 000 photographs Commander Fraccaroli selected his finest Italian and German material: those credited 'Aldo Fraccaroli Photograph' were taken by Fraccaroli himself.

The massive holdings of the US Navy official archives provided the third main group of photographs, and the publishers are indebted to Robert A Carlisle of the Department of the Navy Office of Information for his courteous assistance in the supply of photographs. However, the initial choice and final selection of US photos depended heavily on the advice of Lawrence Sowinski. Few men know the naval side of the US photo archives so intimately or possess such a broad knowledge of which photographs have been published, and we are pleased to acknowledge the importance of this help.

Several other sources were utilised for smaller numbers of pictures and these are fully credited after each caption, but essentially *Camera at Sea* has drawn upon three of the world's largest pictorial archives — one commercial, one private and one official — to put together a unique visual record of the war at sea.

The Contributors

The captions to the photographs in this book were written by a team of internationally famous naval authorities, each identified by his initials in bold type at the end of each caption.
The contributors are:

DAVID BROWN, an expert on carrier aviation and author of *Carrier Fighters, Aircraft Carriers, Carrier Operations of WW II,* etc.

ALDO FRACCAROLI, author of a number of books on the Italian Navy, and owner of one of the best collections of warship pictures in the world.

EUGENE M KOLESNIK, who has worked as an editor on *Jane's,* and is an authority on the Polish Navy.

JACQUES MORDAL, France's leading naval historian, and head of the historical section, Musée de la Marine, Paris.

ANTONY PRESTON, the editor of both *Warship* and *Navy International,* who writes extensively on naval matters.

ALAN RAVEN, who is an expert on warship appearance, and the author of a number of monographs and co-author of the definitive work on British battleships of the WW II era.

JOHN ROBERTS, a fine draughtsman of warship plans, and a much published naval writer, particularly on the subject of naval guns.

LAWRENCE SOWINSKI, a writer on US naval matters and an authority on the US Navy pictorial archives.

ANTHONY WATTS, a naval author specialising in the Japanese Navy.

Any uncredited captions were written by the staff of *Warship.*

1.1 Coming out of a 'hard to starboard' turning, *North Carolina*'s bow rides high as she leaps over a swell. **LS**
USN

1. Warships

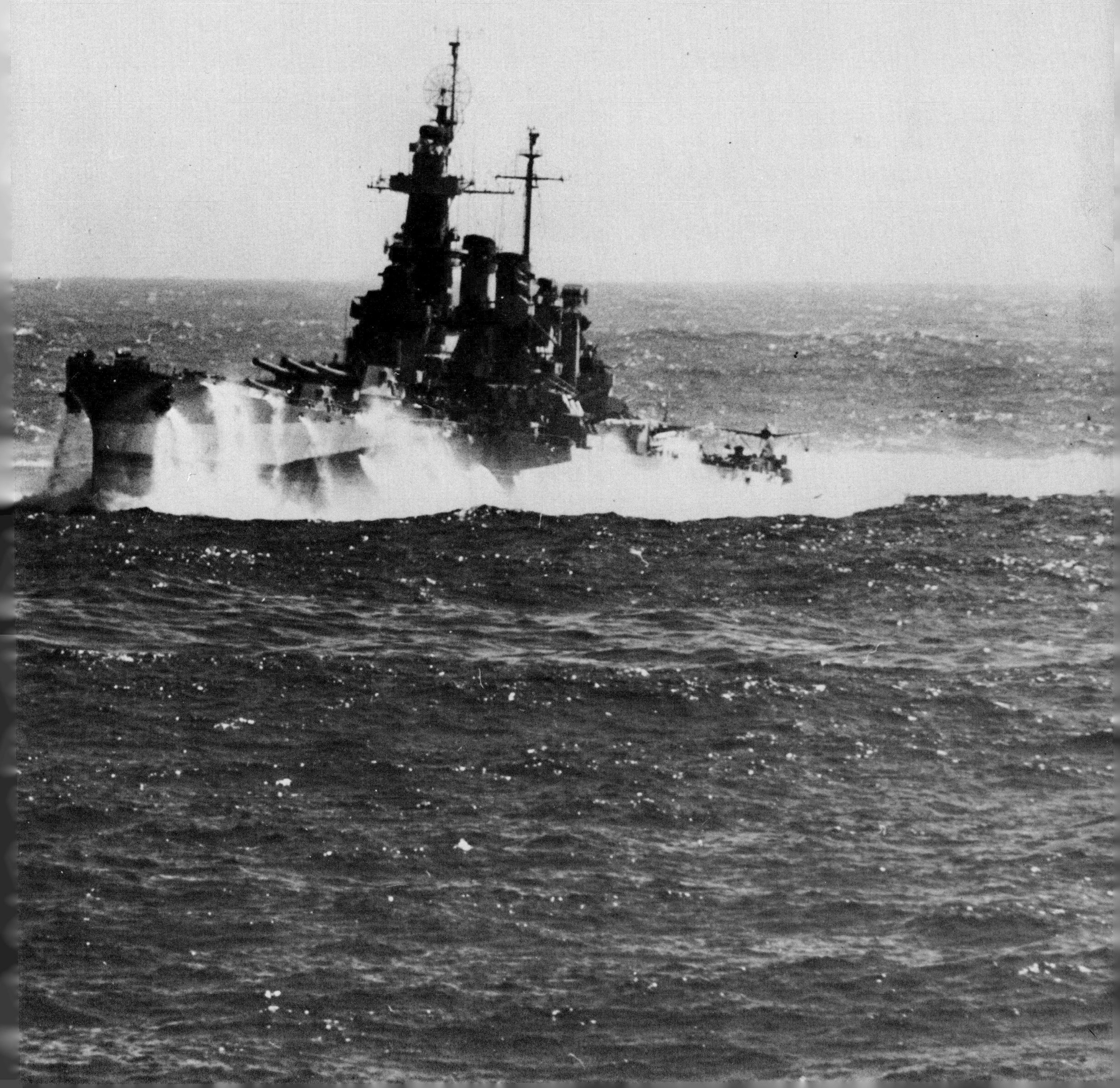

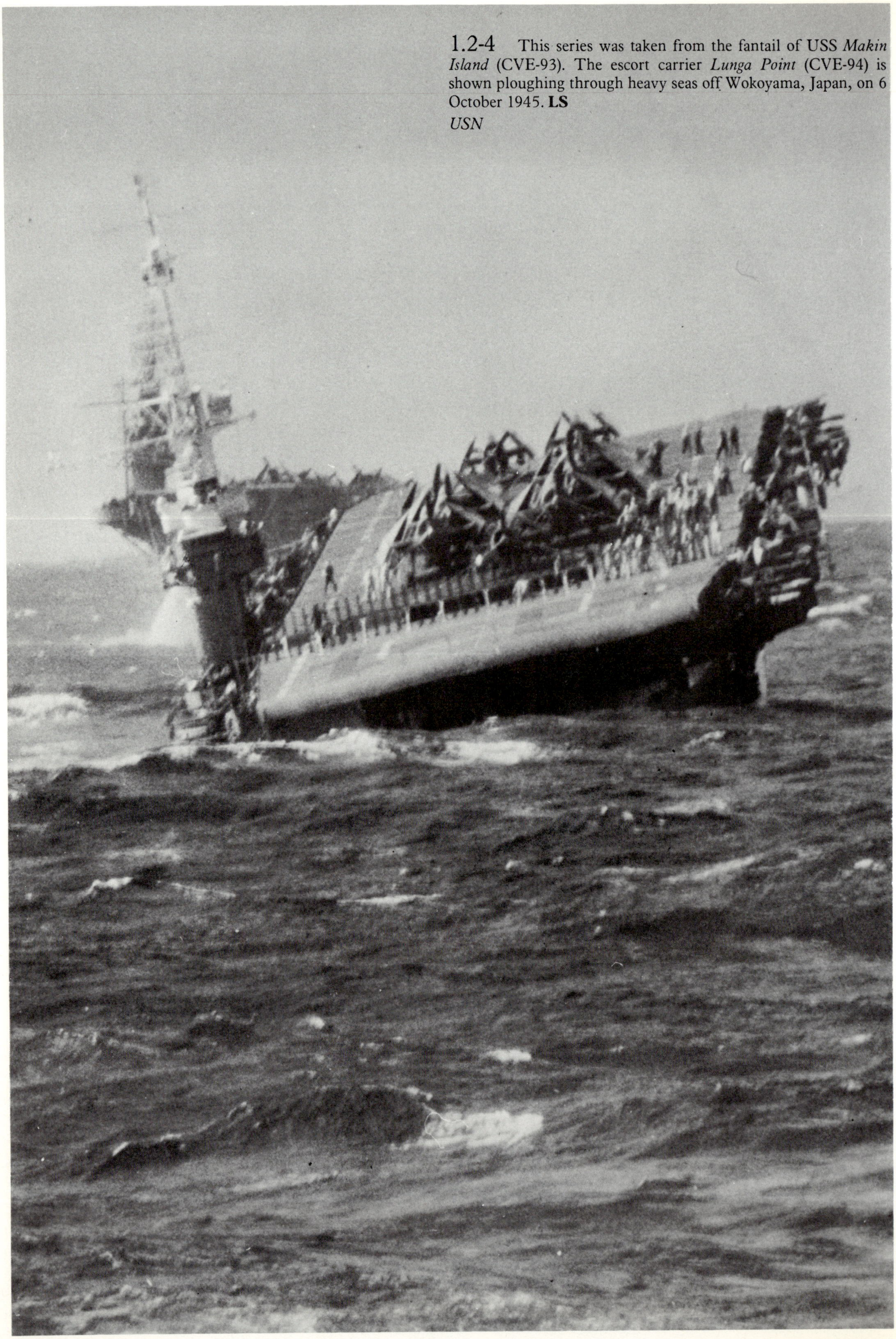

1.2-4 This series was taken from the fantail of USS *Makin Island* (CVE-93). The escort carrier *Lunga Point* (CVE-94) is shown ploughing through heavy seas off Wokoyama, Japan, on 6 October 1945. **LS**
USN

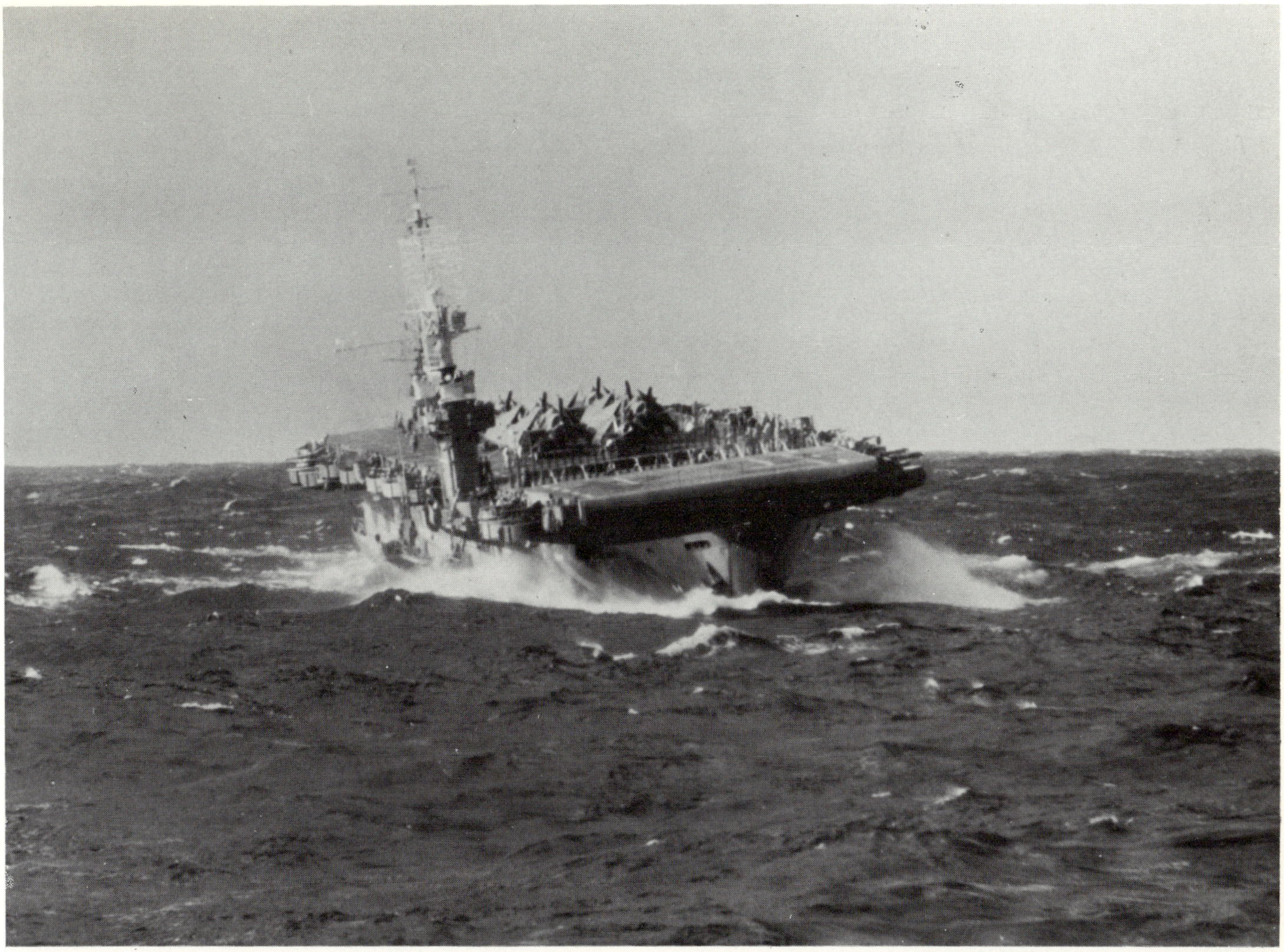
1.3

1.4
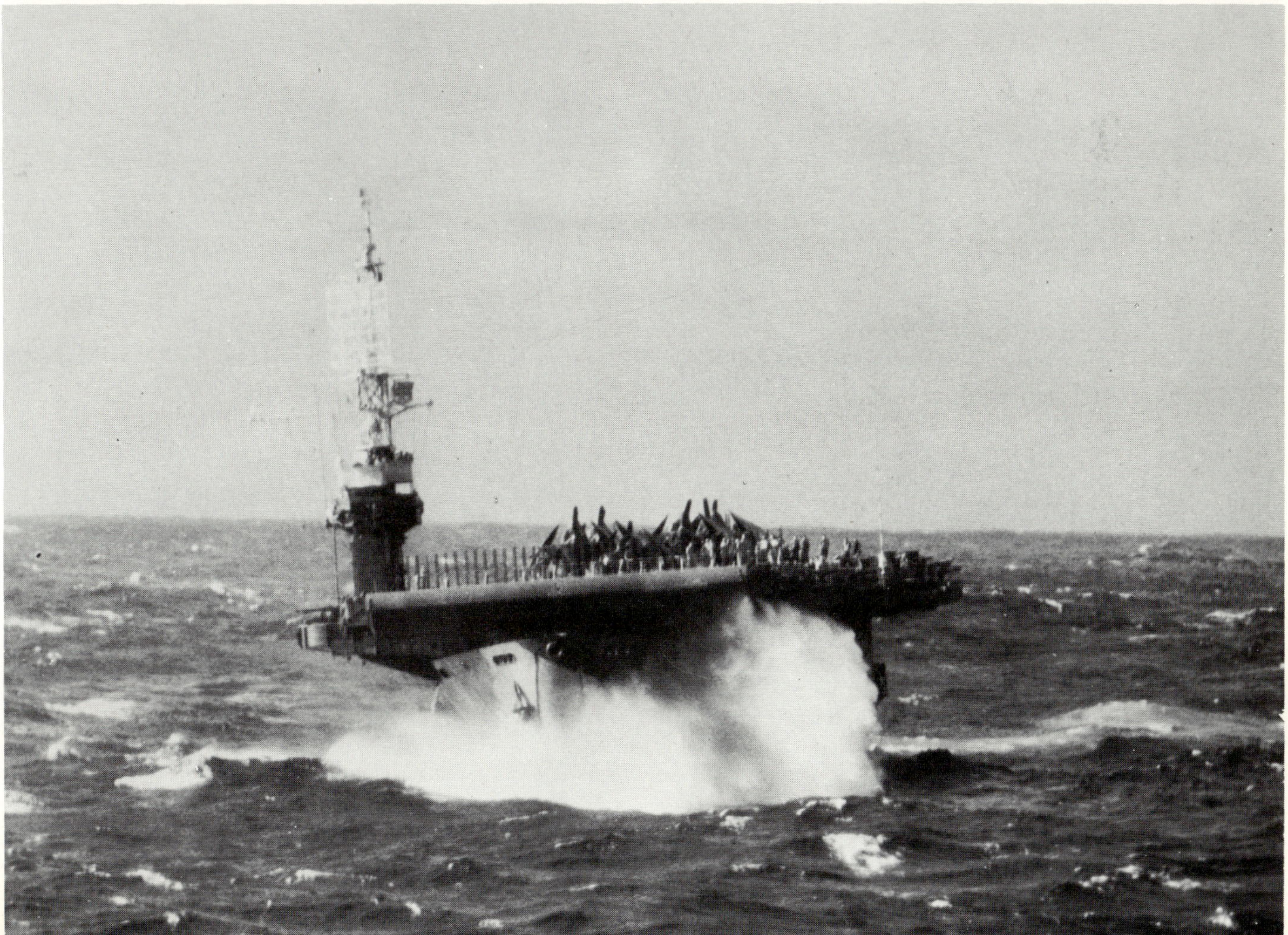

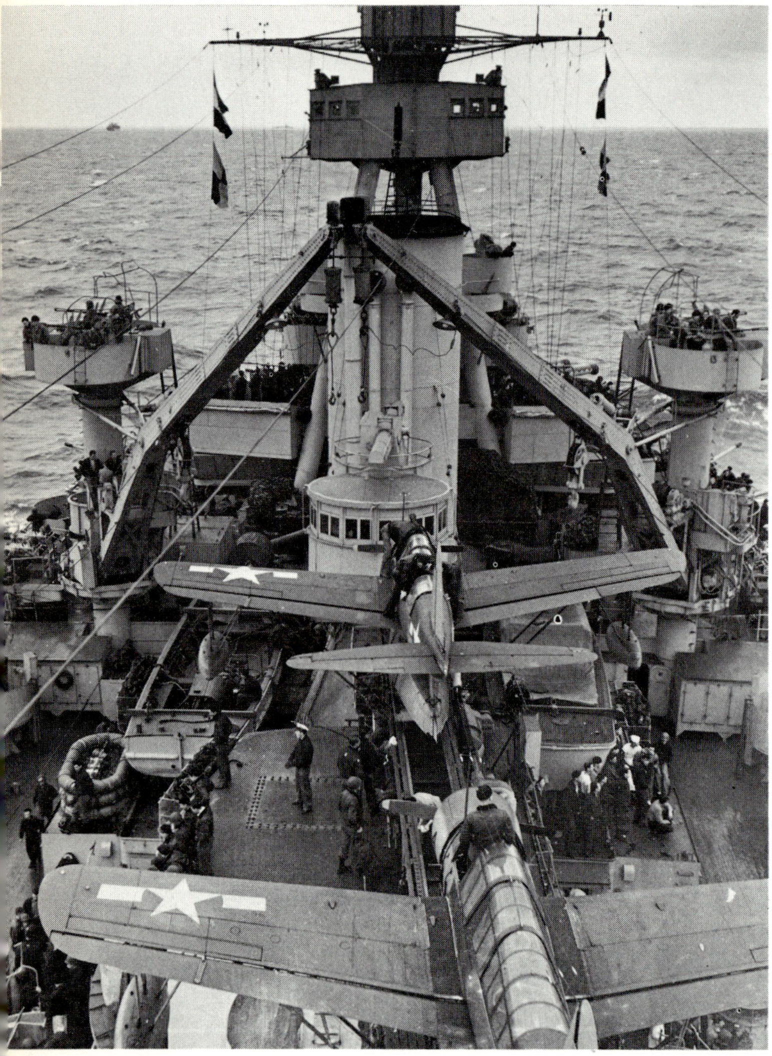

1.5 On board the battleship *Arkansas* in February 1944 while serving on a North Atlantic convoy. Shortly afterwards, the old 5inch guns serving as a secondary battery along the upper deck were removed and a multitude of 40mm and 20mm mountings fitted, so that *Arkansas* served as a bombardment vessel with the capability of giving AA fire to the invasion force during the Normandy landings. **AR**
CPL

1.6 The last and most powerful battleship of the German Navy, the *Tirpitz,* completing in the Kriegsmarine Werft yards, at Wilhelmshaven, in 1940. She was slightly heavier than her sister-ship *Bismarck,* and her AA machine gun armament was increased from the original 16 x 37mm and 16 x 20mm, to 16 x 37mm and 58 x 20mm. Originally she was not fitted with torpedo-tubes, but in 1942 two quadruple mountings were placed on her deck, with a total of 24 (including reserves) 21inch torpedoes. *Tirpitz* was commissioned on 25 February 1941, joined the Baltic Fleet in September of the same year, but in the following January she was transferred to Norwegian waters. She carried out unsuccessful attacks against two British convoys in March 1942, and another operation was interrupted in July 1942 by a Russian submarine attack. The *Tirpitz* destroyed important installations during a raid against Spitzbergen (September 1942), and was always a great menace to British shipping and naval forces. Attacked several times by British midget submarines and aircraft, she was at last sunk in November 1944 by 5.5 ton bombs from 36 RAF bombers, with 1204 casualties. **AF**
Aldo Fraccaroli Collection

1.7 The battleship *Massachusetts* (BB-59) refuels from *Saugatuck* (AO-75), as seen from the carrier *Hornet* (CV-12), 20 April 1945, off the Japanese coast. **LS**
USN

.5

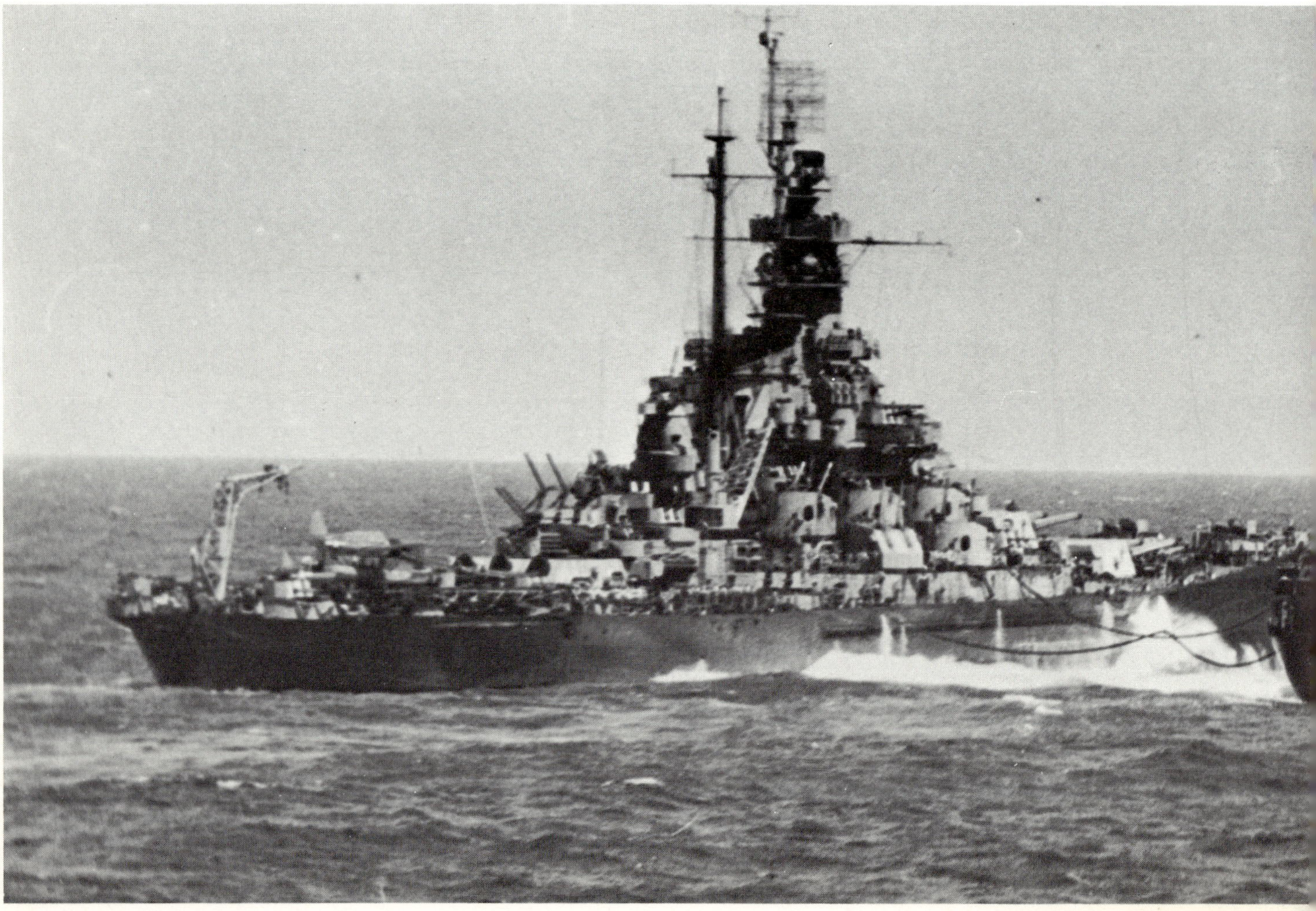

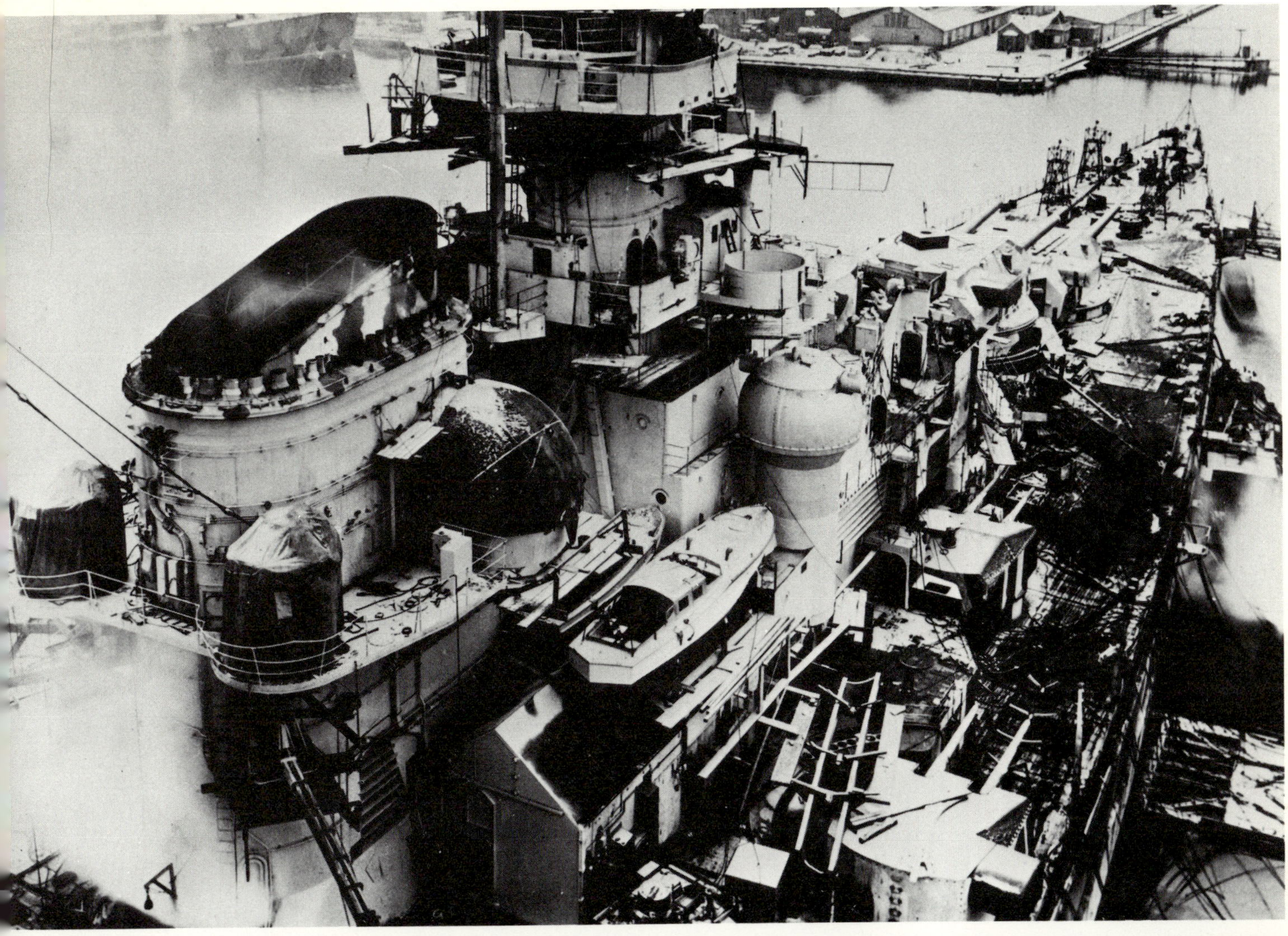

1.6

1.7

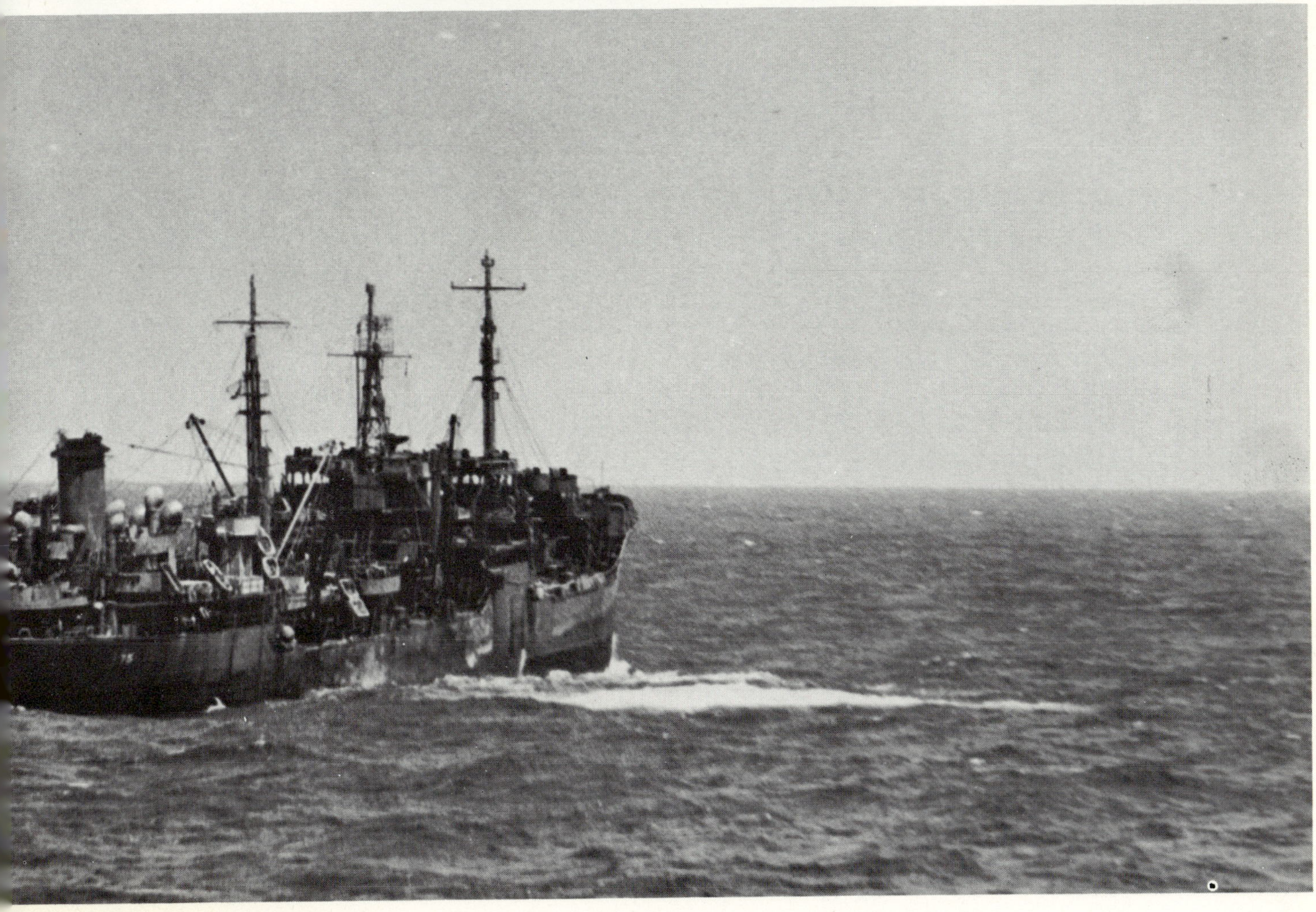

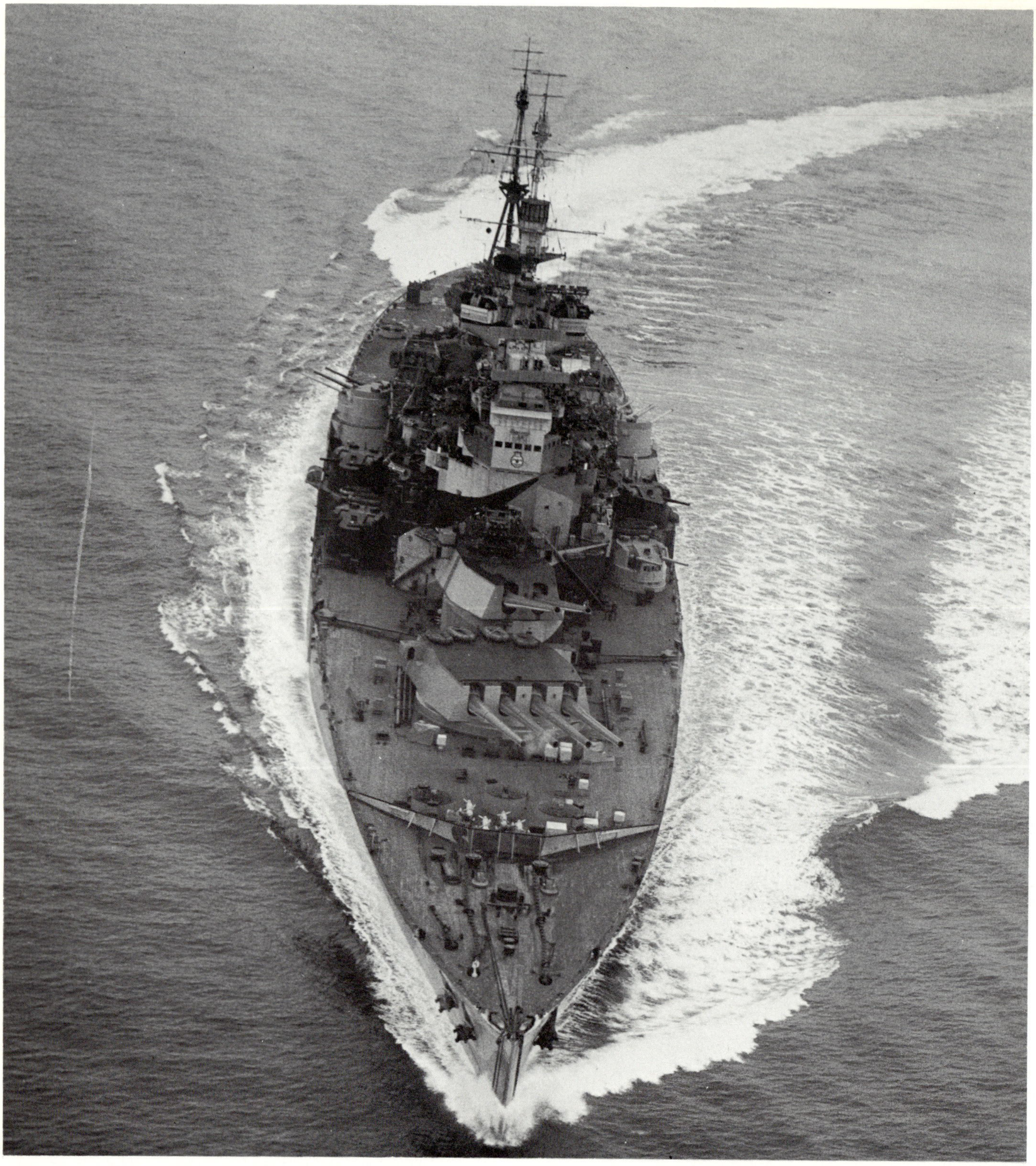

1.8

1.9

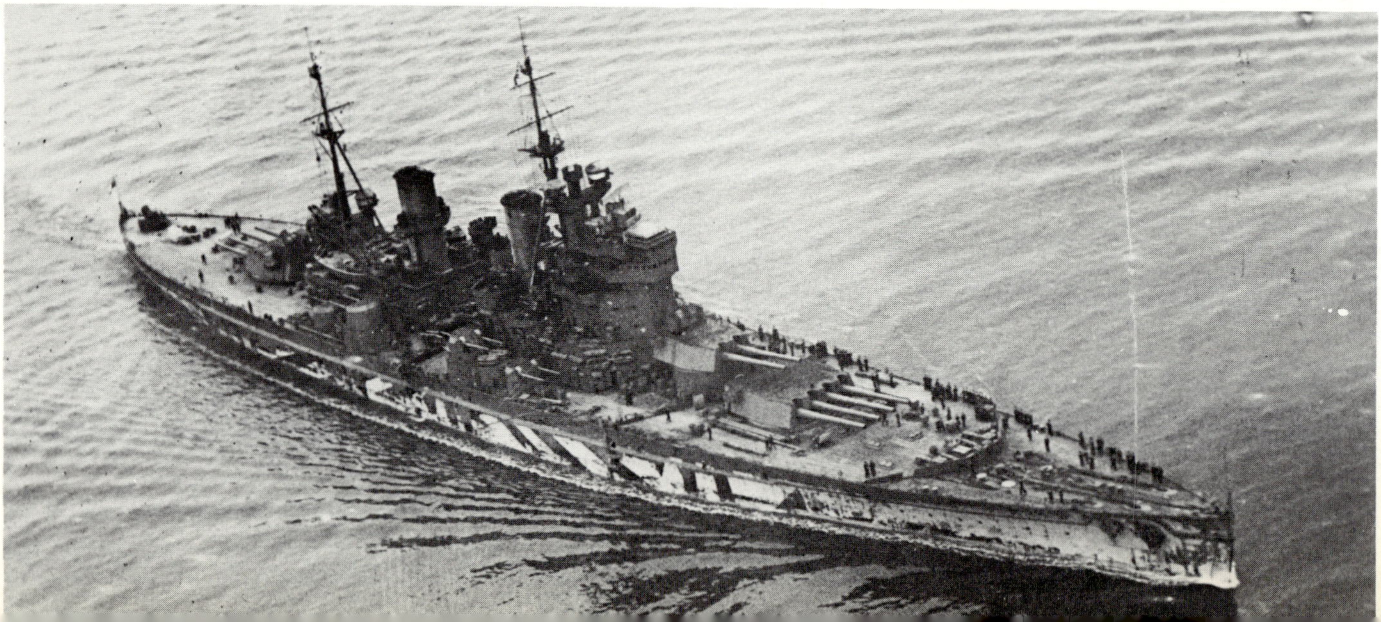

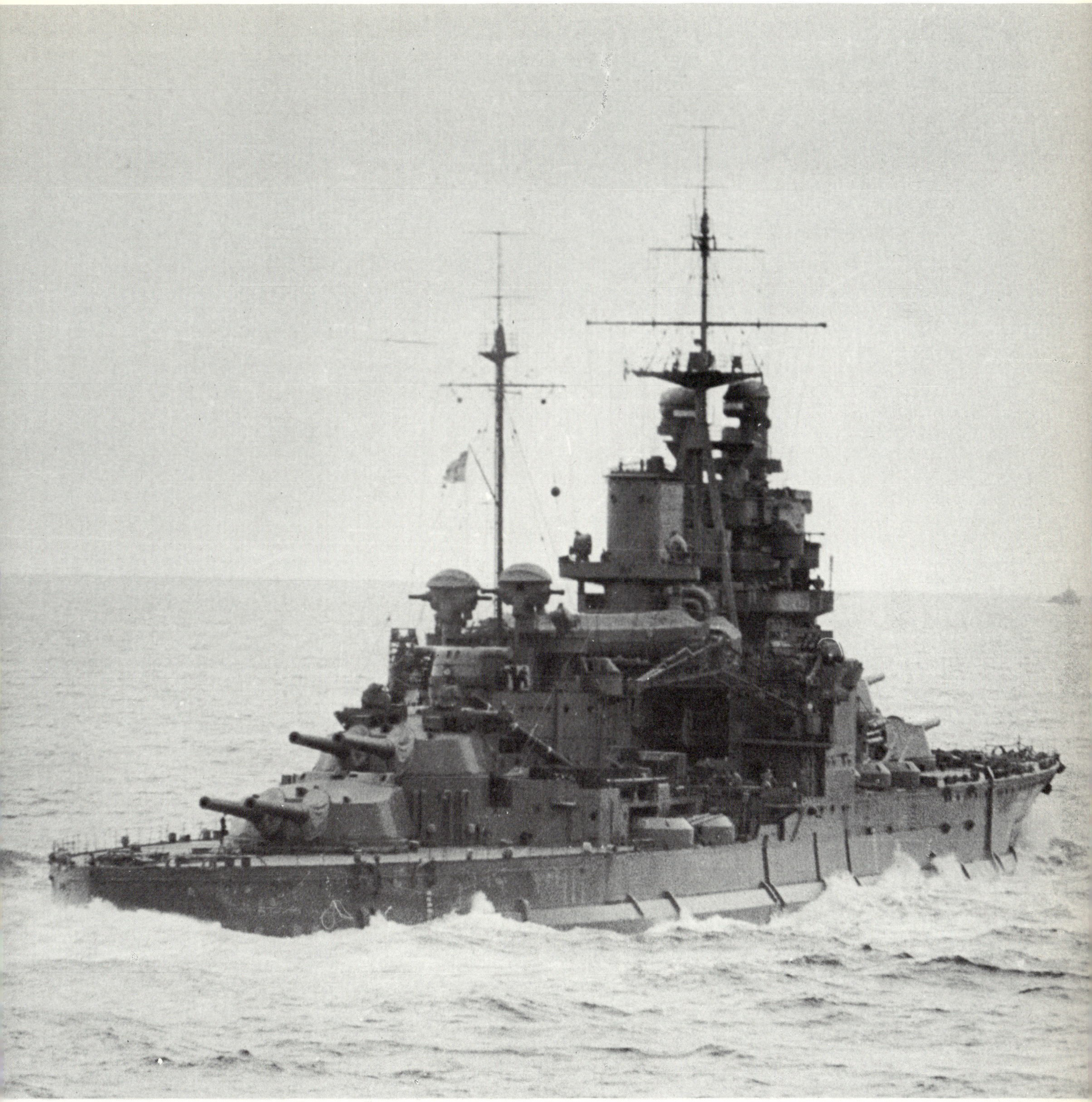

1.10

1.8 The new battleship *Howe* in March 1943, during a demonstration for the Press that included the carrier *Indomitable*. **AR**
CPL

1.9 The battleship *King George V* taken in late 1940 soon after commissioning. This is a rare view since the weathered camouflage pattern was carried for only a few weeks before being painted over in medium grey overall: this was carried out by the end of the year. Only one radar set is fitted, type 279 air warning, with the aerials carried at each mast head. **AR**
CPL

1.10 *Valiant* in August 1940 on passage to the Mediterranean Fleet. This picture shows to good effect the differing heights between the two secondary HACS directors of each pair. Because of the need to position them as close together as possible to avoid their rangefinders touching, they were sited at slightly different heights to allow the necessary few feet of clearance. She carries only one radar set — a type 79Z air warning outfit, the aerials carried at each mast head. She is painted overall in Home Fleet dark grey common to many ships at this time. **AR**
CPL

1.11 The light cruiser *Muzio Attendolo* reached 36.78 knots during sea trials, with 6970 tons of displacement and 121 628 SHP. She was armed with eight 6inch and six 3.9inch AA guns, twenty machine guns of 37 and 20mm, and four 21inch torpedo-tubes (removed in 1943), plus two aircraft and a catapult (all removed in 1943). Commissioned in August 1935, in wartime she carried out 53 missions, steaming 29 061 miles. She was sunk in the harbour of Naples, on Saint Barbara's Day (the patroness of sailors) 1942, by aircraft bombs (the first against Italy by the 9th US Air Force). **AF**
Aldo Fraccaroli Collection

1.12 A view taken from aboard the light cruiser *Emanuele Filiberto Duca d'Aosta,* commonly called *'Aosta'* in the Italian Navy. Astern are the two sister-ships (to each other, but smaller than *Aosta*) *Muzio Attendolo* and *Raimondo Montecuccoli.* All of them were armed with eight 6inch and six 3.9inch AA guns. The *Aosta,* although more heavily protected than the *Montecuccoli* class, attained a maximum speed of 37.35 knots during her sea trials, with 126 159 SHP and 7550 tons of displacement. She took part in the action off Calabria (9 July 1940), the first action of Sirte (17 December 1941), and escorted eleven convoys of transports and troopships to and from North Africa. Under the Peace Treaty, Italy had to transfer her to the Soviet Navy, and under these new colours she was named *Stalingrad* and later *Kerc,* and was laid up about 1957. **AF**
Photograph by Aldo Fraccaroli

1.13 From the beginning of the war (11 June 1940) until Italy's armistice (8 September 1943), Italian warships laid 49 796 mines during 387 missions, of which 45 were carried out by cruisers, 206 by destroyers, 81 by torpedo-boats and 55 by armed merchant cruisers, in addition to the missions effected by the naval minelayers and by the auxiliary ones, plus the minelayer submarines. This view shows three light cruisers laying a barrage. In the foreground: *Bande Nere*; at left: *Attendolo;* right, in the background: *Duca d'Aosta.* **AF**
Aldo Fraccaroli Collection

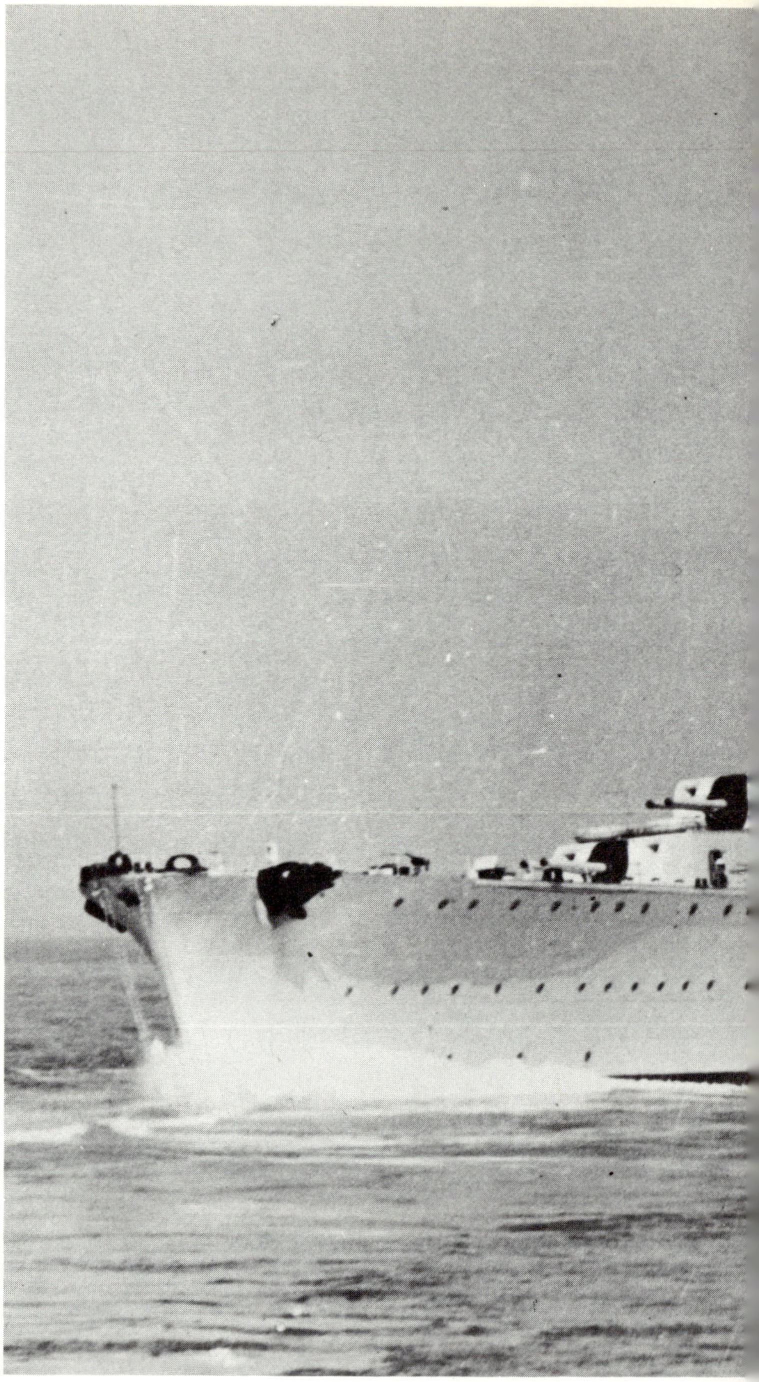

1.11

1.12

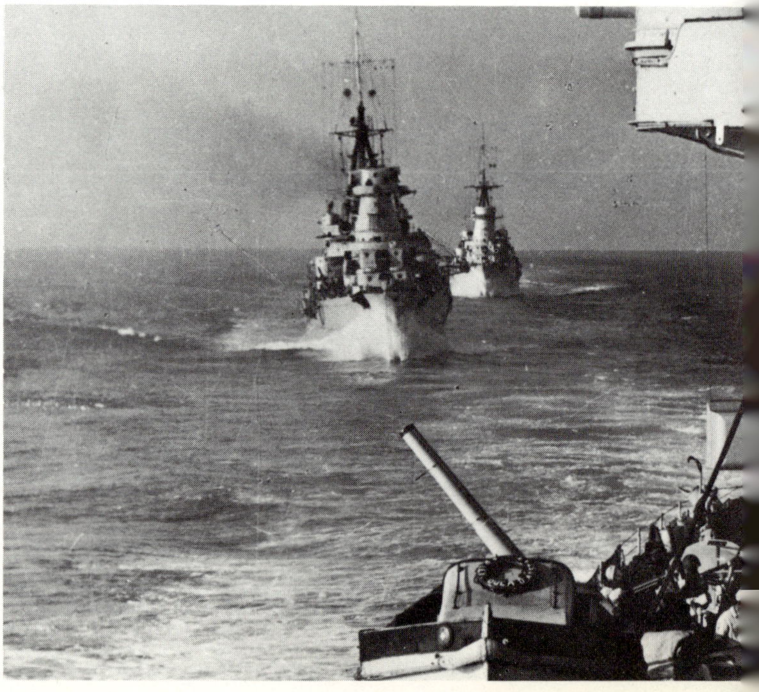

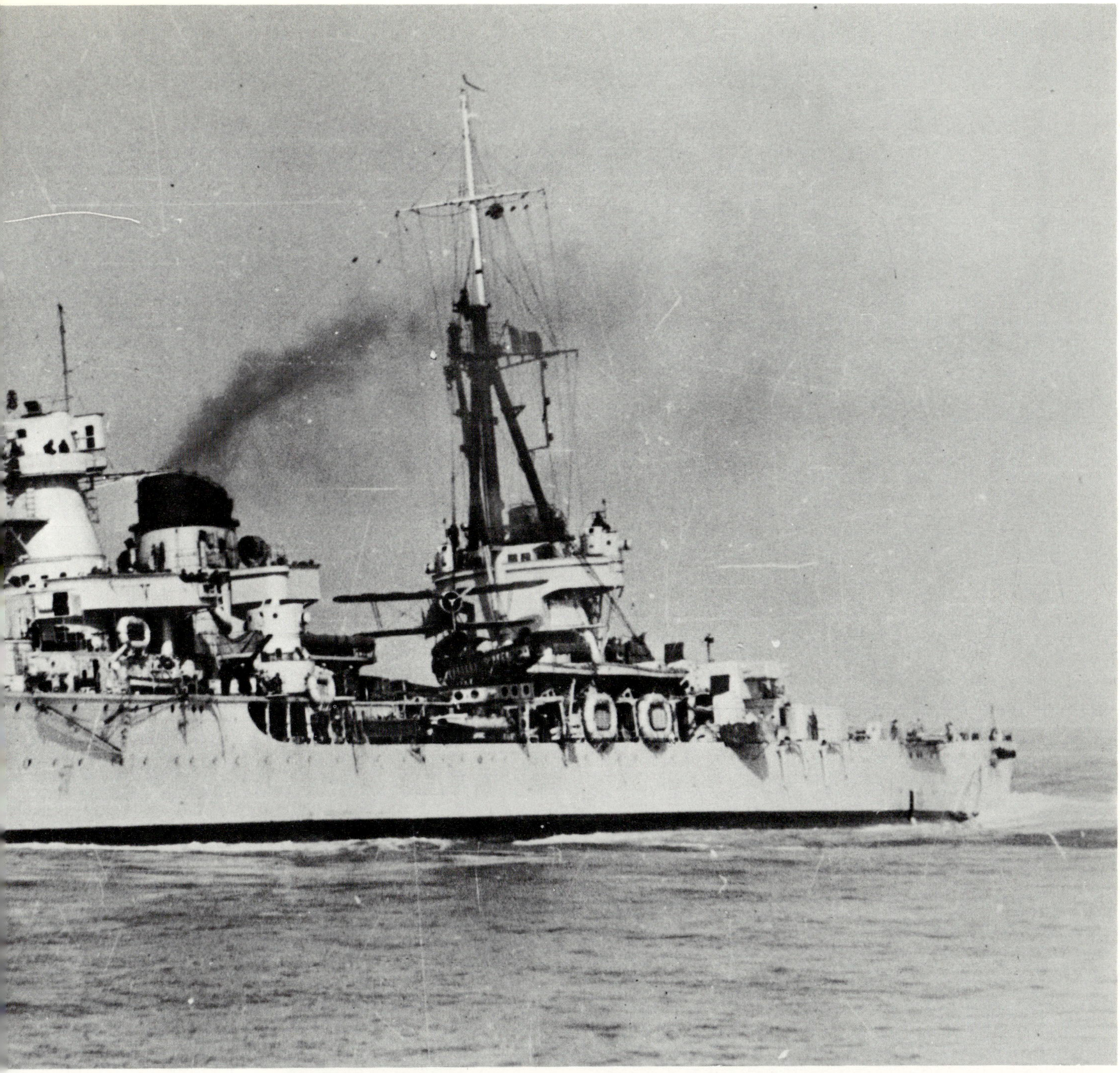

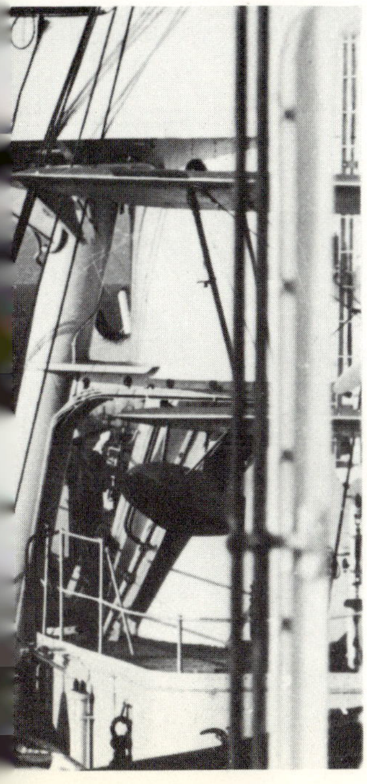

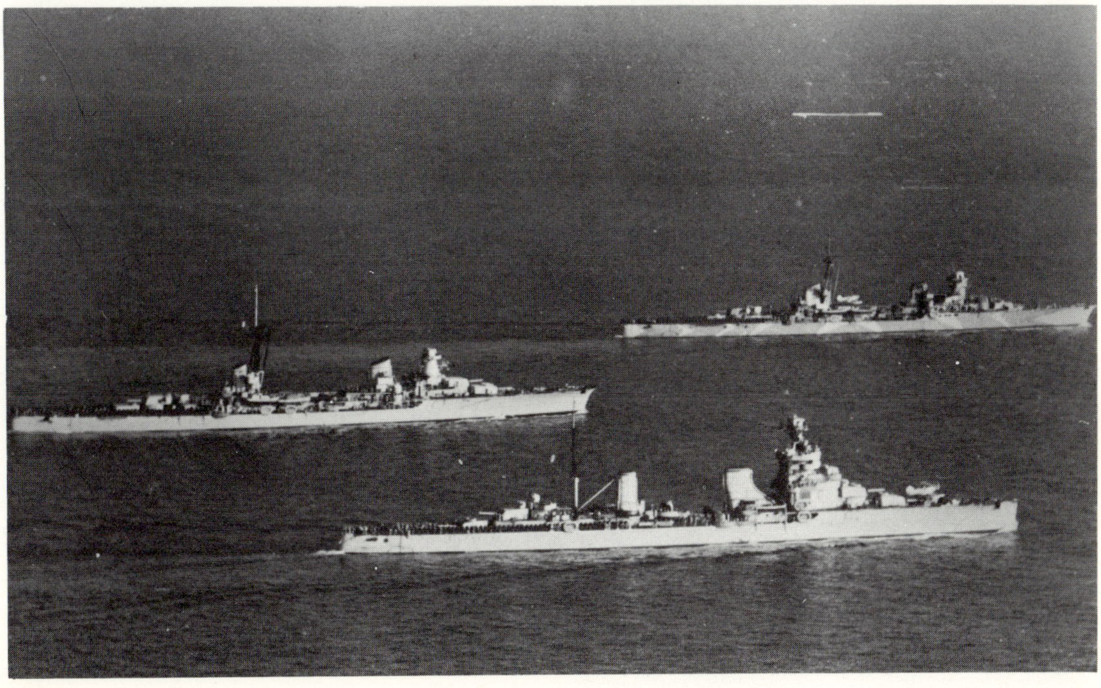

1.13

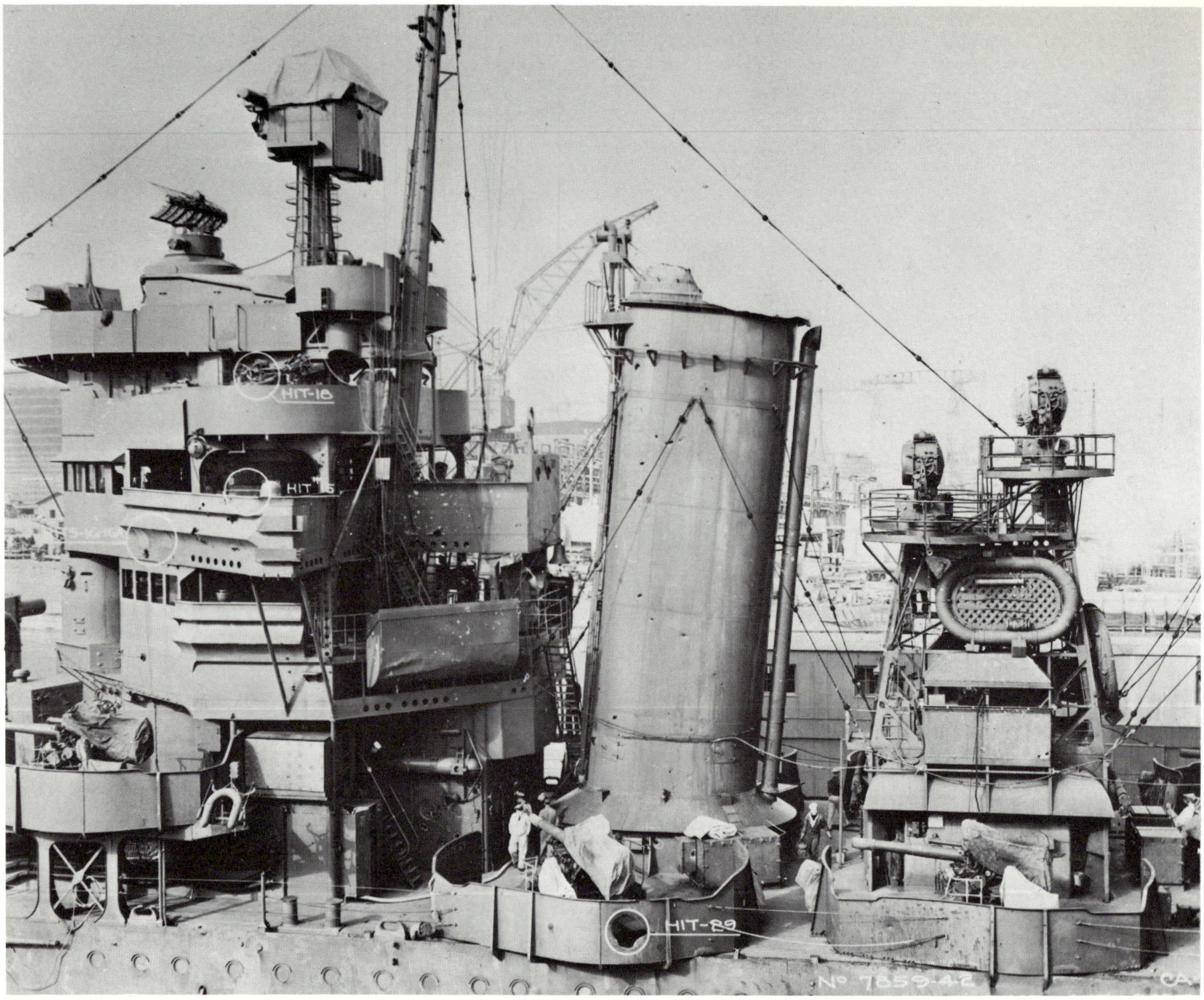

1.14

1.15

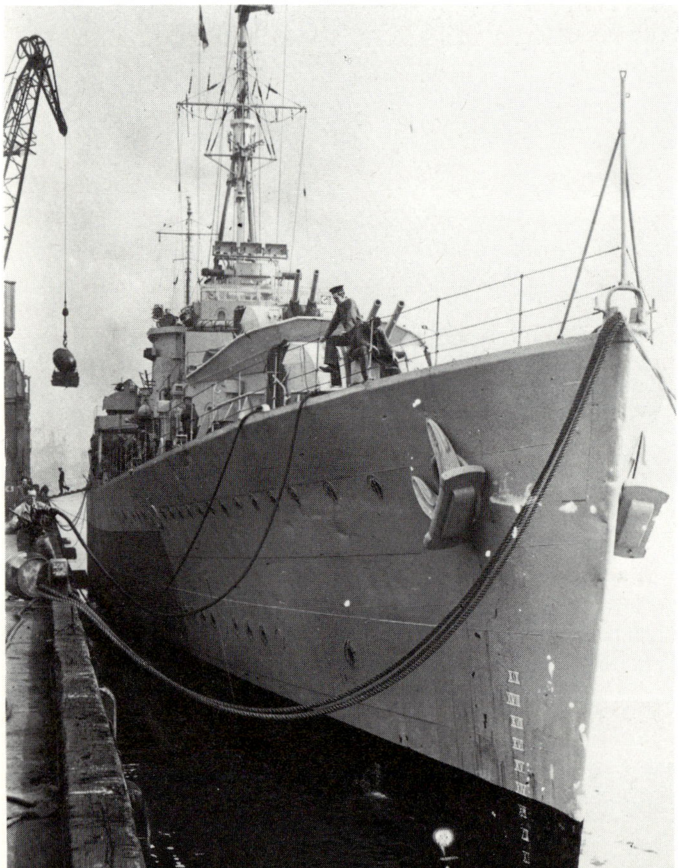

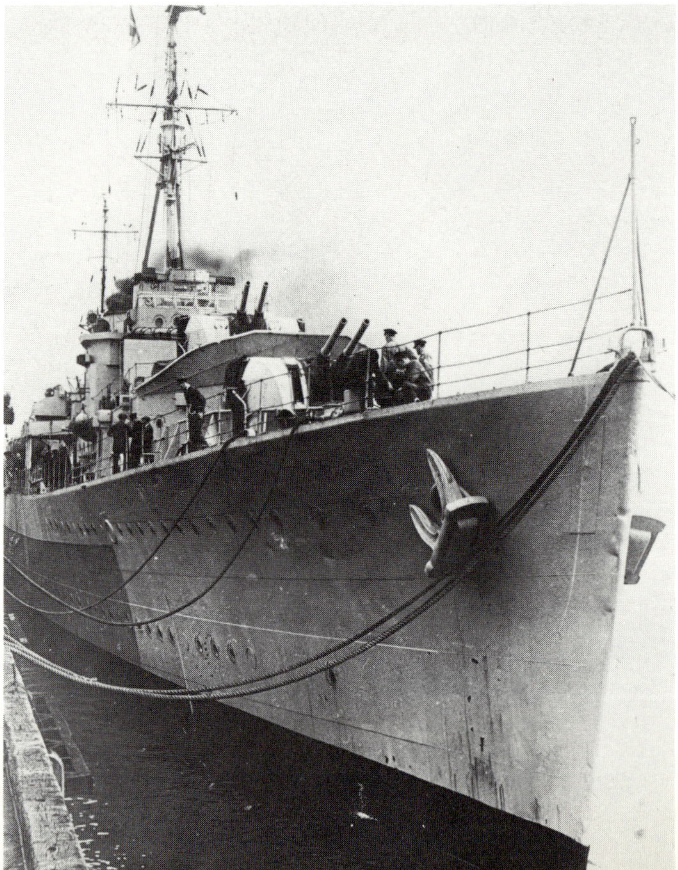

1.1

1.1

1.14 Close-up of heavy cruiser *San Francisco* (CA-38) at Mare Island, California, on 15 December 1942. Although the ship has been cleaned up, some of the 45 hits she received on Black Friday (November 13) are still visible. Several hits were point blank from the Japanese battleships *Hiei* and *Kirishima* (14inch guns). **LS**
USN

1.15-16 The fast minelayer *Manxman* in 1944. The two photographs illustrate very well the art of the wartime censor. The smoke from the funnel has been artificially extended to carry across the radar aerials for type 285 carried on the top of the main gun director, and also deleted is the 'cheese' aerial for the type 276 surface search set, along with its associated IFF (identification-friend-or-foe) aerial immediately below it. However the aerial for the type 291 (air warning) positioned just above the lower fore yard has for some unknown reason been left untouched. The camouflage scheme consists of a dark blue hull panel (B20) with light grey remainder of hull and upperworks (B55). **AR**
CPL

1.17 The heavy cruiser *Admiral Hipper* displaced 18 200 tons at full load and was the first 8inch gun cruiser of the German Navy. The first of a series of three — *Hipper* herself, *Blücher* and *Prinz Eugen* — she joined the fleet in April 1939 and remained in service till 3 May 1945, when she was scuttled at Kiel. She took part in the invasion of Norway, was damaged by the British destroyer *Glowworm,* who rammed her and made raids in the Atlantic, sinking twelve ships. She fought in the battle of Barents Sea and supported the German Army in hindering the Russian advance. **AF**
Aldo Fraccaroli Collection

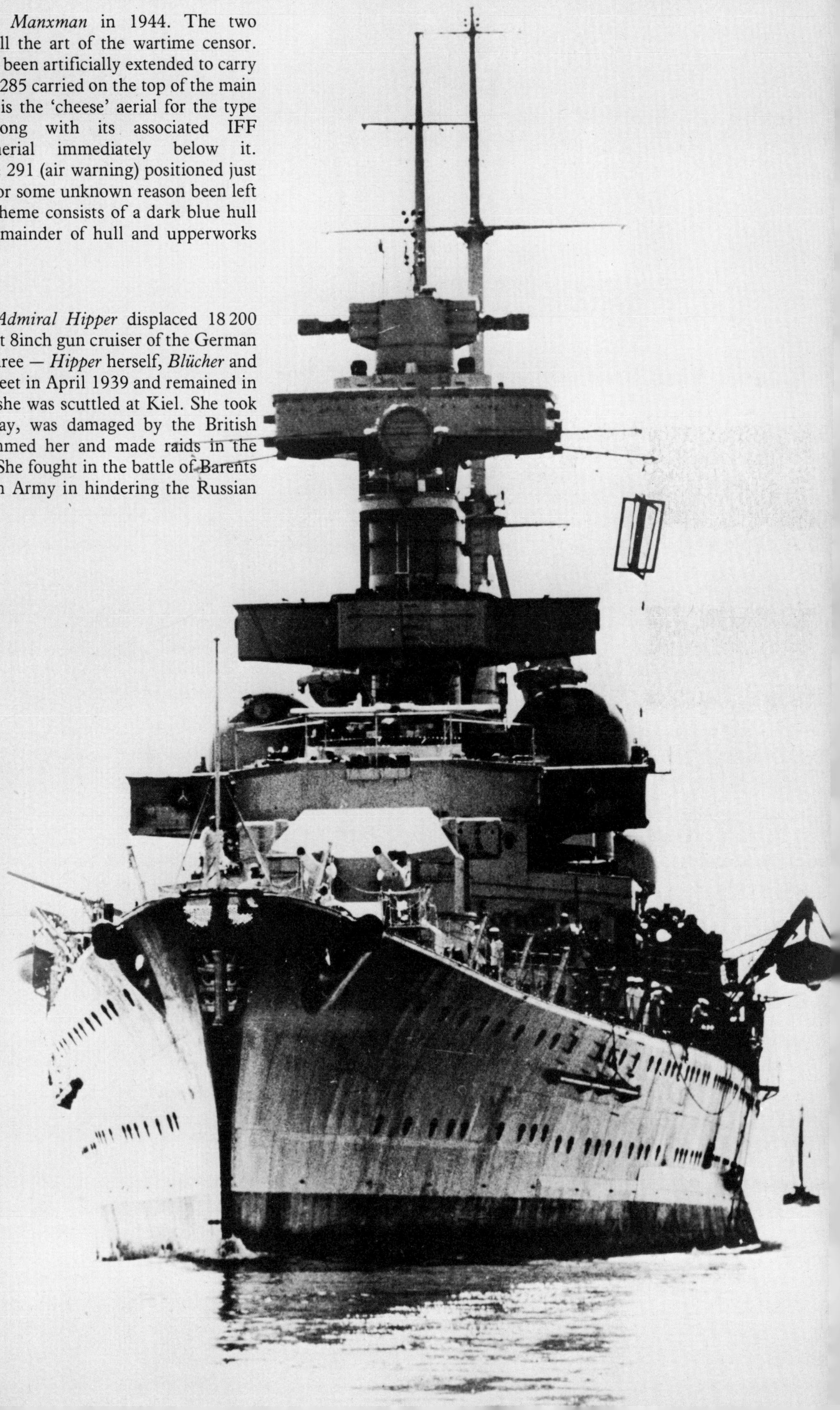

1.20

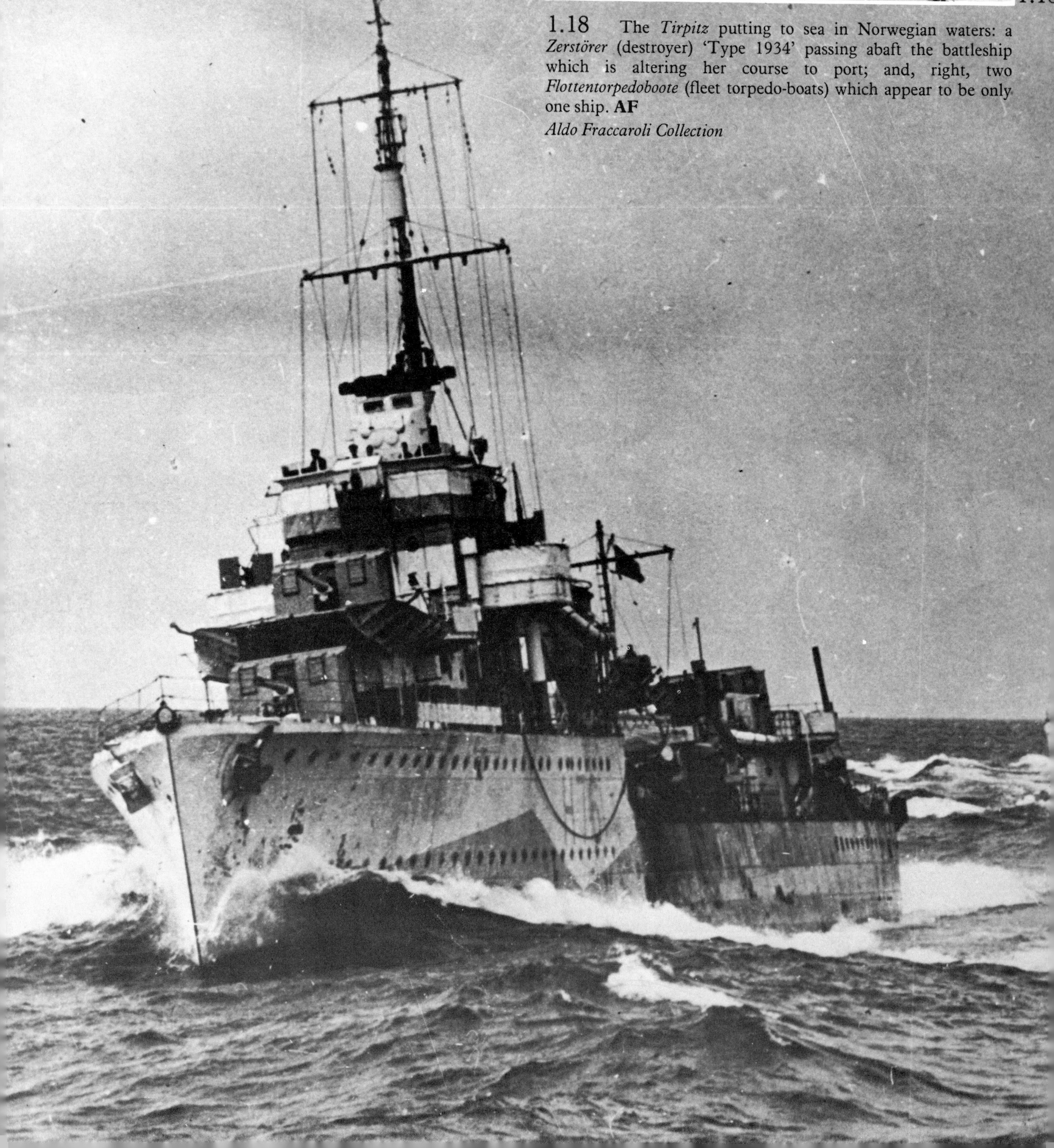

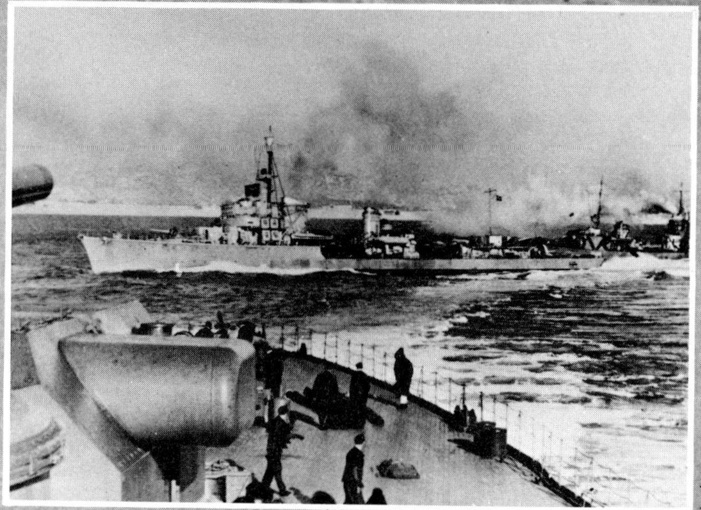

1.18

1.18 The *Tirpitz* putting to sea in Norwegian waters: a *Zerstörer* (destroyer) 'Type 1934' passing abaft the battleship which is altering her course to port; and, right, two *Flottentorpedoboote* (fleet torpedo-boats) which appear to be only one ship. **AF**

Aldo Fraccaroli Collection

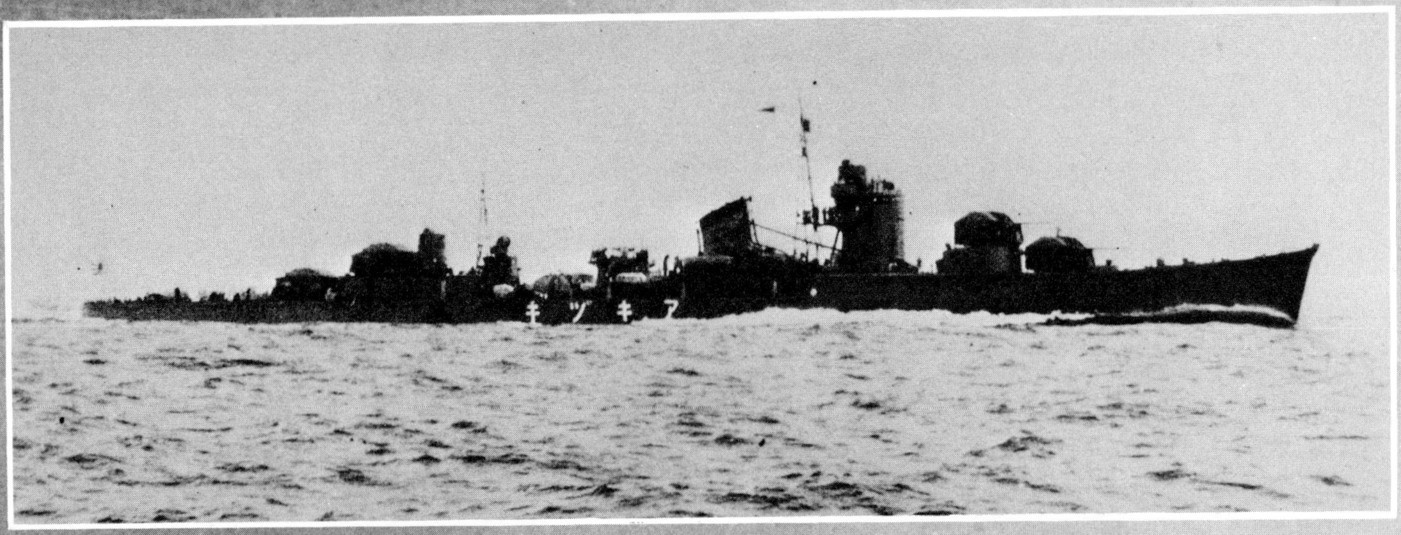

1.19

1.19 The destroyer *Akizuki* (shown above on trials off Maizuru on 17 May 1942) was one of a class of 16 destroyers, three of which were cancelled. They were designed as AA destroyers to accompany Japanese carrier Task Forces. A new AA gun was designed for the vessels with a high rate of fire (25-28 rounds per minute) and a range of 20 000 yards. The guns were mounted in pairs in a gas-tight power-operated turret. The original design showed a vessel capable of providing excellent AA defence for the Fleet, but it was subsequently decided to give the vessels a dual role, and the design was altered to incorporate a quadruple 24inch torpedo-tube mount amidships. Commissioned in June 1942 the *Akizuki* took part in a number of actions including the battles for Guadalcanal during 1942-43, the Battle of the Philippine Sea on 19 June 1944 and the Battle for Leyte Gulf in October 1944, where she was sunk. **AW**
Japanese Navy

1.20 *Fury* leading a group of *N* class destroyers, in 1942 (exact date unknown). *Fury* shows the sort of modification that the older fleet destroyers went through: the old mainmast replaced by a much shorter affair designed to only spread and carry the main W/T aerial leads; type 290 radar at the mast head; 20mm mounts in the bridge wings. However, she is still essentially a fleet boat — witness the company she keeps. **AR**
CPL

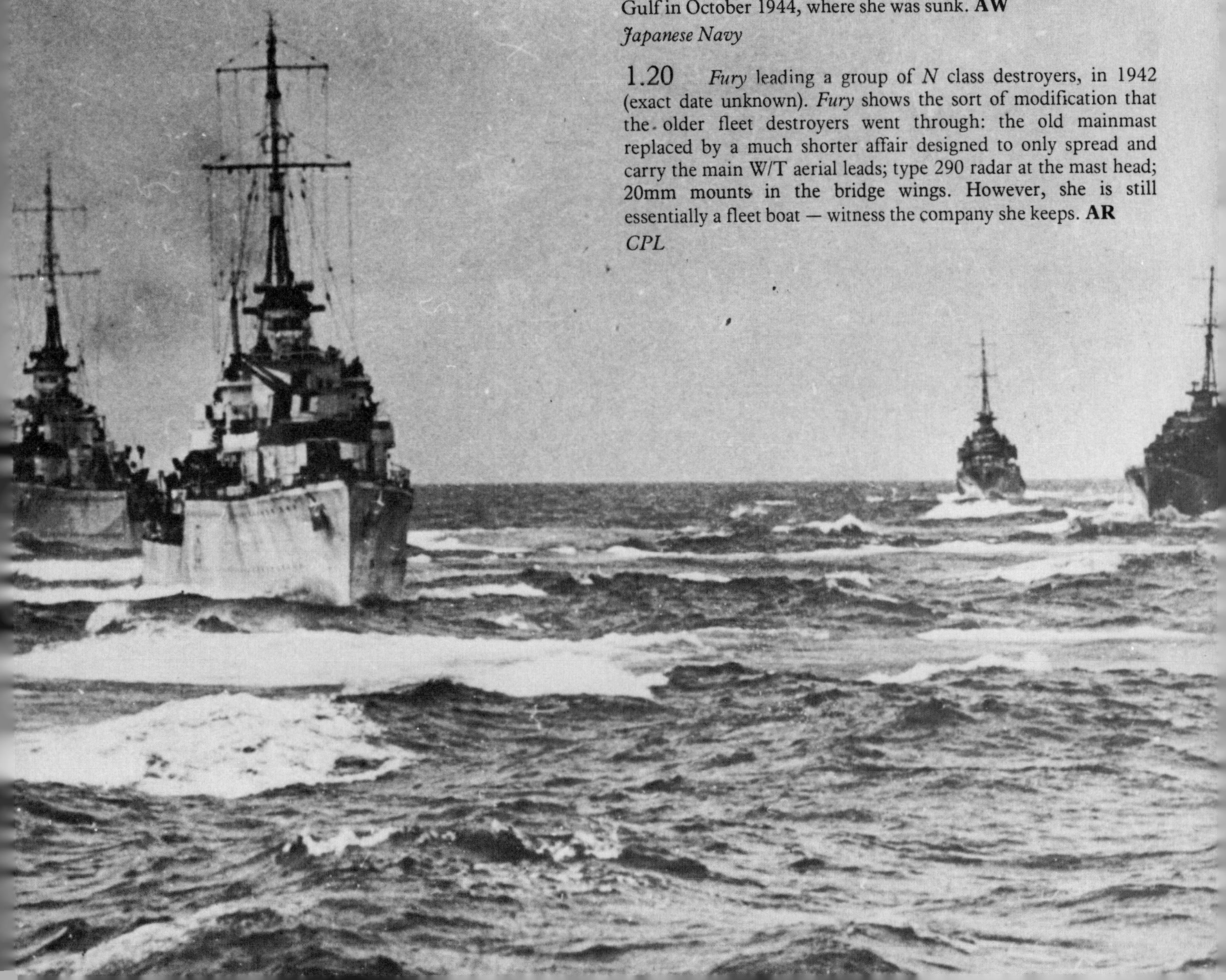

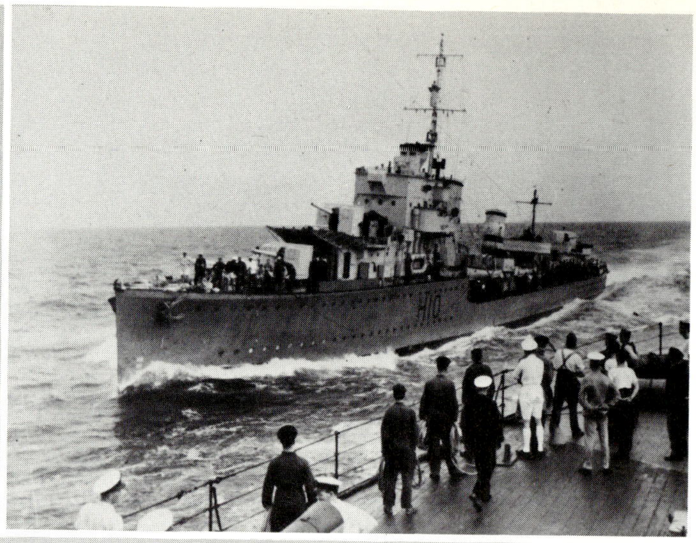

1.2

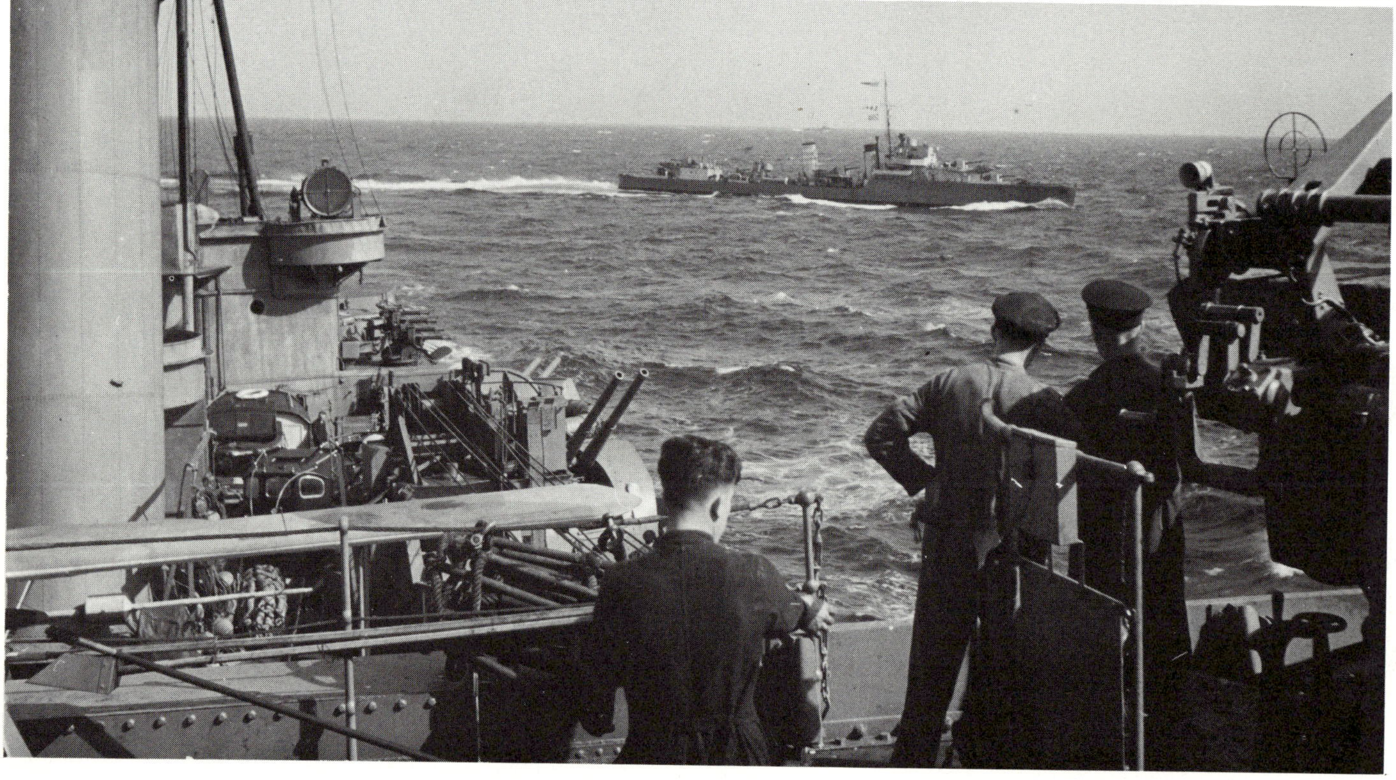

1.22

1.23

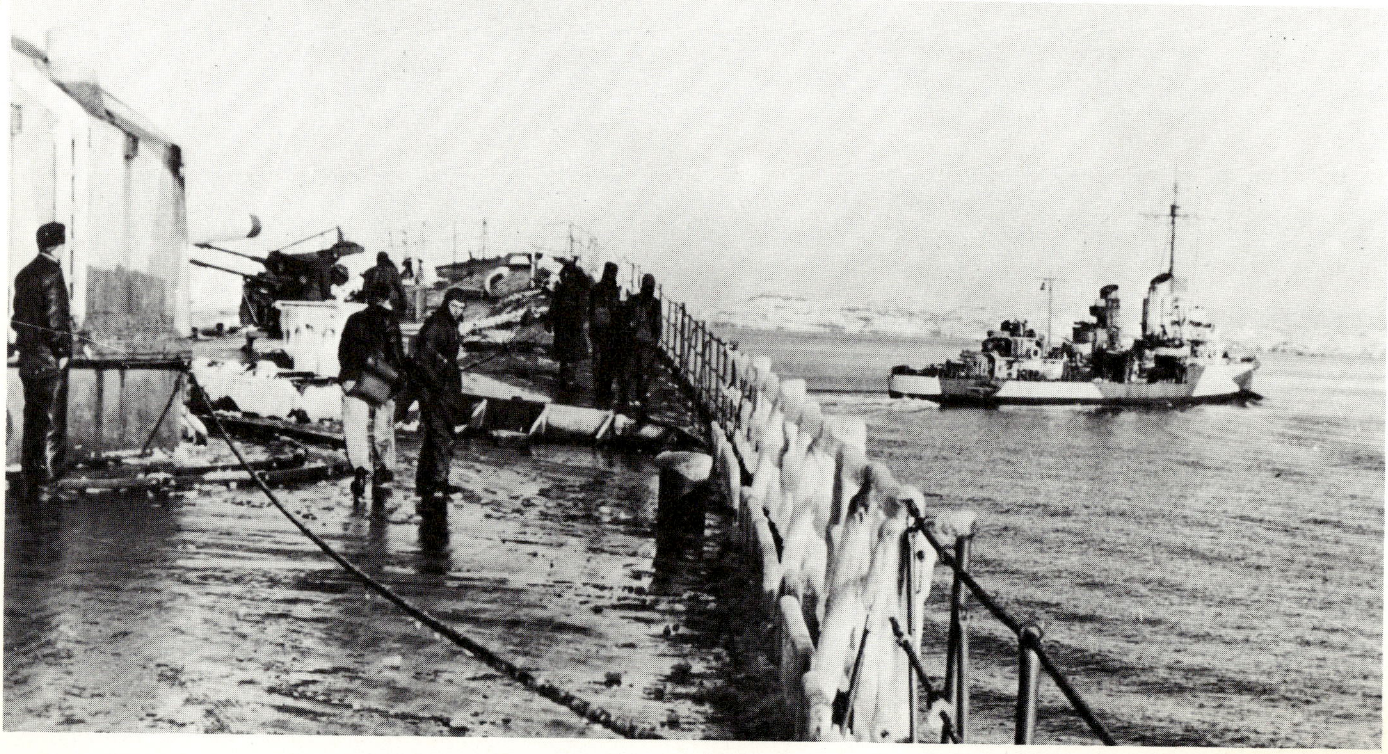

1.21 *Encounter* coming alongside the cruiser *Sheffield* in September 1940. On the quarterdeck of the *Sheffield* a man can be seen waiting to fire a line across the destroyer. *Encounter* has the same sort of modification as *Faulknor* — it will be seen that the ship is without any radar, since destroyers first began to receive this equipment in the latter half of 1940 and then only on newly completing ships. Those already serving on a foreign station had to wait a long time before receiving any. **AR**
CPL

1.22 The destroyer leader *Faulknor* taken from the cruiser *Sheffield* in August 1940 while serving as part of Force 'H' out of Gibraltar. She shows the first modification that this type of vessel underwent — mainmast replaced by short jigger mast and after bank of torpedo-tubes replaced by a single HA 4inch gun. Like many destroyers at this time she is painted a medium grey for the hull with light grey upperworks, and like all leaders in the early part of the war she has a thick black band around her fore funnel to identify her as the flotilla leader. **AR**
CPL

1.23 In Norwegian waters, winter 1942-43. This view shows the icy deck of *Tirpitz* and one of her attendant destroyers. Note, on the bridge of the destroyer, the so-called 'mattress' of her radar aerial. **AF**
Aldo Fraccaroli Collection

1.24 A view of the American destroyer *Butler* of the *Benson/Livermore* class, taken in 1944 from the battleship *Arkansas*. By this period of the war ships of this group were fairly heavily armed with AA mountings. *Butler* has a total of 7 single 20mm mounts and 2 twin 40mm Bofors. She served as a fleet destroyer until November 1944 when she was converted to a high speed minesweeper. **AR**
CPL

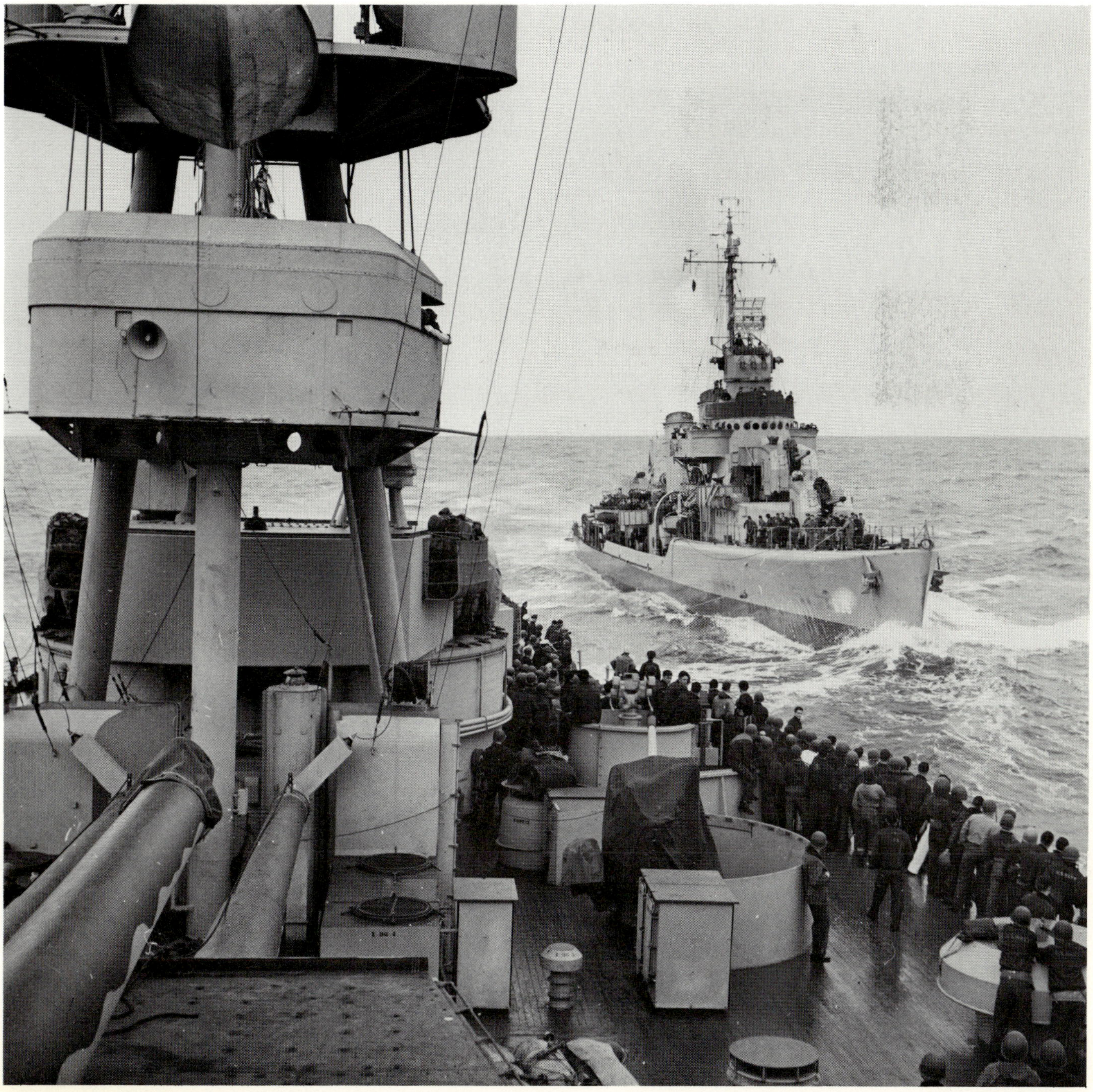
1.24

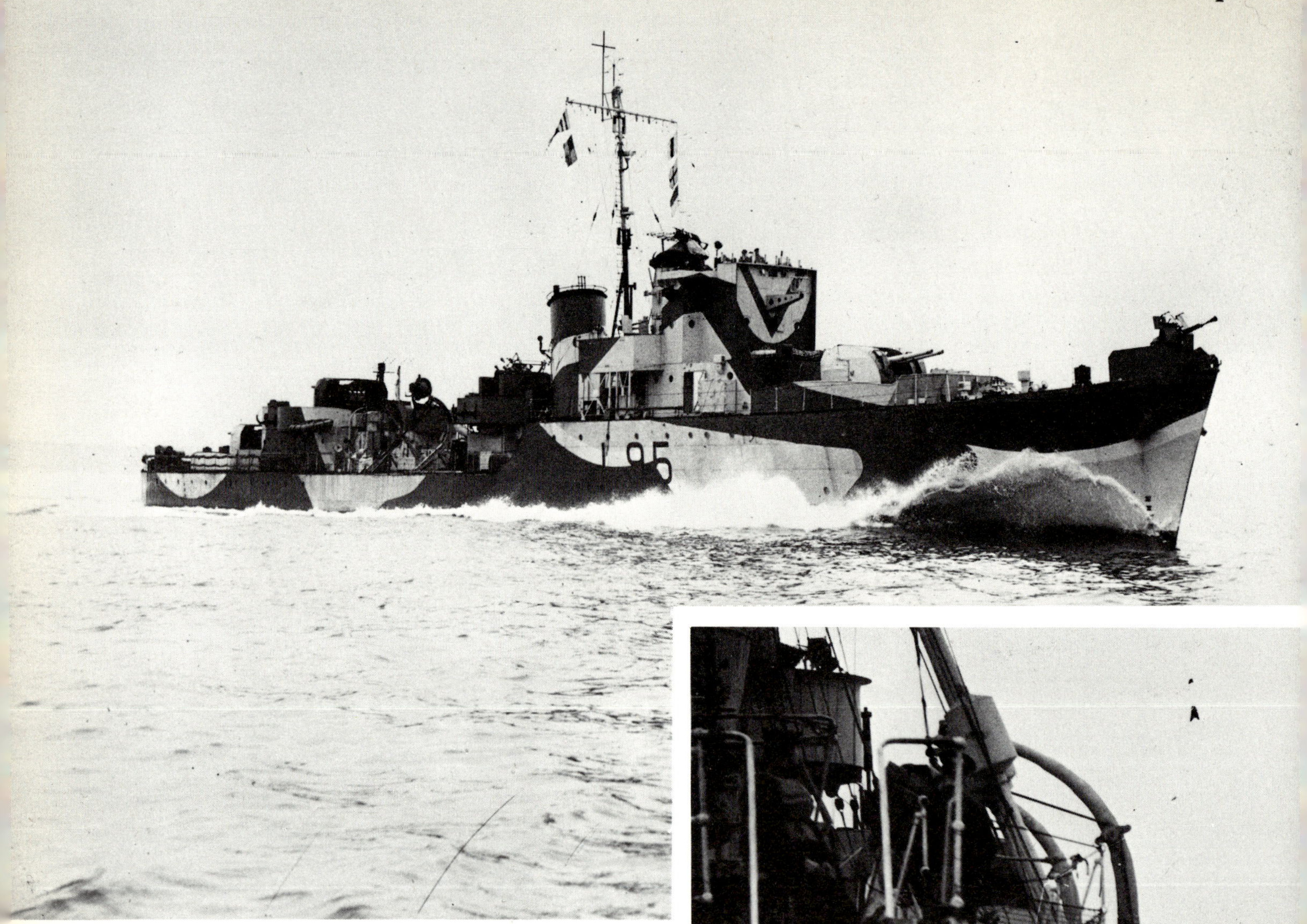

1.25

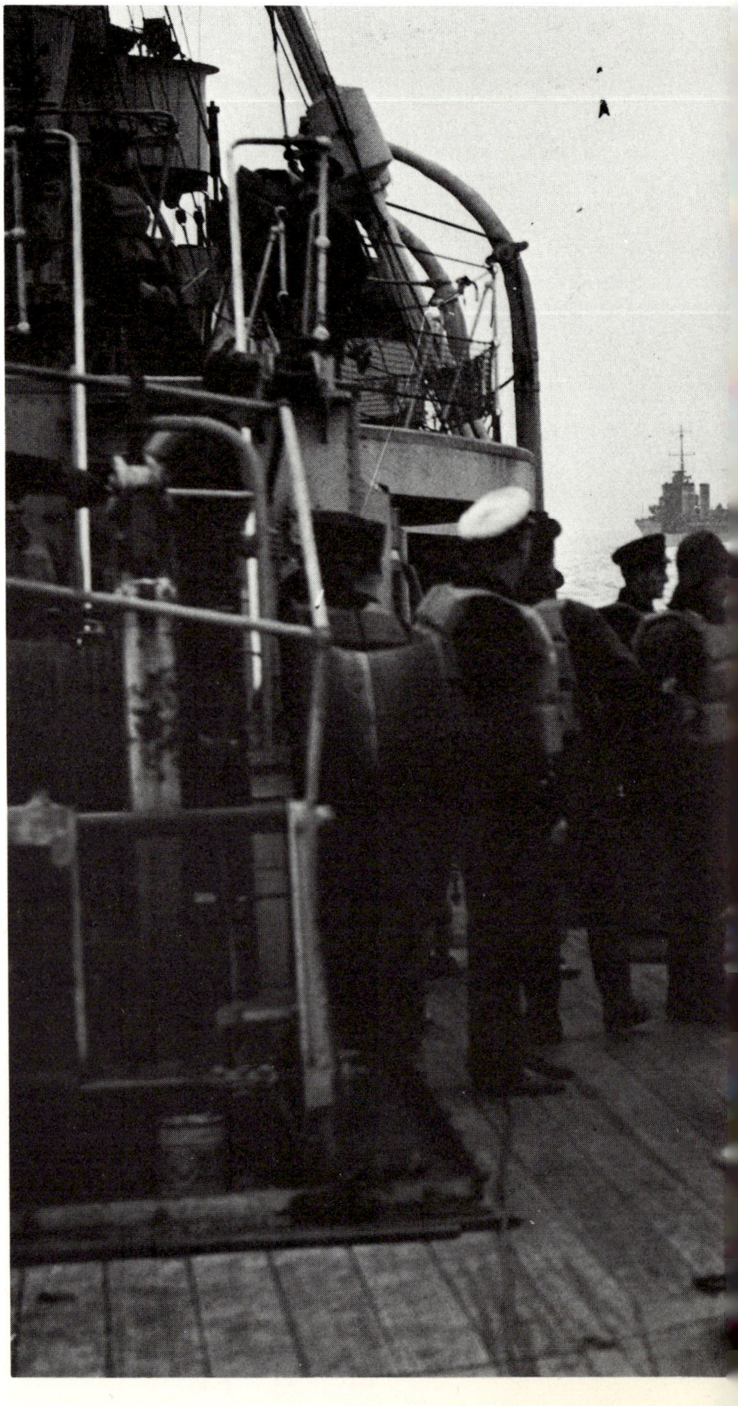

1.25 *Lauderdale,* a *Hunt* Type II, in late 1942 on East Coast convoy work. As well as being fitted with types 285 and 290 gunnery and air warning radar, she has a special TBS (talk-between-ships) Fighter direction outfit standing above the 290 aerial at the mast head. The camouflage is a standard 1942 disruptive type used by several of the class in this period. **AR**
CPL

1.26 *Eglinton,* a *Hunt* Type I, taken in the summer of 1941. There are several reasons for believing the photo was taken at this time: type 286 radar fitted at the mast head only appeared late in 1940; the pom-pom in the bows; the lack of a gunnery radar on the director; all-over one colour, probably medium grey; and lack of single 20mm mounts. **AR**
CPL

1.27 Taken from the deck of the *Halcyon* class minesweeper *Leda* in 1940, this view shows the destroyer *Esk* being led by her sister-ship, *Express.* These two ships of the *E* class were adapted to carry over 60 mines to enable them to provide the Navy with a fast minelaying group if the need arose. To compensate for the weight of the mines, No 4 gun was removed from its place on the quarterdeck as was No 1 gun from the forecastle, along with both sets of torpedo-tubes. Both *Esk* and *Express* had a small refit in mid-1940 which involved the mainmast being replaced by an aerial spreader, and a 3inch HA gun in the after torpedo-tube position, so the photo must have been taken before then. **AR**
CPL

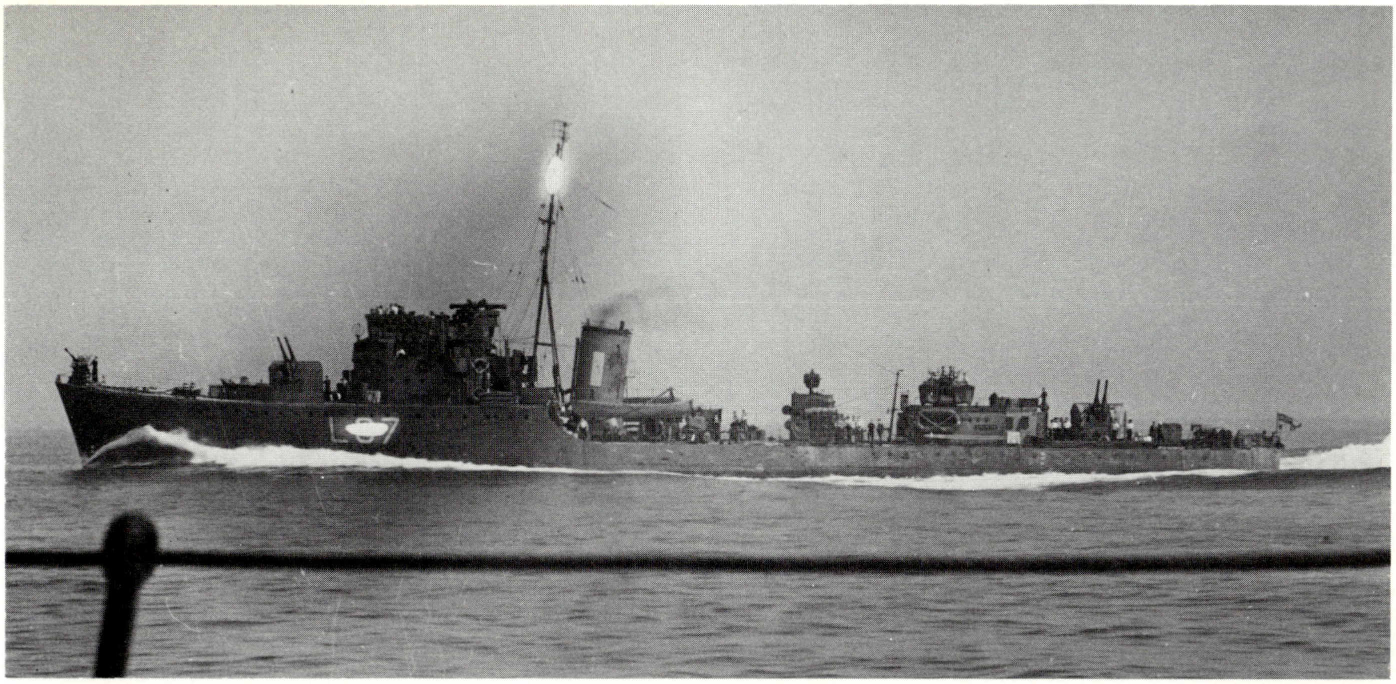

1.26

1.27

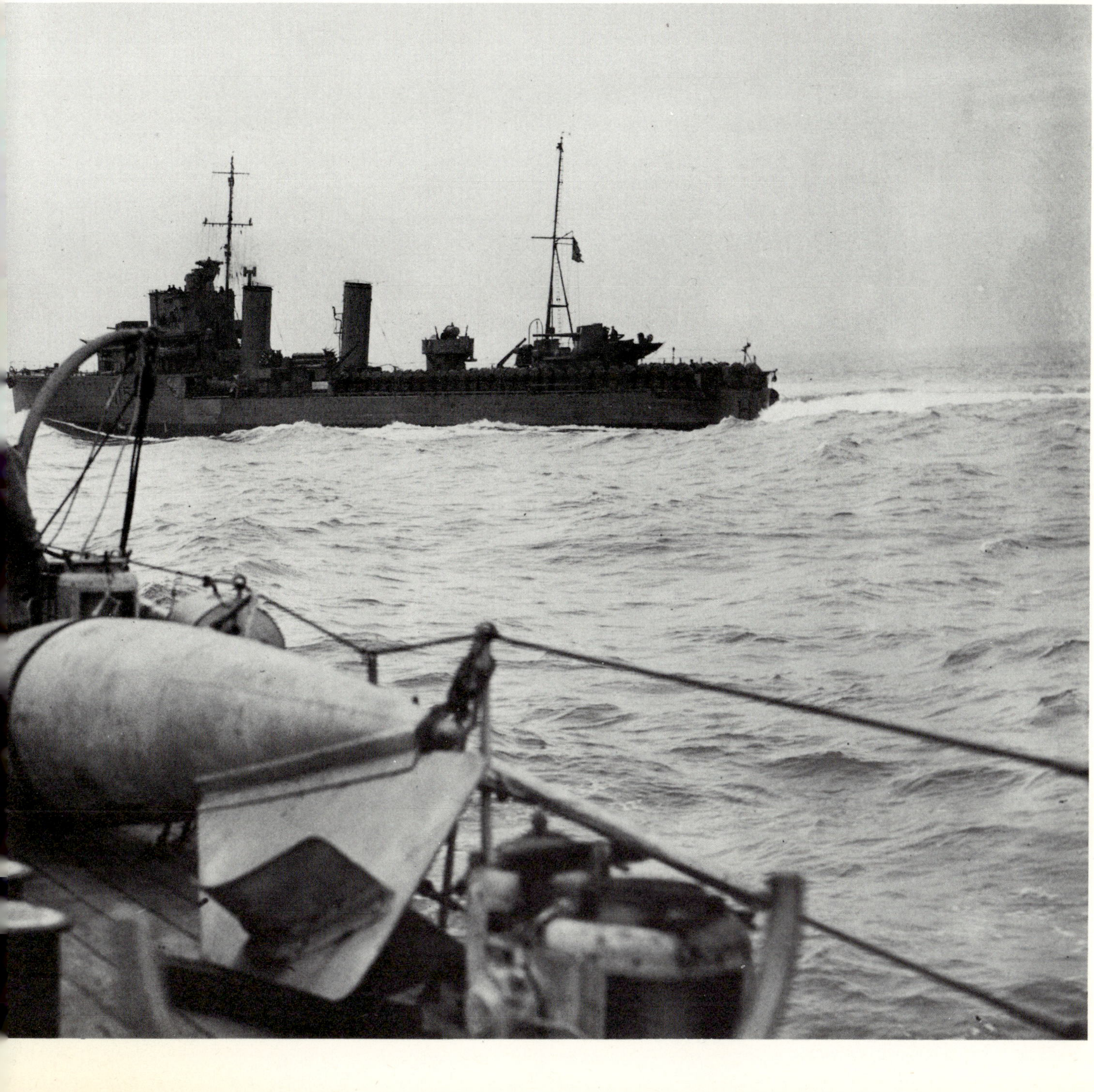

1.28 In 1934 German yards began building large destroyers, displacing 2232 tons standard, armed with five 5inch guns, ten machine guns, eight 21inch torpedo-tubes, and — as usual for German torpedo craft — fitted for minelaying (60 mines); 70 000 SHP machinery achieved a 36 knot contractual speed. Forty destroyers were completed up to 1945; from *Z1, Leberecht Maass;* up to *Z22, Anton Schmitt,* they had a number and a name; from *Z23* onwards they had only the number, 'Z' being for *Zerstörer,* 'destroyer' in German) to *Z39* and *Z43* (because *Z40, Z41* and *Z42*'s construction was stopped in 1942). Gradually the displacement was increased to 3500-3600 tons at full load. This view shows *Z20, Karl Galster* which was launched on 15 June 1938, commissioned on 21 March 1939, and seized by the USSR in 1946. **AF**
Aldo Fraccaroli Collection

1.29 The policy and trend of Italian naval construction before the Second World War was not as well defined as it has been in earlier periods. In fact, during the years of her alliance with Austria-Hungary (1882-1915), Italy built warships designed to fight against French ships, but on 24 May 1915 Italy declared war on Austria, and became an ally to France. From the 1920s onwards, Italy designed fast cruisers and later battleships for specific warfare, namely gun duels with similar British or French ships, whilst the war compelled her to transport soldiers, weapons and supplies to Libya, and to escort the transport ships. The only Italian warships conceived for this type of warfare were the four *Orsa* class escorts and the only subchaser, the *Albatros,* an experimental boat, built in 1931-34. This view shows the deck of *Pegaso,* one of the *Orsa* class escorts. Note the strong armament of depth charges. **AF**
Aldo Fraccaroli Collection

1.30 The destroyer *Shiranui* in dock at Maizuru in July 1942 after being torpedoed by the American submarine *Growler* off the Aleutian Islands. The *Shiranui* was one of the 18 *Kagero* class destroyers. These were heavily armed destroyers mounting six 5inch/50 calibre guns in twin turrets and two quadruple 24inch torpedo-tube mounts. The torpedo mounts (which carried their crew in a completely enclosed turret, as opposed to the open mounts in destroyers of other navies) can be clearly seen fore and aft of the second funnel in the picture. To port and aft of the second torpedo mount can be seen the structure housing torpedo reloads, another feature novel to Japanese destroyers, and which gave them an enormous advantage over Allied vessels. The *Shiranui,* after an eventful career, was finally sunk while escorting a convoy to Leyte in the Philippine Islands on 27 October 1944. **AW**
Japanese Navy

1.31 Two American flush-decked destroyers on their arrival in England in late 1940 after being transferred to the Royal Navy. The majority of the fifty that were taken over entered service in late 1940 and early 1941 in almost their original configuration, dating from the early 1920s, and it was several months before the class began to refit to British standards. Surprisingly the torpedo-tubes shown in the photo were retained (albeit in a reduced number of mountings) until well into 1942 on some vessels. Initial modifications included addition of several depth charge throwers. **AR**
CPL

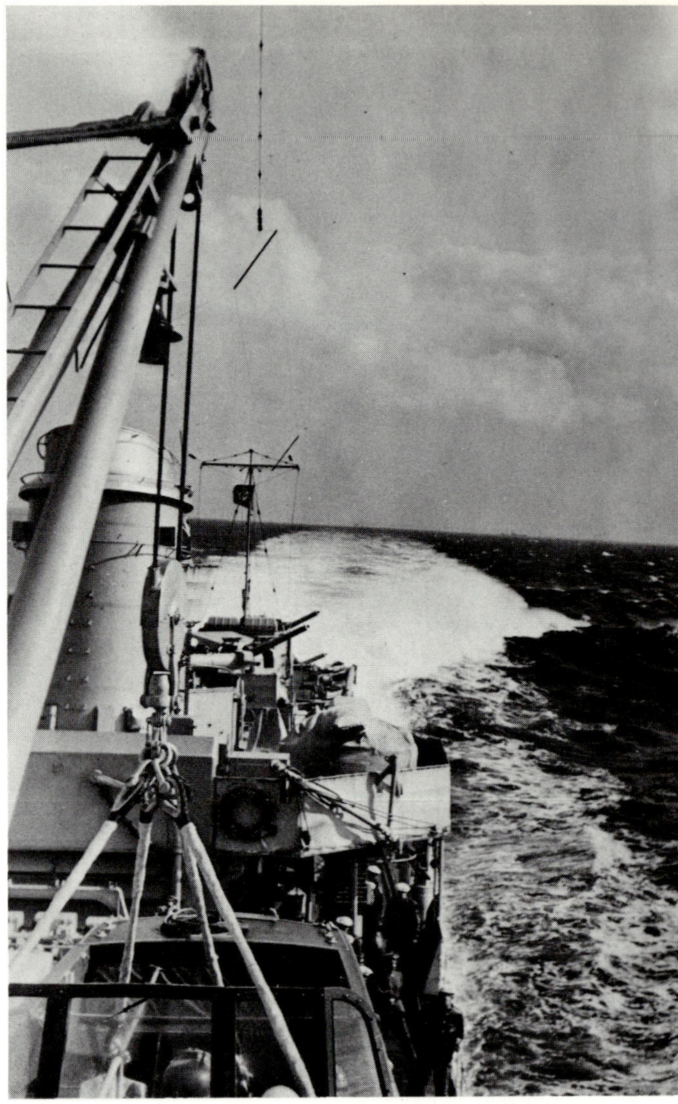

1.2

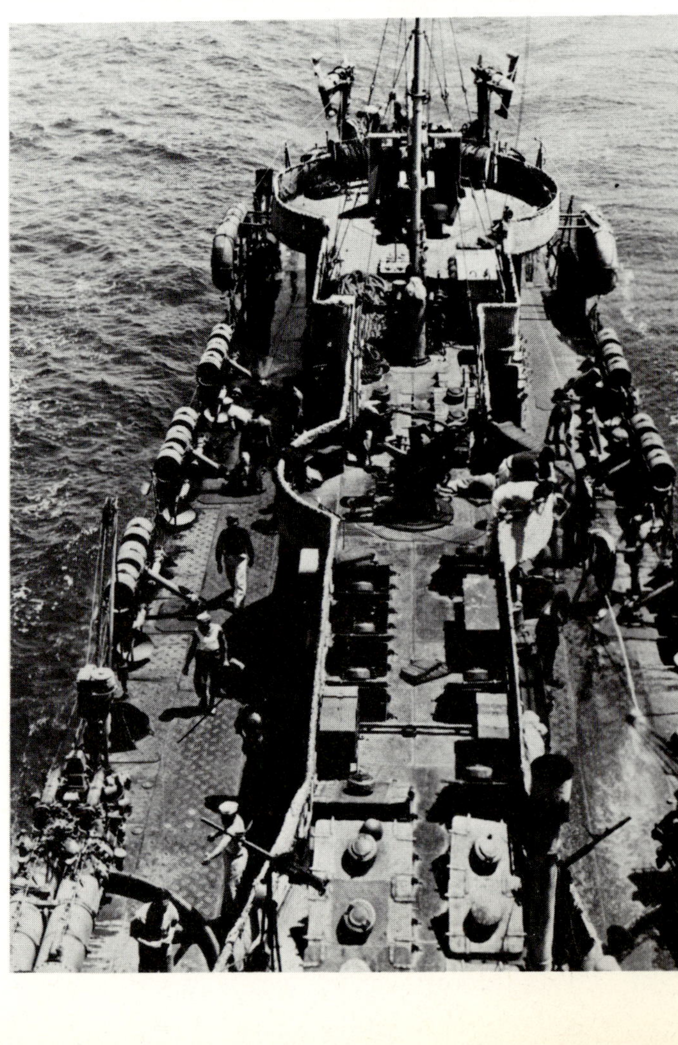

1.2

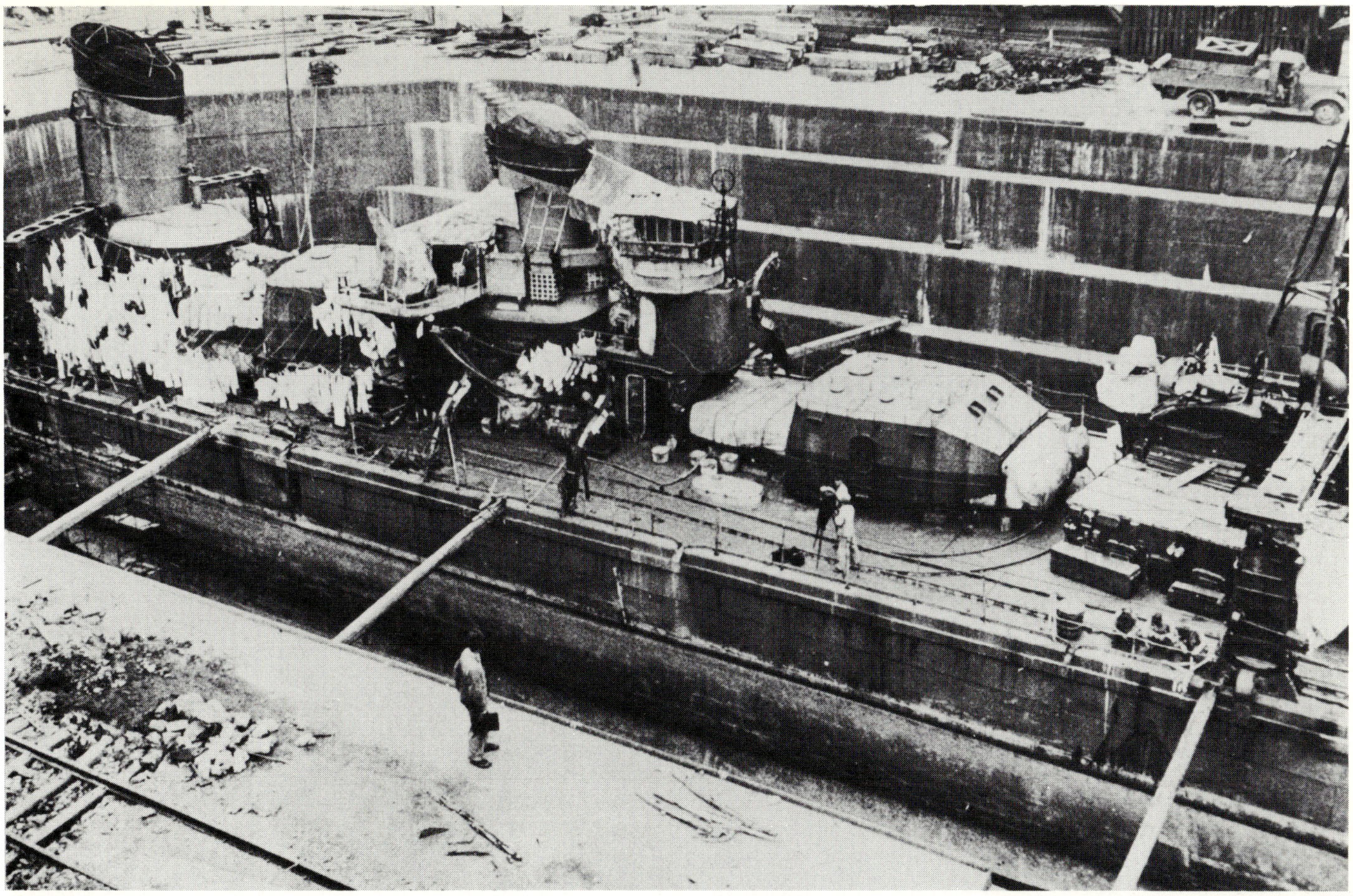

1.30

1.31

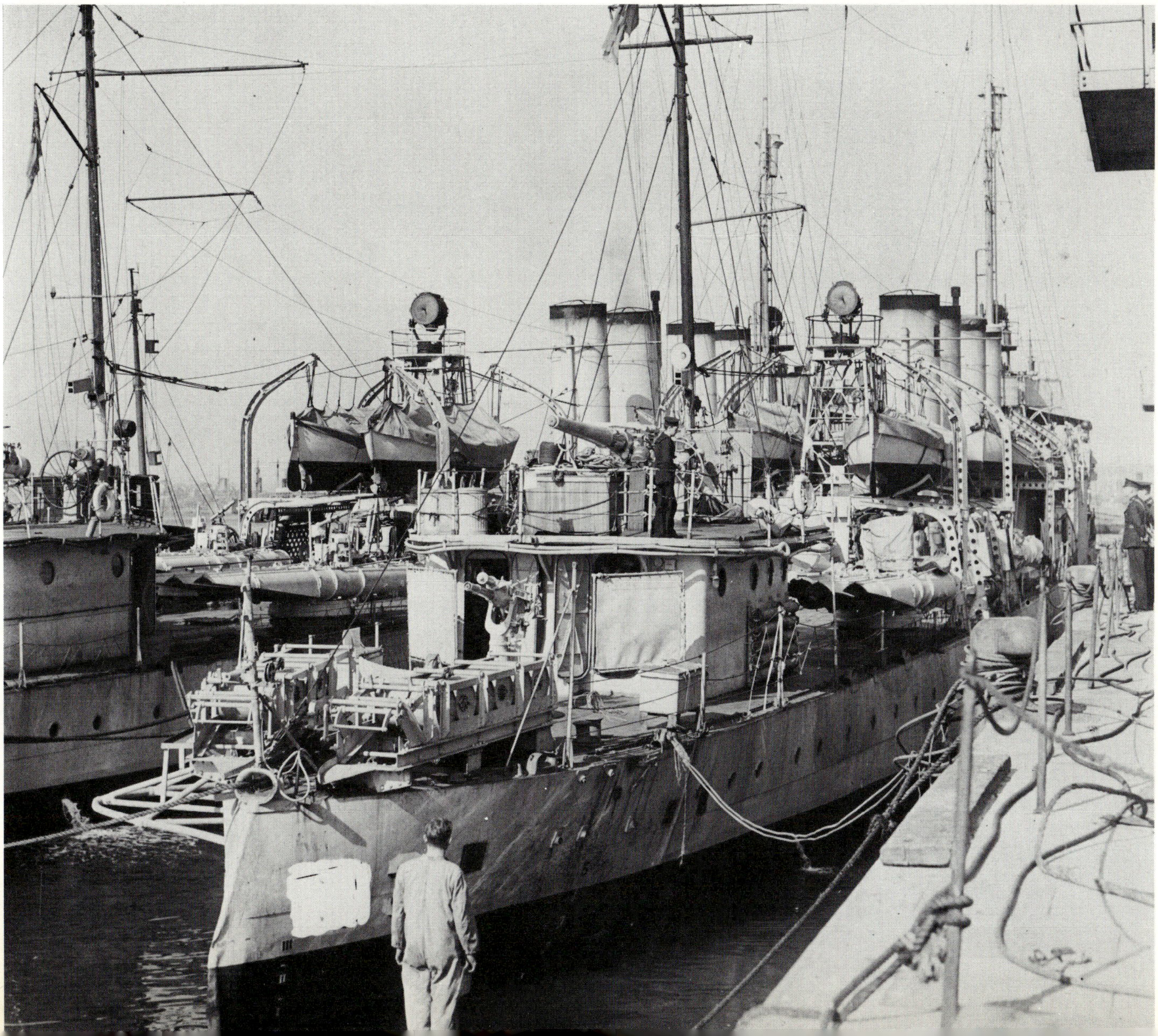

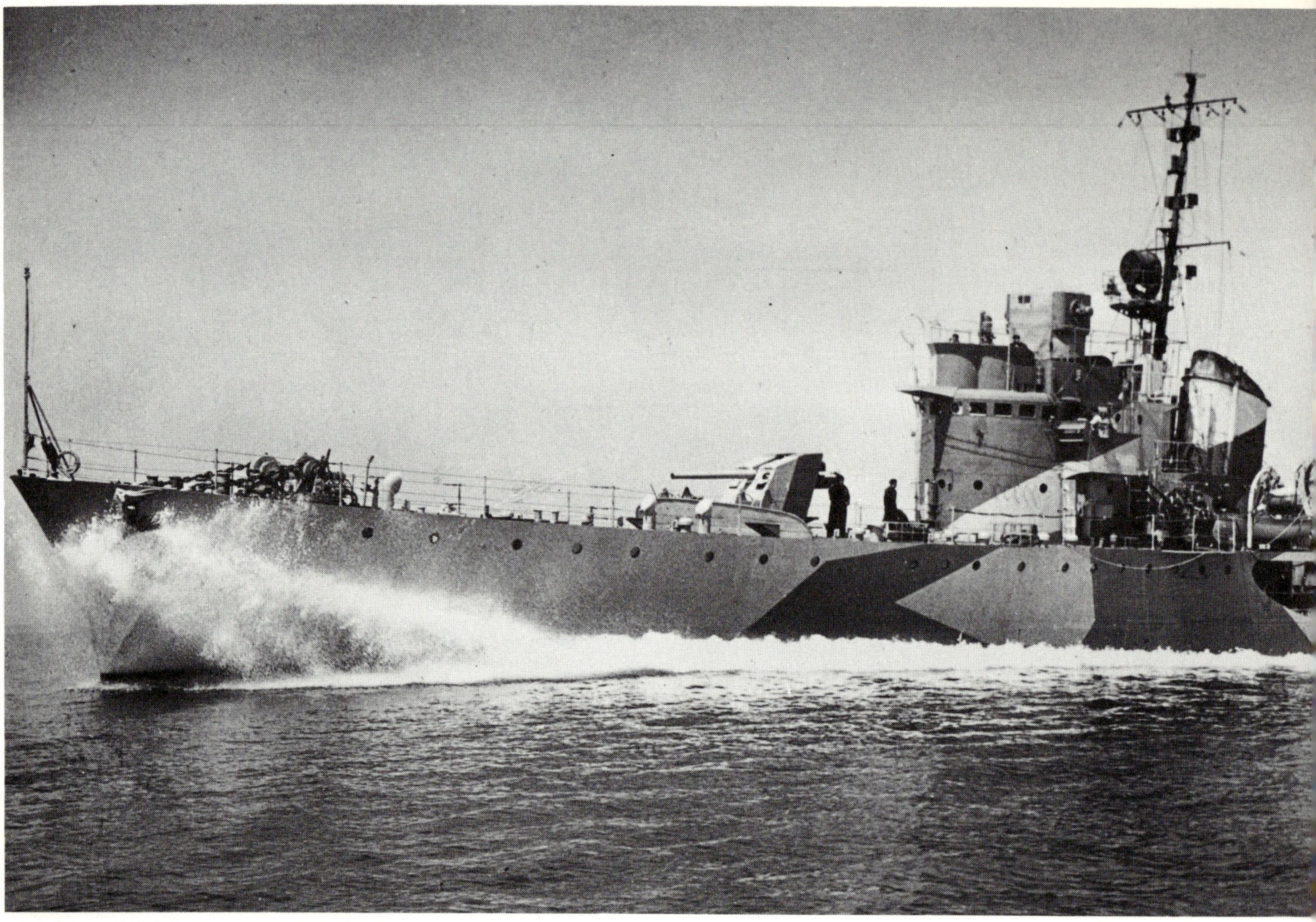

1.32

1.33

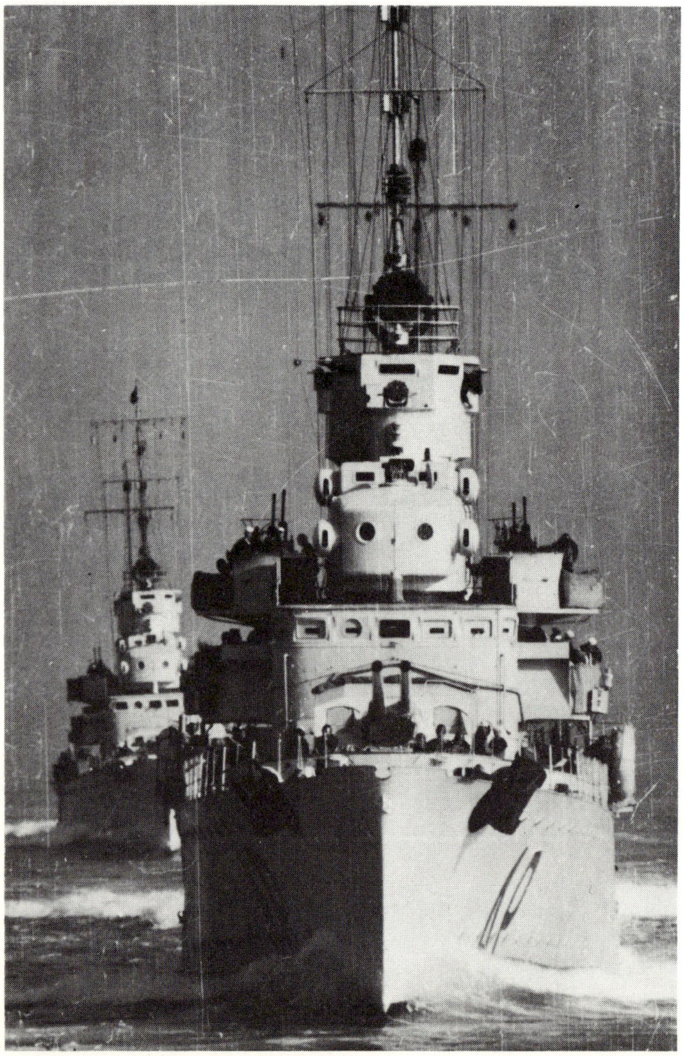

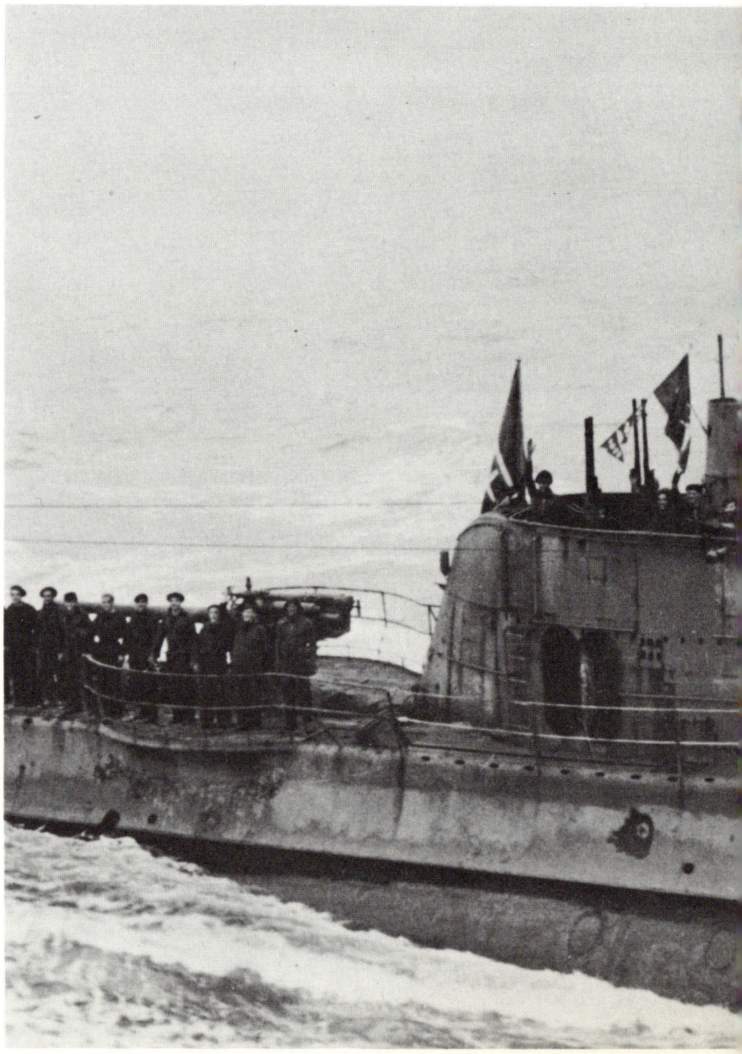

1.34

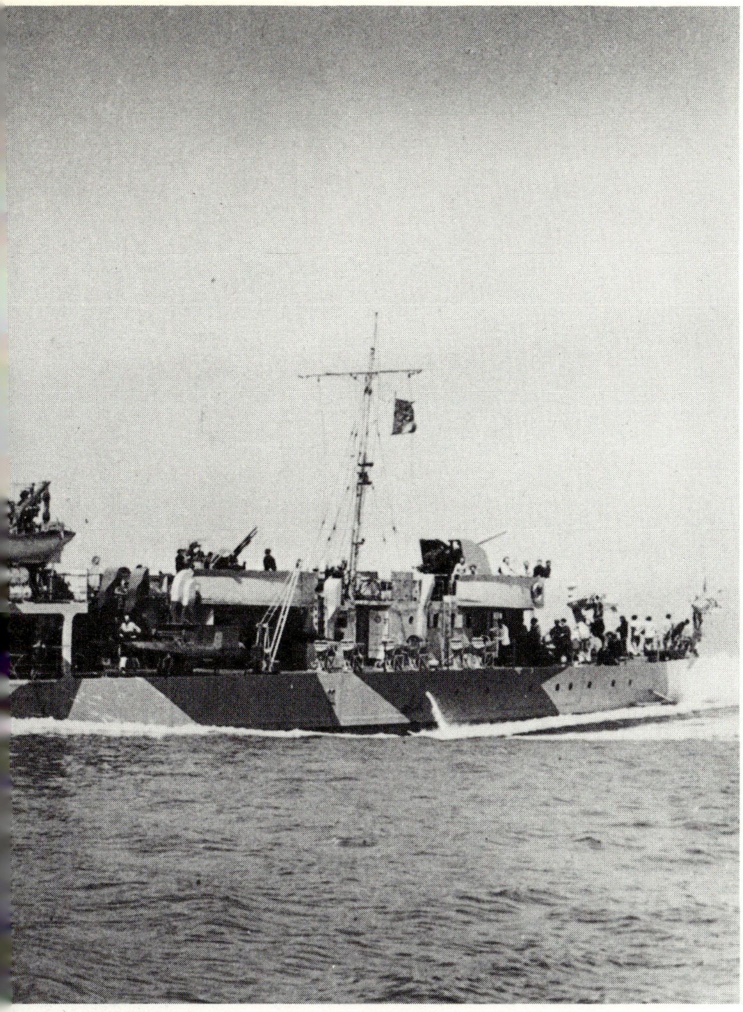

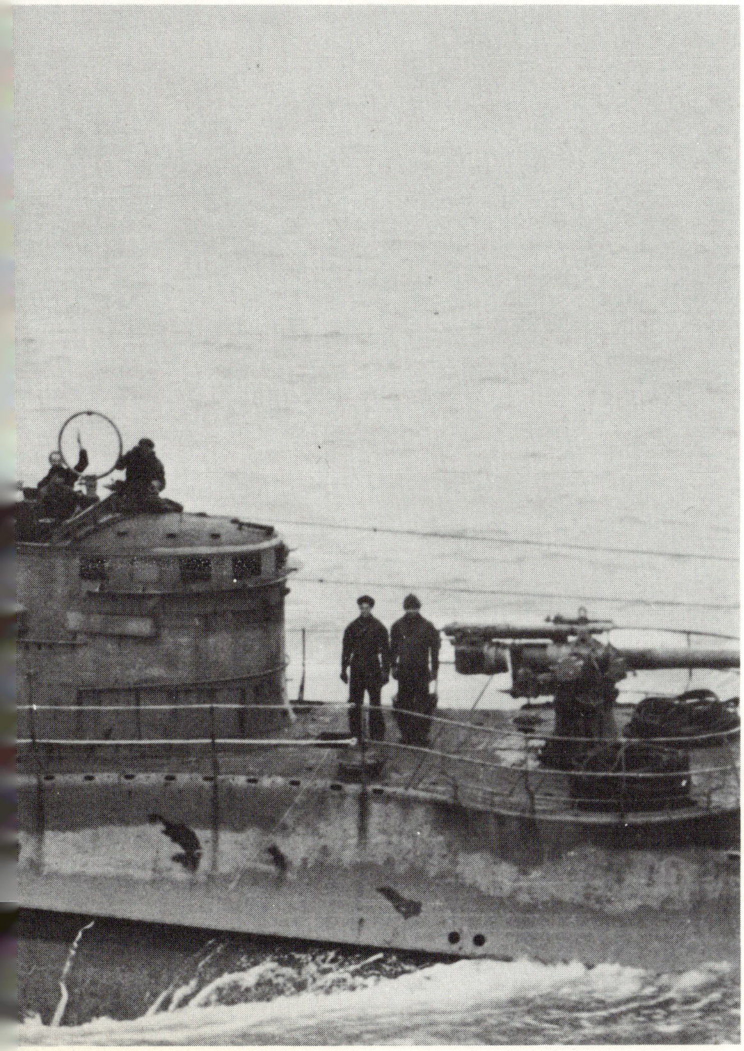

1.32 As the *Orsa* class escorts proved themselves to be excellent seaboats, provided with reasonable independence (for instance, they had an oven, which provided fresh bread daily, while the destroyers and the torpedo-boats employed on escort duties for transport ships had stale bread for their sailors), sixteen other escorts were built during the war. These were called the *Animoso* class, of which we see here the *Ciclone.* Fifteen joined the Italian Navy in 1942-43, while the last *(Intrepido)* was captured by the Germans after Italy's armistice and completed by them. The *Animoso* class boats were about 1700 tons at full load displacement, 25-26 knots, two or three 3.9inch guns, ten to twelve 20mm machine guns, four 17.7inch torpedo-tubes, a large number of throwers and depth charges. **AF**

Aldo Fraccaroli Collection

1.33 The *Soldati* (=Soldiers) class boats were the latest and finest destroyers of the Royal Italian Navy. Their general layout, with a single funnel, derived from the four boats of *Maestrale* class (a remarkable improvement in comparison with the *Dardos* and the *Folgores* of 1929), which had been laid down in 1931 and entered service in 1934. The first series of the *Soldati,* built in 1937-39, comprised: *Alpino, Artigliere, Ascari, Aviere, Bersagliere, Camicia Nera, Carabiniere, Corazziere, Fuciliere, Geniere, Granatiere* and *Lanciere,* of some 2300-2400 tons full load, about 50 000-56 000 SHP and over 40 knots reached during sea trials, with a best sea speed in wartime of about 34 knots. Their armament consisted of four or five 4.7inch guns, eight to twelve 20mm machine guns, six 21inch torpedo-tubes, two to four depth charge throwers, the ability to carry and lay up to 48 mines; 13 to 15 officers and about 200 men. In wartime the AA armament was improved, adding one or two 37mm and some lighter machine guns so reducing to one mounting (only three tubes) the torpedo armament. In this photo *Alpino* is leading, followed by *Fuciliere.* The former was sunk at La Spezia in April 1943, during an air attack; the *Fuciliere* survived the war and was transferred to the USSR in 1950, under the Peace Treaty conditions. During the war, Italy laid down a second series of seven slightly improved *Soldati,* and was able to complete five of them. **AF**

Aldo Fraccaroli Collection

1.34 The submarine *Barbarigo* running along the Gironde river, while returning to her base at Bordeaux, officially called 'Betasom' by the Italian submariners: *Beta* being the phonetic spelling in the Italian Navy of the letter B, initial of Bordeaux; *som,* being the Italian naval prefix for *sommergibile* (= submarine). For instance, *Maricosom* meant: *Mari,* prefix for *Marina* (Navy); *co* for *Comando* (Command, Headquarters); *sommergibili;* that is *Comando (in Capo) della Squadra Sommergibili* (Command-in-Chief of the Submarine Forces).

Barbarigo was one of the nine boats of the *Marcello* class of 1063/1317 tons, 18/8 knots, eight 21inch torpedo-tubes (with a total of 16 torpedoes aboard), two 3.9inch guns and four 13.2mm machine guns. *Barbarigo* was particularly well known because her captain, Commander Enzo Grossi, claimed to have sunk two American battleships in May 1942 and in October 1942. **AF**

Aldo Fraccaroli Collection

1.35 *Atascosa* (AO-66) comes alongside *Lexington* (CV-16) on 25 January 1945. A tricky manoeuvre even in calm weather; underway refuelling required superb seamanship in rough seas. **LS**
USN

1.36 This unusual view of Fairmile 'D' class MTB/MGBs was banned at the time it was taken. The reason is obvious: the 'D' on the far side is in serious trouble and listing heavily to port. What is not known is the cause of the difficulty, but the guns cocked up and the general air of activity suggest battle-damage. Note the heavy armament, a 2pdr forward, twin 0.5inch machine guns port and starboard and twin 20mm Oerlikons aft. The second 'Dog' appears to have a single 6pdr on the quarterdeck as well. **AP**
CPL

1.37 The corvette *Clematis* going to the assistance of a small coaster. This photo was taken in late 1940. She lacks any form of radar and has to rely purely on visual means of keeping lookout, and searching for the enemy, and to this end she has a special lookout position built on to the top of the compass house on the bridge. **AR**
CPL

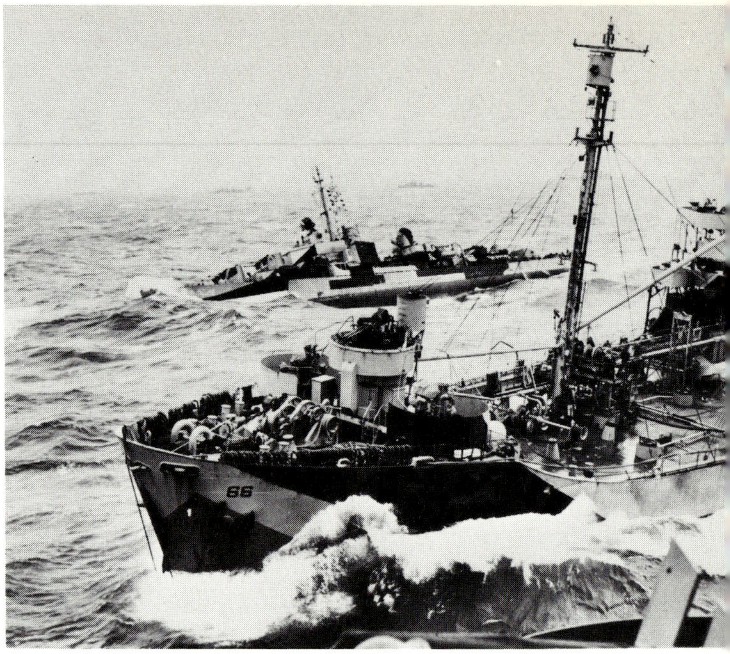

1.35

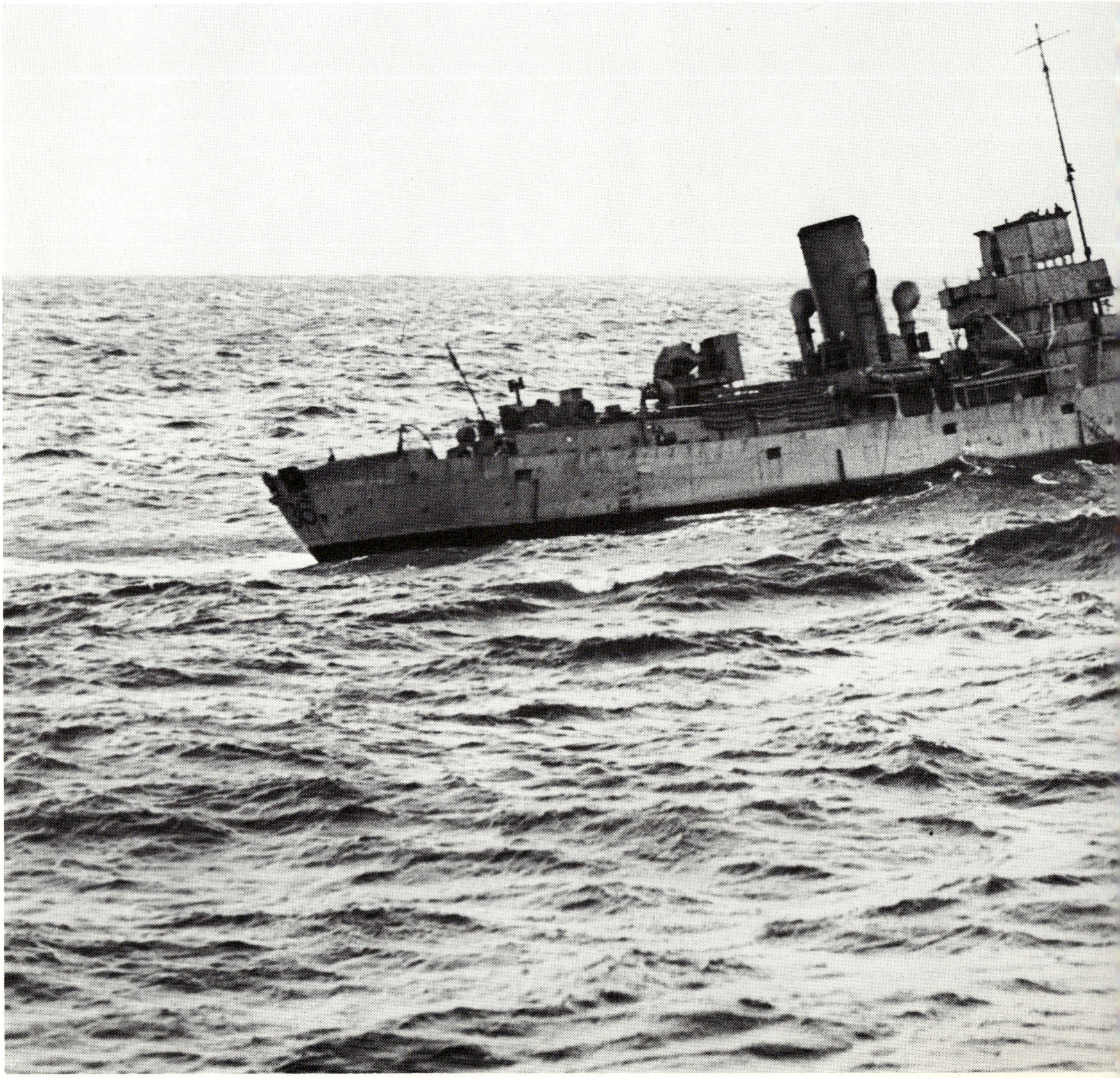

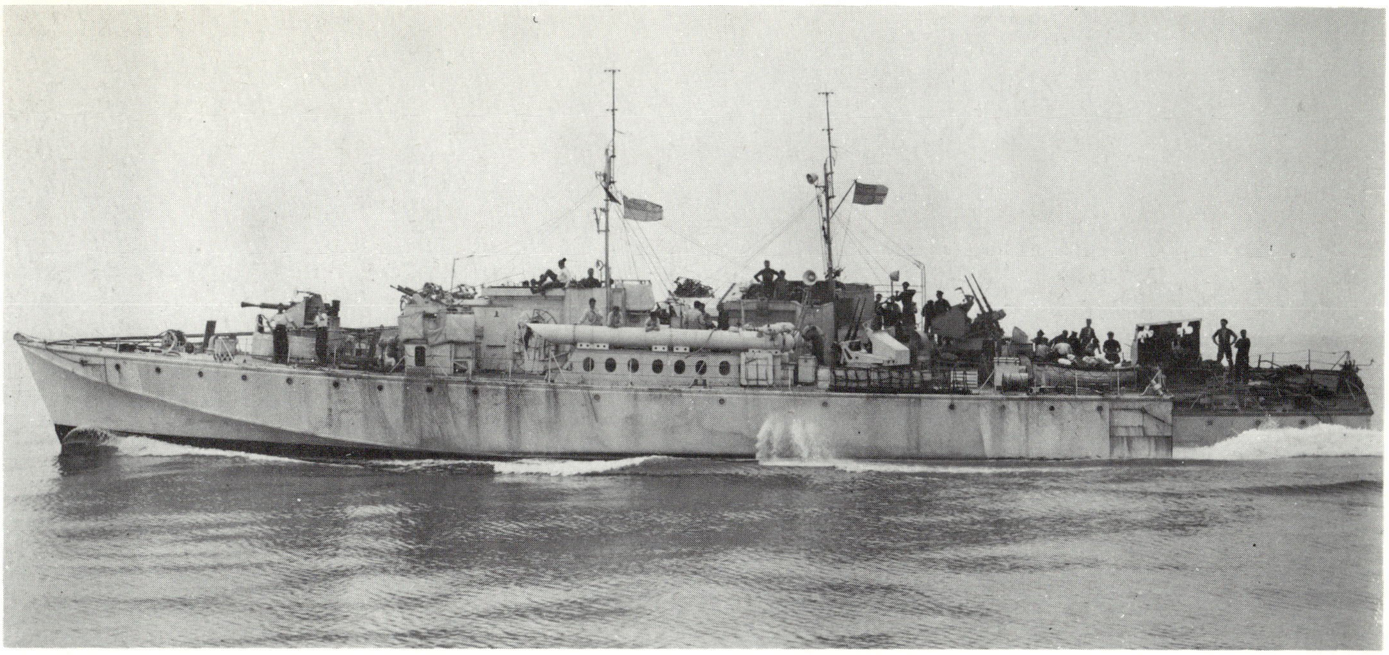

1.36

1.37

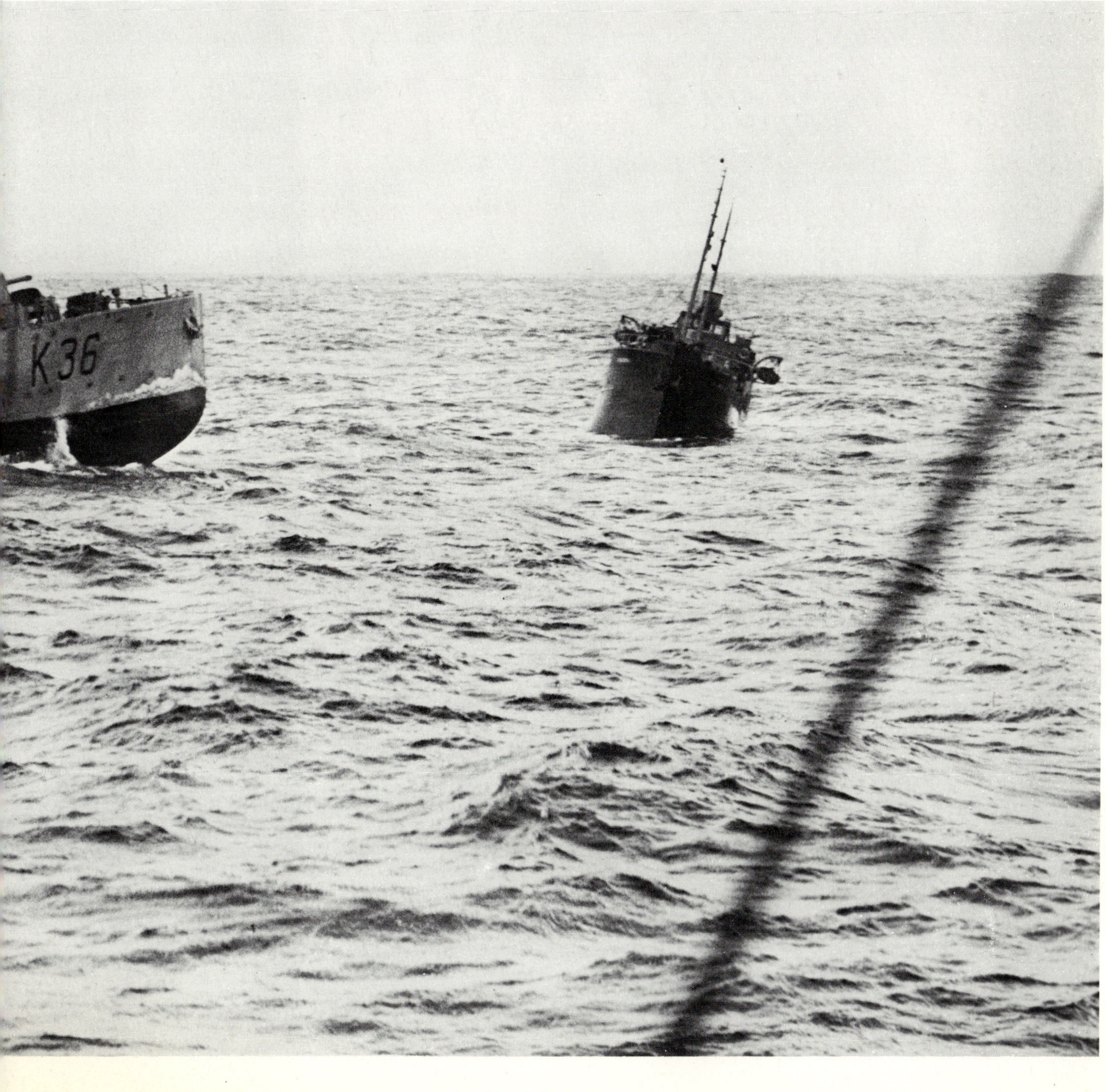

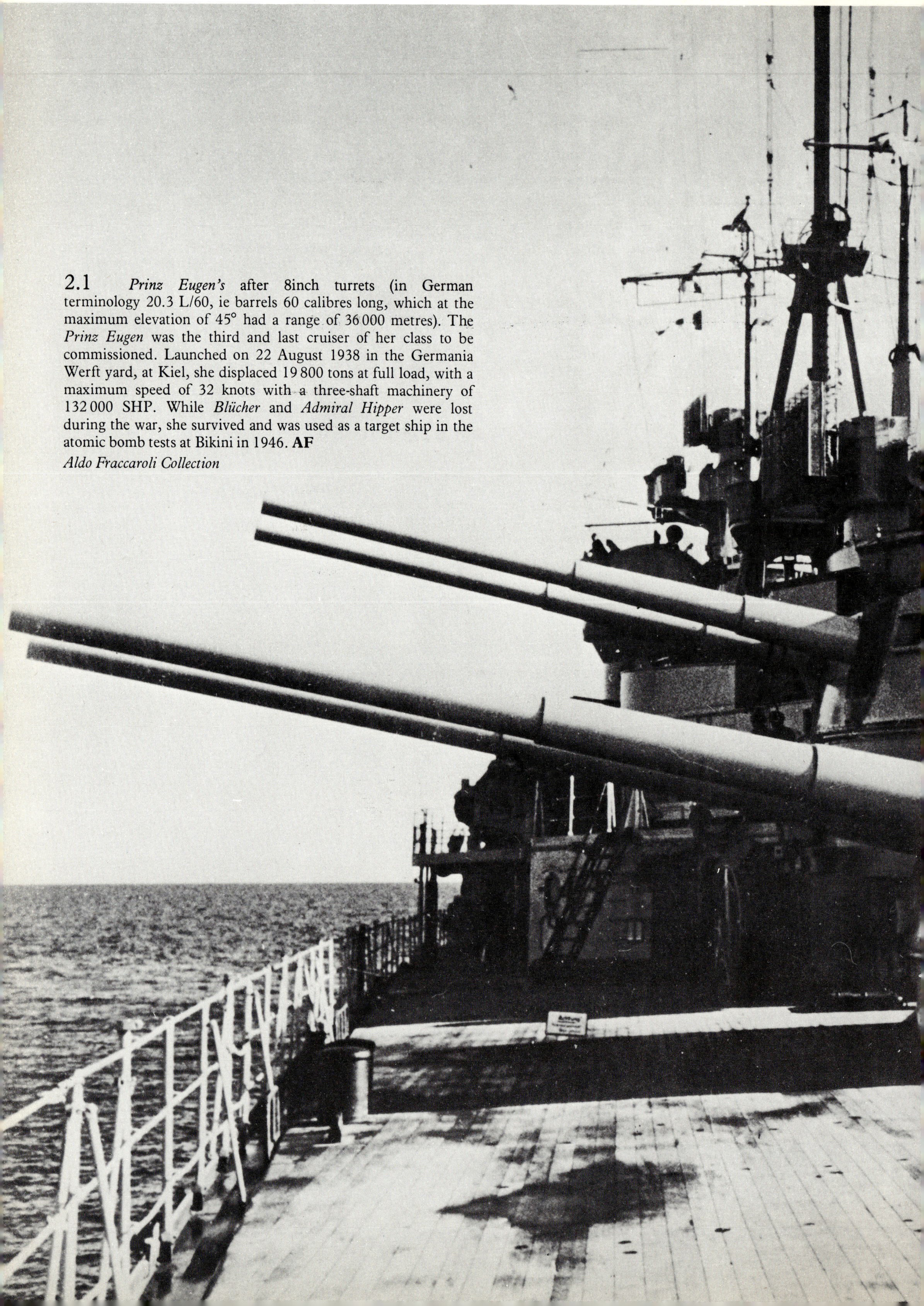

2.1 *Prinz Eugen's* after 8inch turrets (in German terminology 20.3 L/60, ie barrels 60 calibres long, which at the maximum elevation of 45° had a range of 36 000 metres). The *Prinz Eugen* was the third and last cruiser of her class to be commissioned. Launched on 22 August 1938 in the Germania Werft yard, at Kiel, she displaced 19 800 tons at full load, with a maximum speed of 32 knots with a three-shaft machinery of 132 000 SHP. While *Blücher* and *Admiral Hipper* were lost during the war, she survived and was used as a target ship in the atomic bomb tests at Bikini in 1946. **AF**
Aldo Fraccaroli Collection

2. Weapons and Equipment

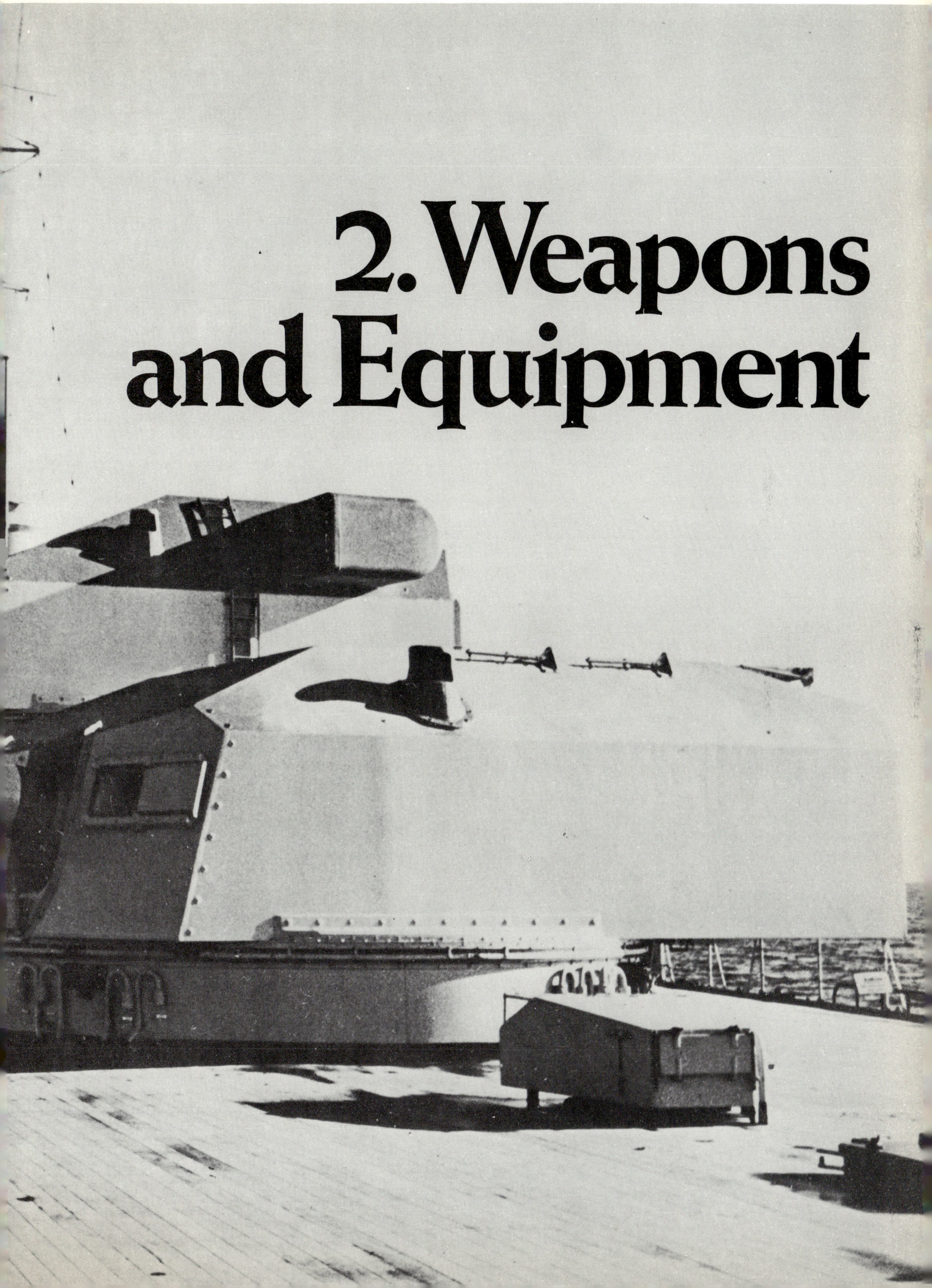

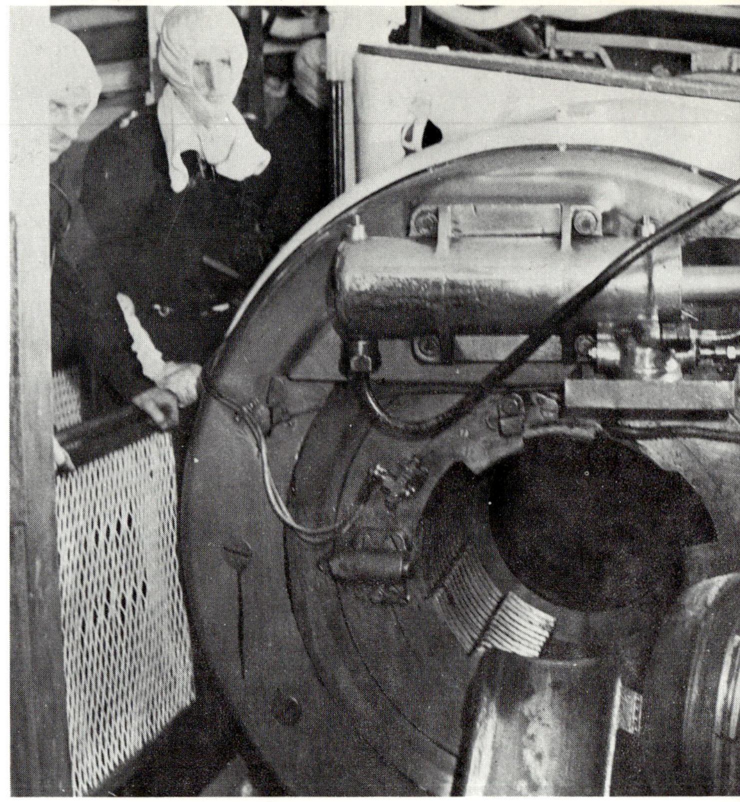

2.2 The breech of one of *Warspite*'s 15inch Mk I guns showing the interrupted screw breech block swung open. The triple radius threads, in three steps, meant that only one twelfth of a turn was required to lock the breech. The mechanism across the top of the breech ring is the hydraulic gear for operating the breech mechanism. The tray at the bottom centre of the breech ring served as a guide for the shell and cordite being rammed into the gun and also protected the threads in the breech ring. **JR**
CPL

2.3 Looking towards the rear of a twin 15inch gun turret from the right side aboard HMS *Warspite,* August 1944. In the bottom right hand corner is the breech block of the right gun in the open position. The breech worker in the lower foreground is inserting a firing tube in the centre of the breech block. The tube, which was like the cartridge of a large bullet, was fired by the electric (or percussion) firing mechanism which in turn set off the main charge in the gun chamber. **JR**
CPL

2.4 'A' and 'B' turrets (*Torre 1* and *Torre 2*, in Italian terminology) of the battleship *Roma,* completing in the 'San Marco' yard of Cantieri Riuniti dell'Adriatico, at Trieste, summer 1942. Note the diagonal stripes (white and red) on the forecastle, the 15inch guns and the conning tower, unhappily not supplied with radar, because Italy was slow developing this aspect of technology. The first radar set aboard an Italian battleship was mounted aboard the battleship *Littorio* in September 1941; her sister-ship *Vittorio Veneto* received her radar set in June 1943; and *Roma,* only in August 1943, a few weeks before Italy's armistice.

A complete triple mounting (turret with guns) of 15inch guns weighed 1559.67 tons, each barrel itself weighing 108.16 tons. In Italian terminology, the 15inch guns were called '381/50', where '381' is the calibre (bore) in mm, and '50' (calibres) is the length of the barrel (19.05 m). The accuracy of fire of Italian ordnance was very inferior to that of German and British guns. **AF**
Aldo Fraccaroli Collection

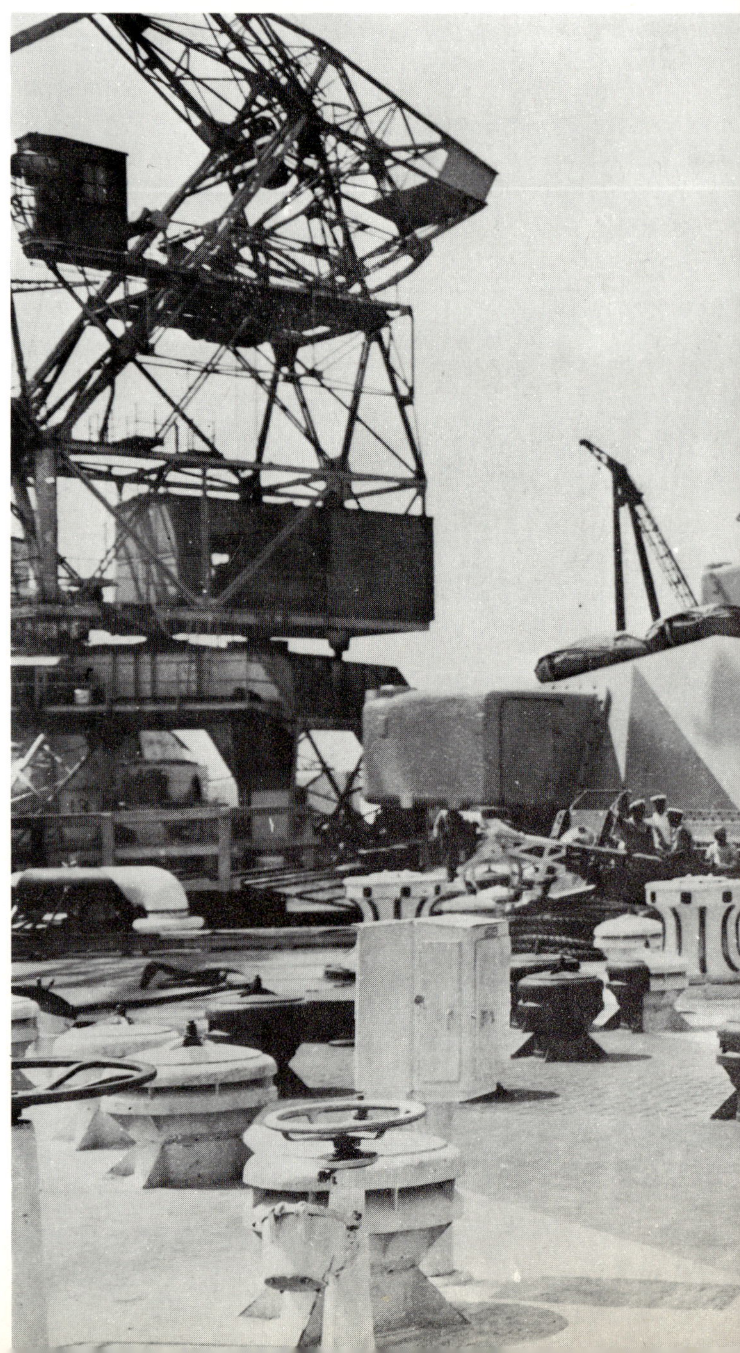

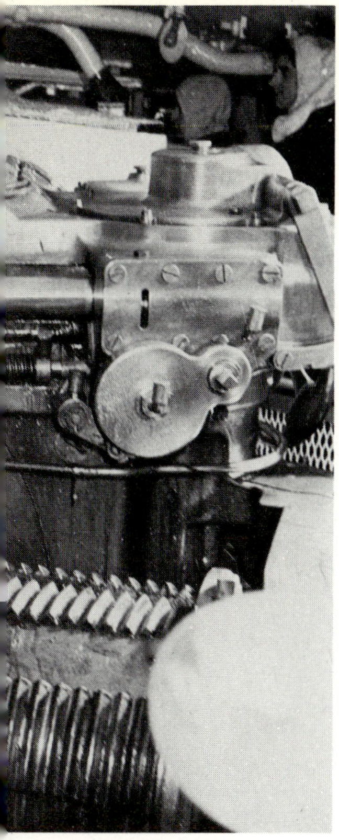

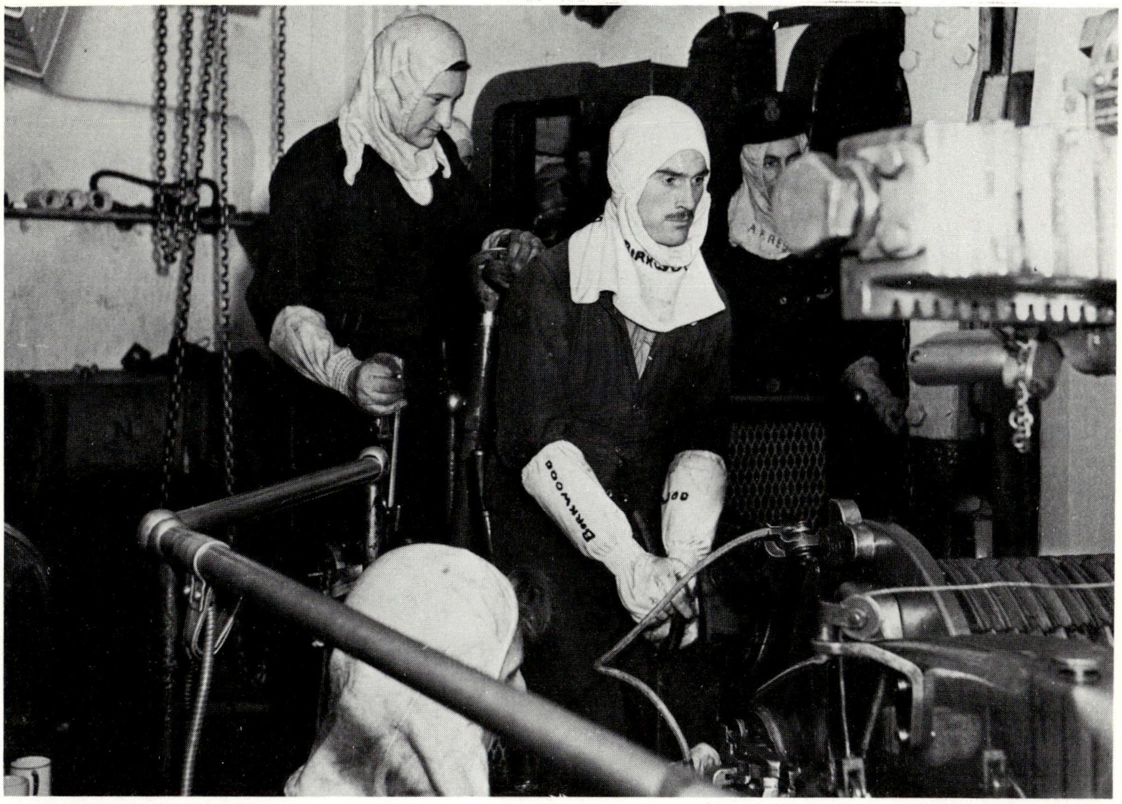

2.3

2.4

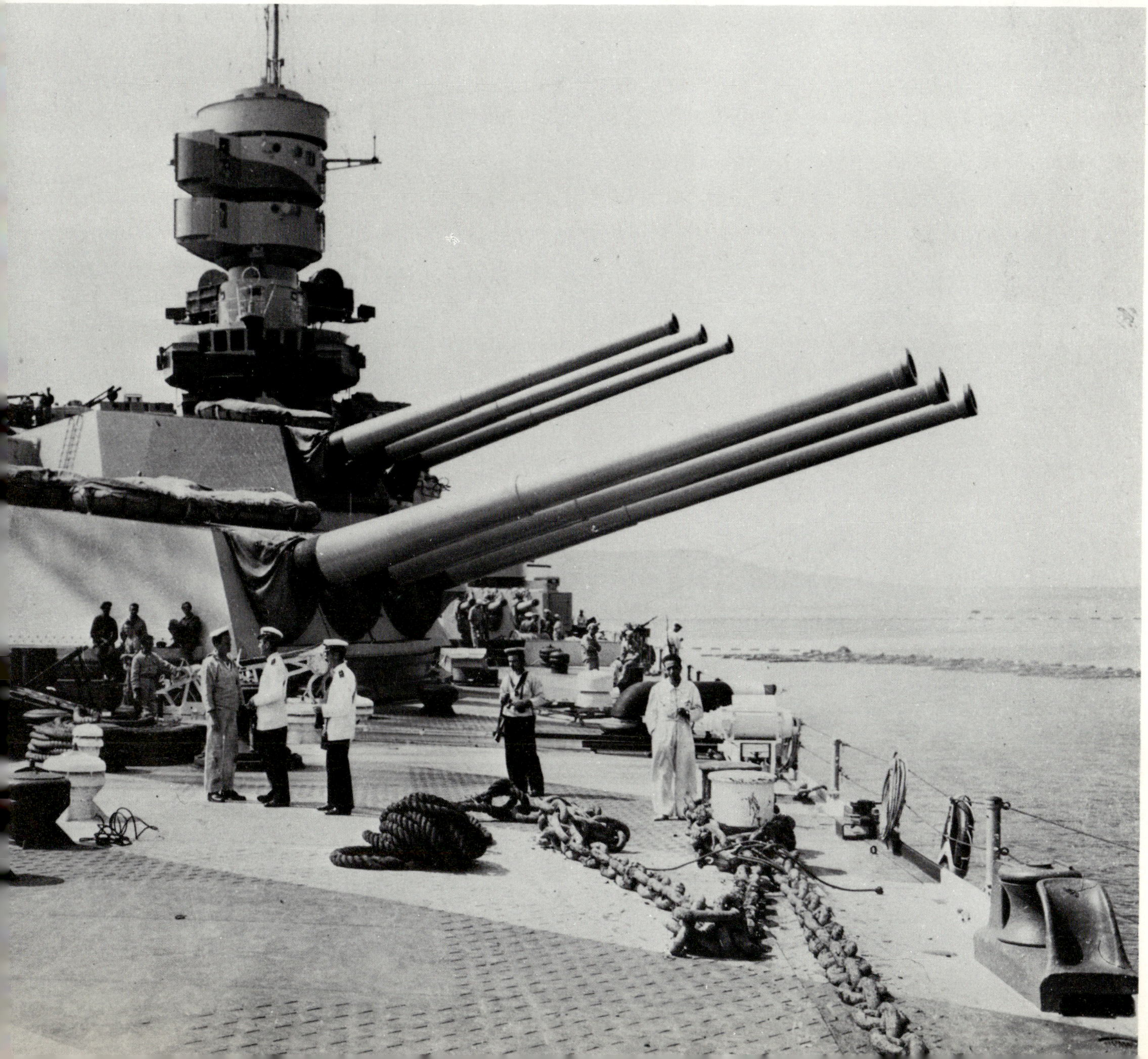

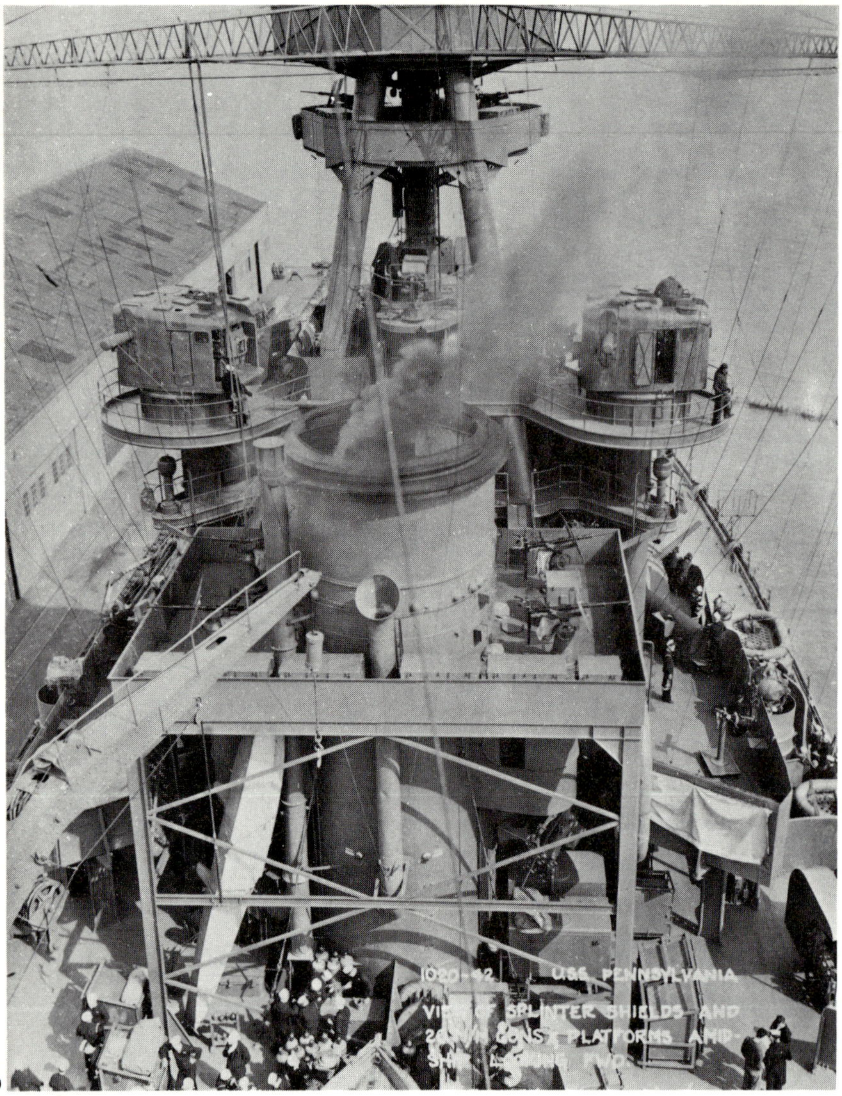
1020-42
PENNSYLVANIA
SPLINTER SHIELDS AND
PLATFORMS

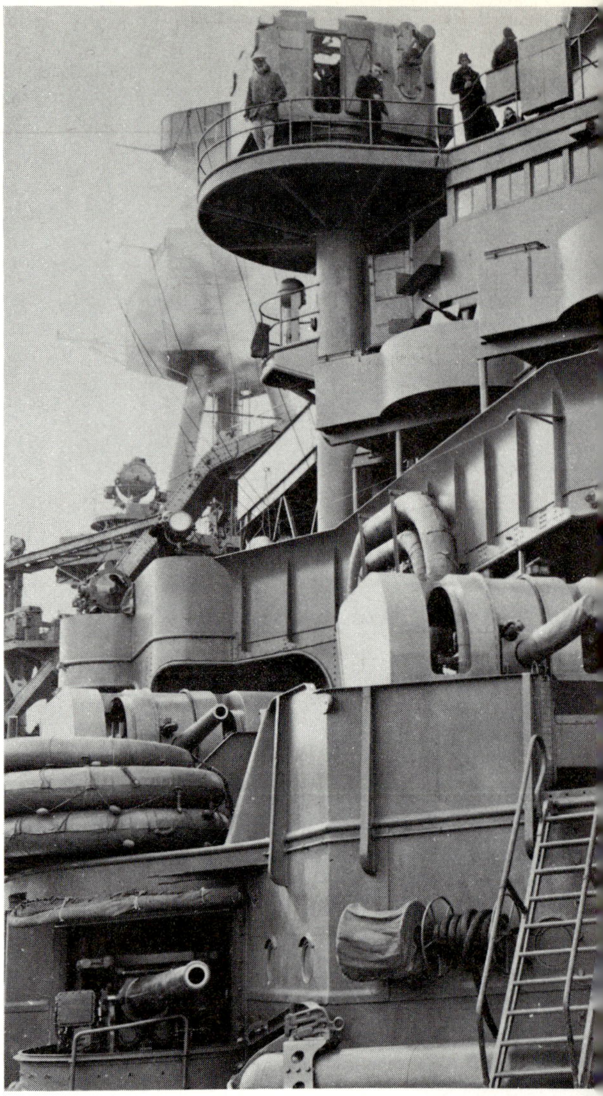

2.6

2.8

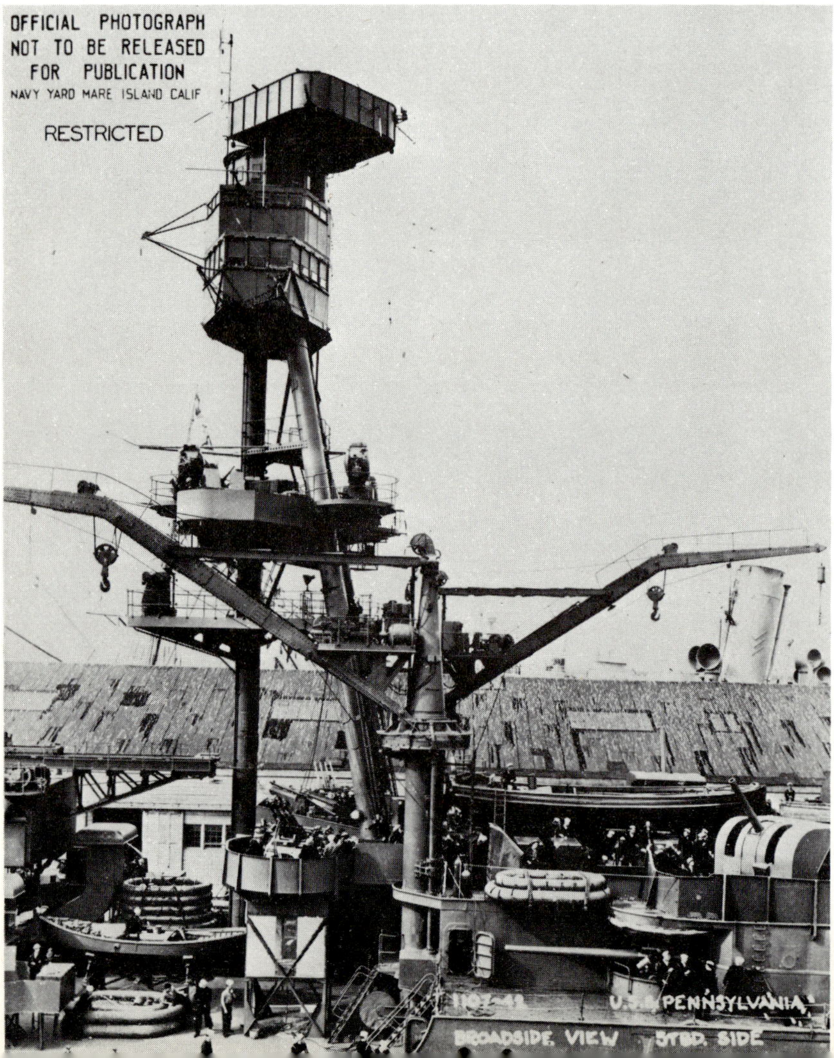
OFFICIAL PHOTOGRAPH
NOT TO BE RELEASED
FOR PUBLICATION
NAVY YARD MARE ISLAND CALIF
RESTRICTED
PENNSYLVANIA
VIEW
SIDE

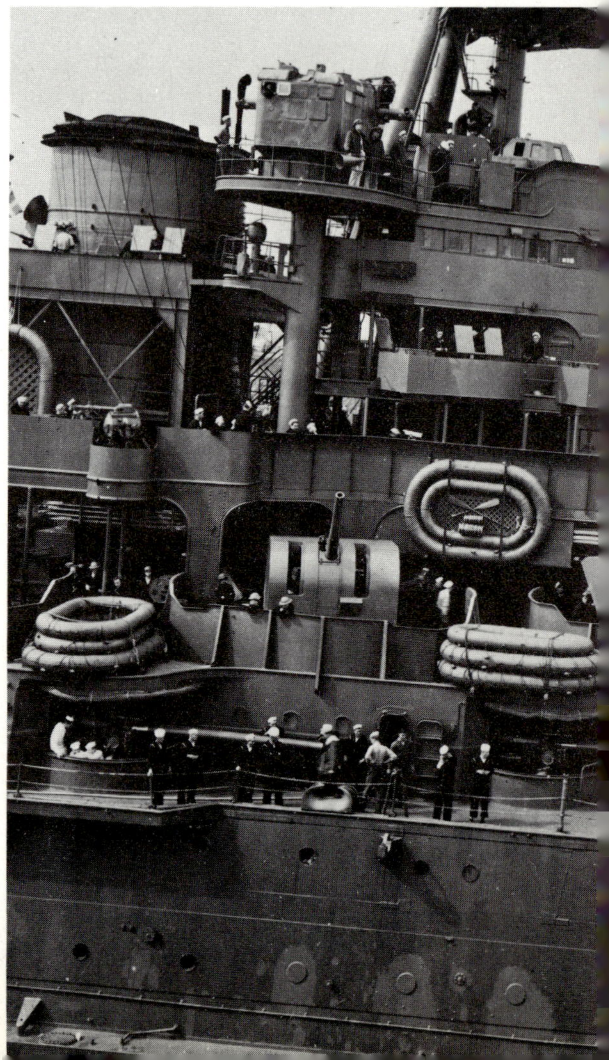

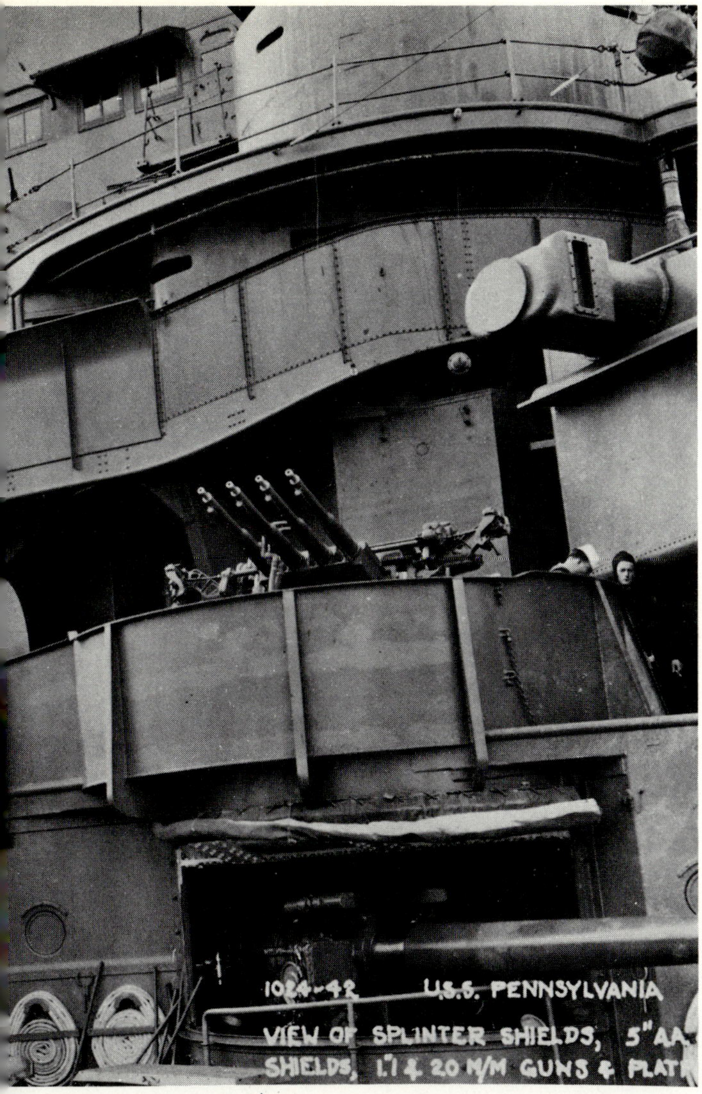

2.5

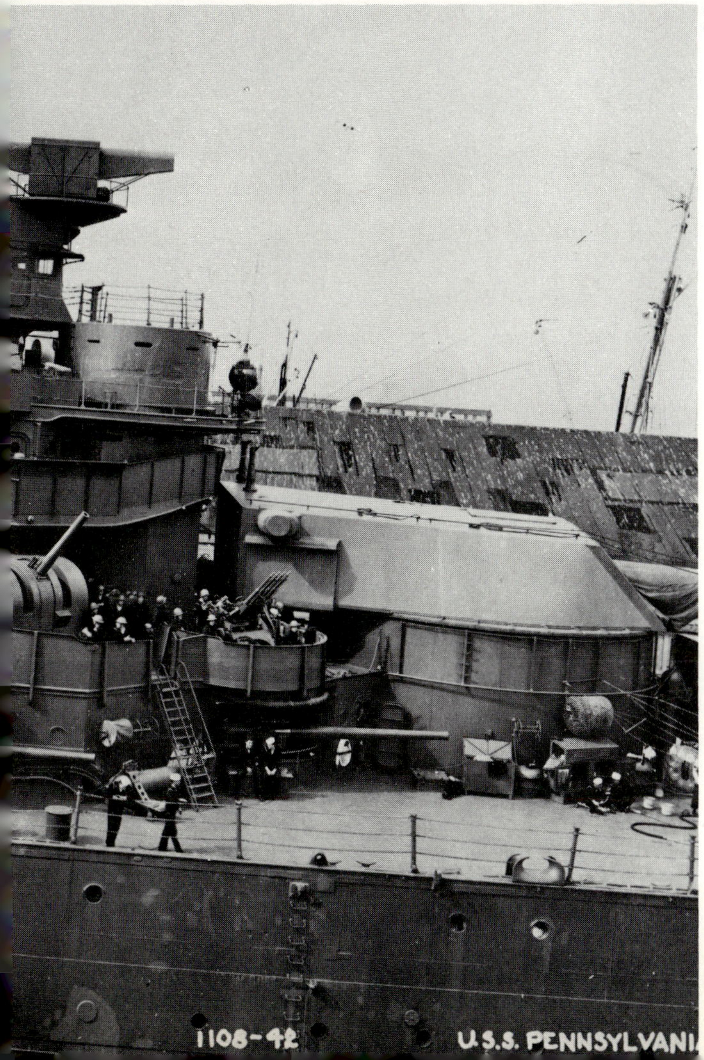

2.7

Four close-up photographs of the USS *Pennsylvania* after refit at the Mare Island Yard in California early in 1942. The ship was not badly damaged at Pearl Harbour and apart from minor repairs the refit was largely concerned with the improvement of her AA defences.

2.5 Taken on 26 February this photograph shows the starboard side of the bridge structure looking aft. At the bottom left and right are two of the 5inch 51 calibre guns of the secondary armament. On the deck above, from forward to aft is a quadruple 1.1inch machine gun mounting and two 5inch 25 calibre, AA guns. Note the paravane at the bottom between the two 5inch mountings. **JR**
USN

2.6 Also on 26 February, the funnel and foremast, viewed from the mainmast, showing six of the sixteen 20mm Oerlikon guns added during this refit. Two can be seen on the platform below the foretop while the other four are fitted on a new platform around the funnel. The Oerlikon mountings are of the hand-raising type in which the cradle was fitted to a central column which could be raised by means of a large handwheel on the fixed pedestal mounting. This allowed adjustment of the trunnion height to suit the elevation at which the gun was being fired, thus avoiding the gunlayer having to crouch at high angles, and to stand on tip-toe at low angles of elevation. Note that the front has been removed from the port secondary armament director. **JR**
USN

2.7 The forward superstructure and 'B' turret on 2 March, showing two more of the new Oerlikon mountings (on the upper conning tower platform); there was of course a matching pair on the port side. The shields on the 5inch AA guns were also added during this refit to provide protection against splinters and strafing. 'B' turret carries three 14inch 45 calibre, Mk I guns which fired a 1400lb shell at a muzzle velocity of 2600 feet per second. The ship carried twelve such guns in four triple mountings. **JR**
USN

2.8 Also on 2 March, the mainmast viewed from the starboard side. On the left 'X' turret is just visible with part of the aircraft catapult, mounted on its roof, projecting to the rear of the mounting. On a raised platform at the base of the mainmast are two of the four quadruple 1.1inch machine gun mountings which the ship carried. These weapons were introduced in the 1930s as close range AA weapons and were equivalent to the British quadruple pom-pom. They were not entirely successful and were superceded by the 40mm Bofors during the early part of the war. The platform at the head of the mainmast carried single 0.5inch machine guns. **JR**
USN

2.9 A view across the forecastle's of two US flush deck destroyers shortly after transfer to the RN in 1940. The guns are 4inch, 50 calibre, of which four were mounted in each ship, one forward, one aft and one in each beam amidships. The shields were fitted only on the forecastle mountings, so it would seem these were intended primarily as weather, rather than splinter, protection. **JR**
CPL

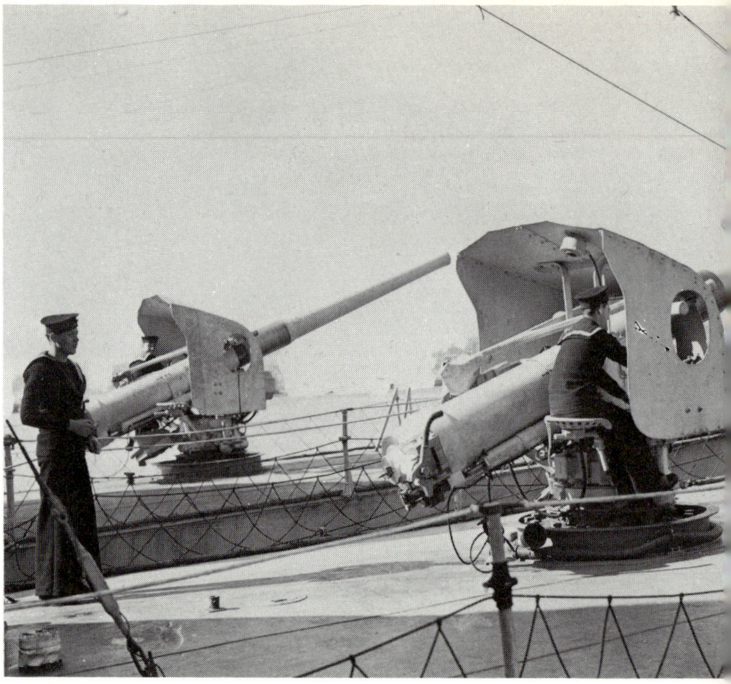

2.10 The port side 4inch gun with its interrupted screw breech open ready to accept the shell and brass cartridge held by the loader (far left). The other members of the crew are (left to right), the sight setter (equipped with voice pipe communication to directing position), the layer, breech worker and trainer. Note the yoke across the top of the mounting which carries the telescopic sights. The brass cartridge case with its 4inch, 30lb shell is visible on the left; this type of ammunition was known as QF (quick firing) in the RN but the USN used the nomenclature RF (rapid fire) reserving the term QF for 'bagged' charges used in fast firing small and medium calibre guns. **JR**
CPL

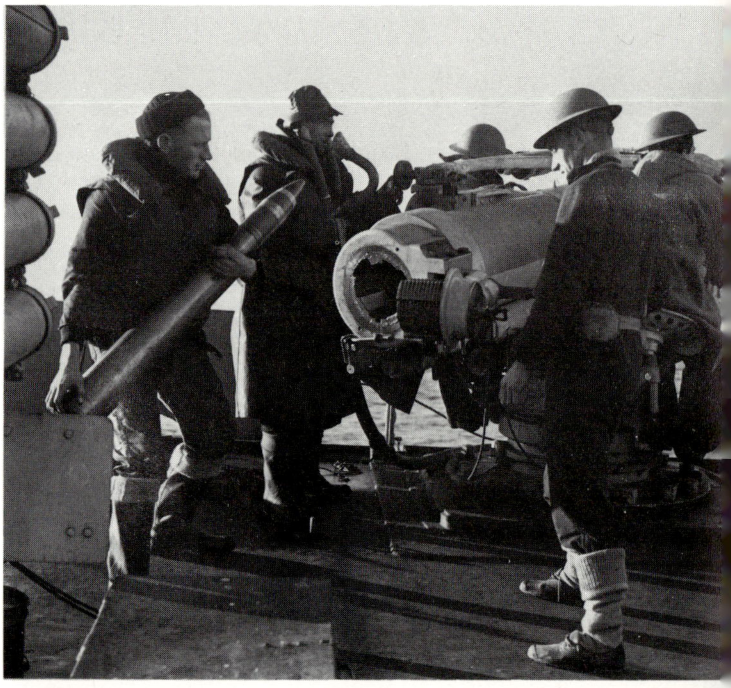

2.11 Ammunition being passed into the revolving base of a twin 4.5inch BD (between decks) Mk II mounting aboard the *Illustrious* in March 1942. The mounting, which carried two Mk III guns, was enclosed by a circular turret and mounted on the deck shown in the photograph — the top of the turret and the guns being above the level of the deck over. The ammunition is 'fixed' QF, the Navy also used 'separate' QF in which the cartridge was separate from the shell. **JR**
CPL

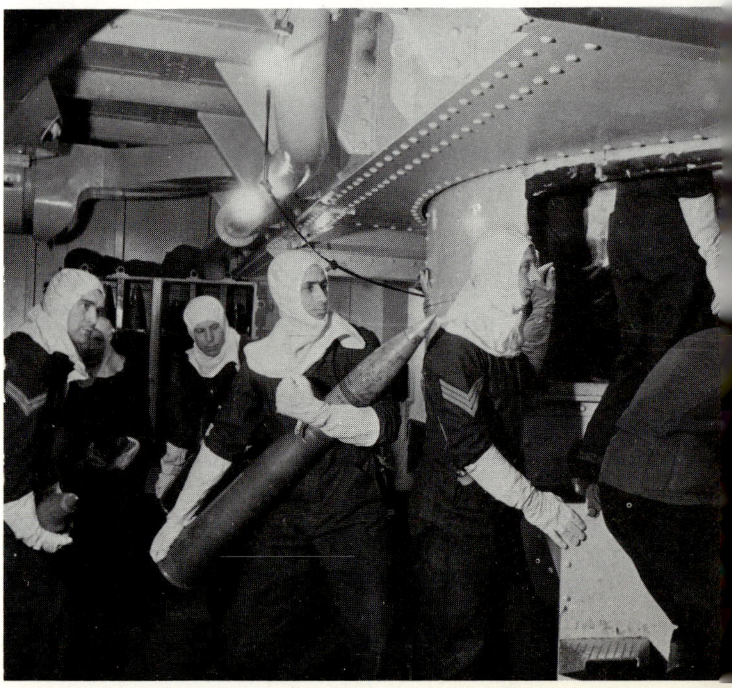

2.12 Gun drill in progress on the forecastle of the destroyer *Whitshed* in 1941. The weapon is a 4.7inch BL (breech-loading) Mk I on a CP (centre pivot) Mk VI mounting which was fitted in the Modified 'W' class, the *Scott* and *Shakespeare* class leaders, and the destroyers *Ambuscade* and *Amazon.* This was the only destroyer gun in service during 1939-45, and the only naval 4.7inch, to employ BL ammunition: ie a separate cordite charge in a silk bag. All other such weapons employed QF (quick firing) ammunition in which the charge was contained in a brass cartridge case. The man on the far left is holding the case which contains the cordite charge and the third from the left is holding the 50lb shell. Like all British Service 4.7inch guns, the true calibre was 120mm (4.724inch). **JR**
CPL

2.13 One of the four twin Mk XIX 4inch gun mountings of the battleship *Resolution* at Gibraltar in 1939. The photograph is unusual in being taken from a position almost level with the deck. This mounting has been raised by the addition of a circular base between the deck and the base plate, normally the base plate was bolted directly to the deck. The equipment mounted on the box at the right hand rear of the mounting is a fuse setting machine. **JR**
CPL

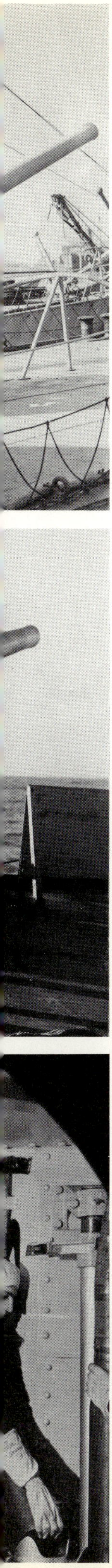

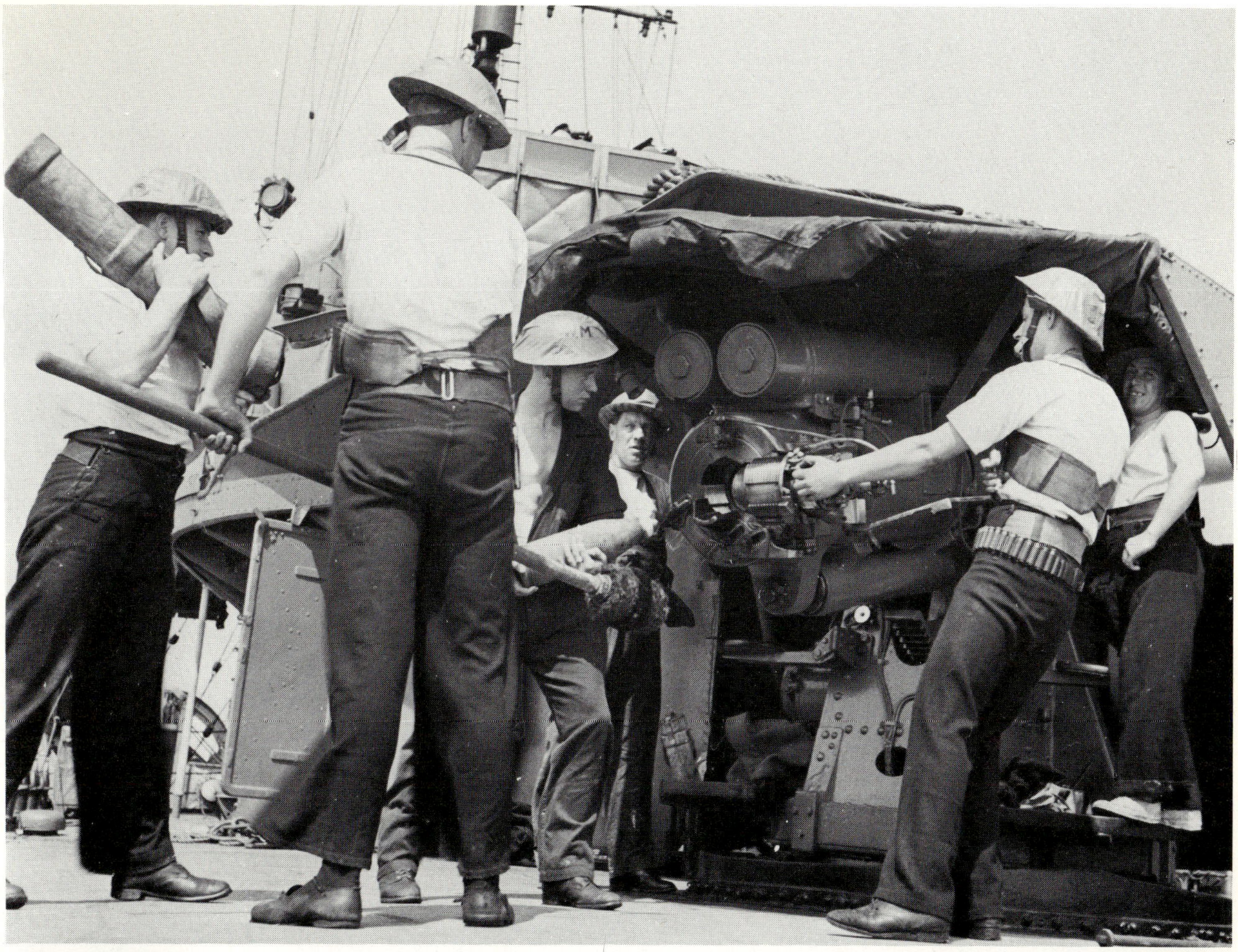

2.12

2.13

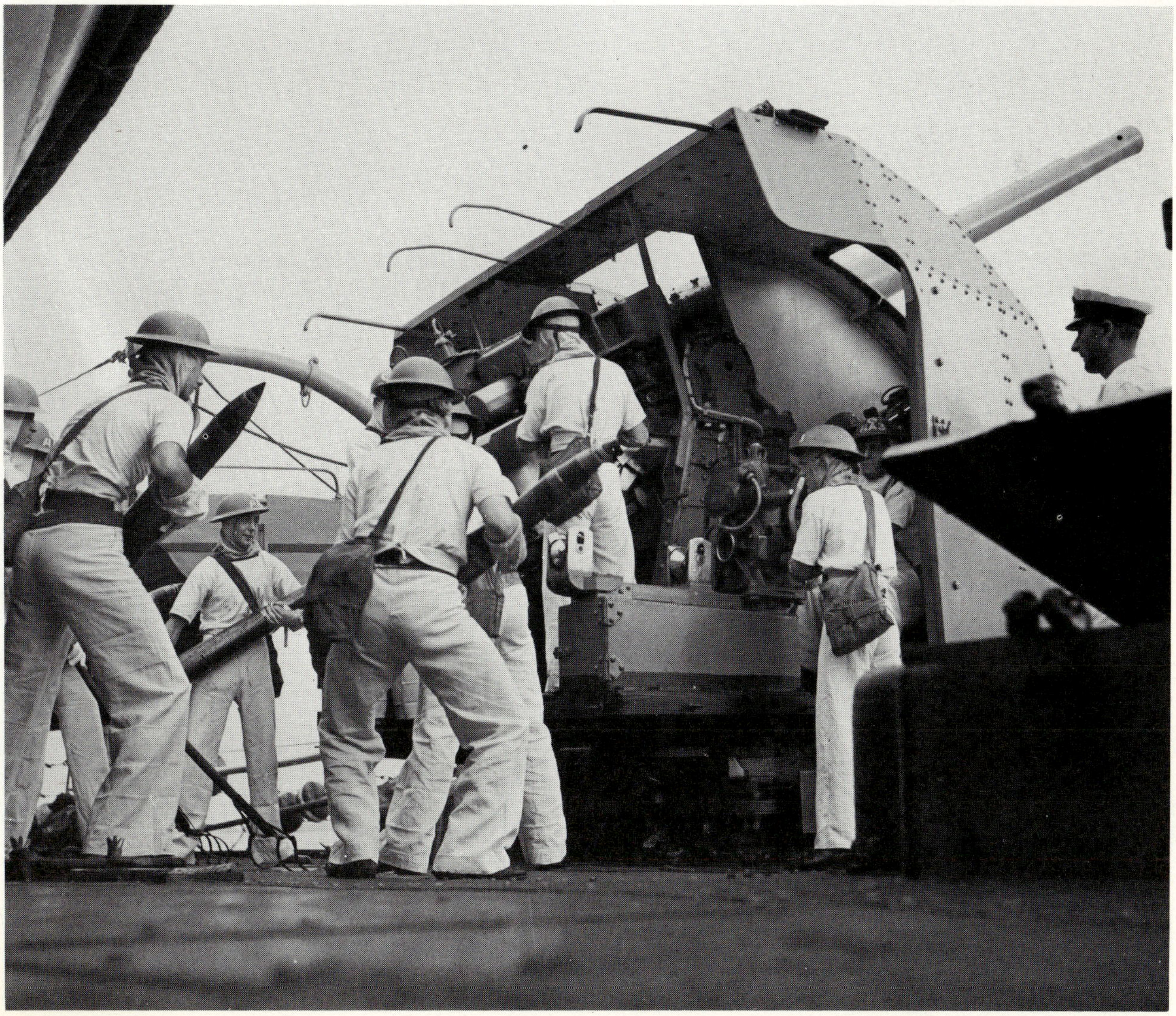

2.11

Three photographs taken on board the aircraft carrier *Indomitable* in the Far East during December 1944/January 1945 when she was the flagship of Rear Admiral Vian.

2.14 A US twin Bofors mounting Mk I viewed from above. The 40mm guns were of 60 calibres length and had a maximum rate of fire of 160 rounds per minute, but this was restricted by the speed at which the guns could be loaded. The Americans also manufactured a quadruple mounting, the Mk II, which was basically two twins on a single platform, and this was also employed by the Royal Navy. A British equivalent of the twin mounting, 'the Mk V Utility Bofors', was introduced late in the war and was employed extensively in the post war fleet. **JR**
CPL

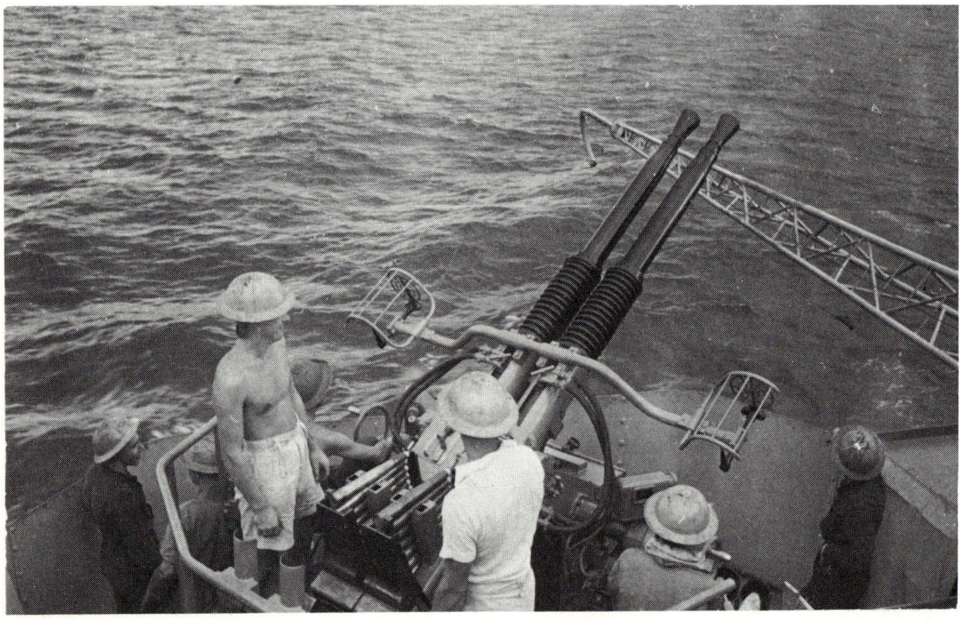

2.14

2.15

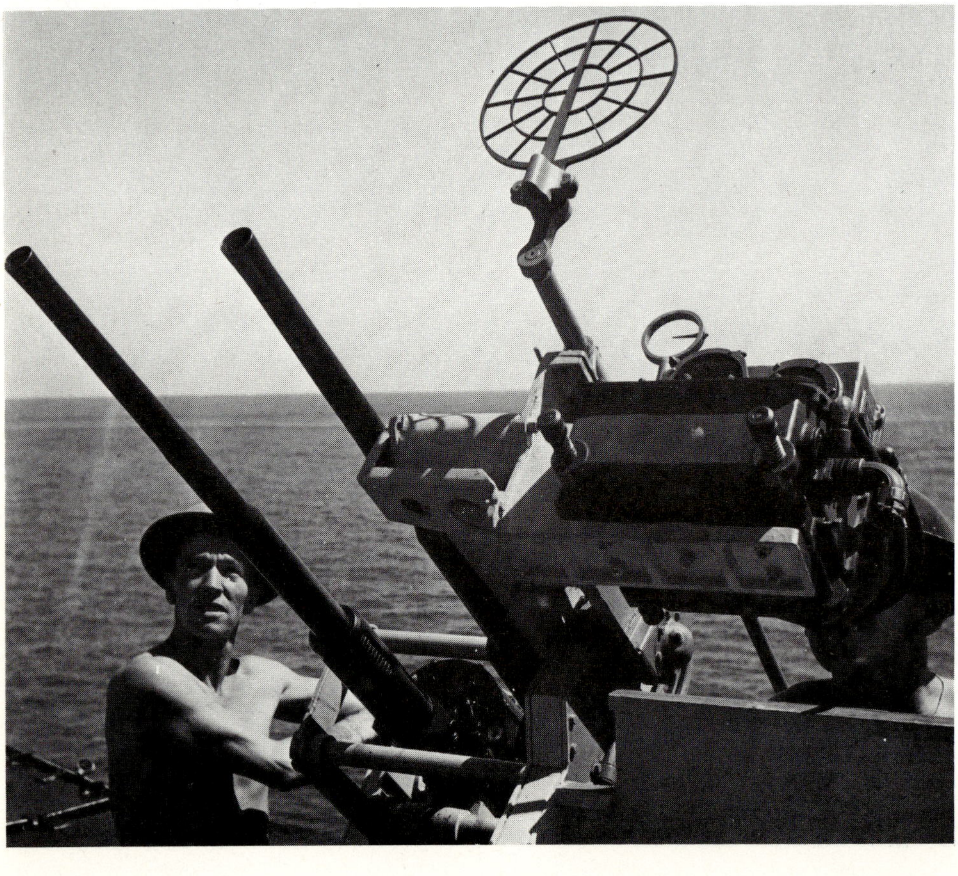

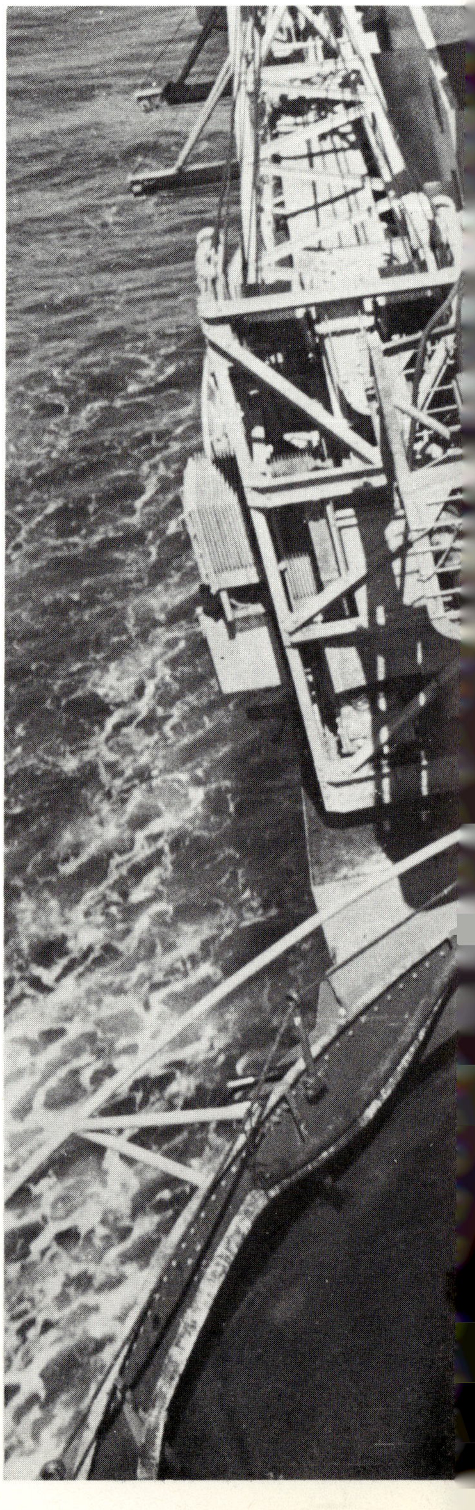

2.15 A twin 20mm Oerlikon Mk V mounting, a weapon first introduced in 1942 and, like the single mounting, fitted in practically every type of vessel in the Navy. Of particular interest in this photograph is the gyro-gunsight, into which the gunlayer is looking. These were fitted to all types of close range AA weapons during 1944-45, priority being given to ships of the Pacific and Eastern Fleets. The gyro sights were considered to be five times as effective as the original eye-shooting sight, the cobweb frame of which can also be seen in the photograph. The second, and only other, member of the crew is the loader. **JR**
CPL

2.16 A view of the Mk VI pom-pom mounting abaft the island superstructure. This mounting is unusual in that it has an enclosed position for the gunlayer on the right side. Its exact purpose is not clear as it seems rather odd to provide protection for the layer, but not for the remainder of the gun's crew. Each gun had a normal rate of fire of 90 rounds per minute giving a total of 720 rounds per minute for the mounting; the maximum effective range was 1700 yards. **JR**
CPL

2.16

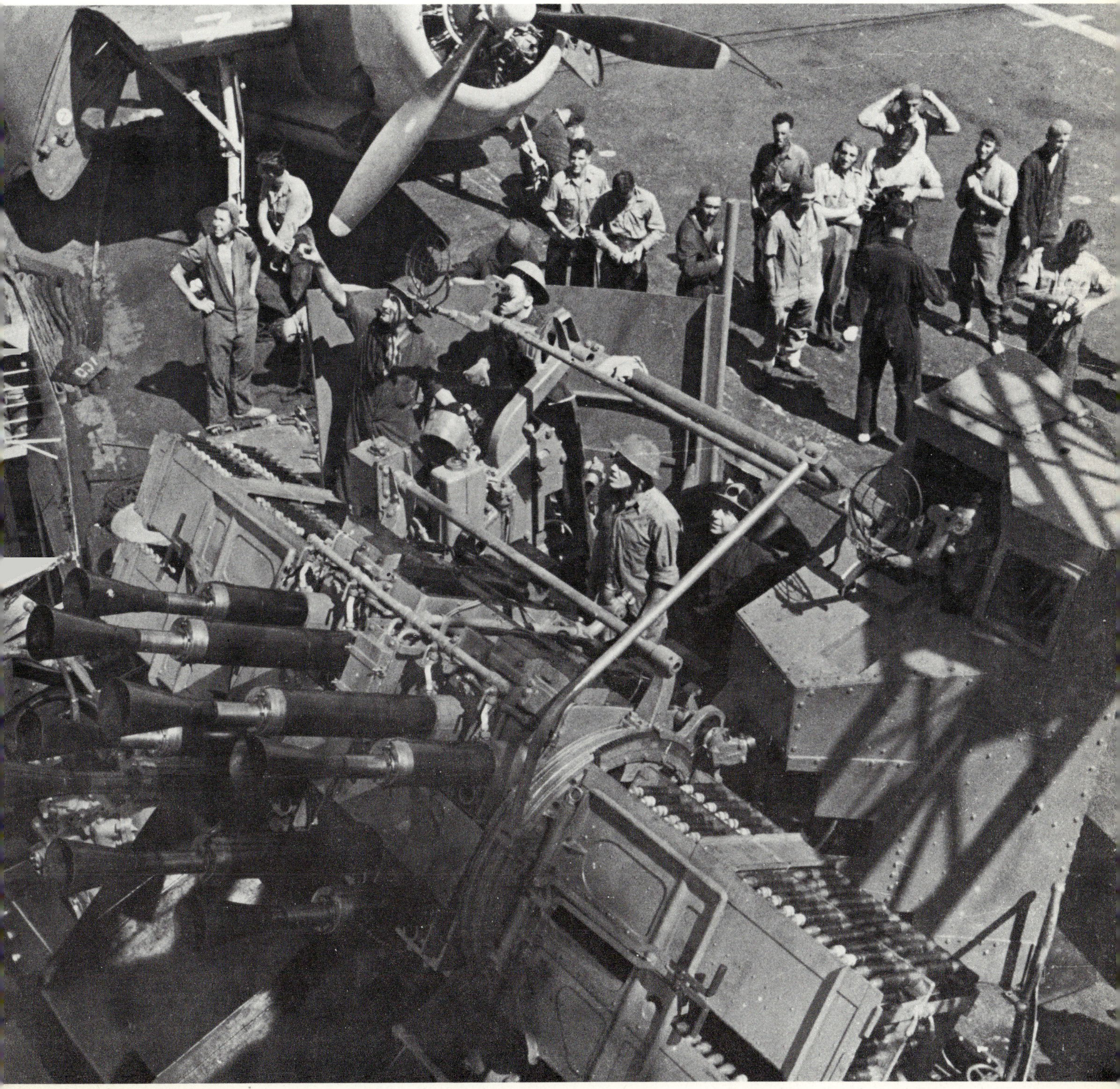

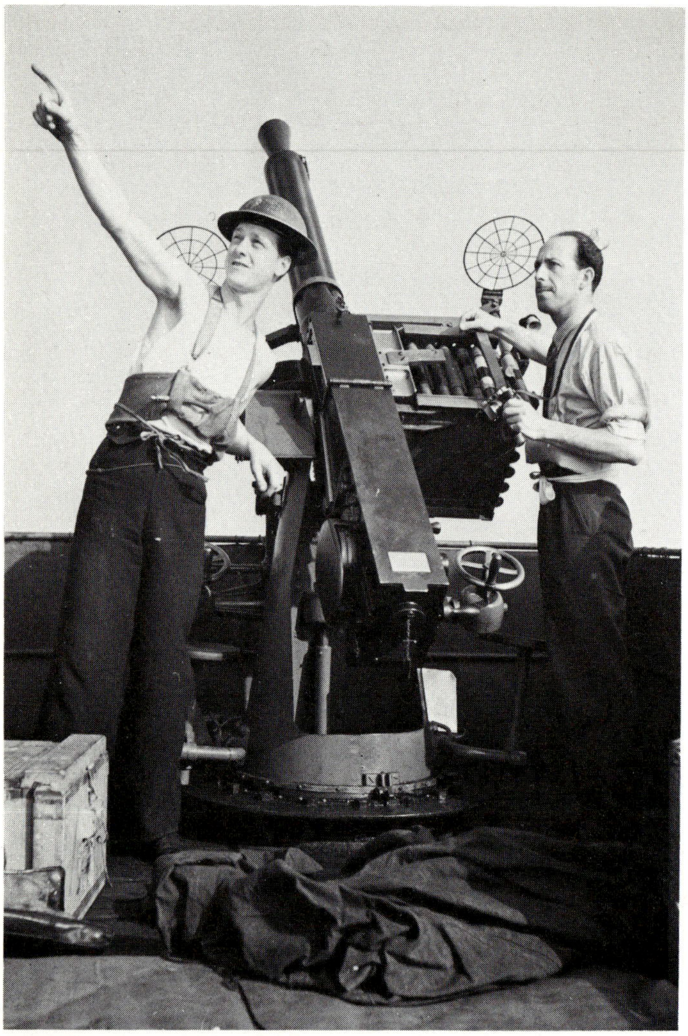

2.17

2.17 A close-up of one of *Whitshed's* single 2pdr pom-poms which illustrates the basic simplicity of the mounting, with its slightly tapered cylindrical pedestal. This basic form of mounting design was typical of those for Vickers small and medium calibre guns. The man with the camera is one of the best-known photographers — Saidman — of the war-time *Illustrated* magazine: he took many of the CPL photos reproduced in this book. **JR**
CPL

2.18 An eight barrel Mk VI, 2pdr, pom-pom mounting on board the *Illustrious* in March 1942. The guns, as in the four barrel mounting, are Mk VIII. Development of this mounting began in 1921 and the first production mountings, the Mk V, entered service in 1930-31. The improved Mk VI mounting followed soon after and was mounted generally in cruisers, battleships and other large ships. Although not a complete success, partly due to an inadequate director, it was a moderately successful deterrent and did well against dive bombers and later in the war against Kamikaze attacks. **JR**
CPL

2.19 A view from amidships looking aft on the *Hunt* class escort destroyer *Lauderdale* while she was escorting an East Coast Convoy in 1941. In the foreground are the four Mk VIII 2pdr pom-pom guns on the Mk VII mounting, which was fitted on a platform abaft the funnel. This mounting was introduced in 1938 for fitting in destroyers and other small ships which could not accept the weight of the eight barrel Mk VI pom-pom mounting. Further aft is one of the three twin 4inch Mk XIX HA/LA (high angle/low angle) mountings which the ships of this class carried. **JR**
CPL

2.18

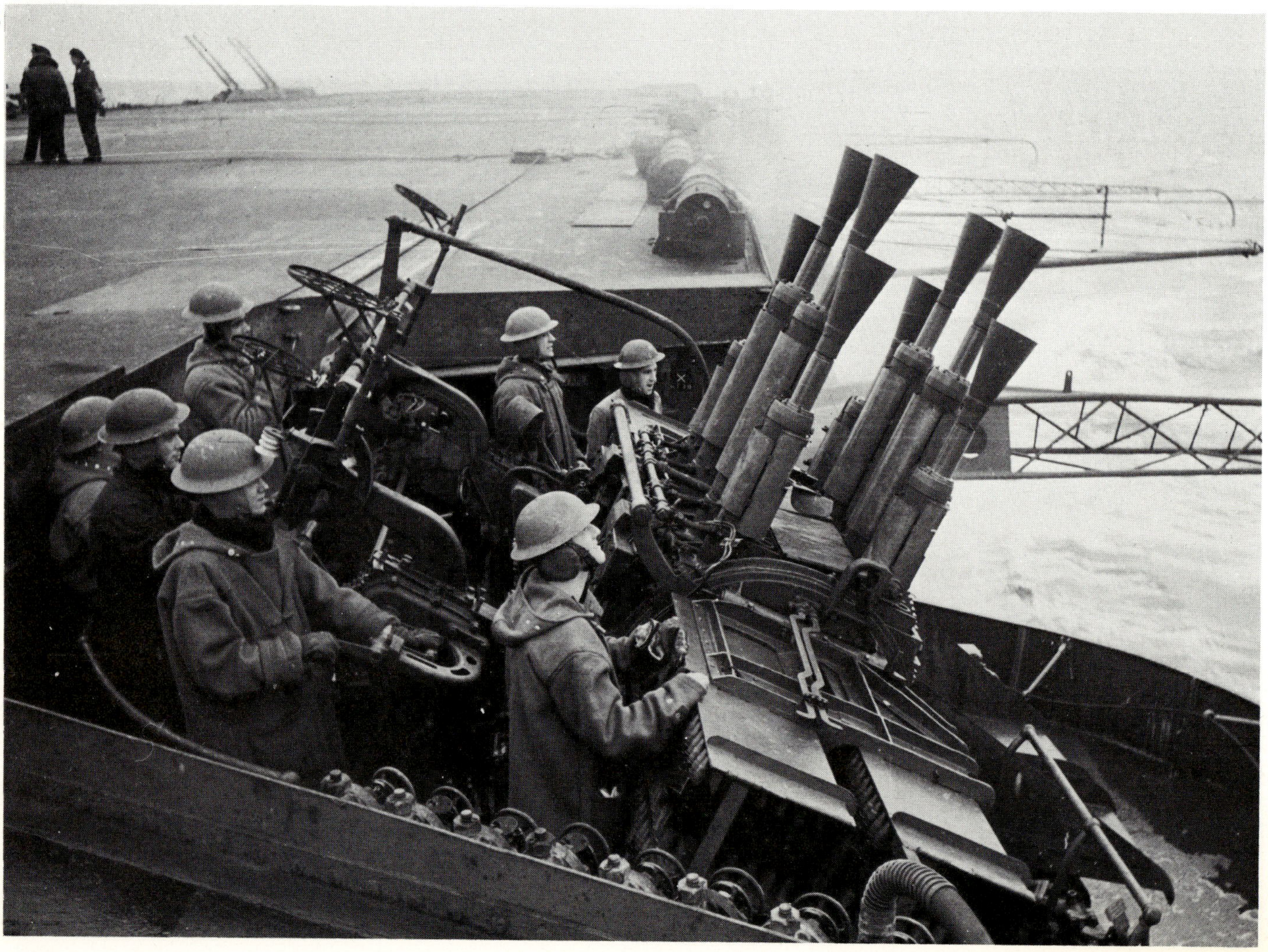

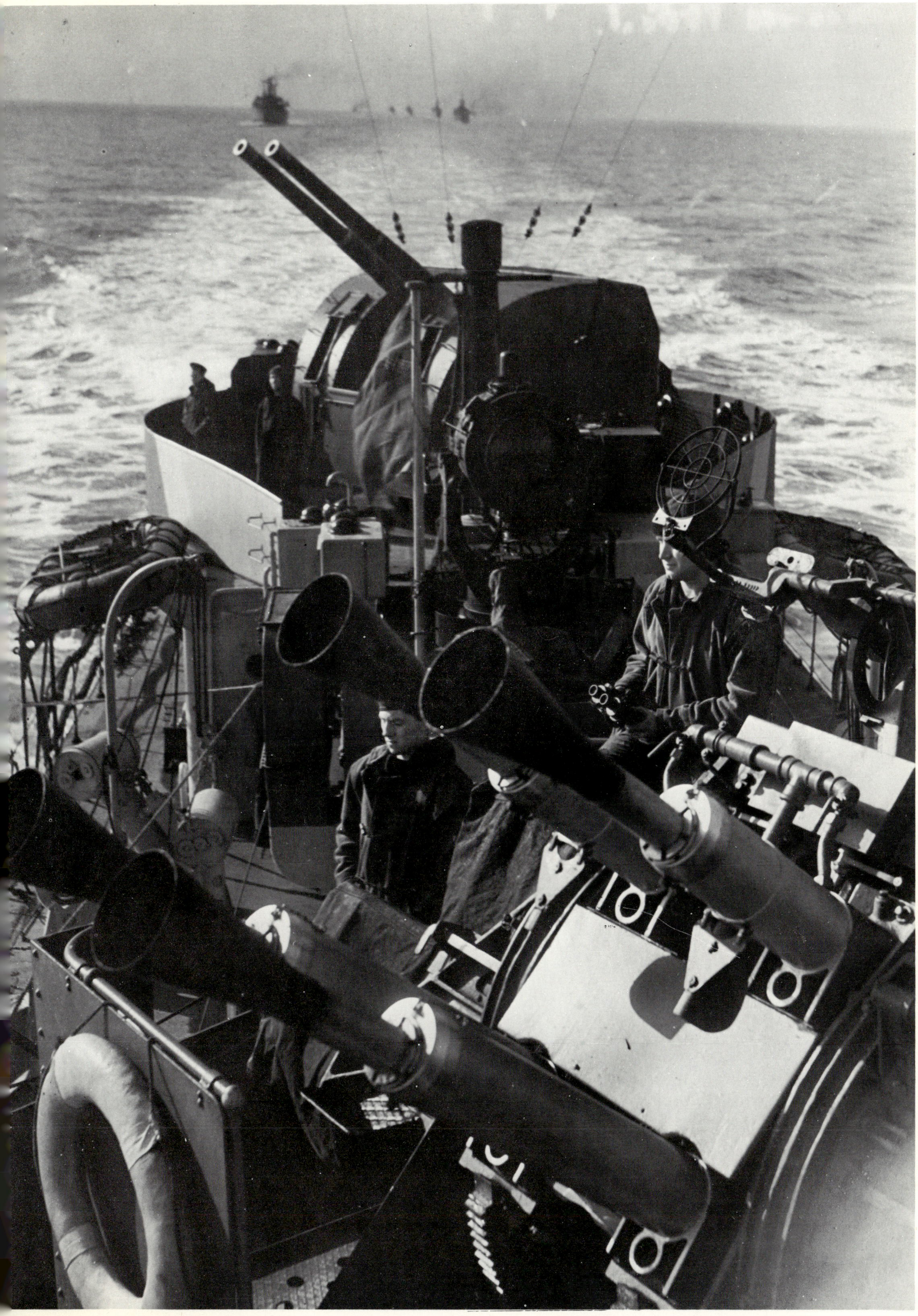

2.19

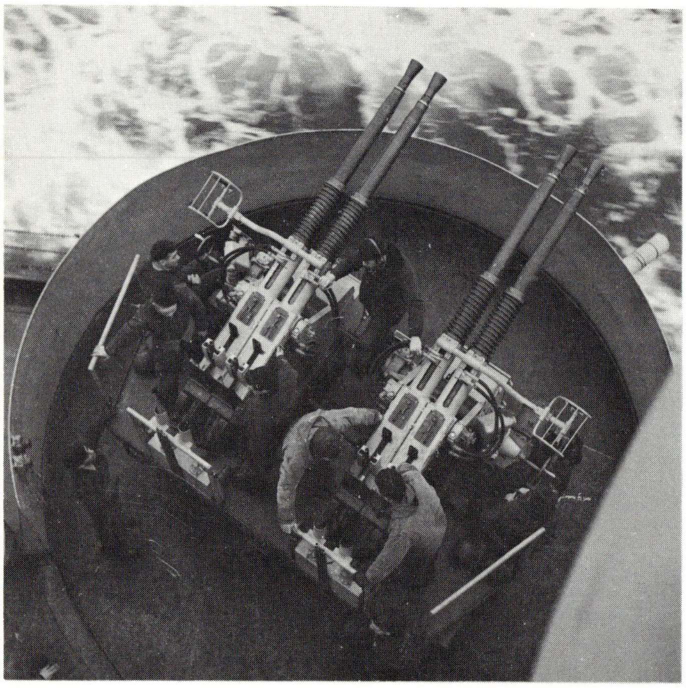

2.20

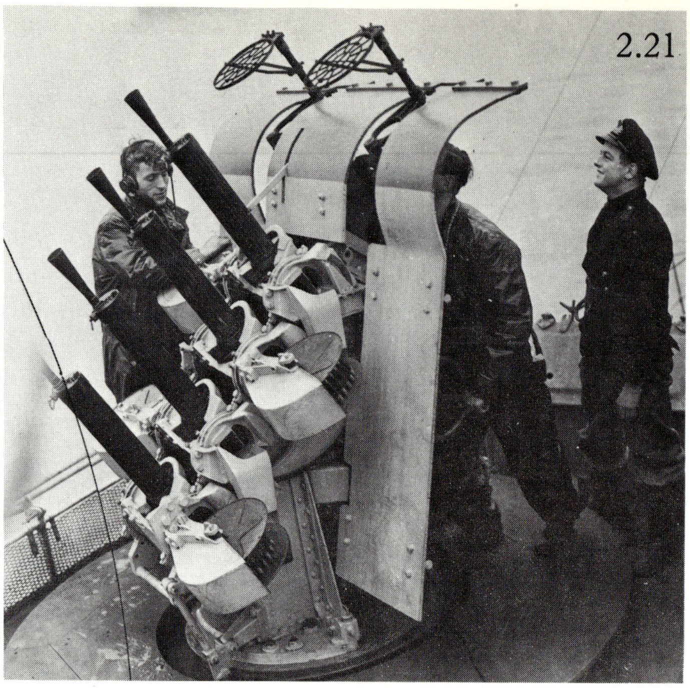

2.21

2

2.23

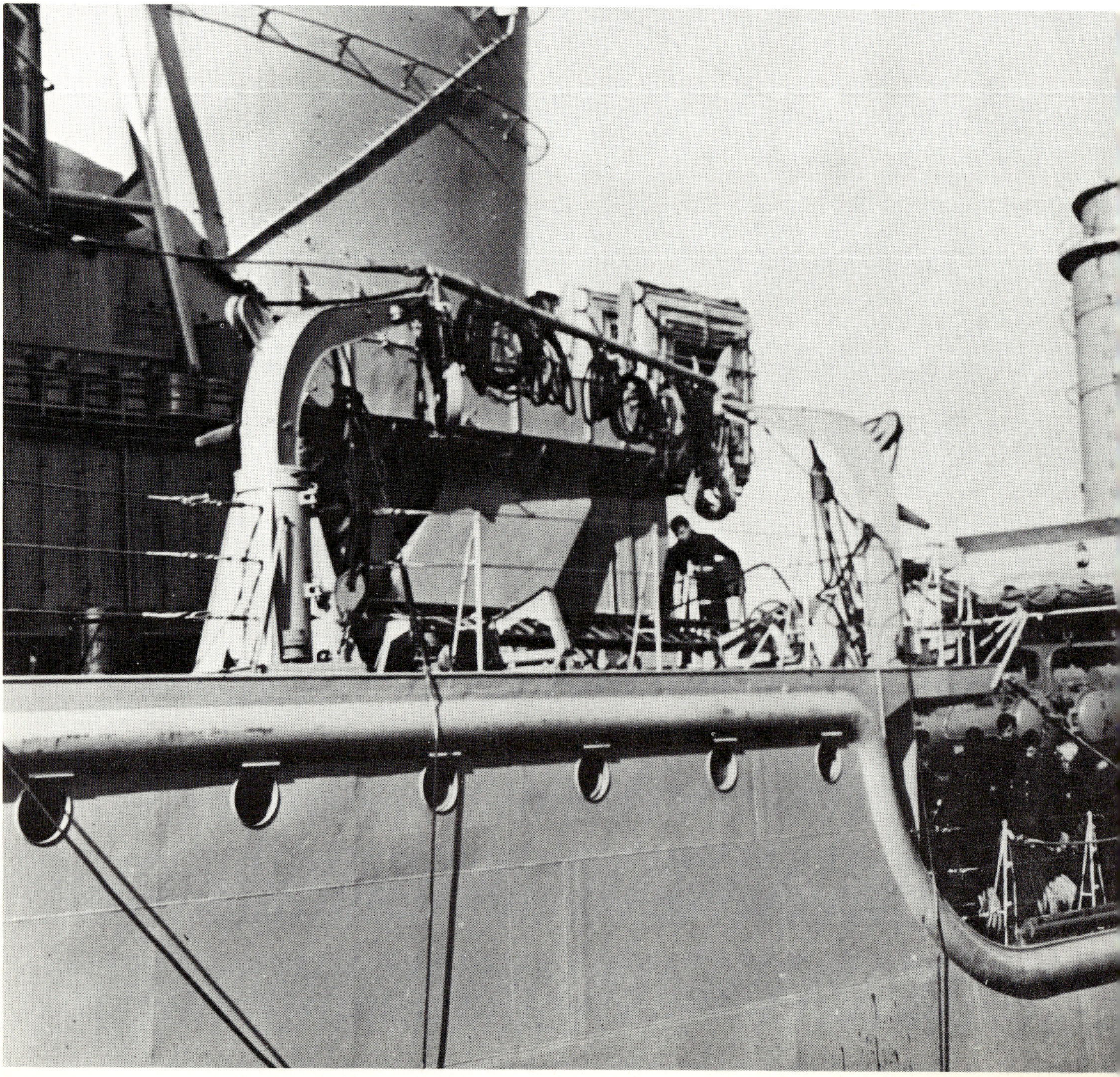

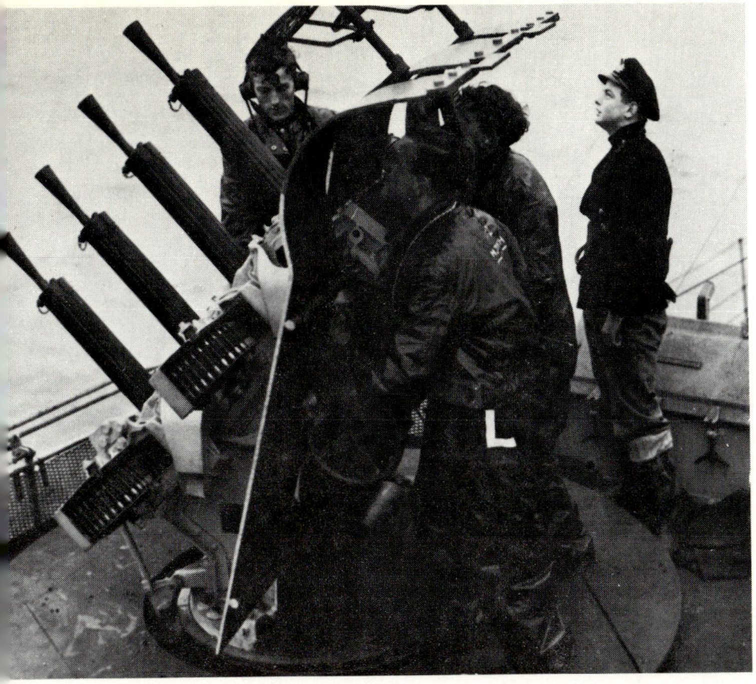

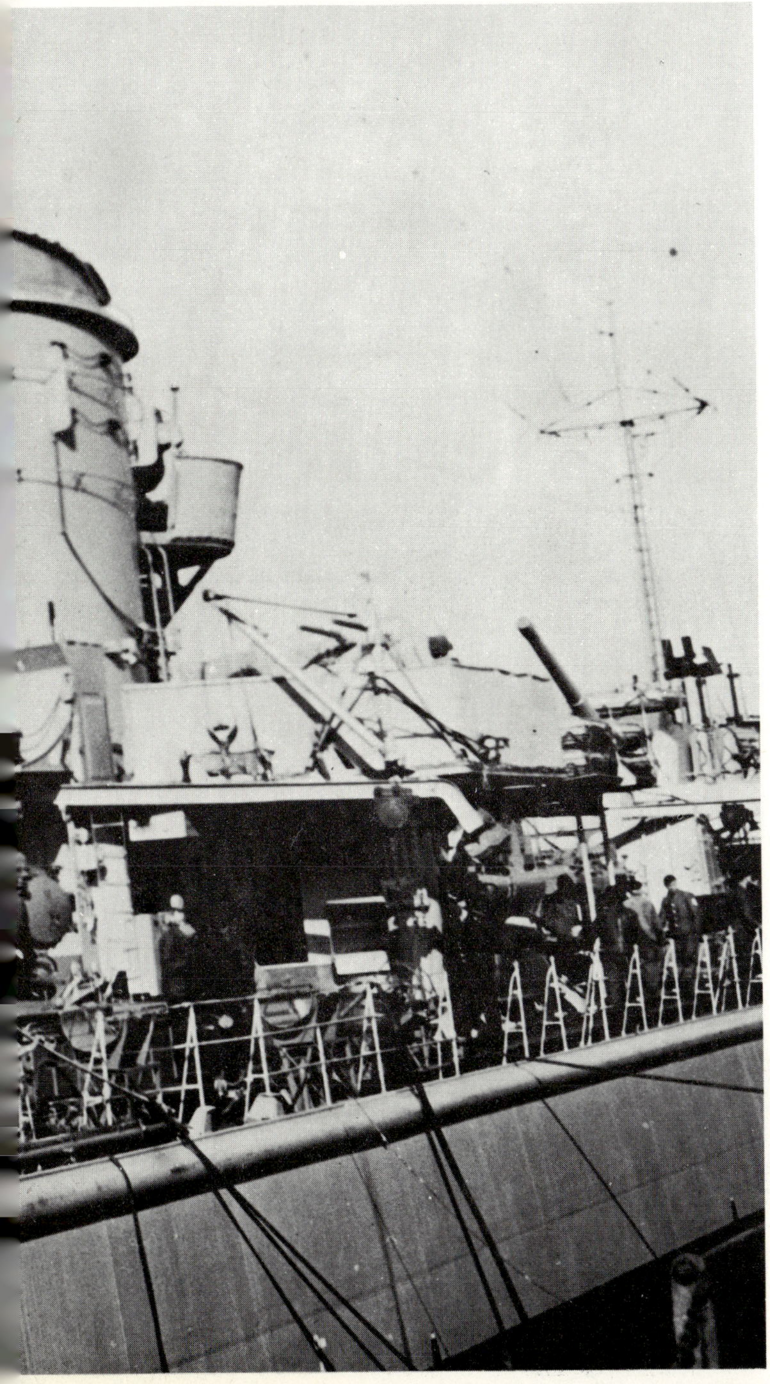

2.20 A quadruple 40mm Bofors mounting Mk II on the US battleship *Arkansas* in 1944. These weapons were virtually doubled versions of the twin Mk I mounting. They were not sophisticated weapons, being designed for rapid production in wartime, but were nevertheless successful. This was in large part due to the provision of a separate, Mk 51, director equipped with a gyro-gunsight to control the mounting by RPC (Remote Power Control). **JR**
CPL

2.21-22 Two views of a quadruple 0.5inch Vickers machine gun mounting on board the *Wolsey* in December 1941. This AA mounting was developed in the late 1920s and introduced into service during the 1930s. Despite its formidable appearance and apparently good performance (700 rounds per barrel per minute and muzzle velocity of 2520 ft/sec) it was not a successful AA weapon. This was largely due to the fact that it fired a solid bullet; the 20mm Oerlikon which superceded it fired an explosive shell and was much easier to handle. **JR**
CPL

2.23 One of the last German destroyers completed during the war at the time of her commissioning. Note the quadruple 21inch torpedo-tube mountings (a total of eight tubes) and the degaussing girdle for defence against magnetic mines. **AF**
Aldo Fraccaroli Collection

2 Weapons and Equipment

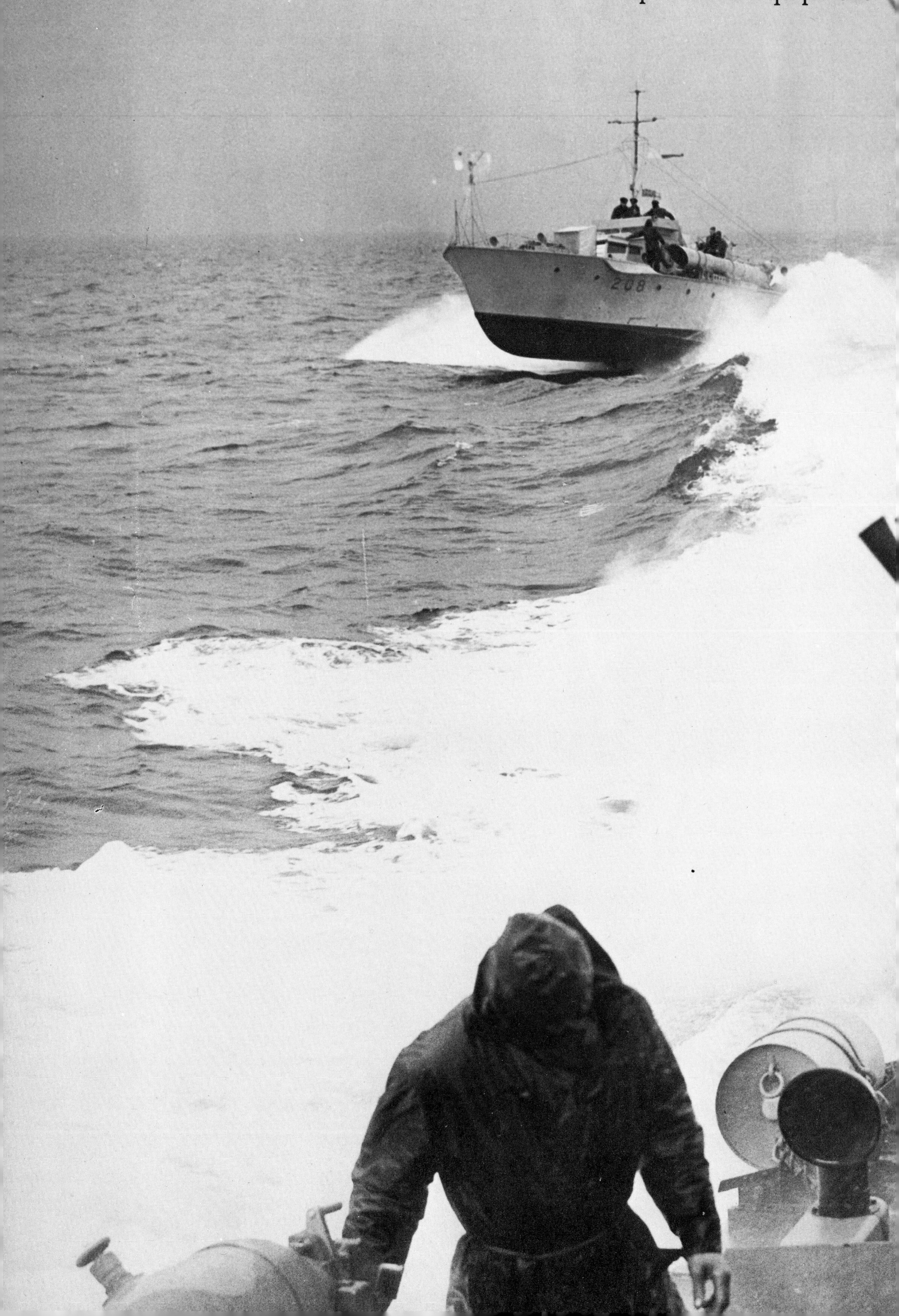

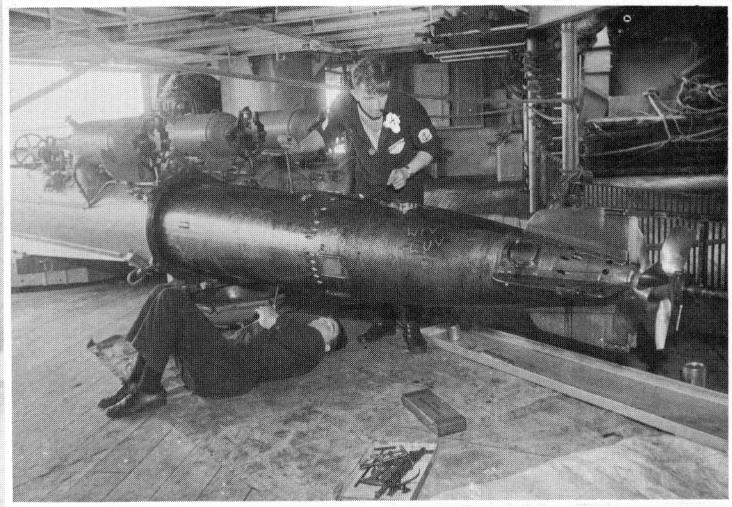

2.24 A twin Mk V 0.5inch machine gun mounting on an MTB. The guns were of the same type as those of the quadruple mounting fitted in larger ships but in this case they were intended for use against surface targets as well as aircraft. The mounting was power operated and controlled by a single man who sat between the guns. The leading vessel (MTB 208) of the three MTB's in the background is of the 'White' type and it is probable that the others belong to the same class. **JR**
CPL

2.25 A TR (triple) Mk VI* torpedo-tube mounting on the *Sheffield* in 1940, showing a 21inch torpedo withdrawn from the left tube for maintenance. The torpedoes were launched by means of a cordite charge contained in the cylinders on top of the tubes. It seems unlikely that the message inscribed in the grease on the torpedo would be appreciated by the recipient. **JR**
CPL

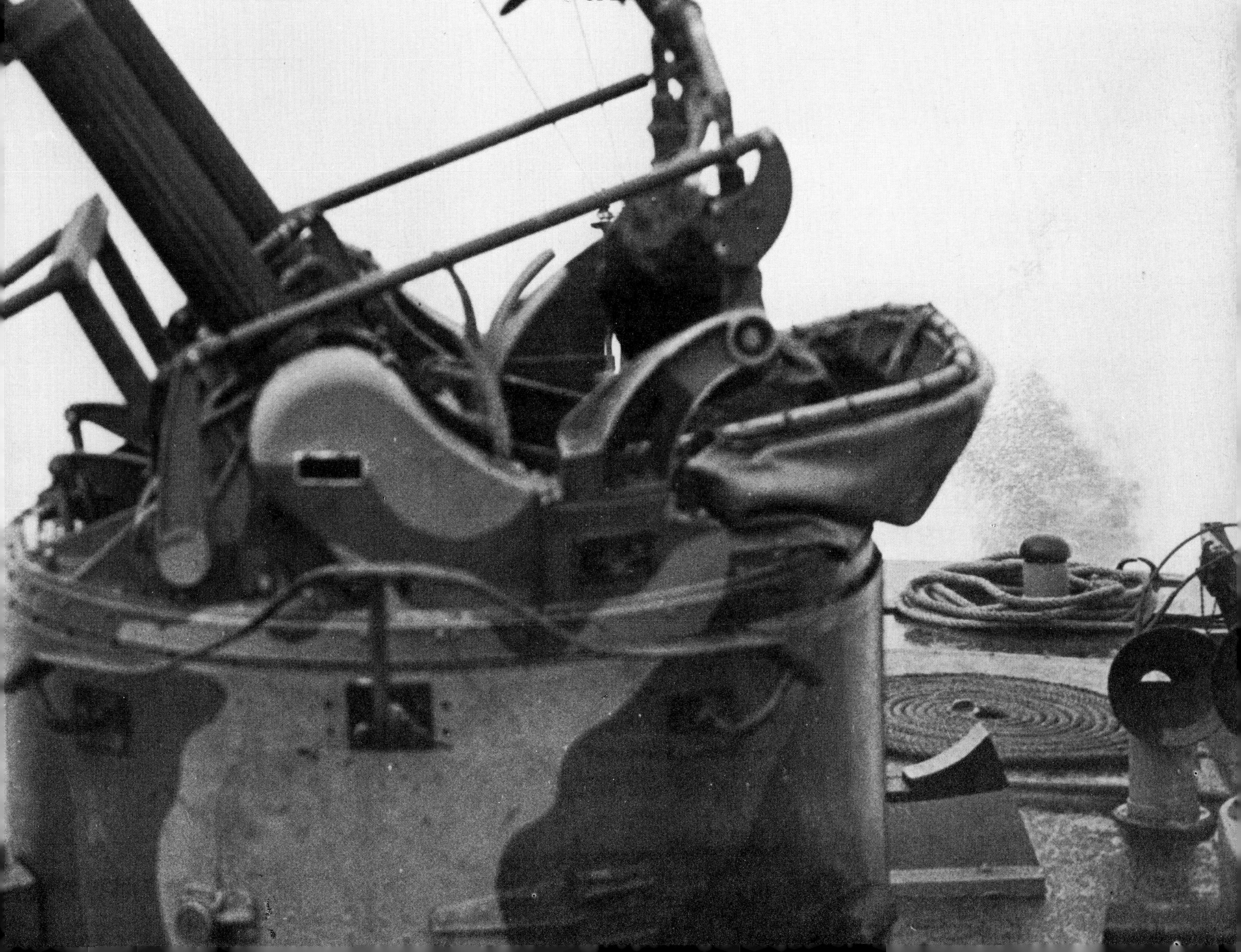

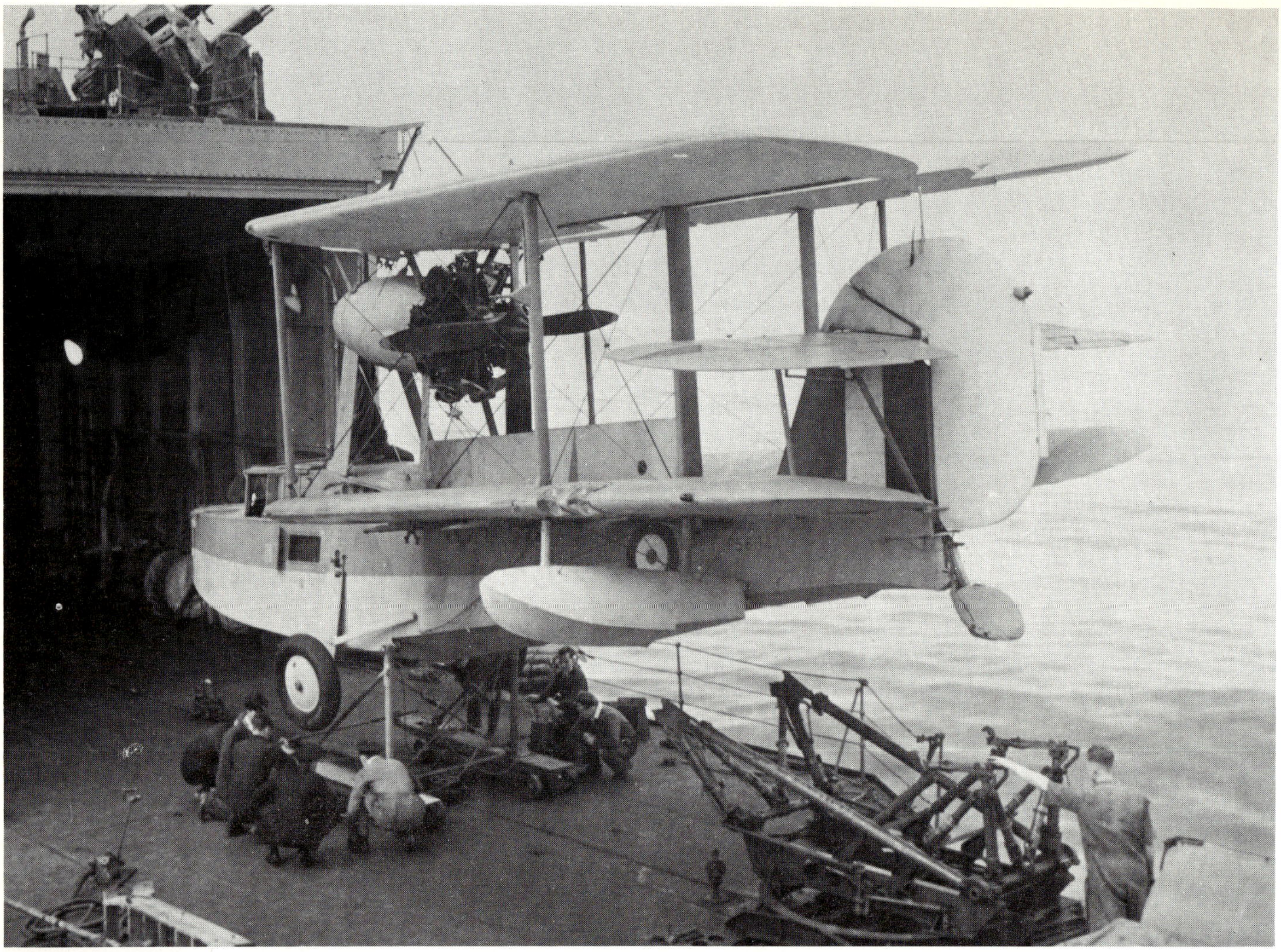

2.26

2.27

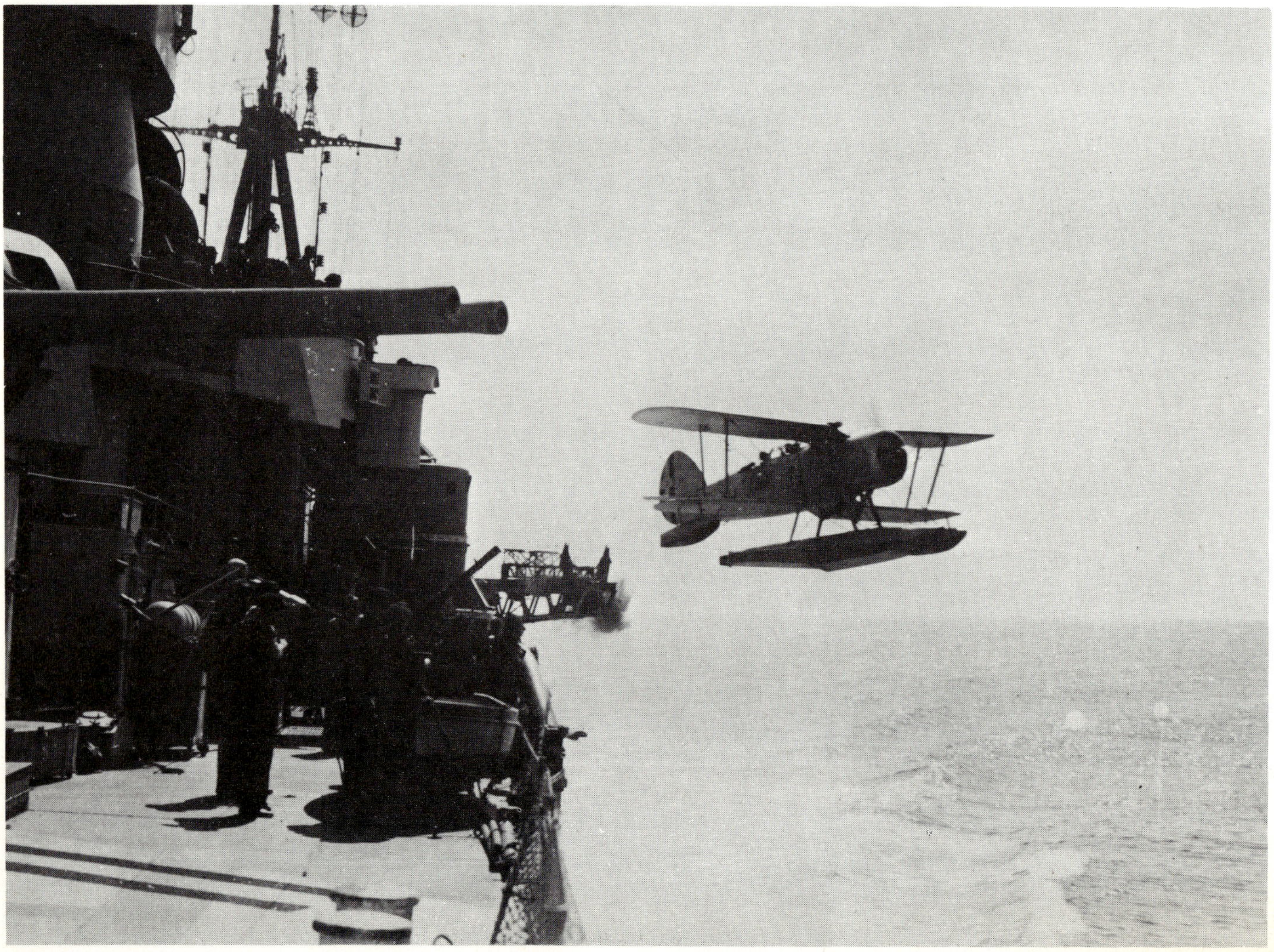

2.26 P5664, HMS *Sheffield*'s Walrus, perched on its handling trolley between the catapult trolley and the starboard hangar. The aircraft is supported on its forward catapult spools and by a strut below the nose; the handling trolley was aligned with the centre of the hangar by means of a guide slot in the deck — the aircraft was thus held rigidly during movement in and out of the hangar and was unable to 'take charge' in strong winds or heavy seas.

Detail on the aircraft includes: the upward-folding inboard section of the trailing edge of the lower mainplane, permitting full aft folding of the wings; the combined tail wheel and water rudder — the fairing was usually removed for operations ashore; the spray deflector ahead of the cabin window; the two under-wing beams to which the bomb carriers were attached; the two-piece four-blade propeller — it was possible to bolt the two pairs of blades together with the pitch in opposite senses, leading to a marked reluctance to fly and severe vibration.

The catapult trolley could be rotated to face in either direction athwartships to launch aircraft, or forward to load and unload aircraft. The distance between the hooks on which the aircraft rested could be adjusted, but the spools on different types of aircraft were situated in nearly the same relative positions, so that the adjustment was slight. The catapult track extended outboard of the ship's side to give a total length of some 90 ft (27 m); this installation could launch the 8000 lb (3640 kg) Walrus at up to 56 knots (65 mph/105 kph).

This particular aircraft had an interesting post-war career. Registered VH-BLD, it was operated as a 10-seat passenger aircraft by Airways Ltd, of Rabaul, New Britain, flying in New Guinea, New Britain and the Solomons Islands between 1949 and 1954. **DB**
CPL

2.27 A 'Ro 43' seaplane being catapulted from the light cruiser *Duca d'Aosta* for reconnaissance duties. The IMAM 'Ro 43' was a small aircraft with a 700 BHP motor and a maximum speed of 290km/h, with an endurance of 590 miles, crew of two (pilot, who was an Air Force officer or NCO; and observer, who was always a Navy officer) and two 7.7mm machine guns. **AF**
Aldo Fraccaroli Collection

2.28 A Vought OS 2U-3 Kingfisher floatplane and catapult on one of the midships 12inch gun turrets of the US battleship *Arkansas*, Februrary 1944. It was a two-seat observation and scout aircraft with a range of about 900 miles.
CPL

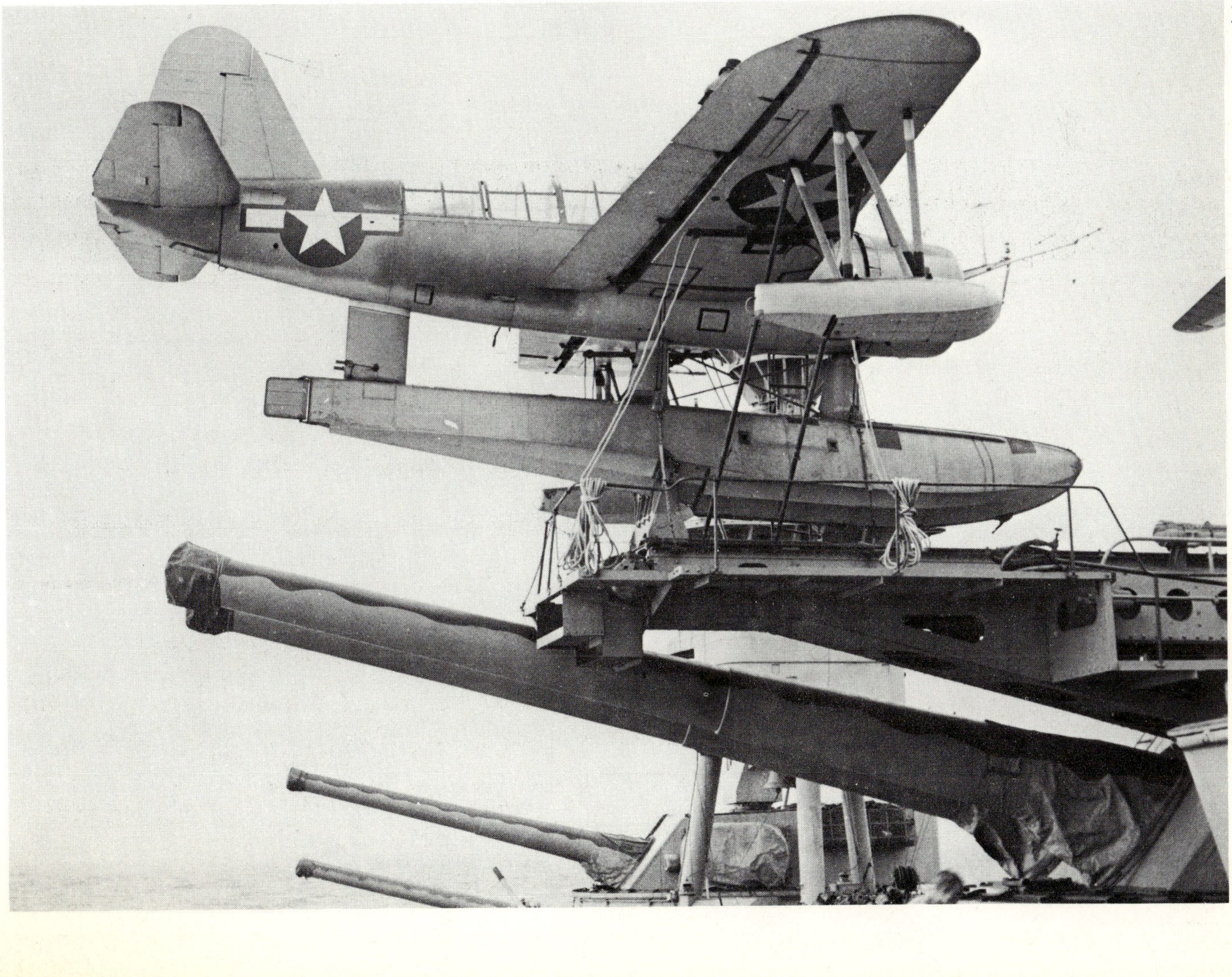
2.28

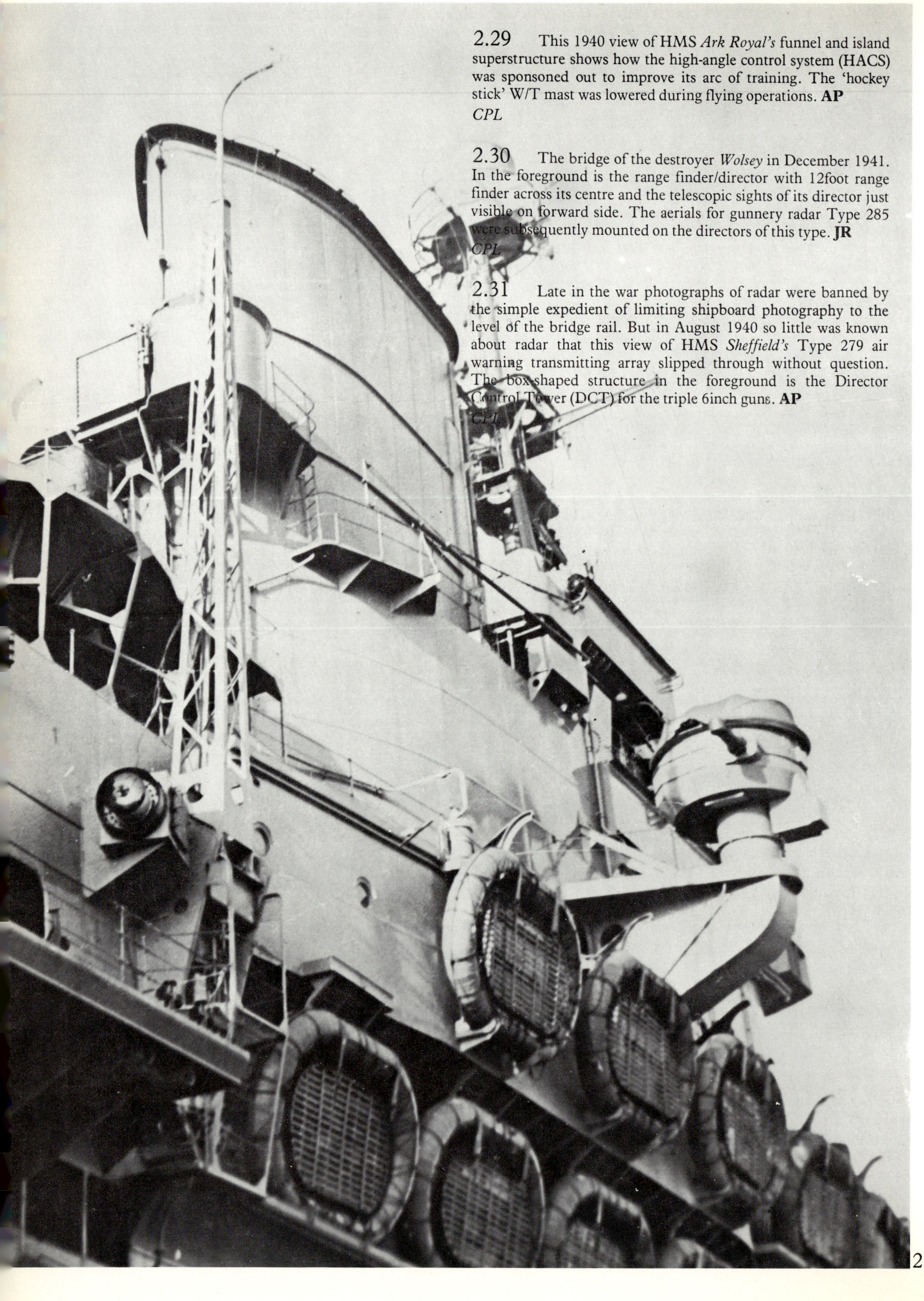

2.29 This 1940 view of HMS *Ark Royal's* funnel and island superstructure shows how the high-angle control system (HACS) was sponsoned out to improve its arc of training. The 'hockey stick' W/T mast was lowered during flying operations. **AP** *CPL*

2.30 The bridge of the destroyer *Wolsey* in December 1941. In the foreground is the range finder/director with 12foot range finder across its centre and the telescopic sights of its director just visible on forward side. The aerials for gunnery radar Type 285 were subsequently mounted on the directors of this type. **JR** *CPL*

2.31 Late in the war photographs of radar were banned by the simple expedient of limiting shipboard photography to the level of the bridge rail. But in August 1940 so little was known about radar that this view of HMS *Sheffield's* Type 279 air warning transmitting array slipped through without question. The box-shaped structure in the foreground is the Director Control Tower (DCT) for the triple 6inch guns. **AP** *CPL*

2.29

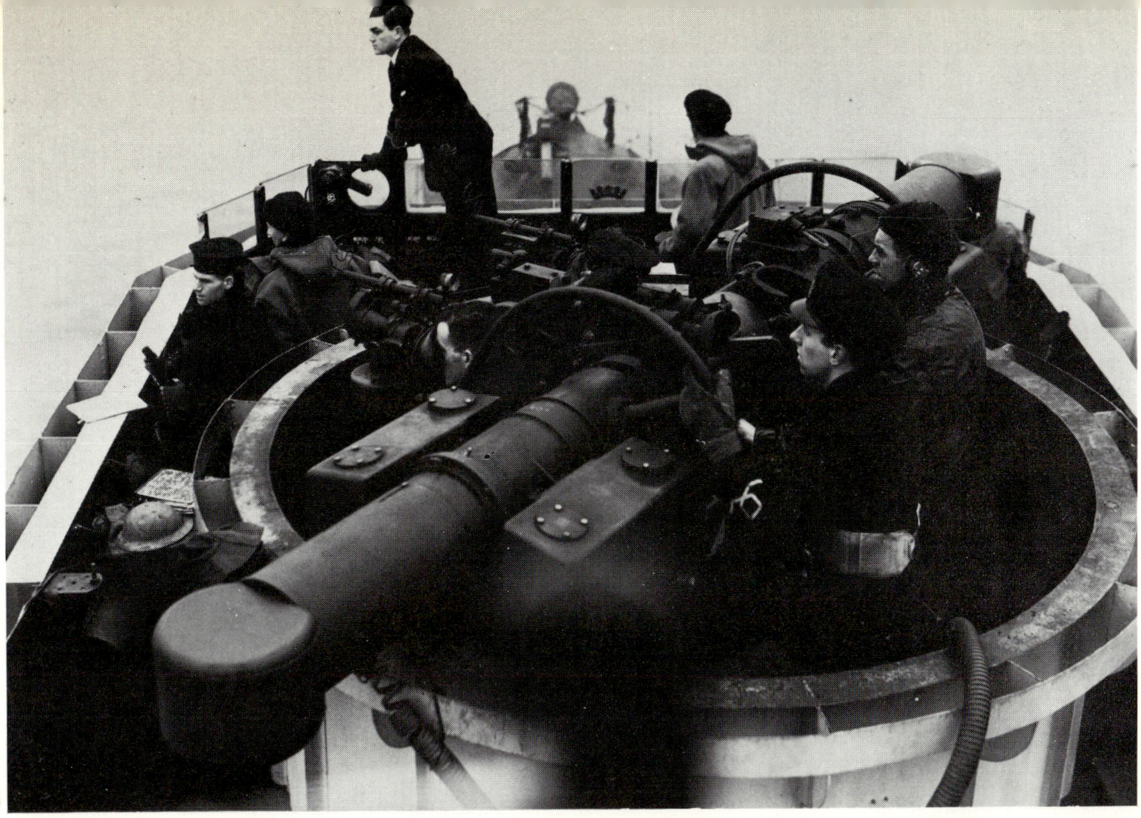

2.30

2.31

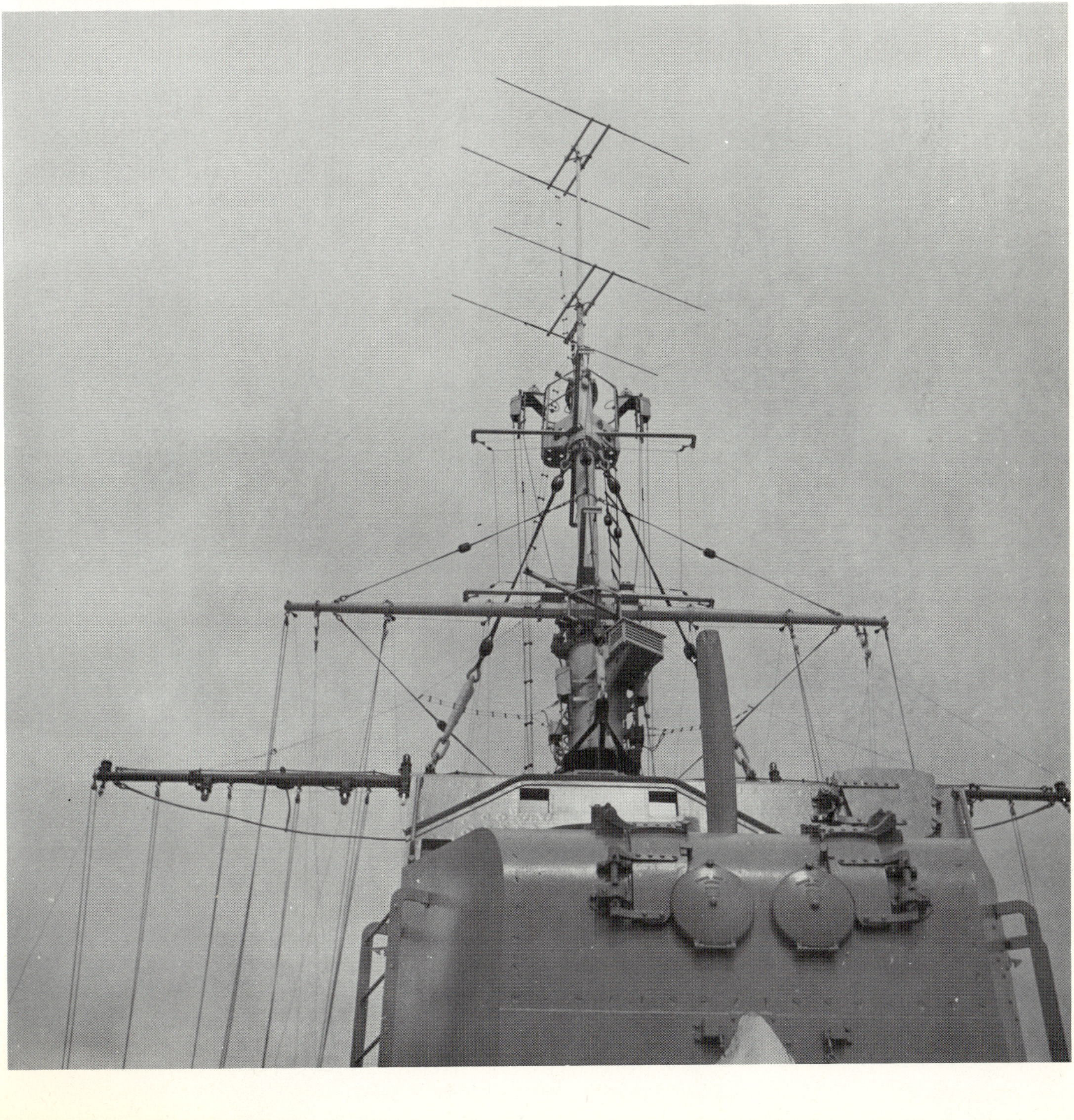

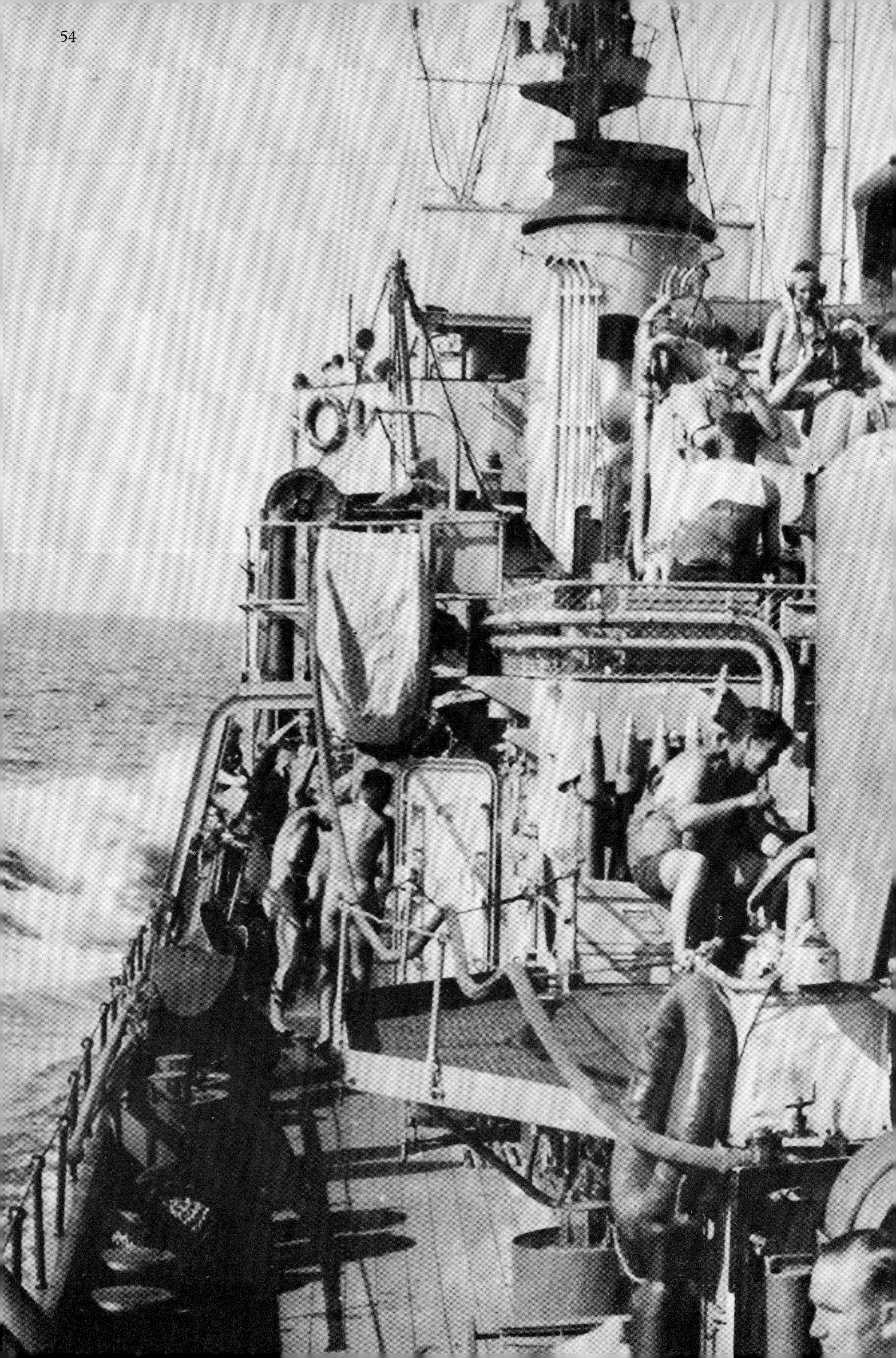

3. Personnel

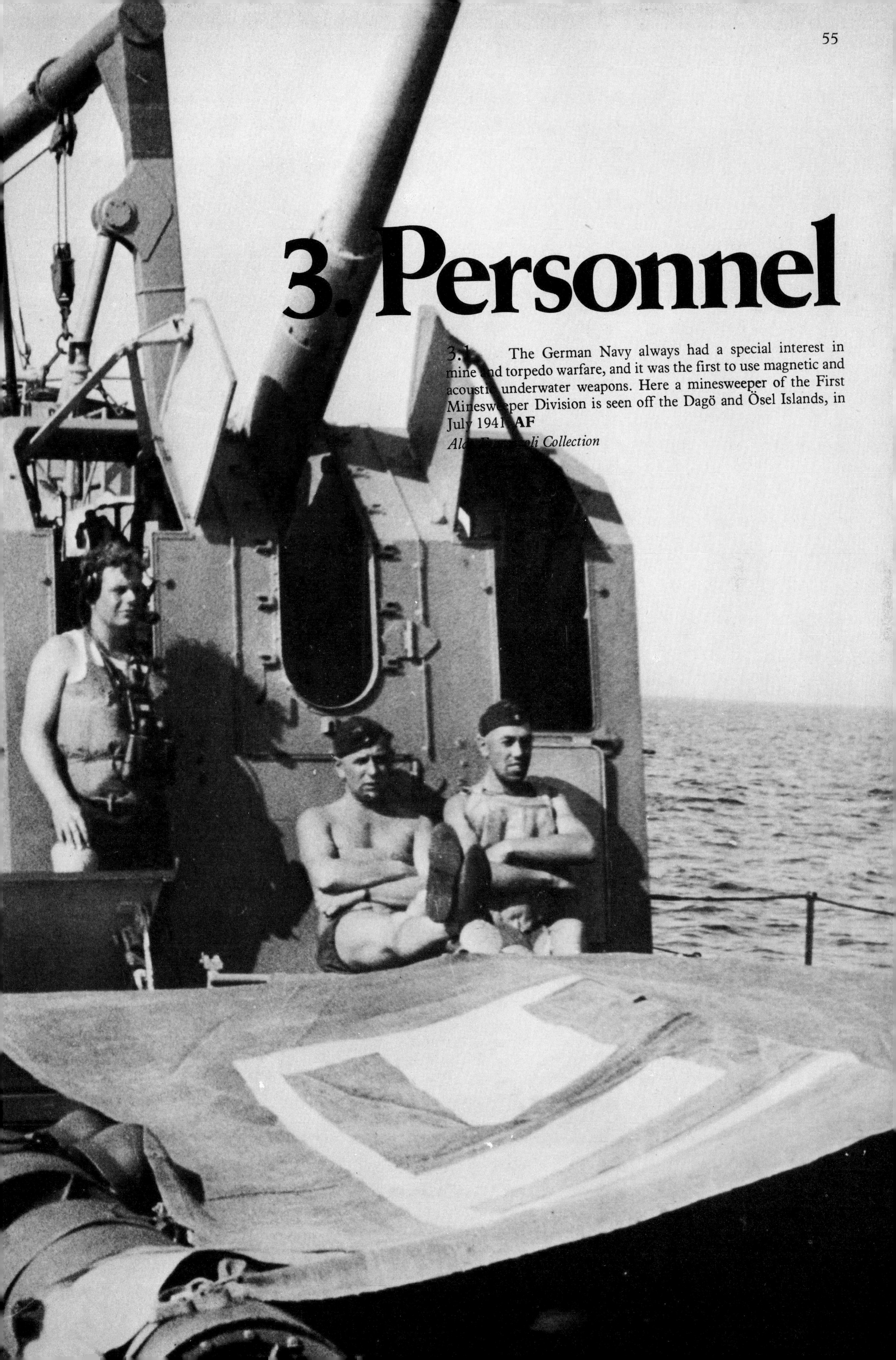

3.1 The German Navy always had a special interest in mine and torpedo warfare, and it was the first to use magnetic and acoustic underwater weapons. Here a minesweeper of the First Minesweeper Division is seen off the Dagö and Ösel Islands, in July 1941. **AF**
Aldo Fraccaroli Collection

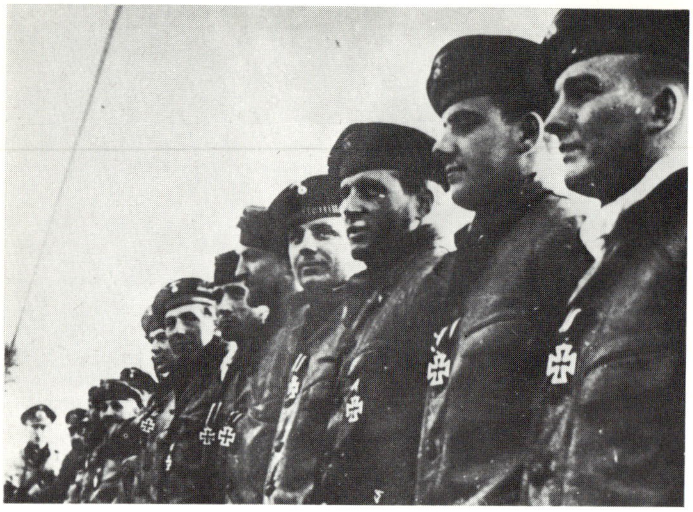

3.2

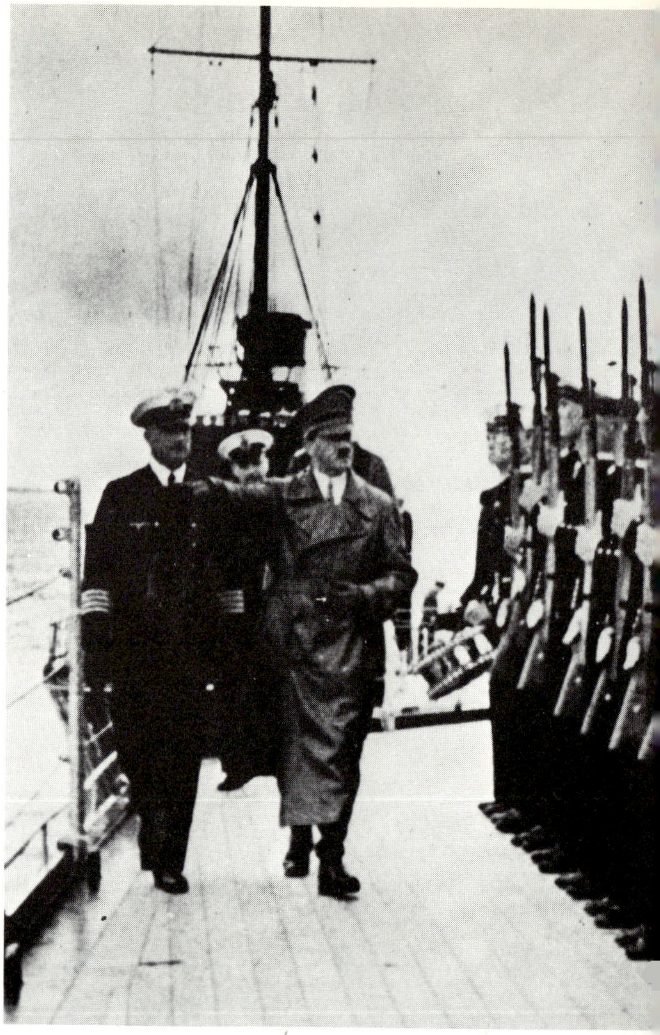

3.3

3.4

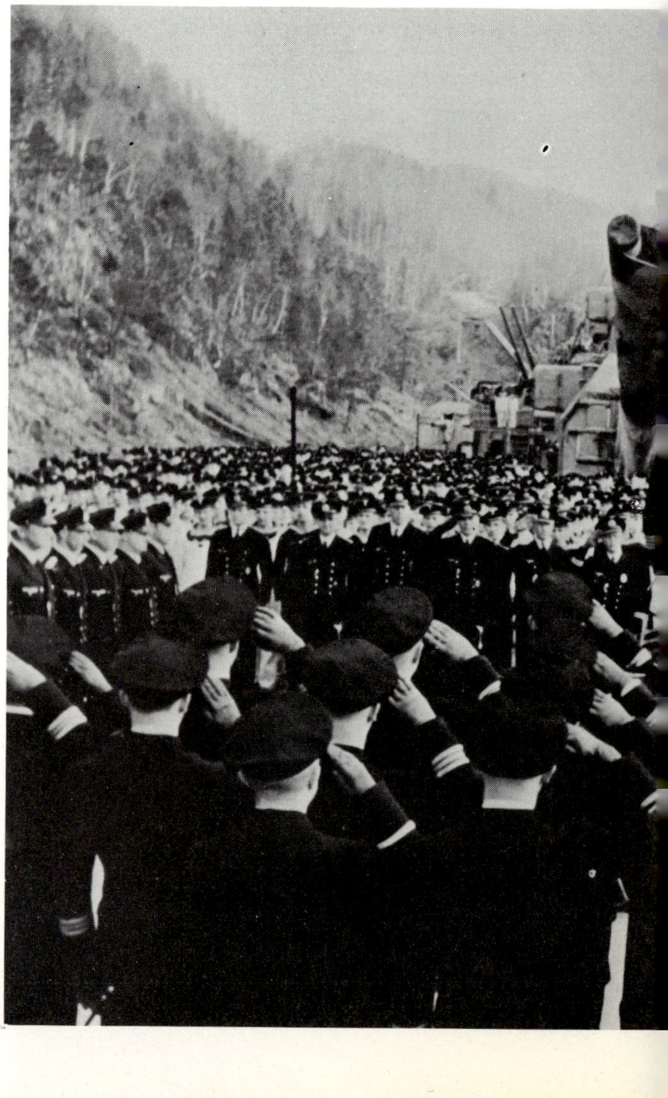

3.2 The crew of Kapitän Leutenant Günther Prien's *U 47* receiving decorations for their exploit in torpedoing HMS *Royal Oak* in Scapa Flow. **AP**
CPL

3.3 The relatively inactive life aboard major surface warships was enlivened by drill and parades. Here the *Führer* inspects a marine guard of honour on board the heavy cruiser (ex-'pocket-battleship') *Deutschland,* soon to be renamed *Lützow.* Hitler did his best to avoid actual trips to sea, and this photograph is taken in harbour. **AP**
CPL

3.4 The *Tirpitz* was a sister-ship to the *Bismarck,* but with some improvements: her full load displacement reached 52 600 tons, and the fuel capacity was 8780 metric tonnes (7900 for *Bismarck).* Her armour was 50+100mm thick on the decks; 320mm on sides; 360mm on main turrets; 350mm on conning tower. The machinery developed 138 000 SHP (designed), but actually reached 163 000 SHP, for 30.8 knots. There were three propellers 4.85m in diameter. The 38.0 L/47 main guns (so they were termed in the German Navy) weighed 109.2 tons each and could fire three rounds per minute at the muzzle velocity of 820.21m/sec at a range of 36 200 metres (AP shell weighed 798kg). This view shows a ceremony aboard the *Tirpitz,* in Fedden fjord, in 1942. After several attacks by British midget submarines and aircraft, the ship was eventually sunk, on 12 November 1944, by special air bombs. **AF**
Aldo Fraccaroli Collection

3.5 The members of the crew of *U 48* after receiving the Iron Cross. Under K/Lt Herbert Schultze and two other COs, *U 48* held the record for Allied tonnage sunk, 310 407 tons. **AP**
CPL

3.6 Part of the secret of the high morale in the U-boat Arm was the way in which the ex-submariner Admiral Dönitz kept personal contact with all his personnel. Here Dönitz congratulates Schuhart of *U 30* for sinking the carrier HMS *Courageous* in September 1939. **AP**
CPL

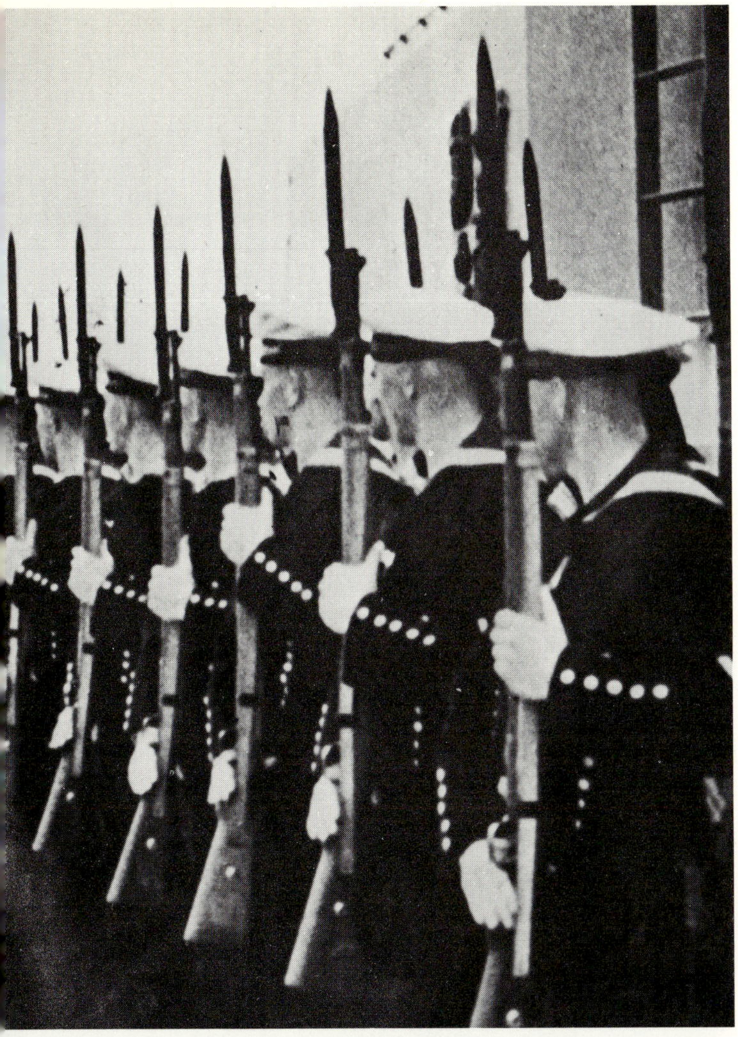

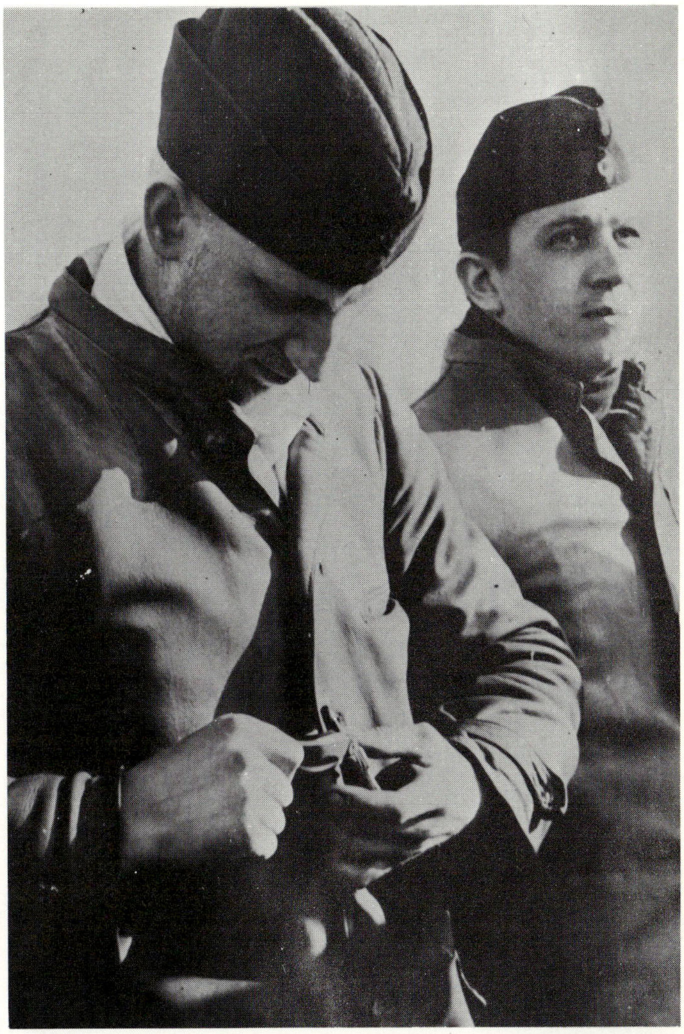

3.5

3.6

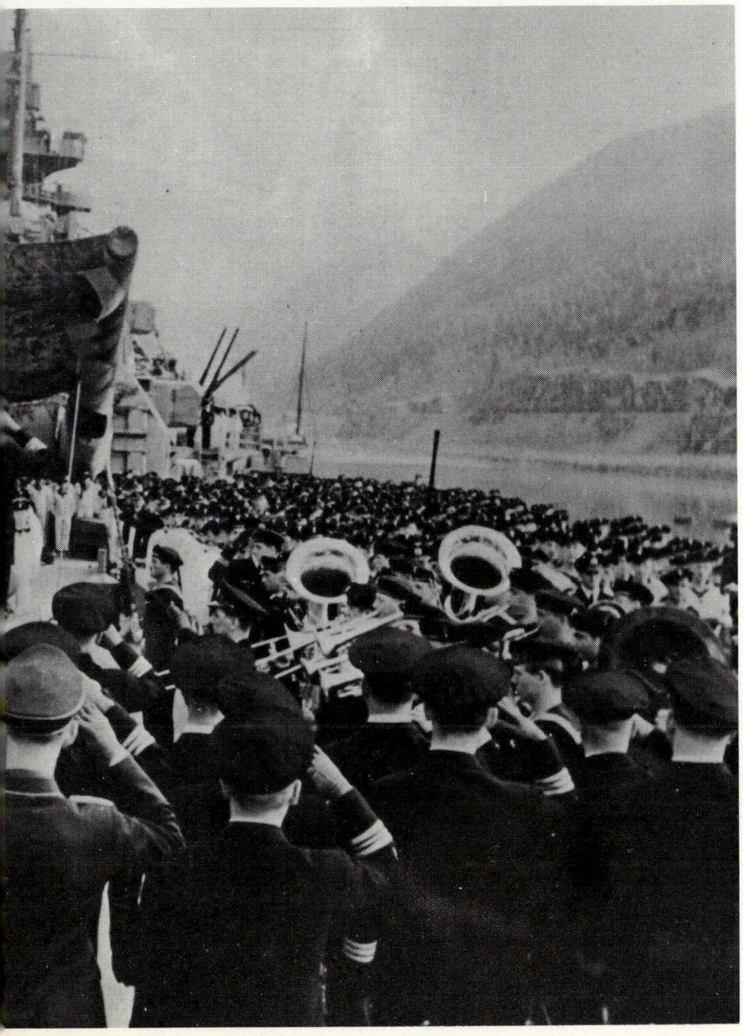

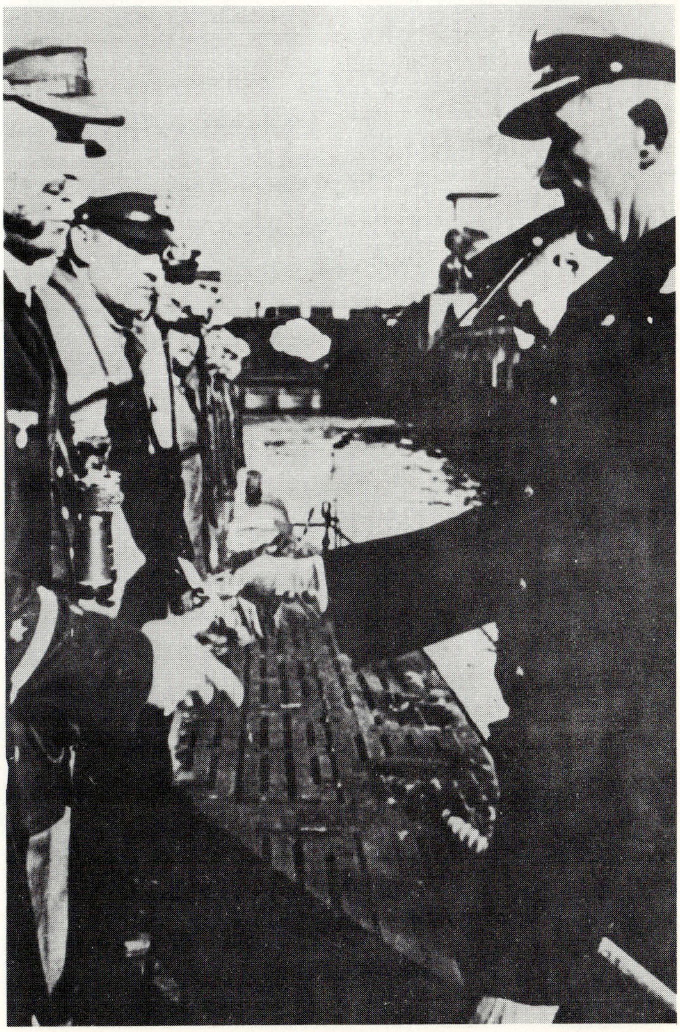

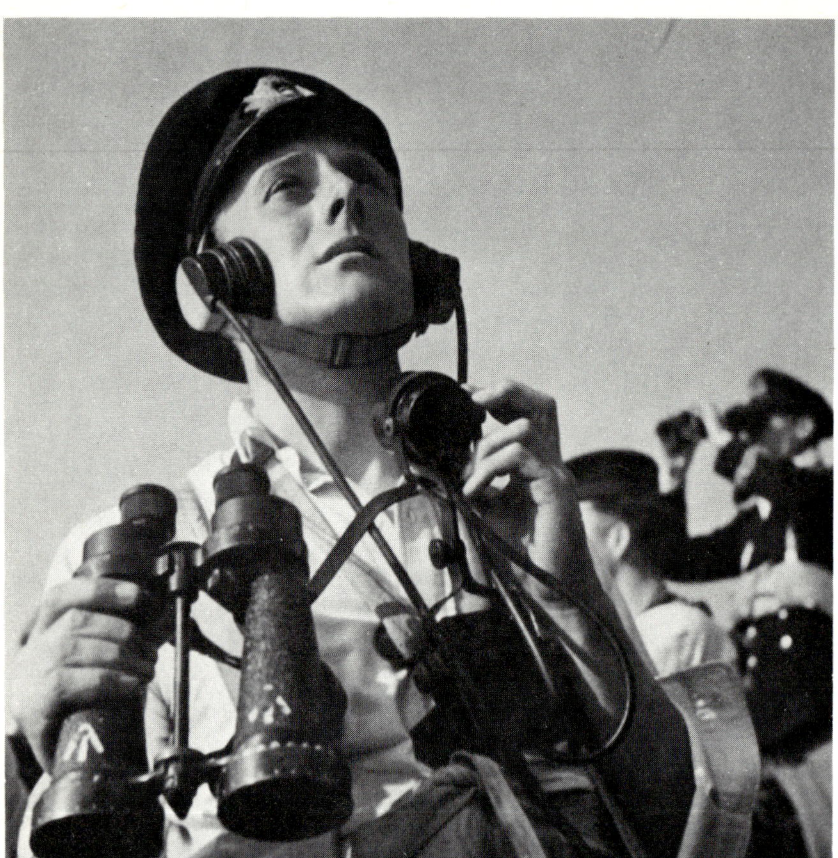

3.7

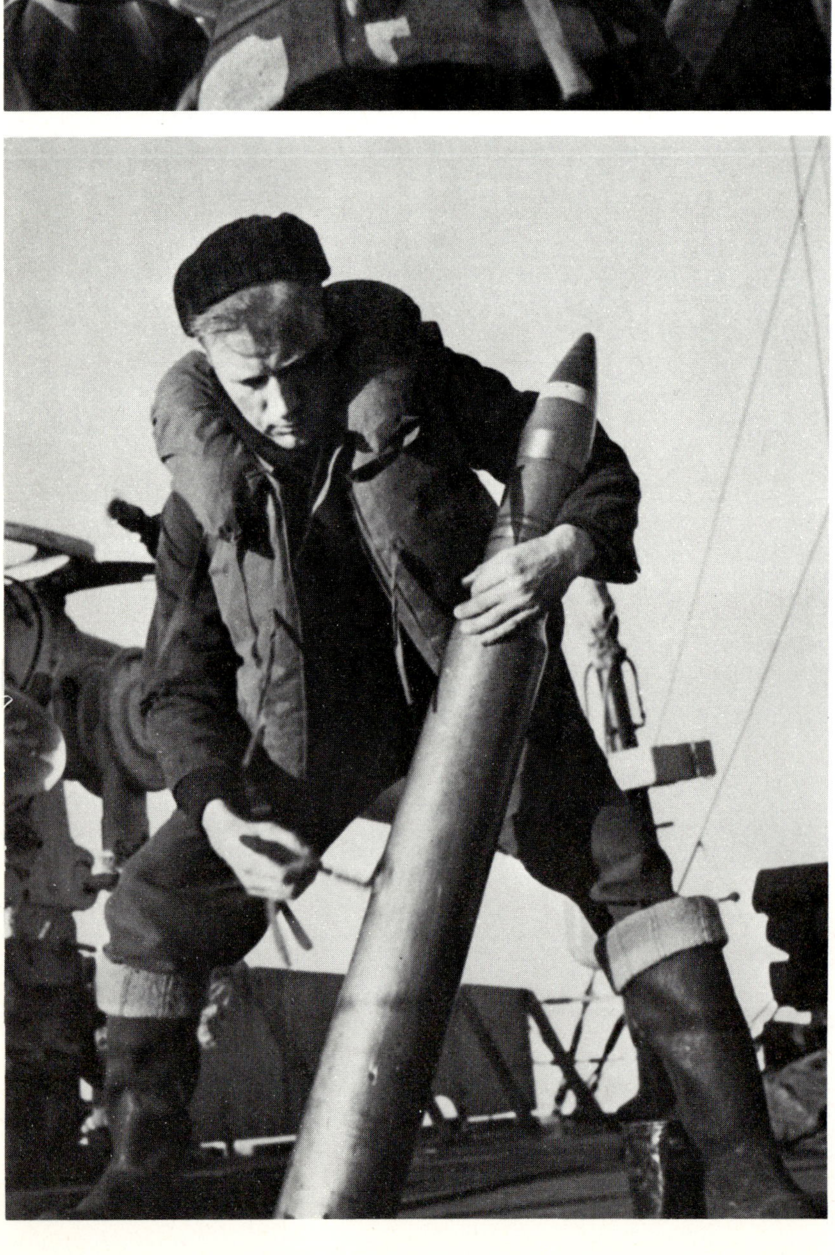

3.9

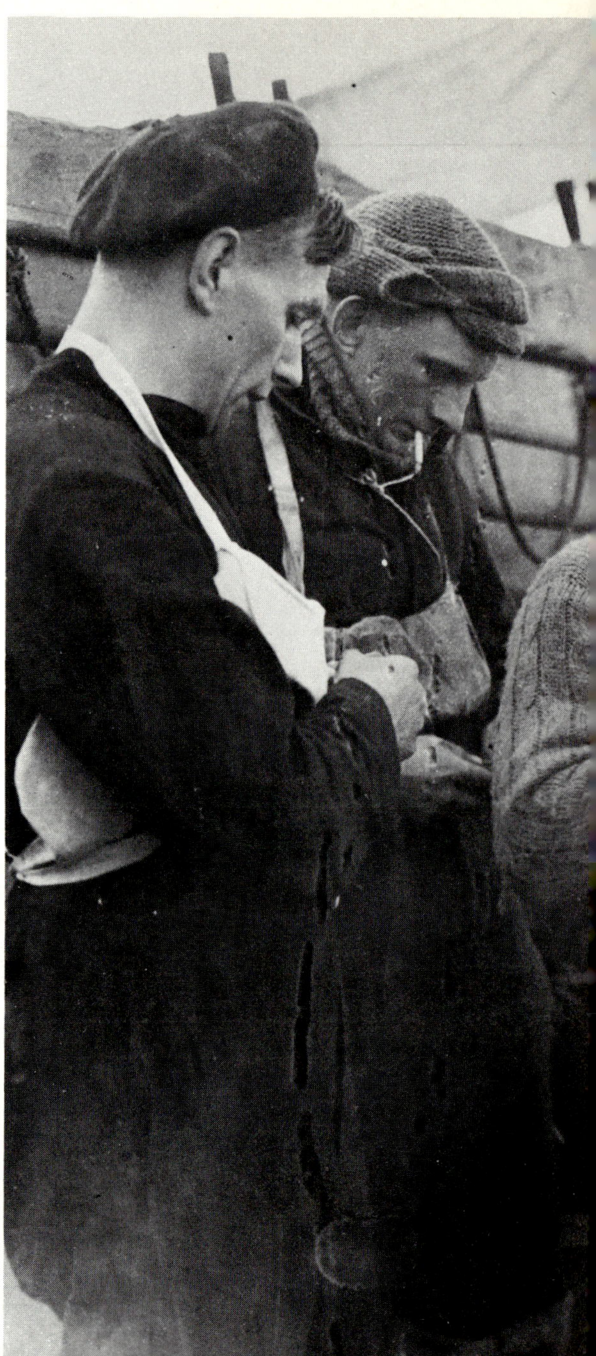

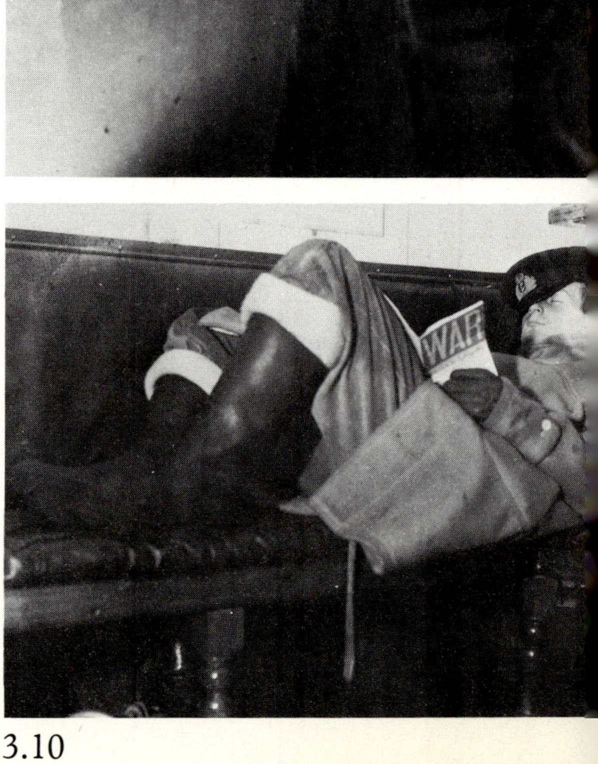

3.10

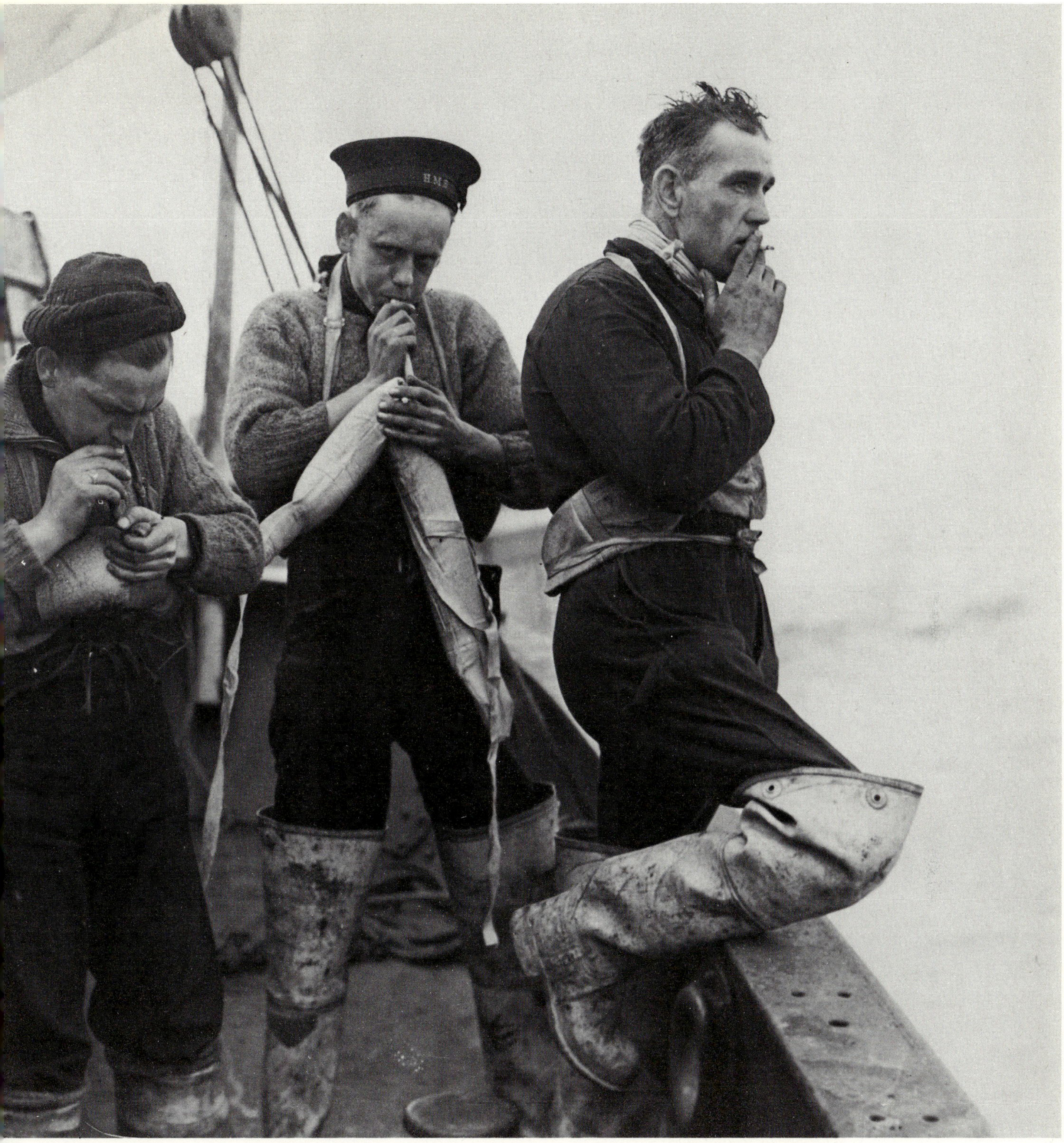

3.8

3.7 The kind of 'posed' portrait much favoured by wartime magazines — the gunnery officer of the escort destroyer *Wolsey,* with headphones for receiving range and bearing data from the high-angle director above the bridge. **AP**
CPL

3.8 In contrast a completely candid shot, epitomising the naval reserve — almost certainly ex-fishermen on board an ex-trawler — these five men relax from the gruelling routine of minesweeping, which was the fate of so much of the fishing fleet. **AP**
CPL

3.9 Greasing a 4inch round aboard a flush-decker to protect it while it lies in the ready-use rack. **AP**
CPL

3.10 Living conditions on the East Coast run — an off-duty officer dozing on HMS *Wolsey*'s wardroom sofa. **AP**
CPL

3.11 Looking aft from HMS *Wolsey*'s bridge in the kind of weather conditions common on East Coast Convoy duty. One can see the quadruple 0.5inch machine guns amidships and the twin 4inch high-angle mounting aft. These 'Wair' conversions were made from old 'V&W' class destroyers in 1938-40 as an interim measure until the new 'Hunt' class escort destroyers were ready. **AP**
CPL

3.12 Except for the warships, this picture could have come from a travel brochure showing the beautiful and peaceful South Pacific. The place is probably Majuro, 27 May 1944. The ships in the background are (left to right): *Bunker Hill* (CV-17), *Enterprise* (CV-6), either *Yorktown* (CV-10) or *Wasp* (CV-18), *Franklin* (CV-13) or *Hornet* (CV-12), an *Independence* class CVL, *Wichita* (CA-45) and another *Independence* class carrier. **LS**
USN

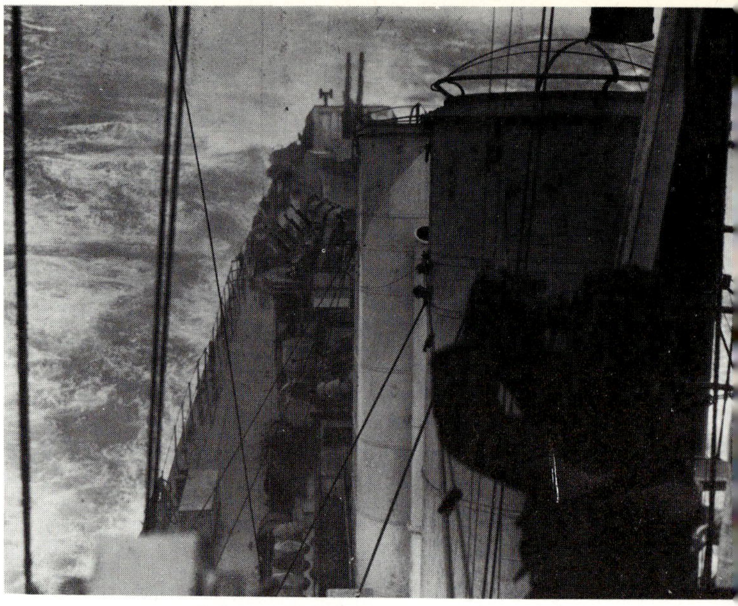
3.11

3.12
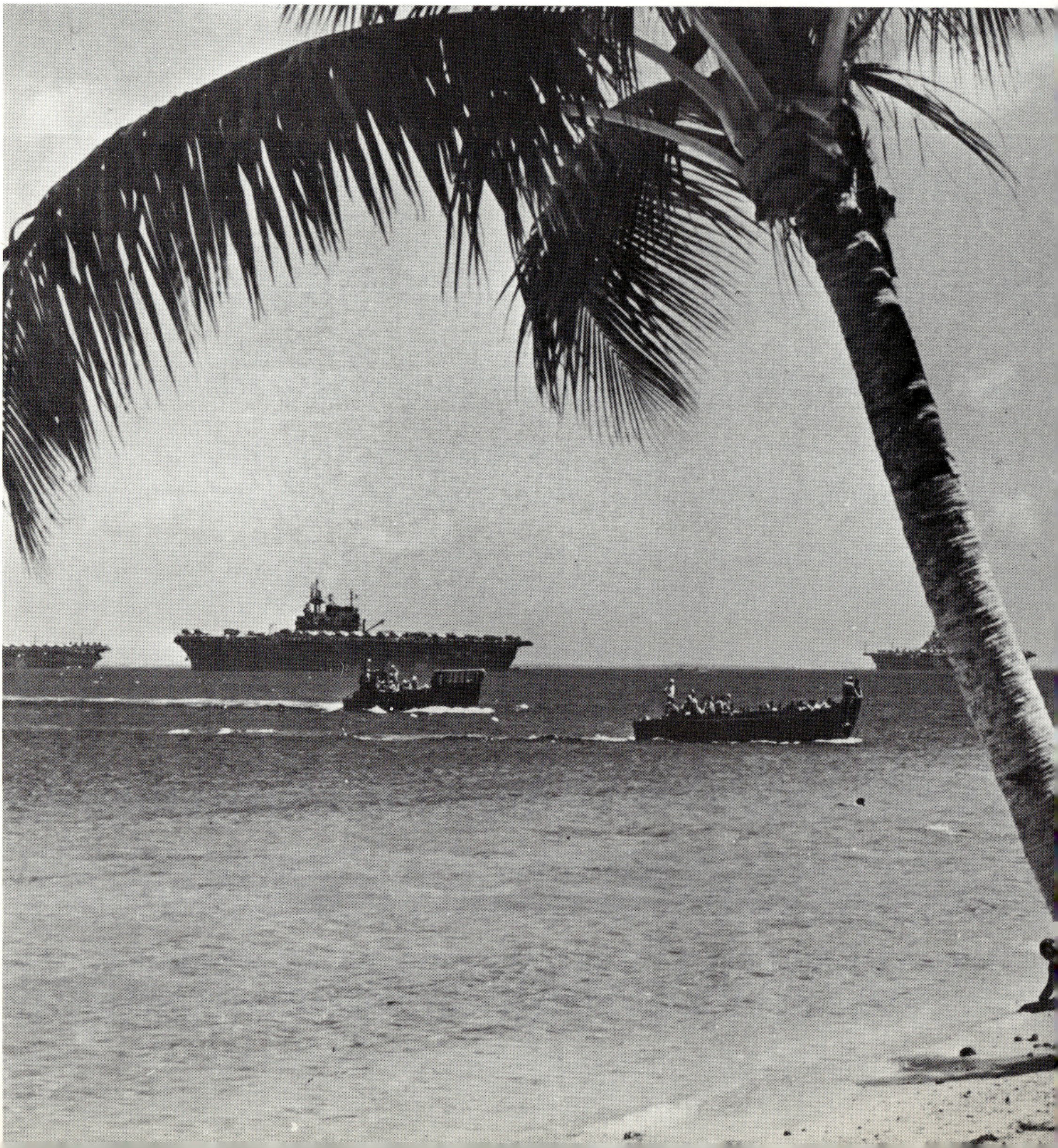

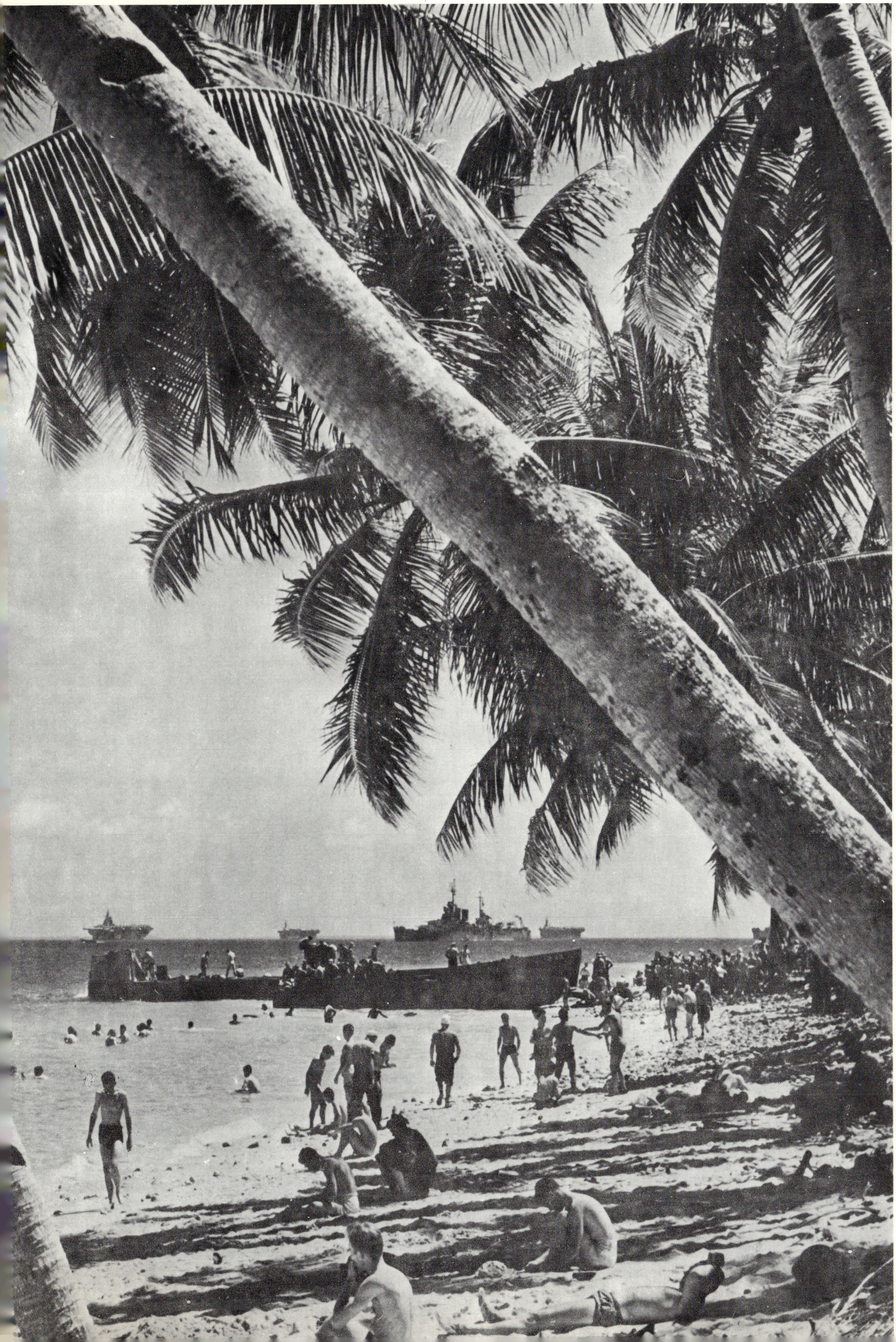

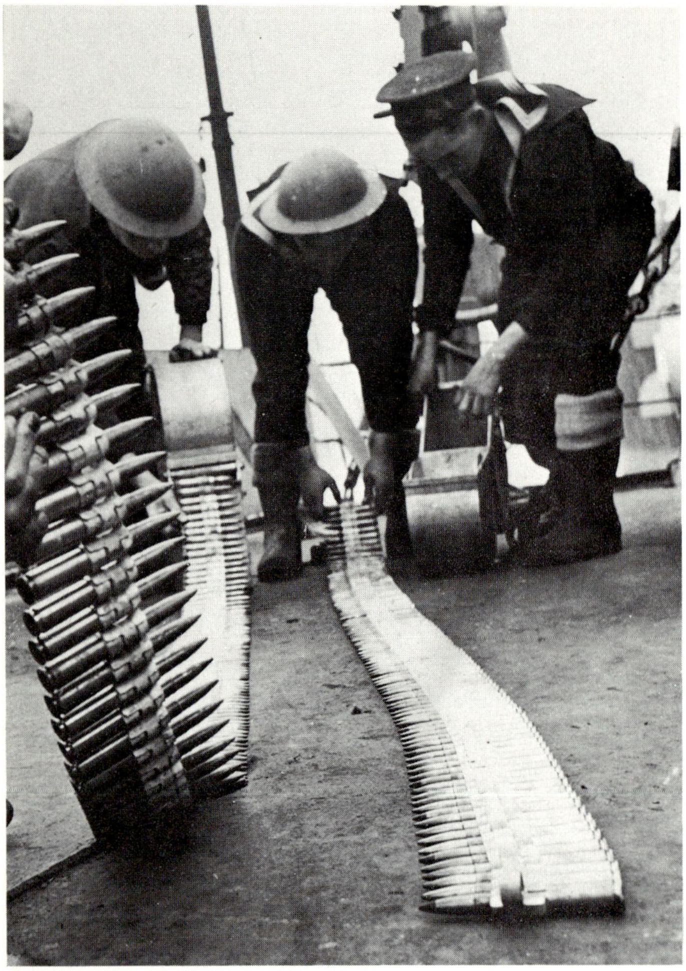

3.14

3.13 Overhauling two Bliss-Leavitt 21inch torpedoes aboard an ex-US flush-decker destroyer. Although the RN was not happy with the design of the torpedo-tube, these 1916-vintage weapons ran reliably after 25 years' service. **AP**
CPL

3.14 Loading 0.5inch belted rounds into drums for the Hotchkiss machine guns mounted as close-range AA armament in the same flush-decker. **AP**
CPL

3.15 A rare view inside the 5inch/51 calibre gun battery of the *Arkansas.* Note how the ready-use rounds are stacked in three tiers on either side of the embrasure. **AP**
CPL

3.16 17.7inch torpedoes and the two double mountings of the torpedo-boat *Lupo,* in the Aegean Sea, May 1942. *Lupo,* the best known torpedo-boat of the Italian fleet (her name had been given to the name-ship and first vessel of a new class of frigates, *Lupo* herself having been commissioned in July 1977) was one of the 32 ships of this class, built between 1933 and 1938. The torpedo-boat *Lupo,* launched from the Cantieri Navali del Quarnaro, of Fiume, on 7 November 1937, displaced 1050 tons at full load, had a speed of 34 knots (about 28 or less in wartime), three 3.9inch guns, eight machine guns, two depth charge throwers, and was fitted for minelaying (20 mines). In May 1941, during the attack on Crete, she was escorting a convoy of light craft with soldiers, for Crete. While trying to defend the convoy, *Lupo* fought gallantly against the powerful force under Rear Admiral Glennie's flag — three light cruisers and four destroyers. During this night engagement she passed between two enemy ships, launched two torpedoes and was hit by 18 shells, receiving only slight damage with some casualties. Her commanding officer, Commander Francesco Mimbelli, attacked British forces on other occasions while protecting her convoys. For instance, he rescued all the German soldiers of the transport *Città di Livorno* in the Aegean Sea on 17 January 1942, literally mooring his ship to the torpedoed transport, until the last soldier passed aboard the *Lupo,* with teutonic discipline, as on a parade ground. While on escort duty with another transport, the *Lupo* was sunk, on the night of 2 December 1942, by a force of cruisers and destroyers. **AF**
Photograph by Aldo Fraccaroli

3.13

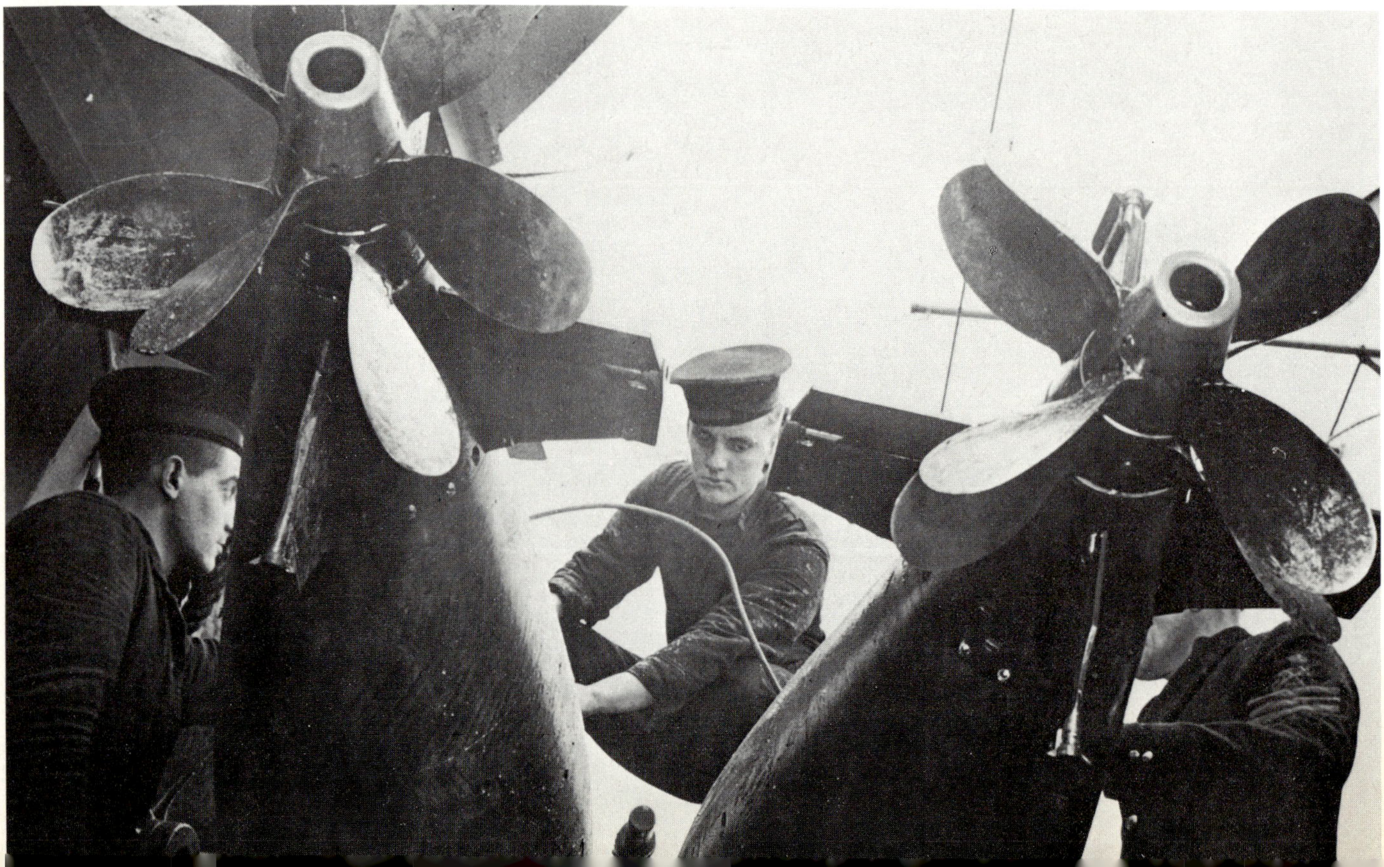

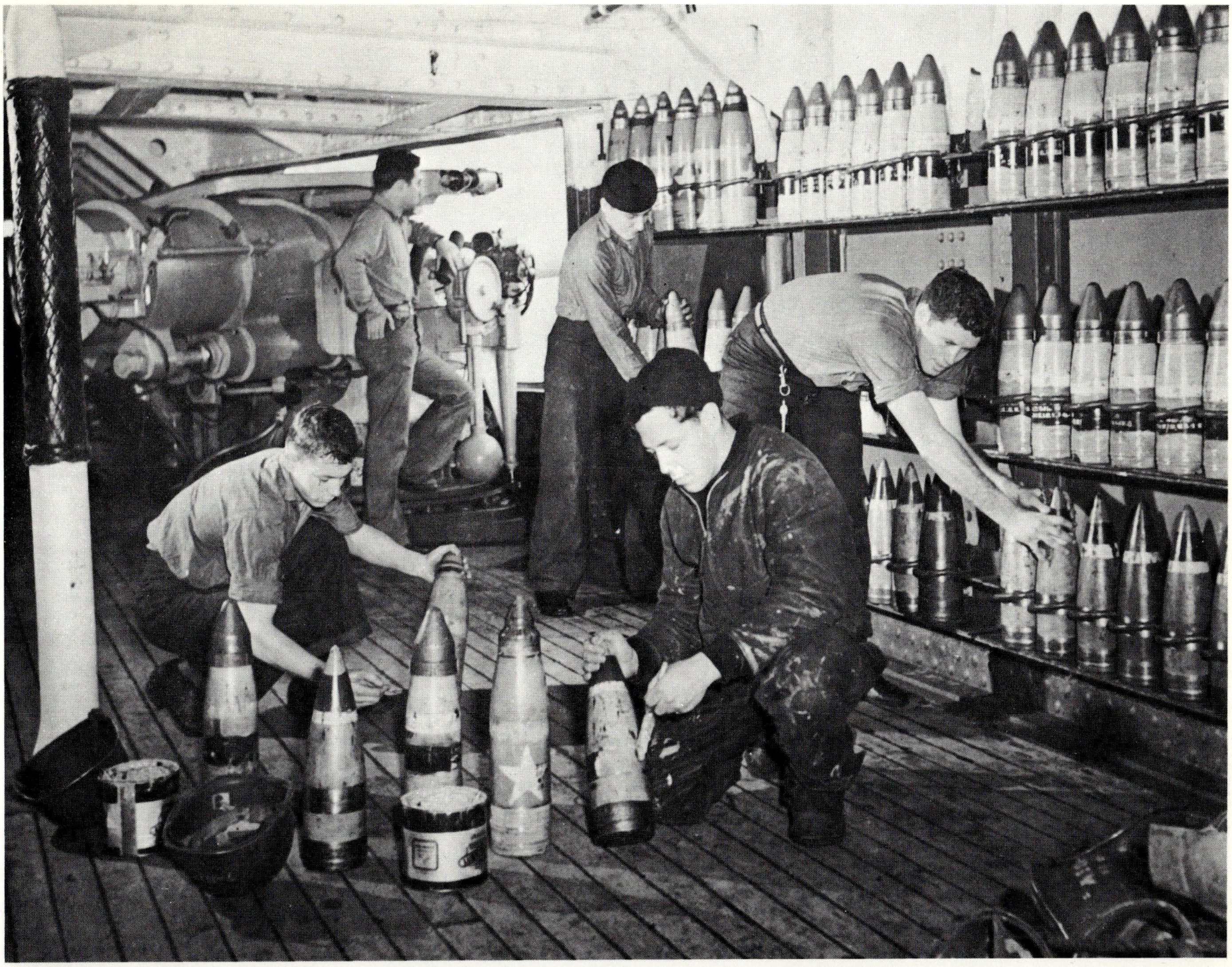

3.15

3.16

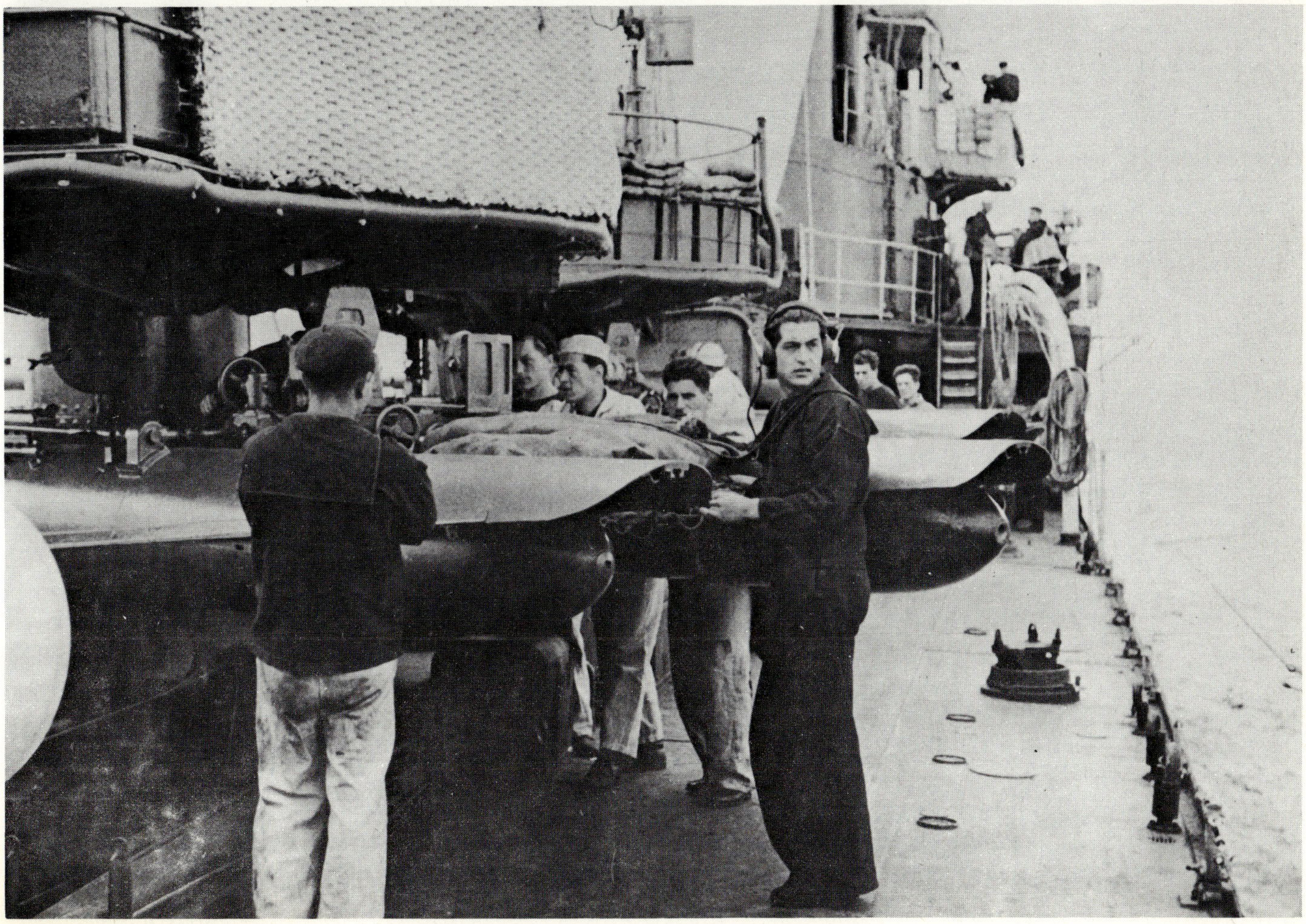

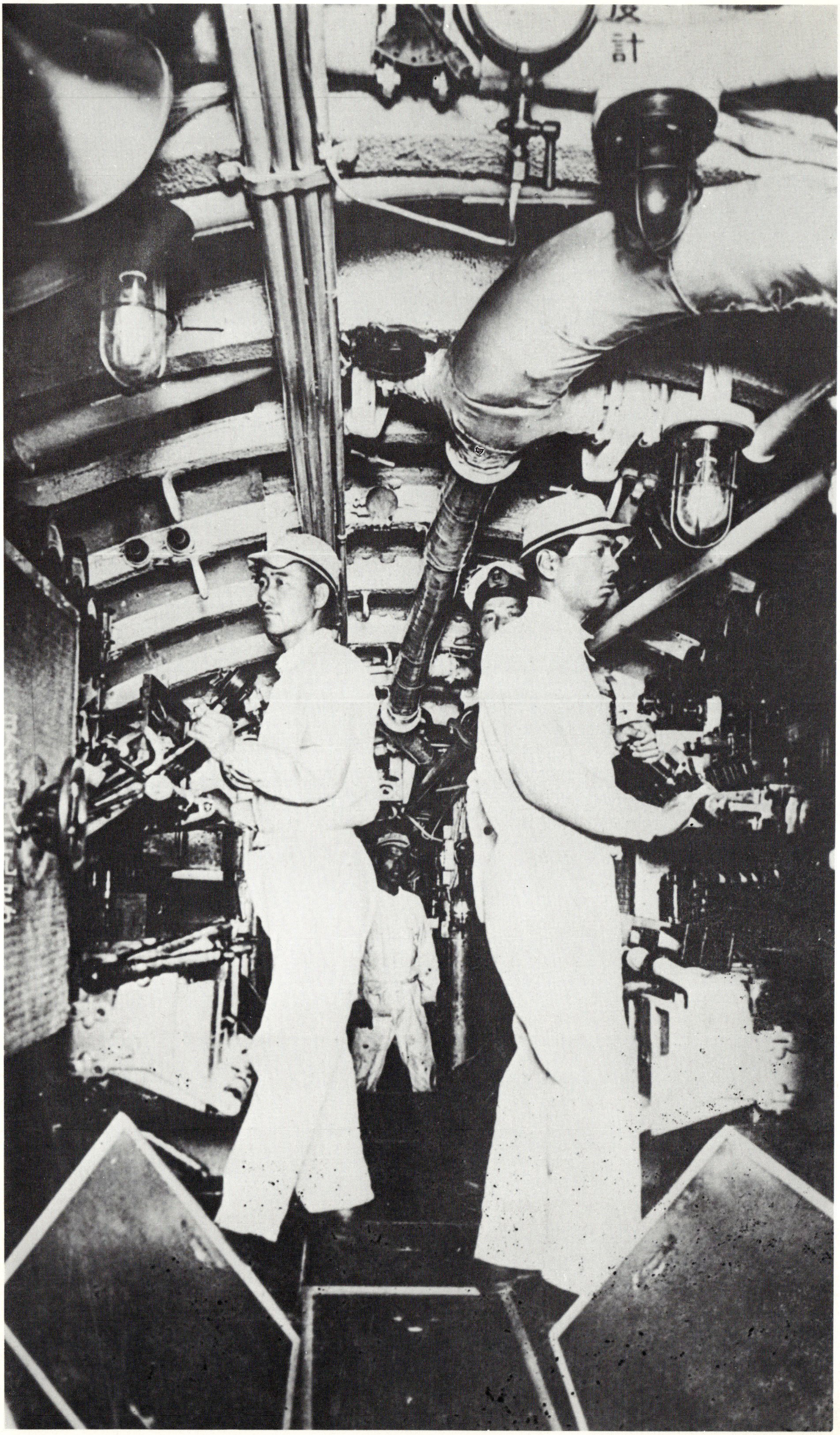

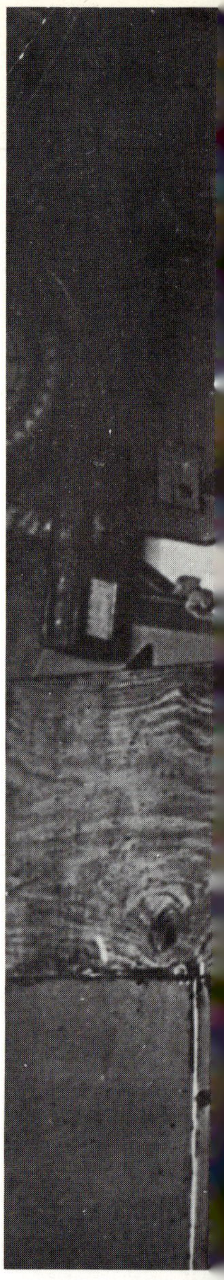

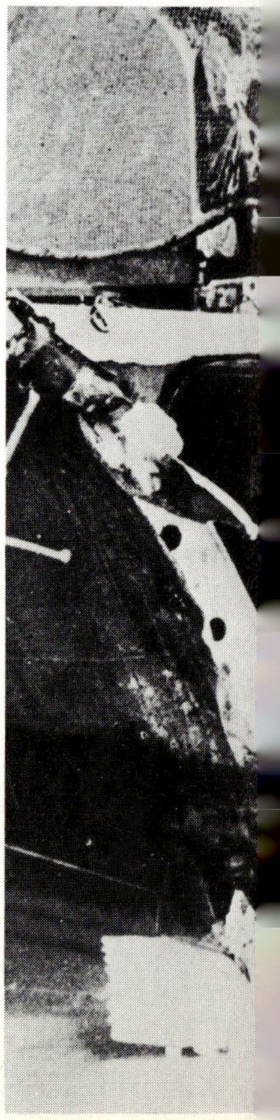

3.17 3.19

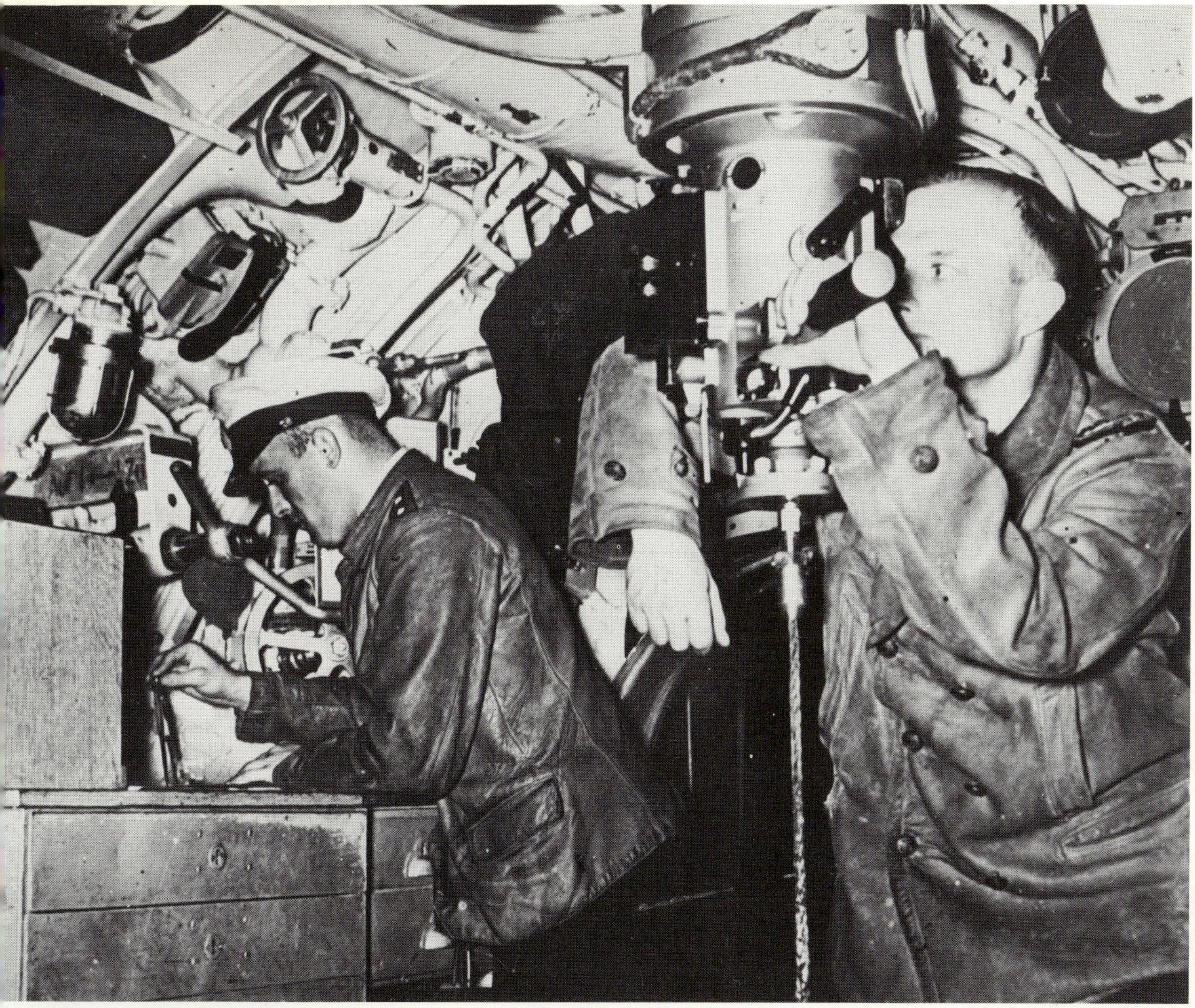

3.18

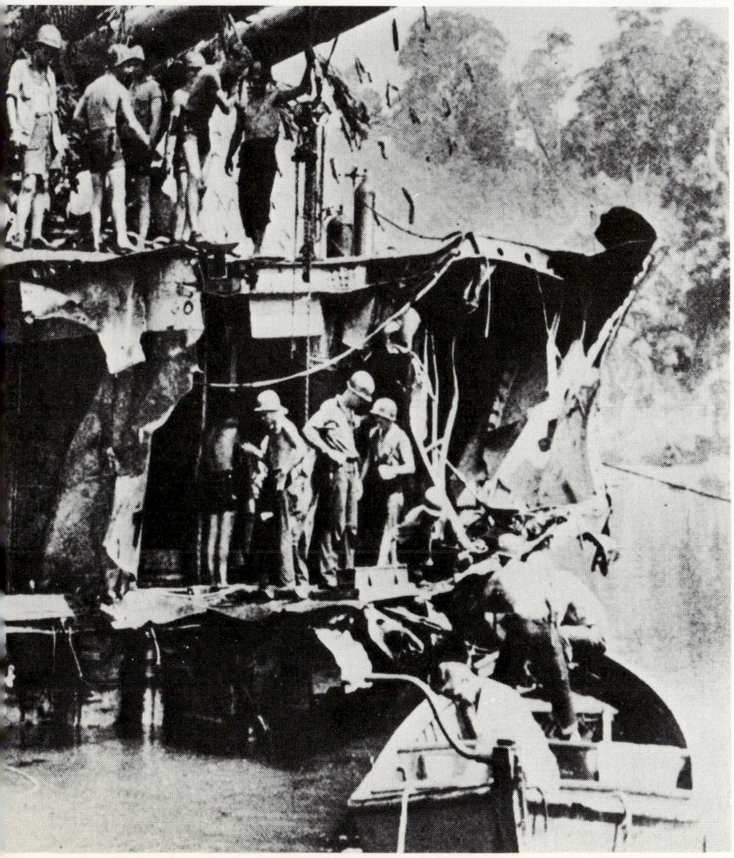

3.17 Two men at the main switchboard of a Japanese 'RO' class medium submarine. **AP**
CPL

3.18 The commanding officer of a U-Boat at the periscope. The all-pervading grease and oil, as well as the primitive washing facilities meant an inevitable relaxation of the regular navy's 'spit and polish'. **AP**
CPL

3.19 *Minneapolis* (CA-36) crewmen inspect damage at Tulagi in the Solomons on 1 December 1942. During the early morning hours an American cruiser and destroyer force had tried to trap a group of 'Tokyo Express' destroyers. Instead, Japanese torpedoes sank *Northampton* (CA-26); hit *New Orleans* (CA-32) and blew up her forward magazines — the foremost turret and entire bow were blown off; *Pensacola* (CA-24) took a torpedo in the after engine room and burned horribly. The flagship *Minneapolis* took one torpedo in the No 2 fire room and one in the bow. The jagged remains had to be cut off. The outnumbered Japanese got away without a scratch to any of their destroyers. **LS**
USN

Vice-Admiral Muselier founded the Free French Navy on 30 June 1940, choosing the Cross of Lorraine for its emblem. In spite of limited equipment, and staff shortage, due to recruitment problems caused by the Mers-el-Kébir tragedy, most of the French vessels which had withdrawn to England were re-armed and taken over by the Royal Navy on 3 July 1940. These vessels included the battleship *Courbet,* which was their base at Portsmouth; the destroyers *Le Triomphant* and *Léopard*; a few escort vessels and anti-submarine craft and four submarines. One of these, the largest of its type in the world, was the *Surcouf.* Lt Commander (capitaine de corvette) Ortoli, was responsible for her re-armament, a tremendous feat in view of the fact that he was obliged to work without any specialised staff.

Under the command of Lt Commander Cabanier, and then of Lt Commander Rousselot, the *Rubis* took part in a successful minelaying operation which was to last throughout the war, and was responsible for destroying about fifteen enemy vessels.

The *Narval,* which had sailed to Malta at the armistice, was lost by a mine in the region of the Kerkenna Islands during her third mission, in December 1940.

Le Triomphant was to represent the Free French Navy on the Pacific front. The *Léopard* together with HMS *Spey* and *Pelican* sunk the *U 136* in the Atlantic in July 1942. The *Léopard* then proceeded to the Indian Ocean, ready for battle when, on 27 November 1942, Reunion Island rallied to the Free French cause. After various escort missions in the Indian Ocean, she ran aground in the eastern Mediterranean on 27 May of the following year.

Without doubt, the vessels with the most distinguished service were the nine corvettes transferred from the Royal Navy in 1941. Six of them served in the north Atlantic. Two were lost: the *Alysse* was torpedoed on 8 February 1942 by the *U 654,* and the *Mimosa* disappeared on 3 June, with her commander, C F Birot and almost the whole crew — only three survived.

The Free French Navy is credited with the destruction of three enemy submarines: the *U 609,* sunk by the *Lobélia,* under the command of Lieutenant de Morsier, on 7 February 1943; the *U 444* and *U 432,* sunk within twelve hours of each other on 11 March 1943 by the *Aconit,* commanded by Lieutenant Levasseur.

Three more corvettes served in the southern Atlantic. In the two years following her re-armament on 19 June 1941, the *Aconit* covered 84 000 miles, escorted 34 convoys through the north Atlantic in 405 days, was engaged in innumerable rescue operations and about ten engagements with the enemy.

Admiral Muselier resigned from his post at the head of the Free French Navy in March 1942, on his return from a successful mission to St Pierre and Miquelon, where he rallied these islands to the French cause. His success was due to an impressive demonstration by the *Surcouf* and three corvettes from Newfoundland.

The *Surcouf* was due to leave for the Pacific Ocean, but collided with an American cargo ship in the Caribbean while making towards Panama. She sank with all hands, including Commander Blaison, on 18 February 1942.

Captain Auboyneau, who at the time was in command of *Le Triomphant* in the Pacific Ocean, was recalled to London and appointed Rear Admiral, thus assuming the functions of national commissioner to the navy. He was to be responsible for uniting the Free French Navy with the African Naval Forces on 2 August 1943, combining under one command all those naval strengths able to take part in the war. Up to this time, out of a total of about 7500 men, the Free French had lost 567 officers and seamen, reported dead or missing. Lieutenant Honoré d'Estienne d'Orves, shot at Mont Valérien on 27 August 1941, was the most illustrious of them all. **JM**

3.1

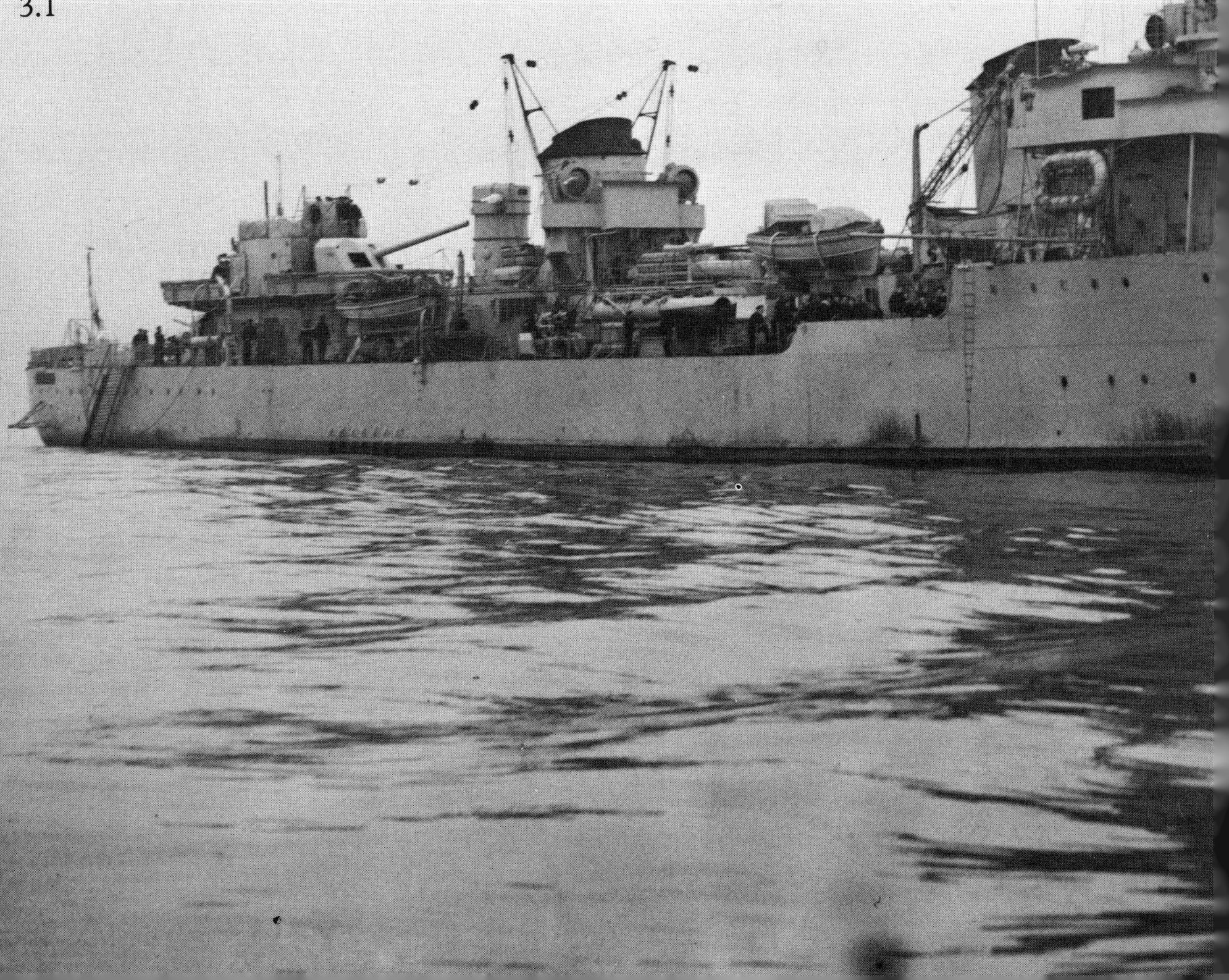

4. Navies in Exile

France

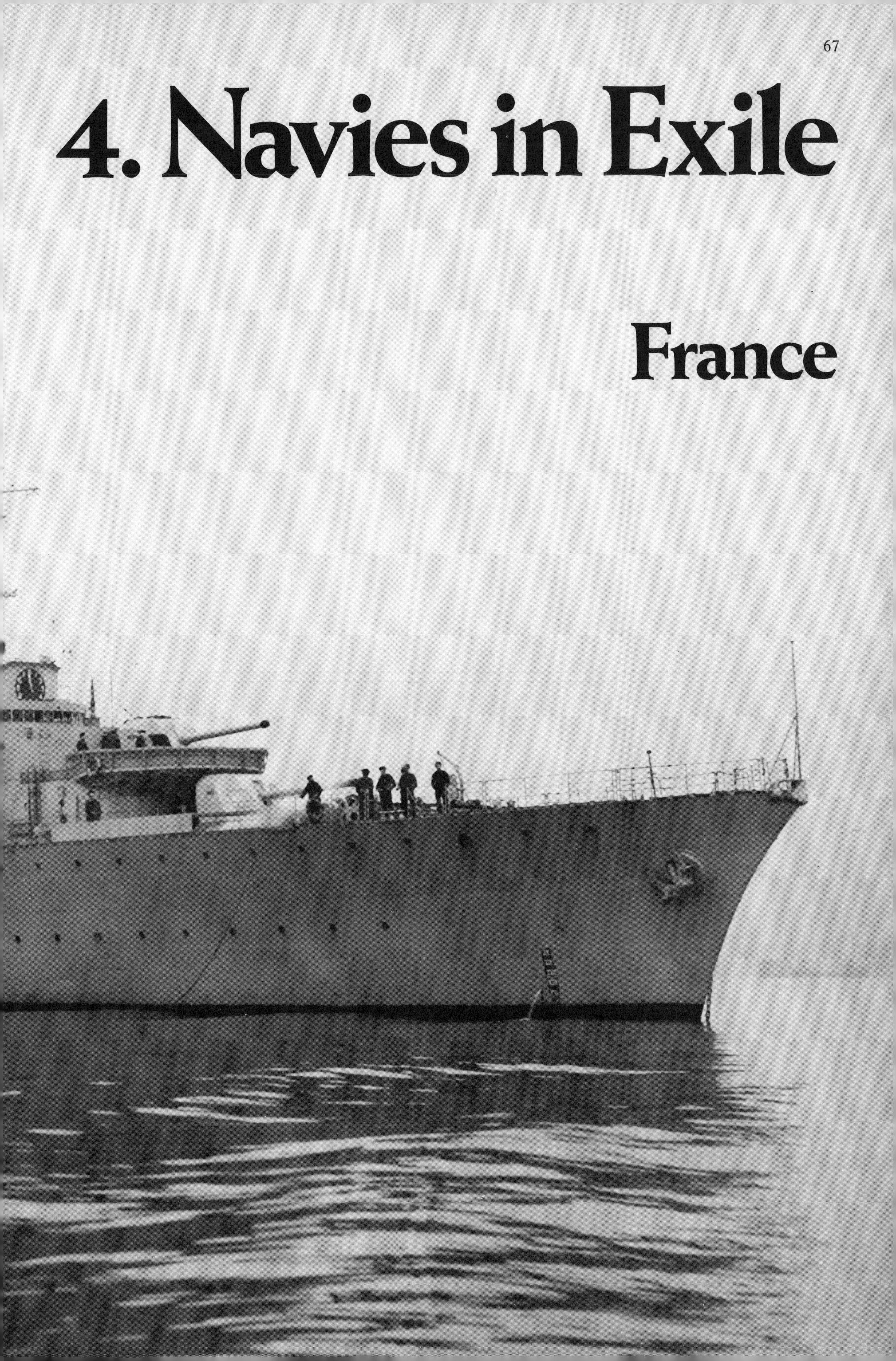

4 Navies in Exile

4.1 *Le Triomphant* was one of a series of six destroyers, belonging to the *Fantasque* class which was part of the 1930 naval programme. She was launched at the shipyards of Chantiers de France at Dunkirk on 16 April 1934. Her trials took place in 1935 and she entered service in the following year.

Displacement	2569 tons standard
Length	132.4m (overall) x 11.08m x 4.8m
Machinery	4 small tube boilers; 2 Parsons turbines; 2 propellers
Horsepower	74 000 (design); 43 knots (maximum)
Crew	220 (peacetime)
Armament	5 x 138mm/50 calibre (single mountings); 4 x 37mm AA (two twin mountings); 4 x 13.2mm AA (two twins); 9 x 550mm torpedo-tubes (three triples); two racks for up to 50 mines.

In April 1940, during an encounter at high speed in the North Sea, *Le Triomphant* was narrowly missed by a bomb. The explosion cracked the propeller-shaft bracket. At the time of the German invasion, the vessel was undergoing repairs at Lorient, but nevertheless managed to reach Portsmouth carrying her shaft and propeller on deck.

She was taken over by the Royal Navy and became part of the Free French Navy. Her damage was repaired while under the command of Commander Auboyneau, and she was then sent to the Pacific under Commander Ortoli, via Panama in mid-August 1941. However, she proved too limited in endurance for this theatre and her equipment was taxed beyond its capacity. On her recall to Europe in December 1943 she was almost lost in a severe typhoon. After her repair and modernisation in the US, she joined the Eastern Fleet in May 1945, and was the first French warship to return to Saigon after the defeat of Japan. **JM**
CPL

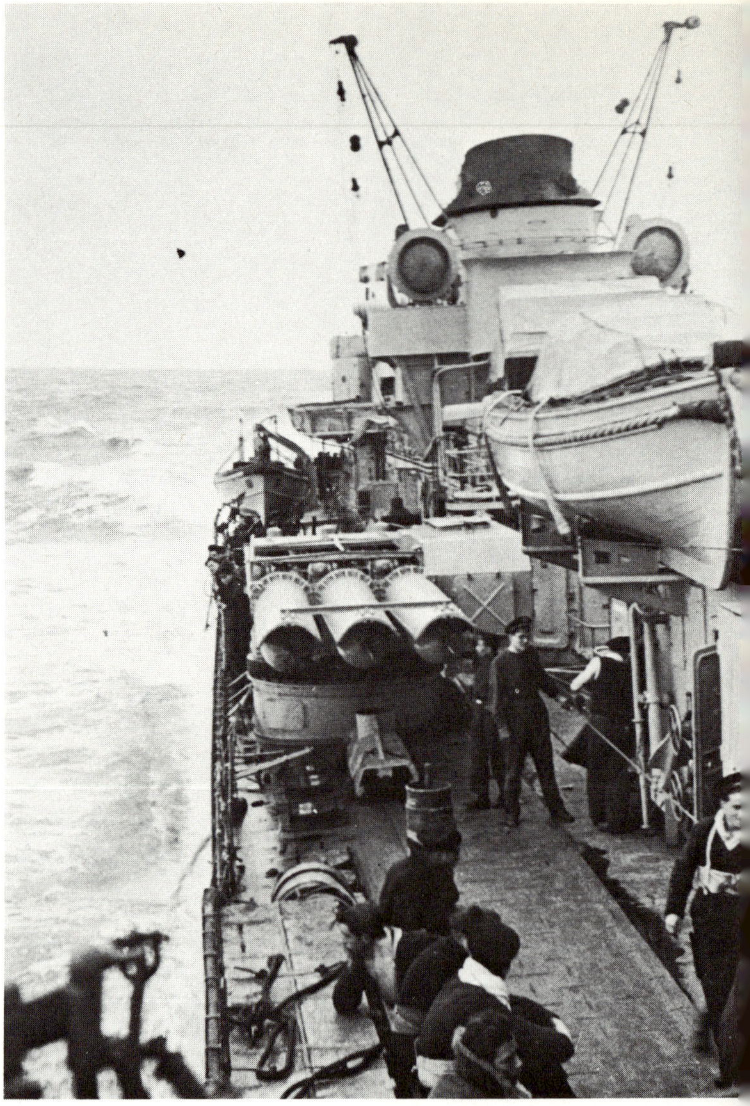

4.2

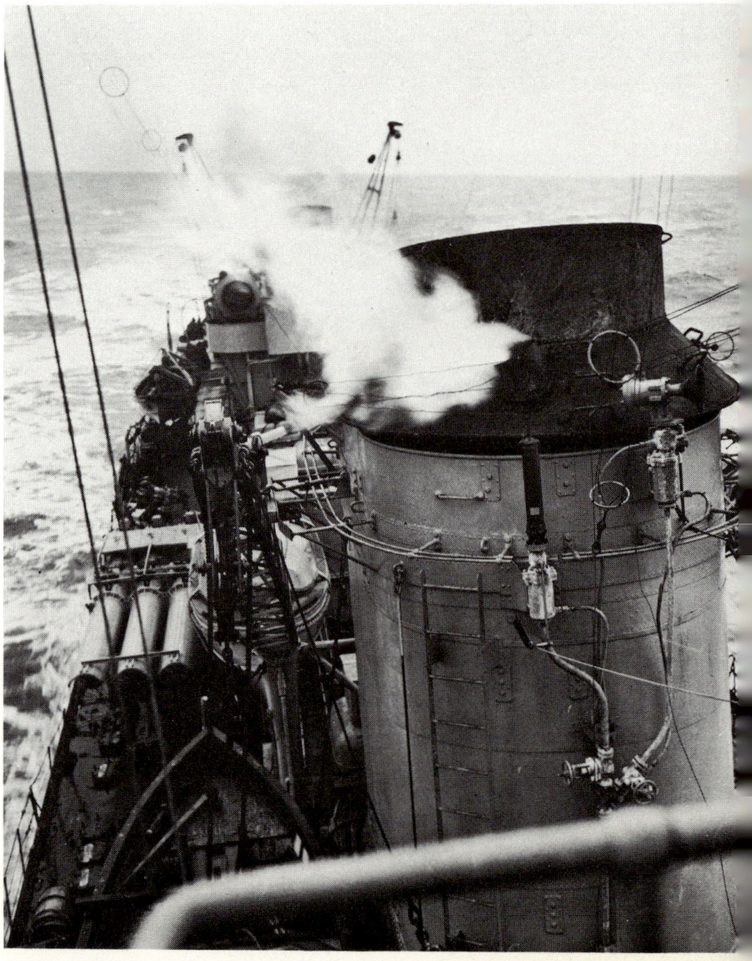

4.3

4.2 A view of the starboard main deck of *Le Triomphant* showing the torpedo derrick and the triple mounting for 550mm torpedo-tubes. There are two reserve torpedoes of the same type at each side. In the background can be seen funnel number two with its searchlight platform and supports for the antennae. **JM**
CPL

4.3 *Le Triomphant* seen from abaft the bridge. From the appearance of the wake the ship seems to be making good headway. **JM**
CPL

4.4 *Le Triomphant* at sea — a view of the bridge and forward 138mm (5.5inch) guns, in the Channel, late 1940. **JM**
CPL

4.5 A view of a 550mm torpedo being placed in its tube aboard *Le Triomphant.* The outer tube of the triple mounting faces aft, at 180° from its normal position, in order to allow the operation to take place. Behind the tubes can be seen the twin mounting for 37mm semi-automatic guns. **JM**
CPL

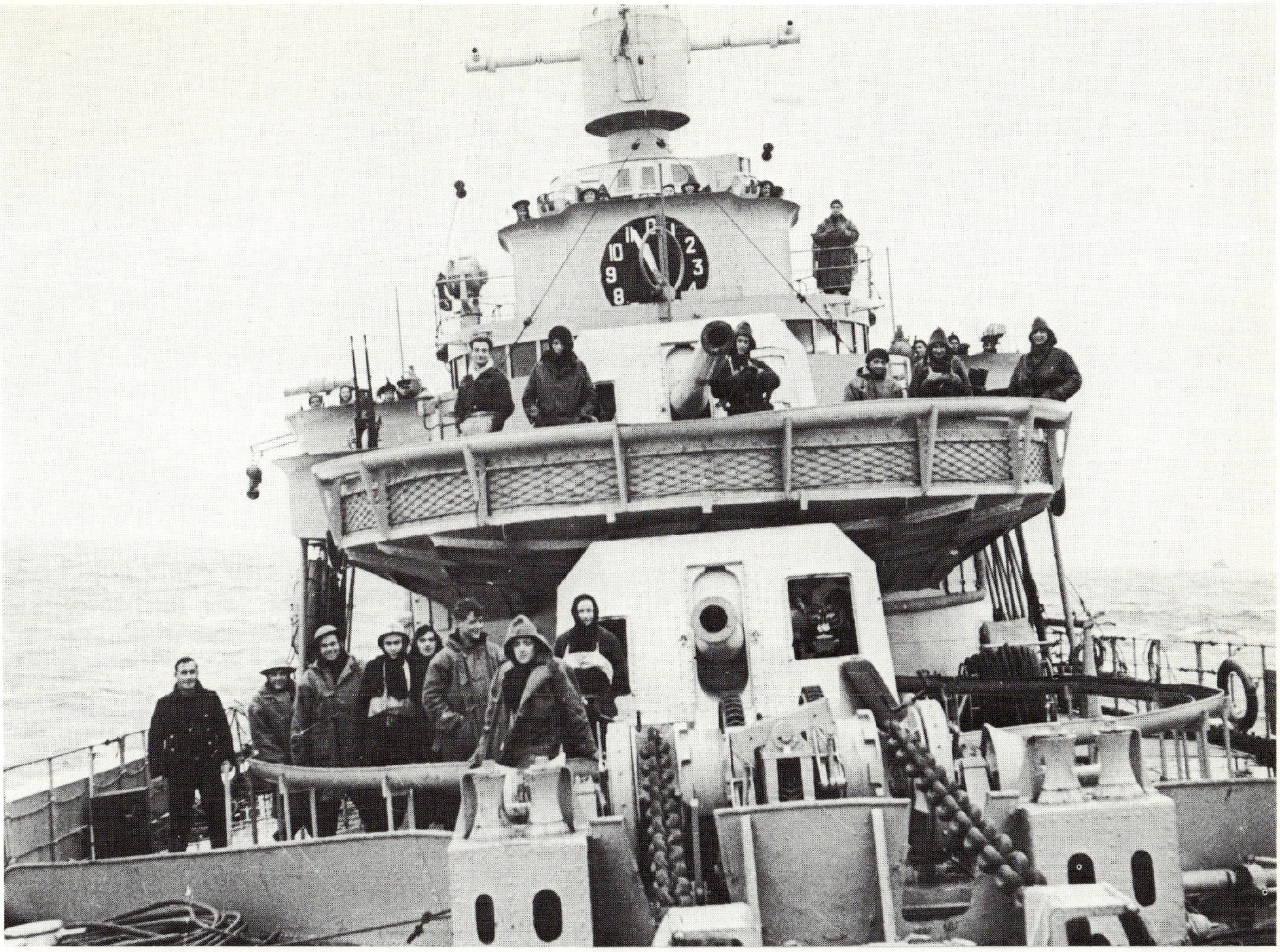

4.4

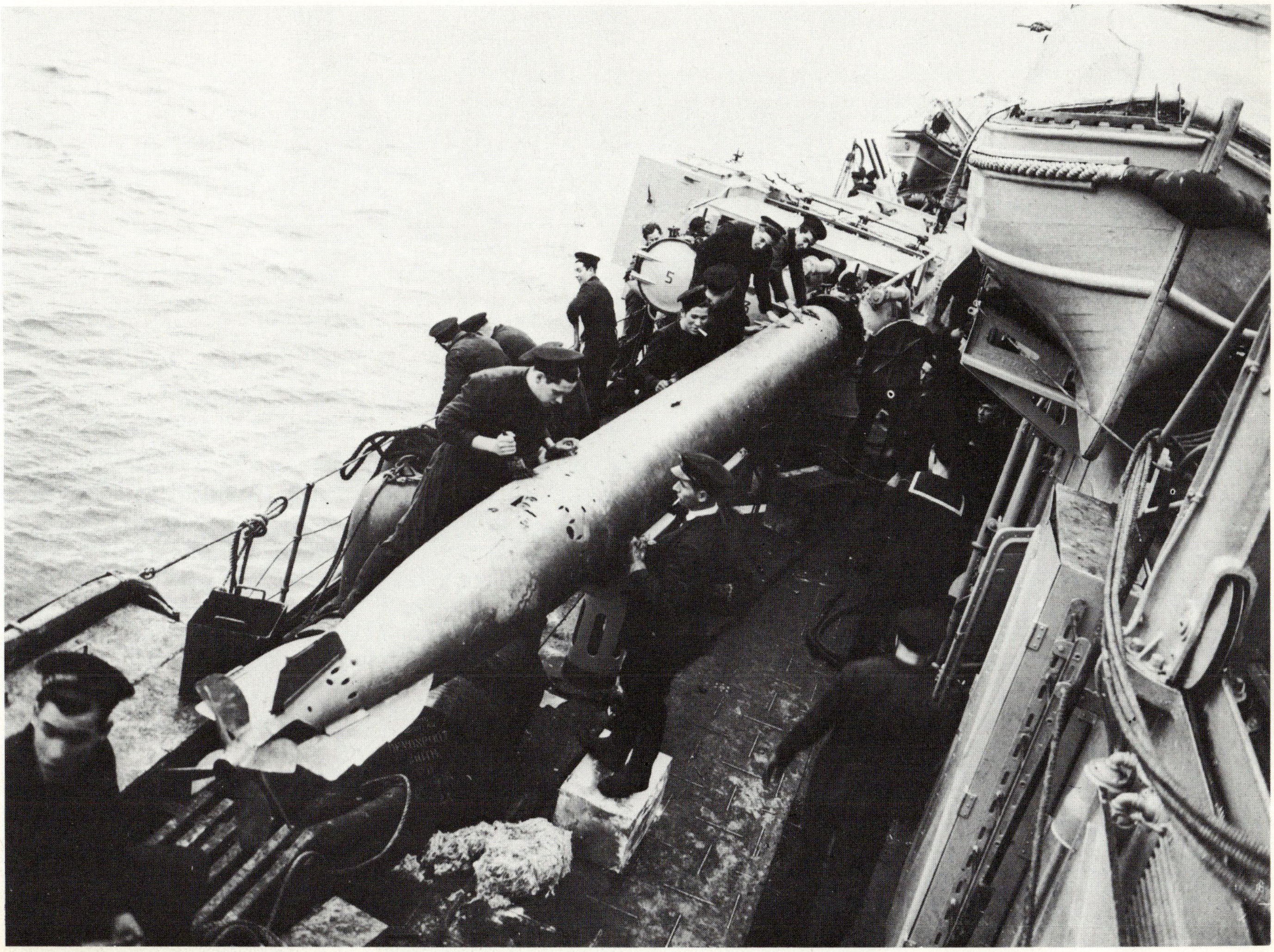

4.5

4.6

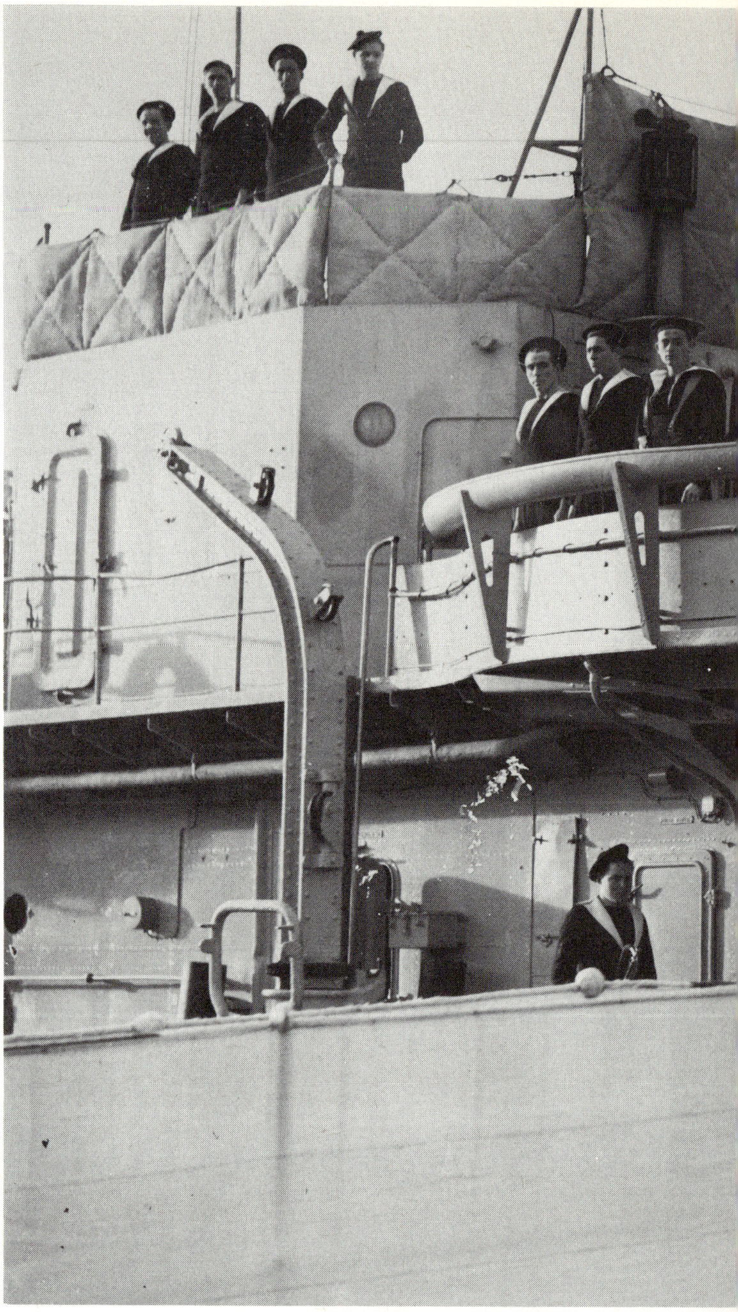

4.6 General de Gaulle and Admiral Muselier on board *Le Triomphant*. Commander Auboyneau, exchanging a few words with Admiral Muselier, Commander-in-Chief of the Free French Navy. **JM**
CPL

4.7 The open compass platform of the destroyer *Le Triomphant*. **JM**
CPL

4.8 The enclosed bridge of *Le Triomphant*. **JM**
CPL

4.9 *Le Triomphant* at action stations with her triple 550mm torpedo-tubes swung out to port. Beside the mounting a twin 37mm anti-aircraft gun can be seen. The anti-aircraft equipment carried by *Le Triomphant* after the modifications carried out in Britain included: one 102mm AA gun replacing gun number IV; two British pom-pom anti-aircraft guns; four French semi-automatic 37mm in two twin mountings; ten 13.2mm heavy machine guns, in pairs. **JM**
CPL

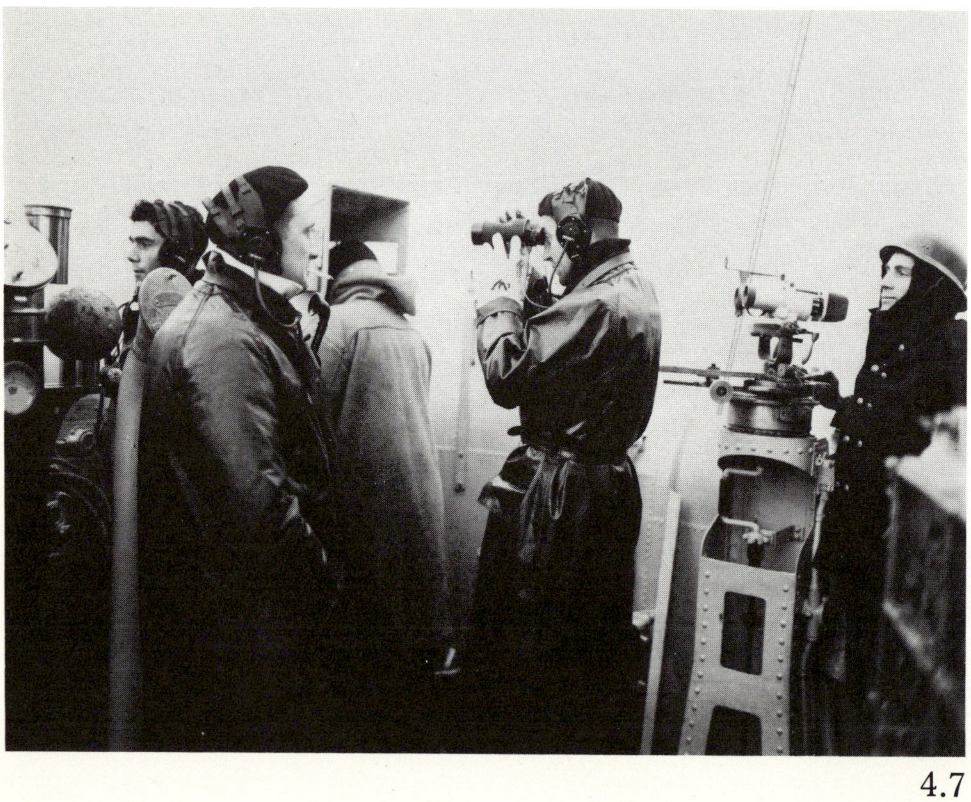

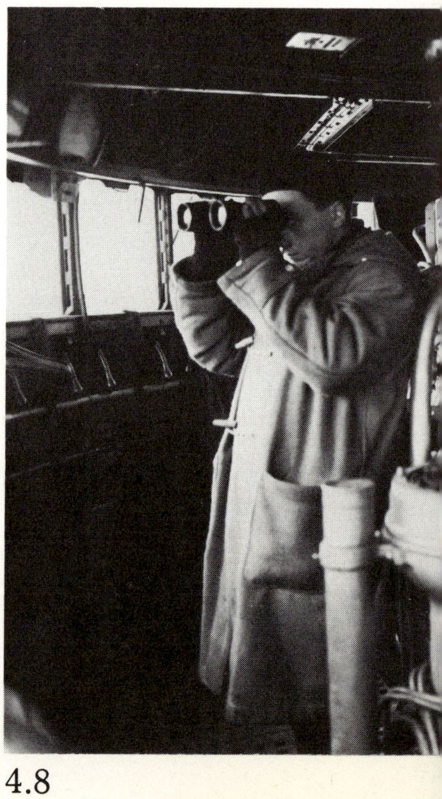

4.7 4.8

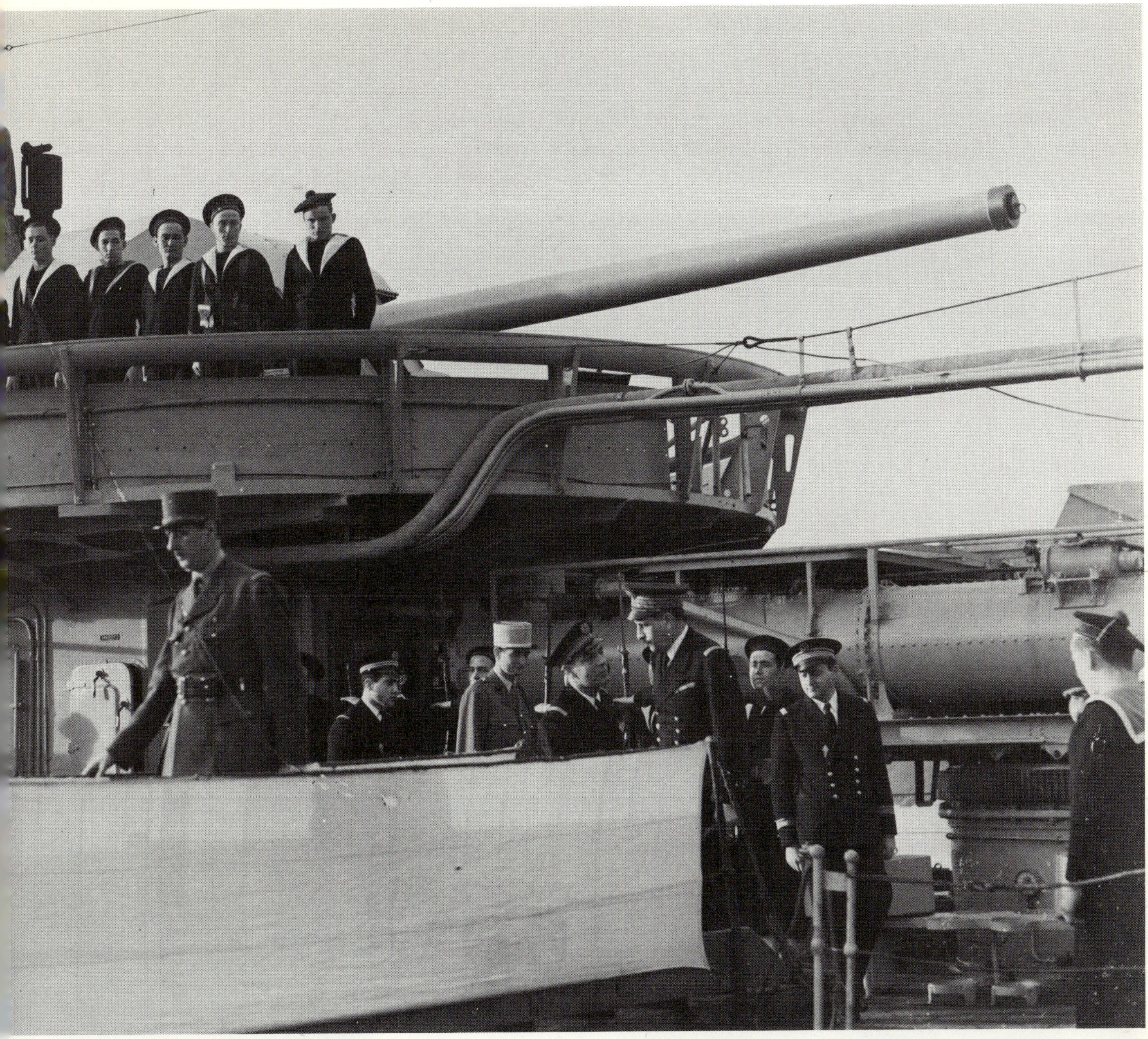

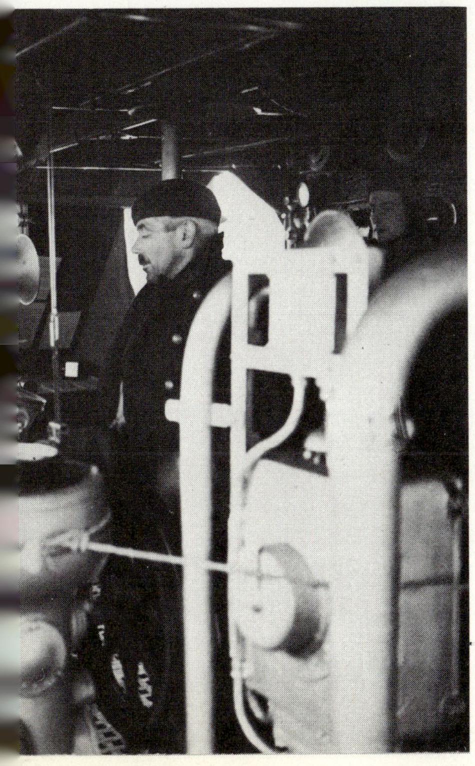

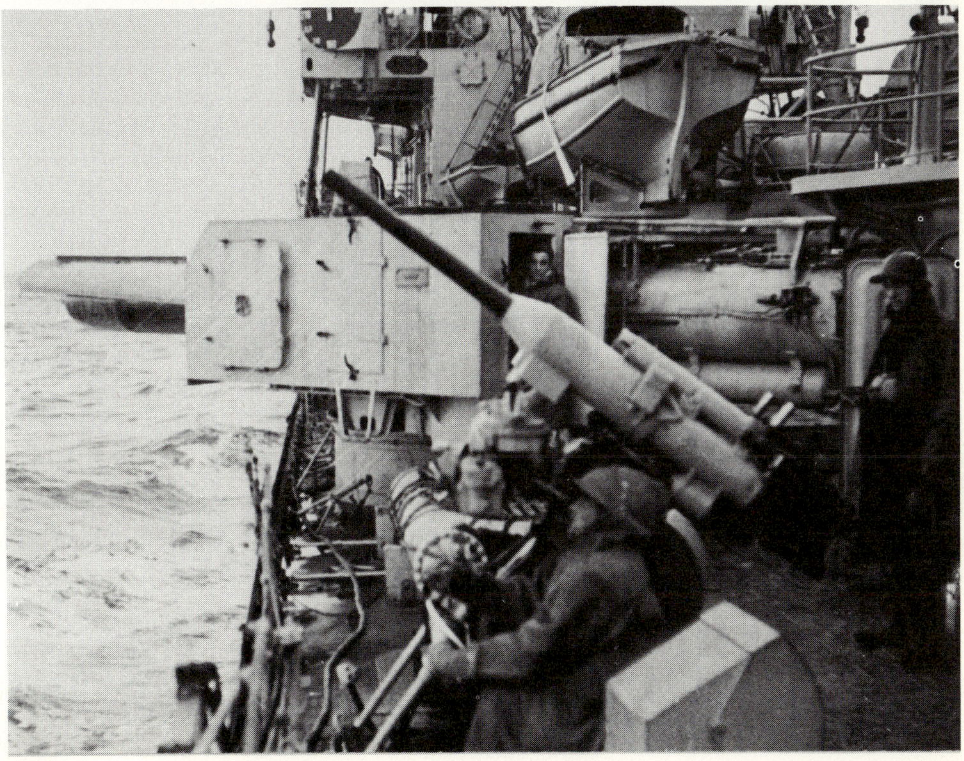

4.9

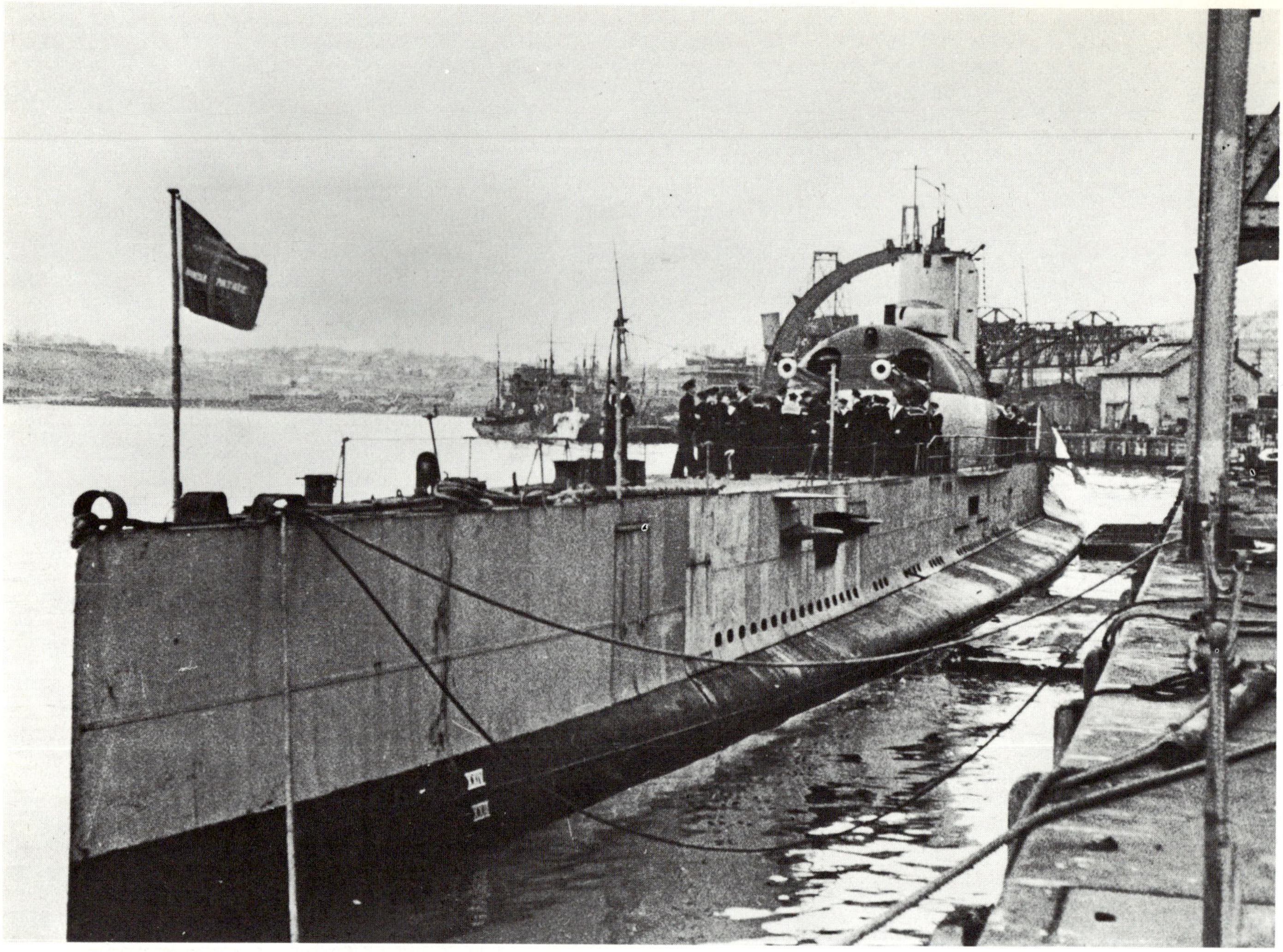

4.10

4.10 The casing of the *Surcouf,* moored in a British port. The flag of the Free French Navy can be seen on the jackstaff. In front of the turret and along the conning tower towards the stern are a group of men dressed for leave.

Surcouf began her service in 1934. Her displacement was 2804 tonnes on the surface and 4034 tonnes when submerged. Her armament consisted of a twin 203mm turret, two 37mm AA guns and ten torpedo-tubes, six 550mm and four 400mm. A Besson MB 411 seaplane was kept in a watertight hangar aft of the bridge.

In 1940 she was the largest submarine in the world. At the time of the German invasion she was at the Brest arsenal with her engines removed. Her miraculous escape to Plymouth was due to Lt Commander Martin and crew. She was taken over by the Royal Navy on 3 July 1940, and her rearmament by the Free French Navy under the command of Lt Commander Ortoli may also be considered as something approaching a miracle.

She disappeared, with all hands, on 18 February 1942 in the Gulf of Mexico after colliding with the SS *Thomson Lykes,* an American merchant ship. **JM** *CPL*

4.11 The four forward 400mm tubes of the *Surcouf* can be seen, arranged in pairs on top of each other. **JM** *CPL*

4.12 The muzzles of the *Surcouf*'s two 203mm (8inch) guns. On submerging, the gun barrels were closed by mechanical means, as shown here. The *Surcouf*'s twin turret equipped with 203mm guns was a great technical success. It was watertight and could open fire as soon as the guns surfaced. This had the advantage of allowing the craft to present a small silhouette. Her guns were supplied with 300 rounds of ammunition, and had a range of 27 000m. **JM** *CPL*

4.13 The minelaying submarine *Rubis* returning to her base at Dundee on 25 August 1941 after an extremely eventful cruise along the Norwegian coast. Under the command of Lieutenant Rousselot she carried out a successful minelaying operation across the entrance to the port of Egersund, and then fired two torpedoes at a small Finnish oil tanker under German escort. The Finnish vessel, the 4360 tonne *Hogland* was consequently sunk.

The *Rubis* had unfortunately operated far too close to her target, and the explosion had destroyed most of her accumulator containers. Unable to submerge, she was soon less than 50 miles from the enemy coast. Any ships that might have come to her aid from Britain were prevented from doing so by the presence of a minefield. All hope of saving her was gradually fading, and seaplanes were being prepared to pick up the crew and scuttle the boat. However, on 23 August, after hasty repairs had been carried out, she set out to join the large naval force sent to meet her by the Admiralty. She was enthusiastically welcomed on 25 August at Dundee.

She was placed at the disposal of the British Admiralty in March 1940, as they were in need of minelayers at the time of the Norwegian campaign. The *Rubis* was present off Trondhjem at the Armistice on 25 June 1940 and was taken over by the Royal Navy on 3 July. She was however returned to Lieutenant Cabanier and her crew on their decision to join the Allies. **JM** *CPL*

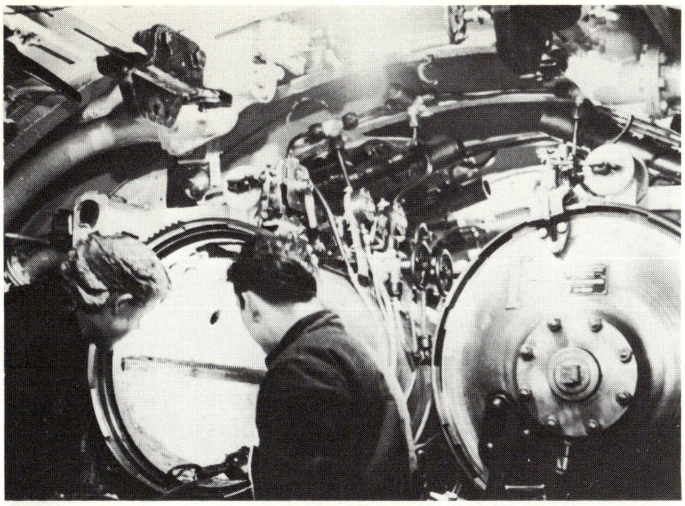

11

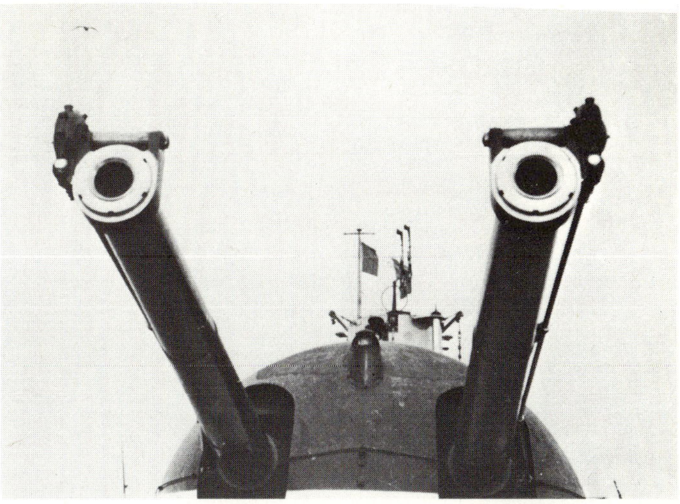

4.12

4.13

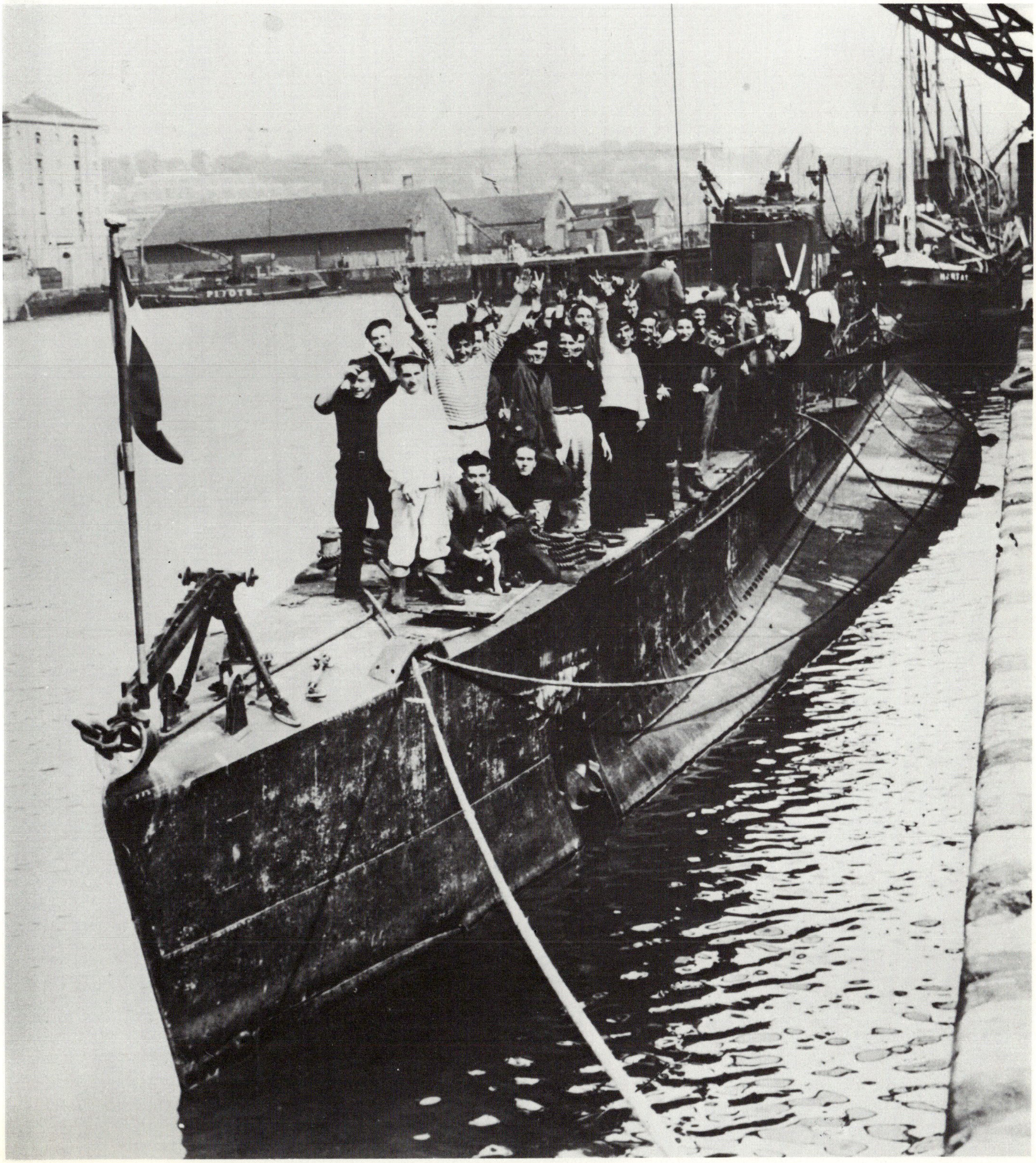

4.14 The French battleship *Richelieu* as completed at the Brooklyn Navy Yard, New York. She escaped during the collapse of France and eventually joined the Free French. Originally intended for spotter aircraft, the fantail is now clustered with quad 40mm AA mounts. **LS**
USN

4.14

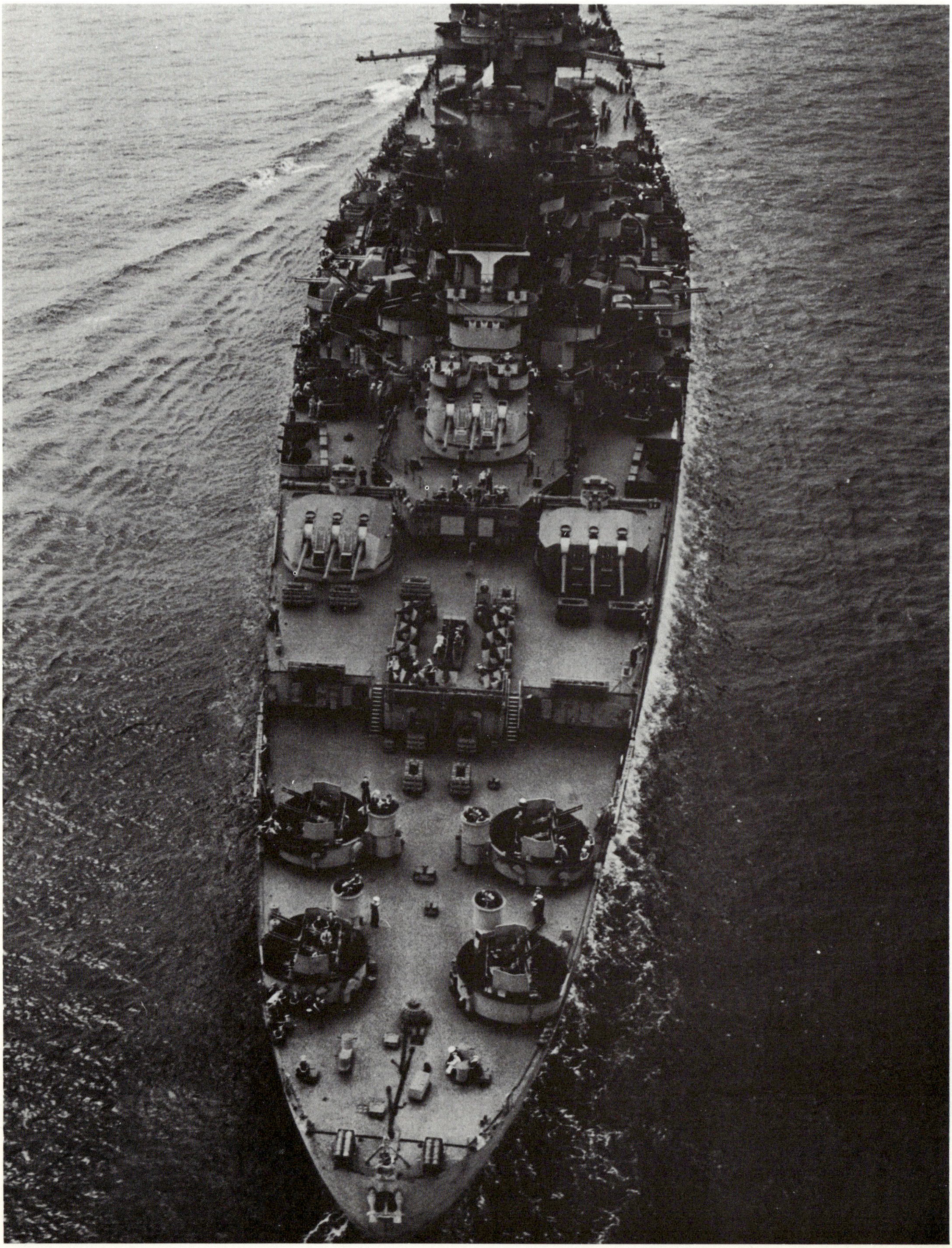

Netherlands

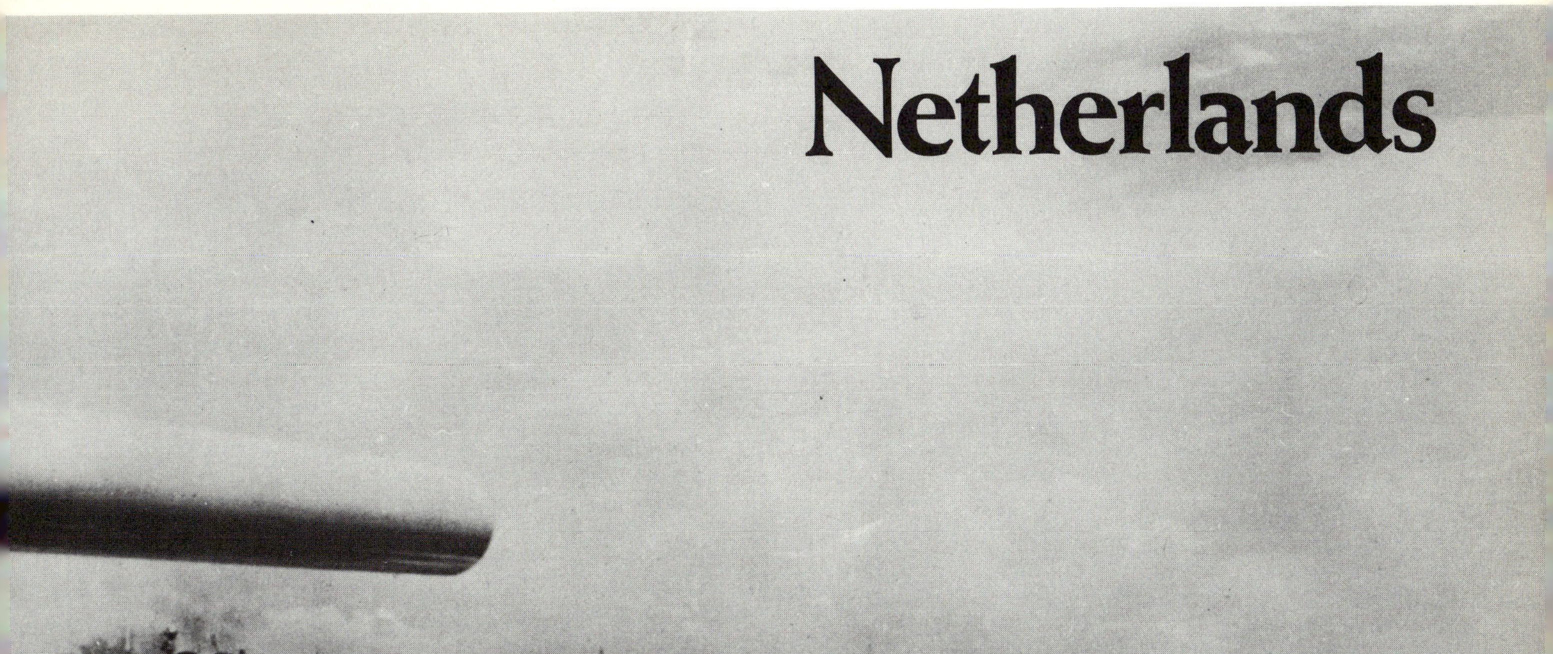

4.15

4.16

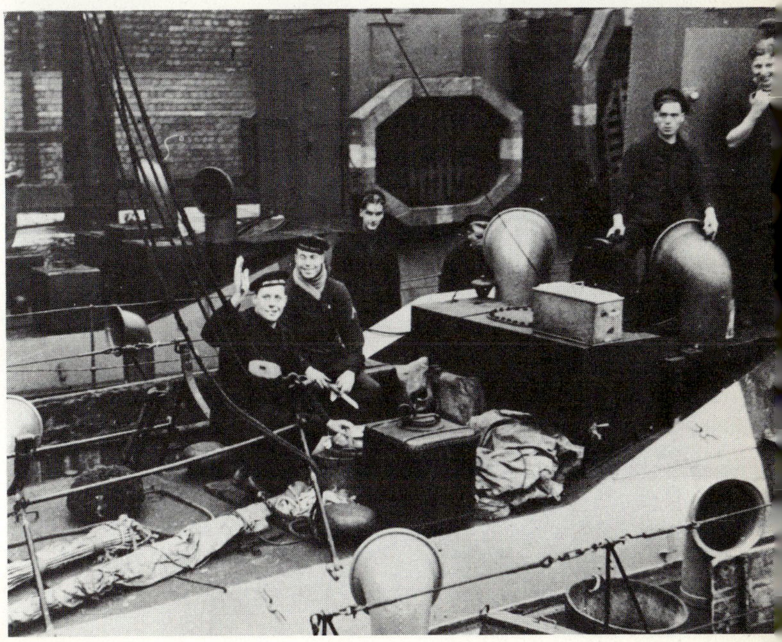

4.15 Ships of the Dutch East Indies Fleet, seen from the quarterdeck of the destroyer *Banckert*. Seven submarines are in the nearest line, with the destroyers *Van Ghent* (GT), *Kortenaer* (KN) and *Piet Hein* (PH) behind, with the cruiser *Java* or *Sumatra* furthest from the camera. **AP**
CPL

4.16 A homely scene on the boiler-room casing of one of the old Dutch torpedo-boats which escaped to England in 1940. **AP**
CPL

4.17 Two torpedo-boats moored, with a third coming alongside. On the left can be seen the after steering position and the binnacle, and on the right can be seen the starboard torpedo-tube and quickfirer. This layout was typical of pre-1914 German torpedo-boats, but these craft were built in Dutch yards. **AP**
CPL

4.18 At sea, with twin Browning water-cooled machine-guns being elevated. This anti-aircraft mounting was presumably installed after the torpedo-boat had arrived in the UK in May 1940. **AP**
CPL

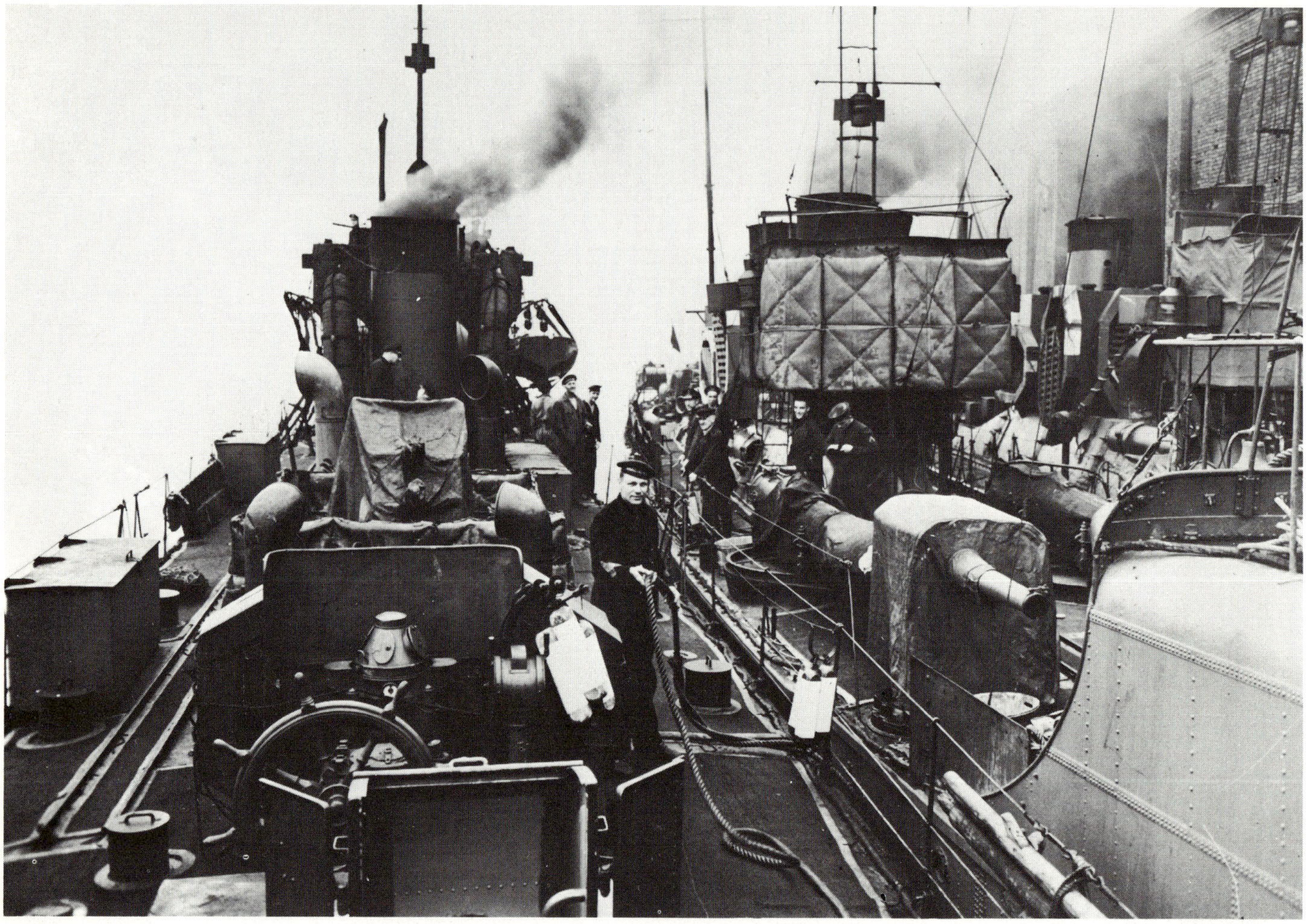

4.17

4.18

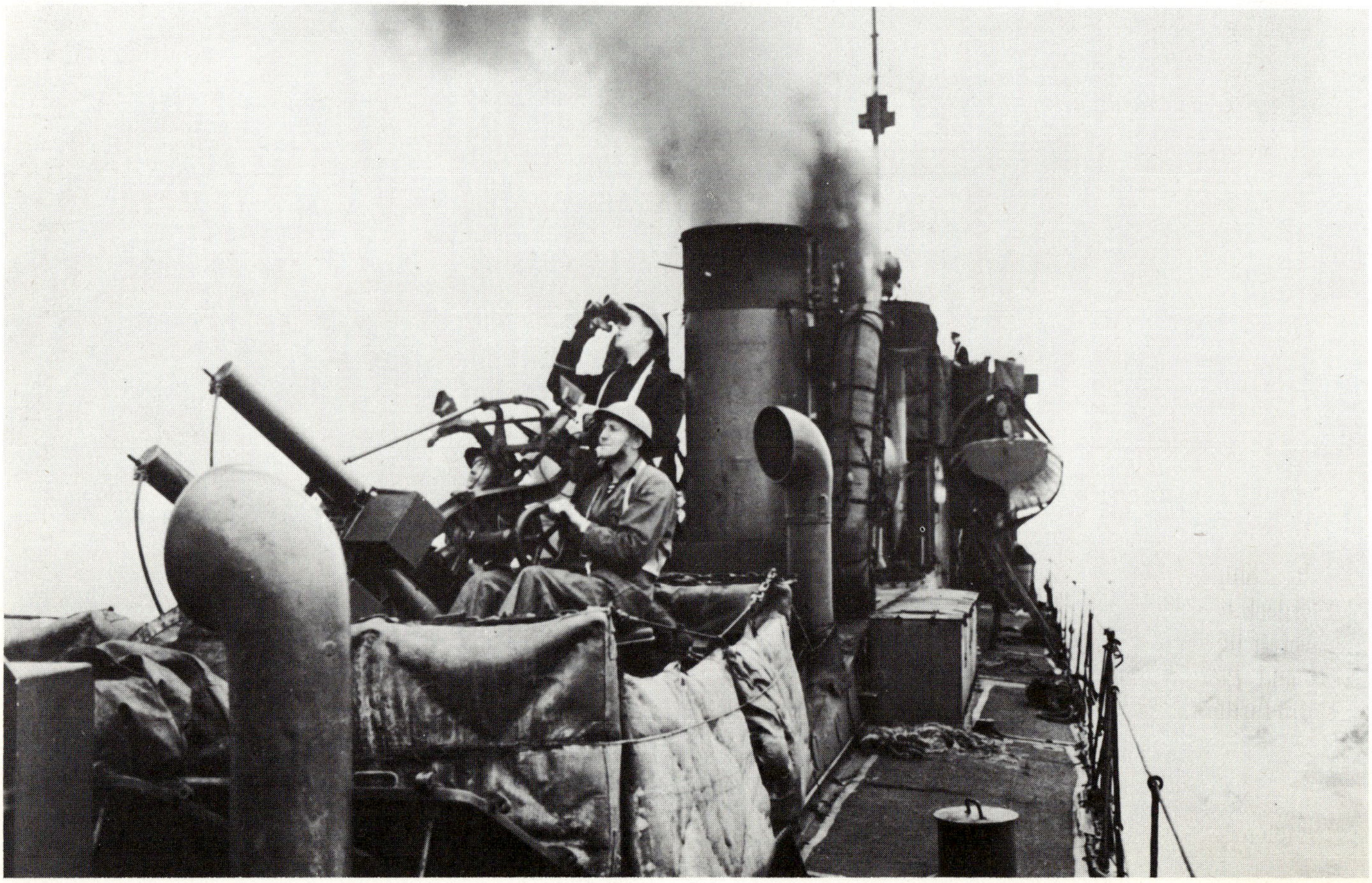

Poland

4.19 The Polish destroyers *Blyskawica* and *Grom* shortly after their arrival in England after the successful completion of operation 'Pekin', the westward dash from Gdynia of the three main fighting units of the Polish Navy. A large print of this photograph reveals an officer on the bridge of one of the vessels watching the cameraman through his binoculars, which probably explains why the negatives for this and other photographs taken at the same time have disappeared. This photograph was salvaged from a battered contact print, and is remarkable for the clarity of reproduction, considering the state of the original. The original forward 4.7inch guns can be seen, but alterations have been made to improve stability, including removal of the prominent funnel cap and the searchlight platform above the bridge. Both vessels were fitted with D Mark V type bow protector paravanes for ice navigation. **EMK**
CPL

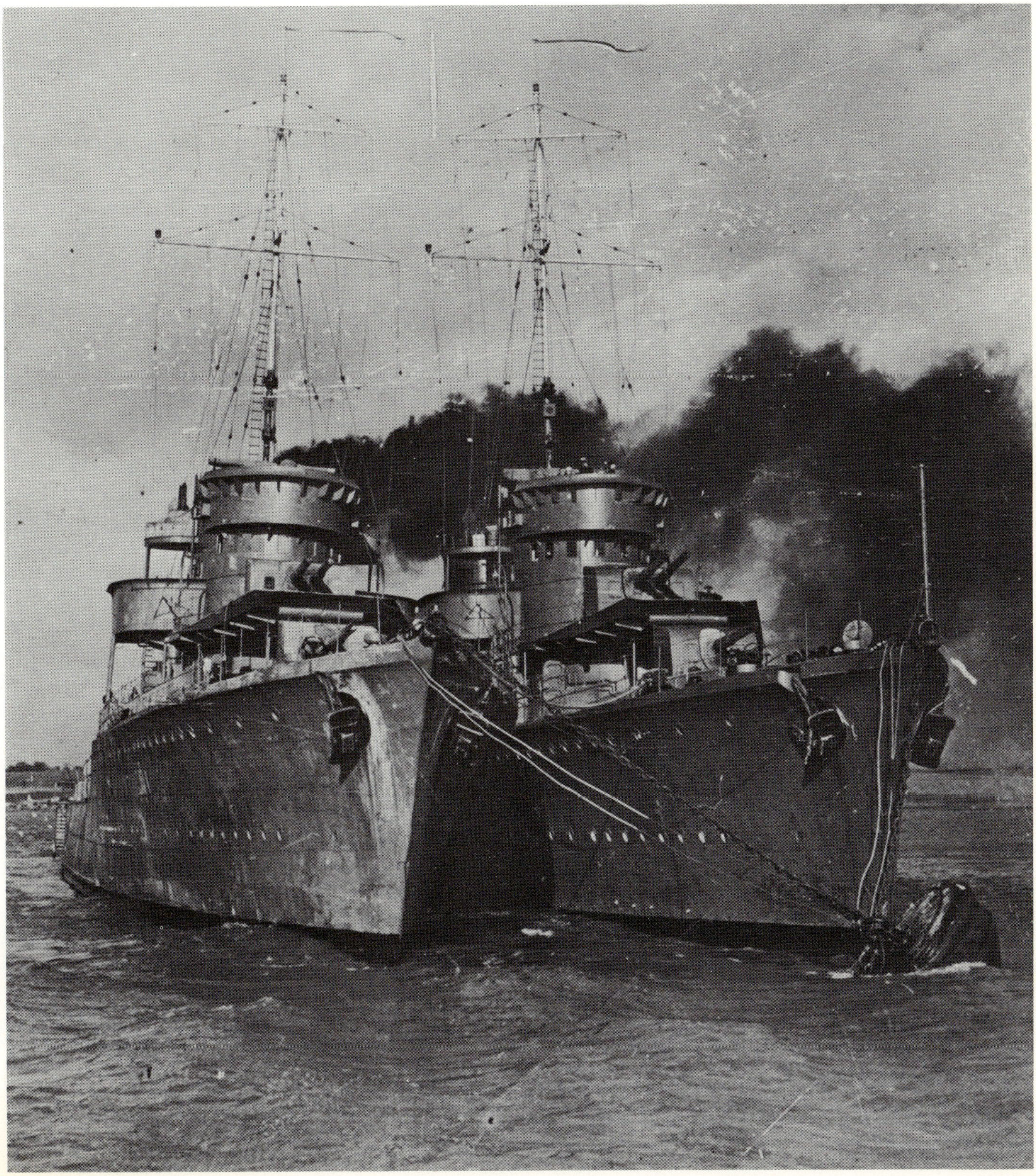

When Germany attacked Poland on 1 September 1939 *Blyskawica, Grom* and the old destroyer *Burza*, the three major units of the Polish Navy, had already departed from the Bay of Gdansk to join forces with and strengthen the Royal Navy. *Burza* was a most valuable ship having a displacement of about 1540 tons and a top speed of 33 knots, while the other destroyers were two of the most powerful ships of their type at that time. The astute and far-sighted move to remove these destroyers from the Baltic before the outbreak of hostilities must be counted not least among the heroic decisions of the war, for it robbed the short coastline of Poland of the greater part of its protection. How well that decision was to justify itself in the wider war could not, at that time, have been known. Therefore what was done was carried out in the blind faith that Britain would fulful her obligations to Poland by declaring war on Germany.

The small destroyer force received the order to execute operation 'Pekin' from Rear Admiral Unrug, Commander-in-Chief of the Polish Navy, at 1.20 on 30 August 1939. The little flotilla set out and passed through the Baltic without interference, but close by the coast of Denmark German light forces were sighted; there was no attack for war had not yet been declared. While in the Skaggerak they were shadowed by German aircraft, but by dusk they were well into the North Sea and the aircraft were seen no more. Eventually all three vessels reached British waters and berthed safely at Leith at about 17.30 on 1 September. It is of particular interest to note that when the commander of the *Burza* opened his sealed orders he learnt that in the event of an attack by a strong force of German ships he was to fall behind and fight it out while the others went on. Commenting on this after the arrival of the ships in Britain, one of the *Burza*'s officers was reported to have said, without showing any trace of emotion, 'You see, they were much faster than us and much more valuable.'

For the 36 days of the 1939 campaign, Poland resisted her aggressor alone and unaided, yet for Poland the war did not end on 6 October with the surrender of General Kleeberg's Independant Operational Group 'Polesie'. It continued without respite until Nazi Germany capitulated in May 1945. *Burza* and *Blyskawica* (*Grom* was lost on 5 May 1940), together with the new vessels of the Polish Navy, continued to fight until the unconditional surrender of Germany to the Allies. Operation 'Pekin' had proved its worth. **EMK**

4.20 A close-up shot showing bridge details of *Blyskawica* (H34) and *Grom* (H71) taken in November 1939. Officers on the bridge of the *Grom* seem to be taking more than a passing interest in the photographer. This photograph, also salved from a small contact print, shows the vessels after alterations had been made to improve stability. (The ships were originally designed for the relatively quiet waters of the Baltic, and with the advent of war they were called upon to work the more turbulent waters of the Atlantic and the North Sea.). Both vessels were built by J Samuel White between 1935 and 1937, and were the fastest ships of their type at that time. During acceptance trials both ships exceeded their design speeds, the top speed of these destroyers being just over 39 knots. The displacement was 2144 tons standard, and 3383 tons full load. The *Blyskawica*'s radius of action at 15 knots was 3573 nautical miles, while that of *Grom* was 3448 nautical miles. **EMK**
CPL

4.21 Grim-faced members of the crew of ORP *Grom* look on in silence as the cameraman takes this shot. In the photograph, probably taken at Harwich early in 1940, a *bosmanmat* or boatswain's mate can be seen standing second from the stern while behind him the Polish Ensign, or *Bandera Wojenna*, can be seen flying in the breeze. For these sailors the winter of the 'phoney' war was as fatiguing and dangerous as any other time during hostilities. *Grom* was tragically lost in action with German aircraft while on the Rombaksfjord patrol on 5 May 1940. Out of her crew of 180 men, one officer and 58 seamen were killed and one officer and 23 seamen were wounded. **EMK**
CPL

4.22 *Jedz dobrze żyj dlugo.* The equivalent in English of: Eat well and live long. The Polish sailor, in his work outfit, tucks into a well-earned meal. On 31 August 1939, Hitler confirmed his decision to attack Poland, and at dawn on 1 September German forces invaded Poland. However, by about 17.30 on that fateful day, the 'Pekin' destroyer flotilla had arrived safely at Leith after an almost uneventful trip from the Baltic. By 7 September the Polish destroyers, eager for action with the enemy, were on patrol off the Scottish coast, and it was not long after that that the *Blyskawica* detected and sunk her first enemy submarine. **EMK**
CPL

4.23 Polish ratings in rather cramped quarters at mess time, apparently enjoying a meal of bread and soup; note the metal mess gear. The seamen nearest to the photographer are wearing sturdy canvas boiler suits, while the ratings in the background appear to be clad in normal uniform. The gunner standing on the right smiles as the mess hand doles out his ration of soup. The gunner can be identified as a *Starszy Marynarz*, the Polish equivalent of leading seaman, from the single stripe on his arm. It is quite remarkable that these sailors look so cheerful and fresh after being on patrol for most of the time since they had arrived at Leith. The record of *Blyskawica*'s first year of service with the British Navy shows that her crew can have had little rest in that time. During that period the *Blyskawica* took part in 27 offensive operations, 1 naval battle, 23 convoys, 3 actions with enemy shore batteries, 56 patrols, 17 engagements with enemy submarines, and 56 attacks by enemy aircraft. It is worth remembering that this period included nine months of the so-called 'phoney' war! **EMK**
CPL

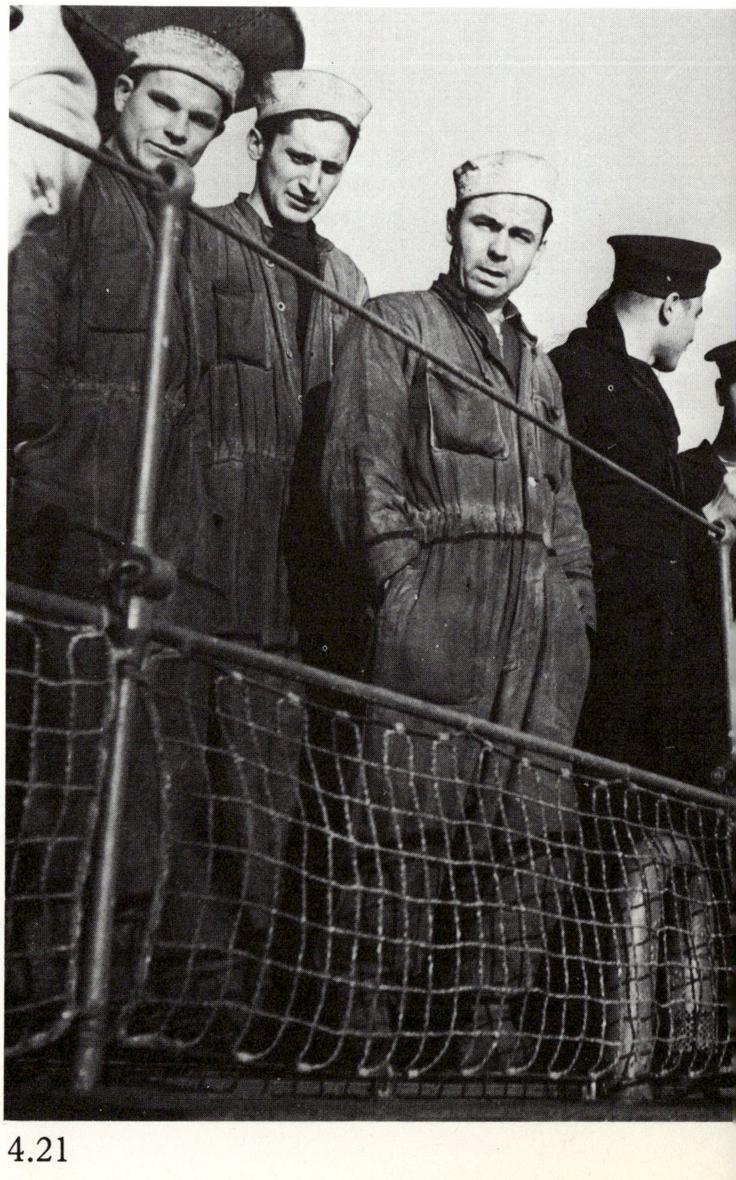

4.21

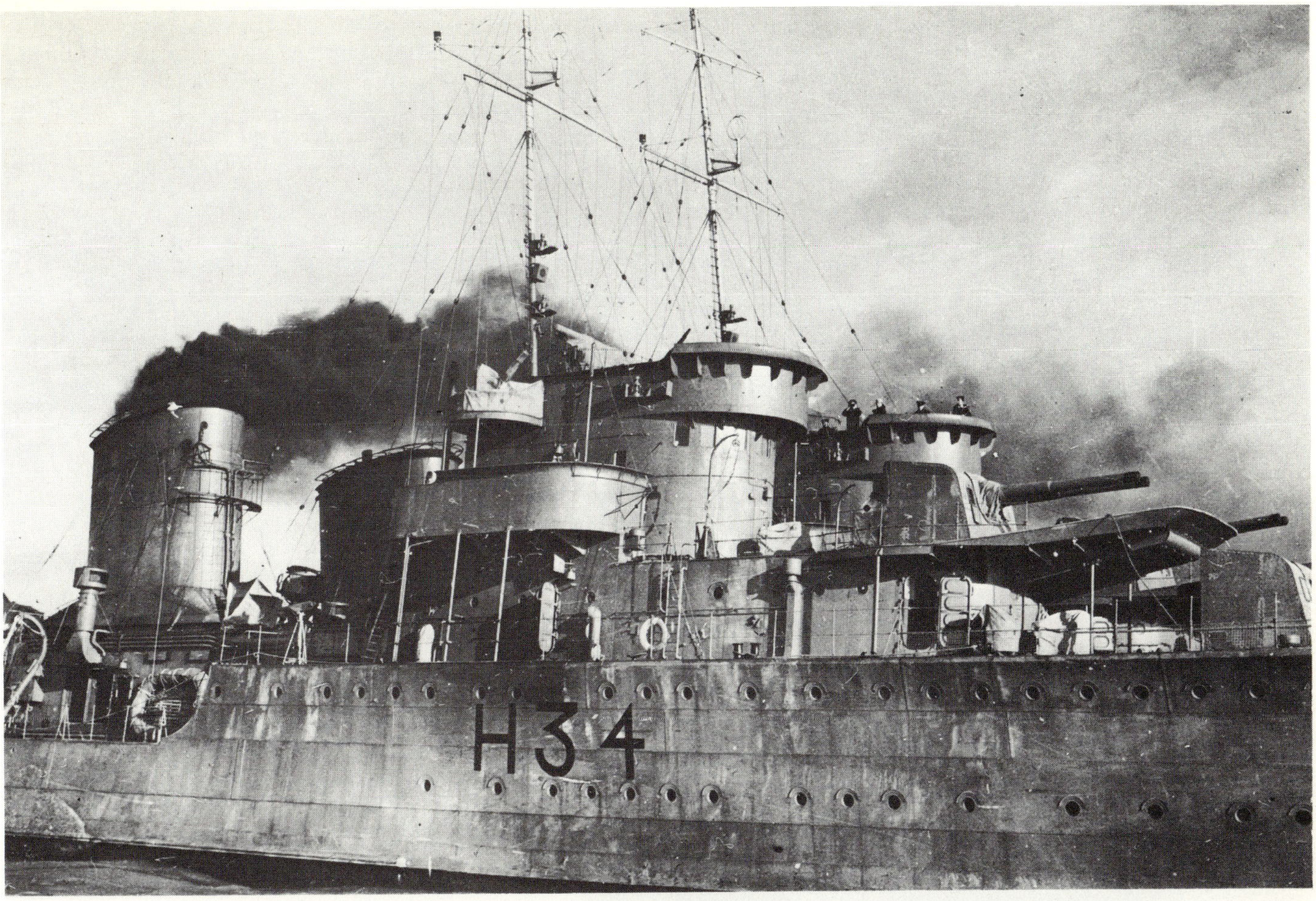

4.20

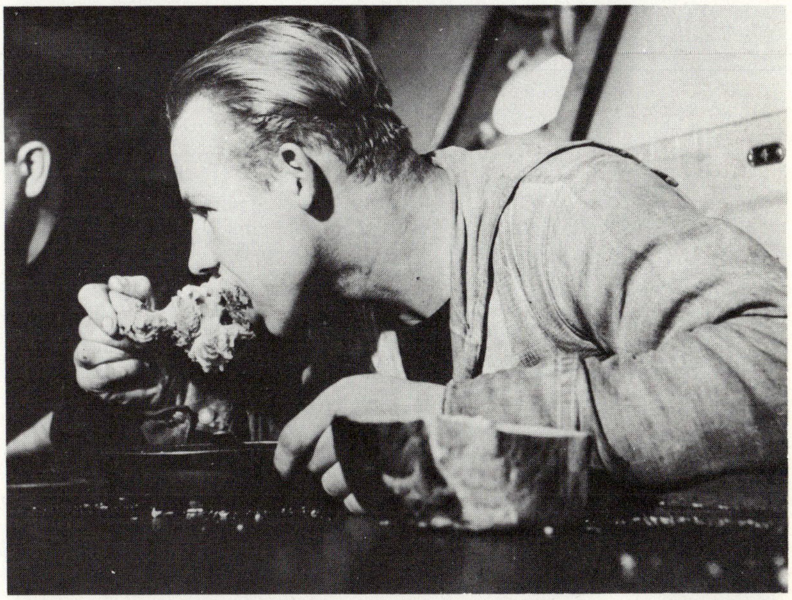

4.22

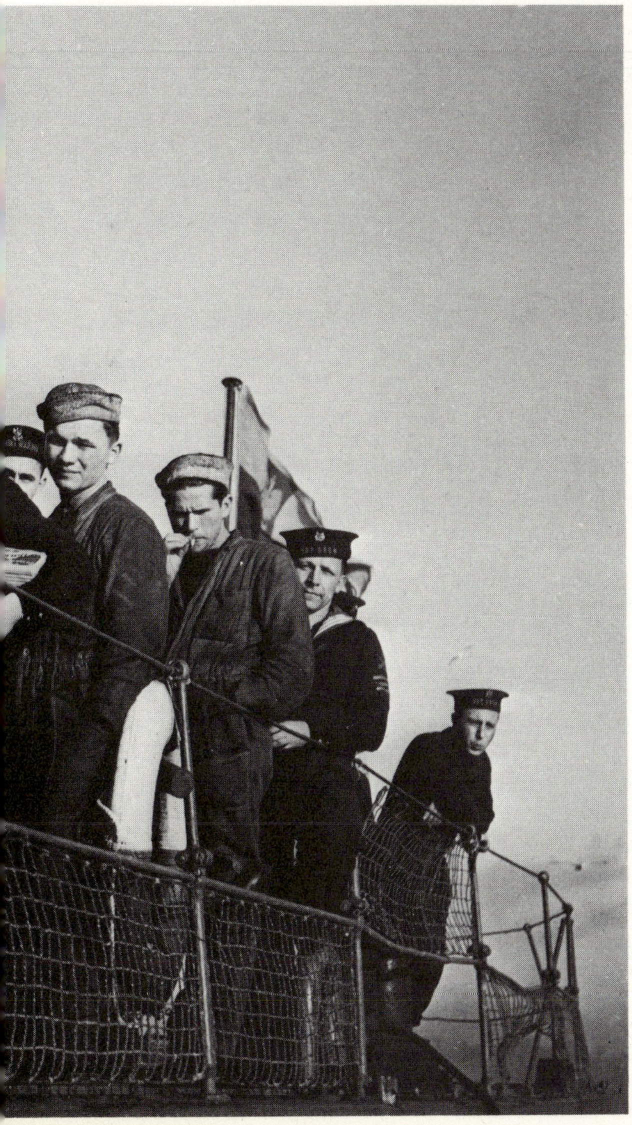

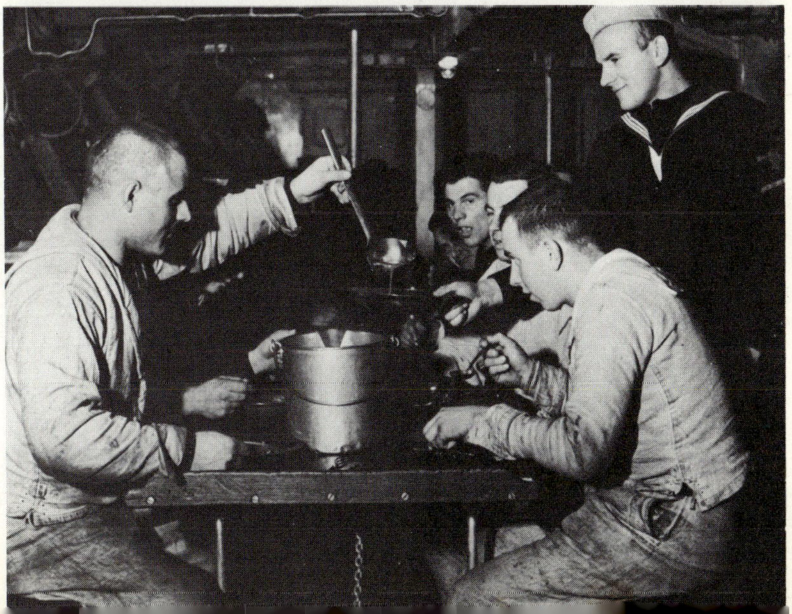

4.23

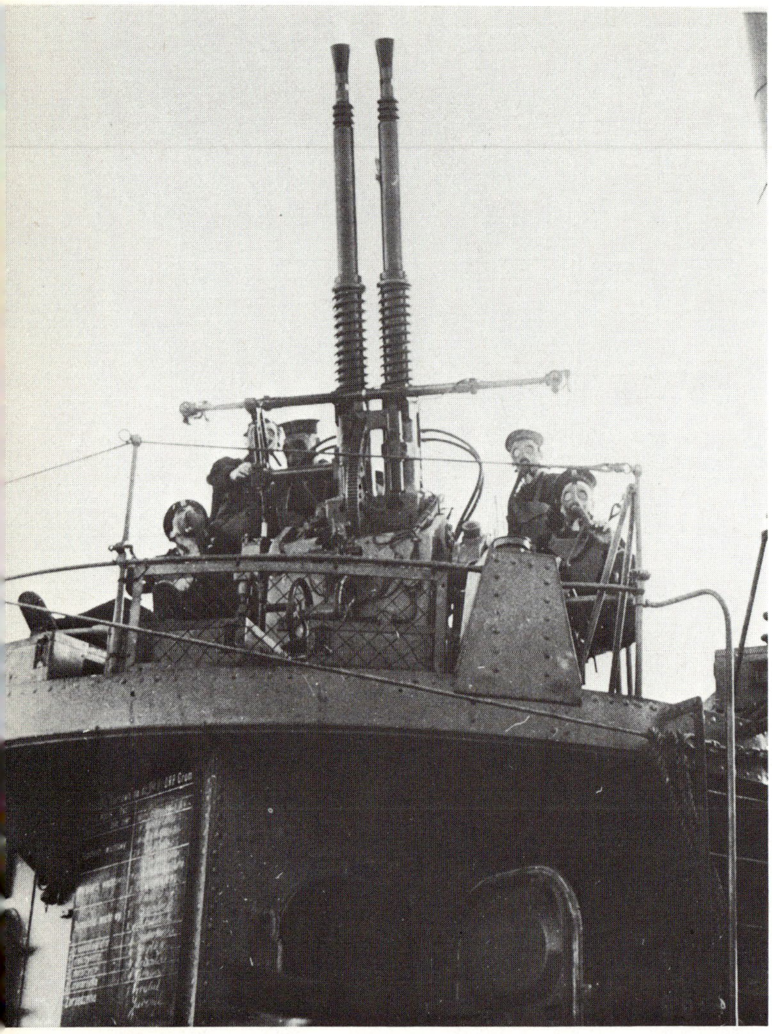

4.24 One of the two twin 40mm AA Bofors mountings aboard *Grom*, with the gun crew wearing gas masks. As completed, both vessels of the *Blyskawica* class carried 4500 rounds of ammunition for their two dual 40mm AA guns. Other types and calibres of ammunition carried included 1388 rounds of 120mm, 19 200 rounds of 13.2mm, and six 533.4mm torpedoes. The vessels could also carry 40 depth charges and 44 mines. Alterations were made to *Blyskawica*'s depth charge stowage in April 1940. This photograph was taken in 1940, probably at Harwich, as were the photographs of the triple torpedo-tube mounting. **EMK**
CPL

4.25 The triple torpedo-tube mounting, showing the aimer's rather exposed position. *Blyskawica* and *Grom* had six 21inch (550mm) torpedo-tubes in two triple mountings. The tubes were fitted with adaptors for 533.4mm and 450mm torpedoes. Both vessels had the after set of torpedo-tubes replaced by a 4inch AA gun in November 1939. In December 1941 the *Blyskawica* had got back her after torpedo-tubes, but in July 1942 she had her two triple mountings exchanged for one set of quadruple torpedo-tubes. After the war *Blyskawica* was handed over to the communist regime in Poland, and she underwent a refit in 1949-50 in which only one set of triple torpedo-tubes was retained. As built, both vessels had two depth charge chutes for 40 depth charges, and mine rails for 44 mines. **EMK**
CPL

4.24

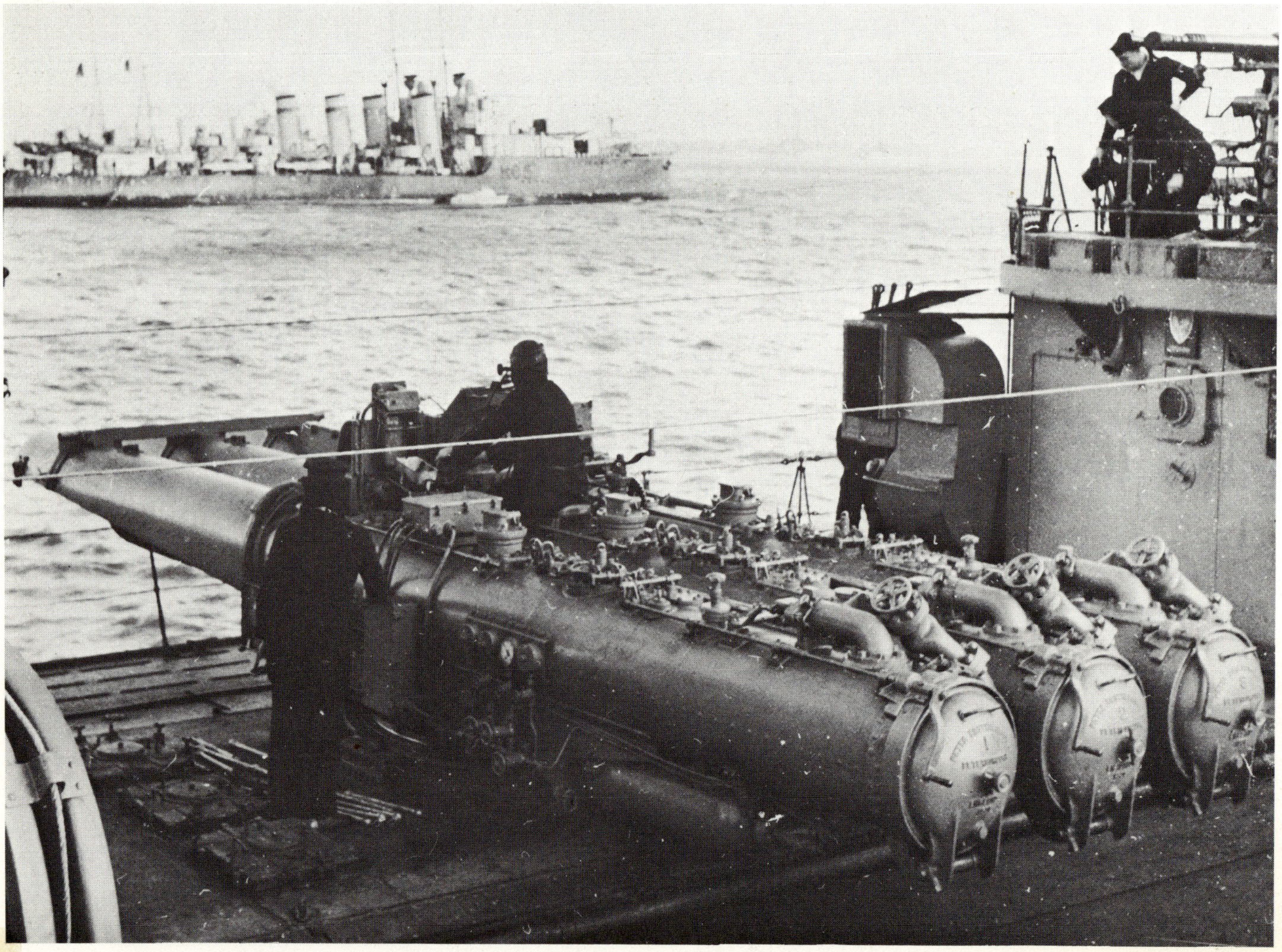

4.2

5.1 The forecastle of the battleship *Nelson* from the bridge just after the end of the war, illustrating the unusual arrangement of the main armament. The three triple 16inch Mk I turrets each weighed 1480 tons and could elevate their Mk I guns to a maximum of 40 degrees. The 16inch gun fired a 2048lb shell at a muzzle velocity of 2700 feet per second, giving a maximum range of almost 24 miles. Six single Oerlikons are mounted on the roof of 'X' turret and an eight barrel Mk VI pom-pom mounting on that of 'B' turret. At the end of the war *Nelson* carried forty-eight 2pdr pom-poms (6 x 8), sixteen 40mm Bofors (4 x 4) and sixty-one single Oerlikons. Several of the latter were removed before this photograph was taken and a few Oerlikon pedestals without guns can be seen on the forecastle abreast 'B' turret and forward of 'A' turret. **JR**
CPL

5. Colour Section

5.1

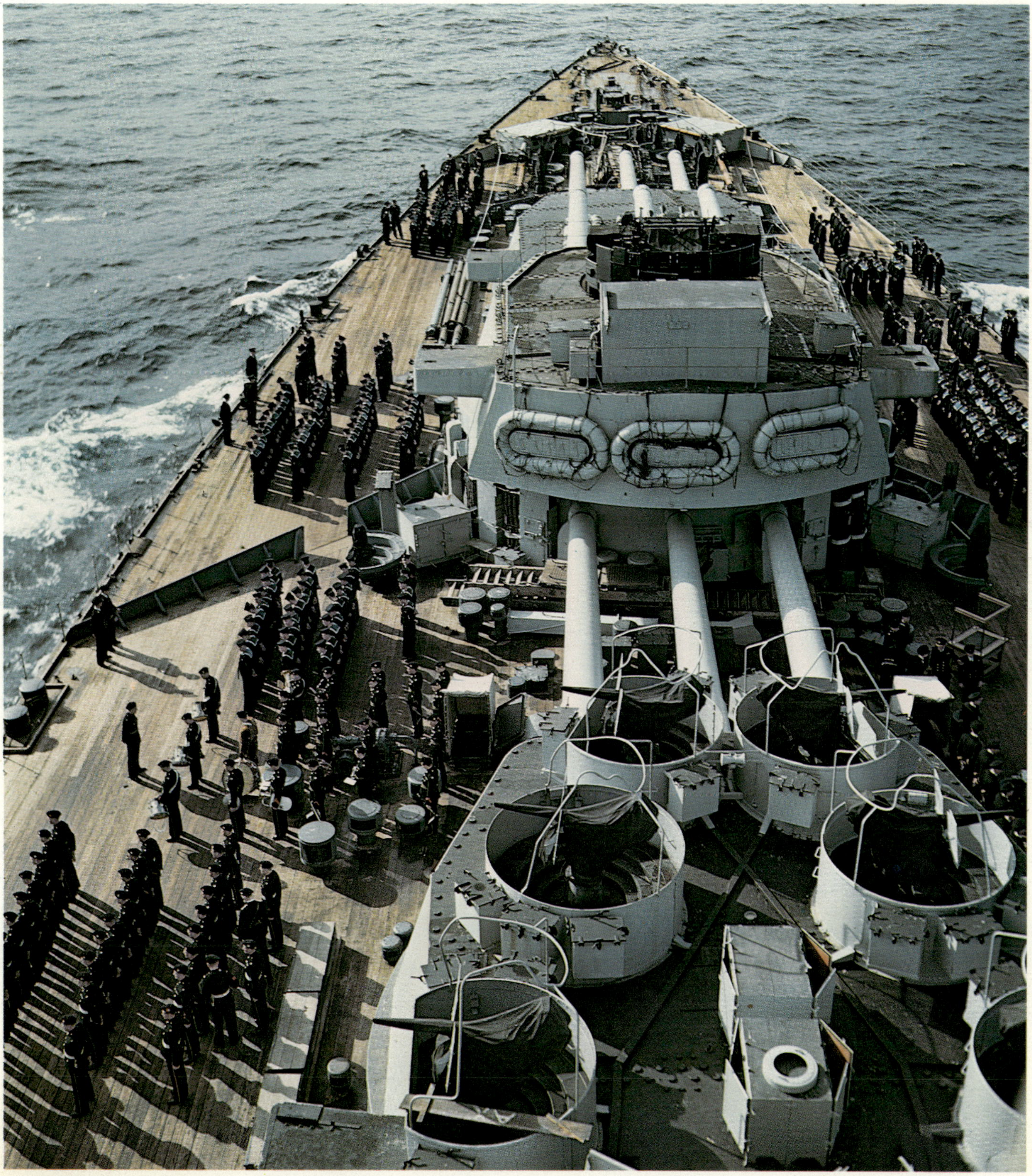

5.2 The *Bismarck* on trials in the Baltic late in 1940. Following an intensive period working up, she sailed in 1941 on her first and only cruise, when she destroyed the battlecruiser *Hood* and in turn was sunk by ships of the British Home Fleet.
Ferdinand Urbahns

5.3 The light cruisers *Leipzig* (foreground) and *Nürnberg* lying peacefully at anchor in Kiel harbour just before the outbreak of war. Not the most actively employed German warships, both cruisers survived the war, *Leipzig* to be scuttled in 1946 and *Nürnberg* to be turned over to the Russians, who commissioned her as the *Admiral Makarov*.
Ferdinand Urbahns

5.4 Taken in the same period as the front jacket photograph — October 1940 — this view from the forecastle of the *Prinz Eugen* shows the forward twin 8inch (203mm) gun turrets and the bridge.
Ferdinand Urbahns

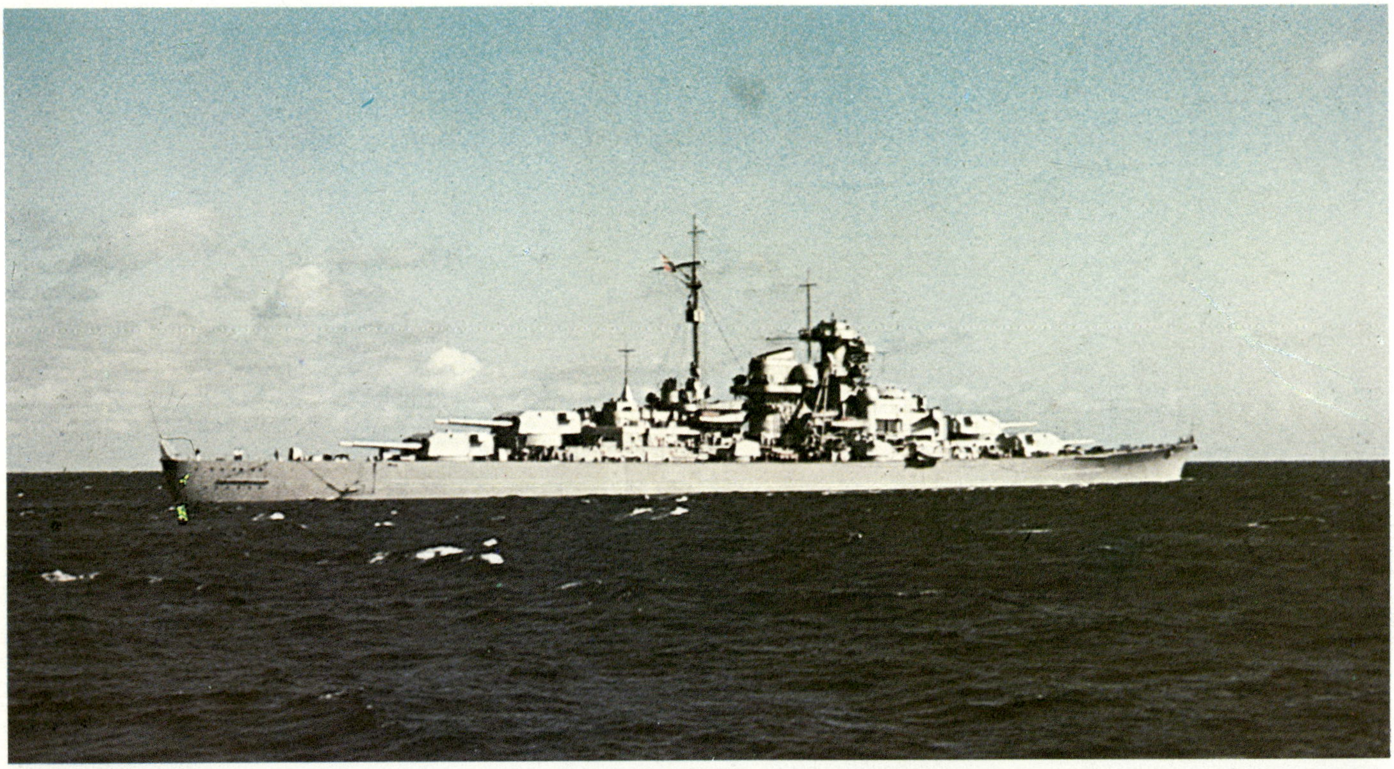

5.2

5.3

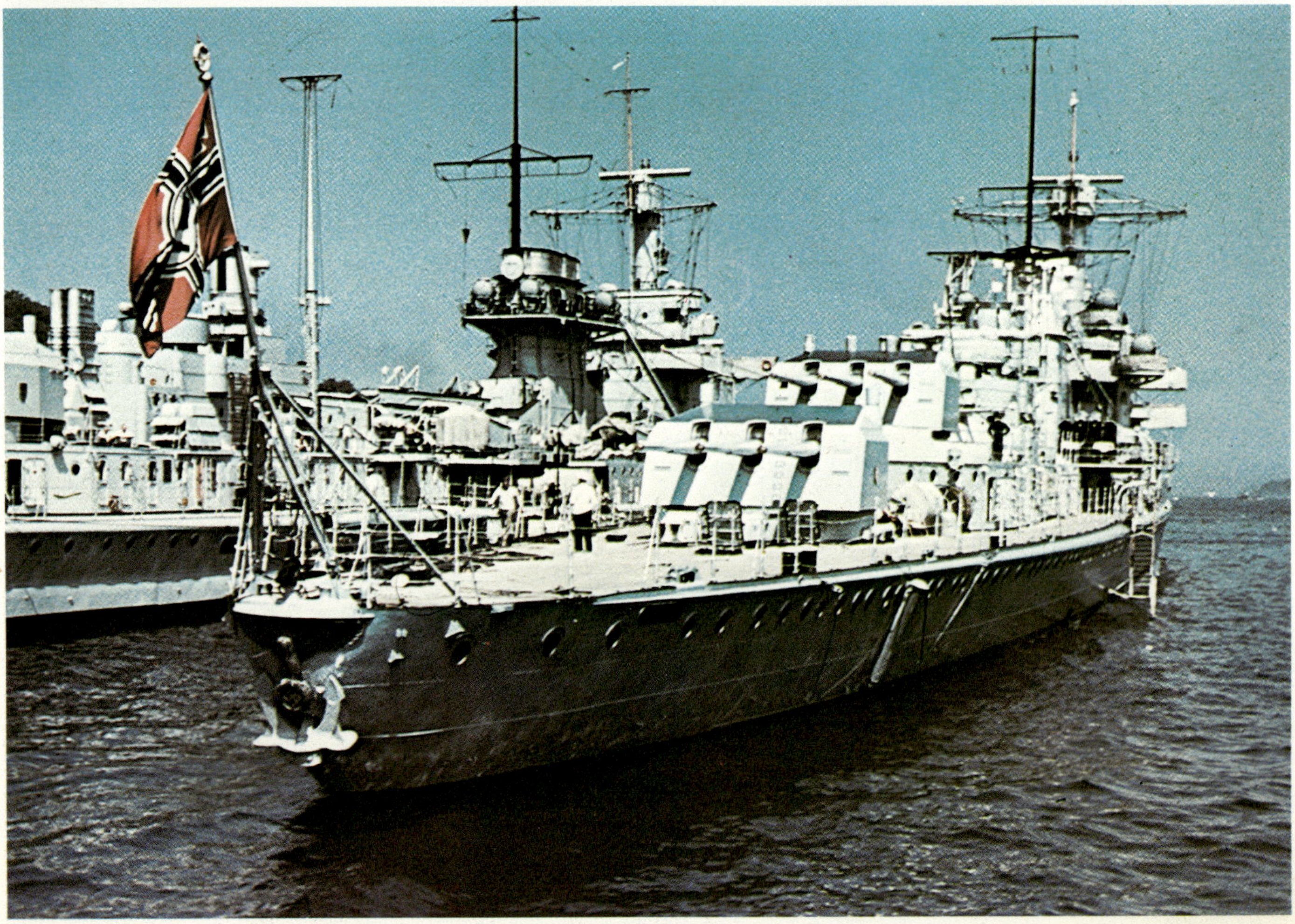

5.4

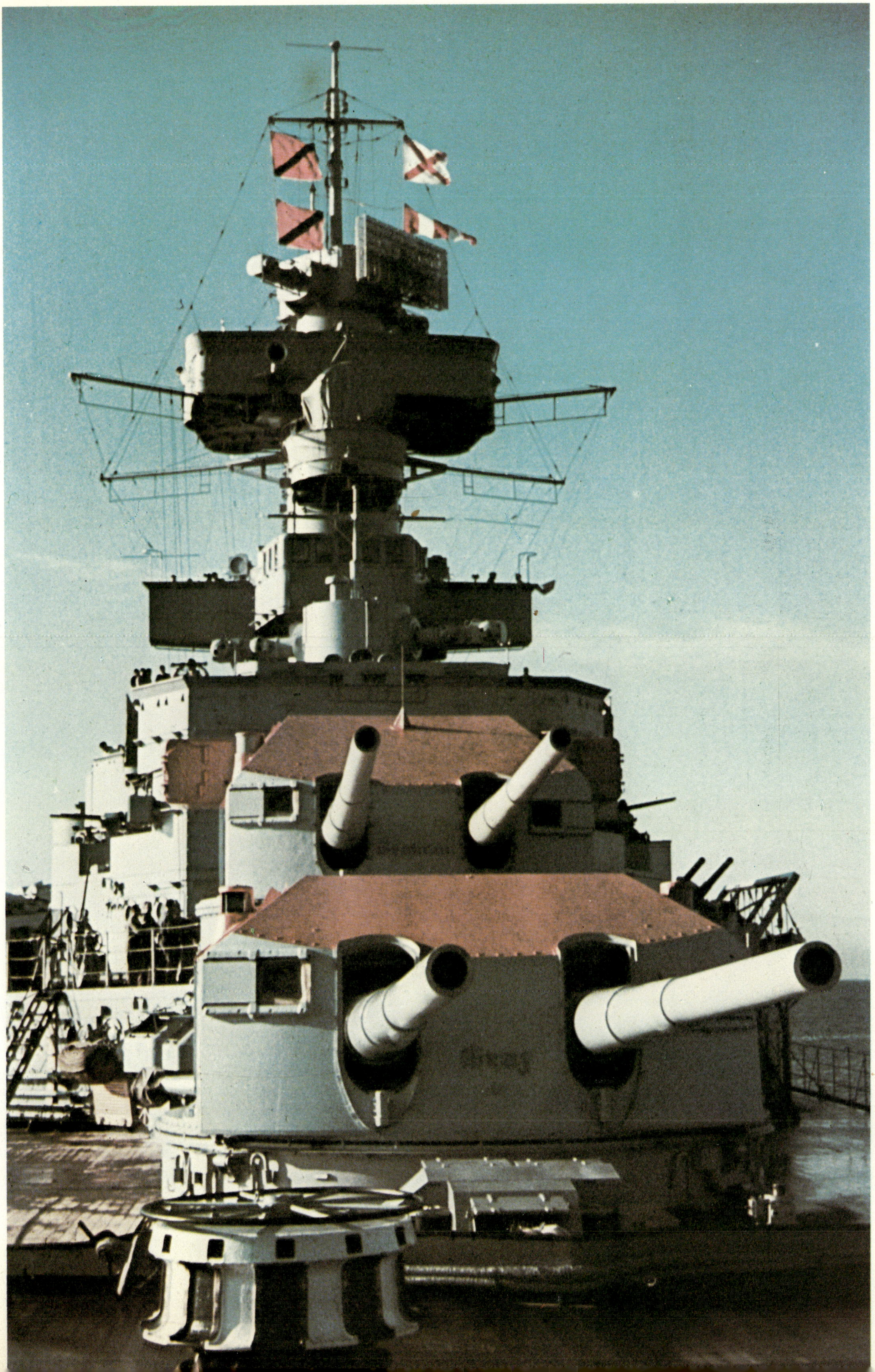

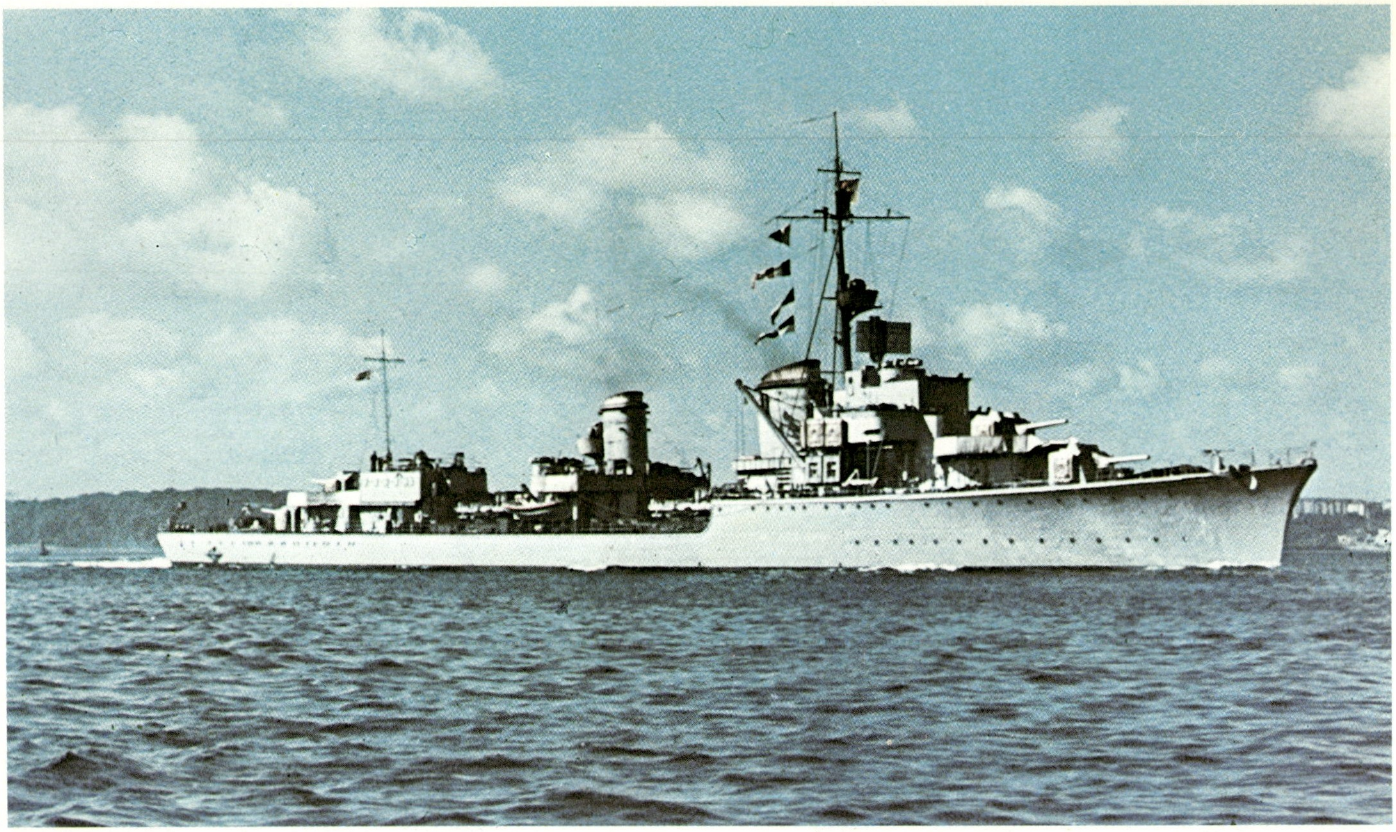

5.5

5.6

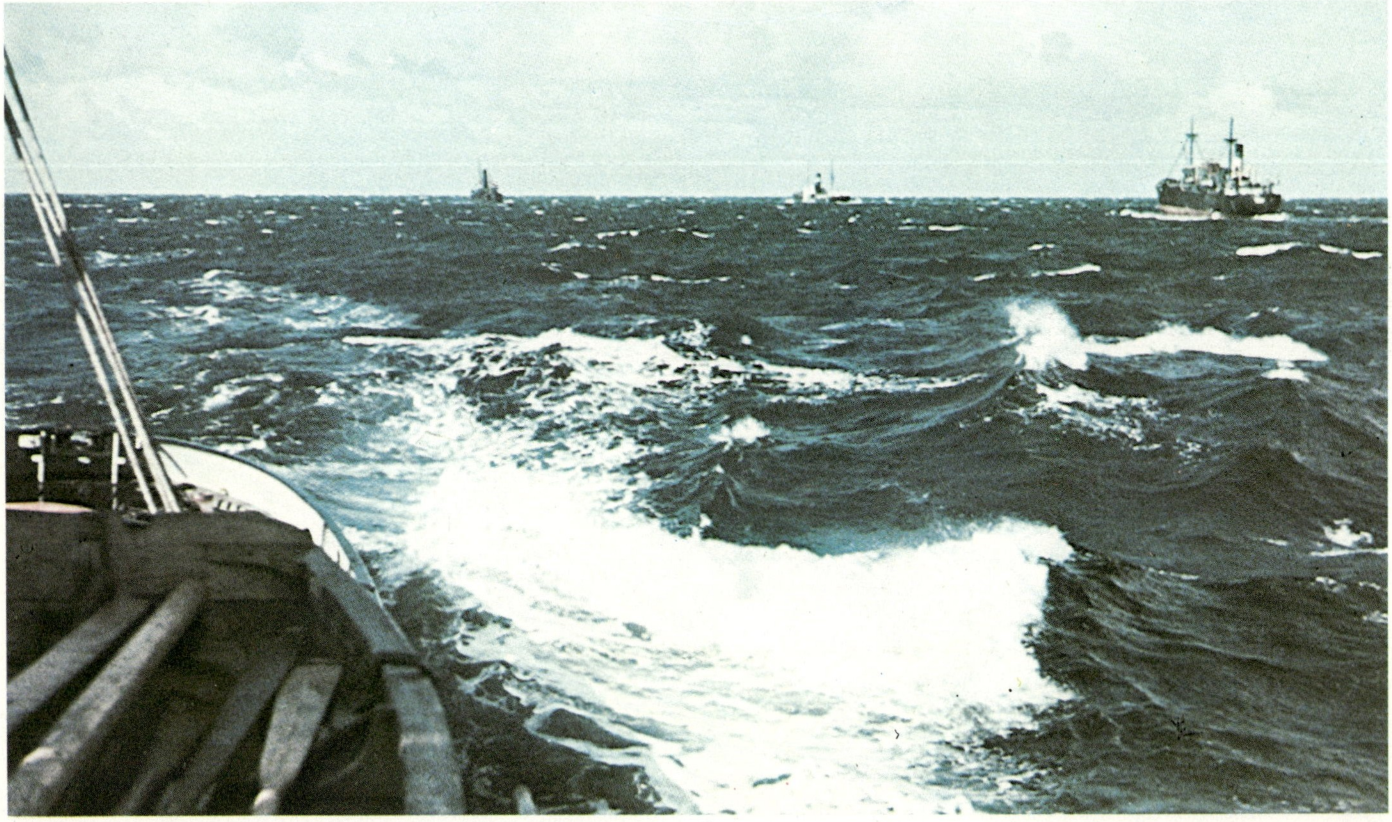

5.5 The 1936A type destroyer *Z28* in September 1941. As a flotilla leader she differed from her sisters in having a large deckhouse instead of the third 15cm mount aft, and two single 15cm guns forward rather than the twin turrets of the other vessels in the group. She was in action against the PQ17 convoy, but was principally employed against the Russians before being sunk in 1945 by British aircraft.

Ferdinand Urbahns

5.6 Although not as large as the vast Allied armadas, the Germans also convoyed their merchantmen, as in this shot taken in September 1940 in a choppy western Baltic.

Ferdinand Urbahns

5.7 In the 'narrow seas' between Britain and Continental Europe, the principal naval threat was not U-boats but E-boats (so-called by the Allies, But 'Schnellboote' — hence S-boats — to the Germans). An early mark E-boat, *S11*, just before the outbreak of war.

Ferdinand Urbahns

5.8 A fine close-up study of an old minesweeper and a camouflaged 'sperrbrecher' — a converted merchantman used for minesweeping and auxiliary roles, Kiel harbour, 1941.

Ferdinand Urbahns

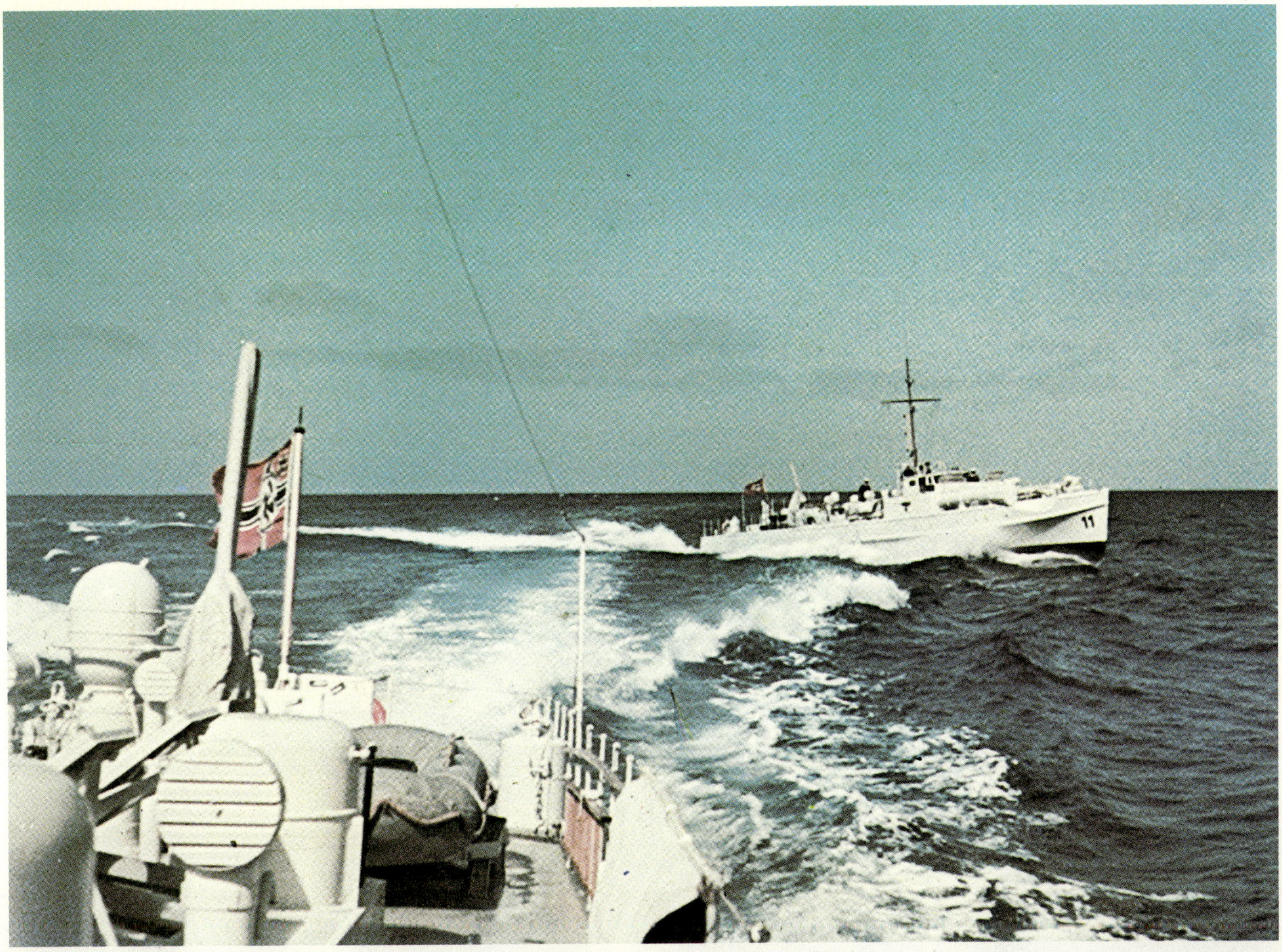

.7

.8

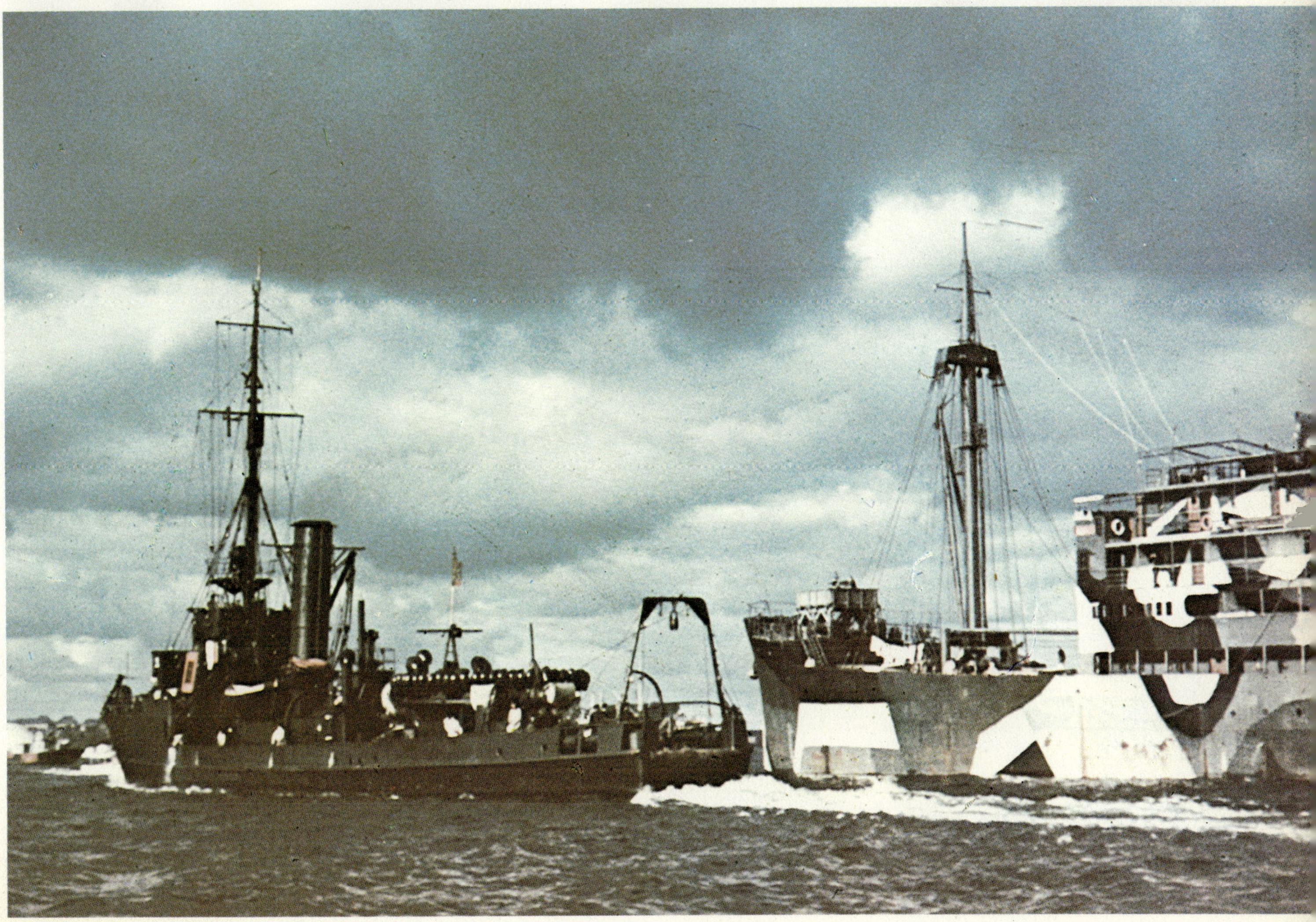

Commercial colour photography started more slowly in Britain than in Germany or the USA, partly because during wartime the film had to be shipped across the Atlantic from the USA to Britain, and shipped back again for processing — running the U-boat gauntlet twice. The following three photos, taken aboard a trawler of the Royal Navy Patrol Service in March 1943, are among the earliest British photos of the sea war.

5.9 The quarterdeck of the trawler with the depth charge crew in action.
CPL

5.10 Most trawlers and auxiliary warships in the Royal Navy had steam reciprocating machinery. Simpler and more familiar to the reservist crews than the diesels which were in such short supply, steam machinery was, nevertheless, hard work — a stoker at work in the trawler's boiler room.
CPL

5.11 The trawler's 'asdic' operator. ASDIC, supposedly named from the initials of the British Anti-Submarine Detection Investigation Committee, later came to be known as Sonar.
CPL

5.9

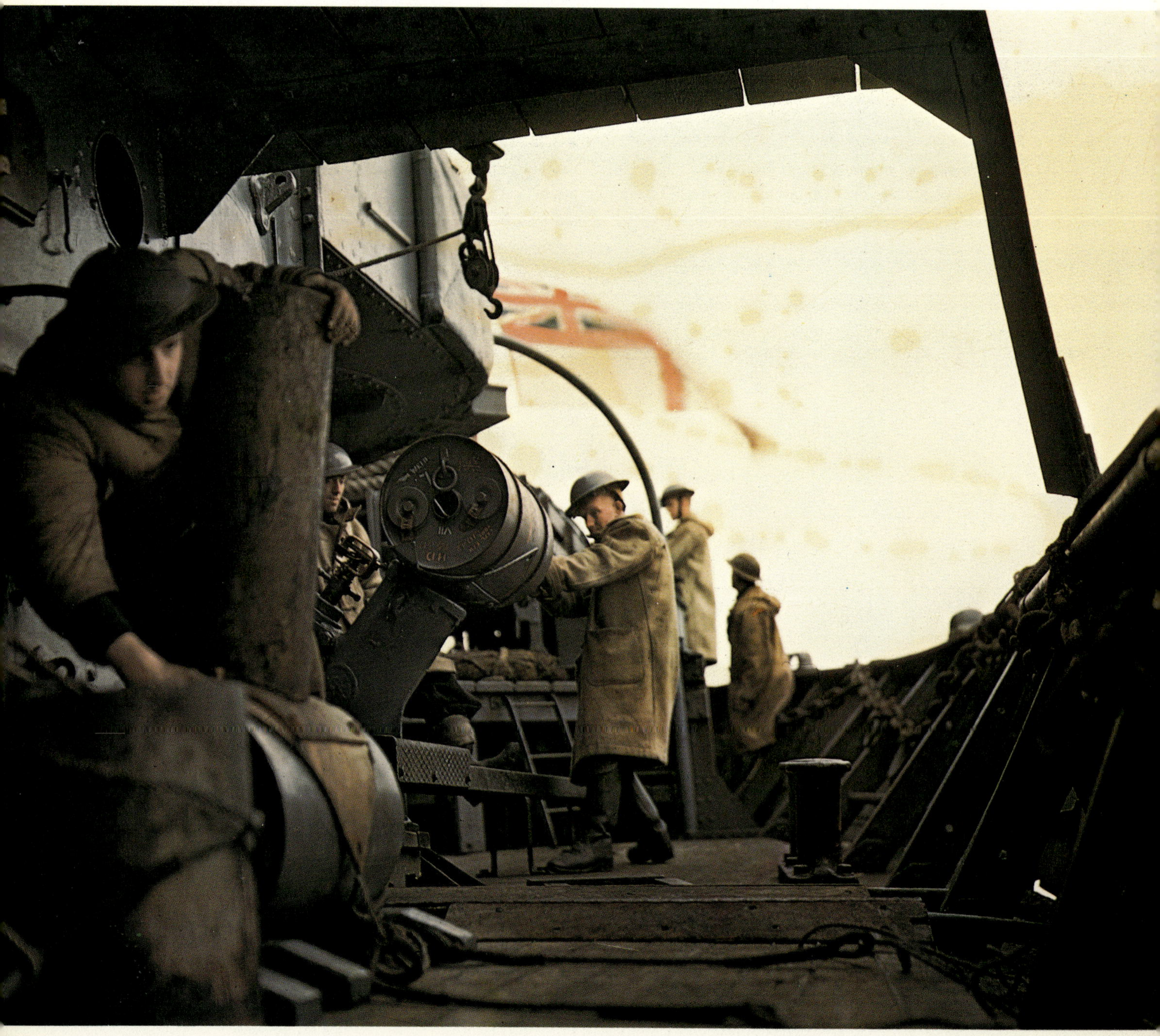

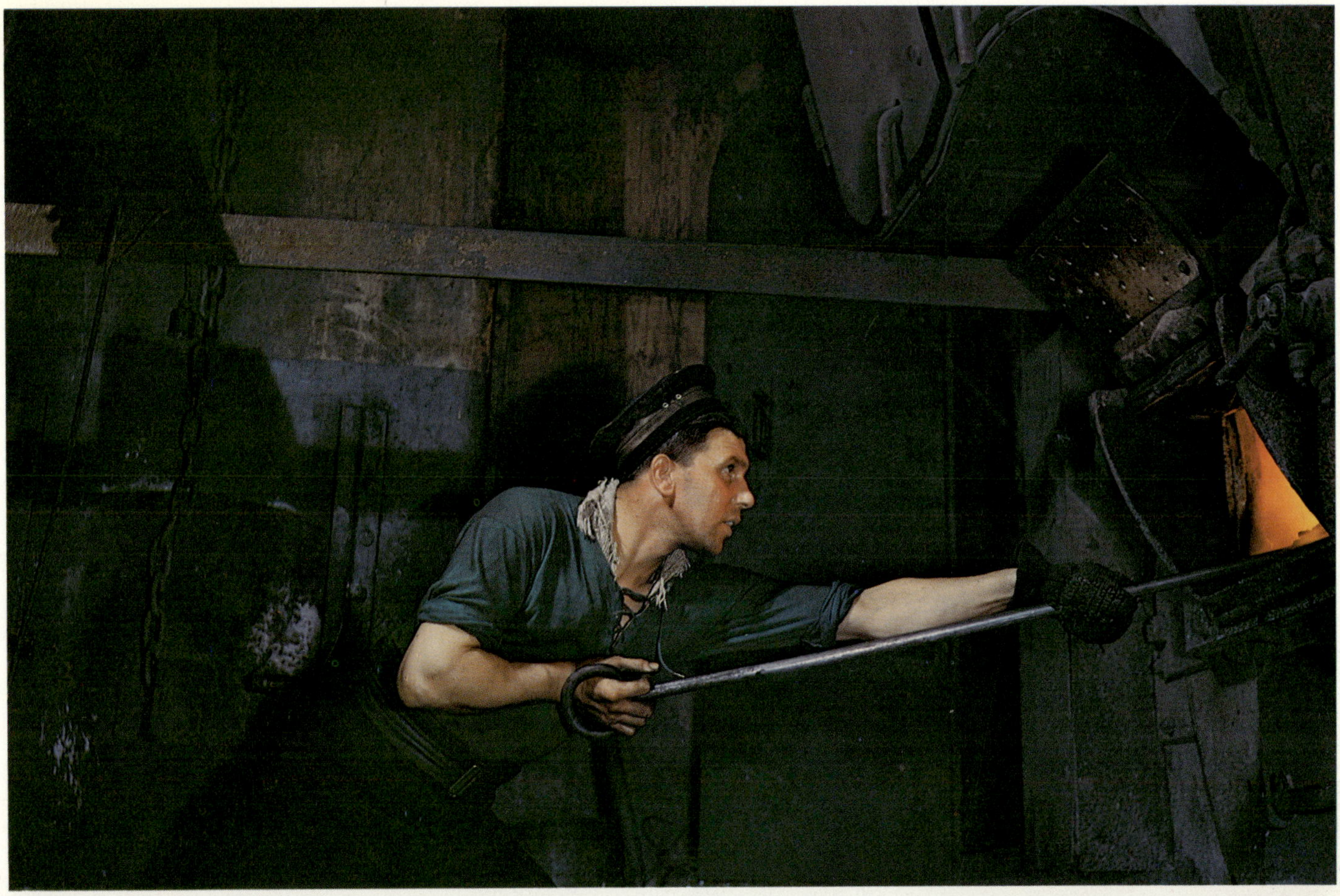

5.10

5.11

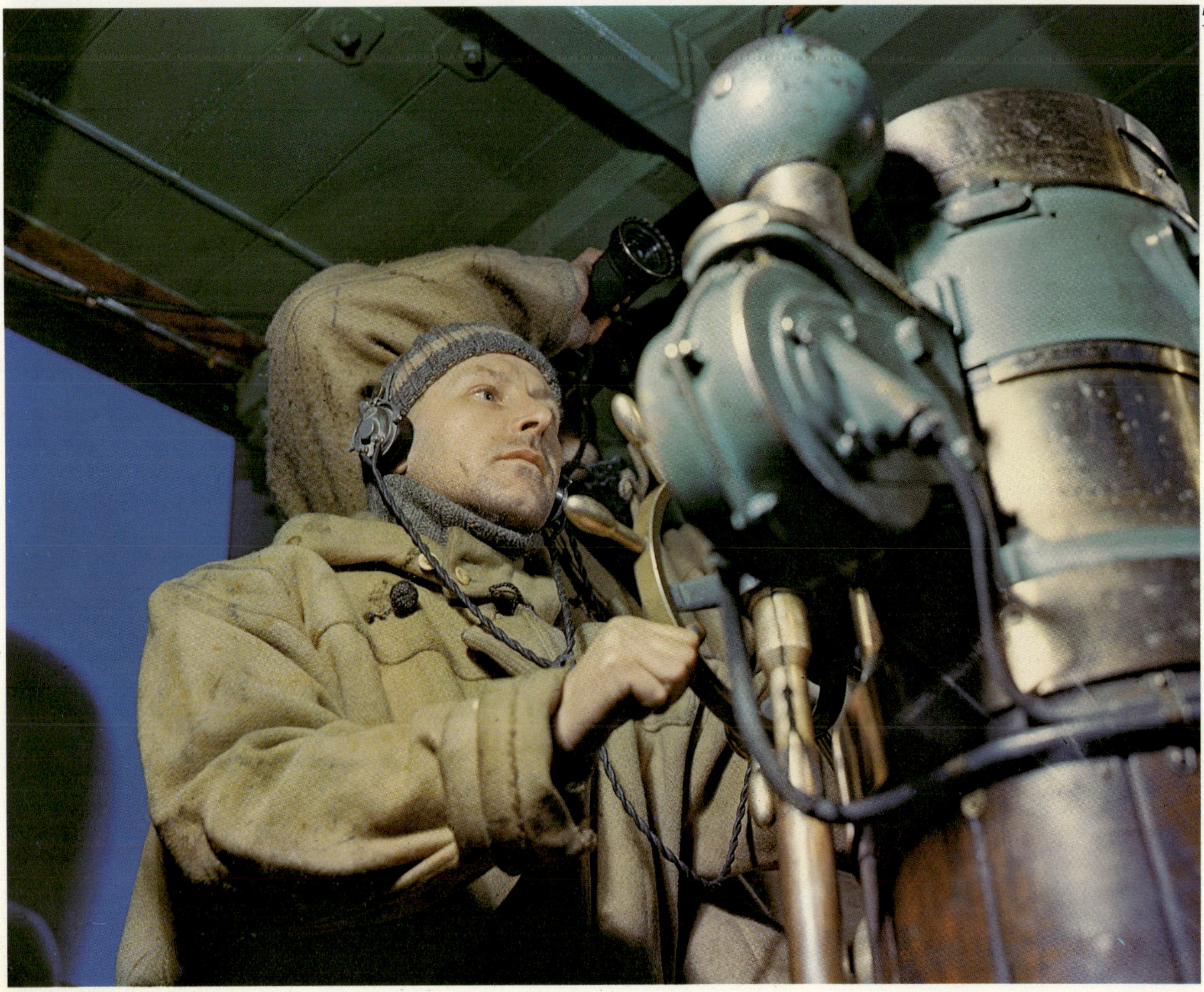

5.12 Submarines of the Third Flotilla alongside the British depot ship *Forth* in Holy Loch, June 1943. The submarines, from inboard outwards, are *Thrasher, Surf,* and the captured *U-570,* here recommissioned as HMS *Graph.*
CPL

5.13 The differences in hull design are apparent in this closer view of the three boats. Although otherwise excellent, the wide flat casing of the U-boat made her slower in crash-diving than her British equivalents. The angled stern torpedo-tubes of the 'T' class boat inboard are very noticeable.
CPL

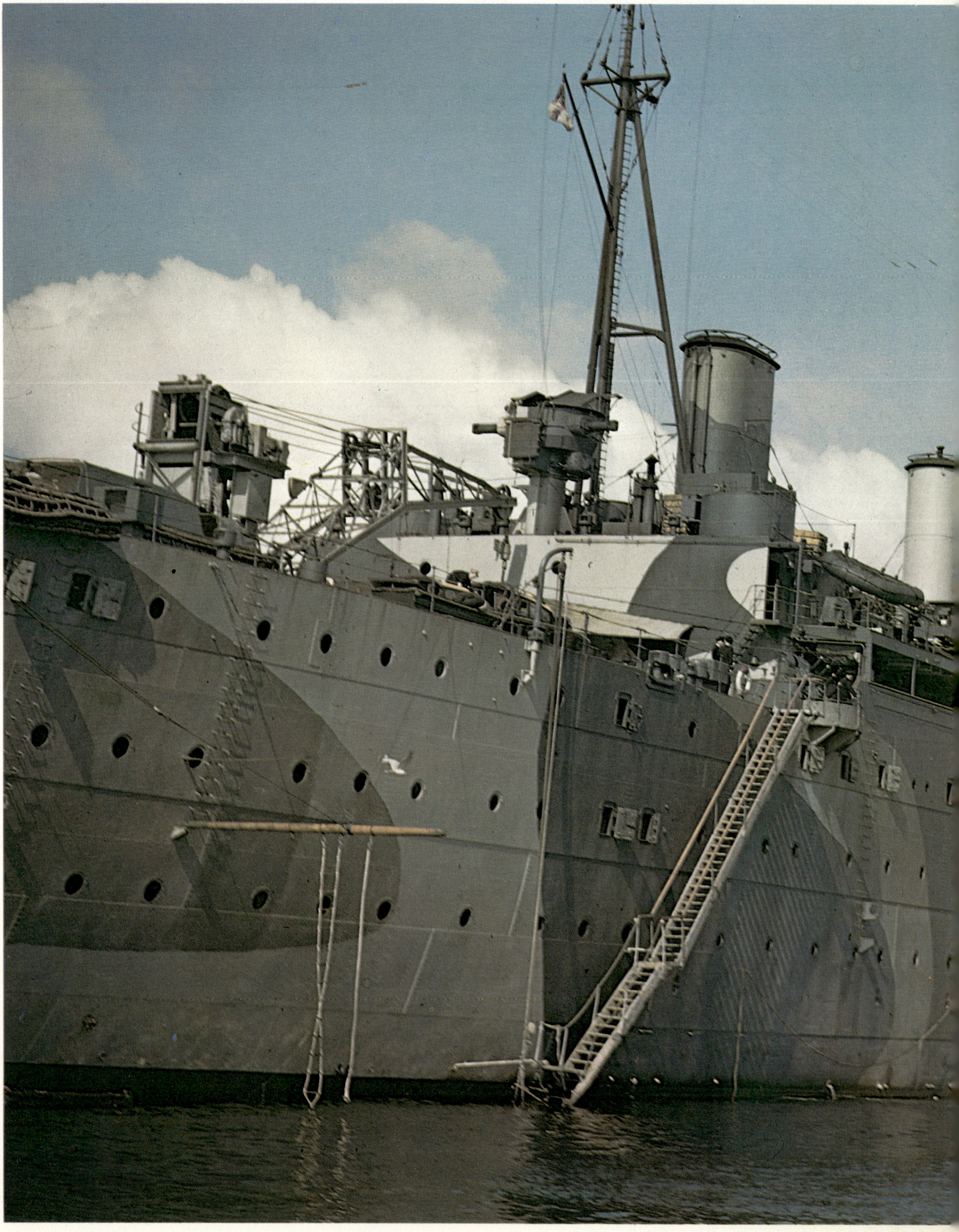

5.13

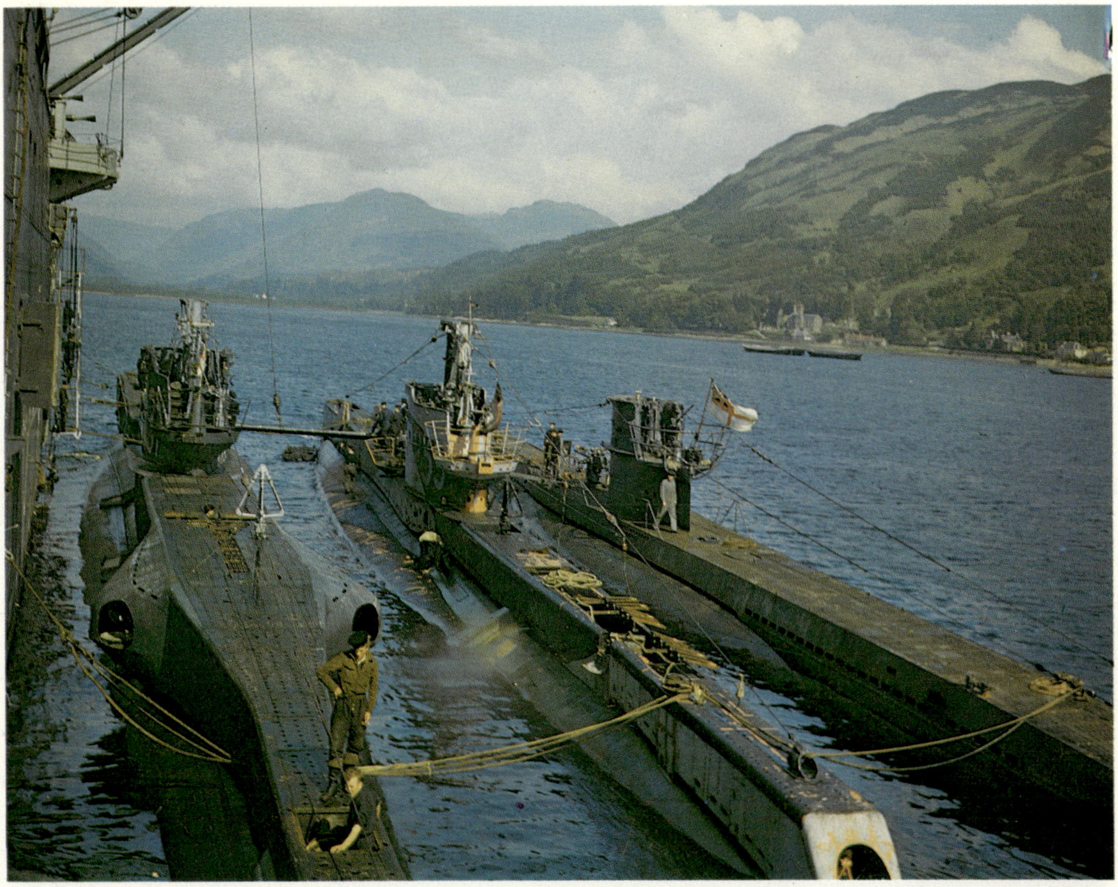

5.12

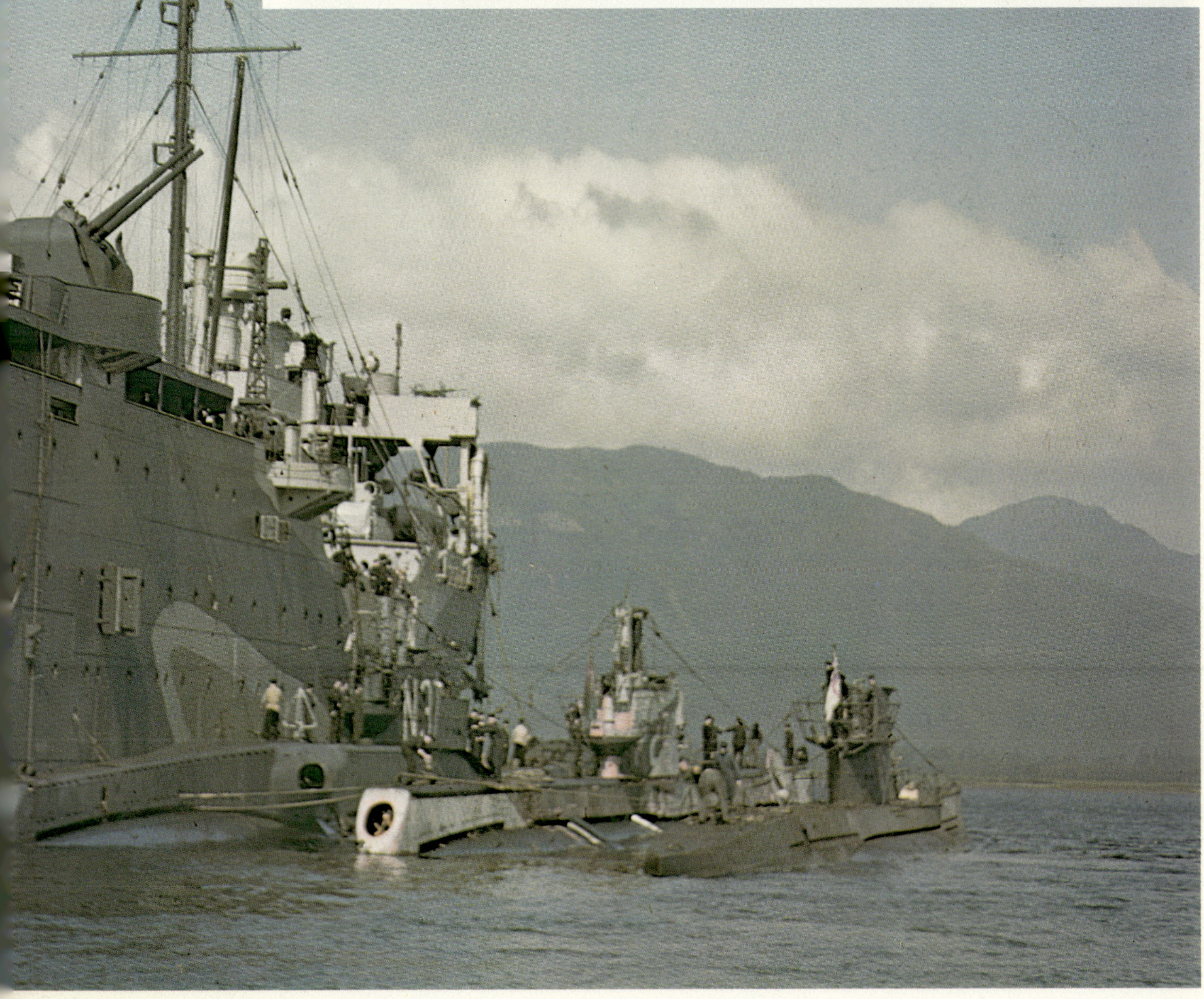

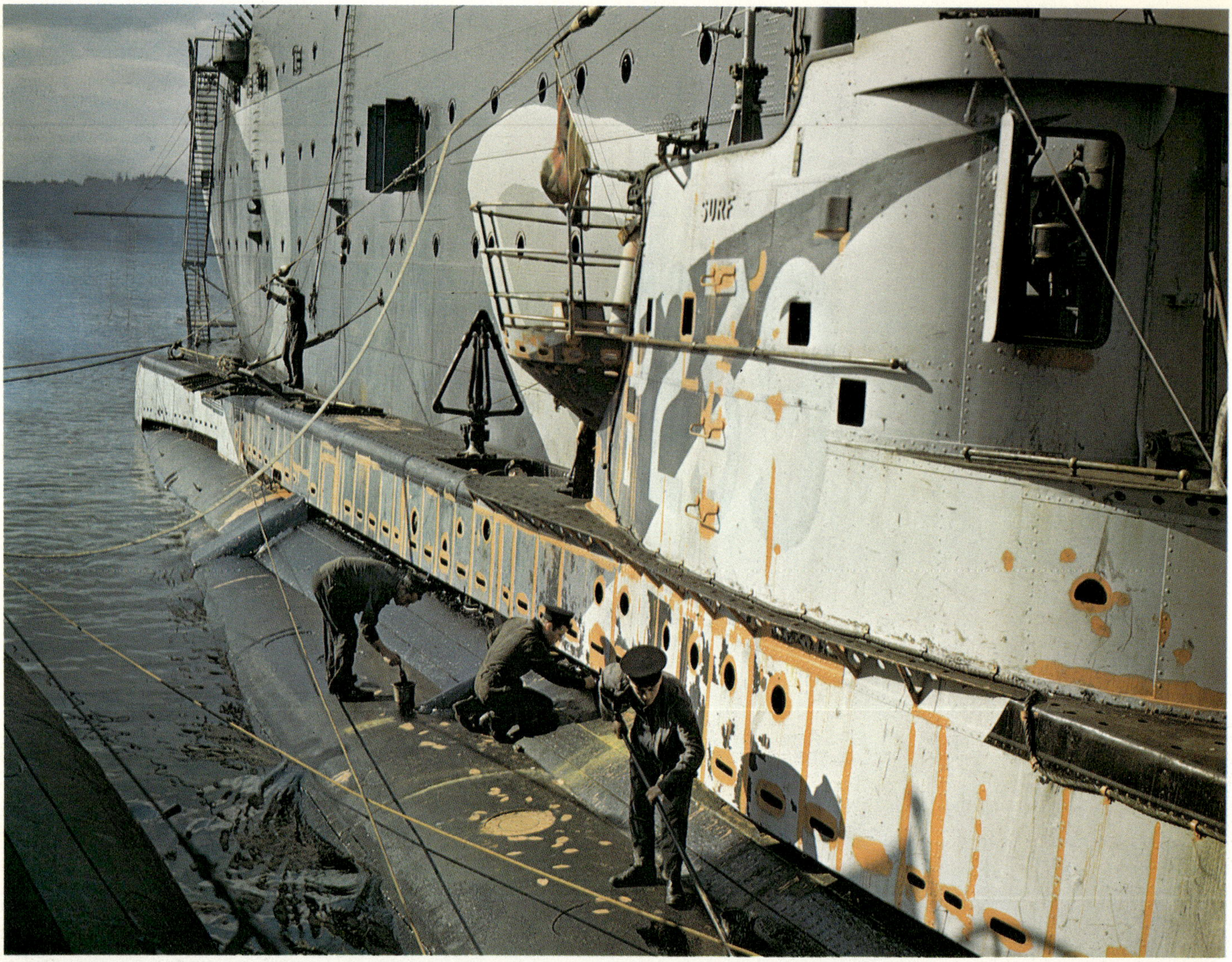

5.14

5.15

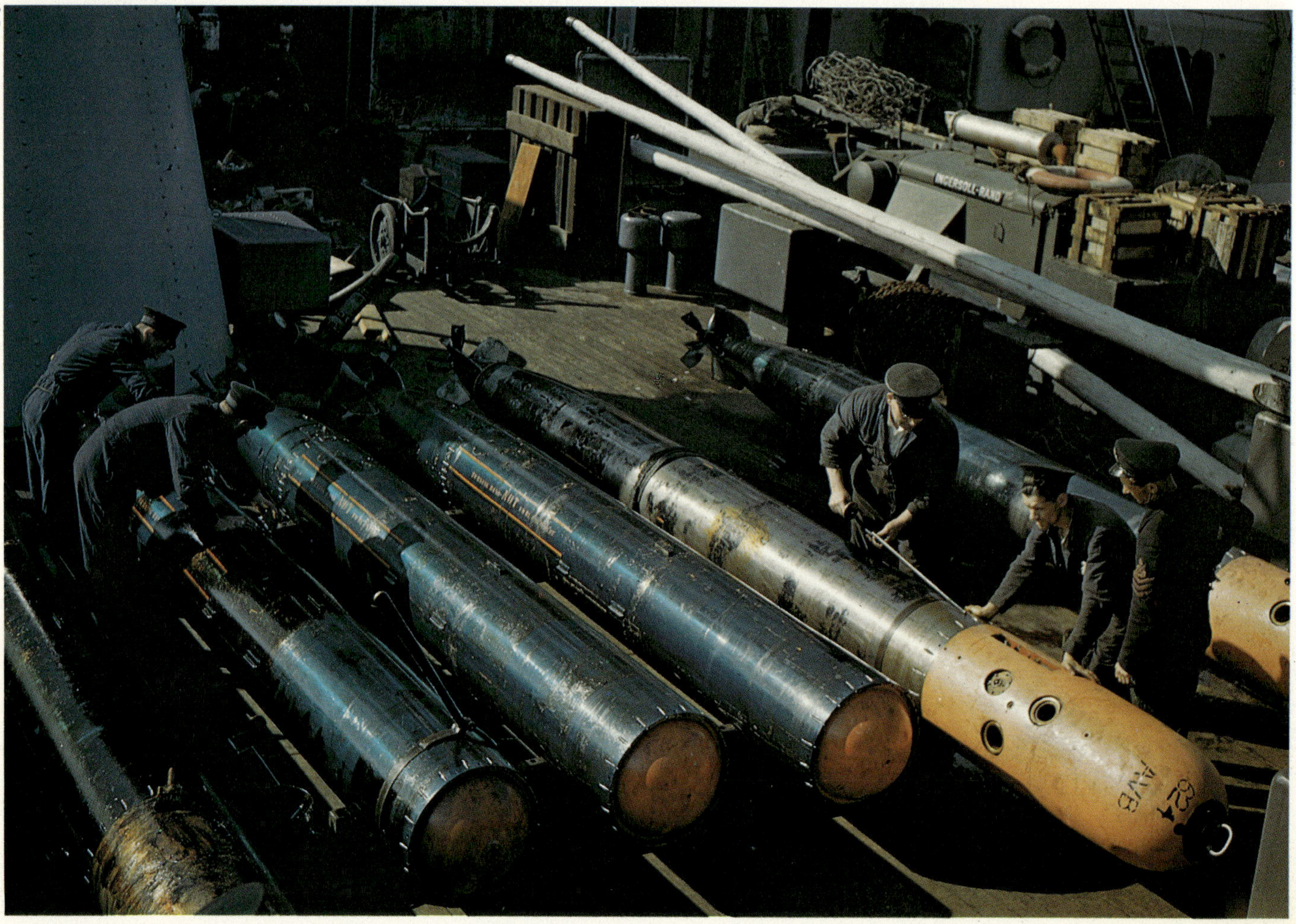

5.14 The *Surf,* a new submarine in June 1943, lying alongside *Forth* preparing for a new coat of paint. The old camouflage is still visible.
CPL

5.15 Fitting warheads to 21inch torpedoes on the main deck of the *Forth.*
CPL

5.16 21inch torpedoes on the deck of the *Forth.* The conning tower and gun of the 'T' class submarine *Truant* can be seen in the background.
CPL

5.16

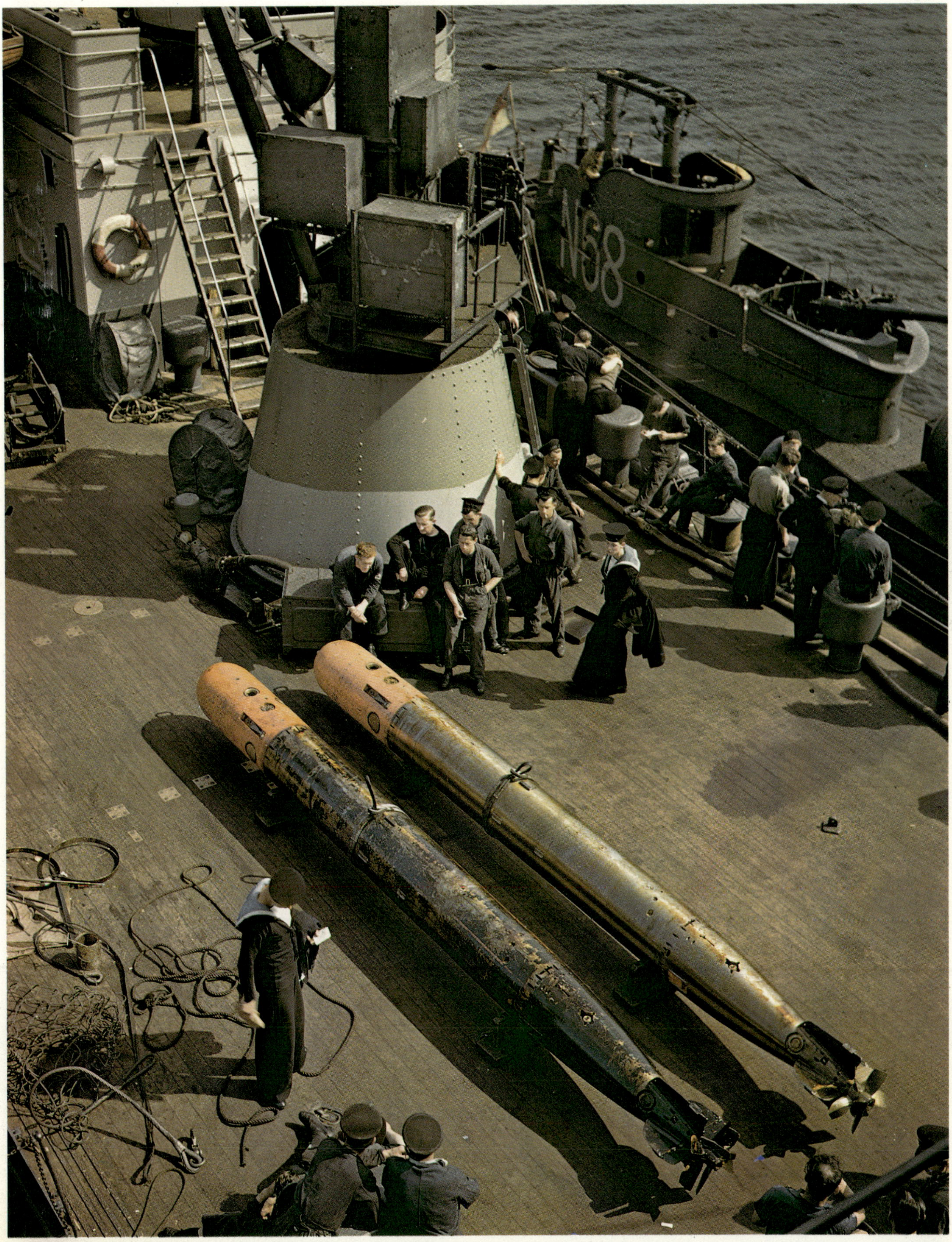

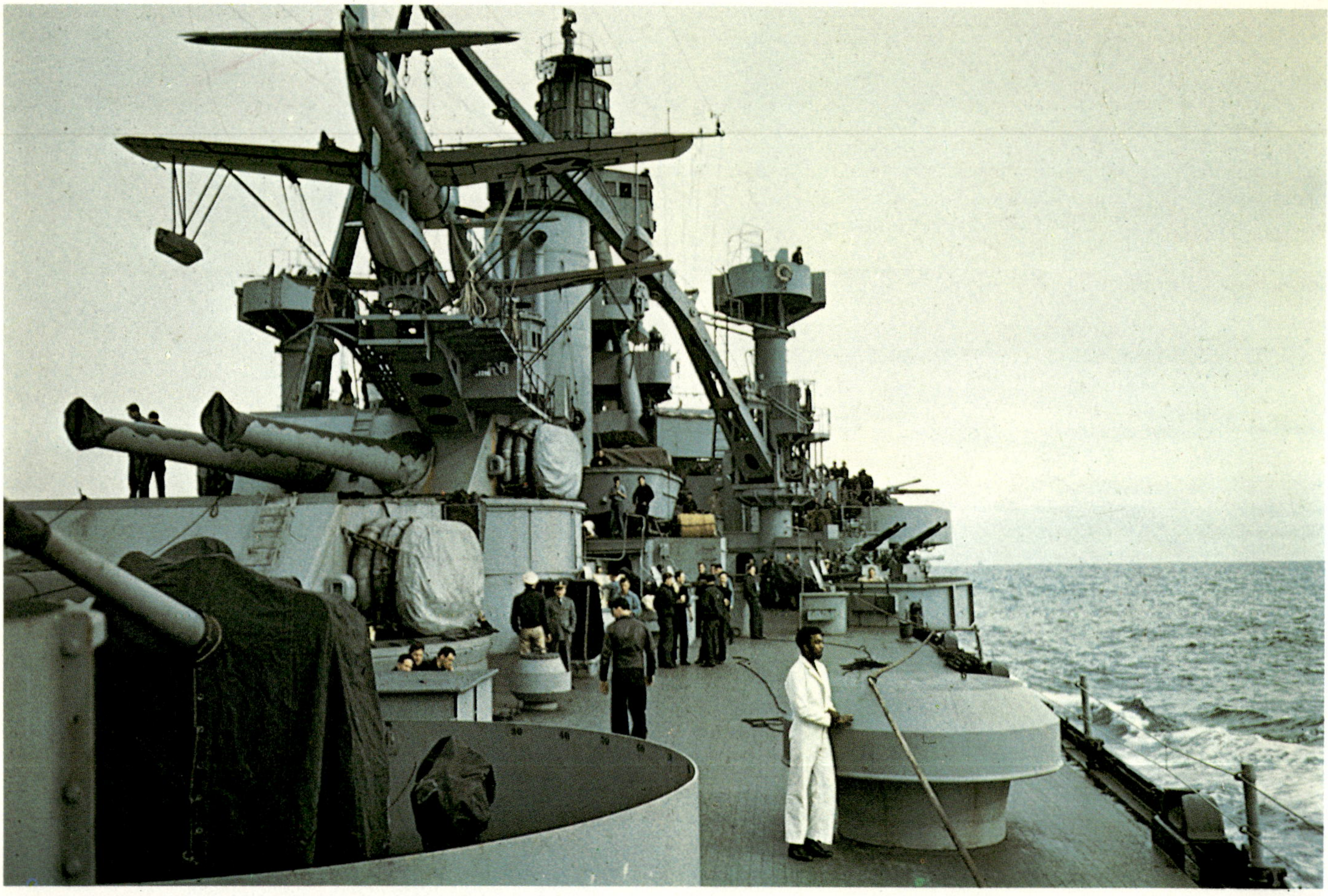

5.17

5.18

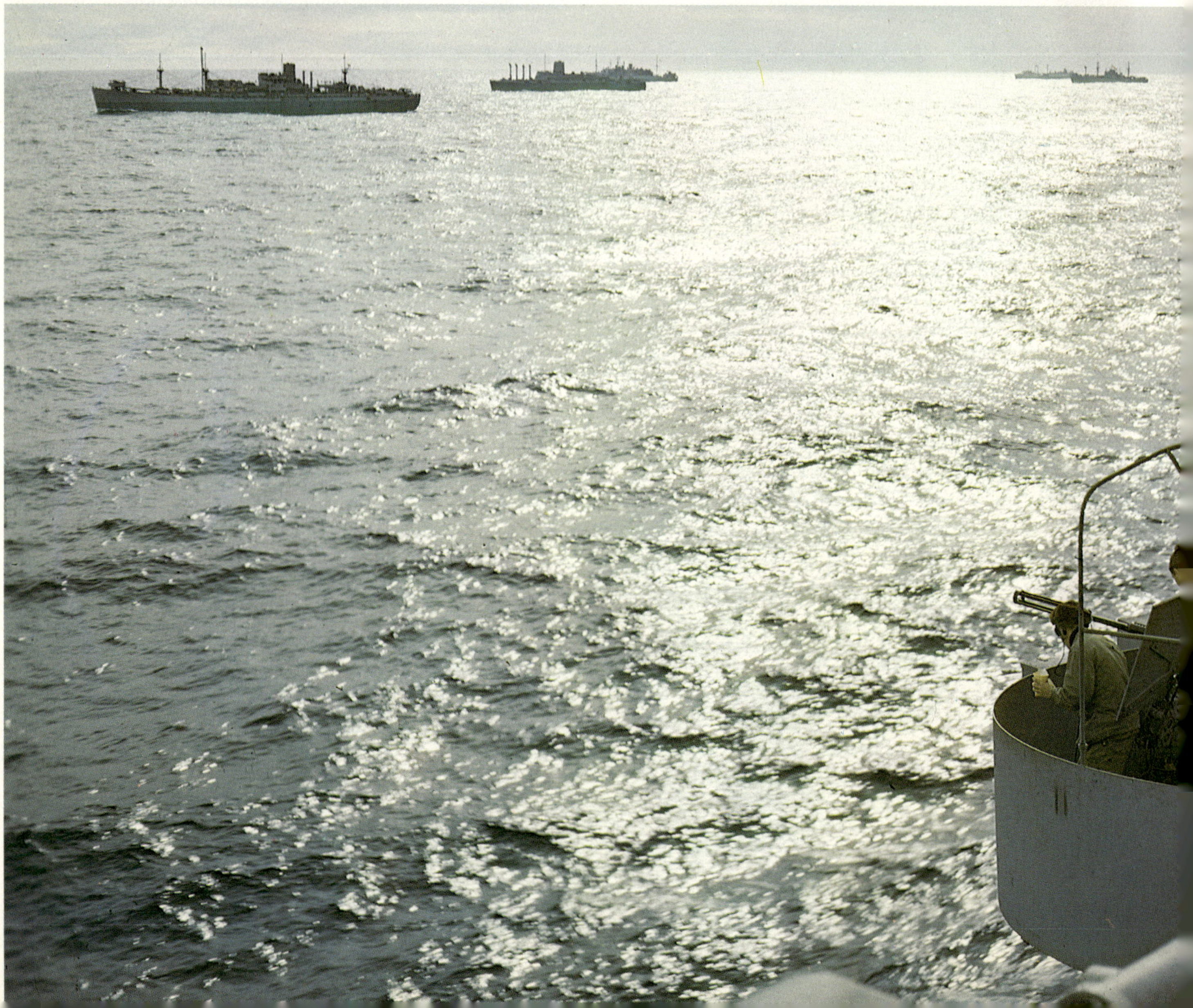

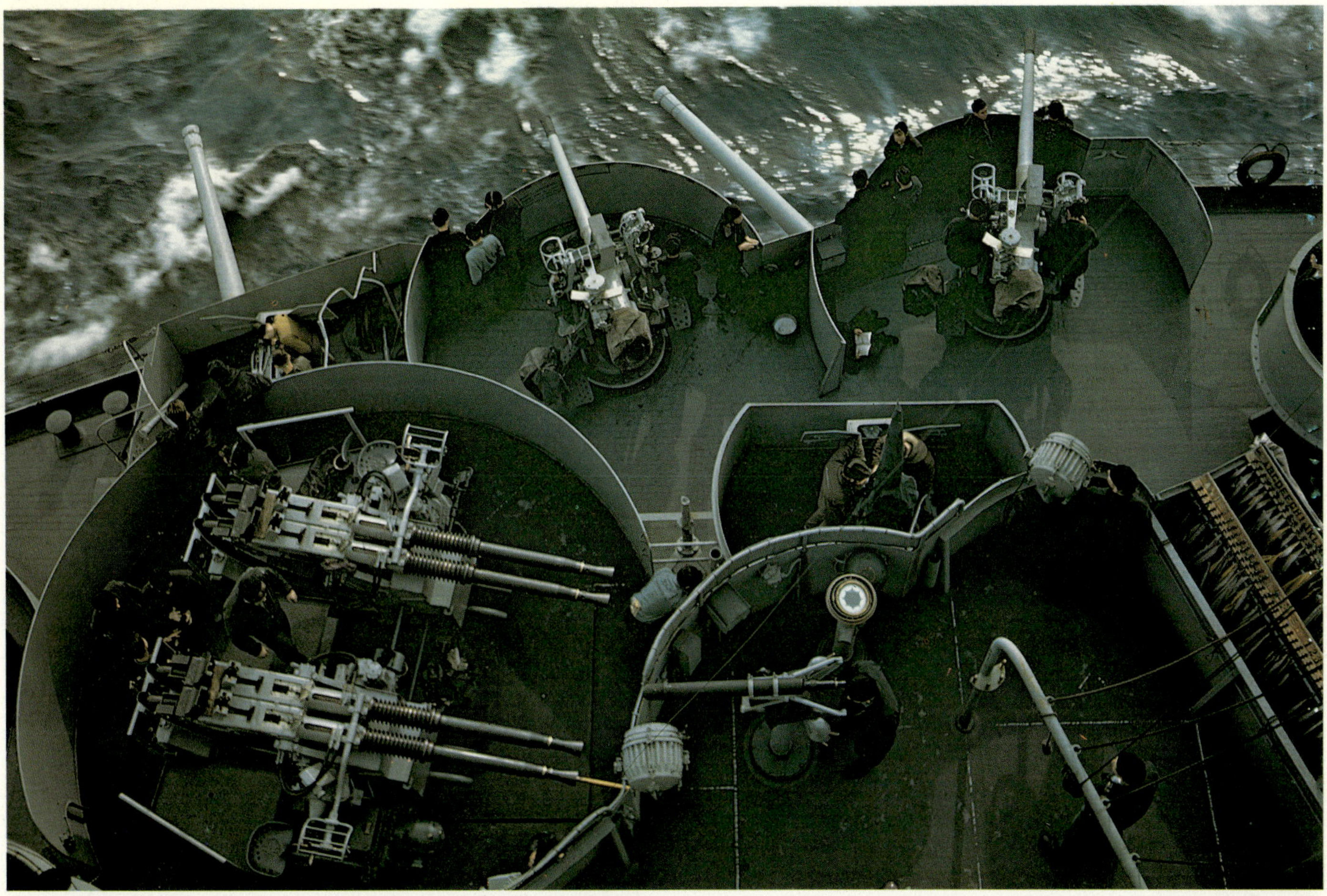

5.19

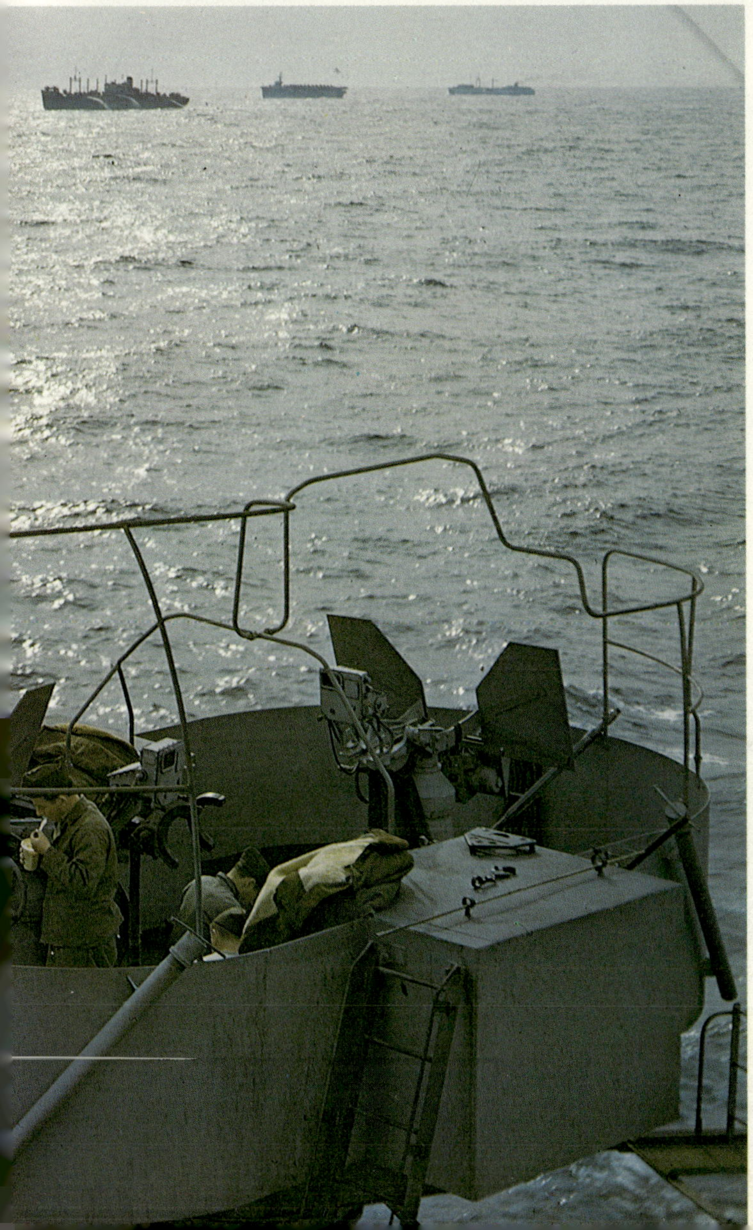

5.17 The US battleship *Arkansas* on convoy duty in the North Atlantic, with the midships pair of twin 12inch gun turrets in the foreground. The floatplanes are Vought OS2U-3 Kingfishers. *Arkansas* was too old to warrant large-scale reconstruction, but during the war she received many additional AA weapons (including the quad 40mm Bofors on the right of the photo) which by 1945 comprised ten 3inch, twenty-four 40mm and more than thirty 20mm guns.
CPL

5.18 Dawn over the convoy *Arkansas* is escorting, February 1944. The convoy left New York for Bangor, Northern Ireland, on 19 January 1944, and was obviously important enough to warrant the protection of a battleship and an escort carrier (right background). In the foreground are two of the ship's 20mm Oerlikon machine guns (one stripped down) behind the elaborate guiderails designed to stop the guns firing into the ship.
CPL

5.19 The forward end of the starboard superstructure of the USS *Arkansas* in 1944. At the ship's side are two 3inch/50 calibre AA guns, and beyond them a single 20mm Oerlikon, protected by a canvas cover. Below the 3inch guns can be seen the muzzles of two of the 5inch guns of the secondary battery. On the raised platforms to the left are a quadruple Bofors mounting and a second single Oerlikon. **JR**
CPL

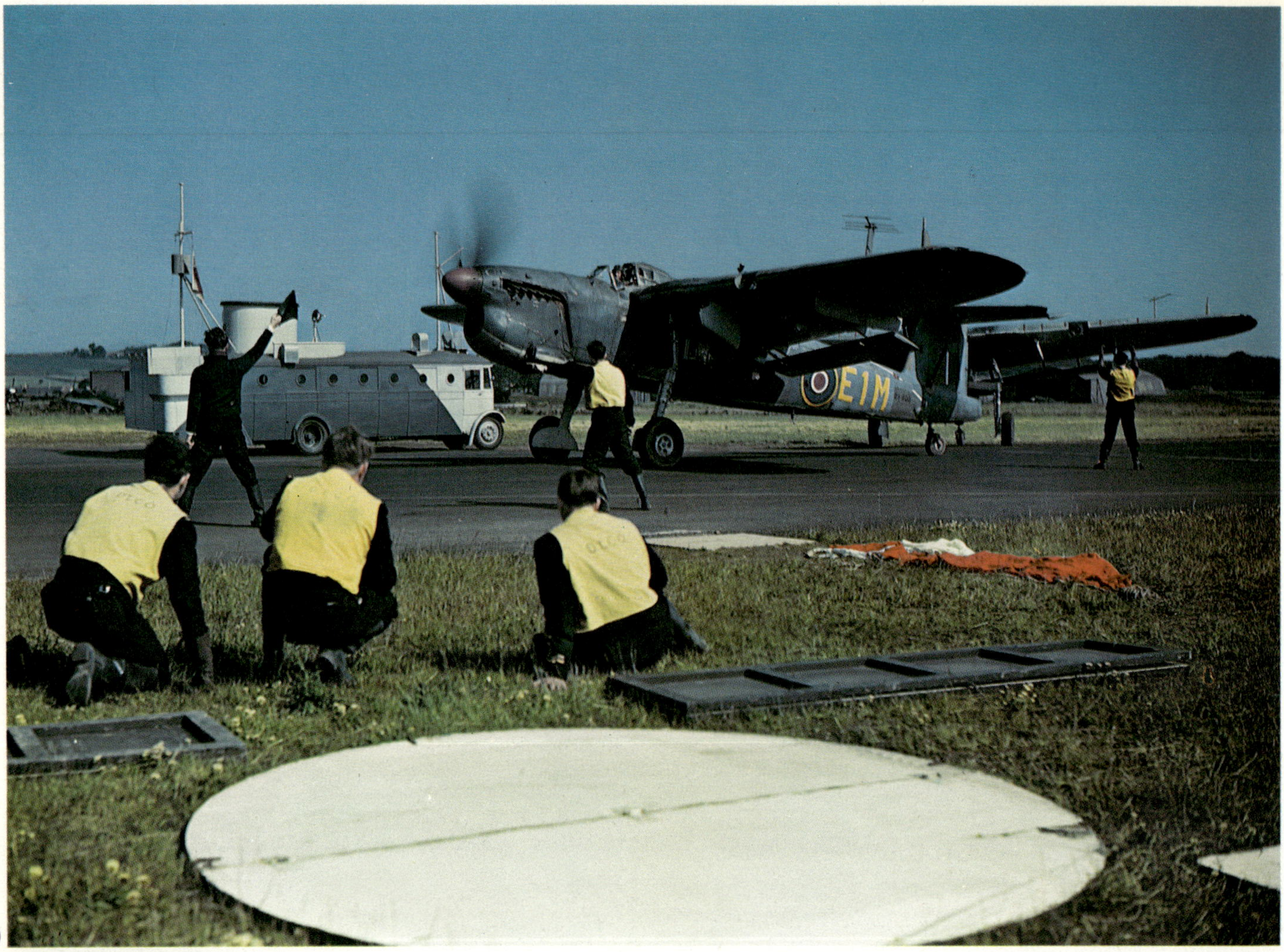

5.20

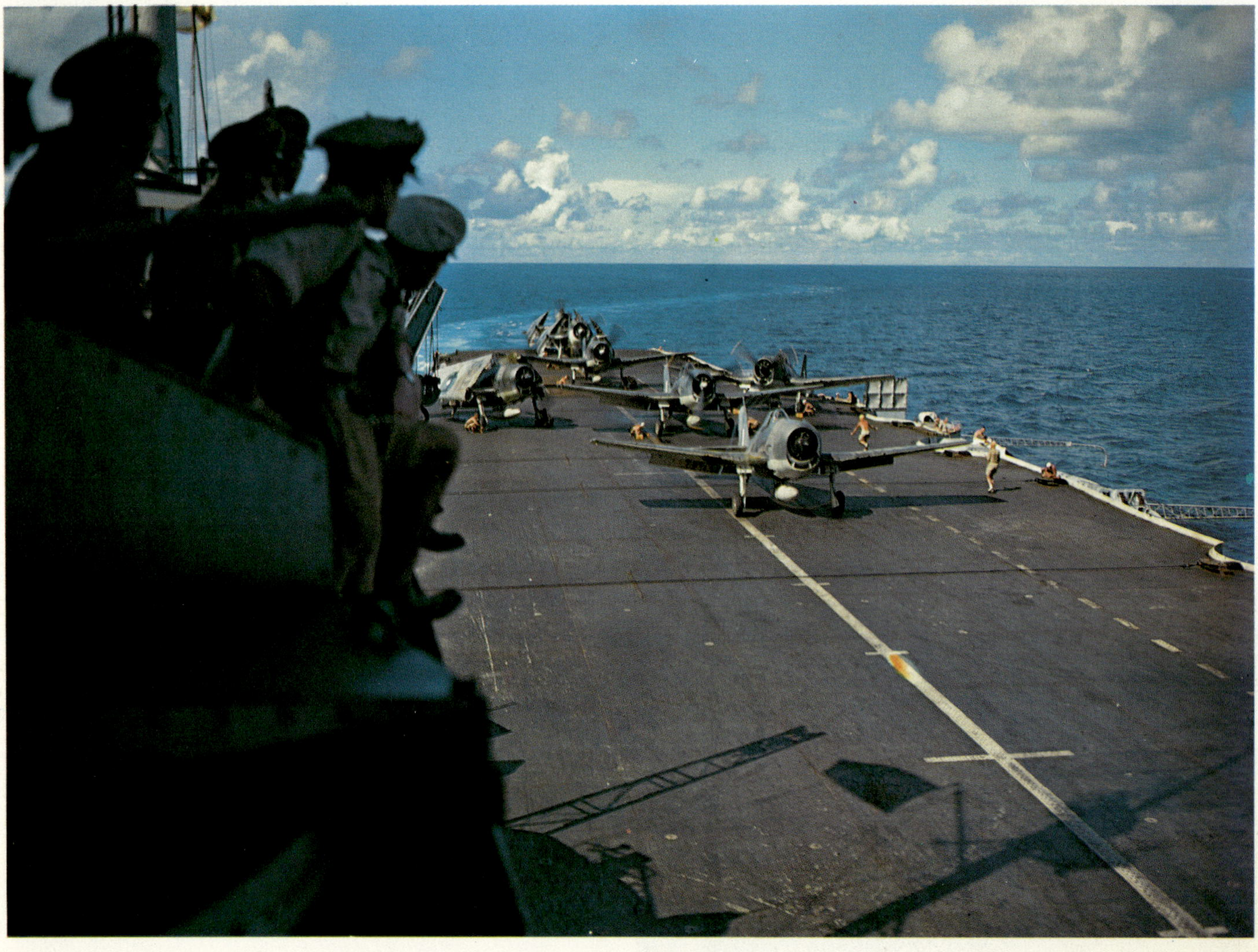

5.21

5.20 The duties of the DLCO were not restricted only to controlling deck landings, but involved all flight deck activity, including the supervision of all aircraft movements on deck and launching aircraft by catapult or free take-off. The DLCOs under training undertook all the duties which their flight deck parties would carry out: two surcoated 'marshallers' are here seen directing a pair of Barracudas up to the 'DLCO', who is already beginning to wind the first up prior to take-off. The curious vehicle in the background is HMS *Spurious,* an Albion bus modified to simulate a carrier island, complete with funnel and mast, and intended to accustom pupil pilots to the obstruction on the edge of the landing and take-off area. **DB**
CPL

5.21 *Indomitable*'s DLCO (standing on the port side of the deck, facing the first aircraft) prepares to fly off four No 5 Fighter Wing Hellcats for Combat Air Patrol (CAP) and two 857 Squadron anti-submarine patrol (ASP) Avengers; the fifth Hellcat is a spare aircraft, manned and started in case a member of the CAP goes unserviceable before take-off. The screen at the port deck edge marks the batsman's landing-on station and was intended to protect him from the wind over the deck and propeller wash from aircraft taxying up the deck after landing. **DB**
CPL

5.22
"When a pilot's not impinging on the barrier,
Or trying his unwilling crew to drown,
If you cannot find him drinking in the Wardroom of the Carrier,
It's safe to bet his head he's crashing down."
Indomitable pilots at readiness — an option not covered in the verse — take the sun in the lee of S I multiple pom-poms. The only article of clothing common to the seven is the Mae West life-saving waistcoat, two are wearing the many-pocketed British flying suits, three have American khaki shirts and slacks, the individual standing appears to be clad in an Engineer Officer's white boiler-suit, but the origin of the rig of the pilot on the extreme left is unknown. **DB**
CPL

5.22

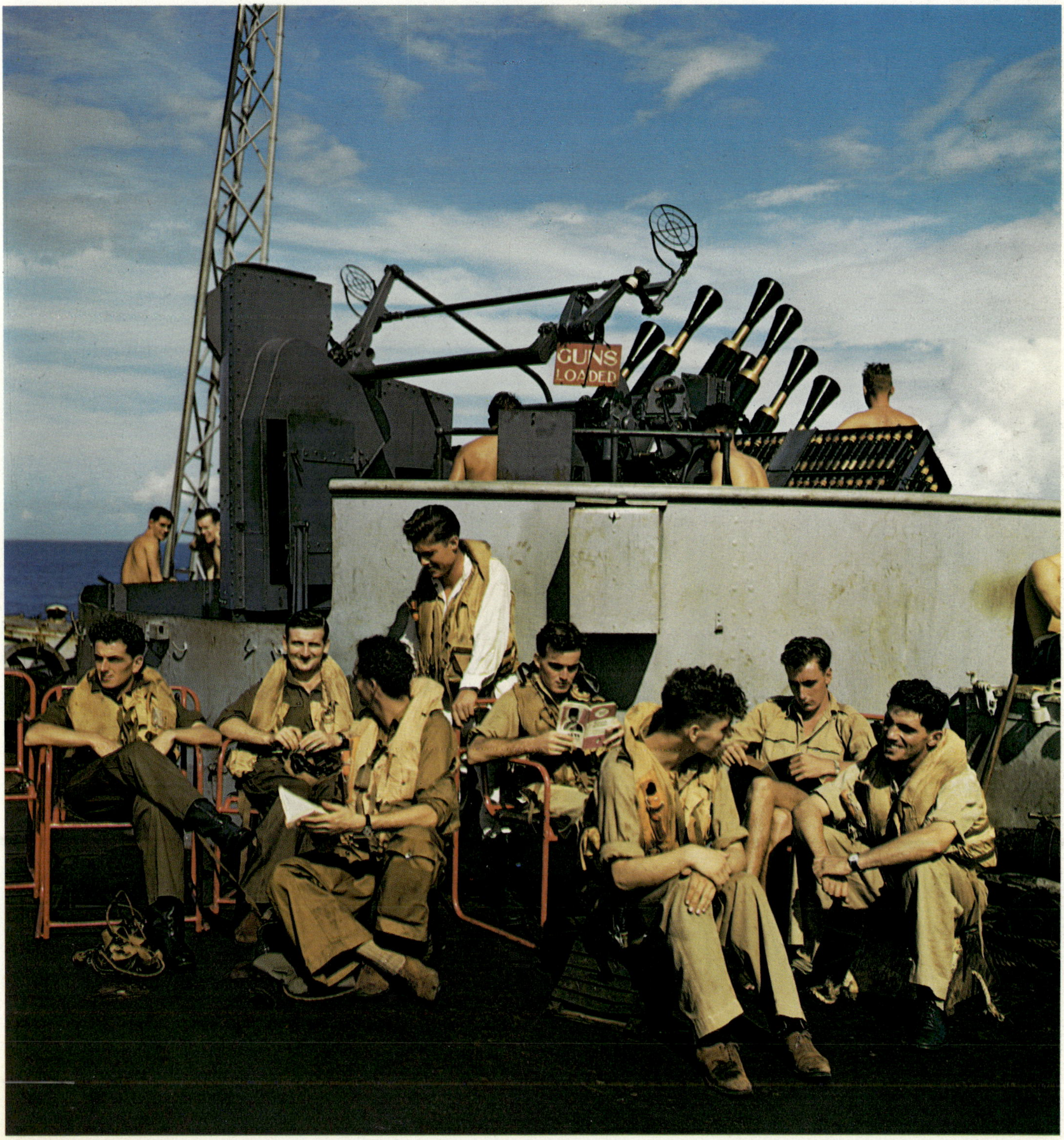

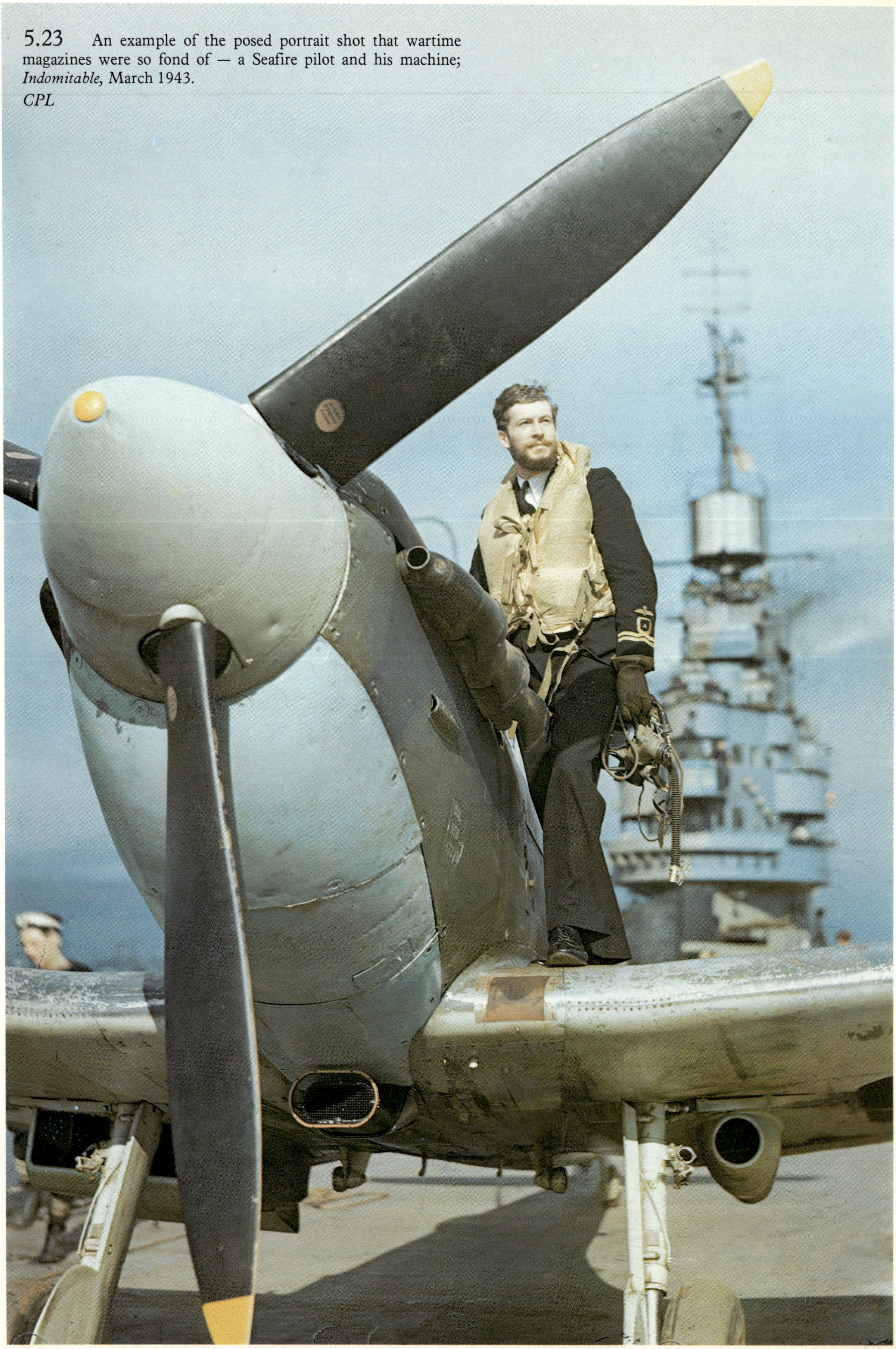

5.23 An example of the posed portrait shot that wartime magazines were so fond of — a Seafire pilot and his machine; *Indomitable,* March 1943.
CPL

6. Naval Air Power

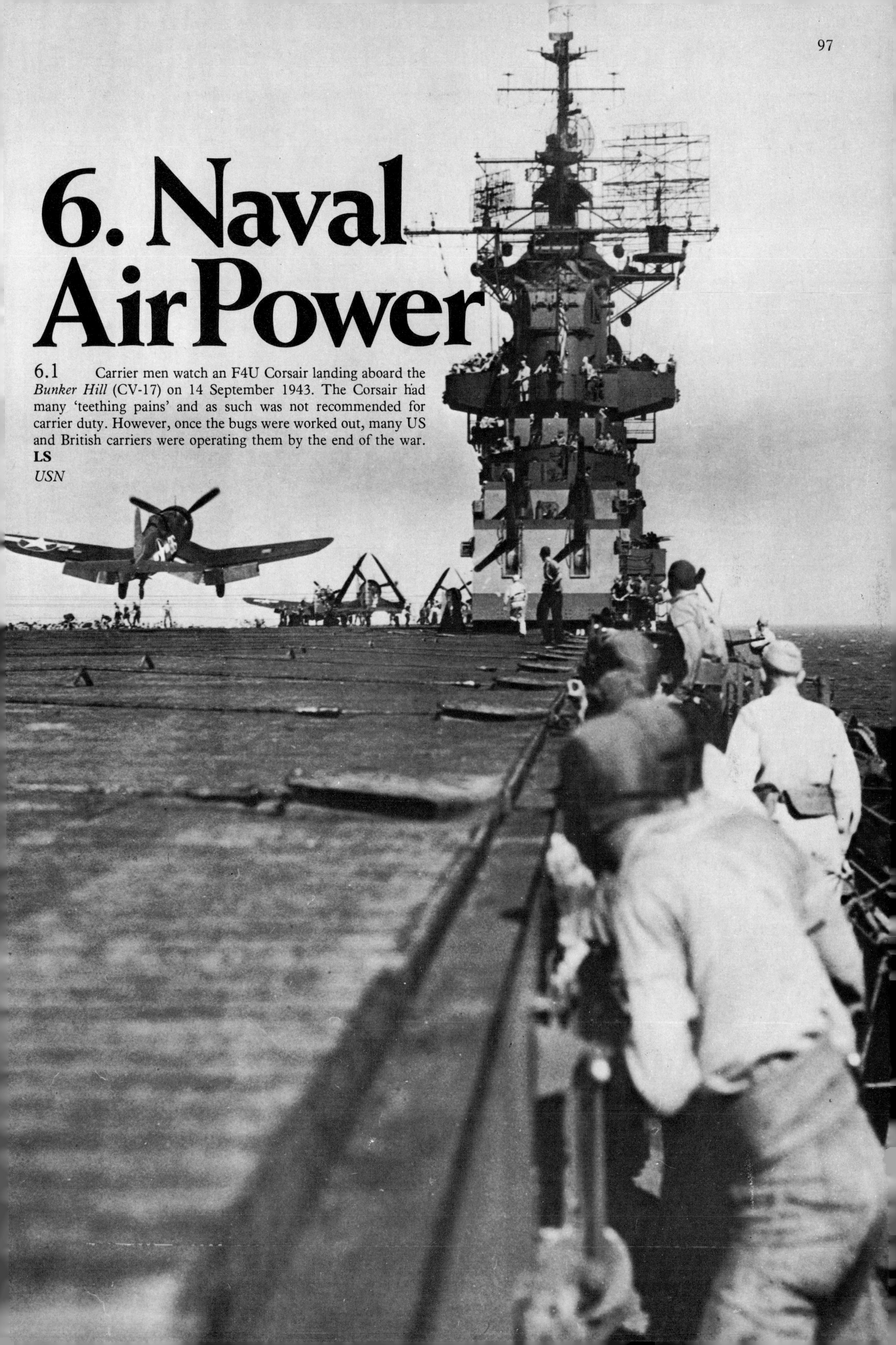

6.1 Carrier men watch an F4U Corsair landing aboard the *Bunker Hill* (CV-17) on 14 September 1943. The Corsair had many 'teething pains' and as such was not recommended for carrier duty. However, once the bugs were worked out, many US and British carriers were operating them by the end of the war. **LS**
USN

6.2 The difference in standard tonnage between *Ark Royal* and *Illustrious* was only 1000 tons, but owing to the greater weight of armour in the latter, and its distribution higher in the ship, a complete hangar deck had to be sacrificed, so that *Illustrious* embarked only 33 aircraft in 1940, compared with *Ark Royal*'s 54. Freeboard was reduced from 60 ft (18.3 m) to 38 ft (11.6 m) at the flight deck, so that the decks appear level although 'Ark' is about 1000 yards to port of *Illustrious.* The islands and foremasts show the influence of improved aircraft control and communications facilities: more than half of *Ark Royal*'s island's bulk is taken up by her large funnel and her somewhat untidy 'layered' bridge structure is relatively small, whereas *Illustrious* is considerably larger, with space for all the necessary command, control and communications 'offices', and the funnel, although longer than *Ark Royal*'s, does not dominate the monolithic island structure. The dustbin-shaped external housing of the type 72 aircraft homing beacon antenna is mounted at the head of *Ark Royal*'s mast, but *Illustrious'* is just above the tripod, permitting the fitting of the radar receiving antenna at the mast head; the lack of suitable positions for radar antennae meant that *Ark Royal* was never to be equipped to control her own fighters at long distances and had to rely upon radar-equipped consorts for warning and fighter direction.

The form of *Illustrious'* fore and aft extremities is of interest: the flight deck was the first of rectangular plan to be seen in the Royal Navy — *Ark Royal*'s was semi-circular forward, the protruding accelerator tracks appearing to give it a 'squared-off' plan; *Illustrious* had only one accelerator, the forward end of which was set well back so that the airflow over the forward 'round-down' would not be disturbed. The same attention to aerodynamic detail resulted in a long, gently-sloping after round-down, the landing area proper not beginning until above the forward end of the quarterdeck. As the war progressed, the after round-down was gradually built up, as was the forward, until by mid-1945 the usable length was 740 ft (225.5 m) — 120 ft (36.5 m) more than in 1940. **DB**
CPL

6.3 On 22 August 1940, a powerful force left Scapa Flow for Gibraltar. Included were the light cruiser *Sheffield (*from which these photographs were taken), the brand-new armoured Fleet carrier HMS *Illustrious* and the equally new *Dido* class AA cruiser *Bonaventure,* and the WWI-vintage battleship *Valiant* and AA cruisers *Coventry* and *Calcutta.* The combination was not remarkable for the blend of ancient and modern but for the fact that all six ships were fitted with air warning radar — the largest force of ships so fitted to be in company up to that time. *Sheffield* and *Bonaventure* were intended to join Force 'H' at Gibraltar, but the other four ships were to pass through the Mediterranean to join the Fleet at Alexandria.

Sheffield, her forward 6inch guns trained to port and at maximum depression to minimise the ingress of sea water, follows the *Illustrious* through a short swell and moderate sea in the Atlantic. The carrier's 'hockey stick' W/T aerials are all raised, as is the windscreen forward of the island — the break in the screen marks the accelerator (catapult) track, which stood proud of the deck and which was, with its fairing plates, some 6 ft wide. The cruiser *Bonaventure* is broad on the carrier's starboard bow. **DB**
CPL

The carrier *Illustrious* was badly damaged by German dive-bombers on 10 January 1941, underwent repairs in the USA between May and November and then proceeded to the United Kingdom for modifications which included the installation of a more up-to-date air warning radar. She did not begin her work-up for operations until early March 1942 and what was to have been a month of training was cut to a fortnight when it was decided to include her in the force despatched to occupy the port of Diego Suarez, at the north end of the island of Madagascar. This series of photographs was taken at the beginning of the air work-up in the Clyde, in the second week of March. **DB**

6.4 The aerofoil shape of the island and funnel is evident in this view, the exaggerated camber on the inboard side being intended to draw the disturbed air and the funnel smoke outboard, clear of the landing area, so as to reduce turbulence over the round-down. The position of the pole mast supporting the type 281 radar transmitter can be clearly seen: it was hardly an ideal situation, for not only did it mask the arc of S IV pom-pom (mounted on the bandstand) but the radar performance was considerably degraded by the 'wooding' effect of the island and the considerable difference in height between the separate radar antennae. In some sectors, maximum range was reduced to about 40 miles (less than half the maximum attainable) and even the subsequent raising of the after antenna to the level of the funnel did little to improve the range. The wartime censor has made a poor job of obscuring the antenna, for the length of the four sets of half-wave transmitting dipoles and reflectors is still obvious. The fighters on deck are the Grumman Martlet IIs of 881 Squadron. **DB**
CPL

6.2

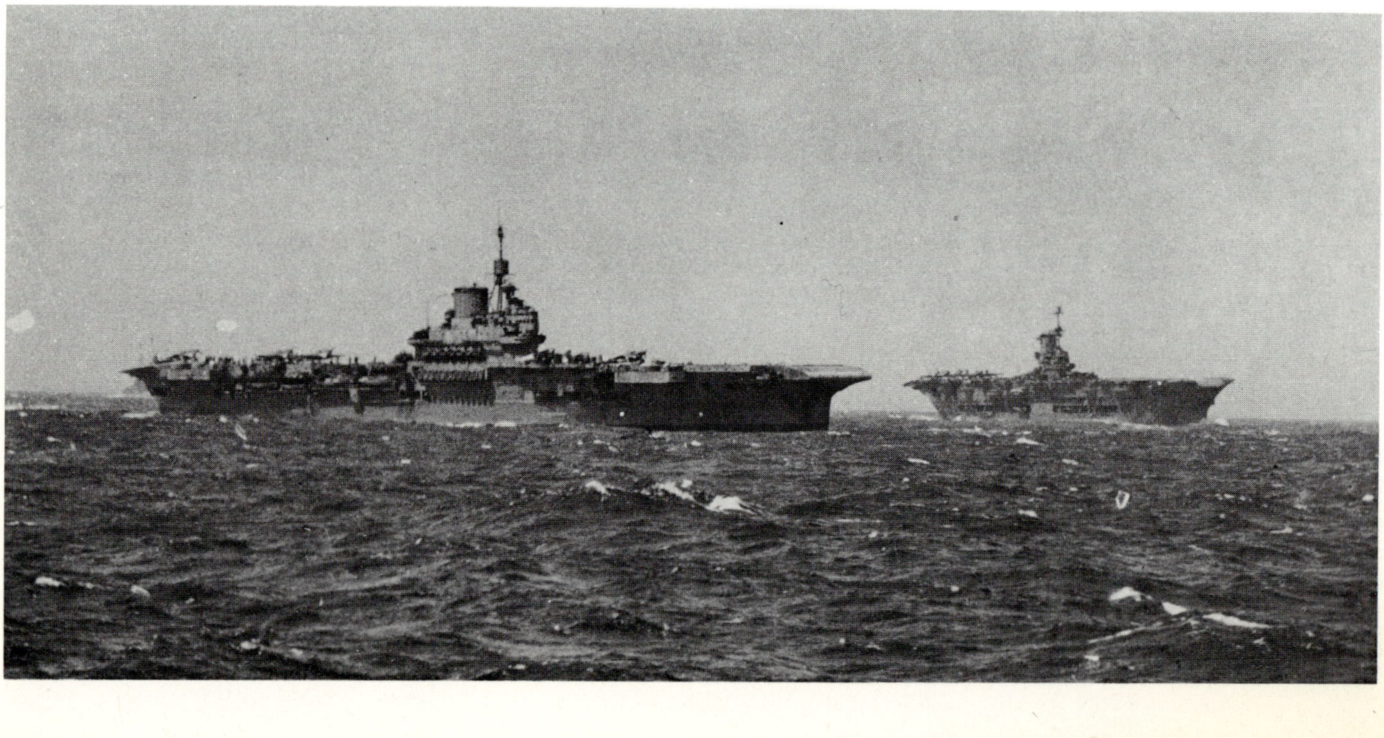

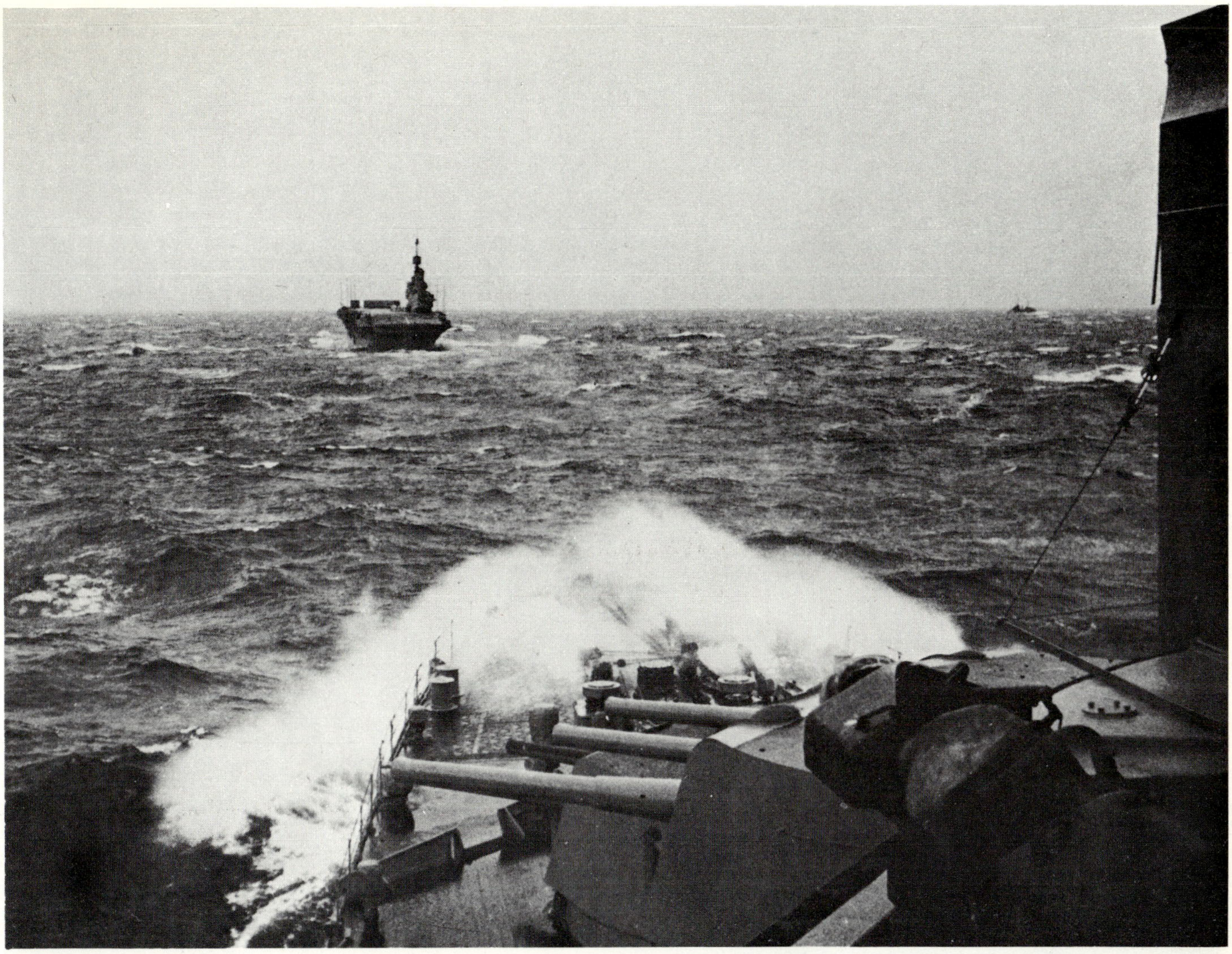

6.3

6.4

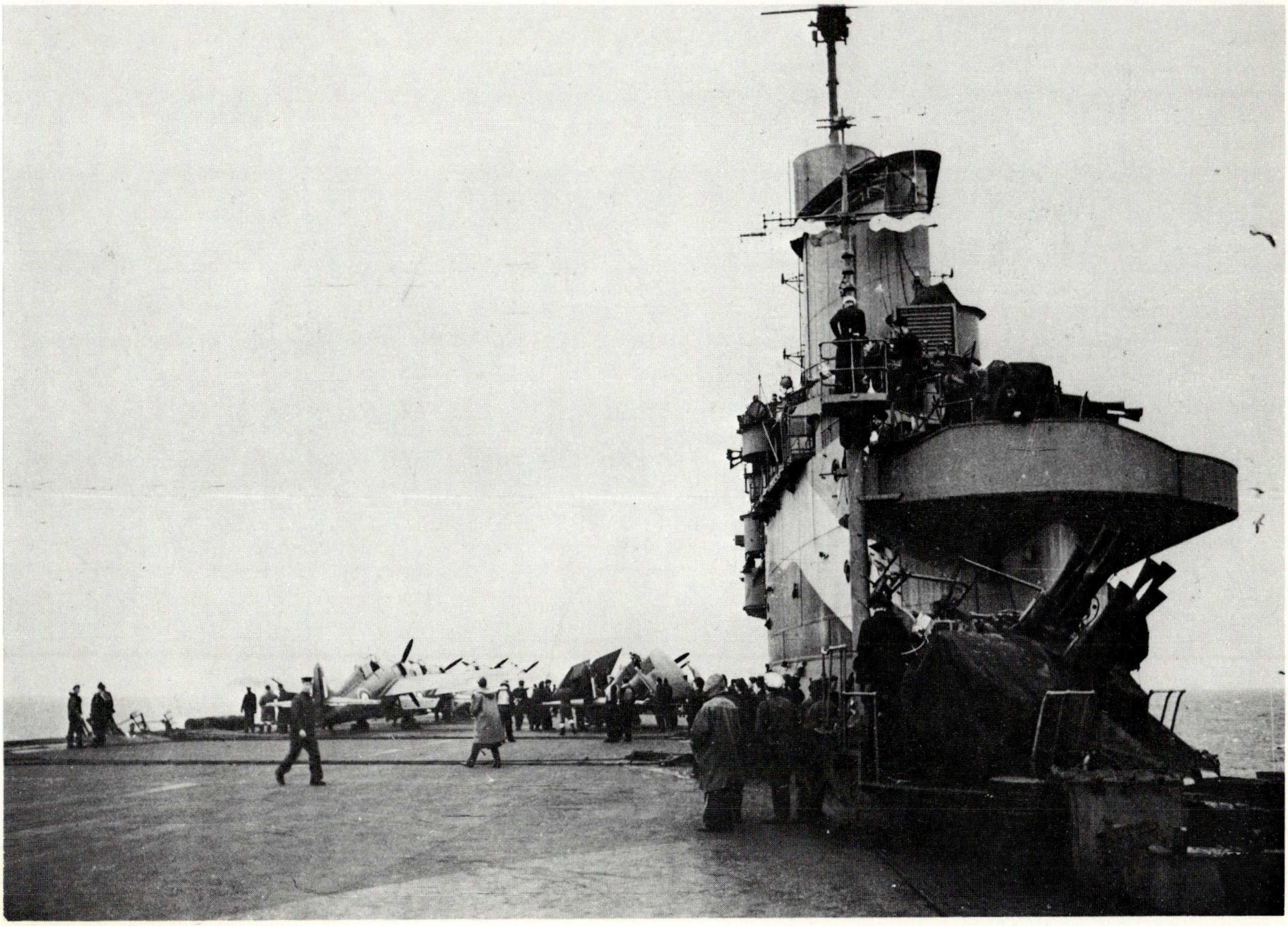

6.5 The censor has done a remarkable, if incomplete job on this photograph: the type 281 transmitter has disappeared altogether, together with a bite out of the Swordfish's propeller. The radar receiver antennae on the Swordfish's outboard interplane strut has also been wiped out, but the 'towel-rail' transmitter of the air-surface vessel (ASV) IIN radar has been left on the leading edge of the upper centre-section. The battery-powered 'dodgem car' towing the aircraft was an acquisition from the stay in Norfolk, Virginia, British carriers having previously lacked any type of flight deck tractor. The method of towing is unusual — tail wheel aircraft were almost invariably towed tail first as directional control was more positive. **DB**
CPL

6.5

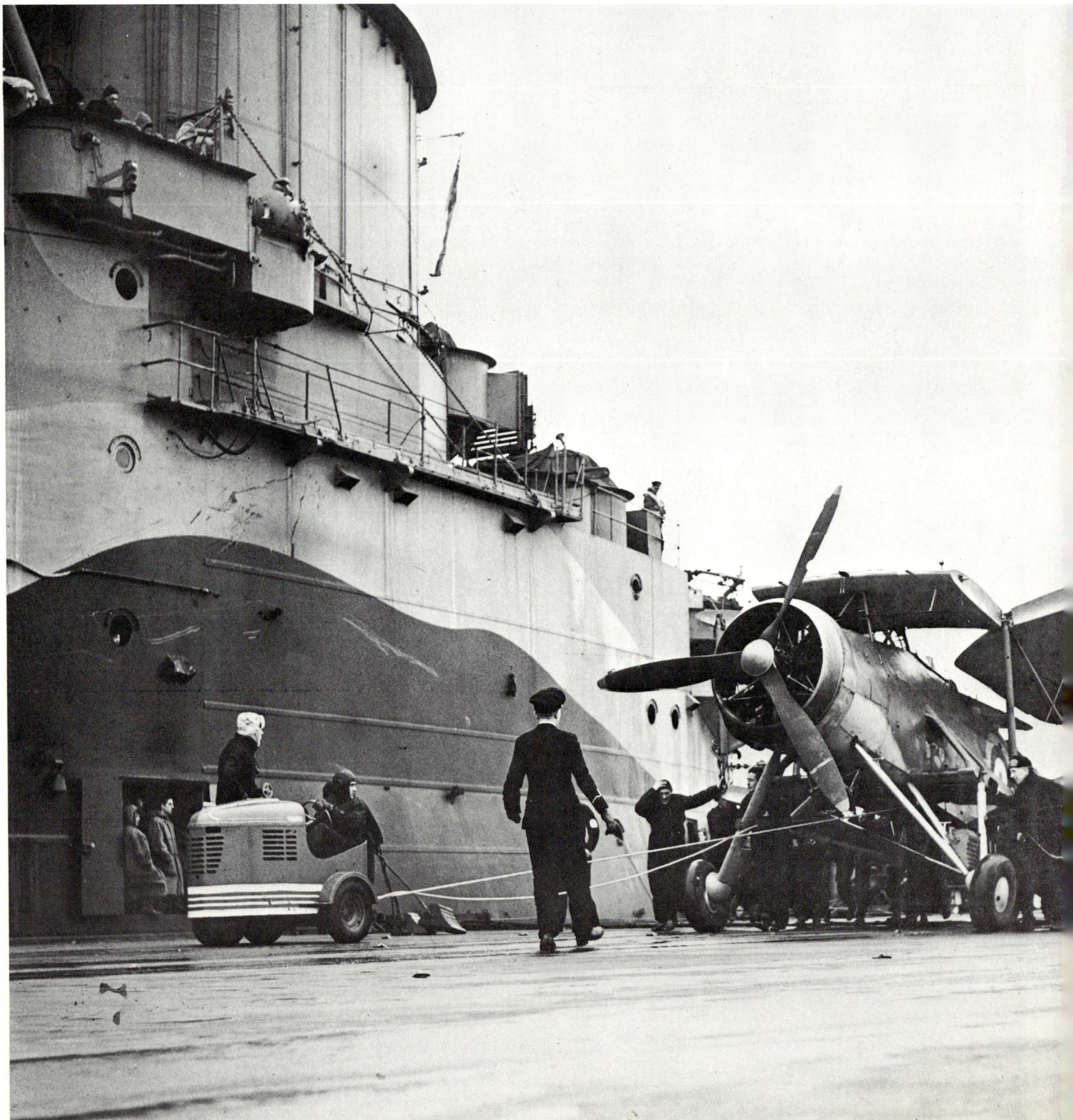

6.6 A Martlet is accelerated off *Illustrious,* weathercocking into the wind which is coming over the port bow, as may be seen by the steam jet on the centreline. The Martlet II, being built to a British pre-Lend-Lease order, was fitted with trolley attachment spigots and the collapsed trolley may be seen at the end of the track, below the port wing-tip of the aircraft. The two objects at the rear end of the track, inboard of the 4.5inch turret tops, are guide-boards for the Martlet's main wheels, to assist in alignment with the accelerator. **DB**
CPL

6.7 The majority of take-offs were 'free', with the aircraft finding the necessary air speed through the combination of engine power, ship's speed and wind down the deck, without recourse to mechanical acceleration. The need for a clear length of deck did, however, limit the number of aircraft which could be flown off: *Illustrious* could range no more than 12 torpedo-armed Swordfish for free take-off at one time under normal wind conditions. Here, one 810 Squadron Swordfish flies past with its hook down as the other (outboard interplane struts cut away by the censor) prepares to take-off. The cylinders down the port deck edge are 'light torpedoes' — buoyant dummies weighted and balanced to resemble the standard 18inch Mark XII aircraft torpedo and intended for dropping in training attacks. The *Town* class four-piper on planeguard duty has type 291 fitted at the foremast head and is still armed with 4inch guns abeam of the fore funnels. **DB**
CPL

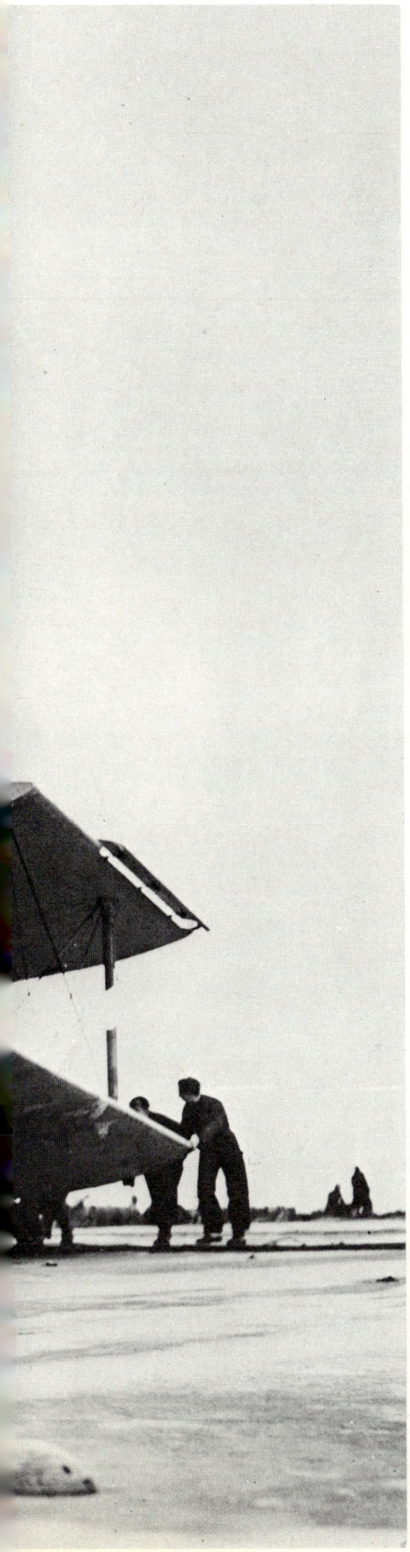

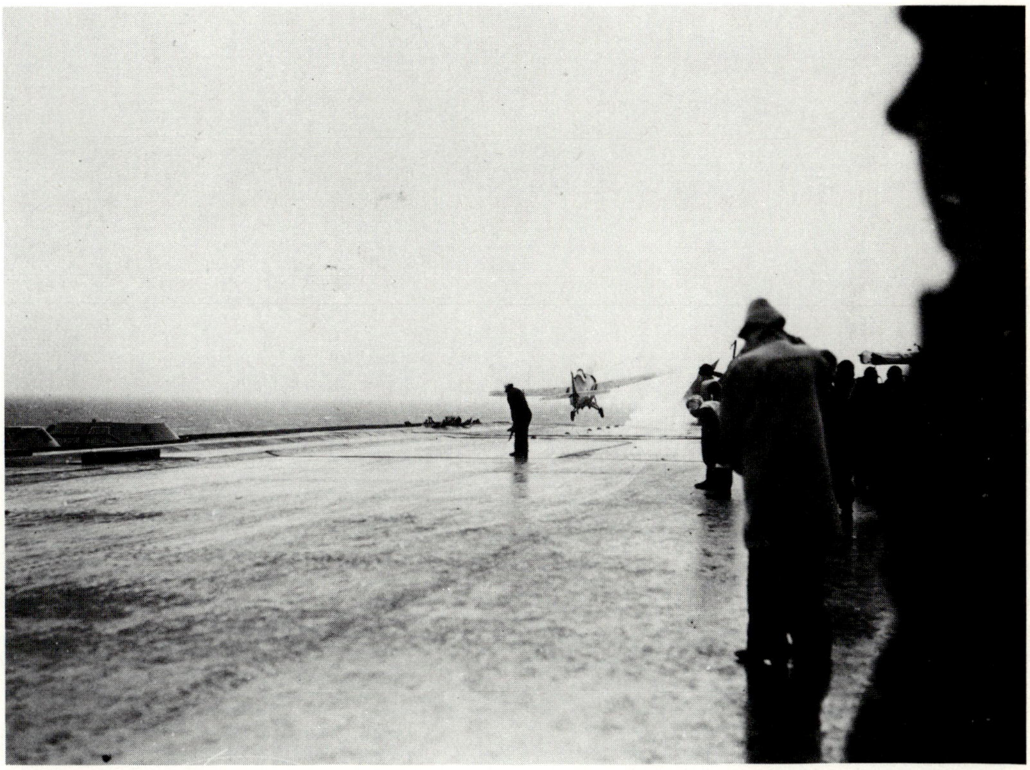

6.6

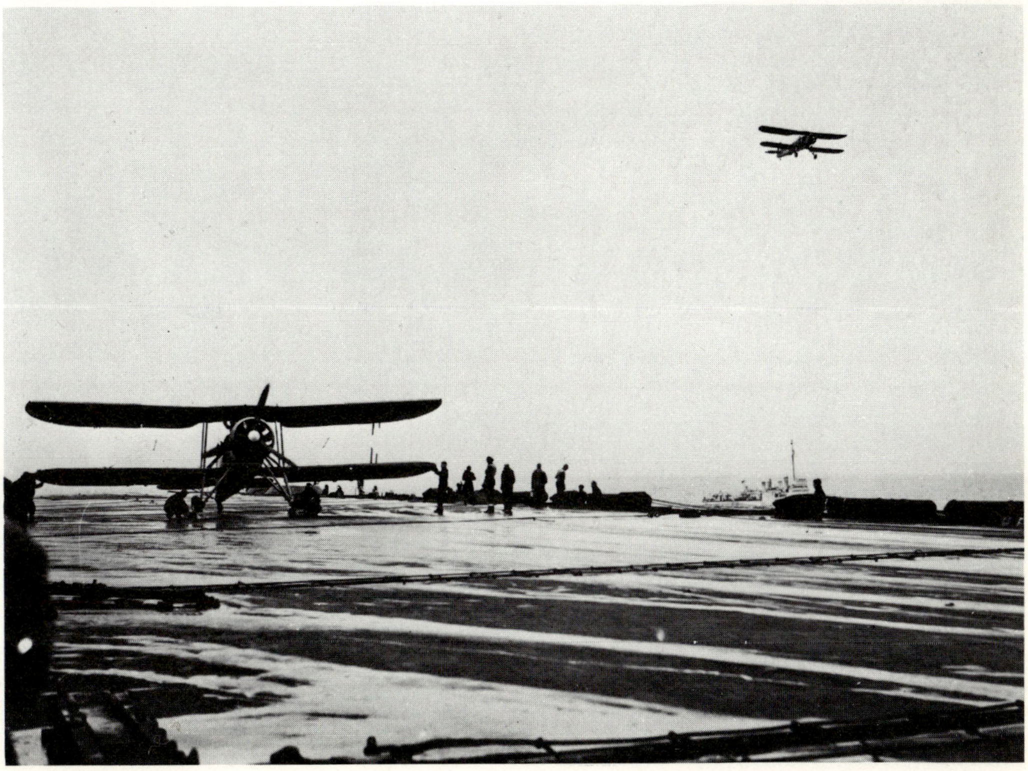

6.7

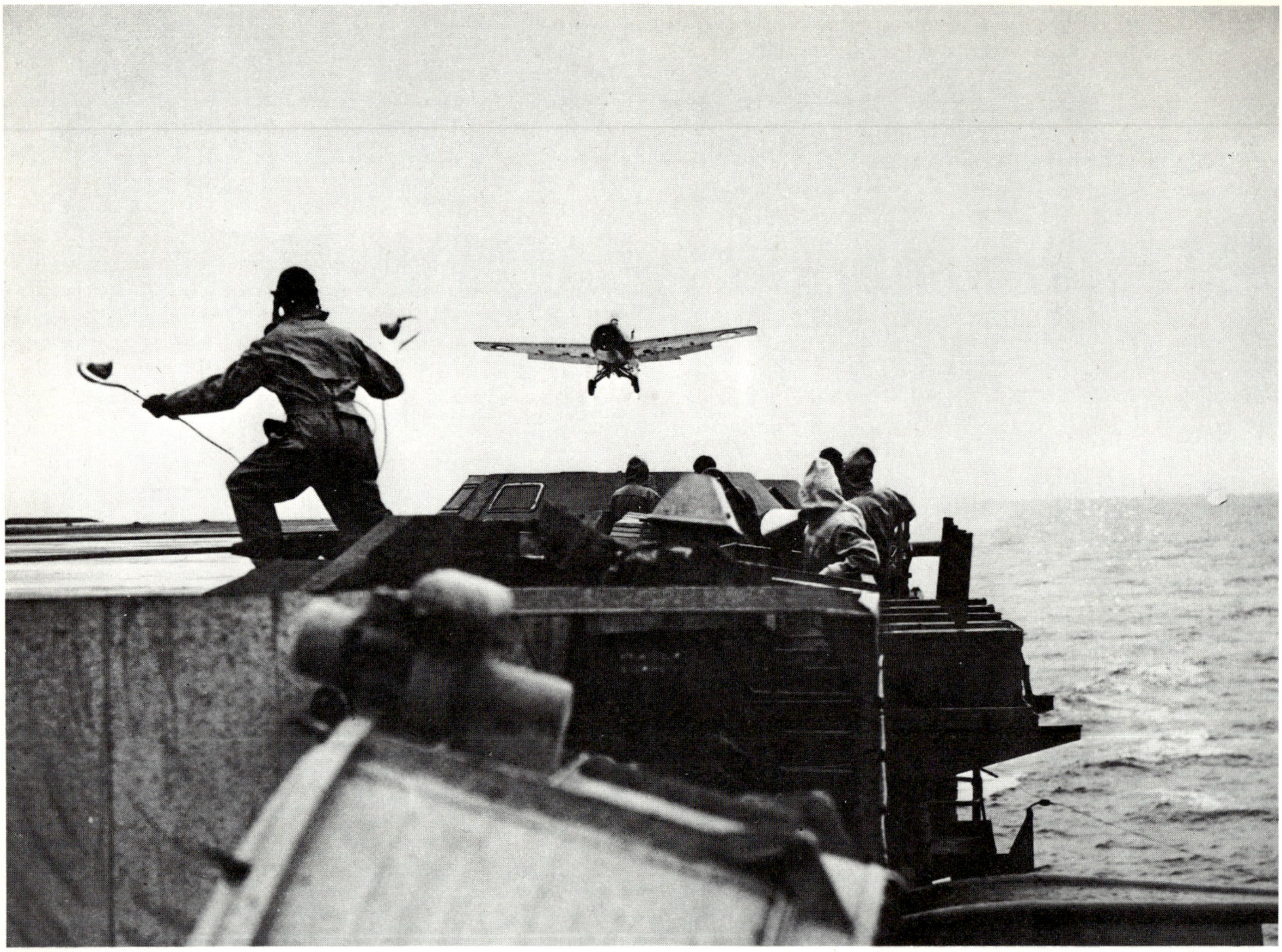

6.8

6.9

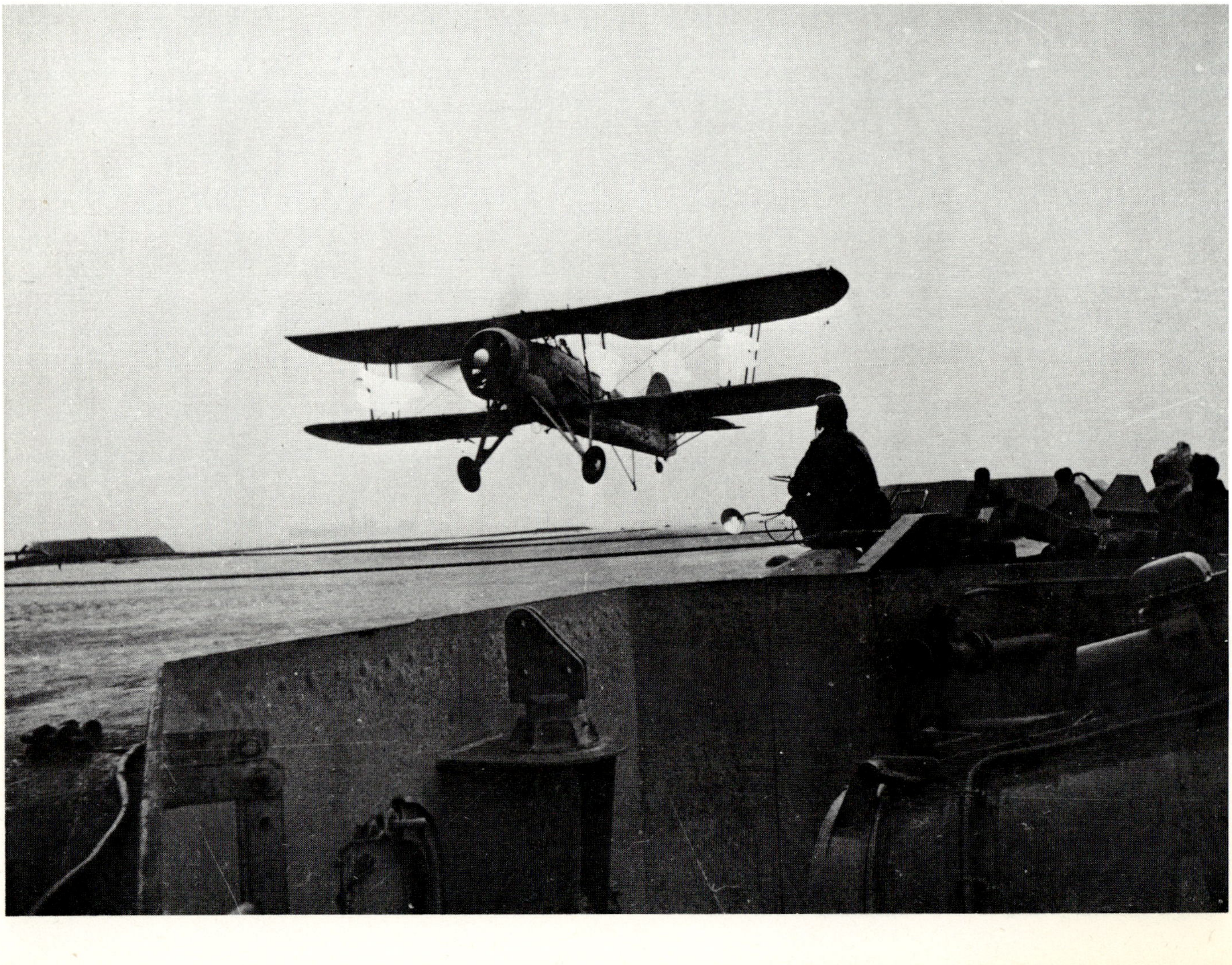

Not until shortly before the war did the Royal Navy adopt the US Navy's idea of using a Deck Landing Control Officer (Landing Signals Officer in the USN) to assist pilots in their approach to the deck. These signals were advisory in the RN and mandatory in the USN, primarily because no formal training in the art was given in the former until 1941, when a DLCOs School was started at RN Air Station Arbroath, Angus. The Commanding Officer was Lieutenant Commander R N Everett DSC RN, who can be regarded as the first British 'batsman', having practised on his fellow Swordfish pilots in HMS *Courageous* and *Ark Royal* in 1938 and 1939. Pilots are conservative by nature and the pre-war generation needed little outside assistance in returning to the deck, so that they saw no need to give the man outside the cockpit the authority to give orders to the man inside the cockpit. As the war progressed, the influx of new pilots, hurriedly trained and despatched to embarked squadrons with few practice deck landings behind them, led to greater importance being attached to the batsmen responsible for getting inexperienced pilots back on to the deck under all conditions.

Two schools of thought on batting technique evolved in the RN. The first, led by Lt Cdr Everett, were known as 'Personality Batsmen', whose idea was to coax the approaching pilot over the round-down by a somewhat theatrical (in the opinion of the other school) display with the bats, adapting the manner of giving the signals to the known or apparent ability of the oncoming pilot. The other, strictly formal, technique was to treat each approach in the same manner, acting as a human semaphore to advise the pilot of errors in his height, speed, attitude and line-up, so that he could make the necessary corrections. The formalists came into their own from 1943, when the increasing number of aircraft to be landed from each mission in the minimum time (upwards of two dozen less than a minute apart in the Fleet carriers by mid-1945) favoured the 'no frills' technique.

Although the actual gestures used by British DLCOs and American LSOs were similar, inter-operability between carriers was complicated by the fact that the interpretation of the signals was in many cases reversed. Thus, both arms raised about 45 degrees meant to a British pilot 'You are low, go high', but to his American opposite number it meant 'You are high, come down'. This led to confusion on occasion, but seldom so near-disastrous as when a RN Seafire pilot, diverting to USS *Essex* in emergency, consciously converted the USN LSO's signals into 'English', unaware that the LSO was already adapting his signals to be read by the British pilot: the landing was perfect, in spite of the Allied desire to see things from the other man's point of view. **DB**

6.8 HMS *Illustrious'* batsmen favoured somewhat unusual 'bats' during 1942, these taking the form of electric lights mounted in reflectors. As may be seen, in their original form they were somewhat unwieldy, with over-long handles and an awkward crook behind the reflector, not to mention the separate cables to each light. In bad light or low visibility, the lights were of considerable assistance to the pilot — in *Illustrious*, however, they were also used in the bright sunlight of the Indian Ocean, modified to be more manageable, with short, straight handles and a single cable to waist level and a third light hung on the DLCO's chest as a reference. **DB**
CPL

6.9 An 829 Squadron Swordfish crosses the round-down after being given the 'Cut' by a different batsman. The 'bowspring' holding the first arrester wire clear of the deck can be seen on the left of the photograph, near the roof of the 4.5inch turret. **DB**
CPL

6.10 A Barracuda II of one of the Easthaven training squadrons in flight over Carnoustie Golf Course, with Barry Camp and the estuary of the Tay astern. **DB**
CPL

6.10

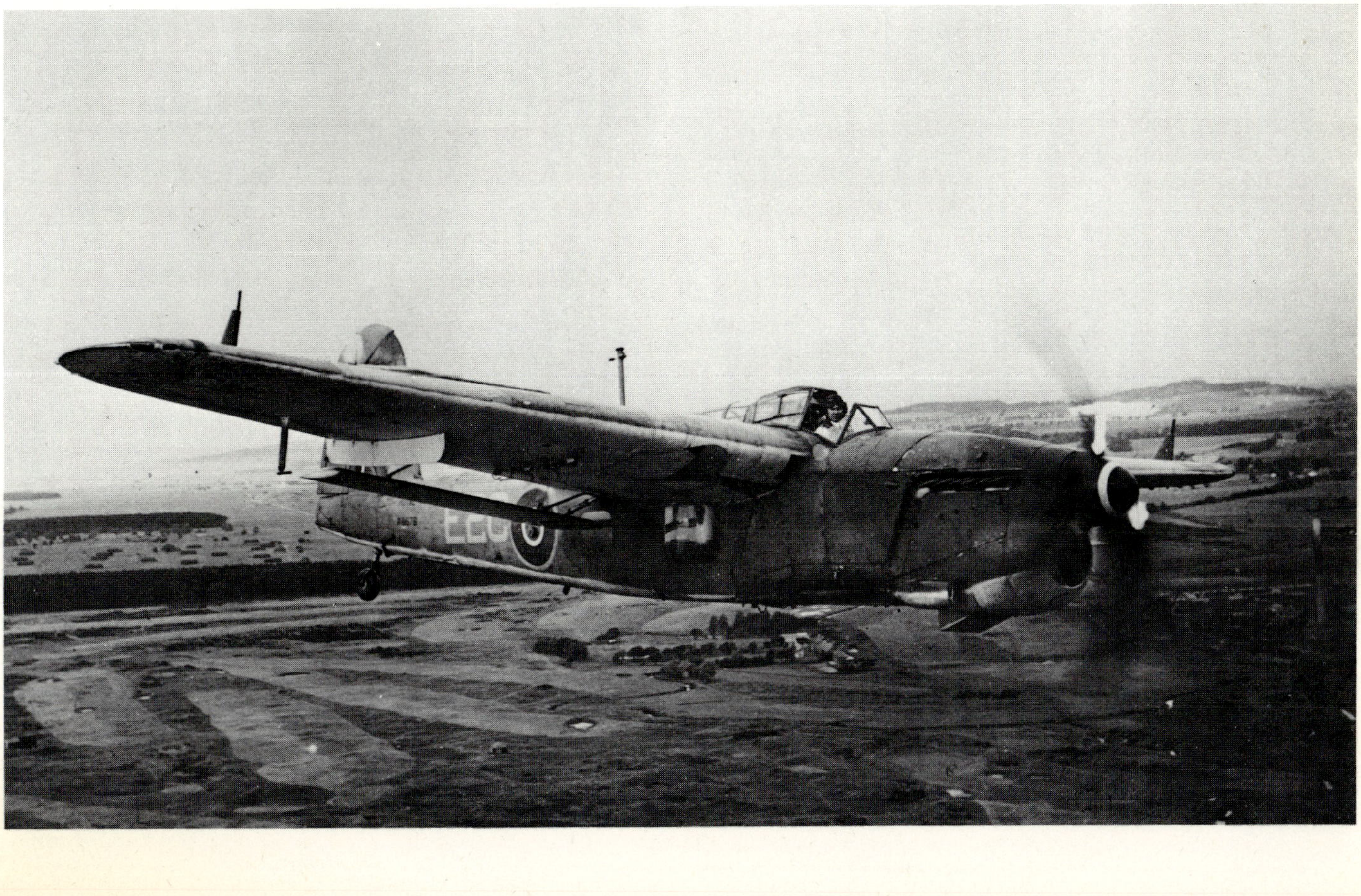

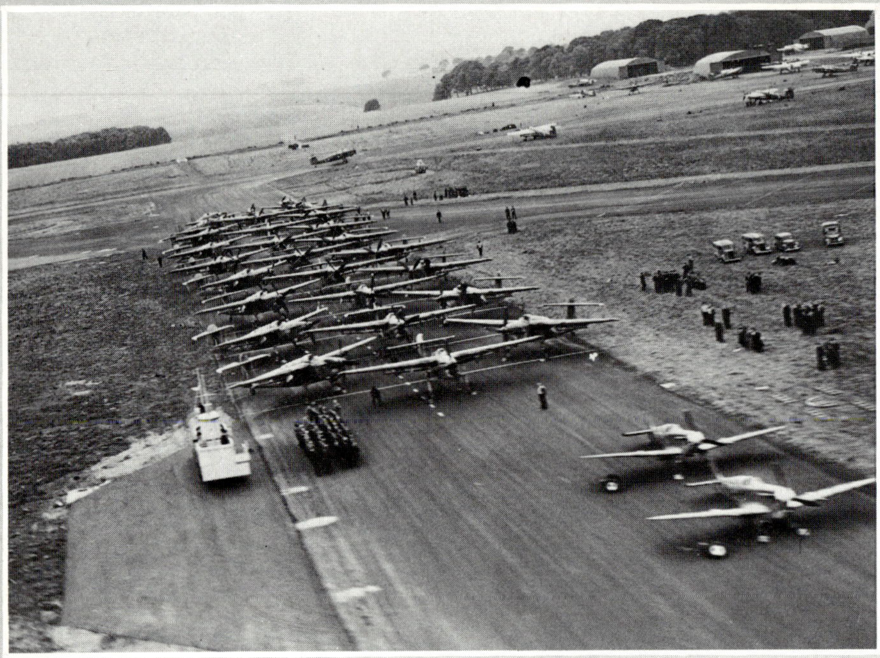

6.11

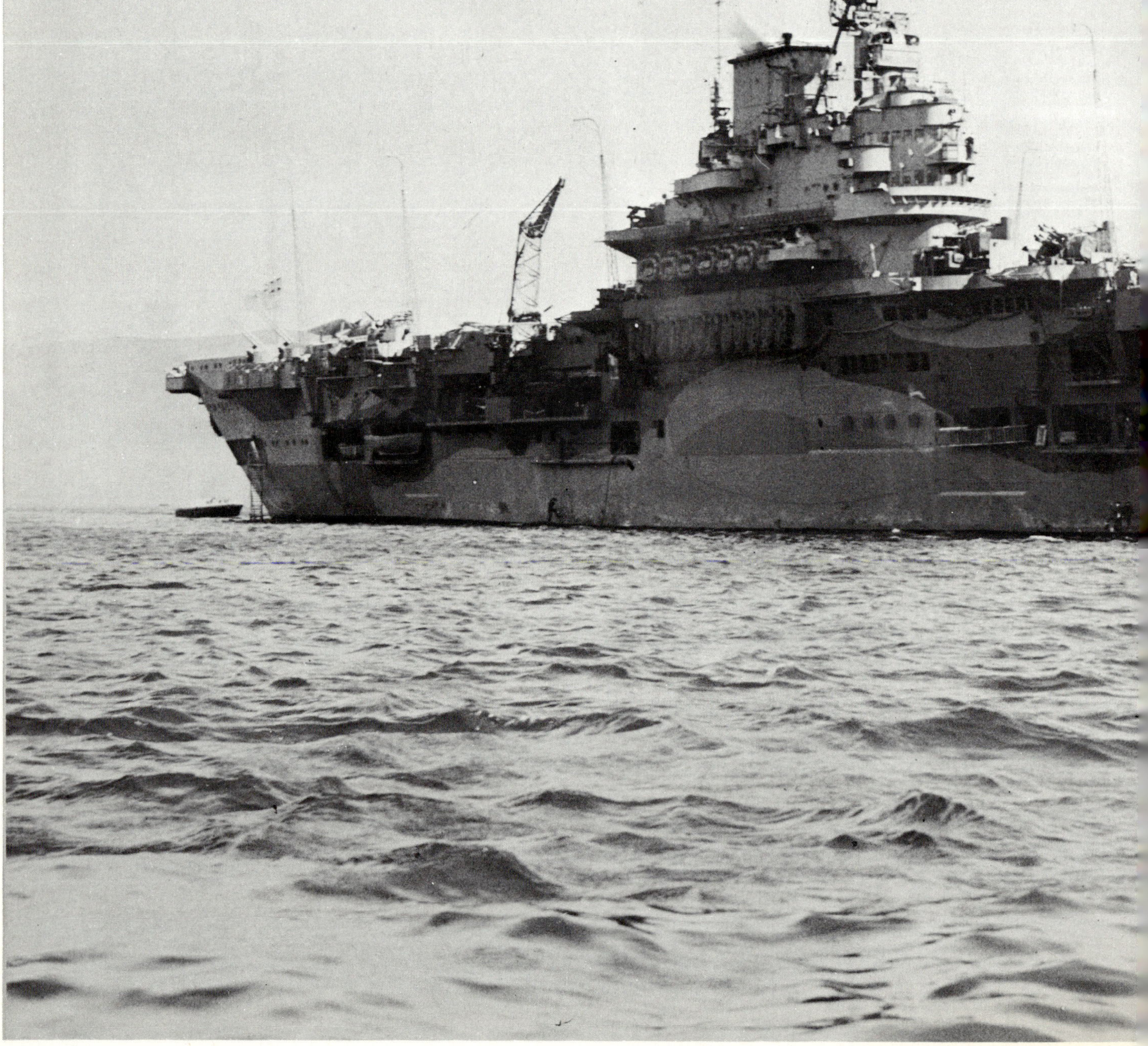

6.11 The DLCO School moved from Arbroath to the nearby RN Air Station at Easthaven in 1943 and in December a special 'Clockwork Mice' unit (731 Squadron) was formed with pilots who had embarked experience; hitherto the courses had batted for torpedo-bomber pilots completing their operational training. One runway at Easthaven was marked out as the 'dummy deck', with a painted centreline and transverse lines representing the arrester wires, and was used by the DLCOs for their airfield dummy deck-landing training ('ADDLs') and also for practising the carrier-type parking and take-offs. In this photograph, 22 Barracudas, 3 Seafires, 2 Fulmars and 2 Sea Hurricanes of 731 Squadron and the two torpedo-bomber training squadrons are ranged for take-off from the dummy deck as the climax of a Press visit. In the background are another 12 Barracudas and a Sea Hurricane. **DB** *CPL*

The *Indomitable* was the fourth armoured Fleet carrier to be ordered and represented an interim stage in the development of British carriers of this type, incorporating a second hangar deck aft to increase the nominal aircraft complement from 36 to 48. As this involved raising the flight deck by 14 ft (4.3 m), some sacrifice had to be made in the form of reduced thickness of the hangar side armour, but the overall length, beam and standard displacement tonnage remained the same as that of HMS *Victorious*, the third of the *Illustrious* class to be completed.

'Indom' spent most of her first commission in the Indian Ocean, but was then moved to the Mediterranean for the August 1942 Malta convoy. Damaged by Axis dive-bombers on 12 August, she was repaired in the USA and was not ready to begin working up new squadrons until March 1943. The initial stages of the work-up, with the Albacores of 817 Squadron and the Seafires of 880 and 899 Squadrons, were conducted in the Clyde areas, where this series of photographs was taken. She subsequently embarked the first squadron of Seafire LIICs (807), bringing her aircraft complement to 40 fighters and 15 torpedo-bombers. **DB**

6.12 *Indomitable* lying at Tail o' The Bank, in the Clyde, with two Seafires parked forward of the island and one Albacore right aft. Since her return from the US, she has been equipped with a more comprehensive radar outfit: with the development of combined transmitting/receiving antennae, type 79 and 281 radar could both be fitted, the former on the pole at the after end of the island and the latter on the foremast, surmounted by the 'X' of the IFF beacon. Immediately ahead of the foremast, below the type 72 homing beacon drum, is one of the four radar-equipped AA fire control directors. Running down the stem, from a hole between the mooring openings, is the chain of the special 'Illustrious-type' paravane gear, with the cable running aft from the 'clump' (immediately below the intersection of the buoy cable with the stem) to the paravane handling space below the 4.5inch battery. When steaming in mined waters, the paravanes were launched, the clump was drawn down to the ship's forefoot and the cable drawn out and down by the paravanes to provide self-defence against moored contact mines. **DB** *CPL*

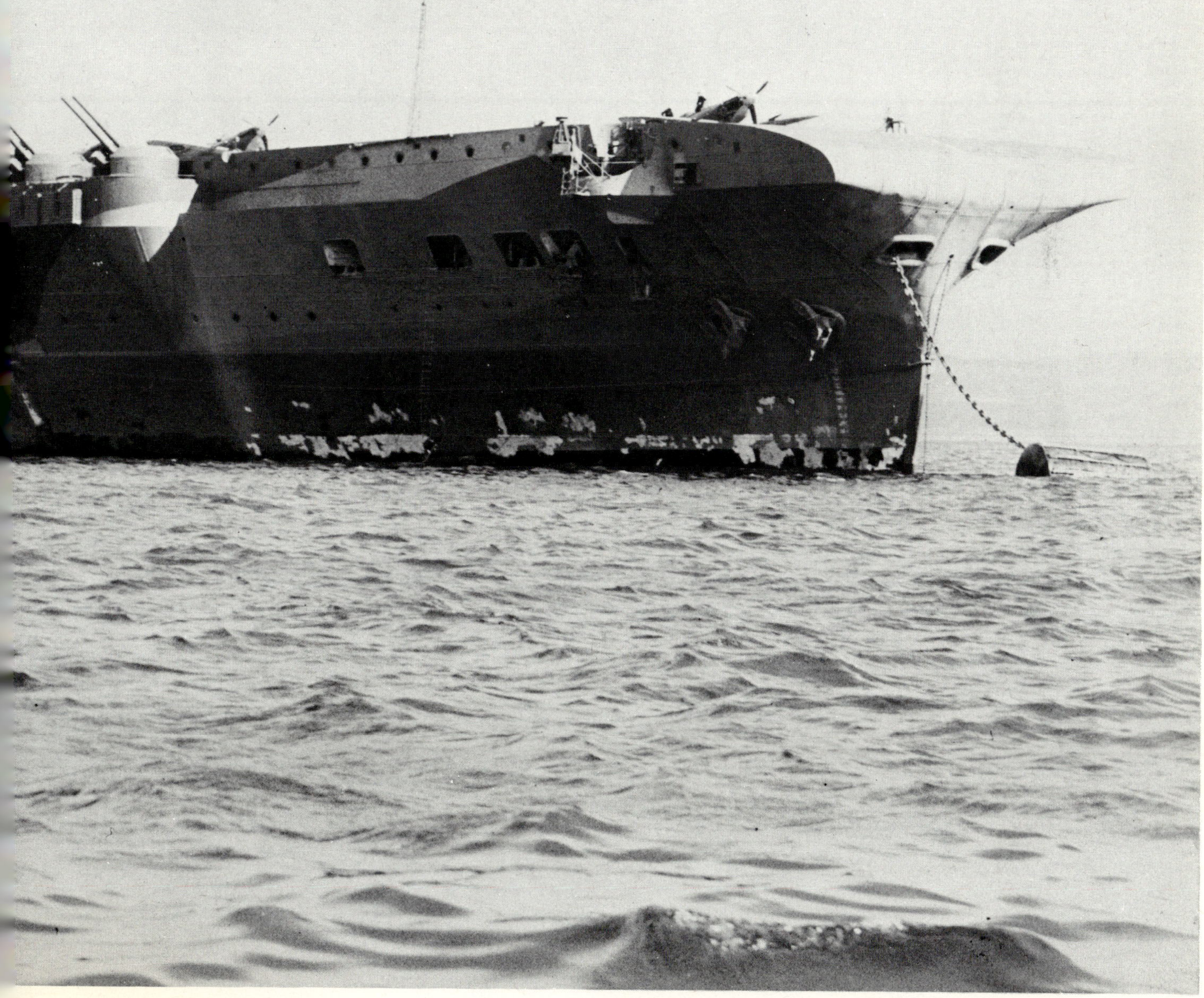

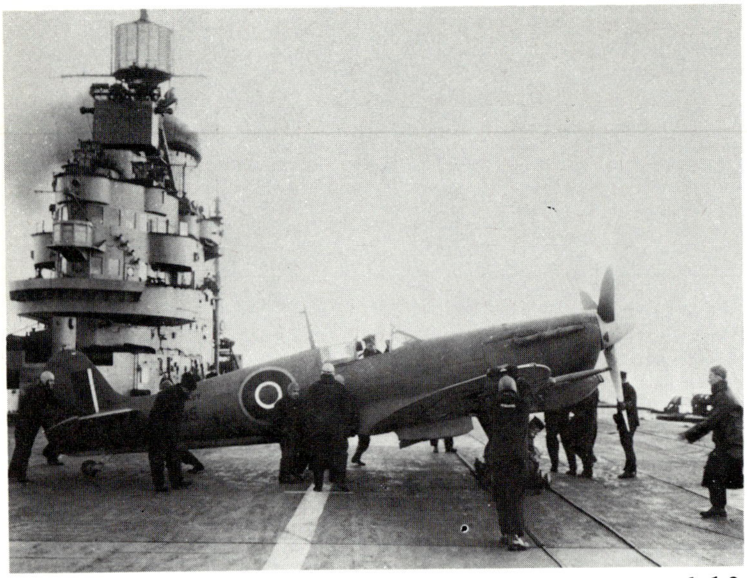

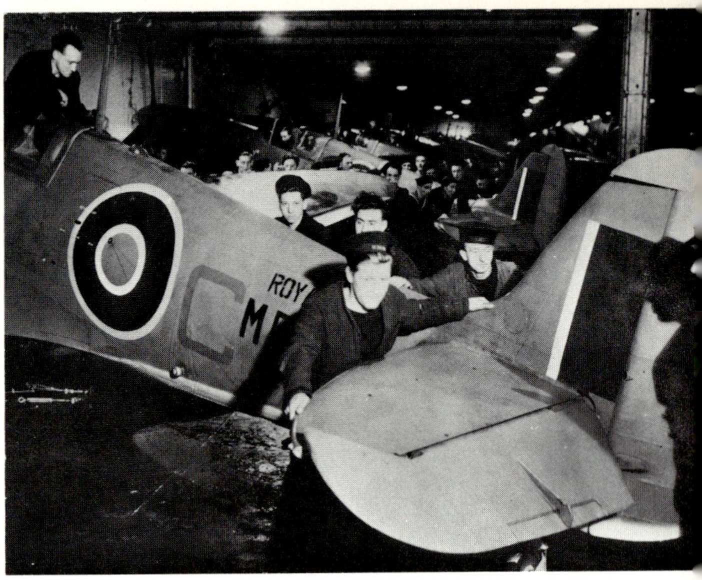

6.13 6.14

6.16

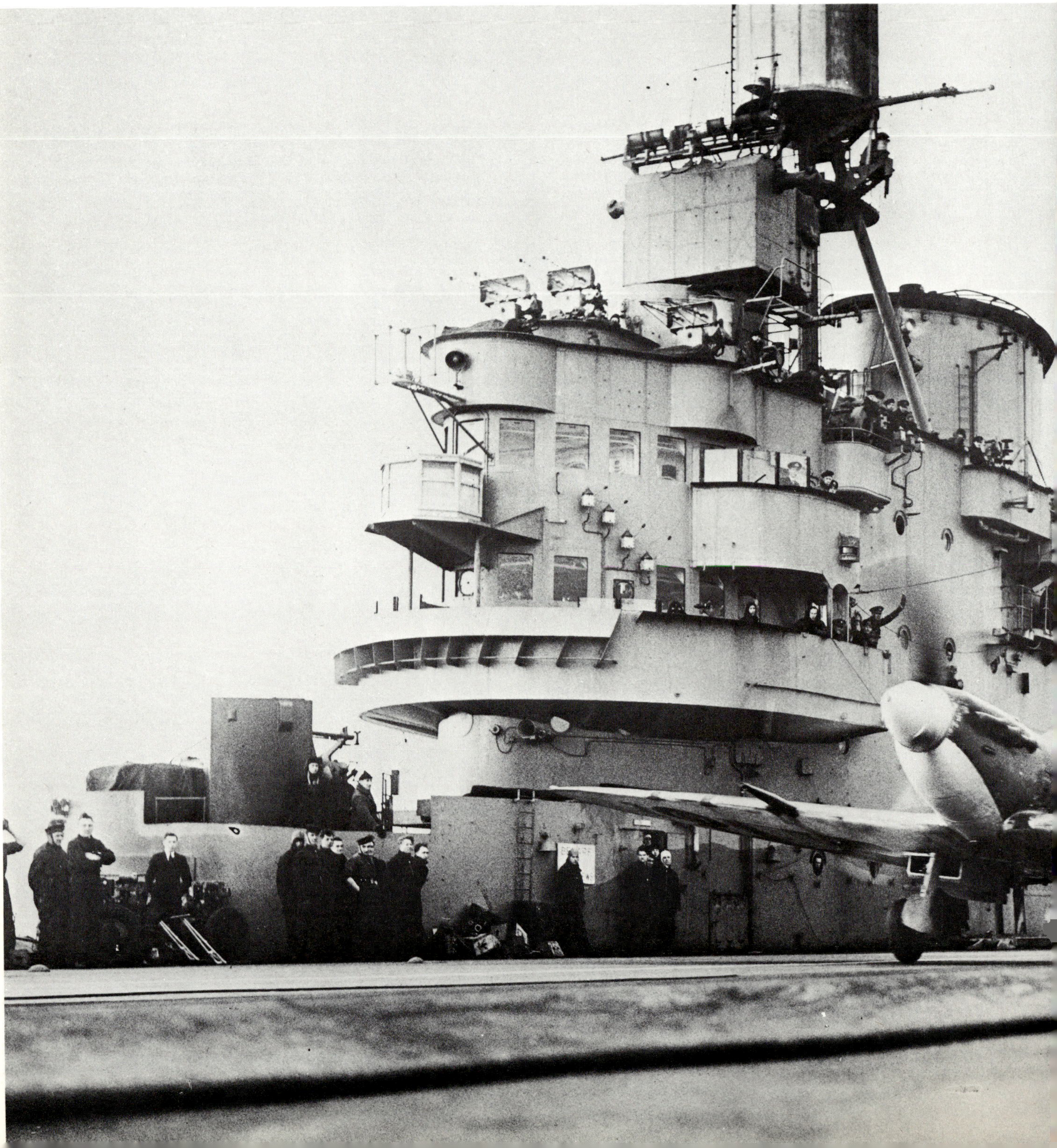

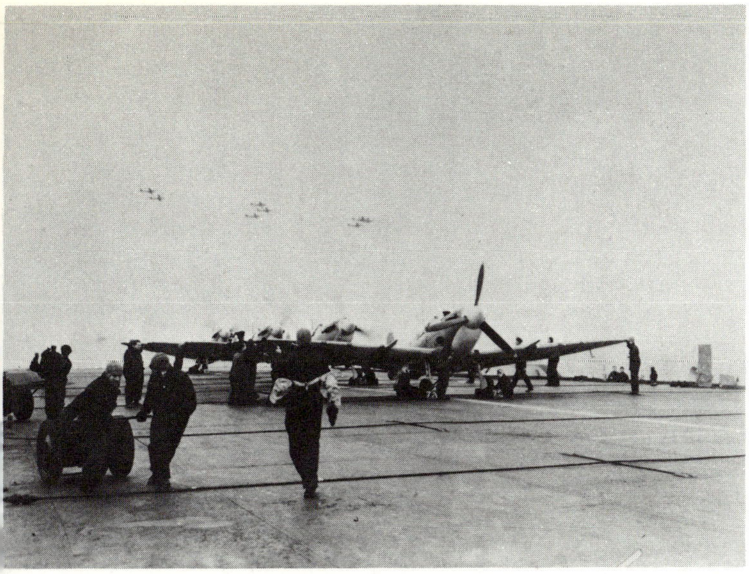

6.15

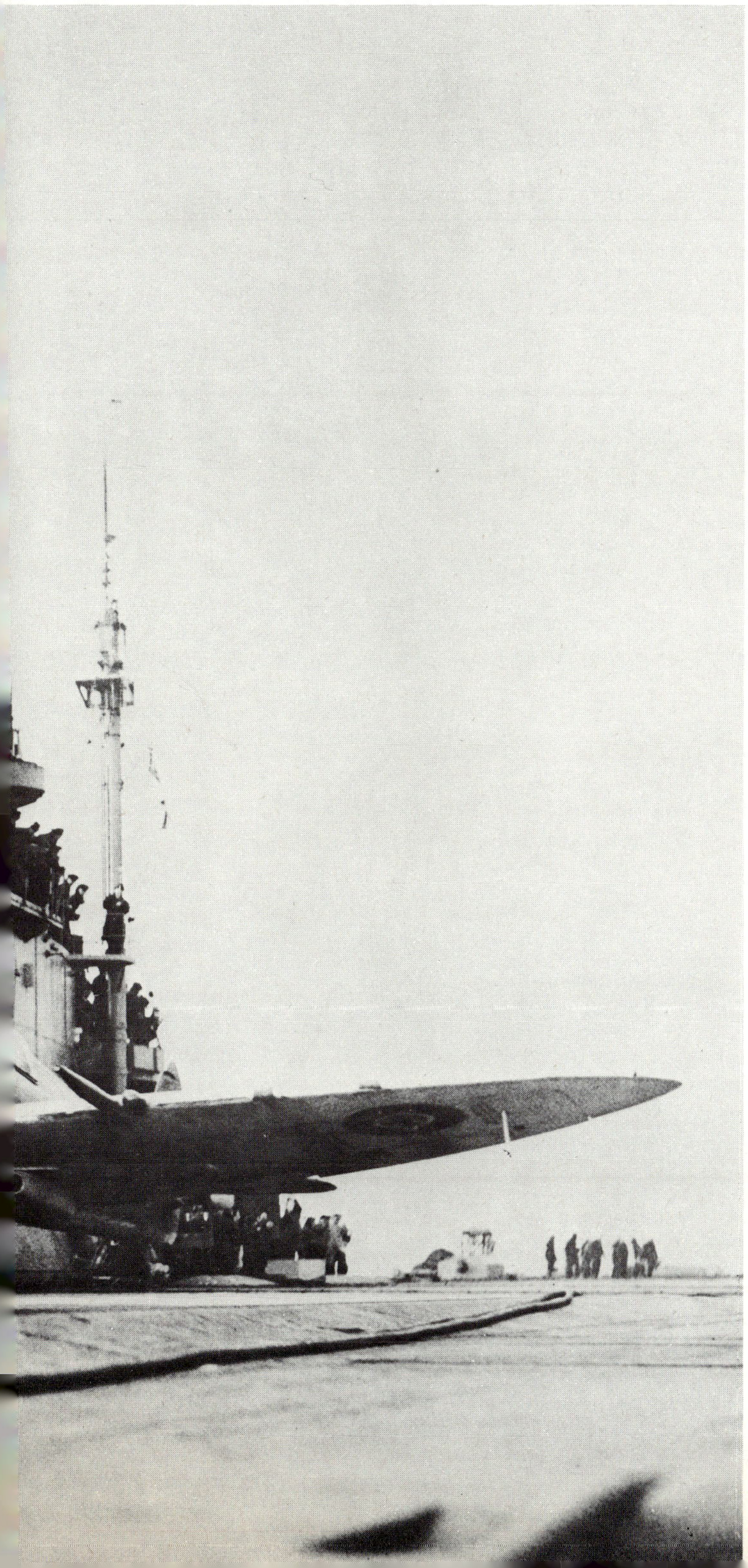

6.13 An important but less obvious difference between *Indomitable* and her immediate predecessors was the enlarged forward lift, with width increased by 50 per cent to 33 ft (10 m). The most important advantage gained was the ability to strike down non-folding aircraft such as the Sea Hurricanes carried in 1942 and the Seafires carried in 1943. These aircraft had to be positioned very accurately on the lift platform, a small trolley being used to manoeuvre the main wheels along a track which extended across the platform fore and aft of the lift at flight deck level and aft of the lift at upper hangar deck level, to guide the aircraft through the opening between the hangar doors; as may be seen, the track was even carried forward over the perforated plates of the wind screen. Once the Seafire IIC of 899 Squadron is on its way down to the hangar, accompanied only by its Pilot's Mate and the lift operator, the flight deck party doubles away smartly to bring the other Seafire forward.

One of the new radars fitted during the period under repair was the centimetric type 273 navigation and surface warning set, whose distinctive protective octagonal 'lantern' can be seen mounted on the face of the island, between the Compass Platform and the Admiral's Bridge. On top of the island, on the Gun Defence Platform below the director, can be seen three type 282 ranging radar antennae for the eight-barrelled pom-poms ahead of the island and on the port beam. Around the pom-pom bandstand can be seen an assortment of mobile servicing equipment, including three of the wheeled trolley-accumulators needed to start the Seafire's Merlin engines. **DB**
CPL

6.14 Once in the upper hangar, the Seafire was removed from the trolley and manhandled into its allocated spot. By stowing the aircraft diagonally, 17 aircraft could be stowed on each side of the 458 ft (139.6 m) hangar, 18 Seafires being visible in this photograph. The upper hangar was divided into three bays, the central bay being isolated when necessary by asbestos curtains to contain any fire which might occur; the central guide post for the after curtain can be seen to the right of the picture. The ends of the fore and aft bays were closed off by armoured doors in action but were usually left open to the lift wells to improve ventilation in the hangar. **DB**
CPL

6.15 Reluctance to start on the part of any aircraft was likely to cause embarrassment, but never so much as when the aircraft concerned was at the head of the range, particularly when it was a non-folding type, like this 880 Squadron Seafire IIC, holding up not only the other three aircraft of the division but also the recovery of the eight Albacores. Note the 'trolley-accs' being pulled up the deck and the collapsed bowspring supports under the arrester wires. **DB**
CPL

6.16 A Seafire IIC makes a flapless take-off in light wind conditions. Under these circumstances, a run of about 450 ft (140 m) would be required, compared with only 280 ft (85 m) 30 knots of wind over the deck. The insect-like antennae of the type 282 radars and the type 285 above the main director stand out particularly clearly. On a sponson between the funnel and type 79 mast can be seen a power-operated twin 20mm mounting. **DB**
CPL

6.17 *Indomitable,* at high speed in a calm sea, recovers the Albacores of 817 Squadron. The three sets of barrier stanchions are abreast the island, the furthest aft rigged as a last-ditch arrester wire to minimise damage on entering the barriers. The Seafire forward of the deck-level pom-poms has a collapsed port main oleo leg and has been pushed out on an outrigger beam; up to five of these outrigger stowages had to be utilised when the third Seafire squadron embarked — an empty outrigger can be seen abaft the island, between the lowered 'hockey stick' aerials. **DB**
CPL

6.18 Albacore '4-K' (BF764) is pushed aft, either to the after lift or to be ranged for the next launch. This aircraft belongs to 831 Squadron, which embarked only for the work-up, leaving at the beginning of May to re-equip with Barracudas. The 'side number' is repeated on the port lower wingtip to simplify identification of the individual aircraft when parked with folded wings. **DB**
CPL

6.19 The Albacore has all too often been dismissed as a 'Swordfish with an enclosed cockpit', but even a cursory comparison with a view of the older aircraft shows that the only true common features were the single-bay biplane lay-out and the fixed undercarriage. The Albacore had a stressed-skin metal monocoque fuselage, small diameter two-row radial engine and cantilevered wings and tailplane; the hydraulically-operated flaps doubled as dive-brakes, to control speed in the torpedo attack approach dive or while dive-bombing. Note the mobile crane — 'Jumbo' — at the rear end of the island. **DB**
CPL

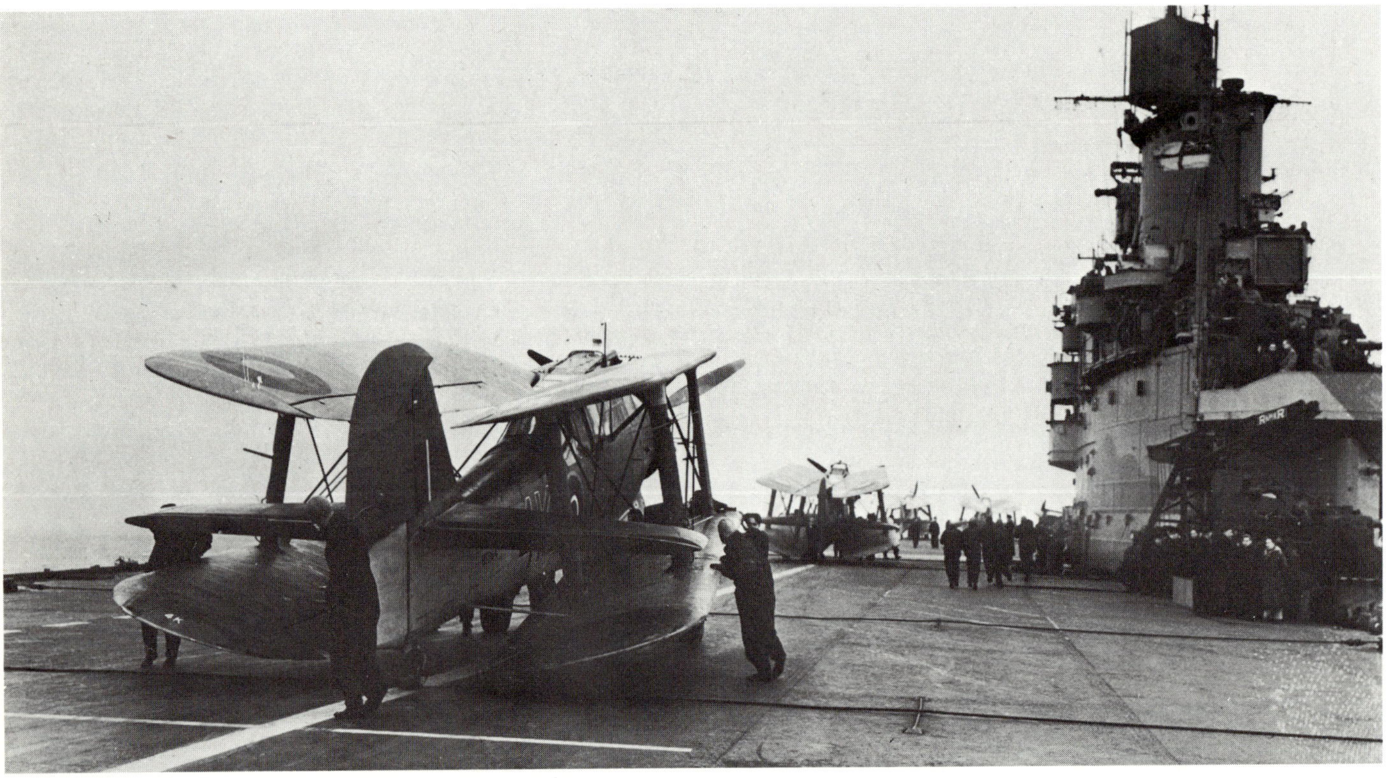

6.18

6.19

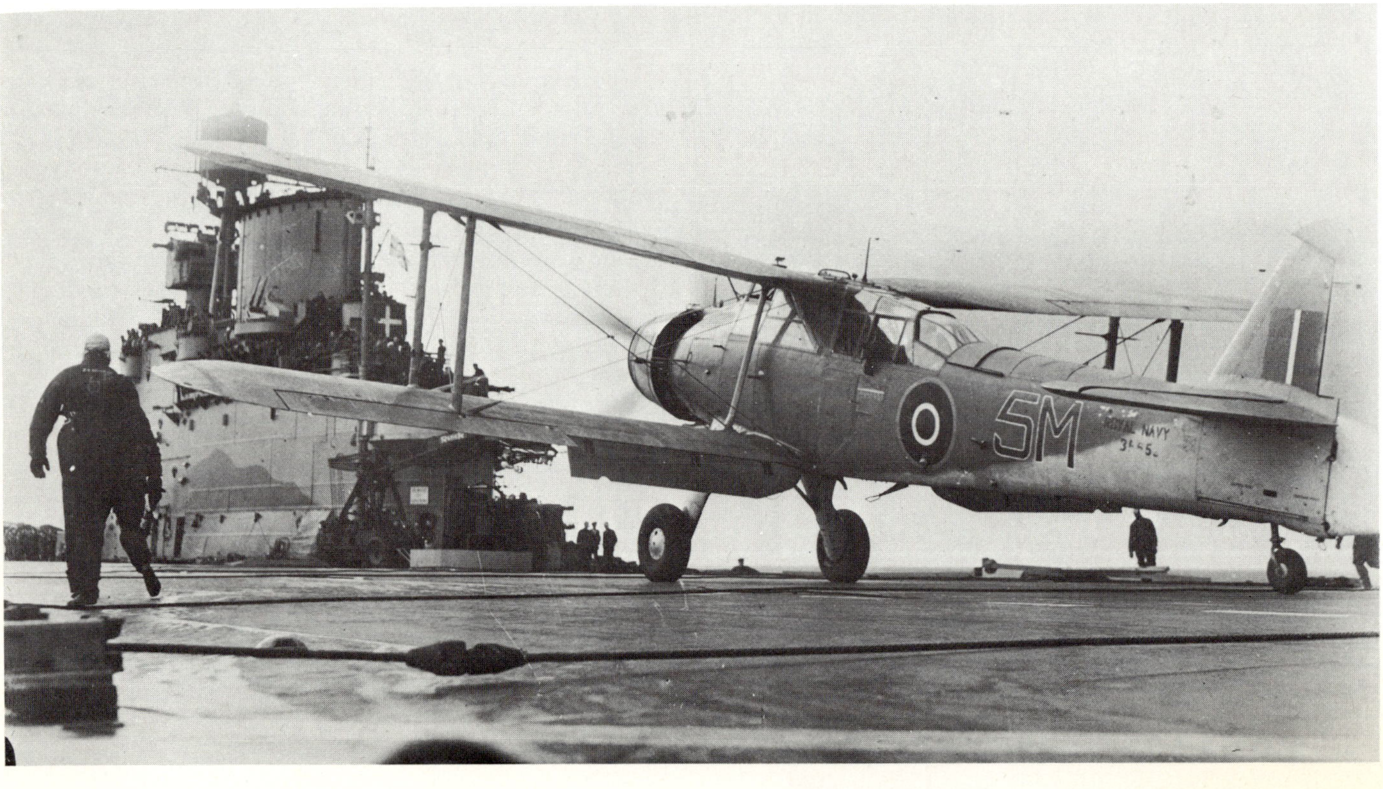

6.17

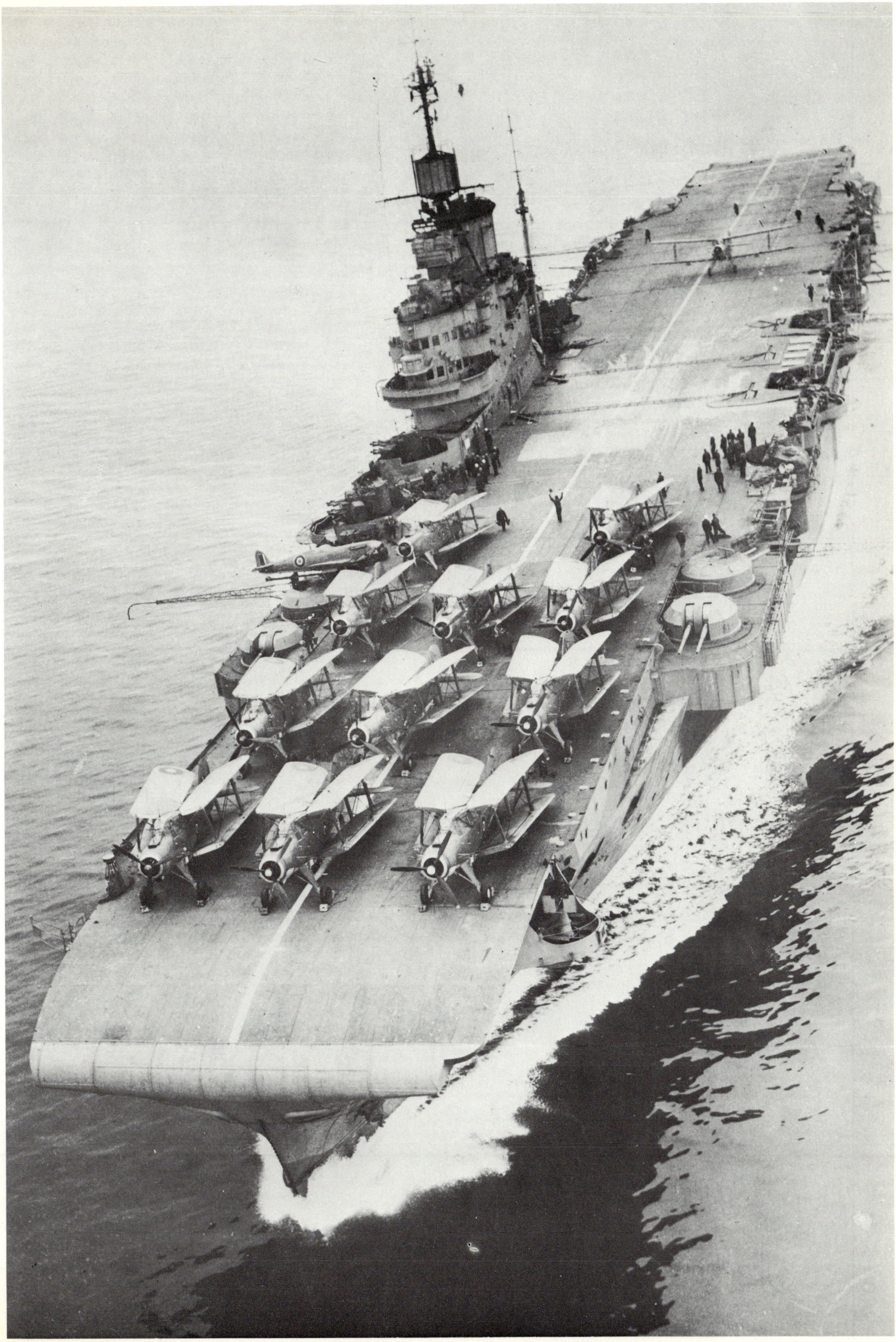

6 Naval Air Power

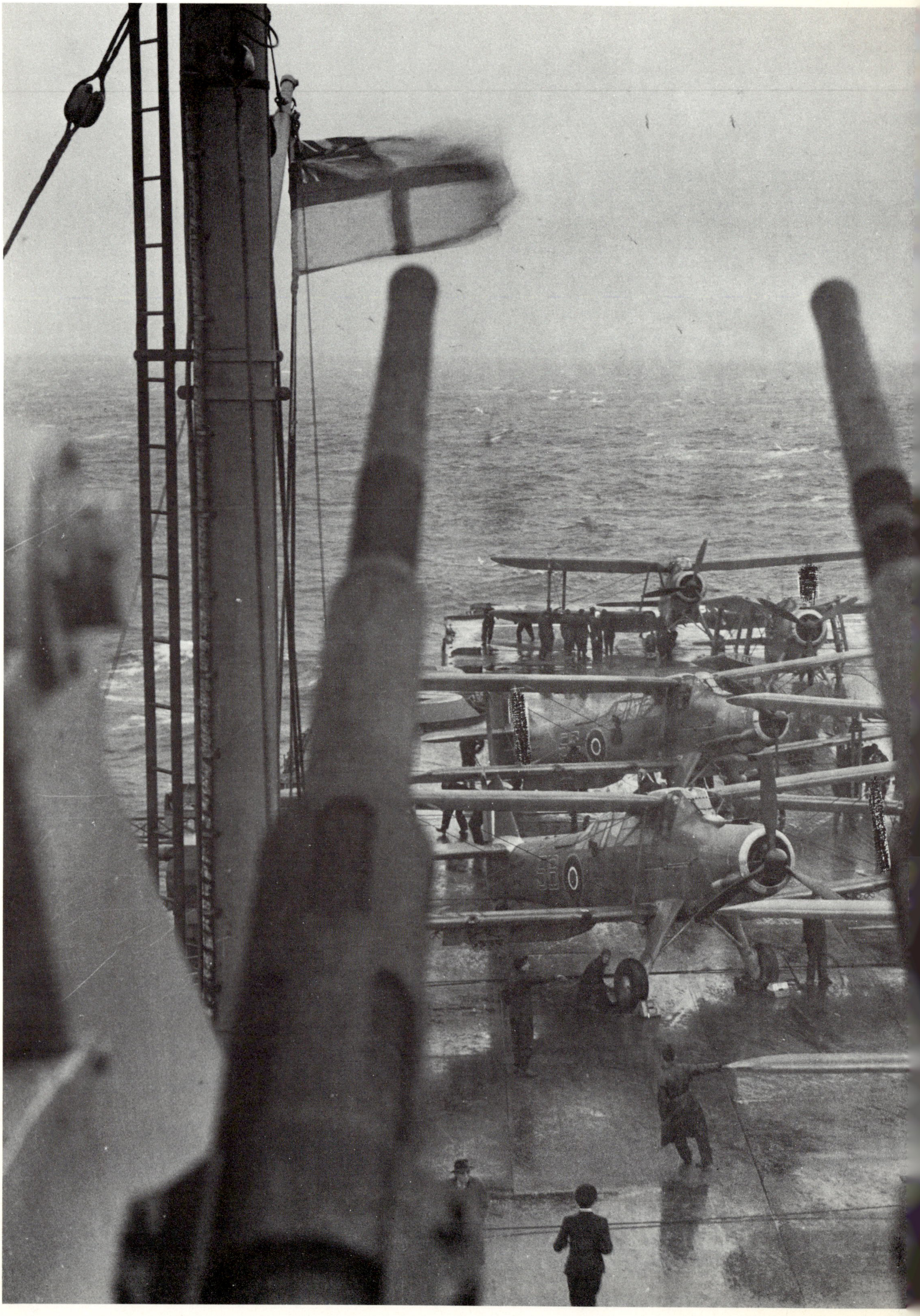

6.20

6.20 A Fairmile 'B'-type motor launch acts as planeguard as *Indomitable* prepares to launch eight of 817 Squadron's 'Applecores' in the wet and windy Firth of Clyde. The censor has blotted out the entire outboard struts of most of the aircraft in order to blot out the upper and lower ASV receiver antennae, but has neglected the transmitters, on the fuselage sides behind the engine cowling. The advantages of the island positioning of the twin 20mm-wide unobstructed arcs and the ability to fire over a full deck park at low angles of depression — are obvious. **DB**
CPL

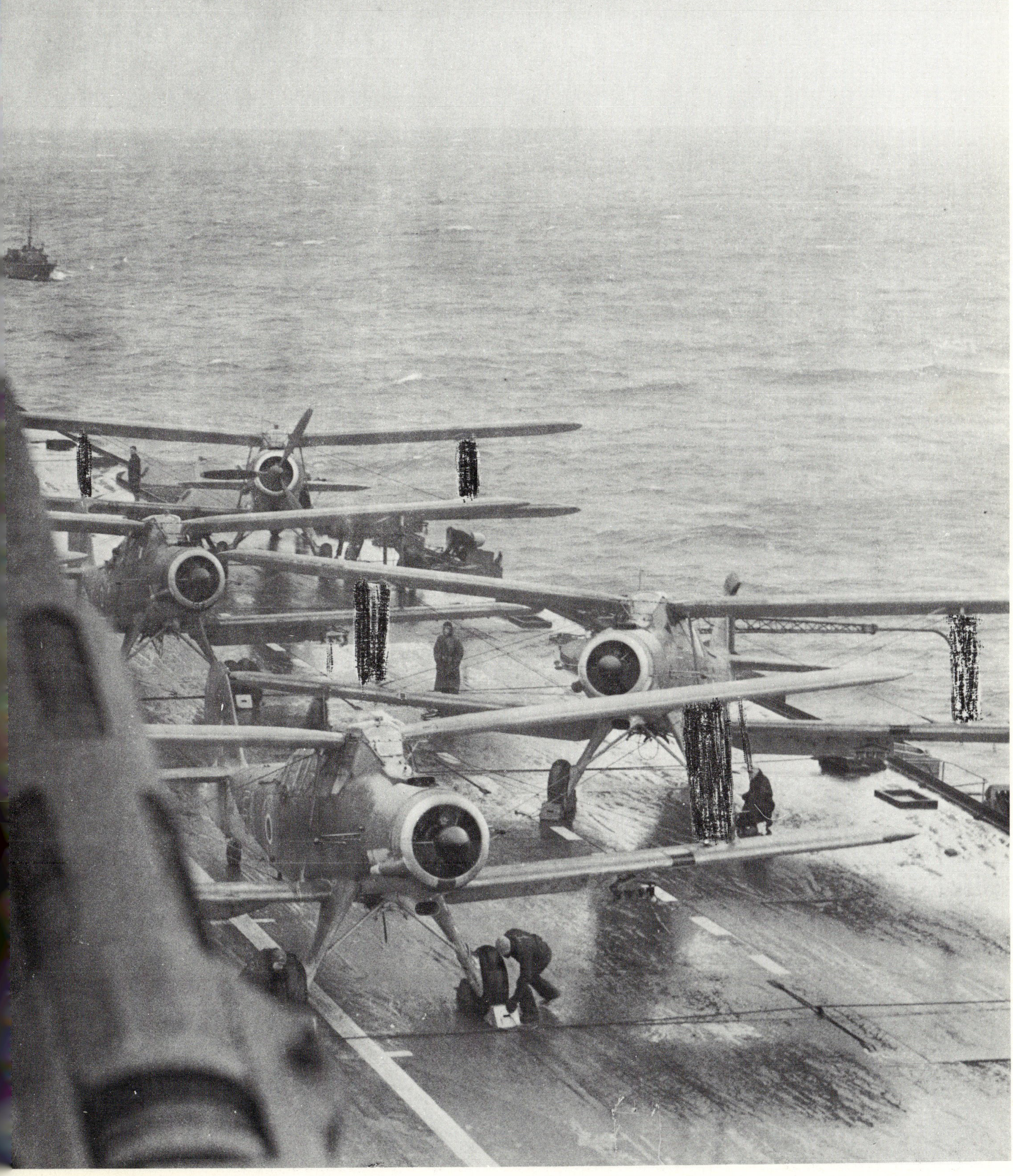

6.21 "Why should the unoffending sky be tainted and corrupted by
This product of a twisted brain that's aeronautically insane?
This violent and hideous abortion, devoid of beauty and proportion,
That Fairey's call the Barracuda; whose form is infinitely cruder
Than any other scheme or plan as yet conceived by mind of man.

To see it stagger into space would bring a blush upon the face
Of the most hardened Pharisee within the aircraft industry.
But I suggest we don't decry this winged horror of the sky,
But keep it 'till the war is won and then we'll all join in the fun.

Festoon the wings with Fairy Lights and wheel it out on gala nights
And so help dispel the rumour that Sea Lords have no sense of humour."

Seen from this angle, and from many others, the Barracuda justifies the words of the Service Trials Unit's verses. The heavy beam and oleo undercarriage, the inboard trailing edge section folded up, complete with flaps, to allow the wings to fold back, the ASV masts and antennae above the wings, the foot-high locking pins and fairings over the wingtips, the boundary-layer fences and handling hoops under the manually folding wings, and the high braced tailplane give the 'Barra' an essentially 'wrong' appearance. **DB**
CPL

6.22 Barracudas of 767 Squadron over Carnoustie in the autumn of 1944. Even in flight the aircraft looked ungainly, but the view from the pilot's and Observer's cockpits was unsurpassed, the latter sitting on the floor amidships with a bow window on either side. The Fairey-Youngman flaps also served as dive-brakes and were an advanced feature to find on an aircraft of this type. Ordered 'straight off the drawing board' by the Admiralty on the Air Ministry's recommendation, the Barracuda prototype had shown considerable promise but the equipment shown to be essential by wartime experience could only be installed at the expense of performance and an increase in weight: in combination, these resulted in a production aircraft which was underpowered and cursed with known structural weaknesses.

The Strike Wings equipped with this aircraft achieved some notable successes off the coast of Norway, damaging the battleship *Tirpitz* and sinking or damaging 32 ships of 62 300 tons for the loss of 3 aircraft to enemy action. Altogether, 419 strike sorties were flown by Barracudas from carriers, a small enough total when it is recalled that more Barracudas were delivered to the Royal Navy than any other type of aircraft — 2570, compared with 2391 Swordfish, the next most numerous type. **DB**
CPL

6.23 A Martlet II's wing-tip 'jury struts' are connected before the aircraft is pushed into the hangar off the forward lift; lying on the port tailplane are the rope lashings used to secure the aircraft to ringbolts in the deck, chocks alone being inadequate to prevent movement, even in the hangar. The individual in the duffel coat with his back to the activity is the lift operator and to his left is one of the lift chains. The door forward of the lift gives access to workshops and also the sickbay, to permit rapid transfer of injured from the upper decks without the need to negotiate steep and narrow companionways and ladders. The full stops following the letters of the Martlet's serial were an odd quirk of the Grumman factory paint shop's staff, who applied them only to aircraft in the 'AM' range (others were A.M. 994, 965 and 974), possibly in the belief that the letters stood for 'Air Ministry'. **DB**
CPL

6.22
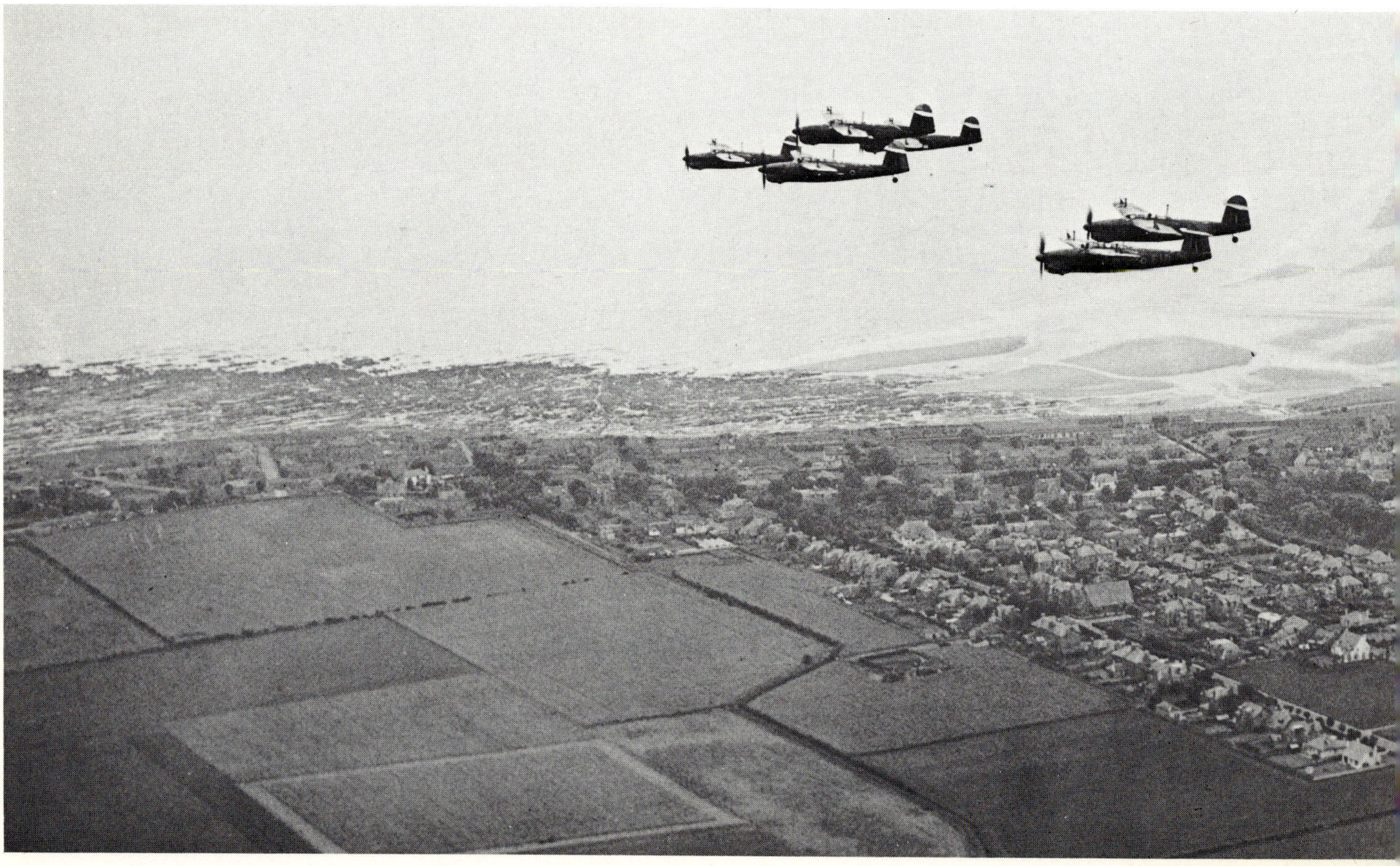

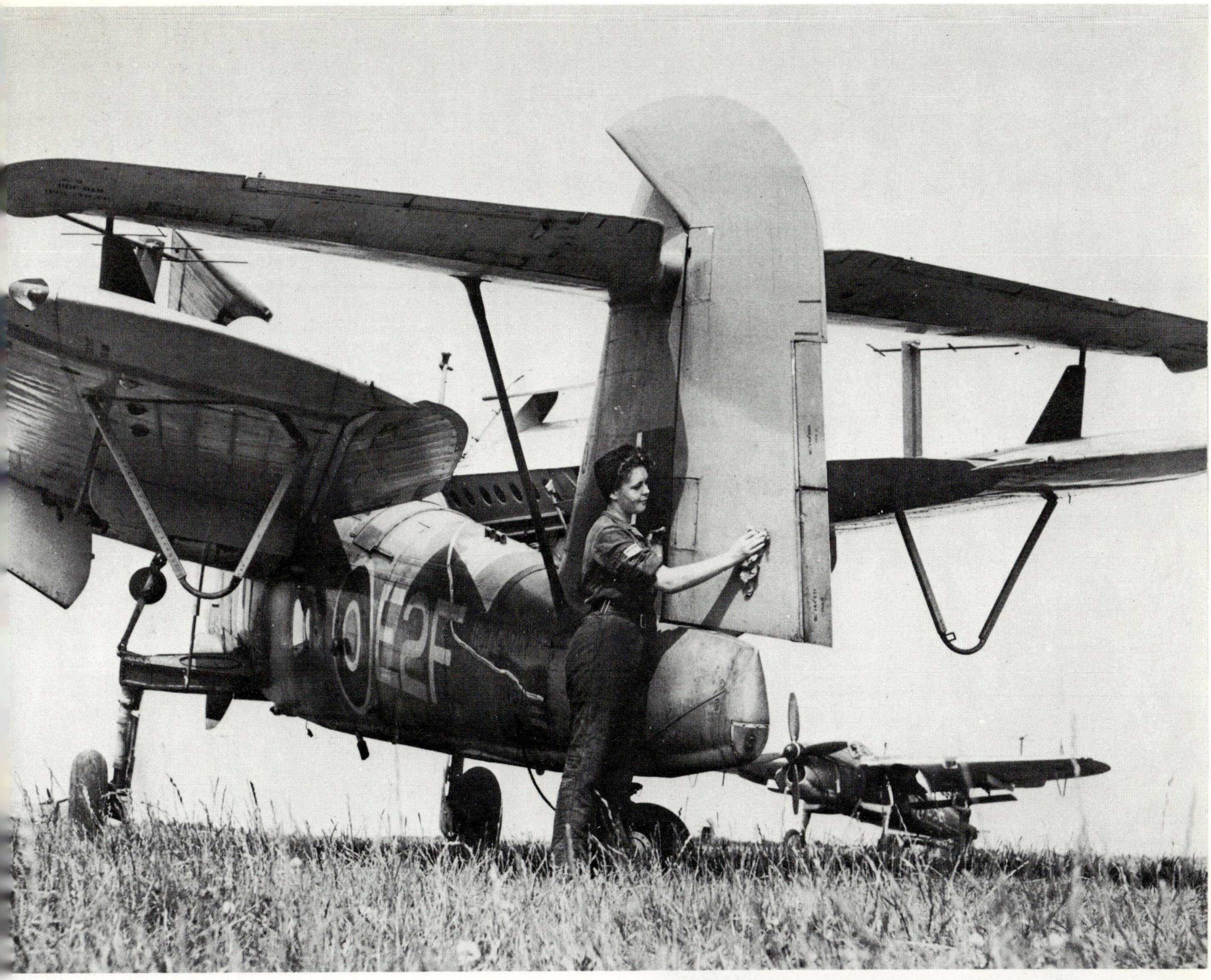

6.21

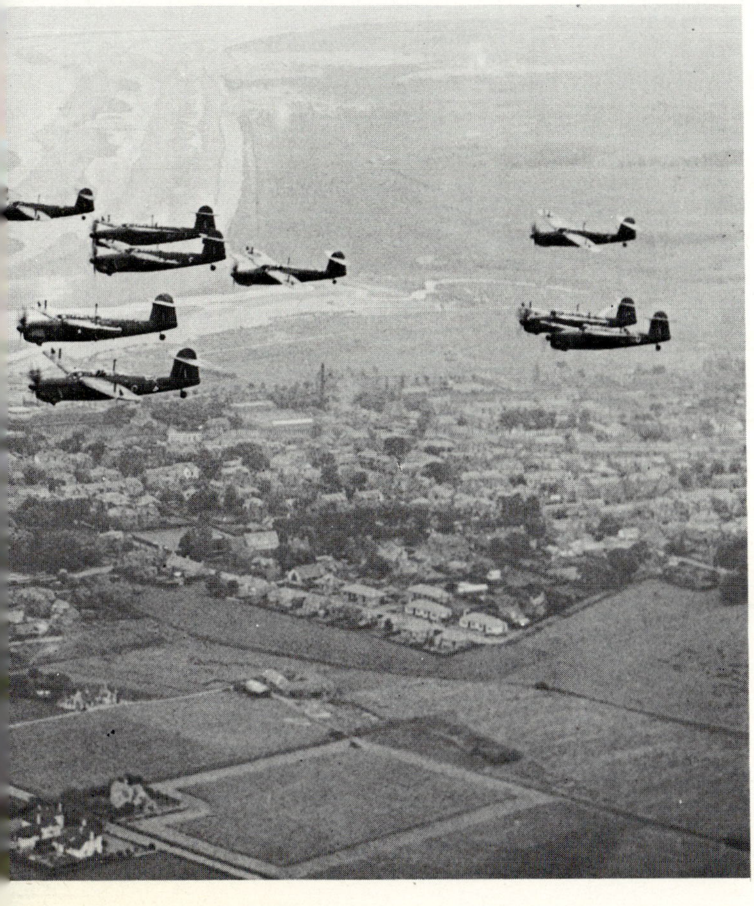

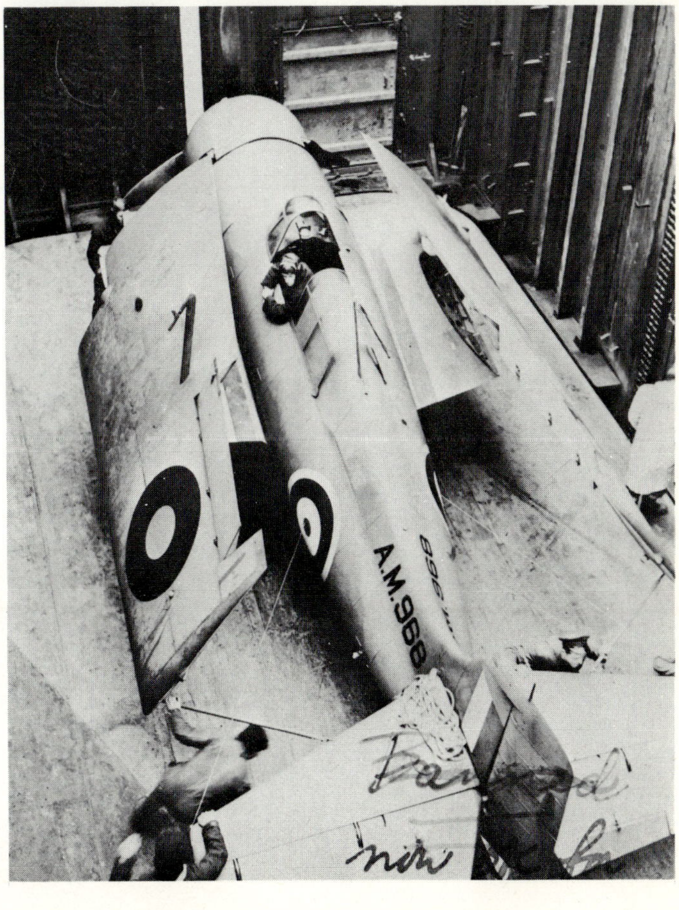

6.23

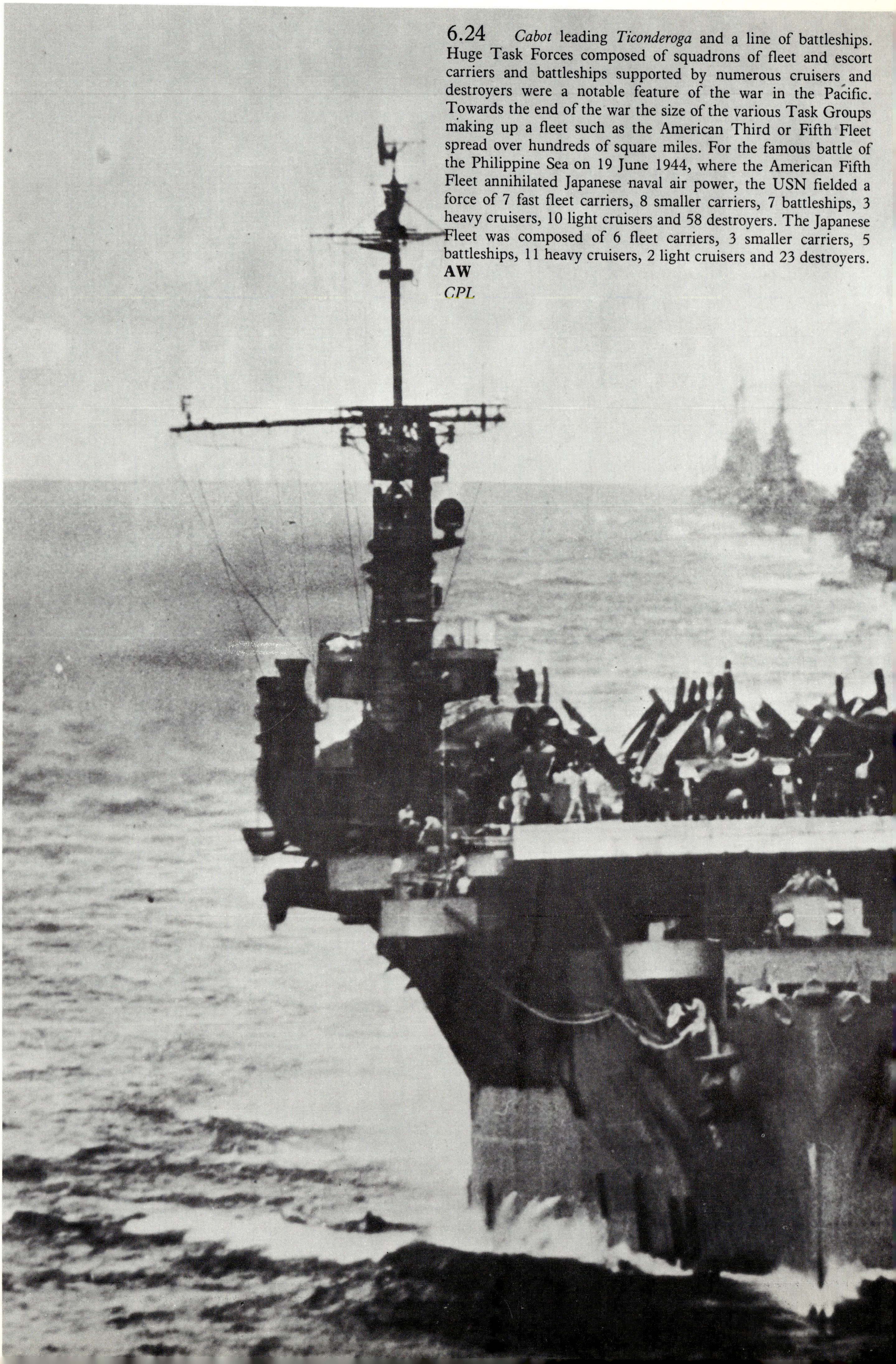

6.24 *Cabot* leading *Ticonderoga* and a line of battleships. Huge Task Forces composed of squadrons of fleet and escort carriers and battleships supported by numerous cruisers and destroyers were a notable feature of the war in the Pacific. Towards the end of the war the size of the various Task Groups making up a fleet such as the American Third or Fifth Fleet spread over hundreds of square miles. For the famous battle of the Philippine Sea on 19 June 1944, where the American Fifth Fleet annihilated Japanese naval air power, the USN fielded a force of 7 fast fleet carriers, 8 smaller carriers, 7 battleships, 3 heavy cruisers, 10 light cruisers and 58 destroyers. The Japanese Fleet was composed of 6 fleet carriers, 3 smaller carriers, 5 battleships, 11 heavy cruisers, 2 light cruisers and 23 destroyers.
AW
CPL

The Pacific

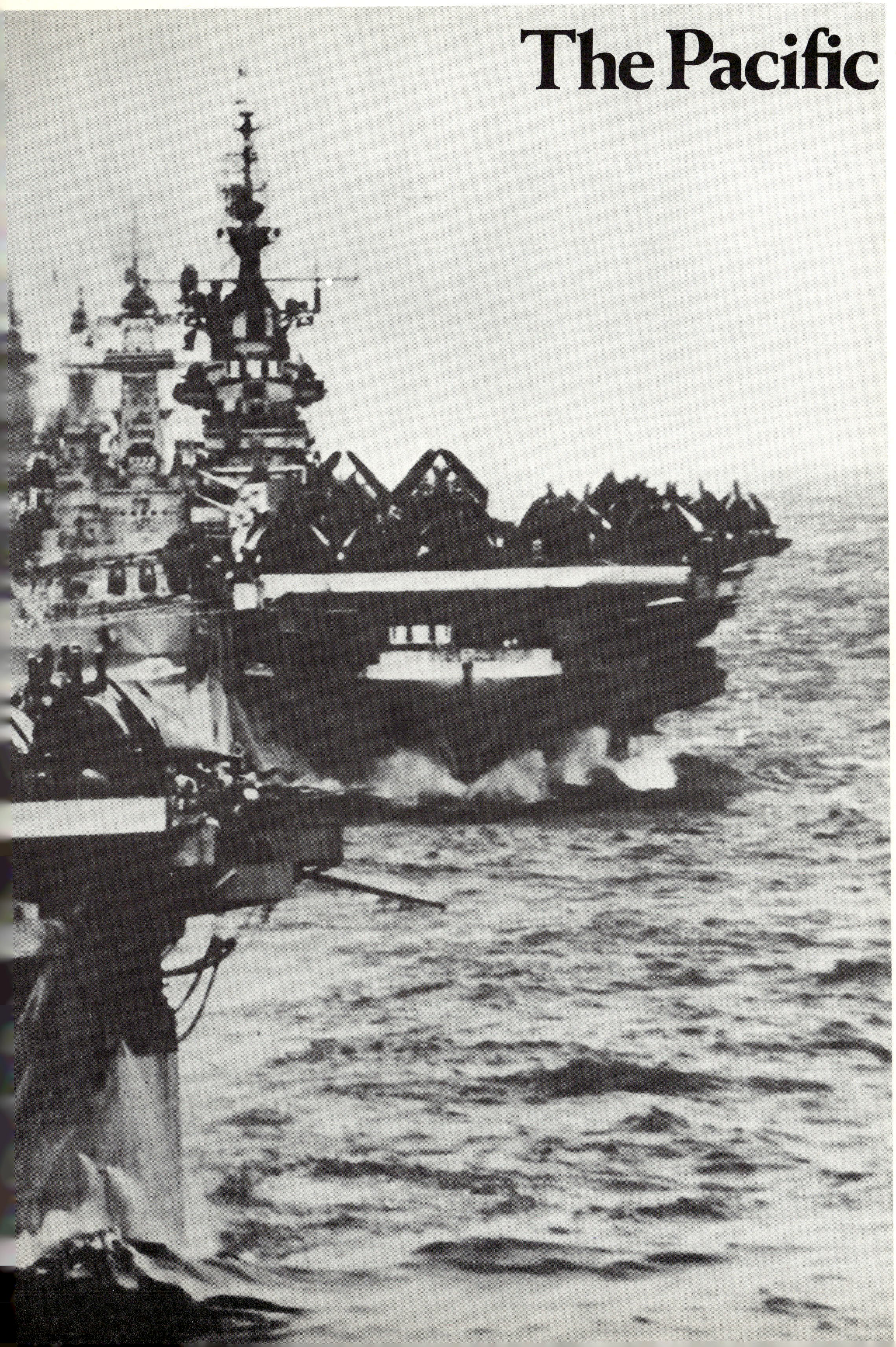

6.25

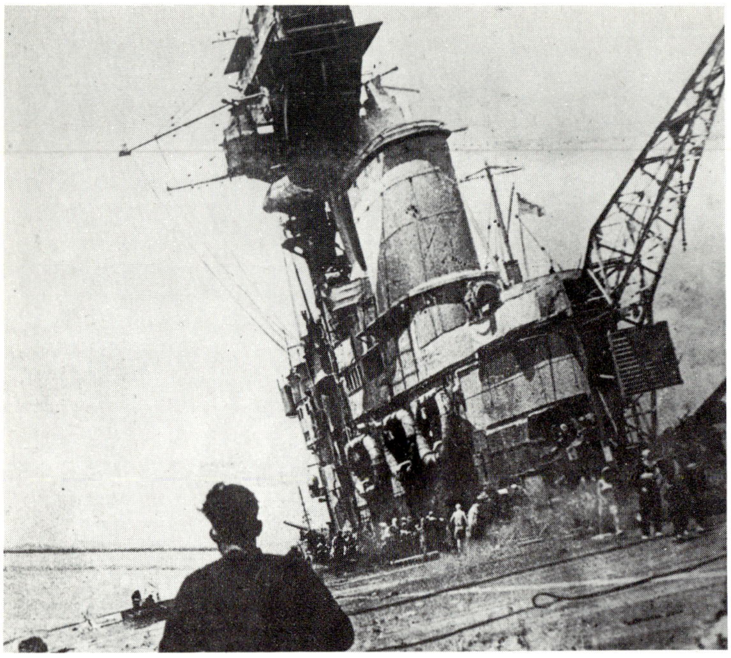

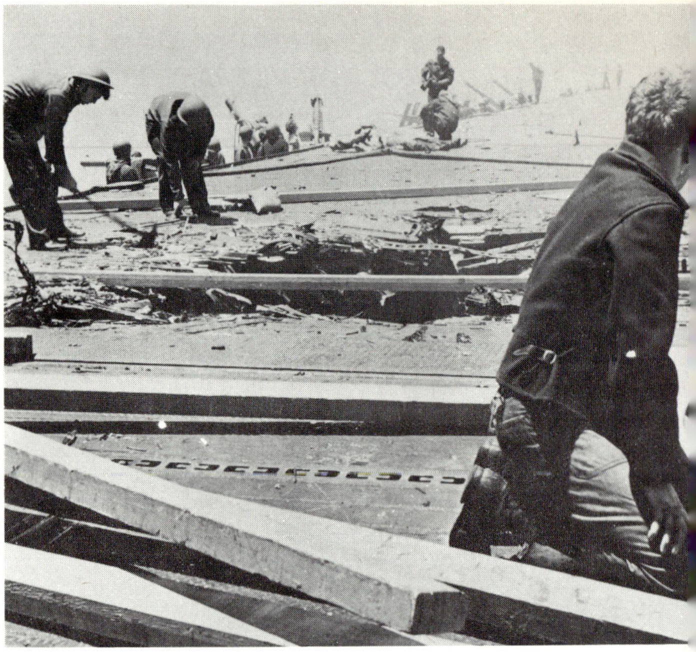

6.27

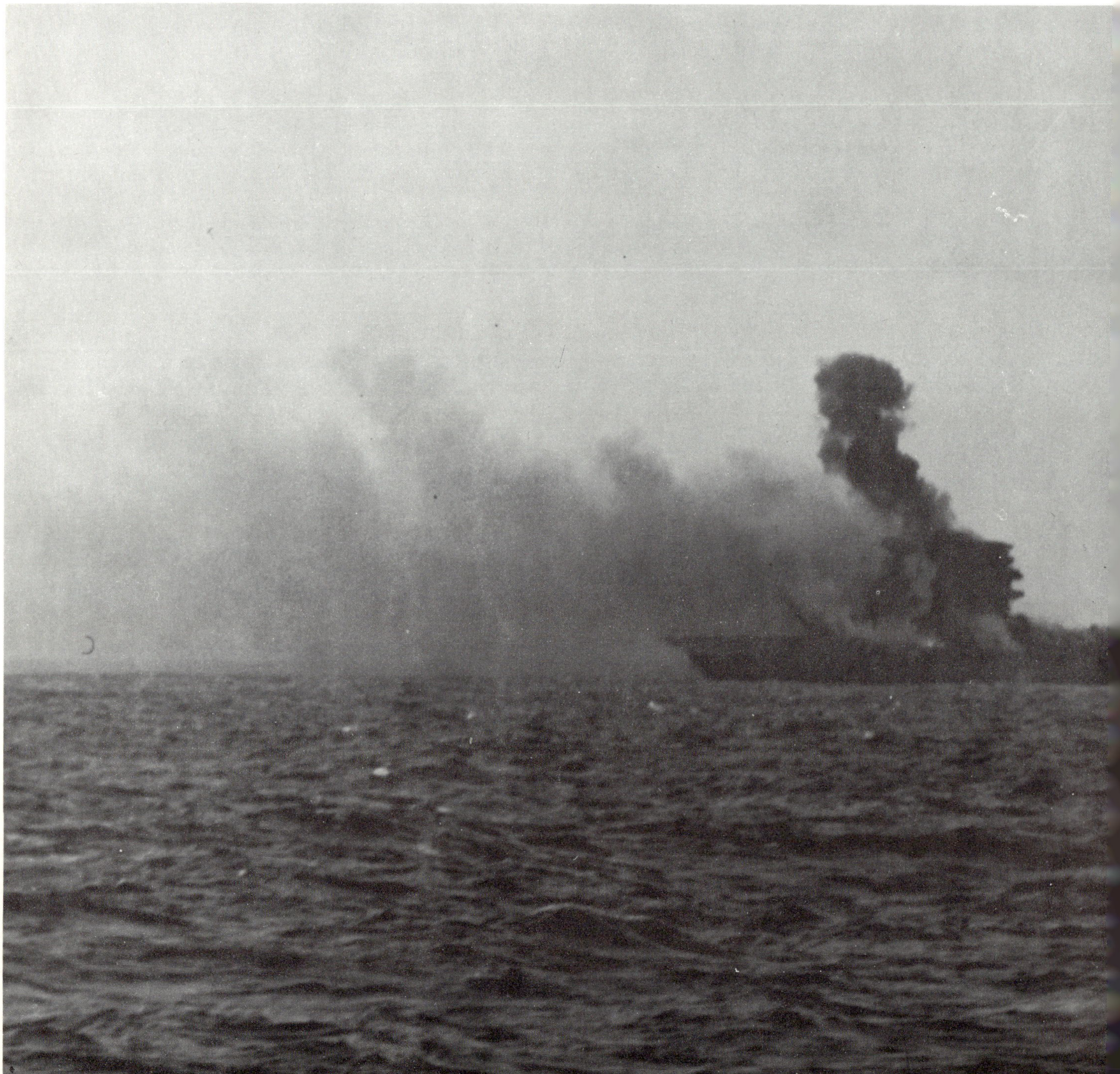

6.25 The loss of HMS *Hermes* on 9 April 1942 was not, in itself, the disaster it appeared at first; certainly not when compared to the loss of the *Prince of Wales* and *Repulse* four months previously in the Far East. The *Hermes* was the world's first purpose-designed carrier and was really obsolete by the outbreak of World War II. She was small and had insufficient speed to enable her to operate satisfactorily with the Home and Mediterranean Fleets. As a result she spent most of her life in the Indian Ocean and Far East. Had she not been lost in all probability she would have been withdrawn from active service by the middle of 1943 for she could not have operated the new generation of naval aircraft coming into service, aircraft such as the Seafire, Avenger, Corsair, Hellcat, etc. HMS *Hermes* joined the Eastern Fleet in March 1942, but was sunk soon after off the coast of Ceylon. A raiding force of over 40 Japanese aircraft from the carriers *Akagi, Hiryu* and *Soryu* found the carrier and sank her with over 40 bombs. The picture, taken by a rating just before 'Abandon Ship', shows the carrier's last moments: lack of panic is very noticeable. *Hermes* was the only British carrier sunk by air attack. **AW**
CPL

6.26 *Yorktown* crewmen begin repairs on the damaged flight deck. The hole was from one of three bombs which hit the carrier during the Battle of Midway, 4 June 1942. A second attack resulted in two torpedo hits which put the ship's stability in jeopardy. Two days later *Yorktown* (CV-5) was being towed from the scene when she was torpedoed and sunk by the Japanese submarine *I 168*. **LS**
USN

6.27 USS *Lexington* (CV-2) belches fire and smoke, 8 May 1942. Six hours earlier she had seemed to successfully survive several bomb hits and from three to five Japanese torpedoes. While on her way home from the Battle of the Coral Sea gas fumes blew her insides out. 'Lex' was abandoned when the fires became uncontrolled. Three hours later, she was still exploding and burning. It took five torpedoes from the *Phelps* (DD-360) to finally send her to the bottom. **LS**
USN

.26

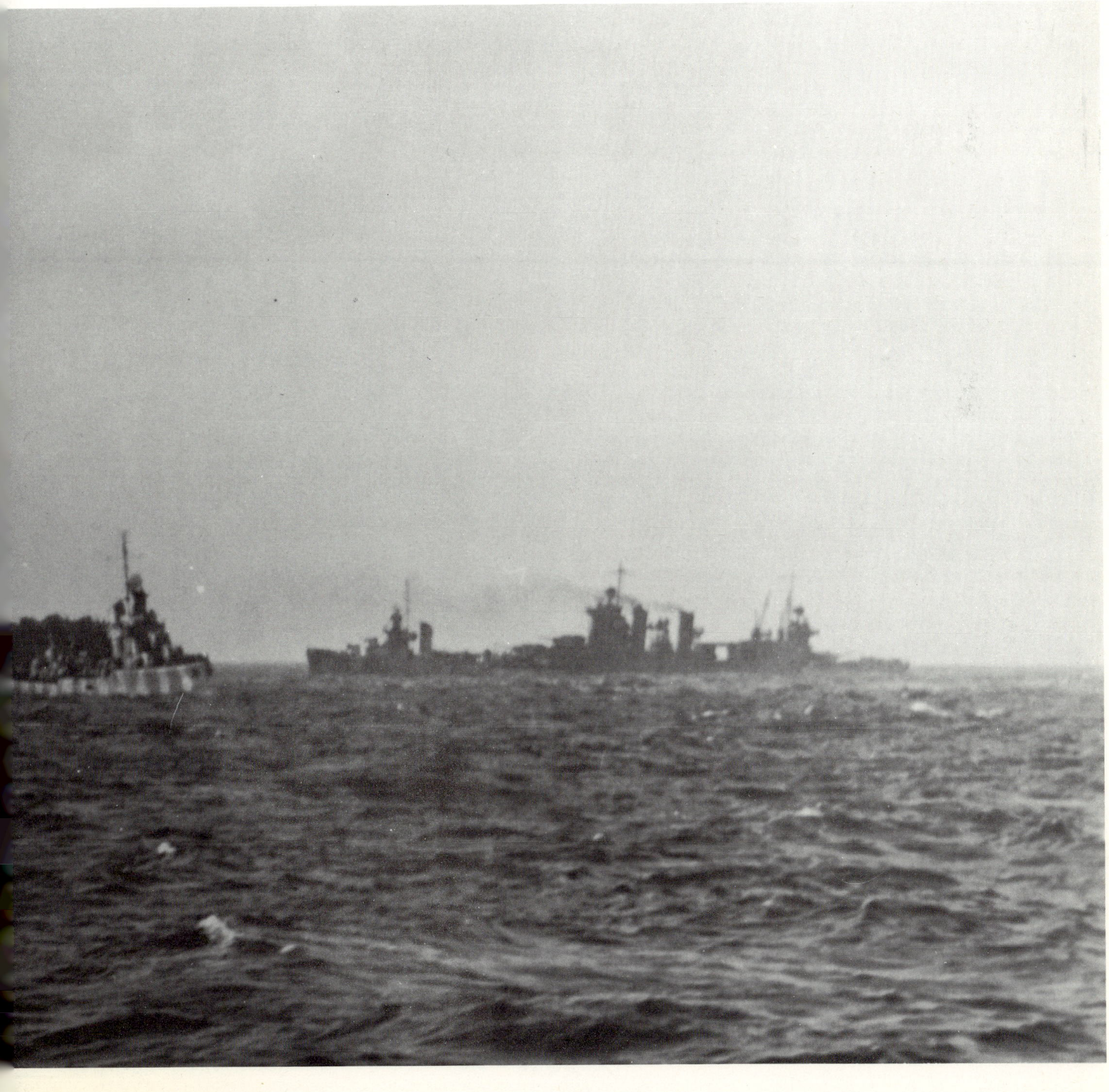

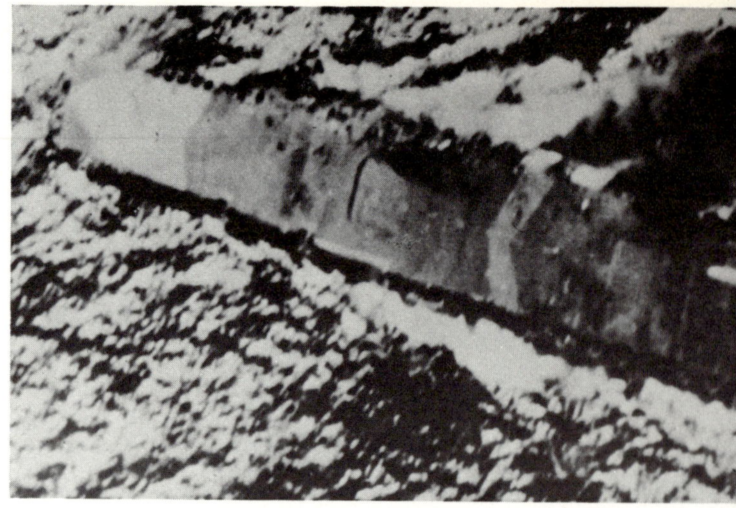

6.28

6.30

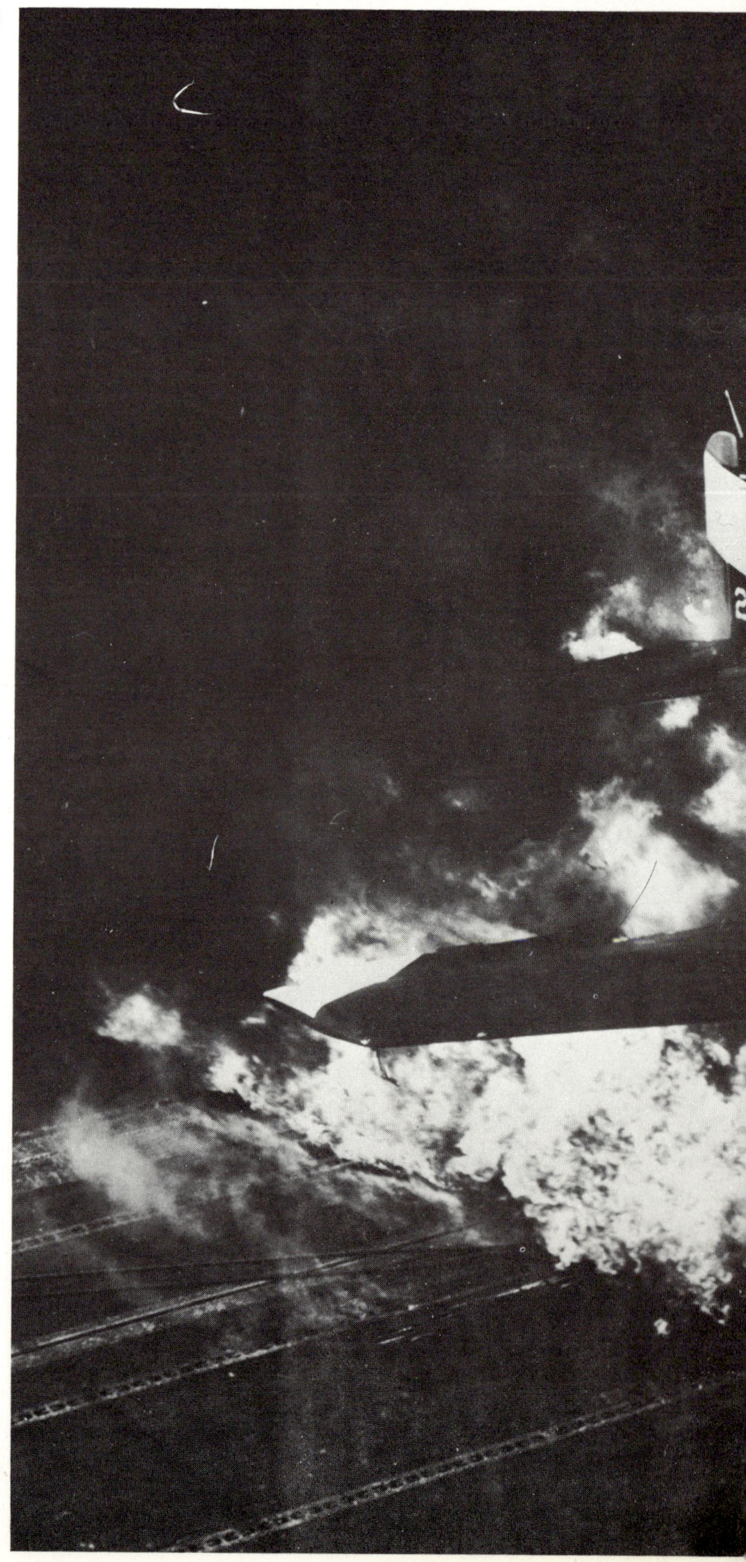

6.28 The aircraft carrier *Zuikaku* under air attack on 25 October 1944 during the battle for Leyte Gulf. The carrier was set on fire by aircraft from the American carriers USS *Essex* and *Lexington* about 220 miles ENE of Cape Engano and heeled over and sank at 1414. The *Zuikaku* was the flagship of Vice-Admiral J Ozawa in command of the carriers. Lacking pilots trained in carrier operations the Japanese decided to use their remaining serviceable carriers as a decoy force to lure the American carrier task force away from its covering position near the American landings at Luzon. This would permit two other large groups of Japanese warships to attack the unprotected American landing forces. The ruse almost succeeded, but failure to follow through the plan and take the ultimate risks necessary led to a Japanese defeat with heavy losses. The picture shows *Zuikaku* just after being struck by a torpedo aft. **AW**
CPL

6.29 Japanese carrier men salute their flag as it is lowered on *Zuikaku* off Cape Engano on 25 October 1944. This marks the end of Japan's finest aircraft carrier as she lists severely to port and settles at the head. *Zuikaku* began the war at the first battle, Pearl Harbor, 7 December 1941, and finished her war during the greatest naval battle in history — the Battle for Leyte Gulf, 25 October 1944. She was the last of the six Pearl Harbor attack carriers to be sunk. During her eventful career she helped sink the US carriers *Lexington* (CV-2) and *Hornet* (CV-8) and many other Allied ships. **LS**
USN

6.30 A fighter pilot escapes from his fire-surrounded F6F, on the flight deck of USS *Lexington* (CV-16). This is one of a series of pictures which show the plane land, the belly tank break loose, spill and ignite. The next picture showed the pilot making it to safety on his aircraft's wings. Note the propeller — it is still turning. Taken 25 February 1945. **LS**
USN

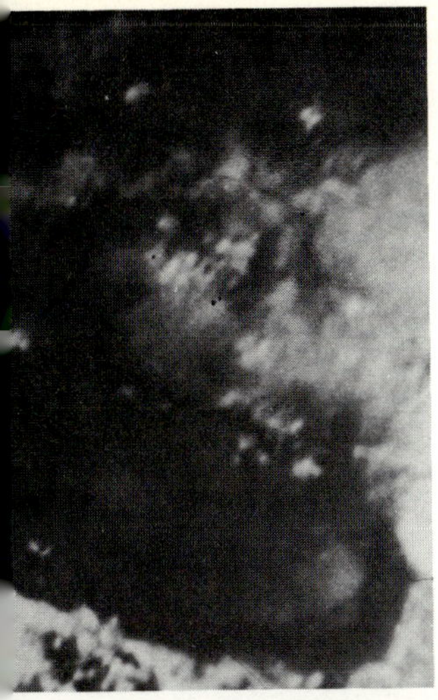

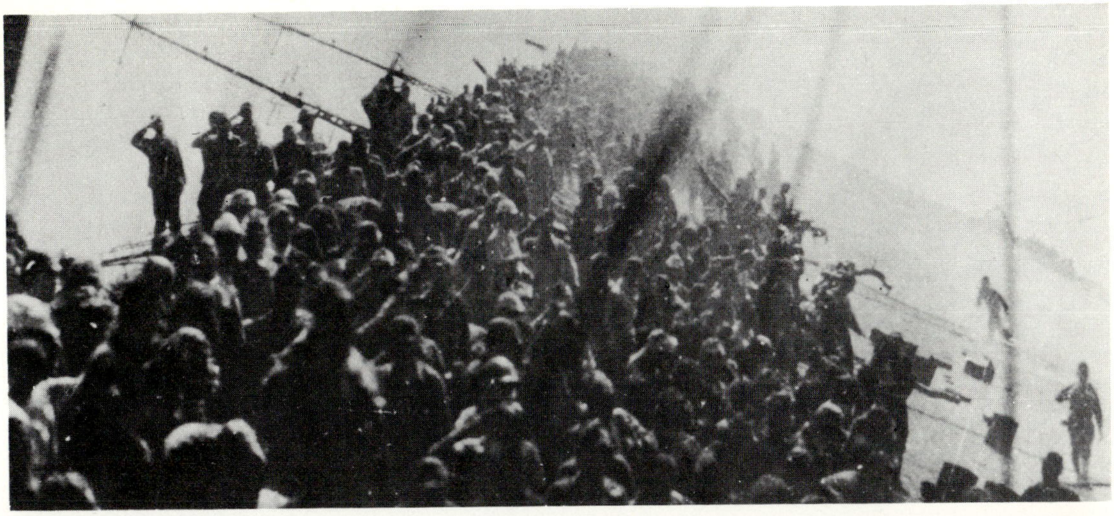

6.29

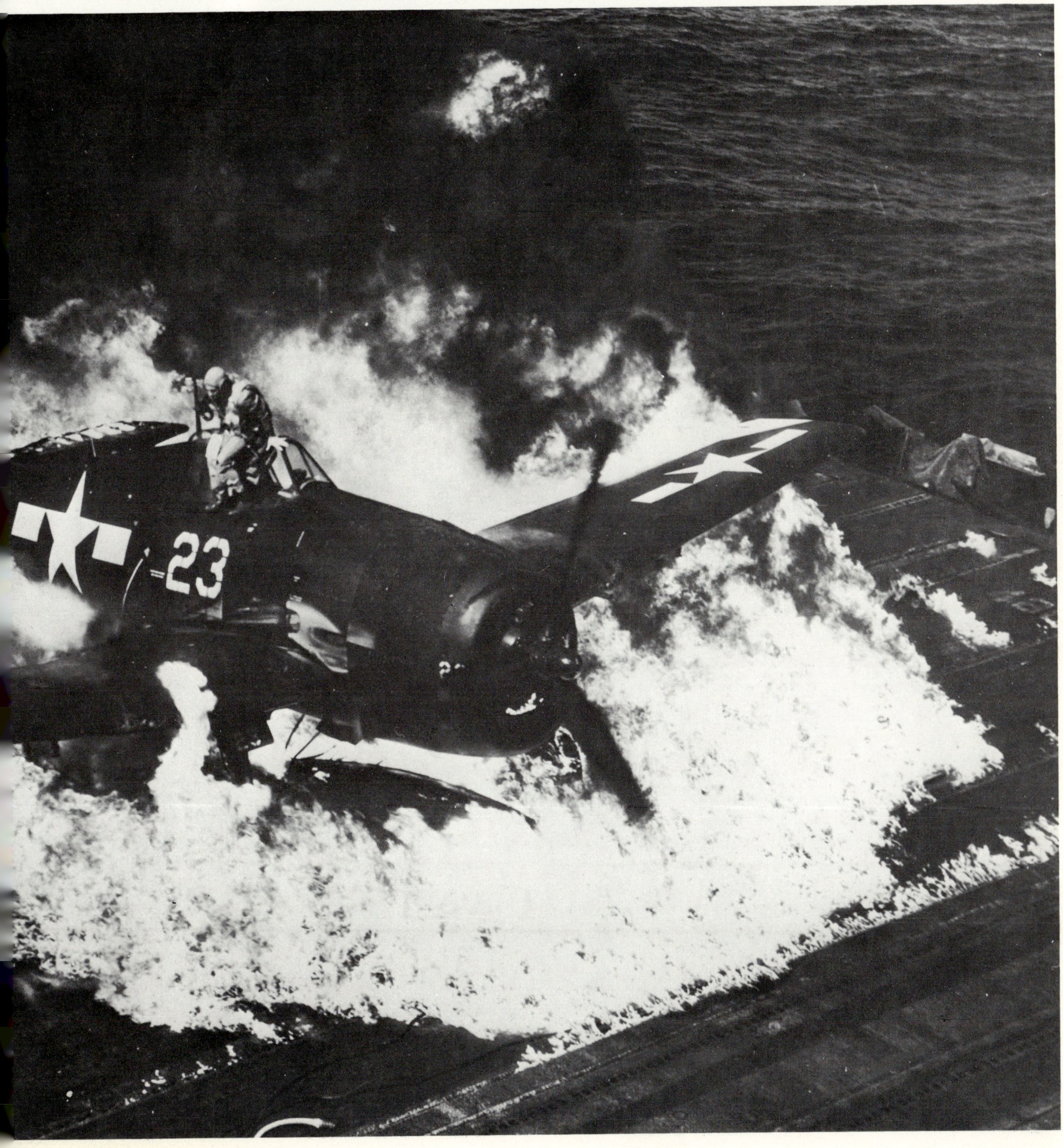

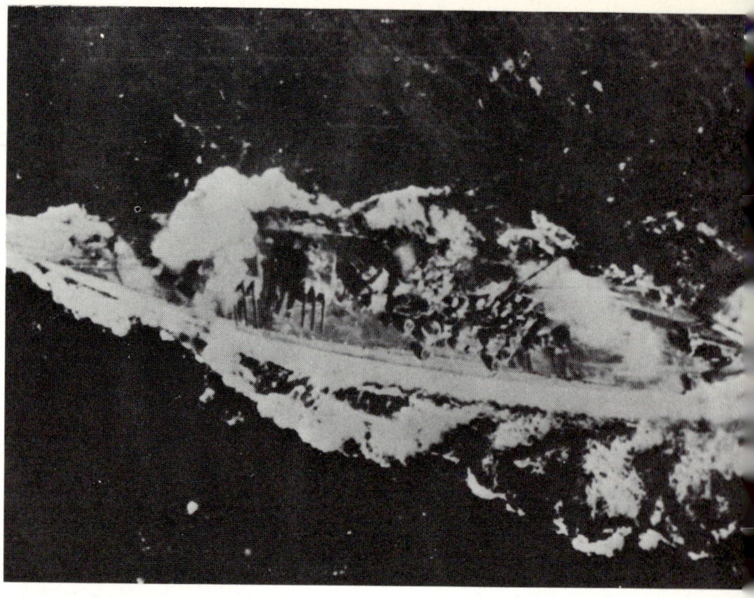

6.31

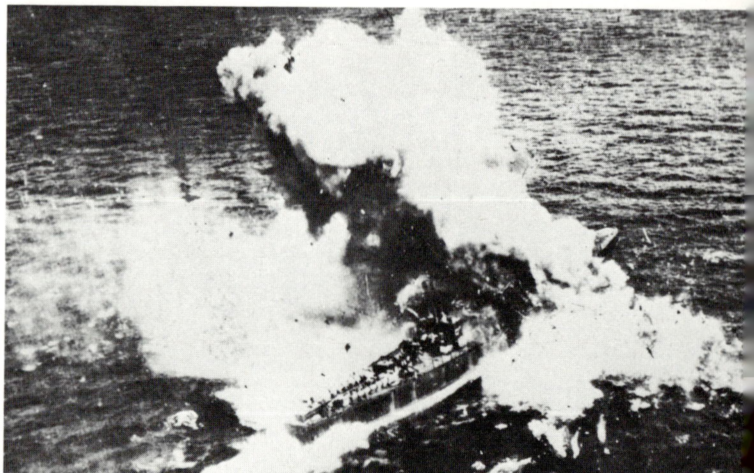

6.32

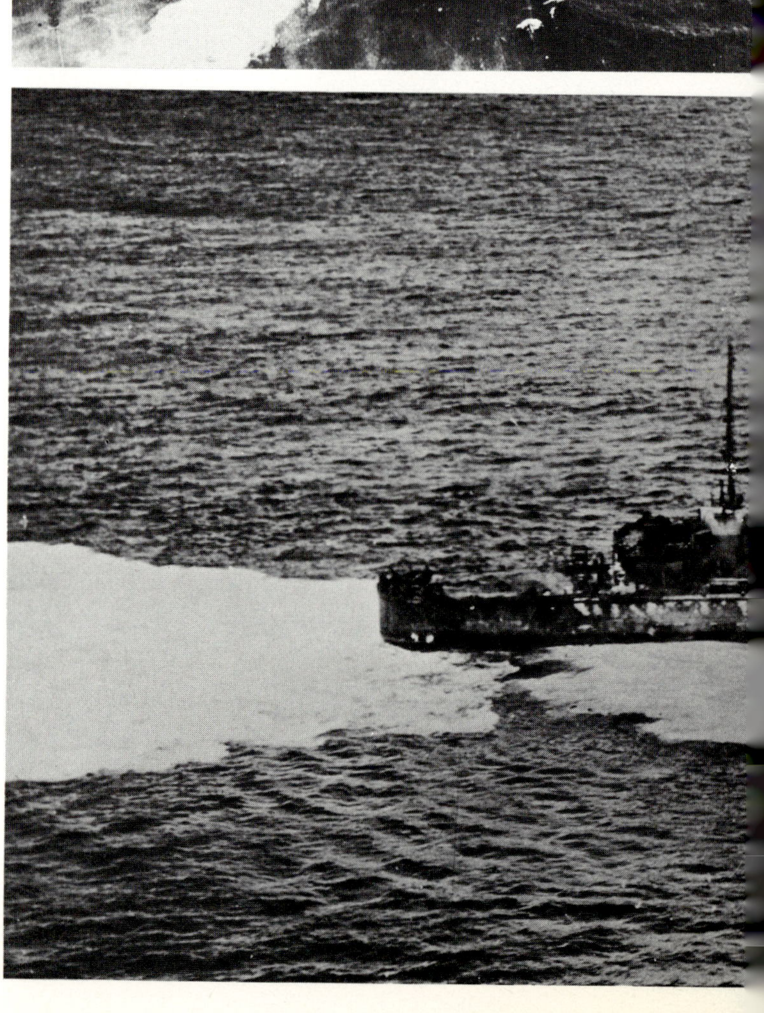

6.31 The battleship *Yamato,* the largest and most heavily gun-armed warship to have been built, under air attack during the battle for Leyte Gulf in October 1944. At the time of the photograph the battleship was under dive-bomber attack from Helldivers in the Sibuyan Sea. In spite of the heavy air attacks mounted by the American carriers against negligible opposition from Japanese aircraft, only two bombs struck the *Yamato,* both on or near 'A' turret which resulted in only slight damage. In the photograph one bomb has just burst near the turret and splinters seriously wounded the Japanese Commander-in-Chief, Kurita's Chief of Staff, Rear Admiral Koyanagi. **AW**
CPL

6.32 The Japanese Type D escort *No 11* bombed and sunk by B-25 bombers of the 38th Bombardment Group USAAF in Ormac Bay on 10 November 1944. The ship was escorting a convoy of empty troopships from Leyte Gulf when attacked; two of the merchant ships were also sunk. The bombers were escorted by P-38 and P-47 fighters which shot down 20 Japanese aircraft attempting to attack the bombers. The following day, 11 November, American naval aircraft from the carriers of TF38 made continuous attacks on another convoy carrying troop reinforcements through Ormoc Bay to Leyte. For the loss of 11 aircraft, four Japanese destroyers, a minesweeper and five transports were sunk with the loss of most of the 10 000 troops aboard. **AW**
CPL

6.33 On 5 November 1944 American aircraft from 11 aircraft carriers of Task Force 38 from the Third Fleet struck the island of Luzon in the Philippines. For the loss of 25 aircraft the Americans destroyed over 400 Japanese aircraft and sank the heavy cruiser *Nachi* in Manila Bay. The picture shows the *Nachi* (one of the four *Myoko* class) frantically manoeuvring 5 miles north west of Corregidor to avoid bombs from aircraft from the USS *Lexington.* The cruiser had been damaged in collision with the *Mogami* at the Battle of Leyte Gulf in October 1944 where she was holed in her port side near the stern, damaging her propellers and reducing speed to 18 knots. She managed to return to Manila for repairs, but after being hit by a number of bombs on 5 November finally sank stern first. **AW**
CPL

6.34 The Japanese destroyer *Mikatsuki* under US air attack, 29 July 1943. With only a handful of anti-aircraft guns she was soon sent to the bottom of the South Pacific. **LS**
USN

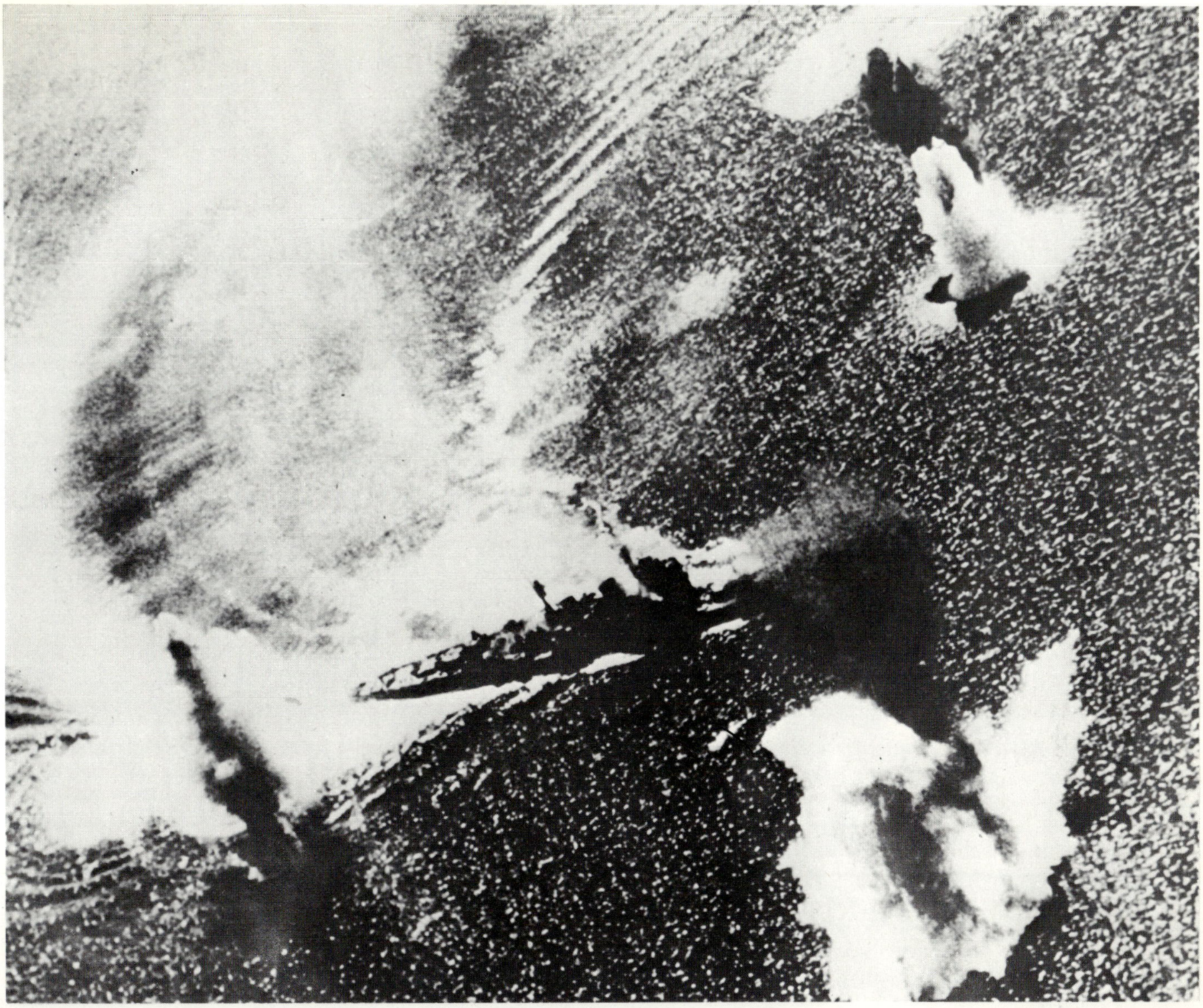

6.33

6.34

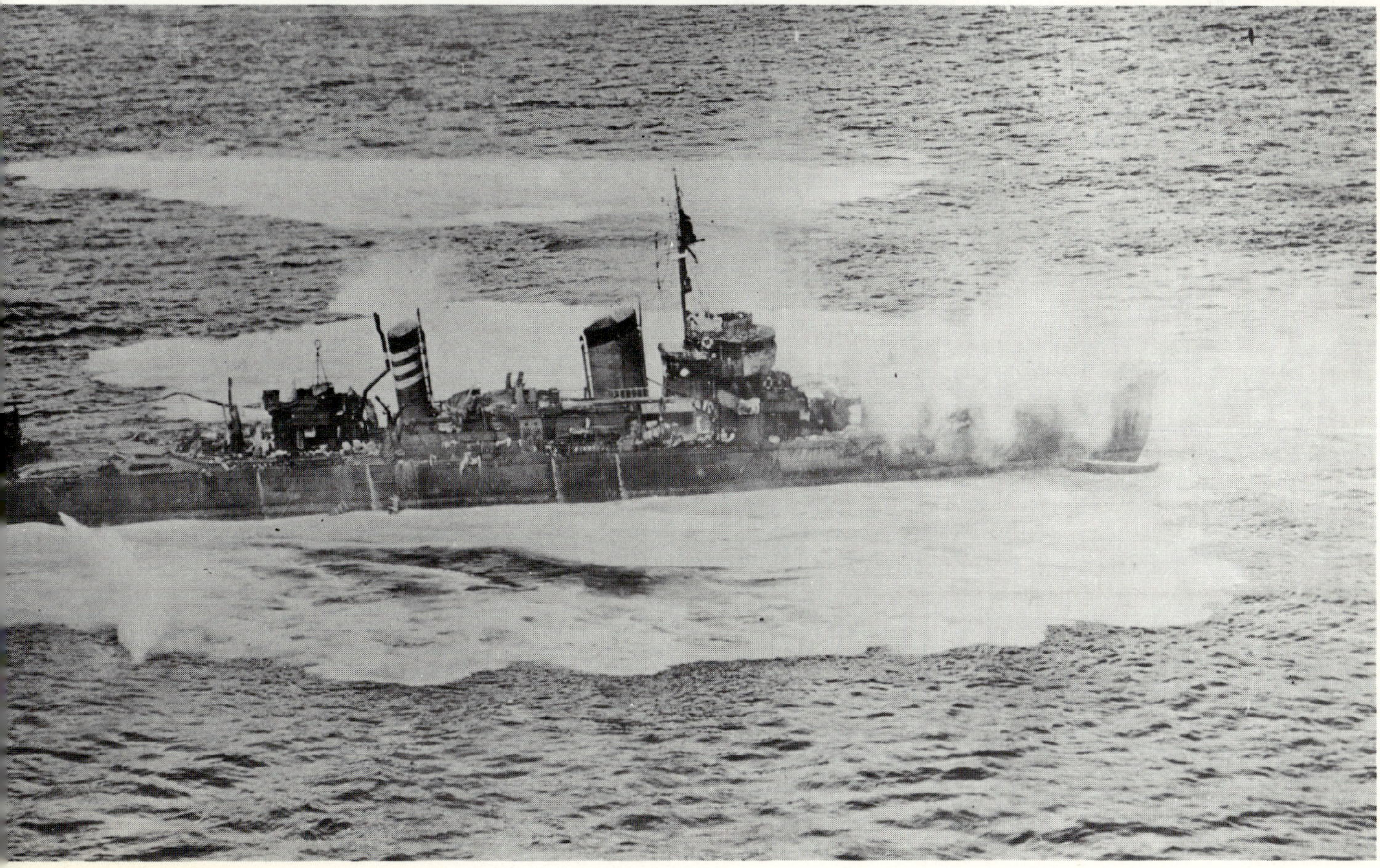

6.35 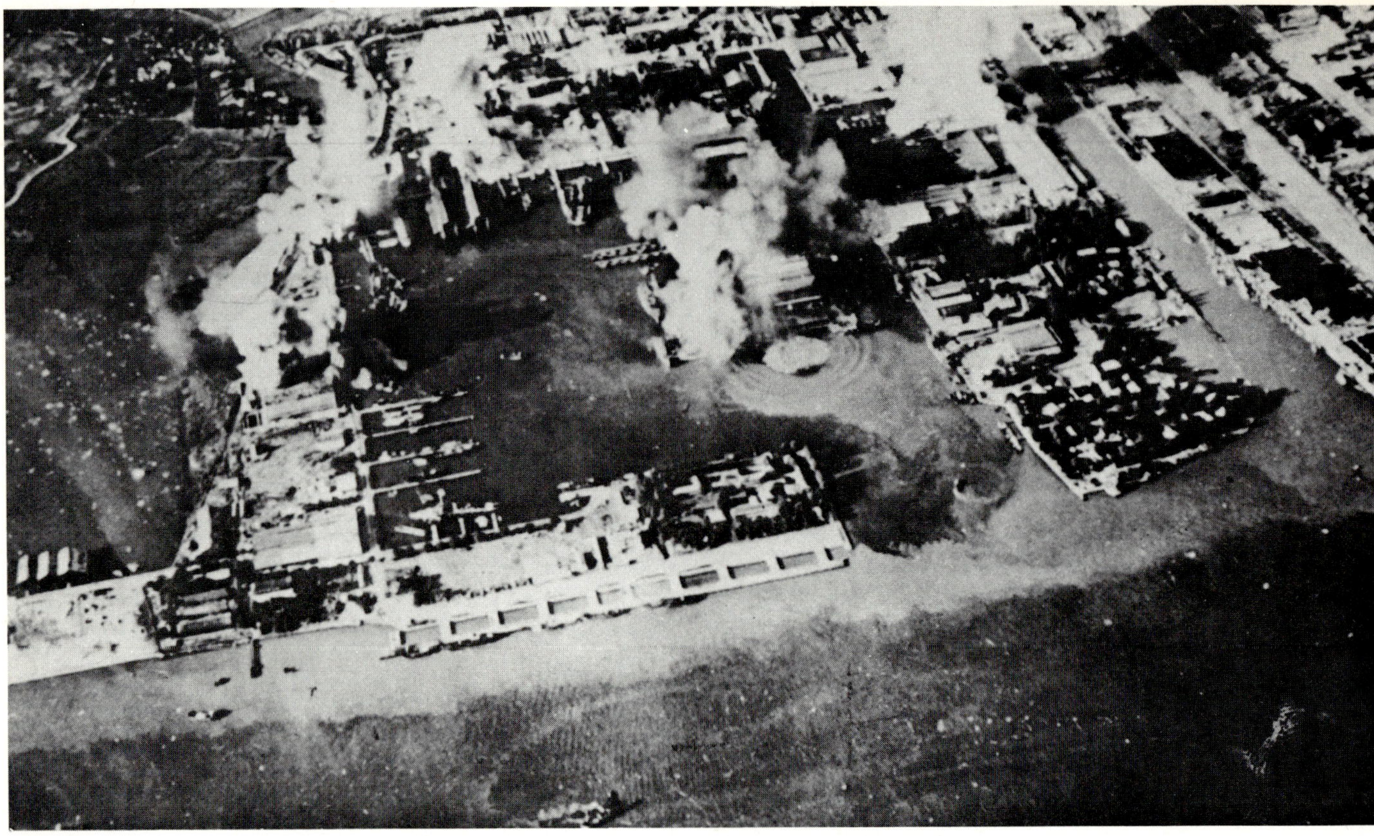

6.35 On 17 May 1944, 45 Avenger and Dauntless bombers and 40 Hellcats and Corsair fighters from the aircraft carriers *Illustrious* and *Saratoga* formed up for a raid on the Java port of Sourabaya. From a position 180 miles south of the target the raiding force headed for the oil refinery and harbour installations meeting no opposition on the way in and only ineffective AA fire over the target. The oil refinery, the only source of aviation fuel on the island, was hit by half the force, while the remainder of the strike attacked the docks and shipping in the harbour. Unfortunately the raid had only minimal success in spite of achieving complete surprise. For the loss of one aircraft (whose pilot was rescued by the British submarine *Tactician*) only one small steamer of 993 tons was sunk, along with 12 Japanese aircraft destroyed on the ground. **AW**

CPL

Indomitable was damaged during her first operation in 1943 — covering the invasion of Sicily in July — and returned to the USA for repairs to extensive hull damage inflicted by an air-launched torpedo. A year elapsed before she was ready to embark an air group. Although the Vought F4U Corsair was the standard fighter aboard the *Illustrious* class carriers, *Indomitable*'s upper hangar lacked the overhead clearance for the 16 ft (4.9 m) folded height of the Corsair and she was therefore given F6F Hellcats which, with the typical Grumman 'twist and fold' mechanism, had a folded height of just under 14 ft. The Hellcat was a very bulky aircraft, however, and only 24 could be stowed in the two hangar bays allocated; the lower hangar and the third bay of the upper were occupied by the 24 Barracudas of No 12 Torpedo-Bomber-Reconnaissance Wing (815 and 817 Squadrons). By accepting a permanent deck park, the strength of No 5 Fighter Wing (1839 and 1844 Squadrons) was eventually increased to 33 Hellcats in May 1945.

Three operations were undertaken with the Barracuda Wing in the autumn of 1944. The 'Barras' were then replaced by the Grumman TBM-1 Avengers Mk II of 857 Squadron; the newer aircraft, of which 21 were at first carried, were able to carry a greater load over a longer distance at a higher speed and were therefore better suited to the nature of operations in the Eastern theatre. To work up with the new type, as well as to deliver a severe blow to Japanese oil production, *Illustrious* and *Indomitable* launched a strike against the Pangkalan Brandan oil refinery in Sumatra on 20 December 1944. This was thwarted by bad weather in the target area and the Avengers were obliged to attack the secondary target — the harbour of Belawan Deli (Medan). A fortnight later, on 4 January 1945, the primary target was heavily damaged by aircraft from *Indomitable, Victorious* and *Indefatigable*, the last-named making her debut in the Far East.

This series of photographs was taken during Operations *Robson* (December) and *Lentil* (January) and depict deck scenes during and after the strikes — the impressive ranges of Hellcats and Avengers launched on the strike days are not illustrated, however. **DB**

6.36 "When the poor old 'O' comes staggering down the flight deck like a porter,
With his canvas sack and chartboard in his hand,
His parachute he wears because 'they' tell him that he oughta'
Hanging round his legs so he can hardly stand."
(Refrain: "A Policeman's Lot")

This 857 Squadron Observer has managed to hand over his 'canvas sack and chartboard' to one of the ground crew and has removed his parachute and seat-type dinghy (life-raft) but still conveys the sense of the parodied verse. In contrast, his Petty Officer Telegraphist Air-Gunner is carrying only an 'electric hat'; the Avenger's turret was too cramped for the wearing of a parachute and the gunner's chance of escape slim if the turret jammed in action when on a beam bearing — his parachute was stowed in the radio tunnel forward of the turret and donned only when the need arose. W-1S (JZ592) is fitted with American ASB radar — a derivative of the British ASV IIN — mounted above the wingtips. **DB**

CPL

6.37 W-1K is manhandled on to the after lift for transfer to the lower hangar as HMS *Victorious* crosses astern of *Indomitable* during the passage out for the successful Pangkalan Brandan strike. *Indomitable* has three arrester wires abaft the lift and one (unrigged) across the platform — as designed, the armoured carriers had only six wires abaft the island, but between three and four were added when the round-down was extended to increase the landing area. **DB**

CPL

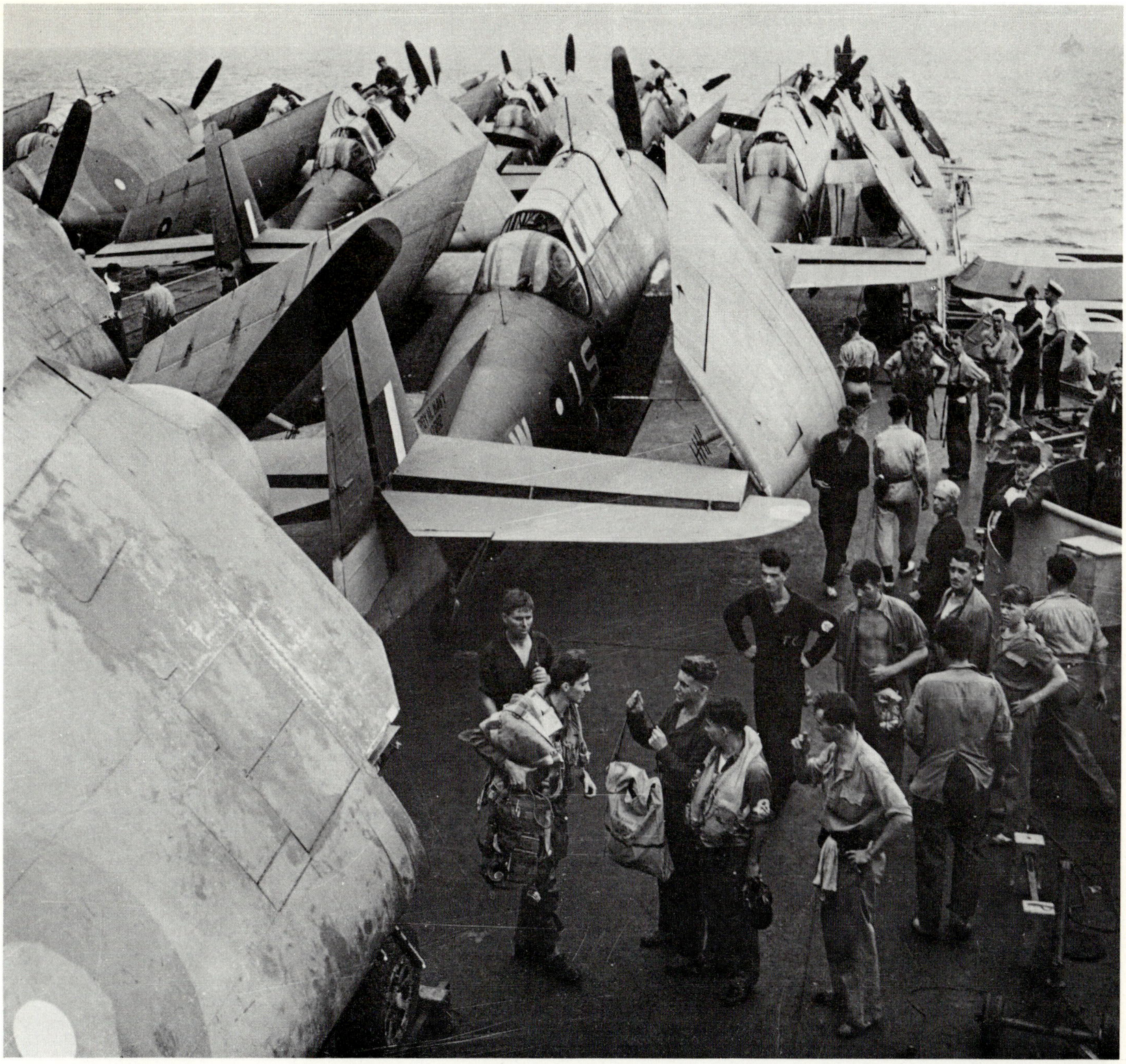

6.36

6.37

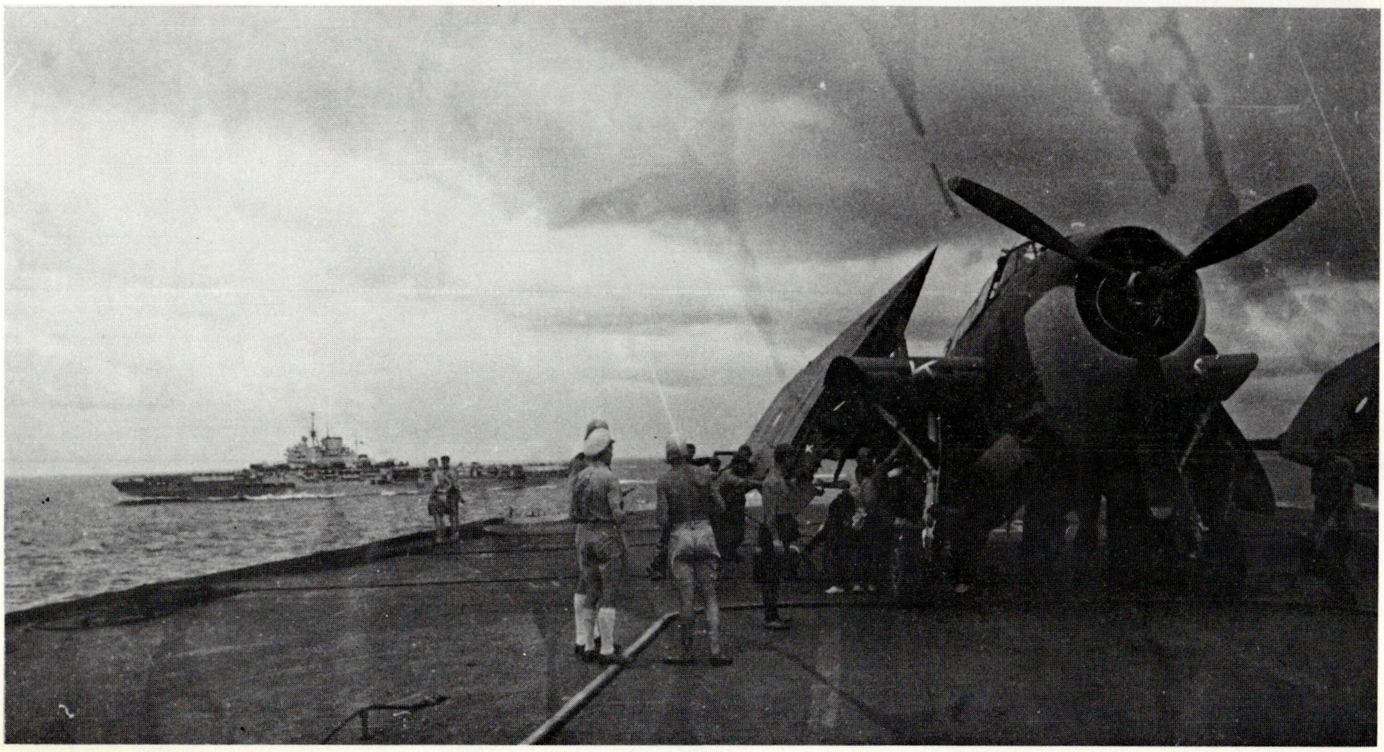

6.38 The DLCO, wearing a US Navy pattern flight deck helmet, strides out across the wet deck to flag off a division of Hellcats for a Combat Air Patrol (CAP) over the carrier force. The after barrier is rigged to be used only in the event of damage to one of the two forward units. **DB**
CPL

6.39 The Hellcats of 1839 Squadron return to *Indomitable* after the strike on Belawan Deli, eight of this squadron having accompanied the Avengers. R-5L (FN362) has taxied outboard, under the guidance of the marshaller standing inboard of the 'hockey stick', to pass around the lift opening into the forward deck park, where two more marshallers, dressed in US Navy rig, await.

R-5N descends the lift with engine still running and the handling party double out from the island and the port catwalk to push back the unlocked mainplanes of R-5R (JV100), destined for the deck park via the port side of the deck (although the Hellcat's folding gear was hydraulically operated, manual assistance speeded up the procedure). His marshaller, wearing a waist-type life-preserver, is standing on one of the white lines painted alongside the catapult track to assist in the alignment of aircraft being launched by the tail-down towed technique. **DB**
CPL

6.40 Aircrew unable to reach the island access door between the raised forward barriers watch the approach of an 857 Squadron Avenger; note also the member of a gun's crew dressed in anti-flash gauntlets and helmet. The British barrier rendered from the top of the support, necessitating solid barrier stanchions to take the load; American barriers were held up by light 'knock-down' supports which were intended to collapse when the barrier was engaged, the wire paying out from the deck. A spare barrier net is hung on the cleats on the side of the island by the forward barrier. **DB**
CPL

6.41 The old CAP lands on as soon as the new CAP and ASP have taken off and 1844 Squadron Hellcat R-6F (FN383) is marshalled into the forward park, its bespectacled Pilot's Mate standing by (extreme left). **DB**
CPL

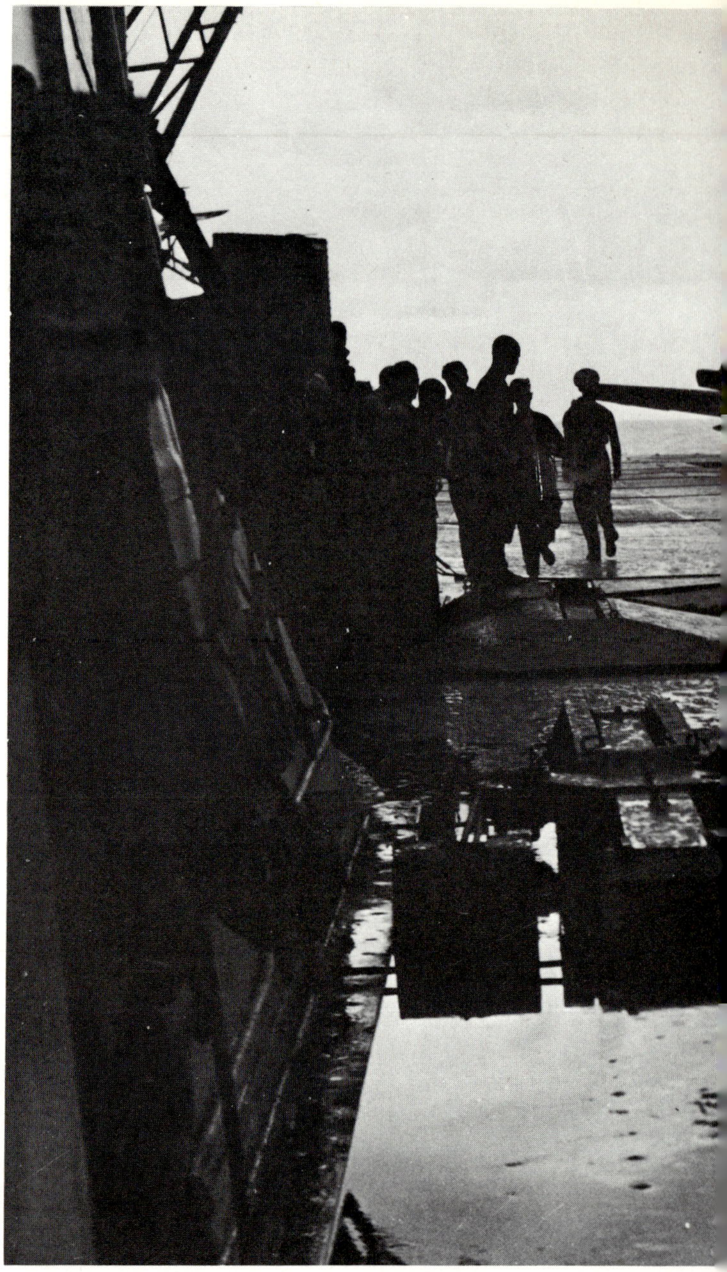

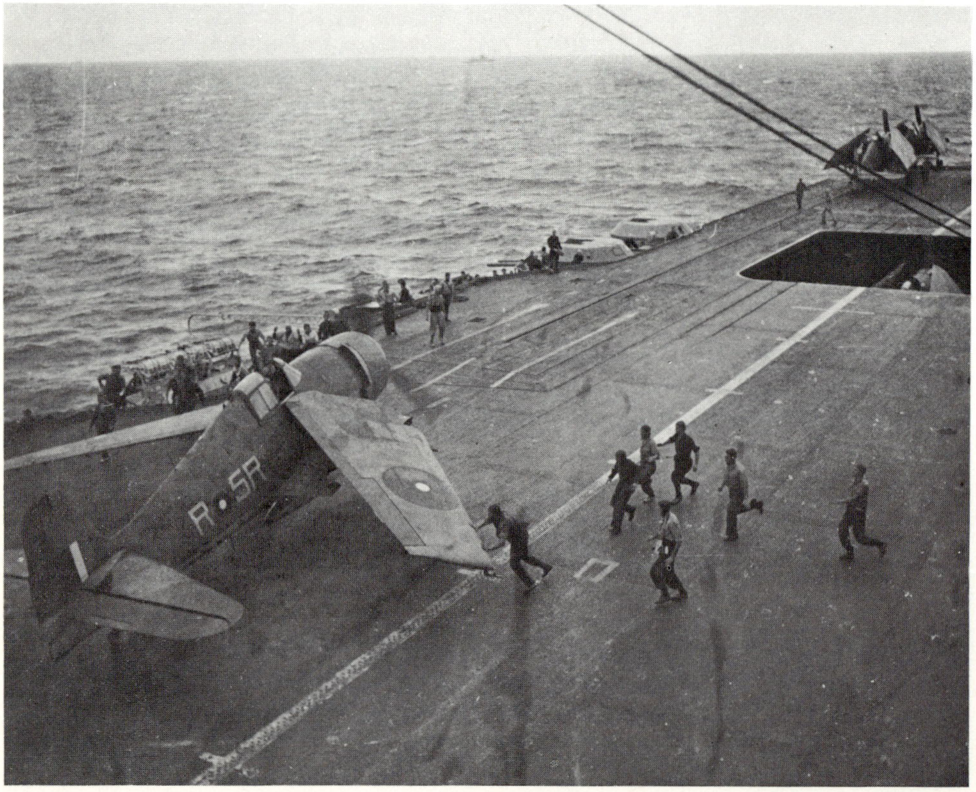

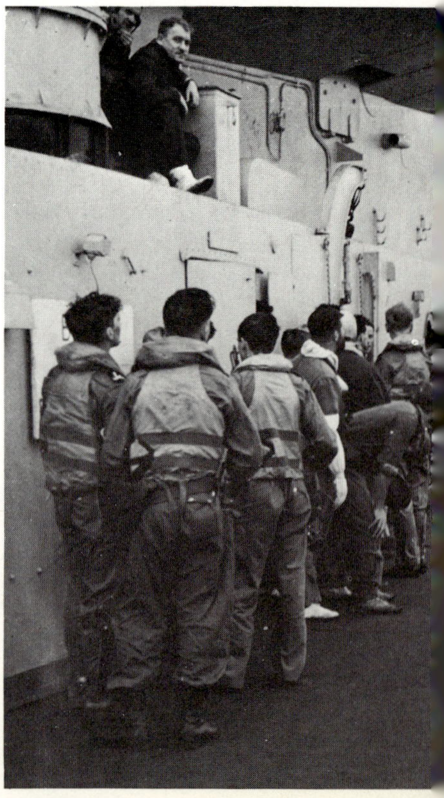

6.39 6.40

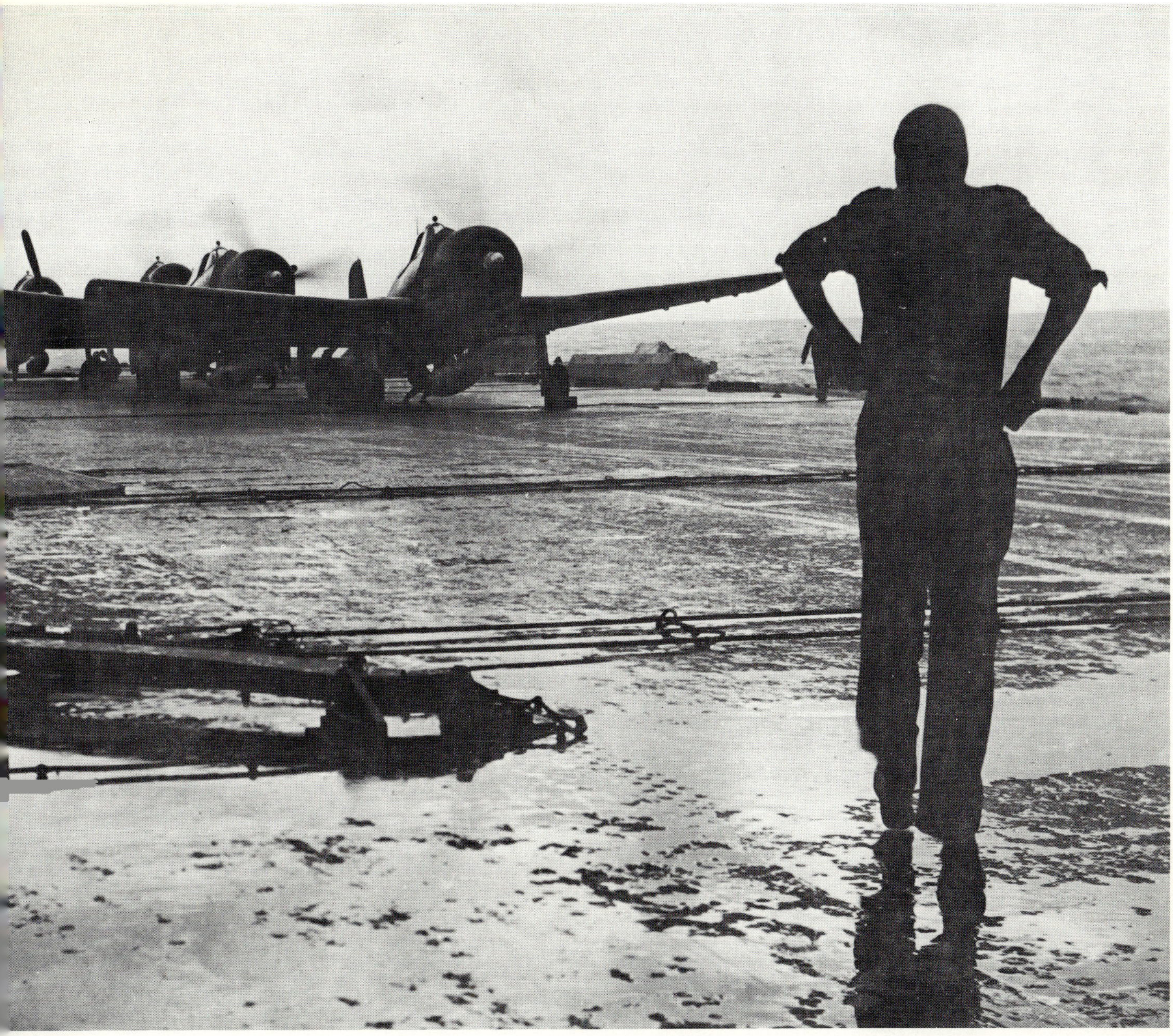

6.38

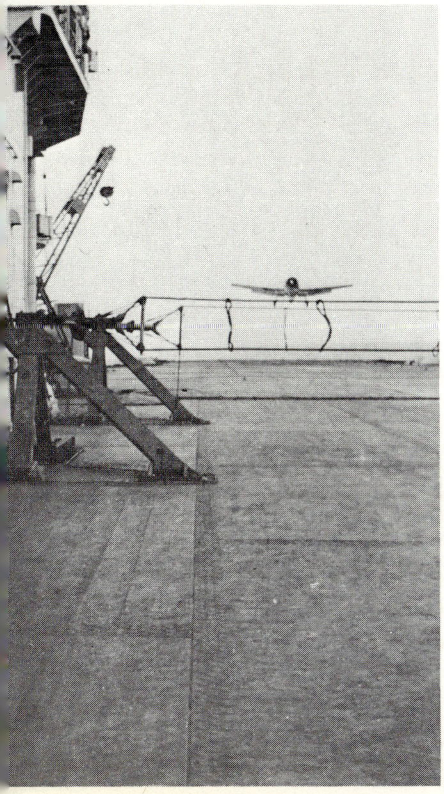

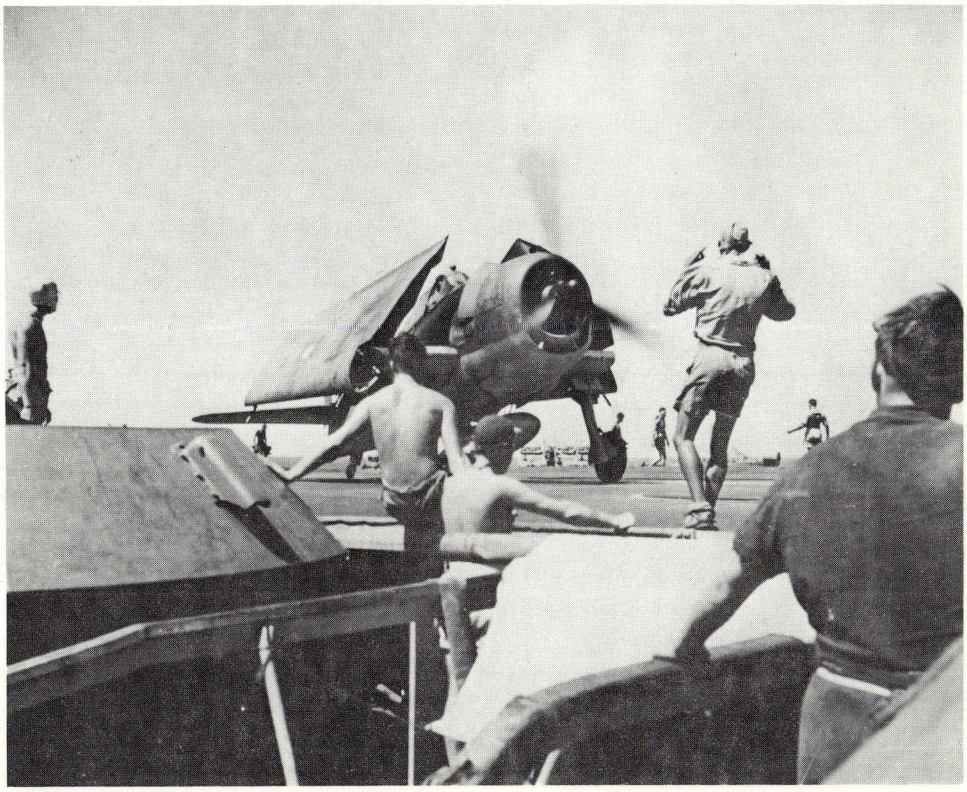

6.41

6.42 Avenger W-1Z and Hellcat R-6F are pushed aft for re-spotting. The RN modified the TBM-1 to station the Observer in the glasshouse, complete with chartboard, radar and communications equipment; the third crew member in the US Navy TBF/TBM was a radioman, located in the 'tunnel' below and ahead of the turret but able to crawl through into the empty space behind the pilot. The Observer's open canopy can be seen abaft the radio mast; this aircraft appears to be fitted with a camera gun immediately forward of the windscreen.

The saving in manpower possible with tractor power is evident — W-1Z needs a dozen 'coolies', a cockpit brake number and a tail wheel arm number for the move, whereas R-6F is attended only by its two chockmen, brake man, the 'dodgem car' driver and his passenger. In the background is *Victorious,* her Corsairs and Avengers ranged for the next day's strike. **DB**
CPL

6.43 R-5P (FN432) of 1839 Squadron has help in folding its wings on return from a CAP sortie. The lift is not in use as so few aircraft are involved in this recovery, so that the forward park will not get overcrowded. **DB**
CPL

6.44 R-6F is parked to starboard of the lift. The fighters used the American adjustable 'dumb-bell' chocks, whereas the Avengers had British wedge-type chocks. The 125 Imperial gallon centre-line drop-tank was carried on all missions and gave the Hellcat a combat endurance of over four hours and a combat radius of action of 350 miles but reduced maximum speed by about 20mph. **DB**
CPL

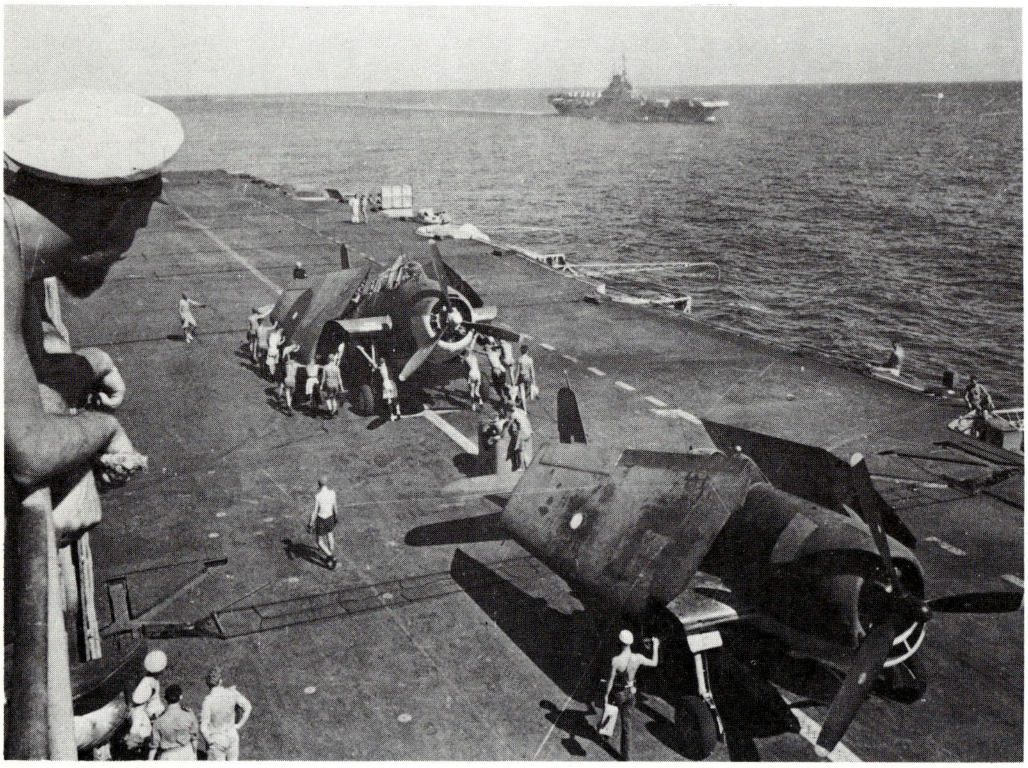

6.42

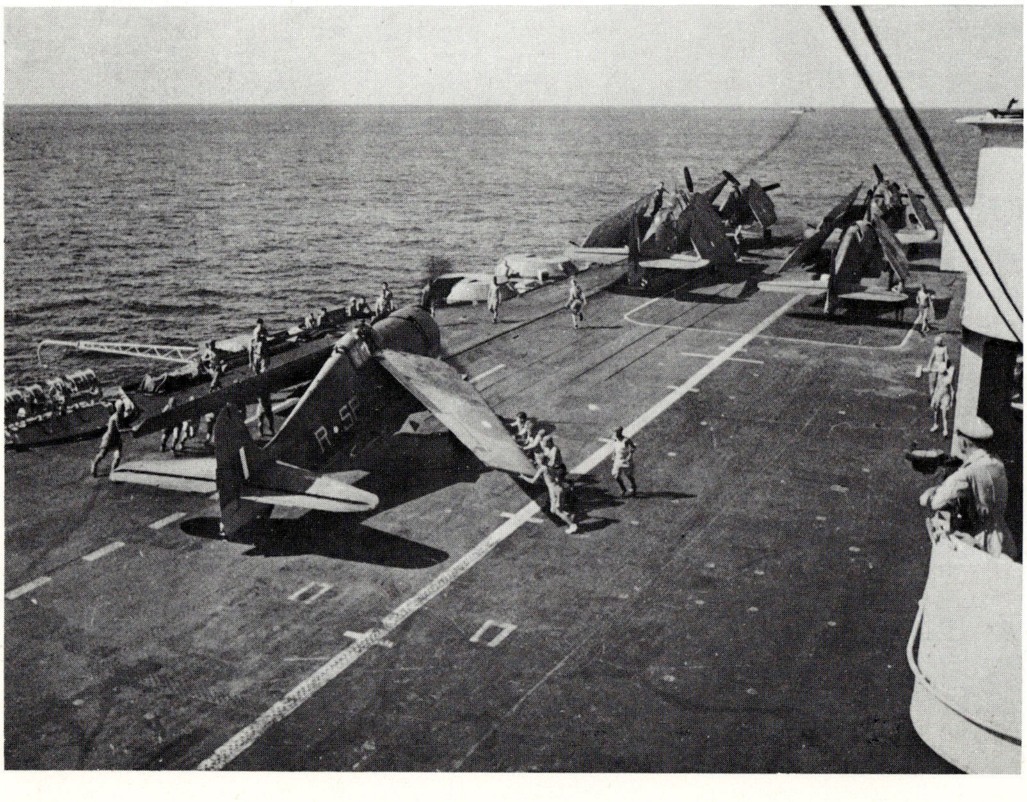

6.43

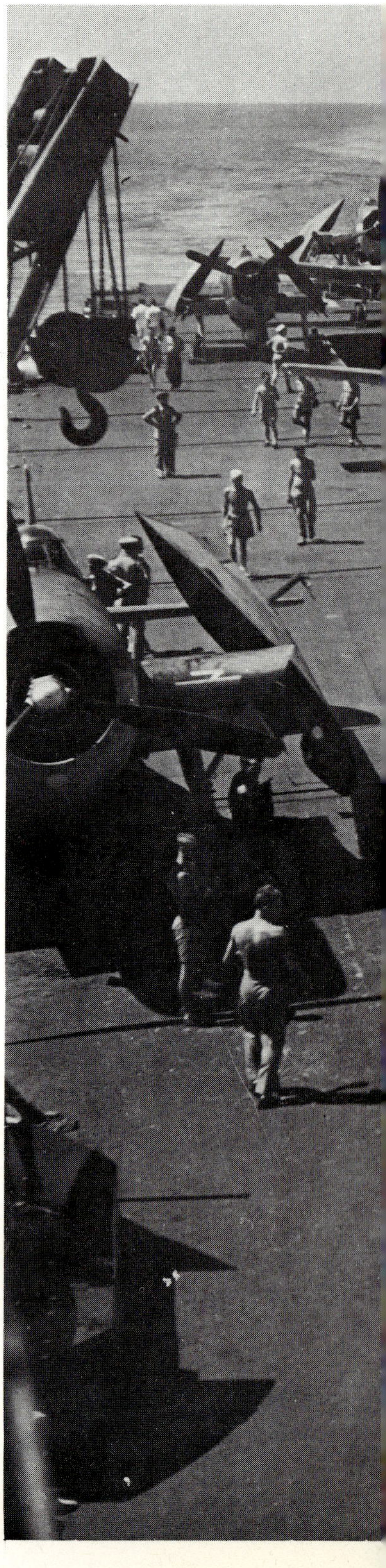

6.45 Once the next range had been spotted, the flight deck party and aircraft maintenance personnel on deck could indulge in deck hockey — a game which was liable to 'break out' whenever there was even a short break in flying activity and played with such fervour that players have been known to rush off the sides of the pitch after the rope quoit! The fighters at readiness on deck are, however, all attended by their two chockmen and Pilot's Mates. In this view, as in the others, a third mast can be seen stepped on *Victorious*, outboard of the funnel: this supports the American 'YE' Ultra-High Frequency homing beacon — a more compact aid than the Type 72 and one with a far superior performance. **DB.**
CPL

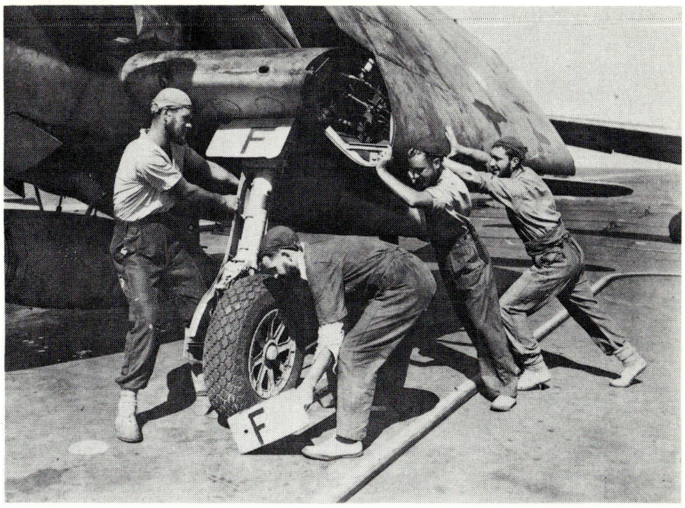

6.44

6.45

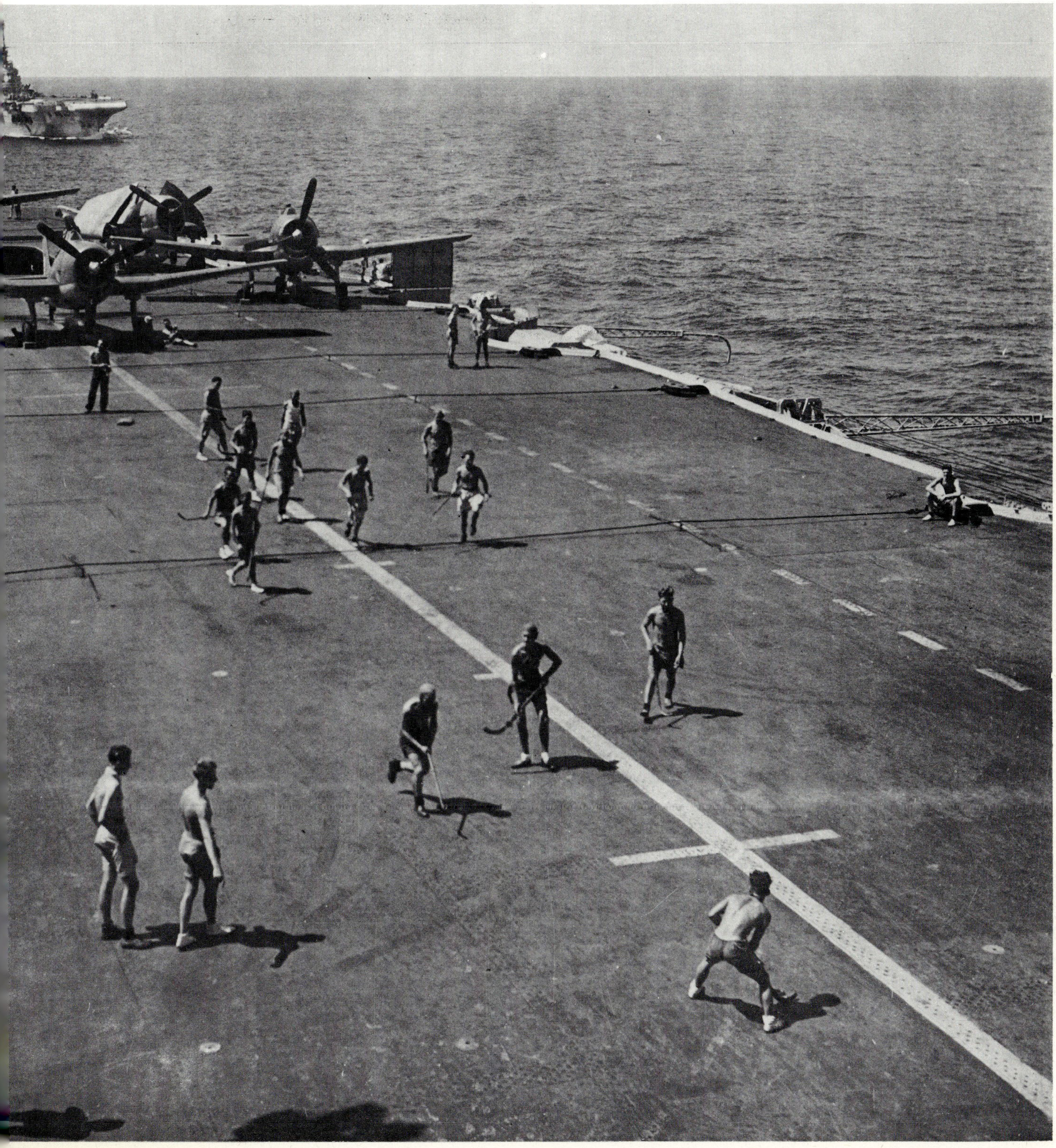

6.46 *Victorious* seen from *Indomitable*'s round-down — any sense of tranquility should be dispelled by the extent of the bow wave, indicating a speed of at least 20 knots. **DB**
CPL

6.47 Carrier and aircraft crewmen examine SBD Dauntlesses as they land aboard the new *Lexington* (CV-16). The planes have just returned from a strike mission. **LS**
USN

6.48 A 'Lex' pilot is pulled to safety from what would have been certain death. On 21 May 1943 this F4F Wildcat missed the arrestor while landing. The pilot attempted to veer off but his engine stalled. Evidently his tail hook caught on something and snapped the aircraft against the port side catwalk. In this 'nose straight down' position, the plane when worked free would have gone straight to the bottom. Several *Lexington* (CV-16) crew (right) are standing by with an additional safety line. **LS**
USN

6.46

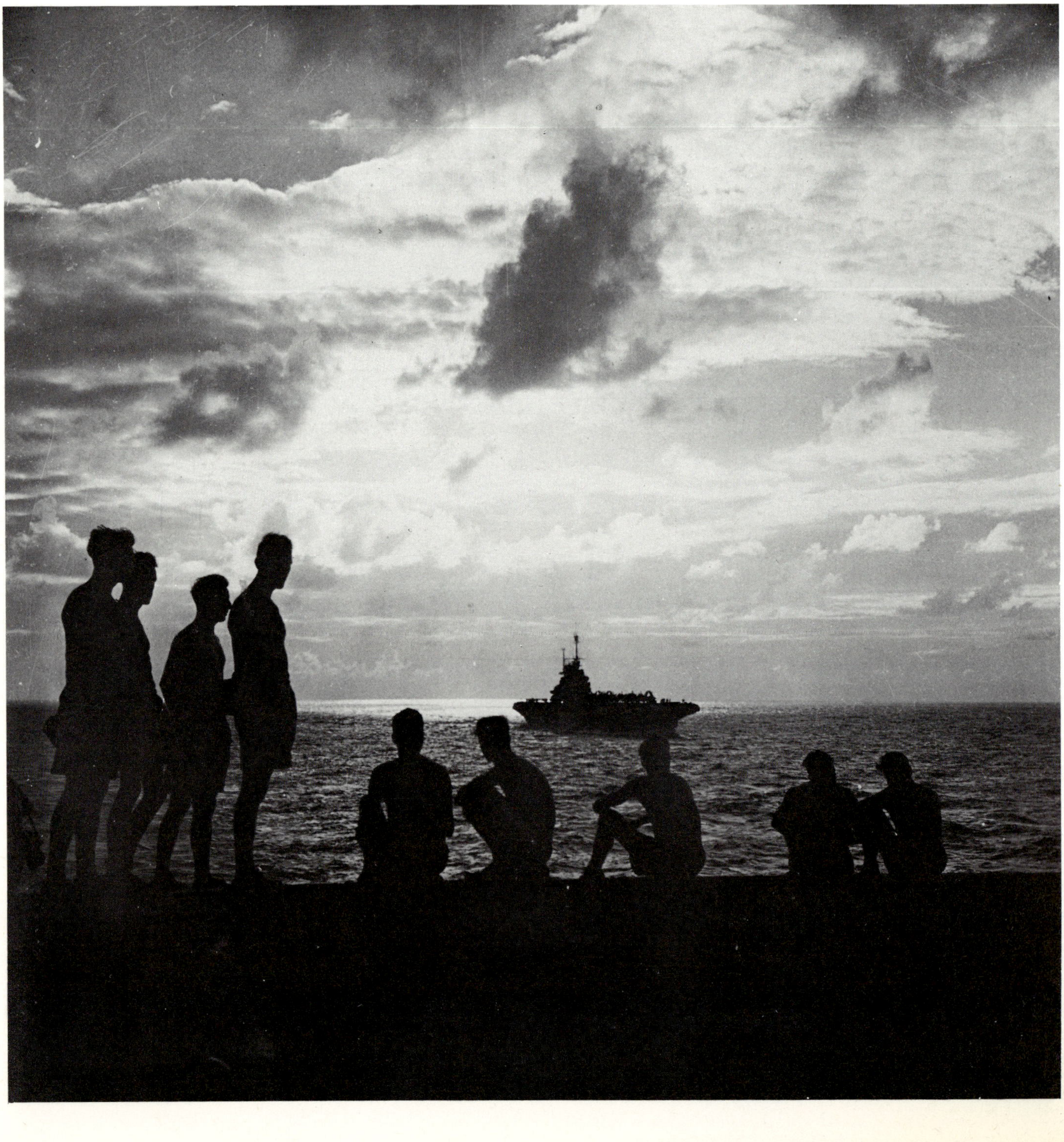

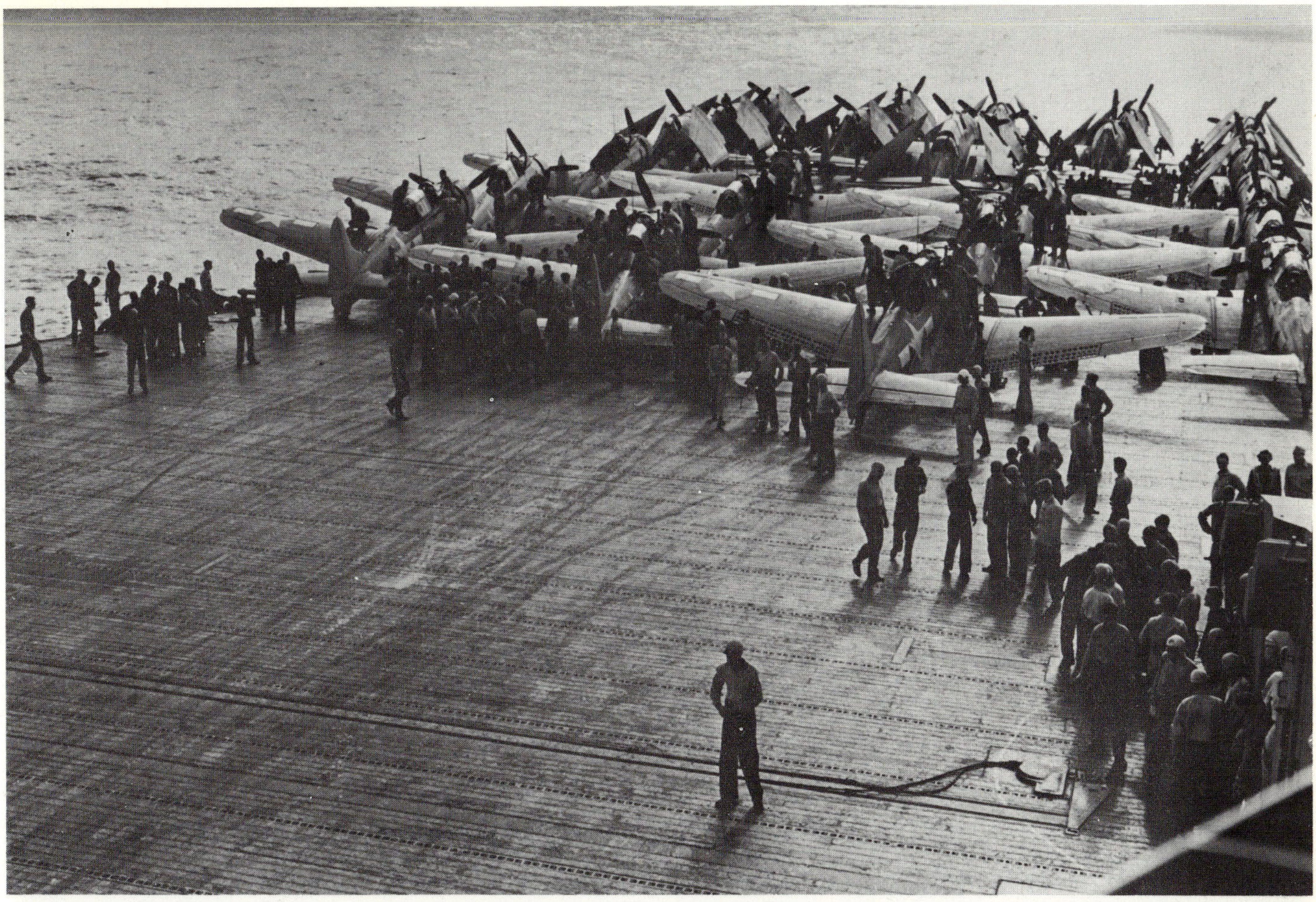

6.47

6.48

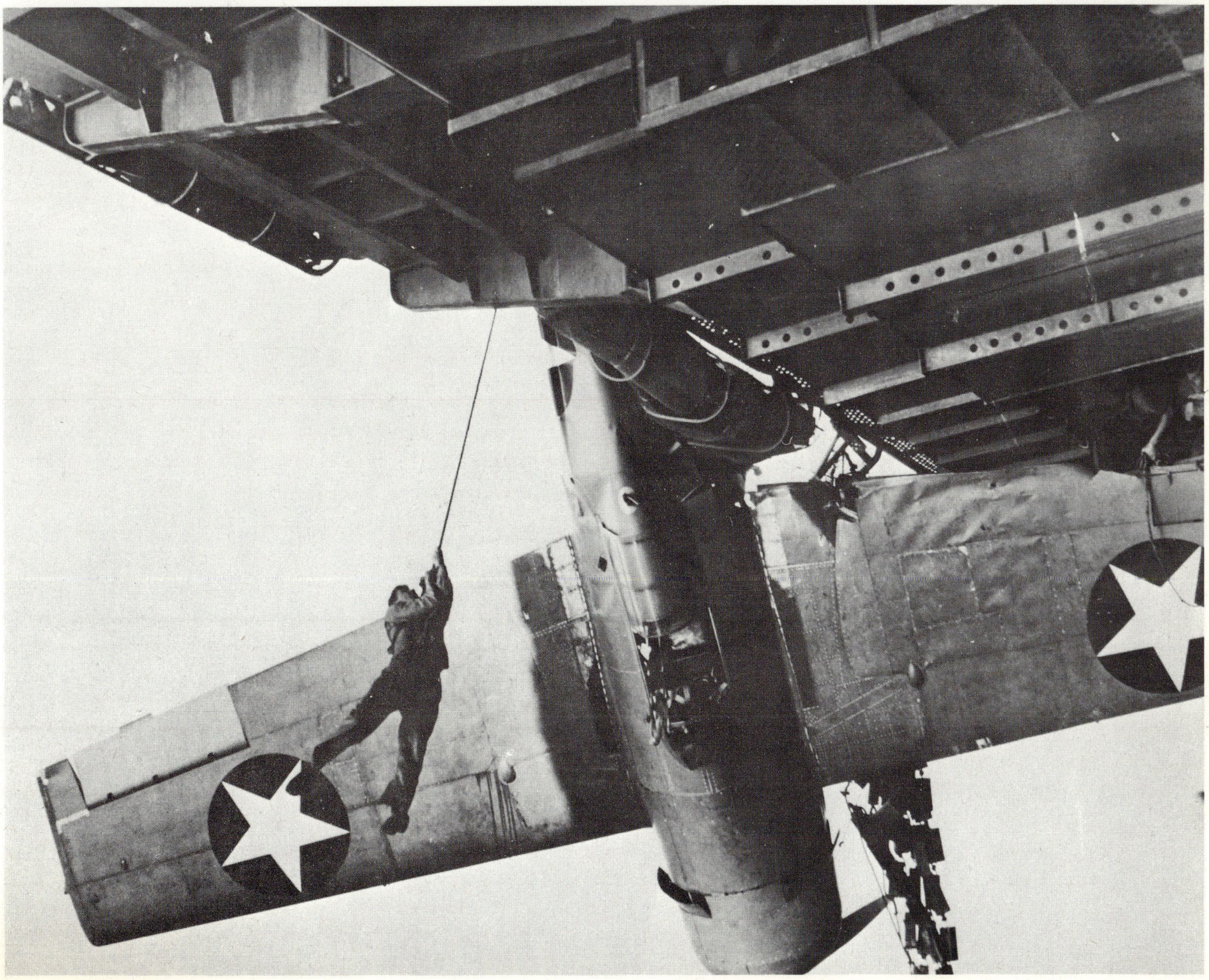

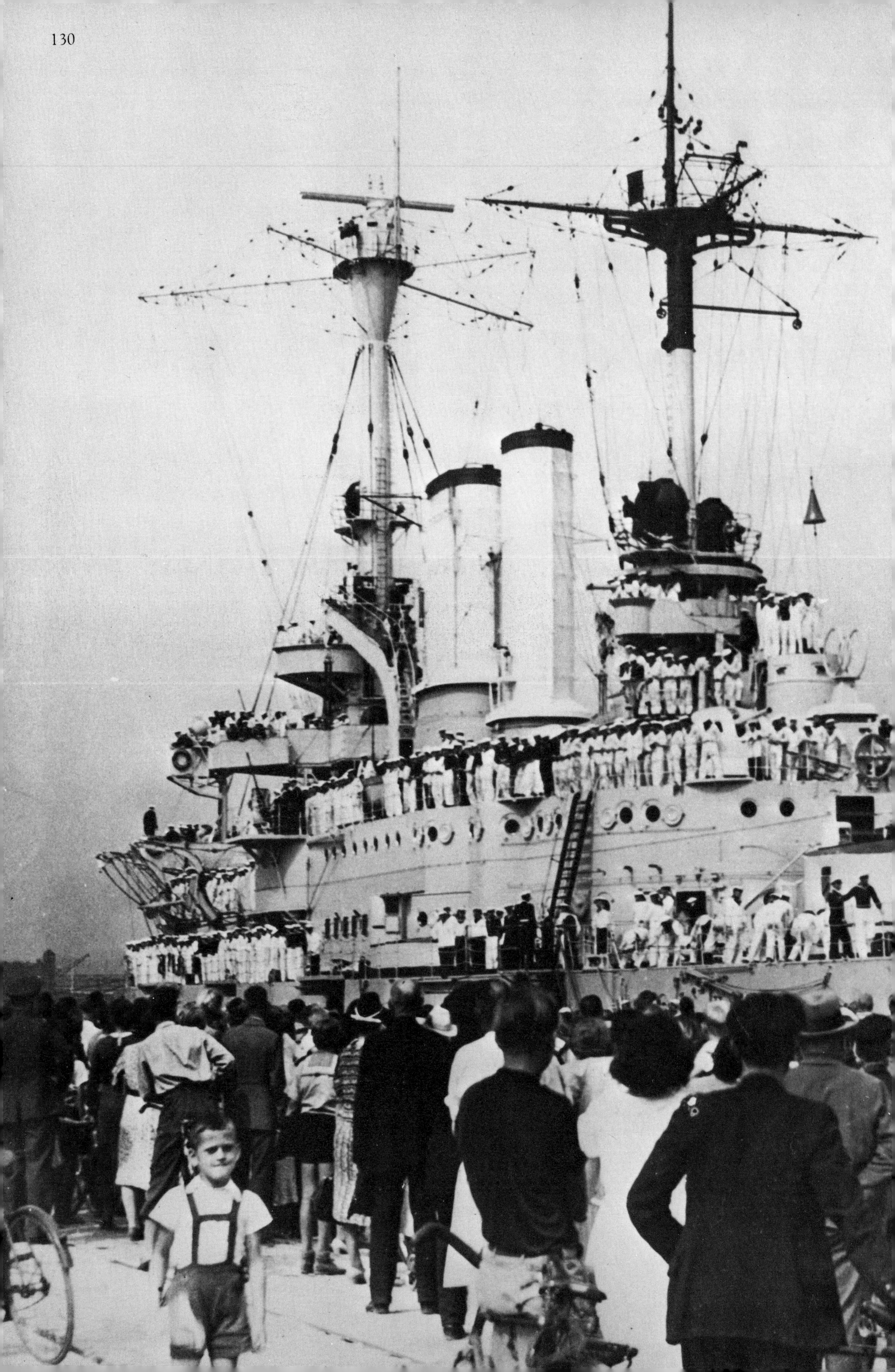

7. Operations

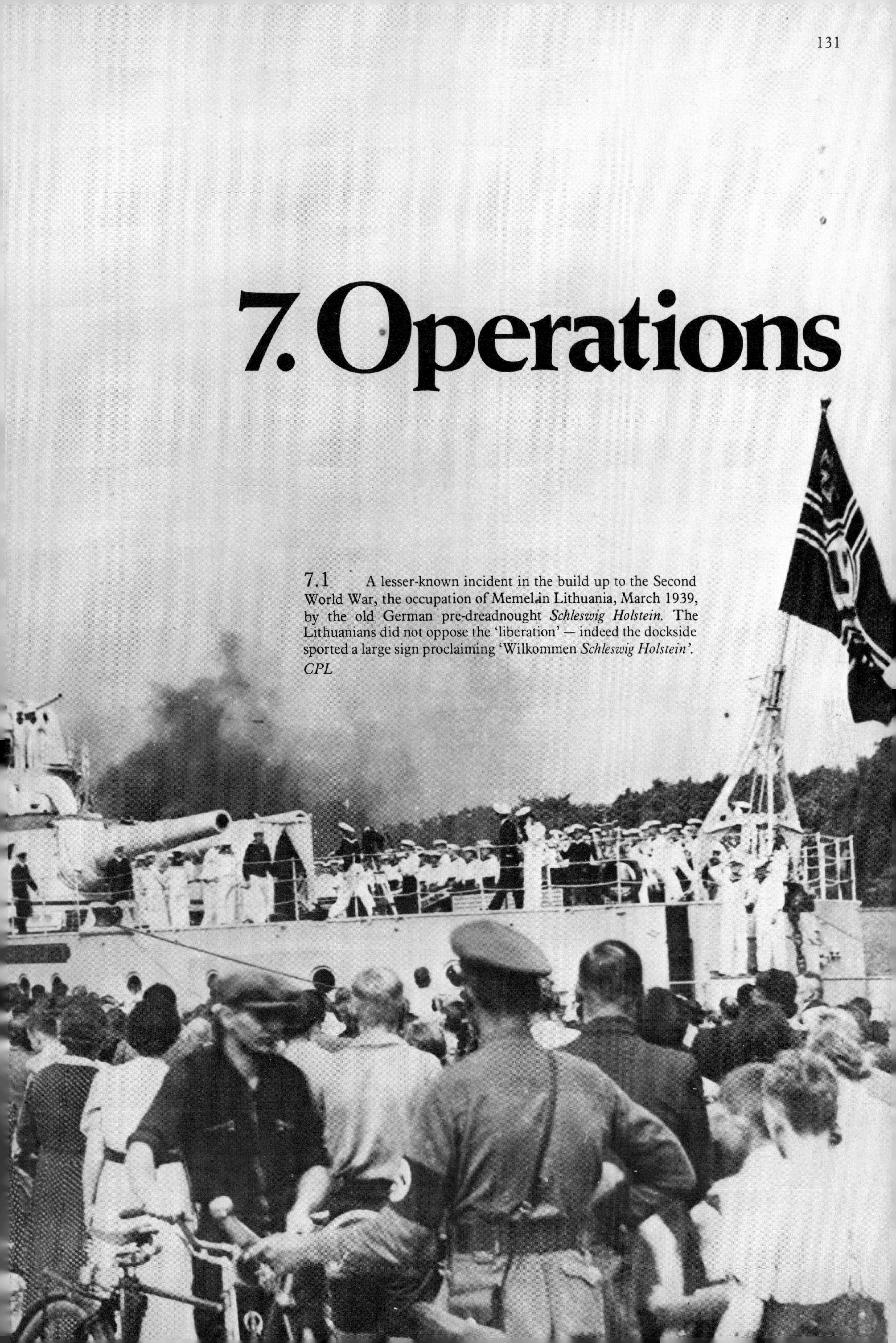

7.1 A lesser-known incident in the build up to the Second World War, the occupation of Memel in Lithuania, March 1939, by the old German pre-dreadnought *Schleswig Holstein.* The Lithuanians did not oppose the 'liberation' — indeed the dockside sported a large sign proclaiming 'Wilkommen *Schleswig Holstein'.*
CPL

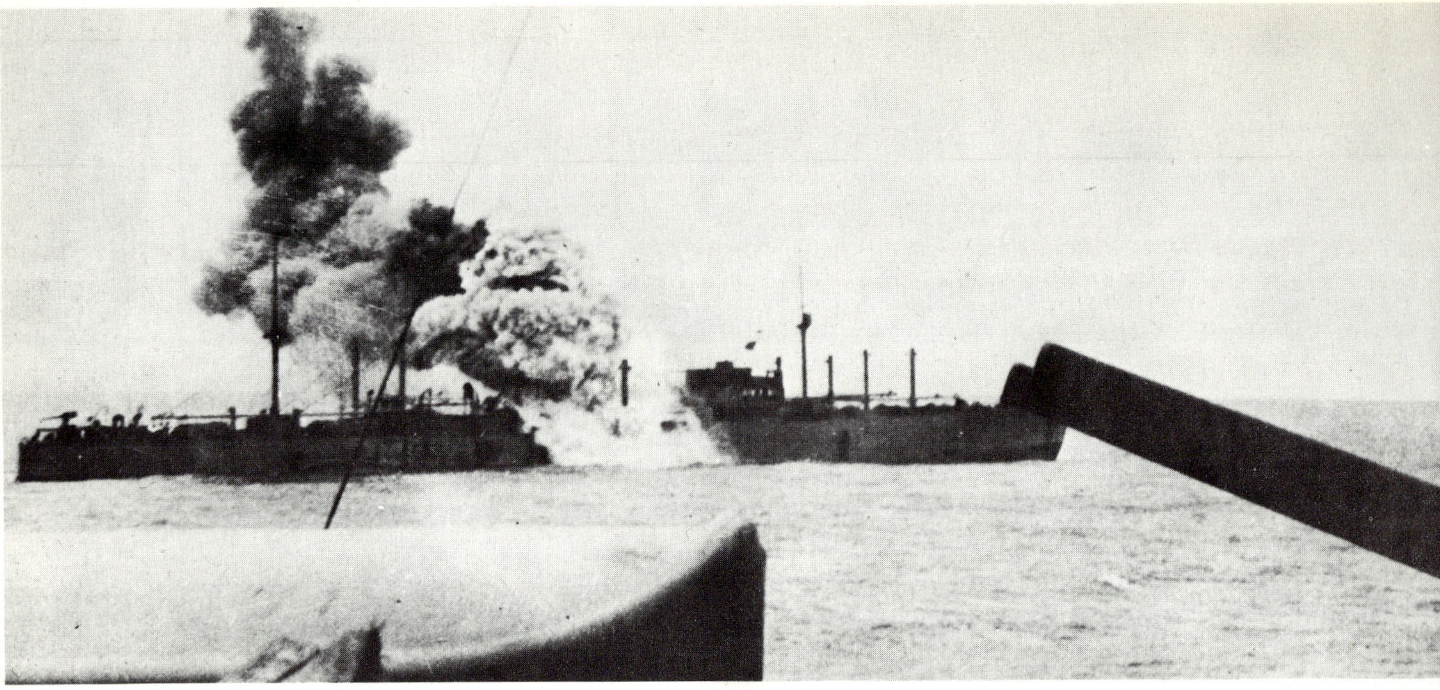

7.2

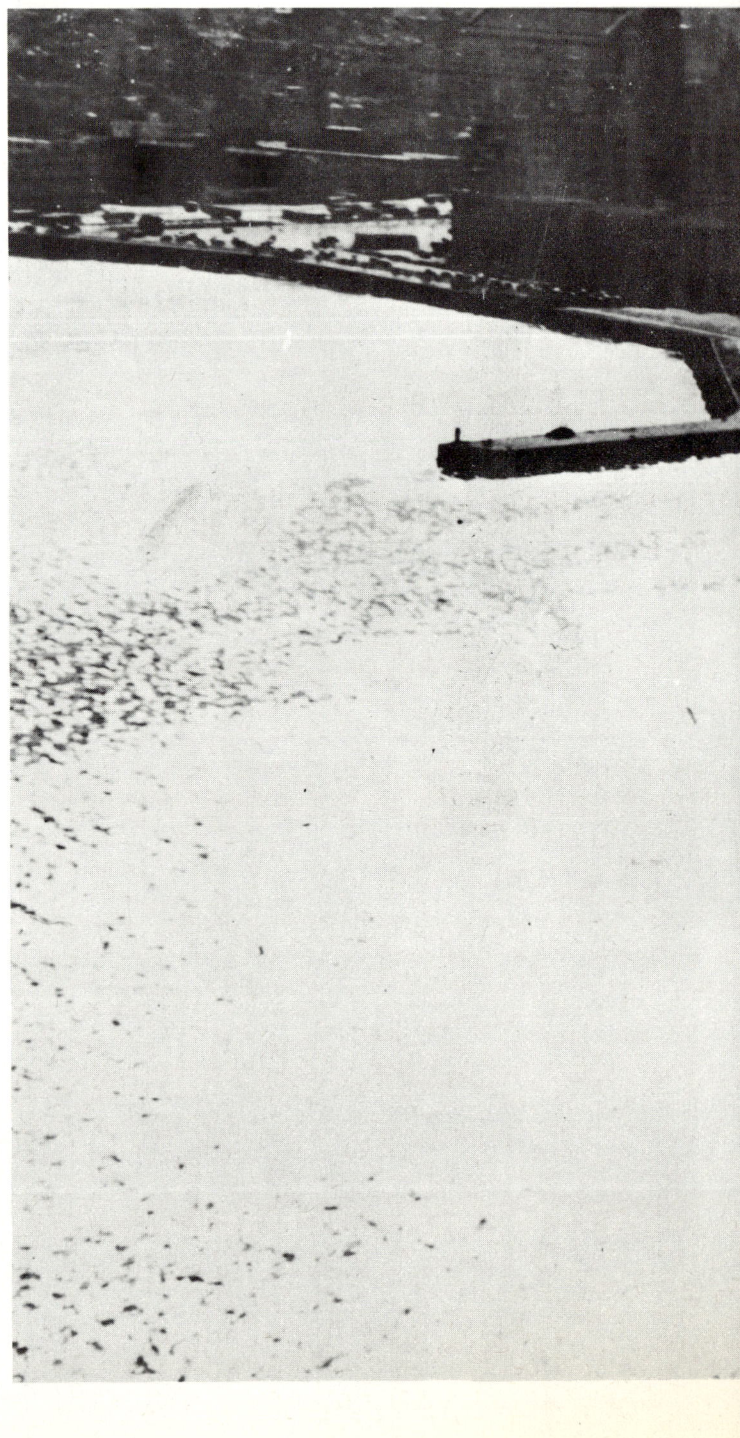

RIVER PLATE—THE FIRST NAVAL BATTLE

7.2 On 2 December 1941 the *Graf Spee* caught her seventh victim, the SS *Doric Star*. After being boarded she was torpedoed. **AP**
CPL

7.3 Between 16 and 17 October 1939 the ex-British prize *Huntsman* (right) transferred her prisoners and stores to the *Graf Spee*'s supply-tanker *Altmark* (left), before being scuttled. **AP**
CPL

7.4 Sailors of the 'pocket battleship' *Admiral Graf Spee* watch the British tramp *Ashlea* sink on the morning of 7 October 1939. This was one of her first victims. **AP**
CPL

7.5 The *Admiral Graf Spee* in Montevideo after the Battle of the River Plate, on 14 December 1939. Although by no means out of action, she was low on ammunition and had faulty machinery and needed repairs before she could put to sea. **AP**
CPL

7.4

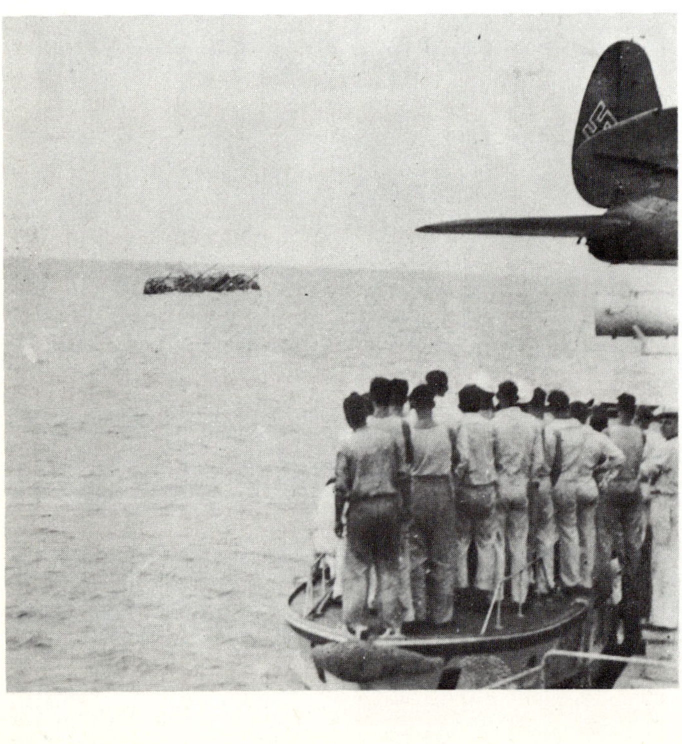

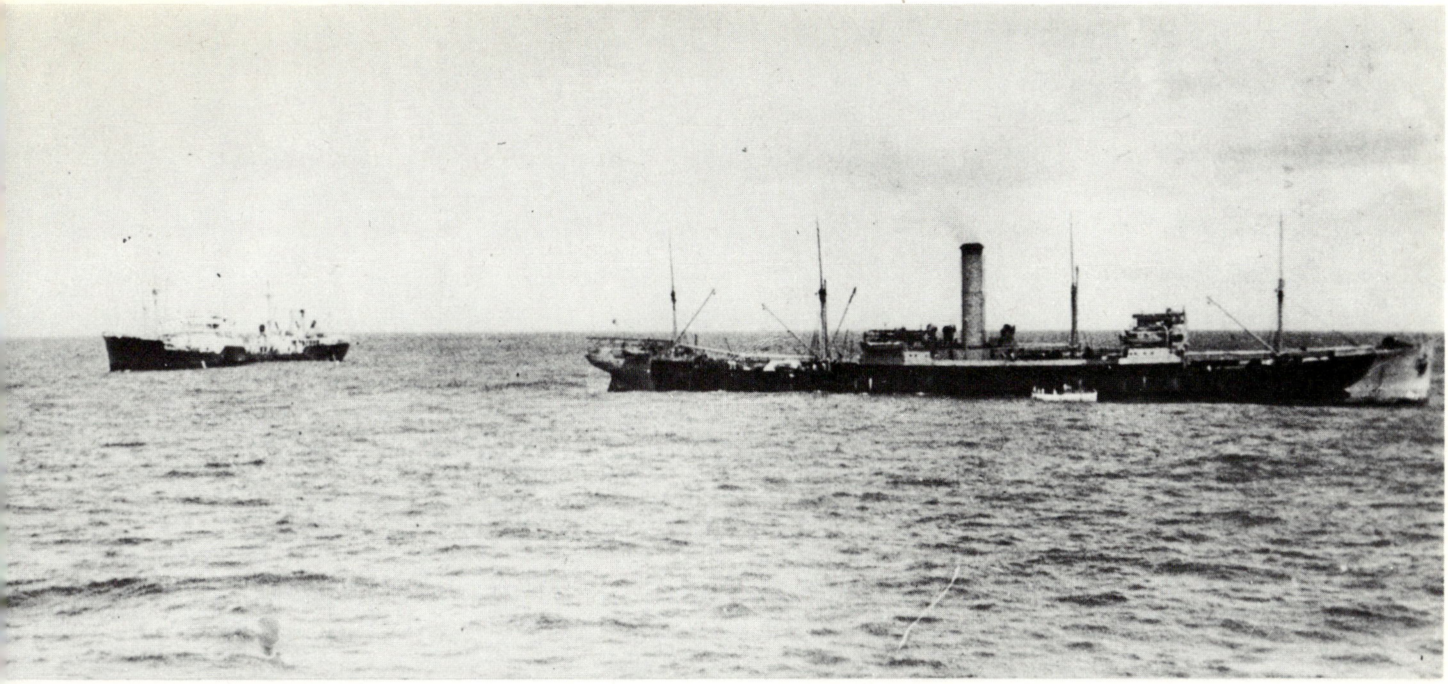

7.3

7.5

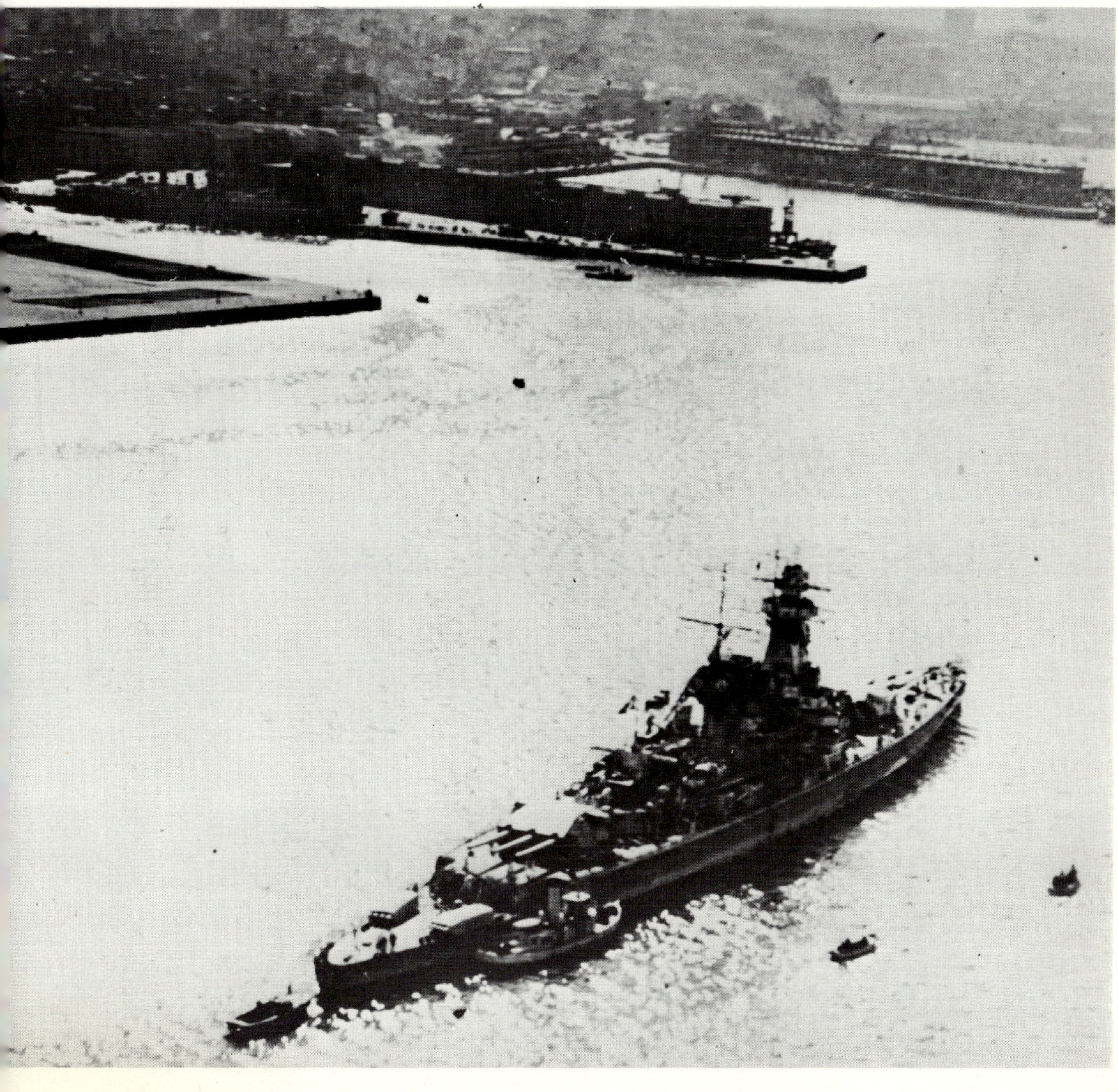

7.6 Many photographs were taken of the scuttled wreck of the *Graf Spee* but this is one of the most dramatic. This port broadside view shows how the massive funnel was blown to starboard, with smoke pouring out of the superstructure, probably from burning fuel. The control tower has already been gutted. **AP**
CPL

7.7 The battle-scarred *Exeter* returns to a hero's welcome from Devonport Dockyard. Note that she is painted in a two-tone grey camouflage scheme, and that the wrecked forward 8inch turrets have been repaired. The tall pre-war topmasts would have been struck some time before the battle. **AP**
CPL

7.8 HMS *Ajax,* Commodore Harwood's flagship, escaped with less damage than the *Exeter,* but she too had a pair of 6inch turrets knocked out. The wings of her Fairey Seafox floatplane can be seen forward of the searchlight platform and mainmast in this rare photo of the damaged ship after the battle. **AP**
CPL

7.9 HMS *Exeter*'s fore funnel, pitted and scarred by shell-splinters from the *Graf Spee*'s 11inch shells. **AP**
CPL

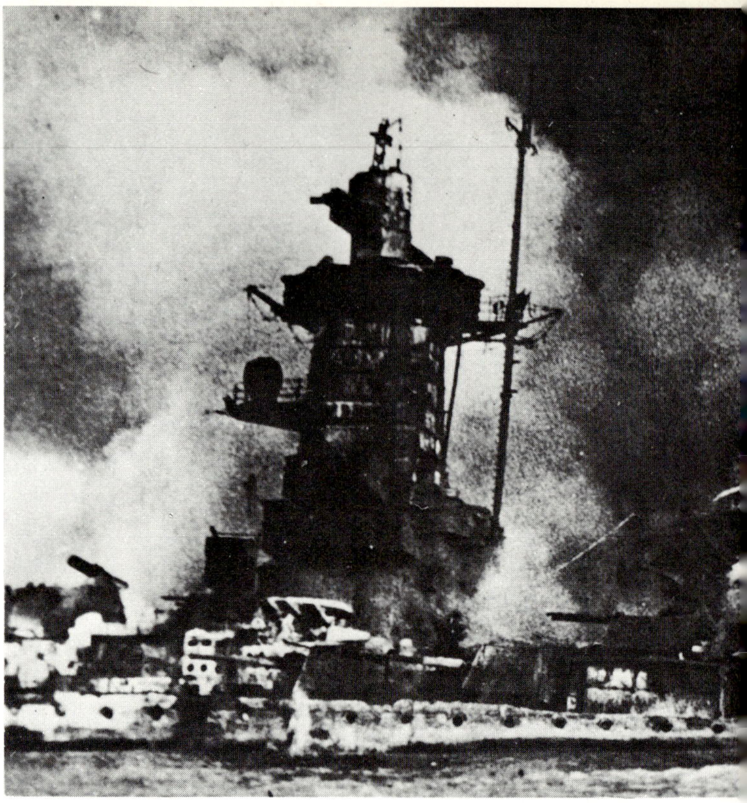

7.7

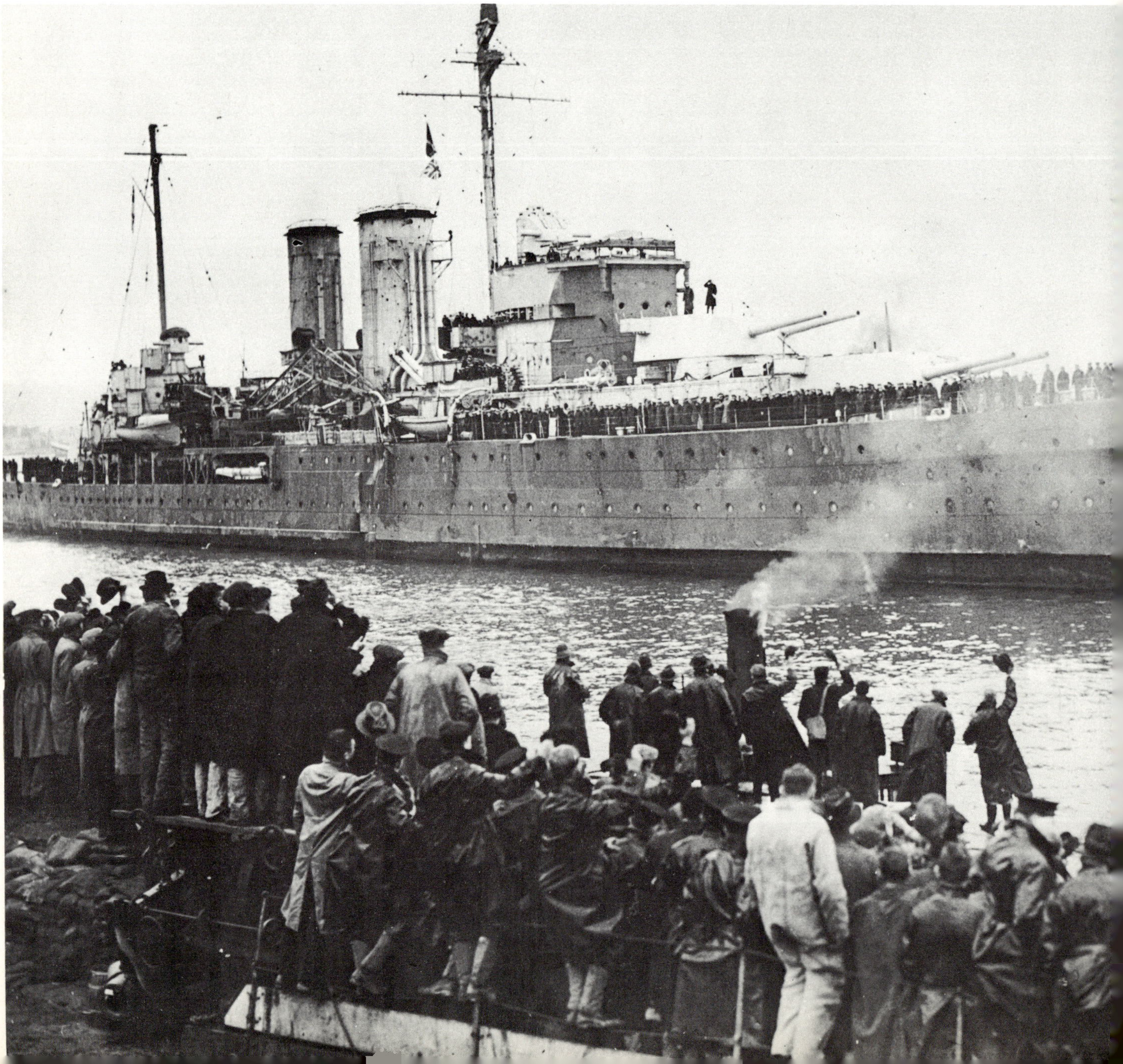

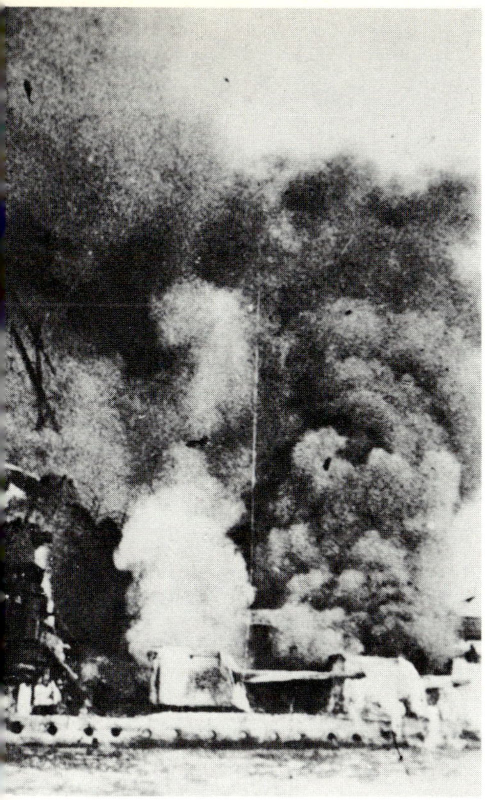

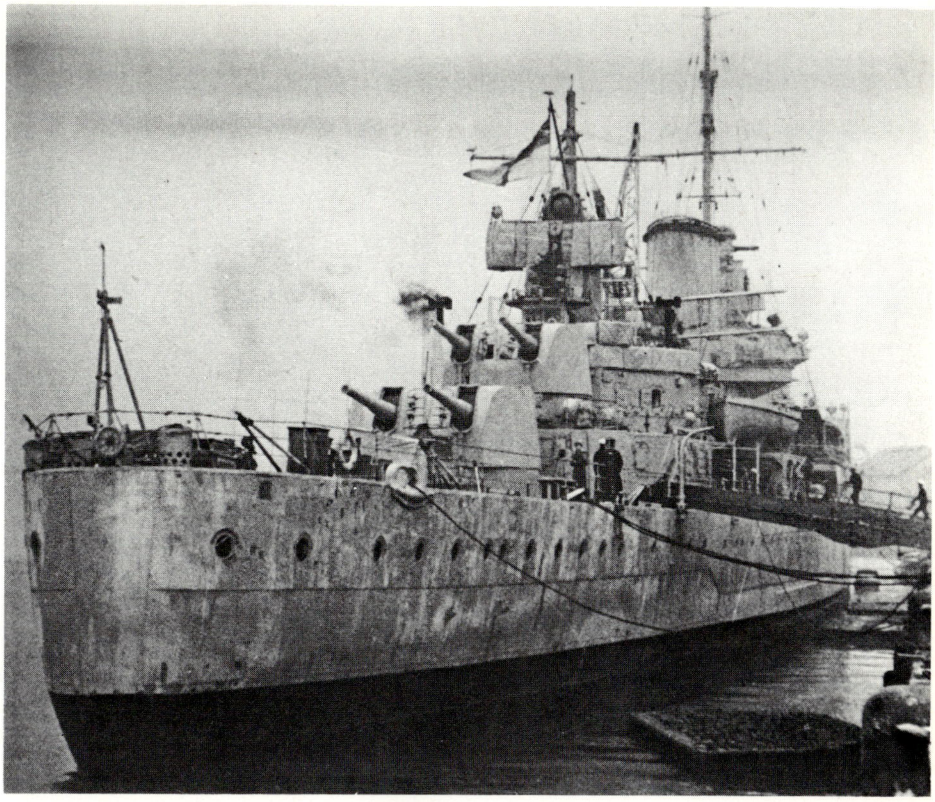

7.8

7.9

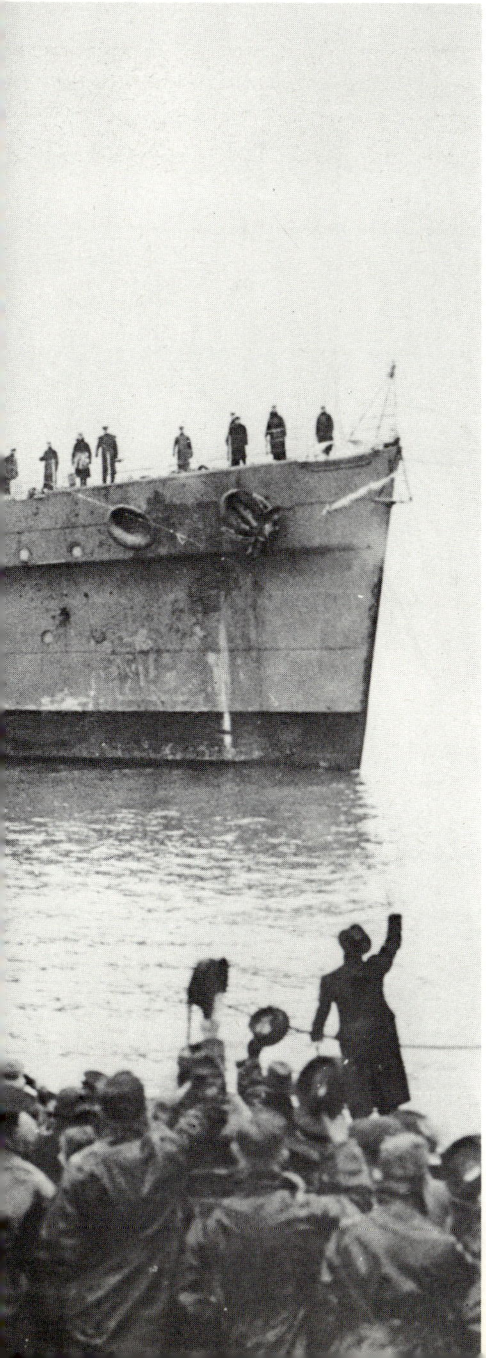

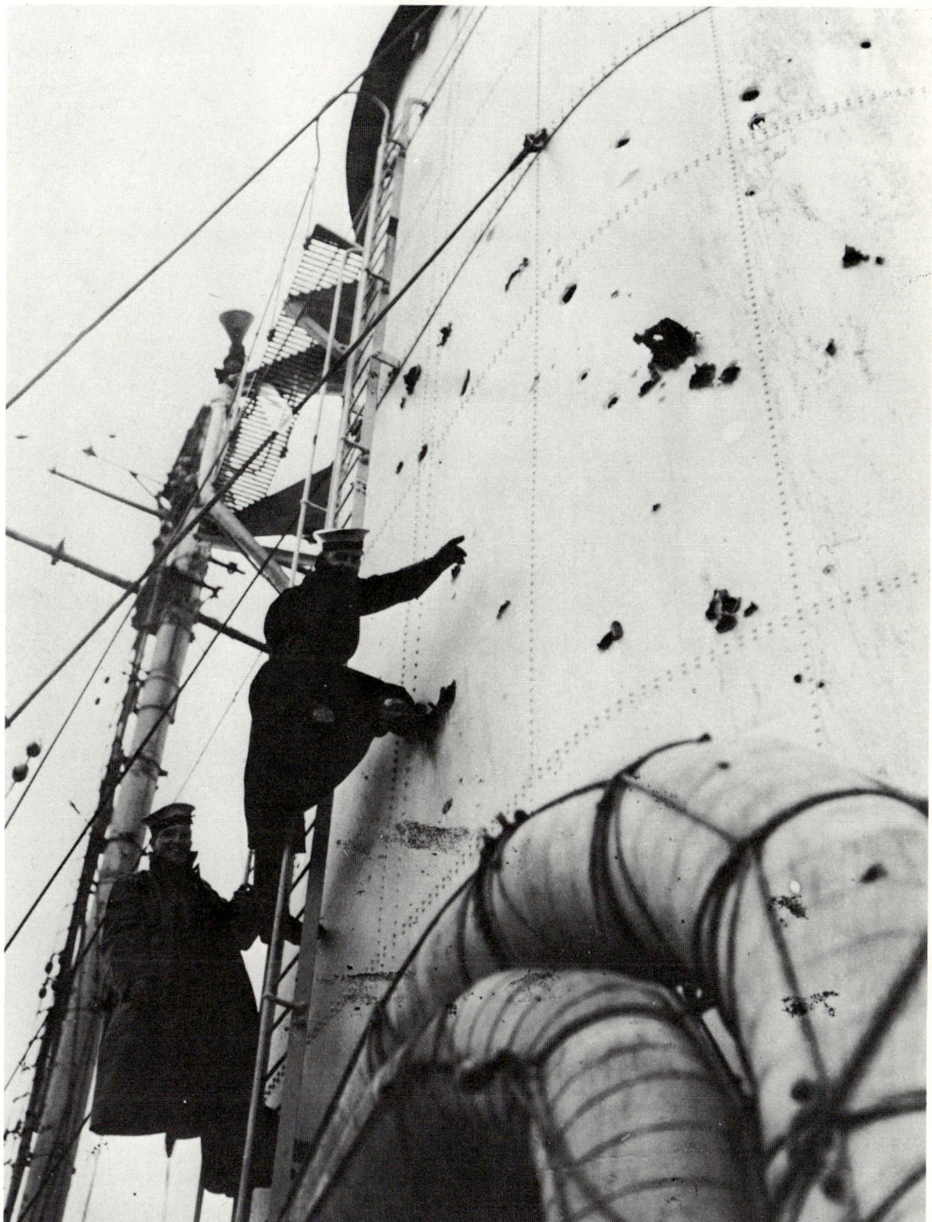

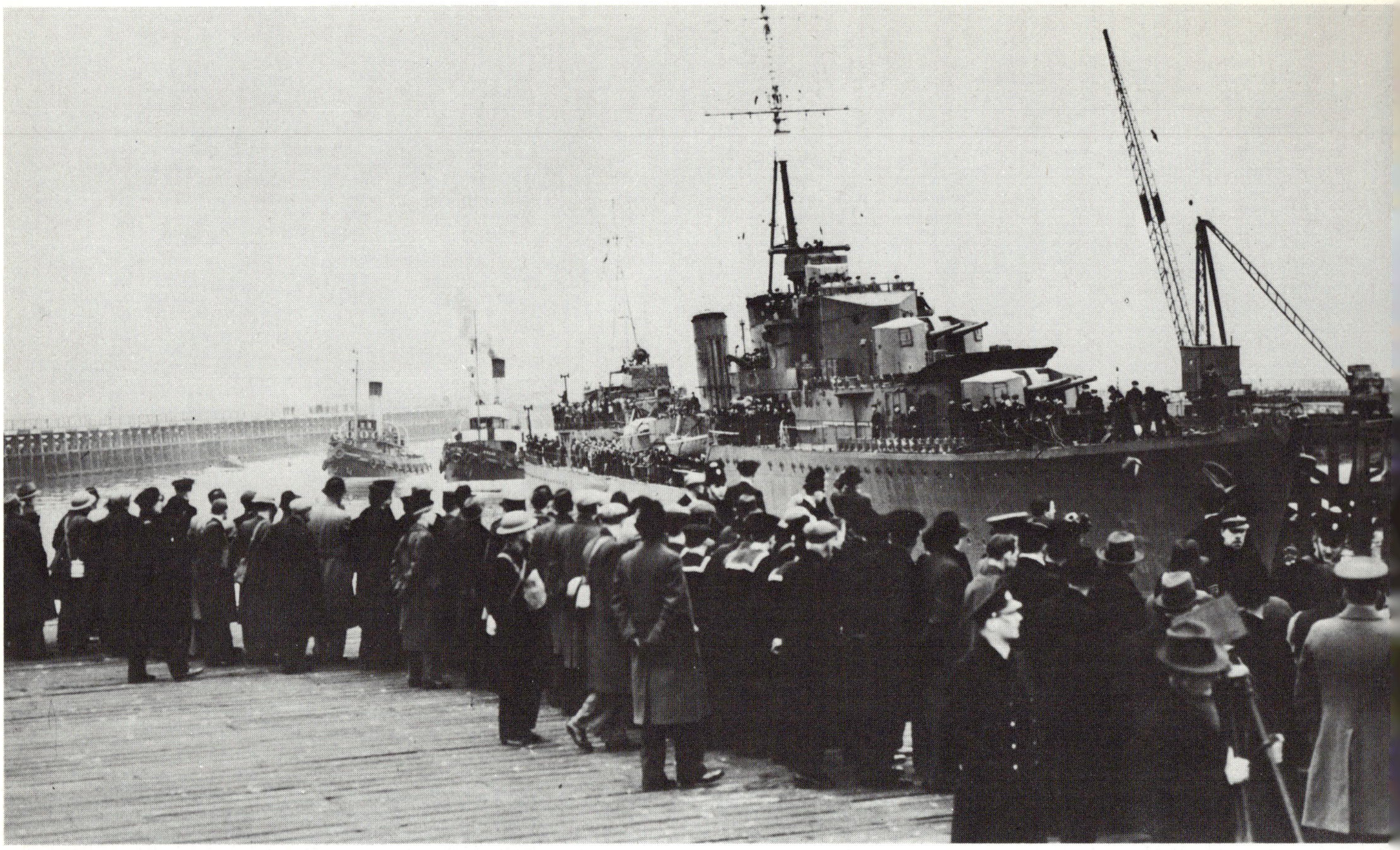

7.10

7.11

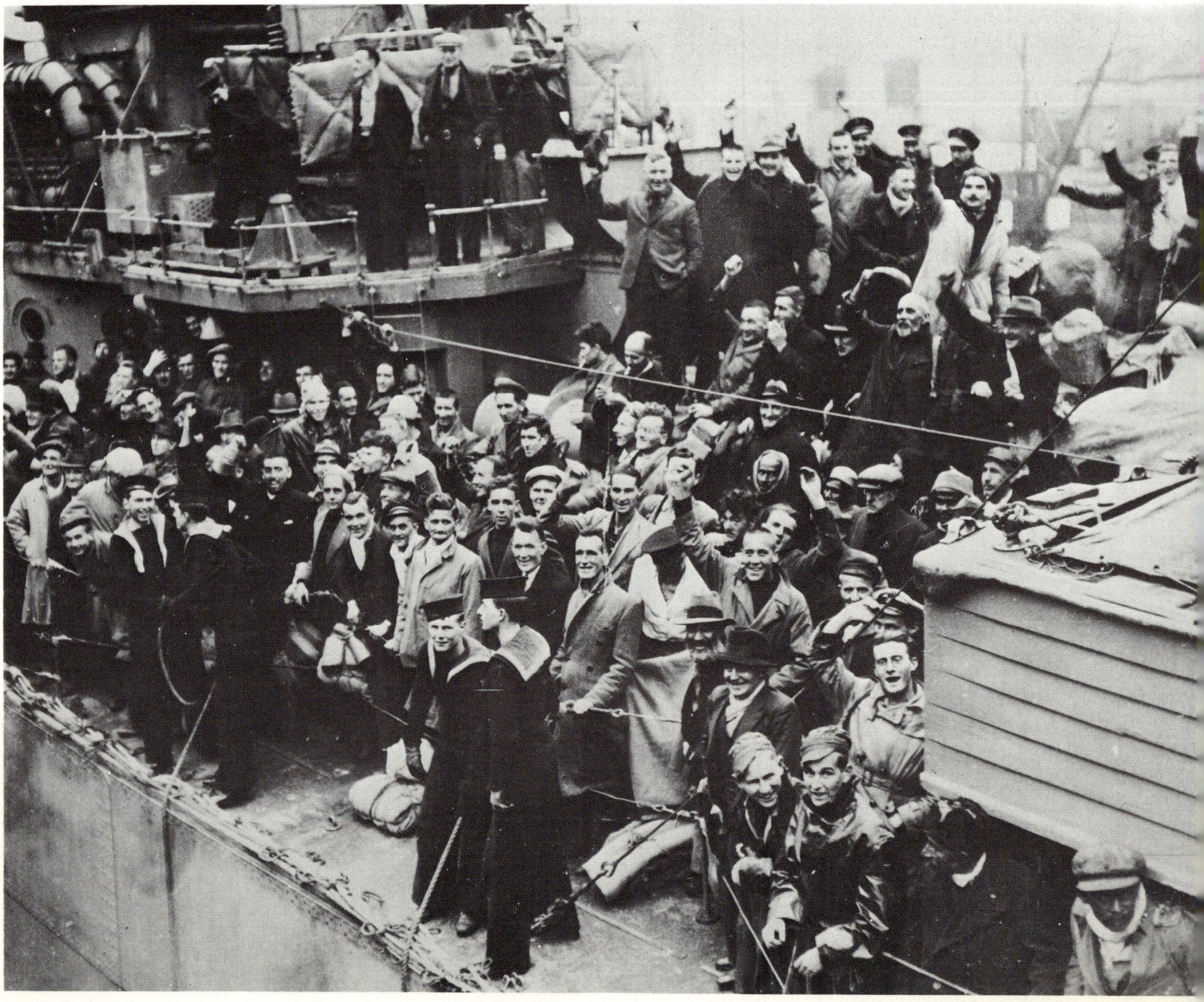

7.10 The final chapter in the *Graf Spee* story was the rescue of the British prisoners from the supply-tanker *Altmark* in Norwegian territorial waters. The destroyer *Cossack* returns to Leith with her decks packed with 300 merchant seamen and officers. The destroyer is still painted in Home Fleet grey, has no pendant number, but carries a black band on the forefunnel to indicate that she is a flotilla leader. **AP**
CPL

7.11 A crowd of ex-*Altmark* prisoners gathered in the *Cossack*'s waist, on the pom-pom platform and even on the quadruple 21inch torpedo-tubes. **AP**
CPL

7.12 The invasion of Norway — Operation *Weserübung* — was a large operation which required nearly all the German surface and submarine forces. For Narvik: ten large destroyers (one of which is shown in this photograph) carrying 2000 Alpine troops, and the battleships *Scharnhorst* and *Gneisenau* as the covering force; for Trondheim: the heavy cruiser *Admiral Hipper* and four large destroyers carrying 700 troops, plus one tanker and three supply ships; for Bergen: the light cruisers *Köln* and *Königsberg,* three minor vessels, seven motor torpedo-boats, one depot ship carrying 1900 troops, one tanker and three supply ships; for Christiansand and Arendal: the light cruiser *Karlsruhe,* three torpedo-boats, one MTB flotilla, one depot ship, four merchant transports with 1100 troops; for Oslo: the heavy cruisers *Blücher* and *Lützow* (ex 'pocket battleship' *Deutschland*), the light cruiser *Emden,* three torpedo-boats, eight minesweepers, two whalers (auxiliary sub-chasers), 2000 troops, two tankers, five supply ships; plus, the supplies to be sent in the following days, totalling 23 transports, carrying another 14 500 troops, 1900 horses, 2800 vehicles, 8200 tons of material; for Egersund: four minesweepers. In addition: air landings at Stavanger (two battalions with *Flak* — AA guns and machine guns), one tanker and four transports; four minelayers and four minesweepers west of the Skagerrak; and nine groups of *U-boote,* comprising 35 boats, sent off the Norwegian coasts, to the Orkneys-Shetlands area and to the eastern end of the Channel. **AF**
Aldo Fraccaroli Collection

7.12

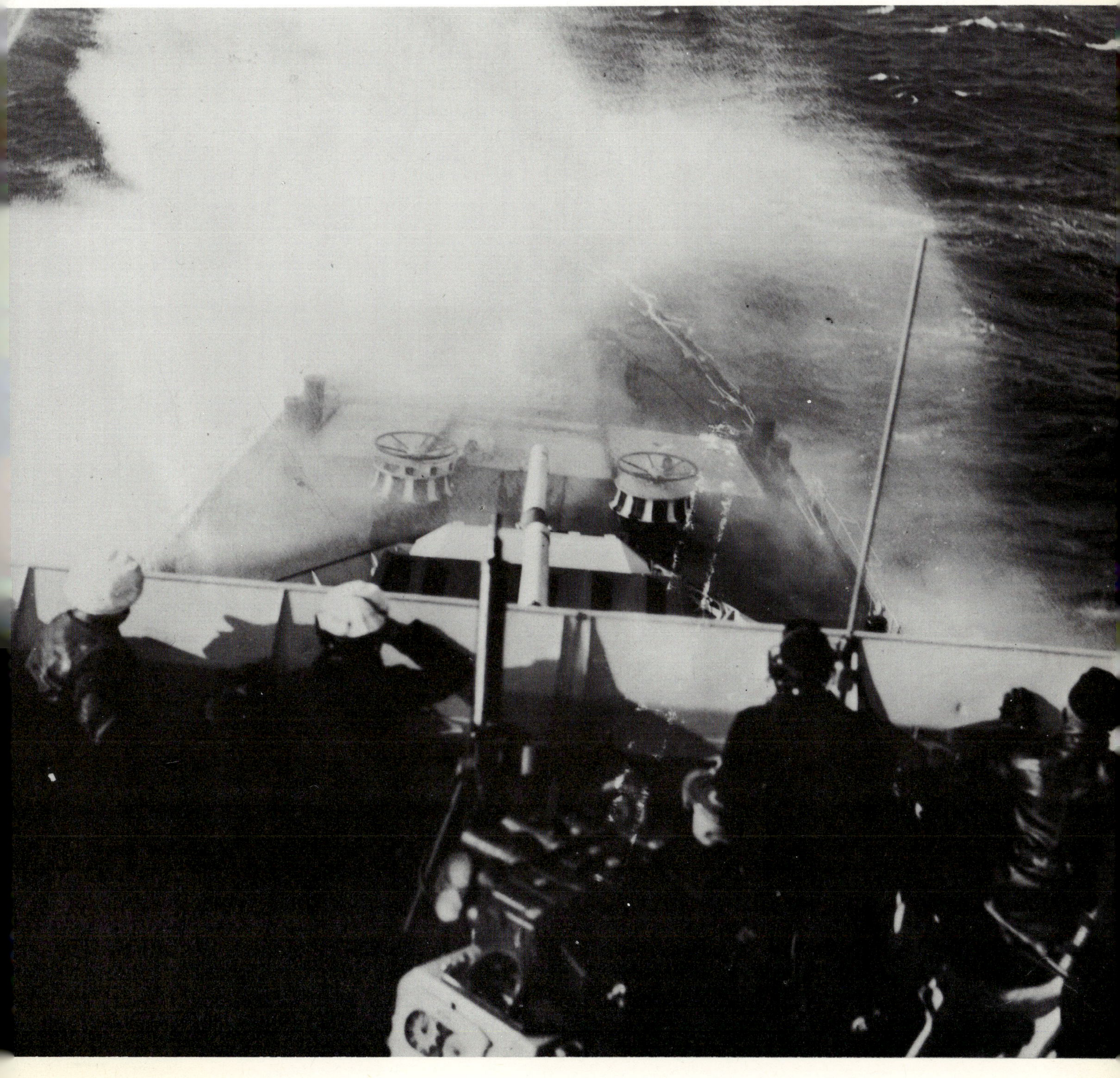

7.13

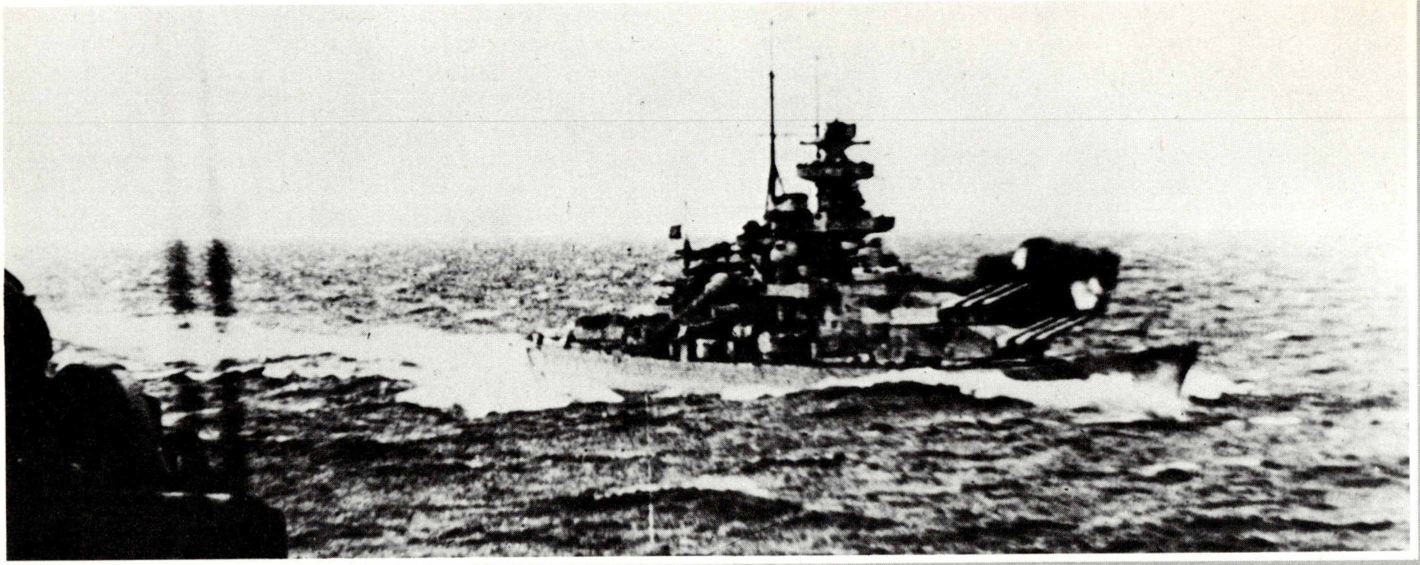

7.13 On 4 June 1940 a German squadron comprising the battleships *Scharnhorst* (Admiral Marschall's flag) and *Gneisenau,* the cruisers *Admiral Hipper* and four destroyers began an operation for easing the British pressure on the German forces at Narvik. During the mission, the squadron hit with gunfire (8 June) the tanker *Oil Pioneer* and her escorting trawler, *Juniper,* and the empty troopship *Orama,* all of which were sunk. Later the squadron sank the aircraft carrier *Glorious* and her attendant destroyers, *Ardent* and *Acasta,* the last of which was able to launch a salvo of torpedoes, one of which hit the German flagship, making a hole of 12 x 14 m through which the hull was flooded with 2500 tons of water. This photograph shows the *Gneisenau* firing her 280mm guns (54.5 calibre) at HMS *Glorious.* **AF**
Aldo Fraccaroli Collection

7.14 This view, taken from aboard the battleship *Tirpitz* (of which the 380mm fore turrets and the conning tower can be seen) and the light cruiser *Nürnberg* in autumn 1941. The *Nürnberg* was the last light cruiser built during a period from 1921 to 1935: she displaced 8380 tons at full load, had a speed of 32 knots, and an armament of nine 5.9inch and six (later eight) 3.5inch AA guns, eight 37mm and a number of 20mm machine guns, twelve 21inch torpedo-tubes (which were reduced to six in 1941). **AF**
Aldo Fraccaroli Collection

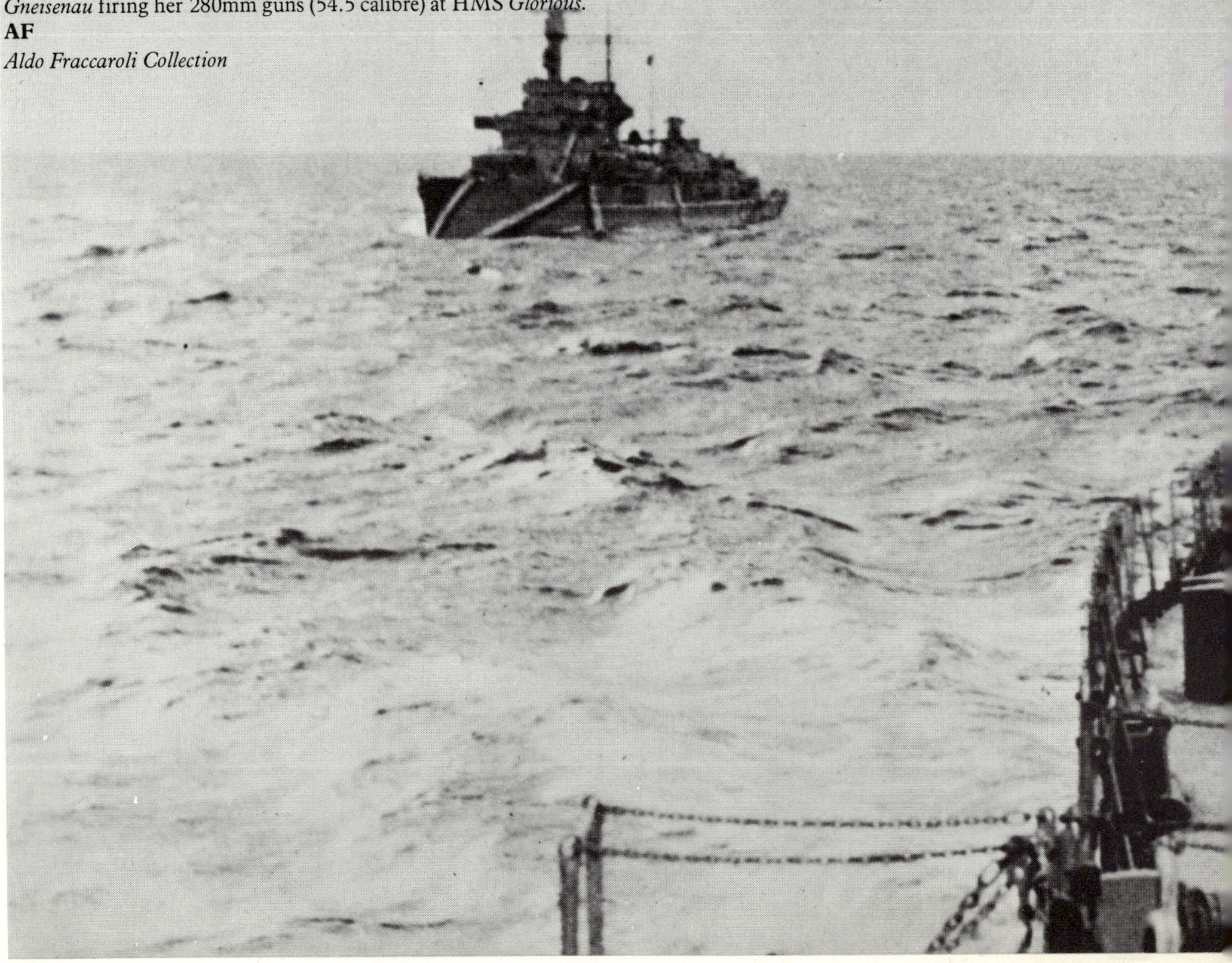

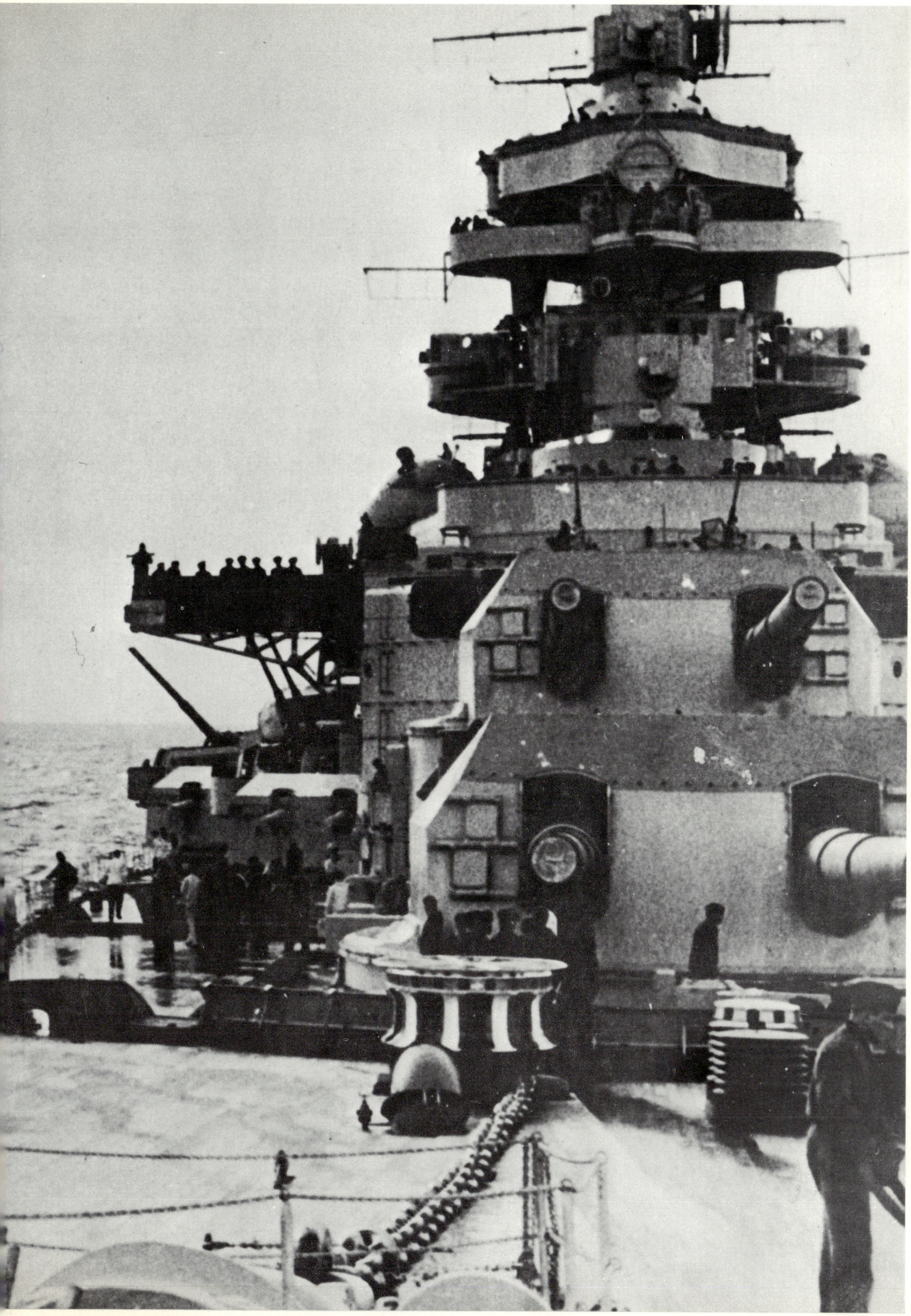

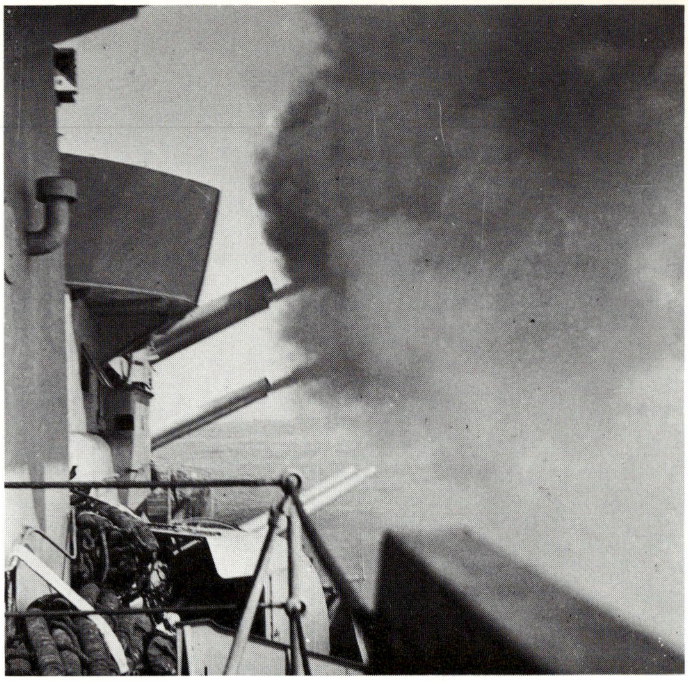

7.15

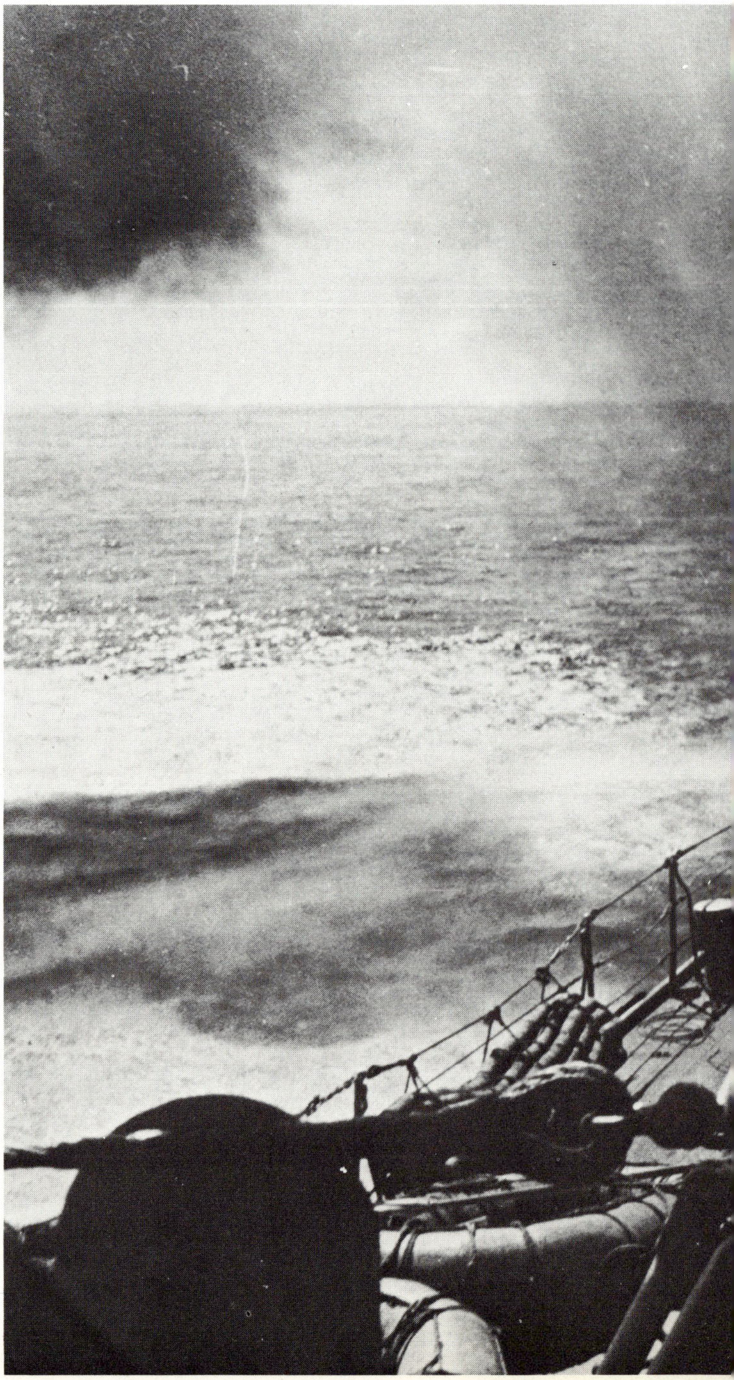

Three photographs taken on board the battleship *Warspite* during the bombardment of Brest on 25 August 1944. It was on this day that she had rejoined the bombardment force having just completed repairs necessitated by mine damage received on 13 June. These repairs were only sufficient to make her operationally fit as a bombarding ship, and she had one propeller shaft, one boiler room and 'X' turret out of action (these last two were due to earlier damage received off Salerno in 1943 when she was hit by a glider bomb) plus numerous minor defects.

7.15 Looking forward along the starboard side a fraction of a second after the left guns of 'A' and 'B' turrets have fired. As modified the 15inch guns fired a 1938lb shell at a muzzle velocity of 2600 feet per second. In the foreground is one of her four twin 4inch Mk XIX HA/LA (high angle/low angle) mountings. **JR**
CPL

7.16 The forecastle from the bridge showing the four 15inch Mk 1 guns of 'A' and 'B' turrets. These guns and mountings were among the most successful and efficient heavy ordnance ever manufactured and saw front line service from 1915 to the early 1950s. In the 1930s they were 'modernised' by the provision of new ammunition and by raising the elevation of the guns from 20 to 30 degrees which increased the maximum range from 23 700 yards to 32 200 yards. Two single 20mm Oerlikons were mounted on the roof of each of her four twin 15inch Mk I mountings. **JR**
CPL

7.17 Looking aft along the starboard side during the bombardment: note that 'Y' turret is in action but the inoperative 'X' turret is still trained fore and aft. Just visible in the shadow of the right foreground, on what was the catapult deck, are three single Oerlikons added in 1942 (together with another three on the port side) when the catapult was removed. At the after end of the forecastle deck are two twin Mk V Oerlikon mountings which replaced the singles in those positions (port and starboard) in June 1944. **JR**
CPL

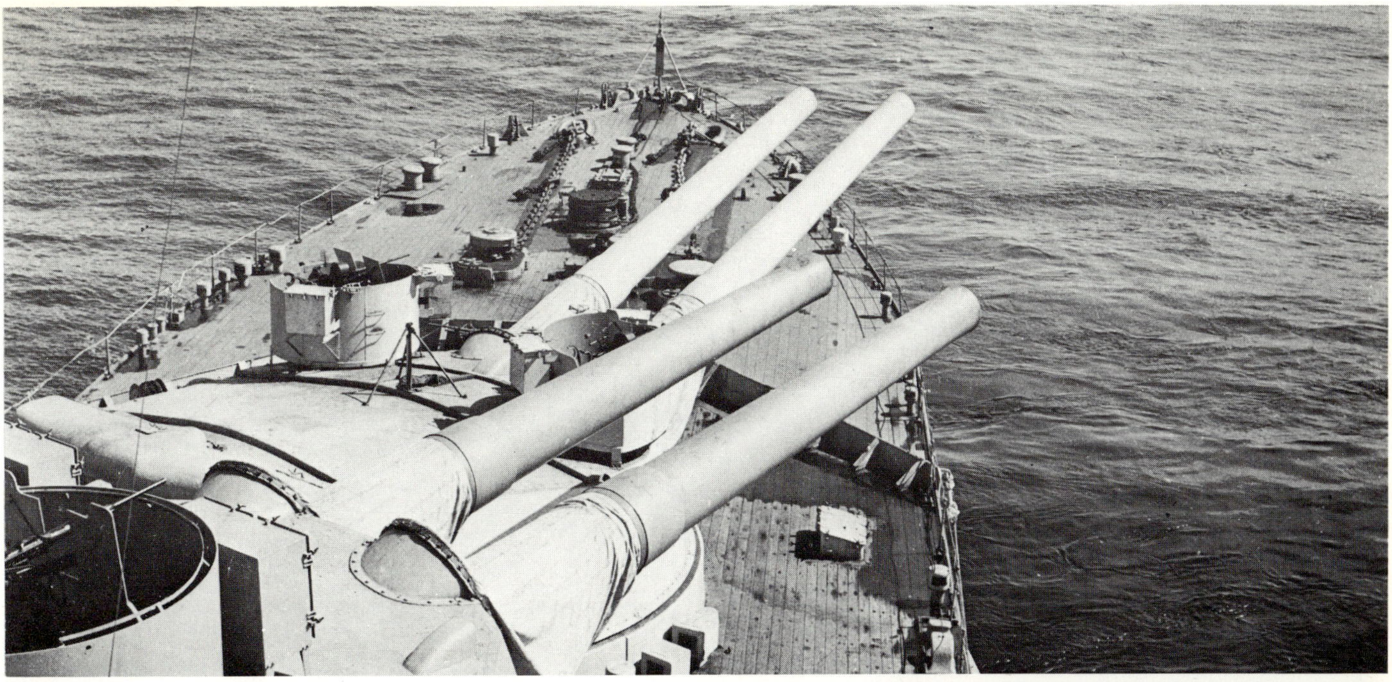

7.16

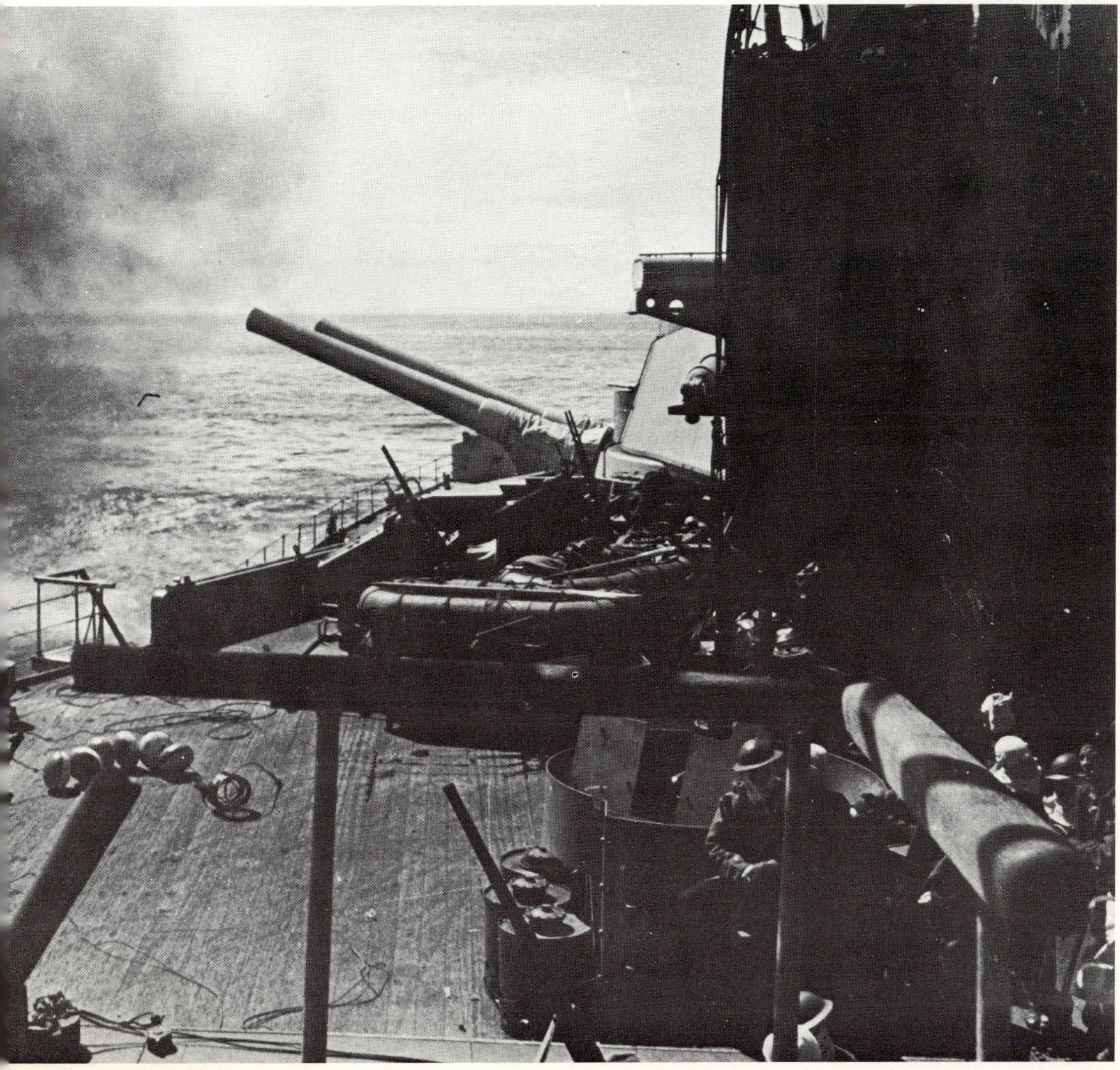

7.17

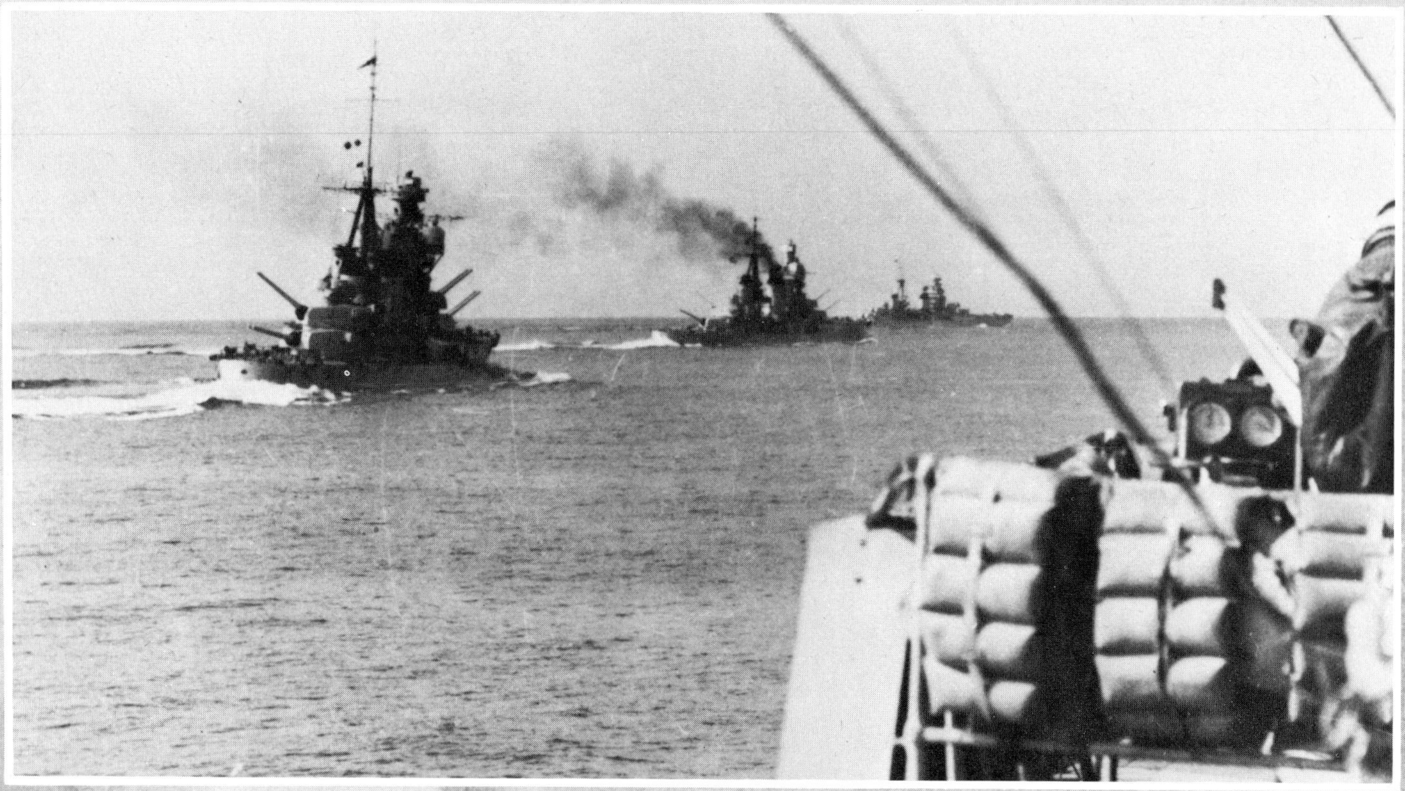

7.18

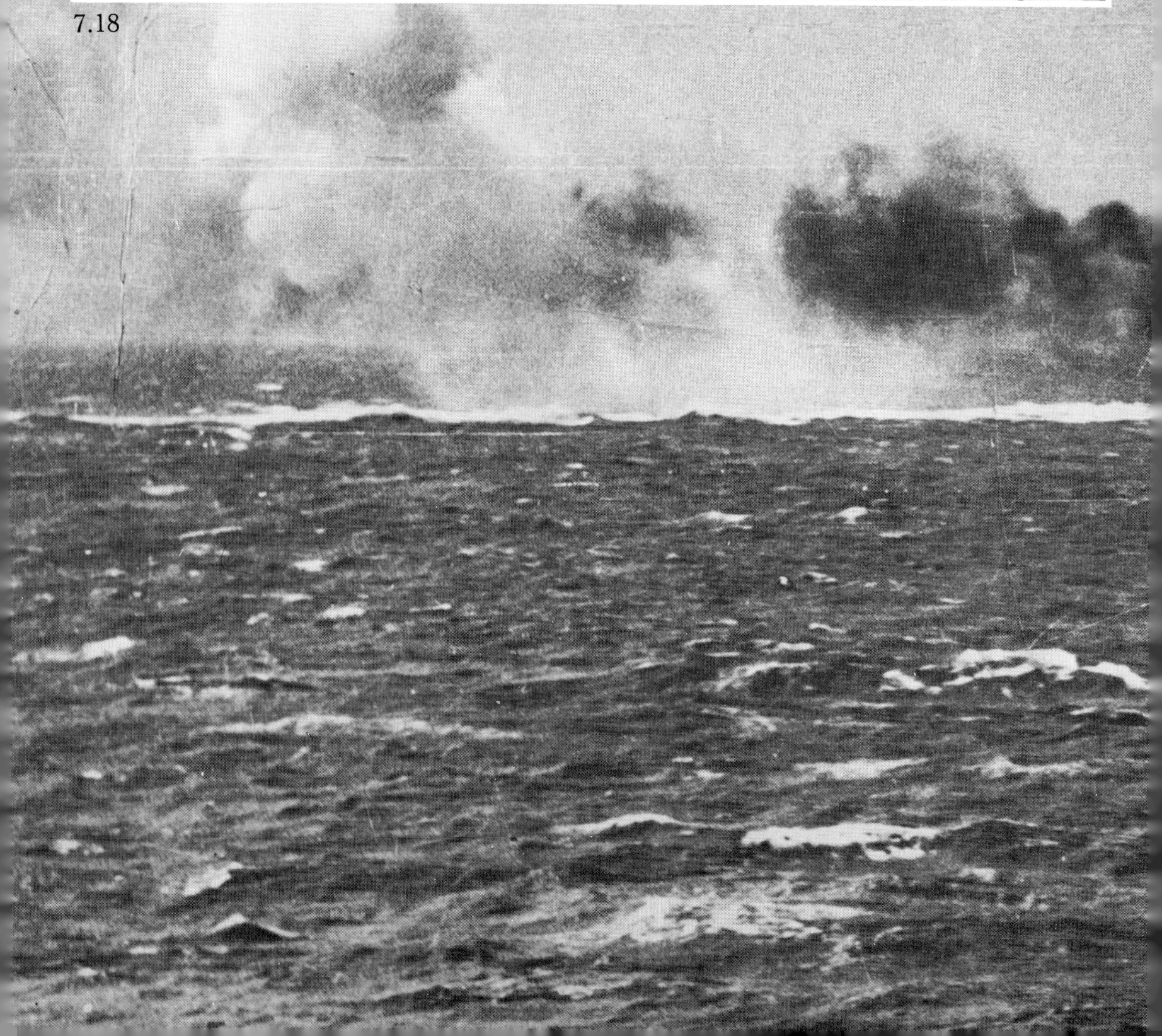

The Mediterranean

7.18 The First Cruiser Division of the Italian Fleet during exercises in autumn 1940. Left to right, they are *Fiume, Gorizia* and *Zara* (plus *Pola*), heavy 8inch gunned cruisers of about 14 400 tons at full load. Built from 1929 to 1932, they were good sea ships, sufficiently fast (practical best sea speed, 29 knots, but during speed trials, with a light displacement, they exceeded 35 knots, while designed for 32), armed with eight 8inch and twelve 3.9inch AA guns; no torpedo-tubes; two aircraft. They were well protected, but obviously 15inch projectiles from the British battleships were too much for them, and during the night of 28-29 March 1941, *Fiume* and *Zara* were crippled and sunk in the action off Cape Matapan, followed by *Pola,* which had been struck that evening by an aircraft torpedo, and later by two other torpedoes launched by British destroyers. **AF**
Photograph by Aldo Fraccaroli

7.19 The second Battle of Sirte, 22 March 1942, originated in an attempt by the Italian fleet to intercept a British convoy from Alexandria to Malta, under the escort of five light and AA cruisers, eleven destroyers and six escort destroyers, under Rear Admiral Philip Vian's command. The first Italian group, comprising the heavy cruisers *Gorizia* (Rear Admiral Angelo Parona's flag) and *Trento,* the light cruiser *Bande Nere* and four destroyers, sighted the British forces and, supported by the battleship *Littorio* (Admiral Angelo Iachino's flag), escorted by three destroyers, attacked them. Vian's tactical manoeuvres were very able, and his well-trained ships repeatedly dashing from the thick smoke screens threatened the Italian forces with torpedo attack. They were provided with radar, while there were no radar sets aboard the Italian vessels. However, Iachino succeeded in delaying the arrival of the British convoy at Malta, and only two of the four British transports entered the Grand Harbour, because two of them had been sunk by Italo-German air attacks: the other two were sunk in the harbour, and only 5000 tons of supplies (out of a total of 25 000) could be safely discharged. Two British destroyers were also sunk in harbour, but two Italian destroyers were lost in a violent storm, while returning to Taranto. Here *Gorizia* is seen at speed during the action. **AF**
Photograph by Aldo Fraccaroli

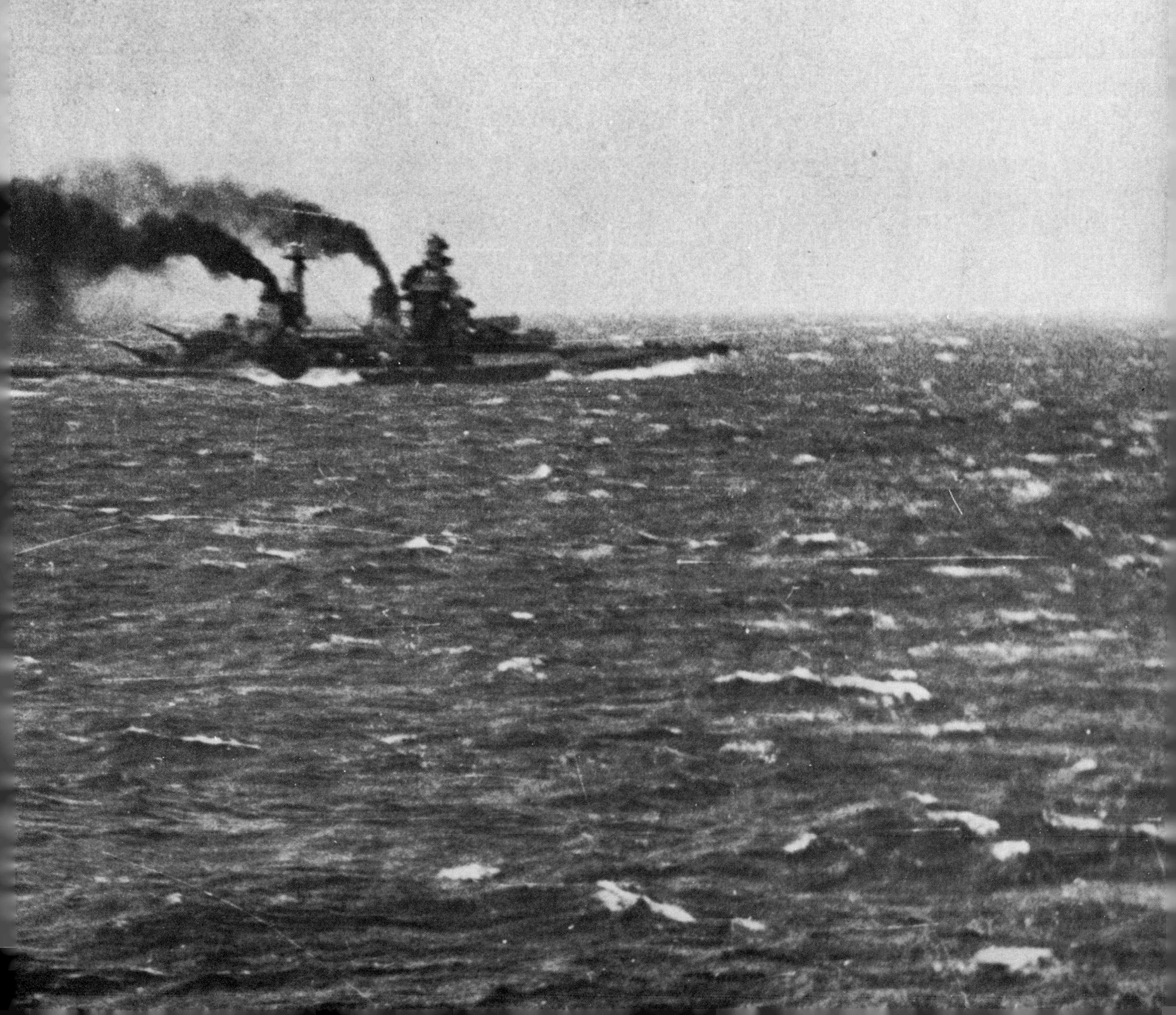

7.20

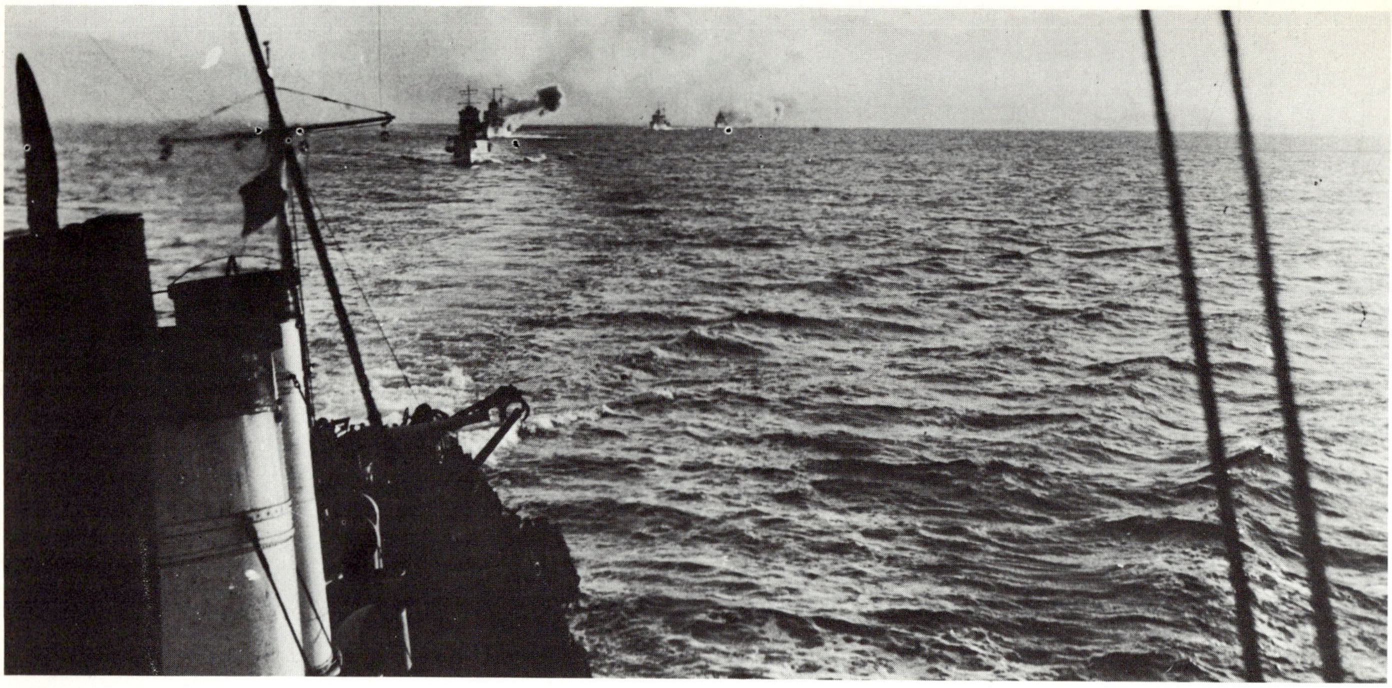

7.21

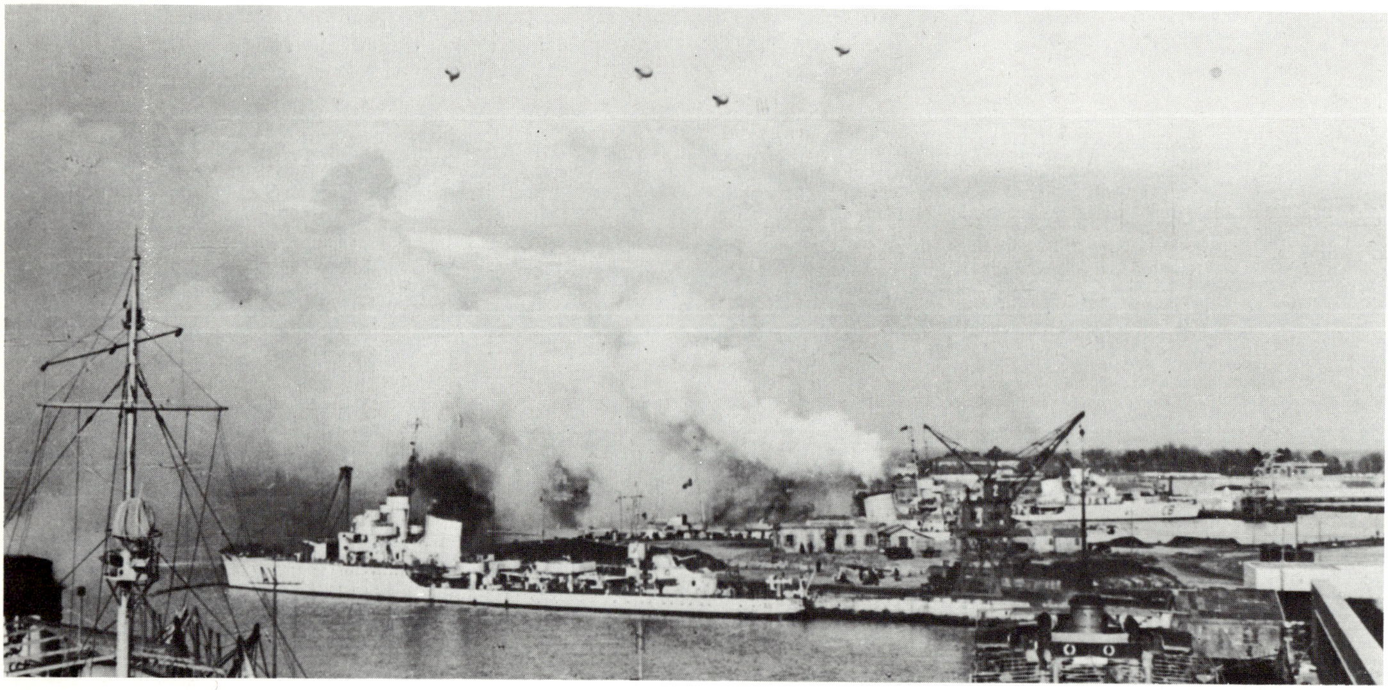

7.22

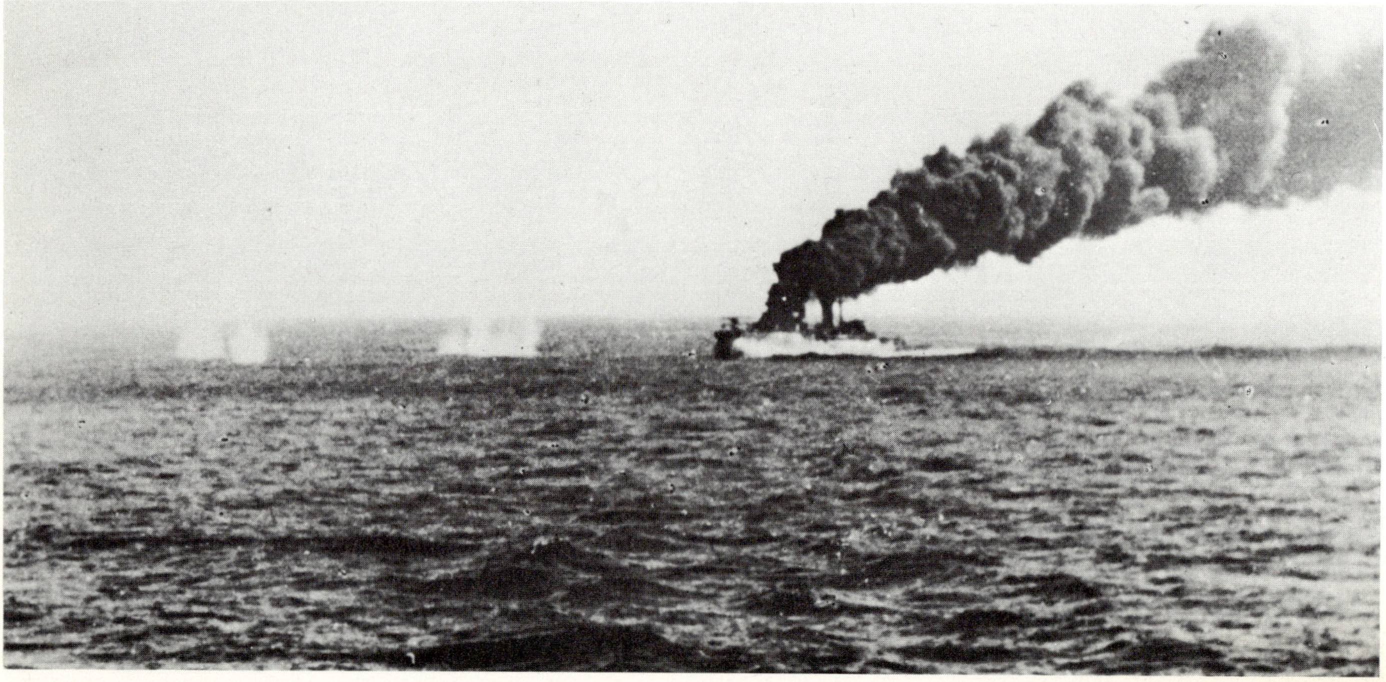

7.20 A unique photograph of the first bombardment against the Greek positions in the North East of Corfu, carried out on 28 November 1940, by six destroyers and torpedo-boats. The photograph, taken from aboard the old torpedo-boat *Bassini*, shows, in order: the torpedo-boat *Prestinari*, destroyers *Pigafetta*, *Riboty*, *de Recco* and *Pessagno*, which fired some 1600 rounds of 120 and 102mm shells. In all there were 13 important bombardments against Greek positions (in which four cruisers also took part, in addition to twenty destroyers and eight torpedo-boats), the last of which was on 4 March 1941. **AF**

Photograph by Aldo Fraccaroli

7.21 In wartime, the naval bases and the more important harbours of Italy were supplied with 1531 sets of smoke-laying apparatus between April 1941 and June 1943. In this photo, taken in the harbour of Messina (where 117 smoke-layers had been fitted), three *Soldati* class destroyers are also producing smoke: *Aviere* (foreground) and *Carabiniere* (background), plus an unidentified destroyer in the centre. Above them some of the twelve balloons of the AA barrage can be seen. **AF**

Photograph by Aldo Fraccaroli

7.22 Perhaps the unluckiest action for the Italian fleet in the Second World War was the battle off Cape Spada (Crete), on 19 July 1940. The two cruisers of the 2nd Cruiser Division, *Bande Nere* (flagship of Rear Admiral Ferdinando Casardi, Captain Franco Maugeri) and *Colleoni* (Captain Umberto Novaro) engaged, at 6.27 on that day, four British destroyers at 17 500 metres. The conditions were ideal for the Italian fast cruisers — armed with sixteen 6inch and twelve 3.9inch guns, against sixteen 4.7inch guns, no radar aboard the British ships, no enemy aircraft, no submarines, no mine barrages. Only the sunlight was against the Italians, for this meant that their admiral had not been able to gain a favourable tactical position. The occasion was exactly that for which this type of cruiser had been built: that is, as an anti-destroyer cruiser. But no Italian hit was scored in this first part of the action. Later, the cruiser *Sydney* (eight 6inch and four 4inch guns, 32½ knots nominal speed, compared to the 37 of the Italian cruisers, which however were four years older) and a fifth British destroyer joined the battle, and *Colleoni* was hit and stopped, and at last struck by torpedoes launched by destroyers *Ilex* and *Havock*, which sank her. **AF**

Aldo Fraccaroli Collection

7.23 When *Roma* was actually ready for sea service, in November 1942, the Italian Navy had a battle squadron composed of three large and fast battleships: *Littorio*, *Vittorio Veneto* and *Roma*, which may be seen in this view, taken during the winter of 1942-43. They displaced about 43 000 tons at normal load and more than 45 000 tons at full load; had a main armament of nine 15inch guns (maximum range: 42 000 metres for AP projectiles, 44 640 for HE shells), twelve 6inch guns, twelve 3.5inch AA guns, four 4.7inch starshell guns, twenty 37mm and 28 to 32 20mm machine guns. Their maximum practical sea speed was 28 knots. The armour was exceptionally strong for an Italian ship (14 669.8 tons in total, or 37.2 per cent of the weight of the *Littorio* in light conditions), with 375mm on side, 207mm on deck, 260mm on conning tower, 350mm for main calibre turrets and 280mm for medium calibre turrets. **AF**

Aldo Fraccaroli Collection

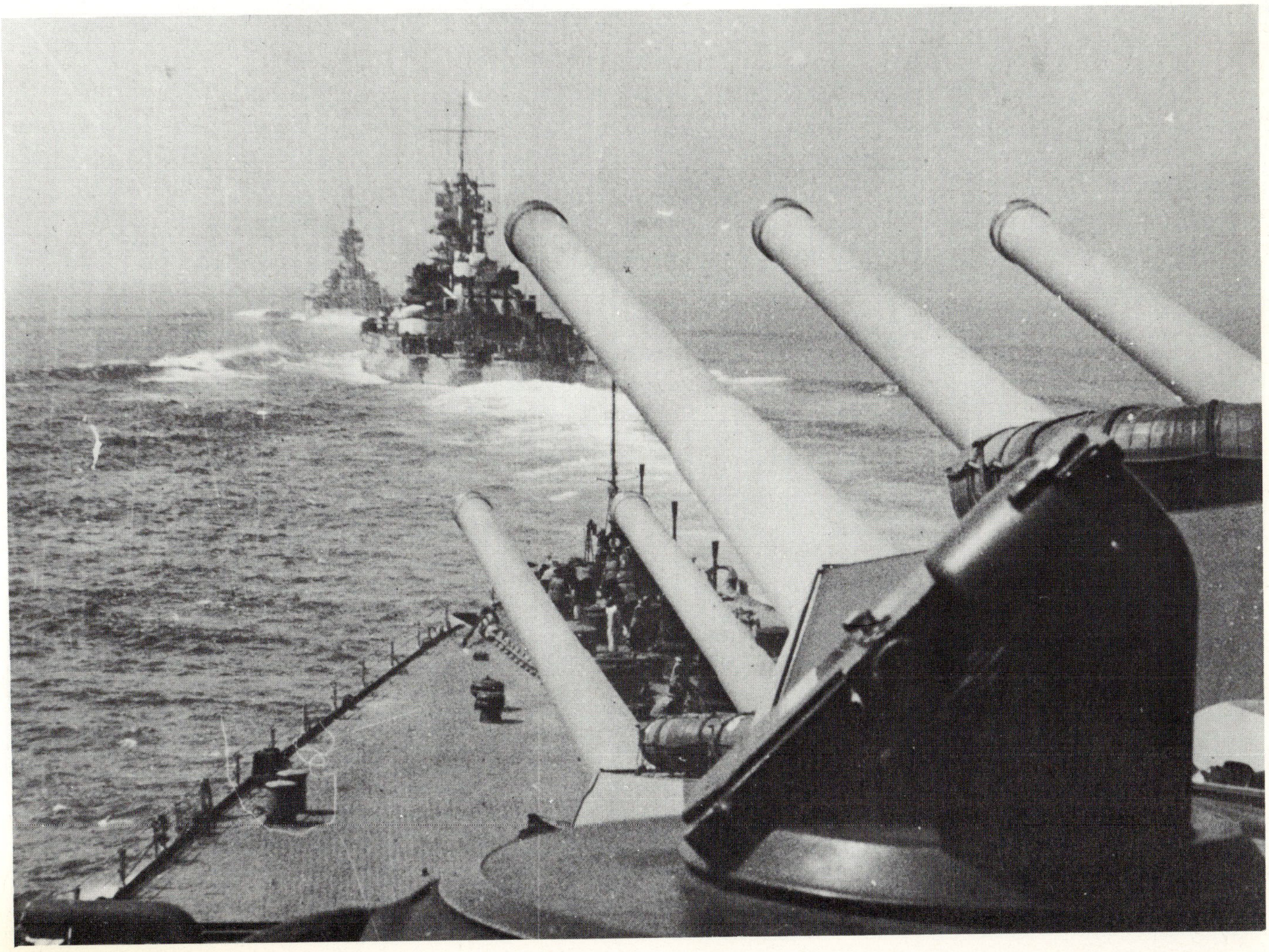

7.23

7.24 HMS *Legion* picks up non-essential members of the *Ark Royal*'s ship's company in the late afternoon of 13 November 1941. Apart from the toppled crane (to the right of and below the white-topped AA director) and a few displaced Carley Floats, there is little obvious damage above the waterline, in spite of the violent 'whip' caused by the torpedo's explosion. The destroyer is equipped with a type 291 small ships' air and surface warning set at the mast head and type 285 AA fire control radar on the director — *Ark Royal*'s only radar was that carried by her Swordfish. **DB**
CPL

Successful attacks by aircraft on large warships at sea were not as common as popularly believed. One of the best executed operations of the war was *Fliegerkorps X's* strike against the British aircraft carrier *Illustrious* off Malta on 10 January 1941. **AP**

7.25 The first photograph shows a bomb falling astern of the *Illustrious,* while her 4.5inch guns and pom-poms blaze away. **AP**
CPL

7.26 Seconds later the 23 000 ton ship reels under the impact of three 1000 kg armour-piercing bombs. She should have been sunk, but her deck-armour and sound fire-precautions saved her. **AP**
CPL

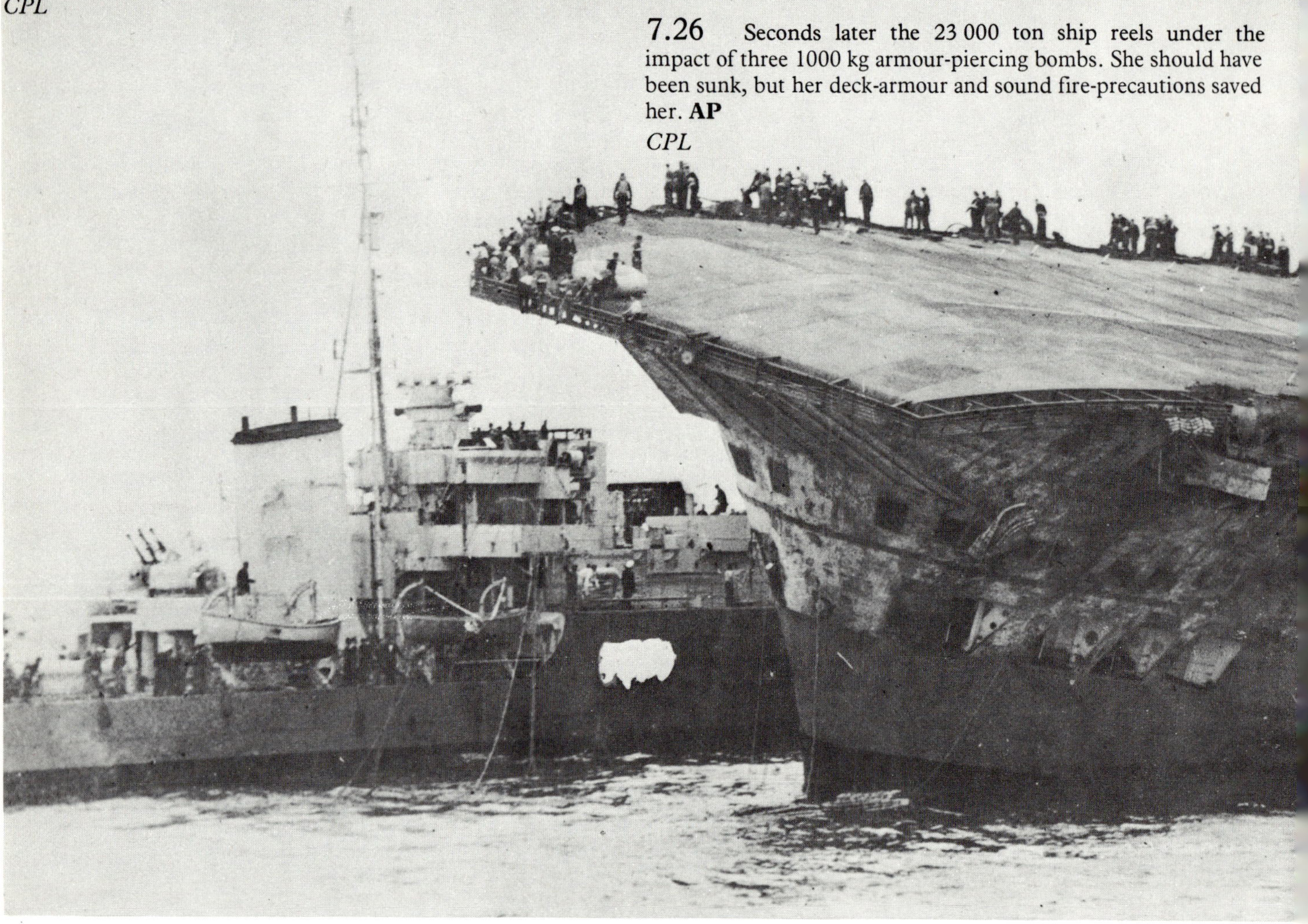

7.24

7.25

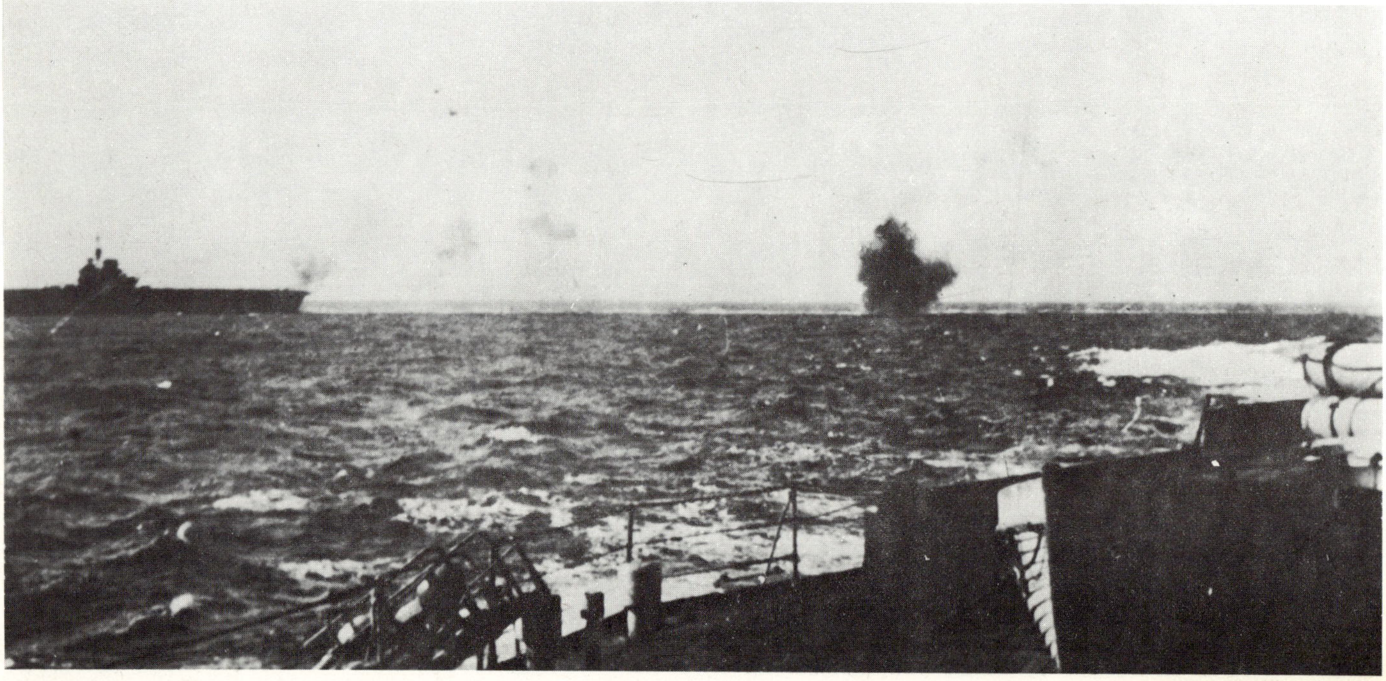

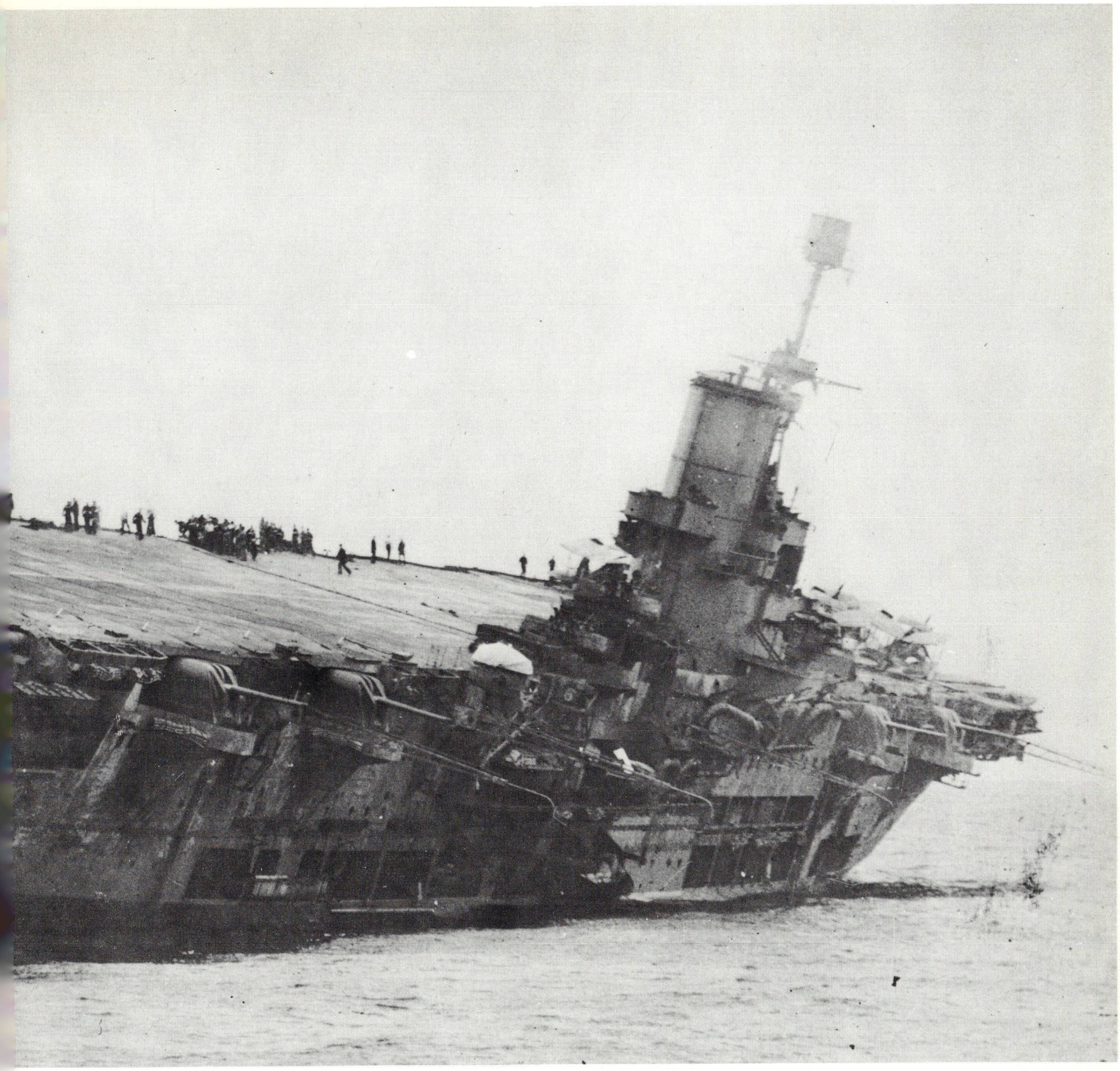

7.26

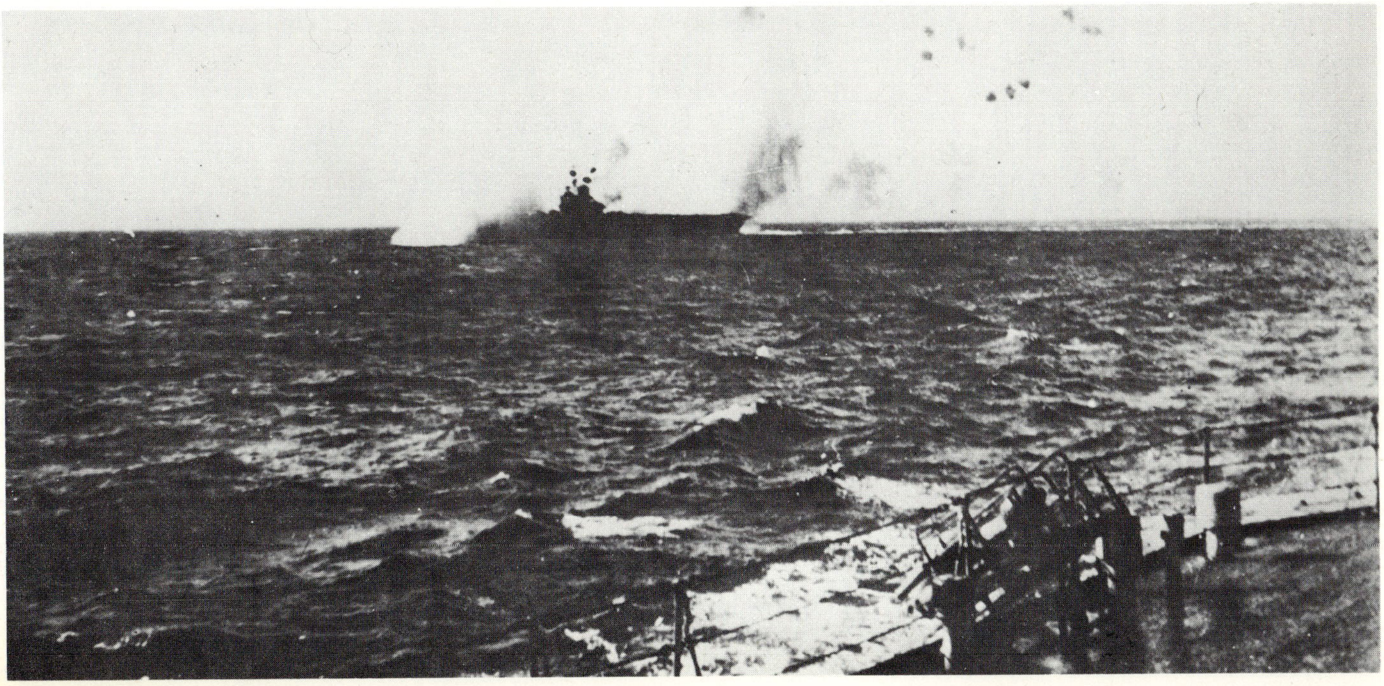

7.27 The French Fleet anchored at Mers-el-Kebir just before the British attack. Left to right: *Dunkerque, Provence, Strasbourg, Bretagne* and *Commandant Teste.* **AP**
CPL

7.28 The *Strasbourg* is seen shifting her berth. In the confusion she was able to get up steam, but she was the only major warship to escape from Mers-el-Kebir. **AP**
CPL

7.29 The battlecruiser *Strasbourg* gets under way against a backdrop of explosions from the stricken battleship *Bretagne.* **AP**
CPL

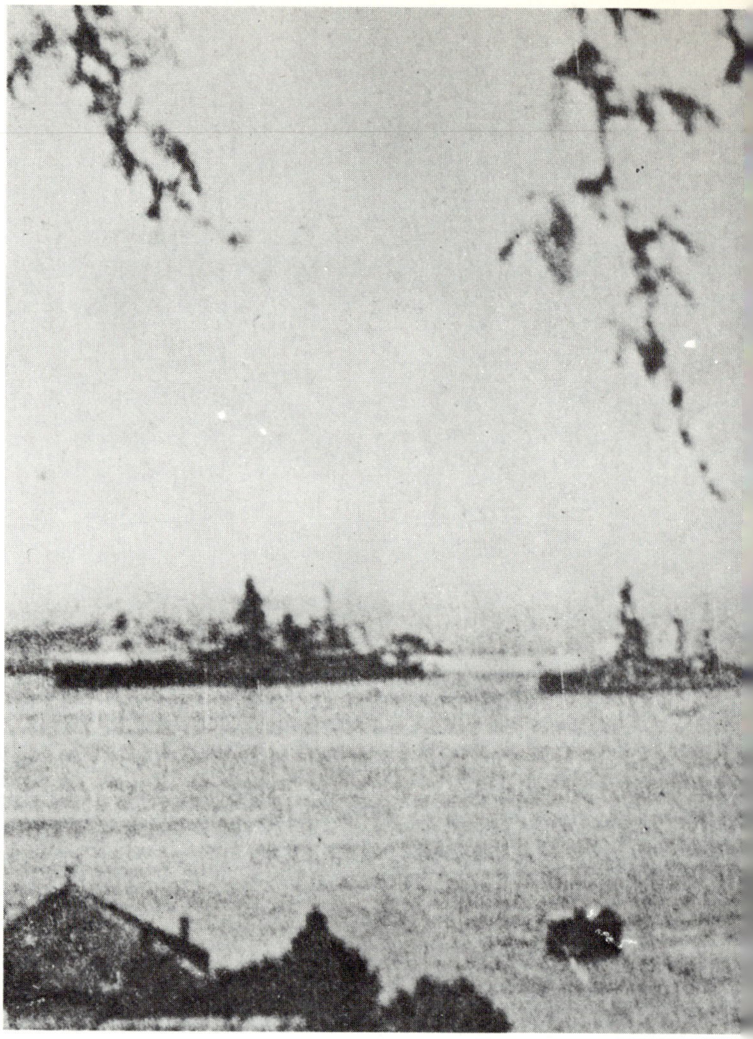

7.28

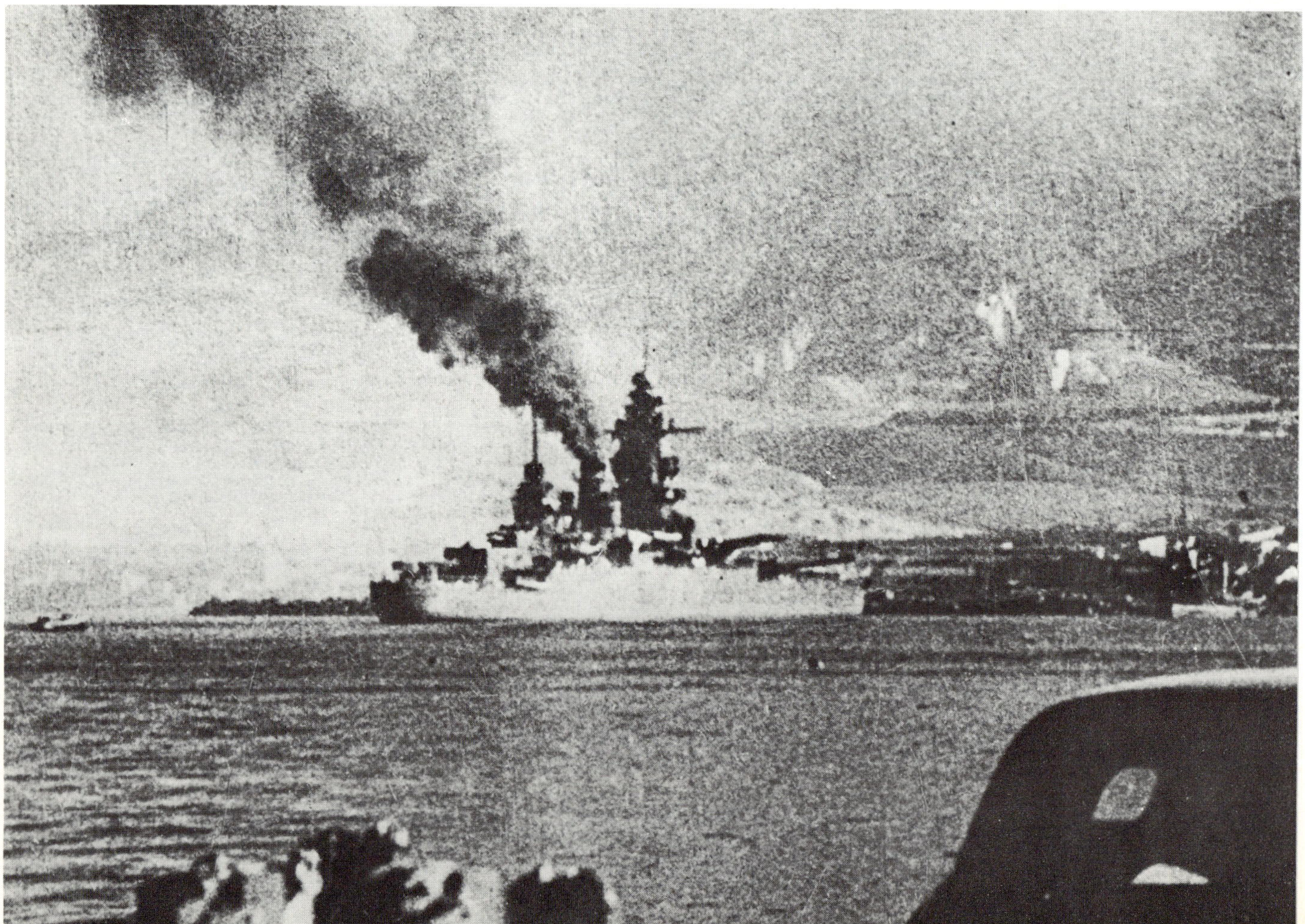

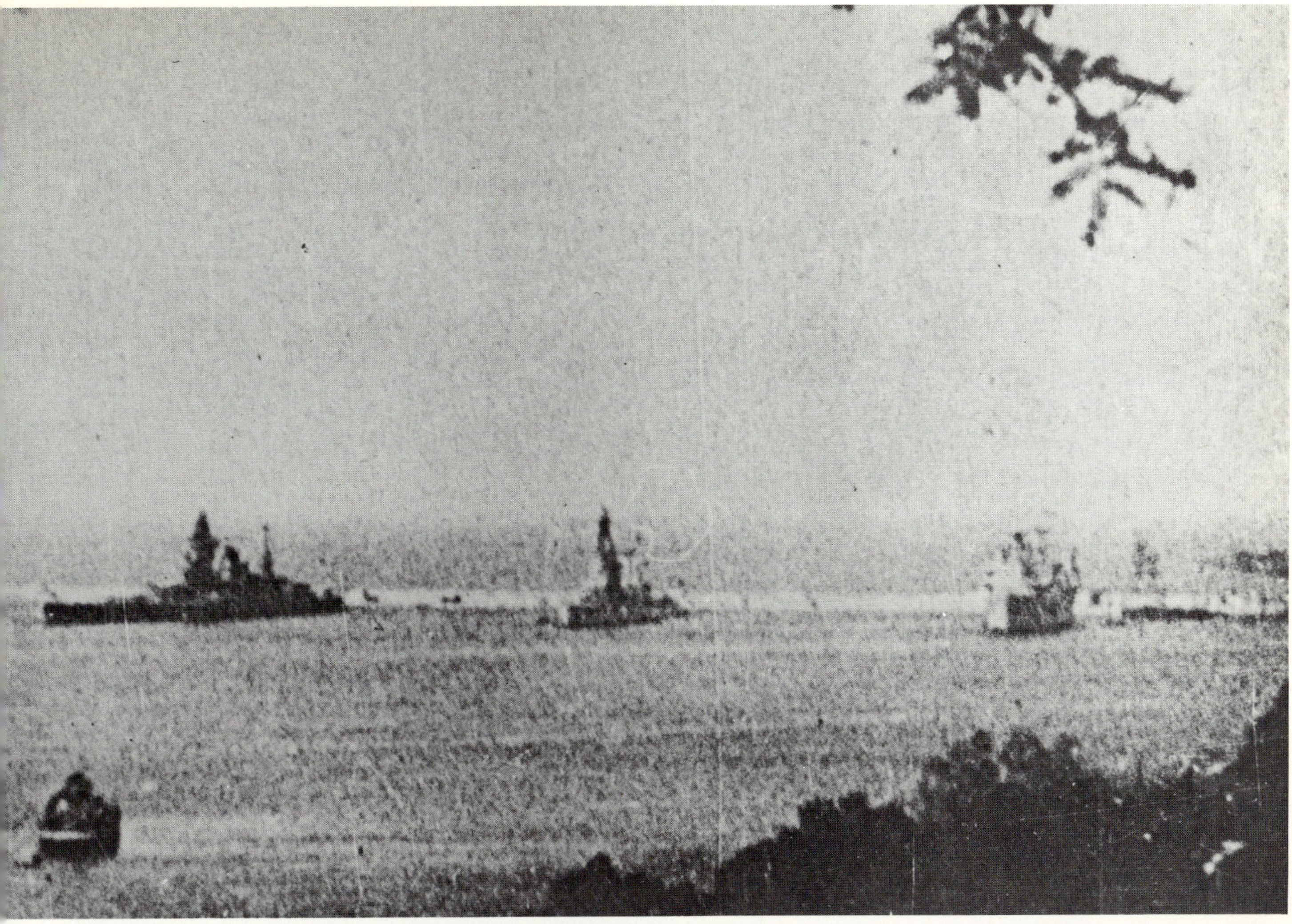

7.27

7.29

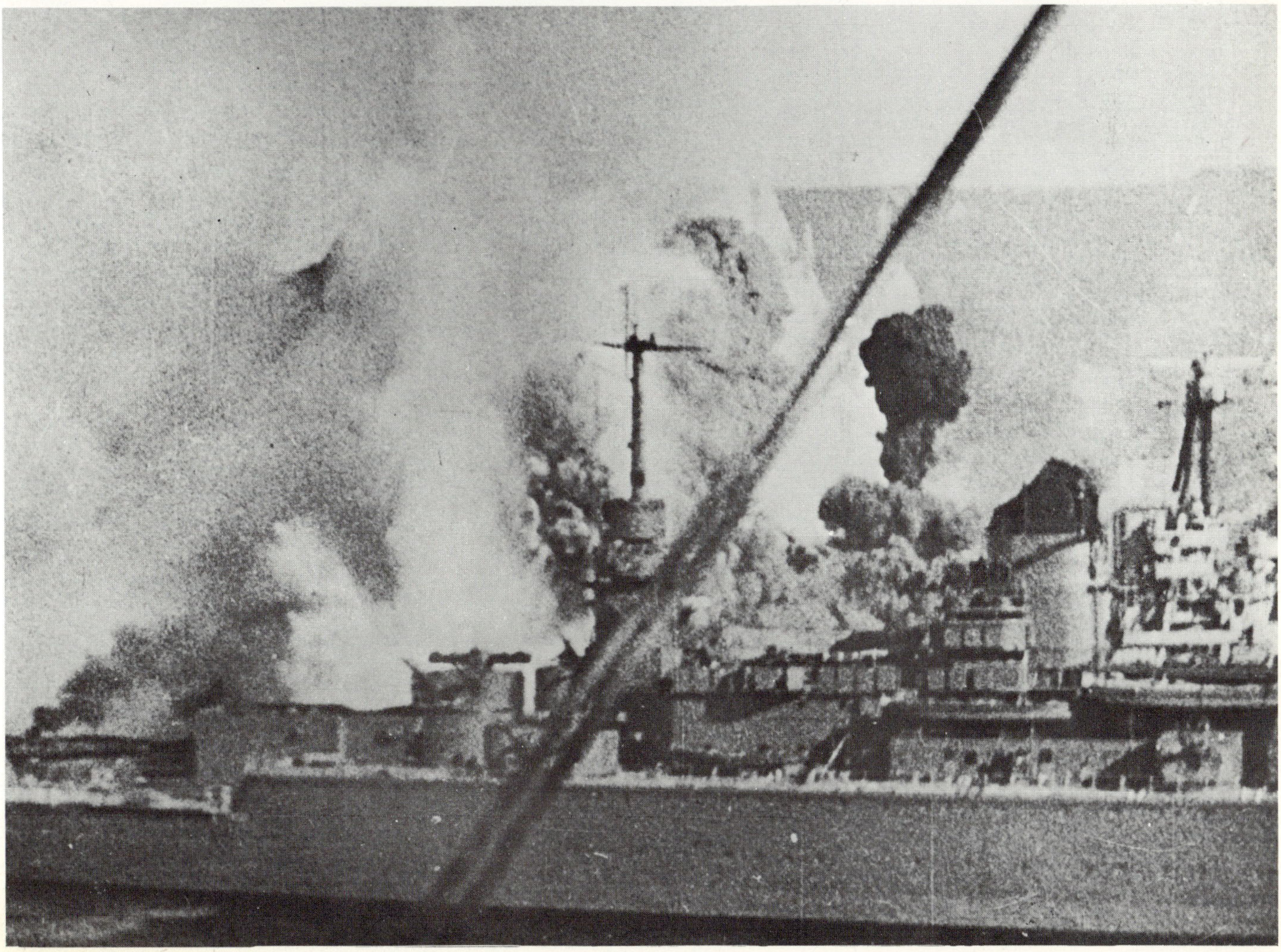

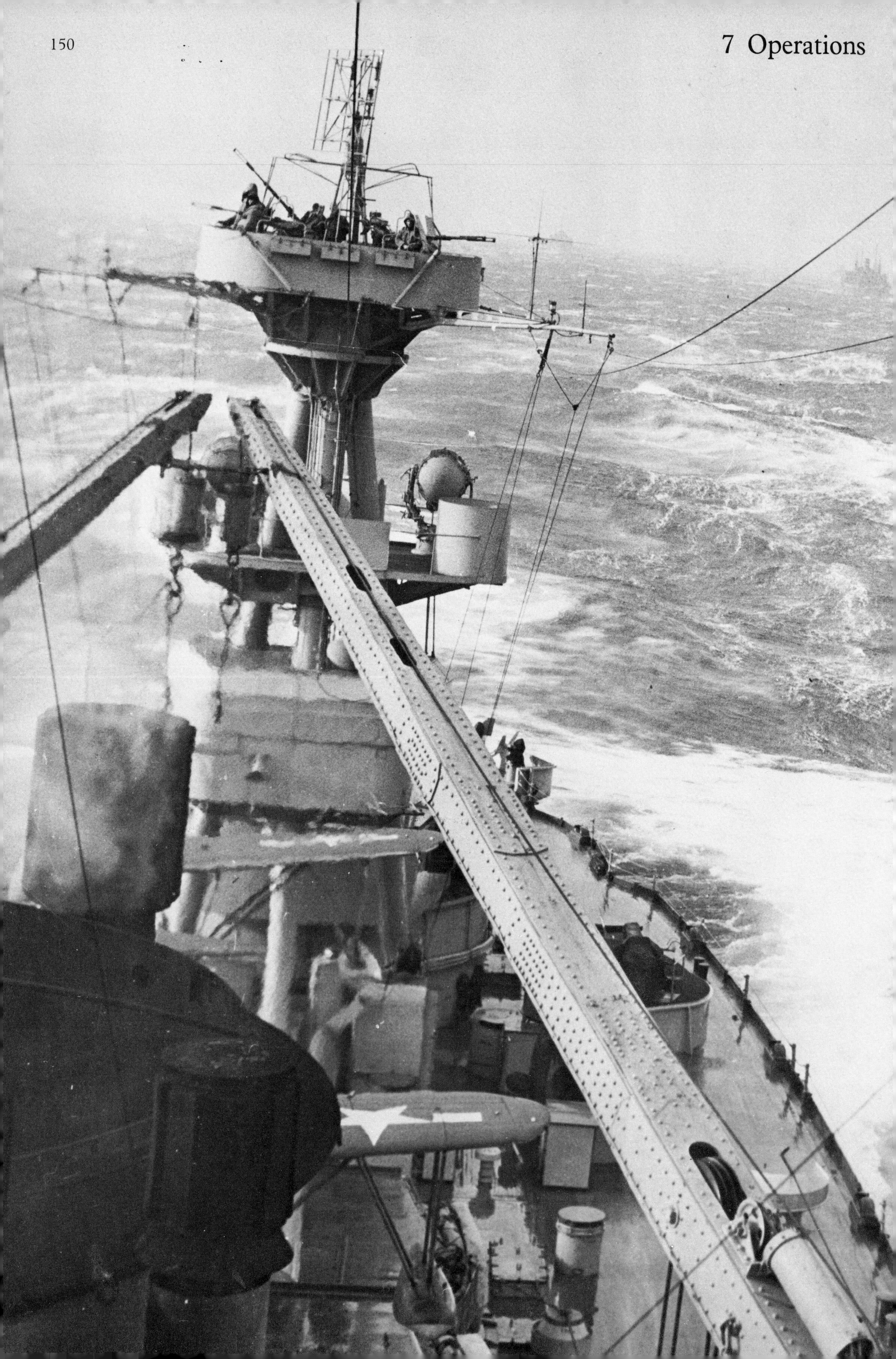

Convoys

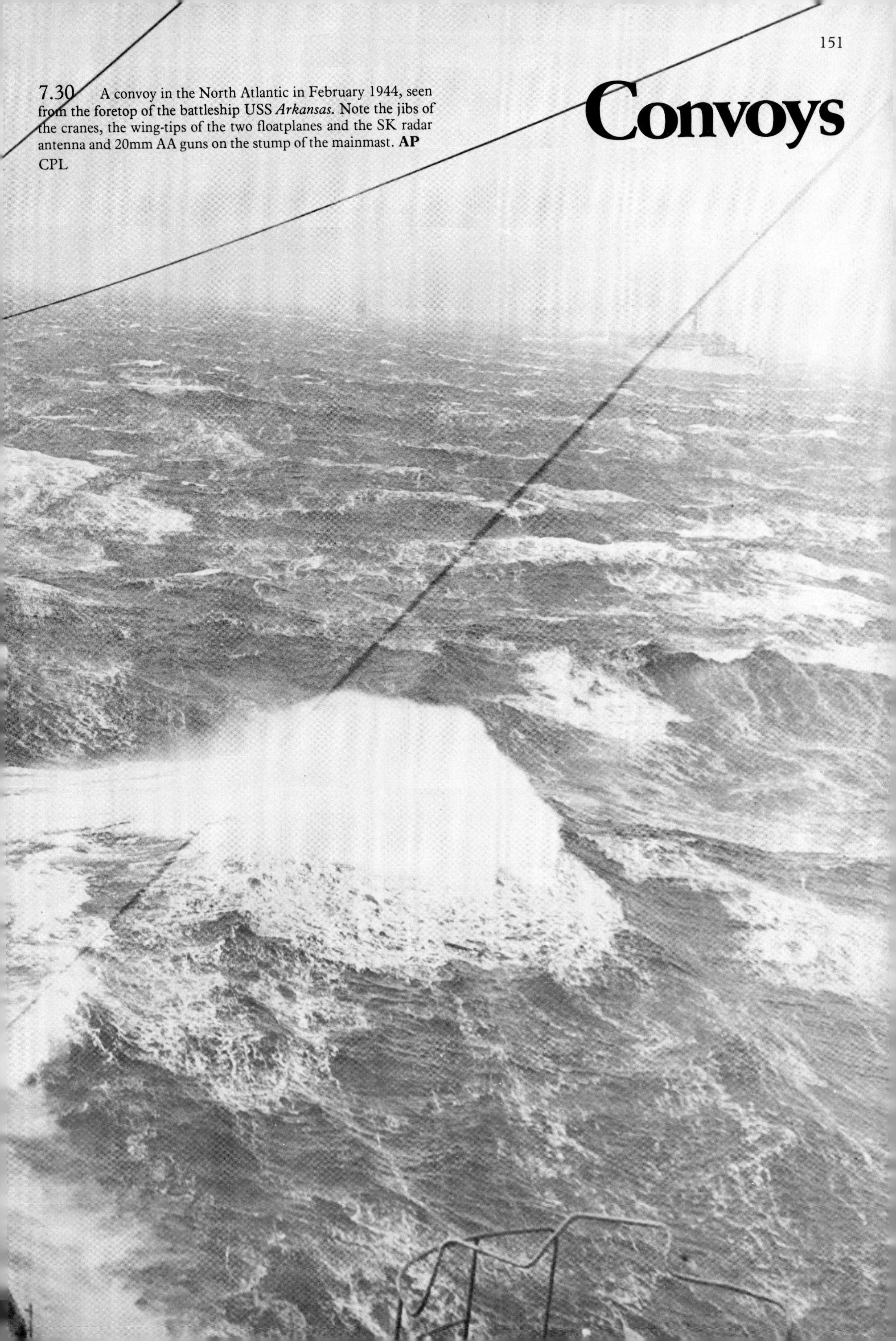

7.30 A convoy in the North Atlantic in February 1944, seen from the foretop of the battleship USS *Arkansas*. Note the jibs of the cranes, the wing-tips of the two floatplanes and the SK radar antenna and 20mm AA guns on the stump of the mainmast. **AP** CPL

7.31 The engine-room telegraph and wheel in the tiny enclosed wheelhouse. The US Navy preferred closed bridges, whereas the Royal Navy kept the open bridge as it gave the CO a better view and consequently more chance of dodging air attacks. **AP**
CPL

7.32 The slender forecastle of the 'flush-decker' buried in spray, with the 4inch gun and the footstrips barely visible. **AP**
CPL

7.33 HMS *Battler,* a Lend-Lease Escort carrier, arrived in the United Kingdom at the end of 1942 and began her work-up in the Clyde a couple of months later, after modifications to her aviation fuel system, radar and communications outfit, Fighter Direction and Operations Rooms, and the addition of extra ballast. The protective cover over the centimetric type 271 surface search radar is ahead of the lattice mast and the turning gear for the type 79 air warning and control radar can be seen towards the rear of the platform above the lattice. A mixture of American and British 'tin hats' is being worn by the handling party around the Swordfish, which is armed with an 18inch Mark XII torpedo; this weapon was carried only in the Trade Protection Escort carriers and was never used in anger by their Swordfish. The censor has most skilfully removed not only the ASV IIN antenna from the port outboard strut but also the upper centre-section leading edge transmitter antenna. The dotted lines across the flight deck are the metal drains to carry water off the uncambered wood plank deck. **DB**
CPL

7.31

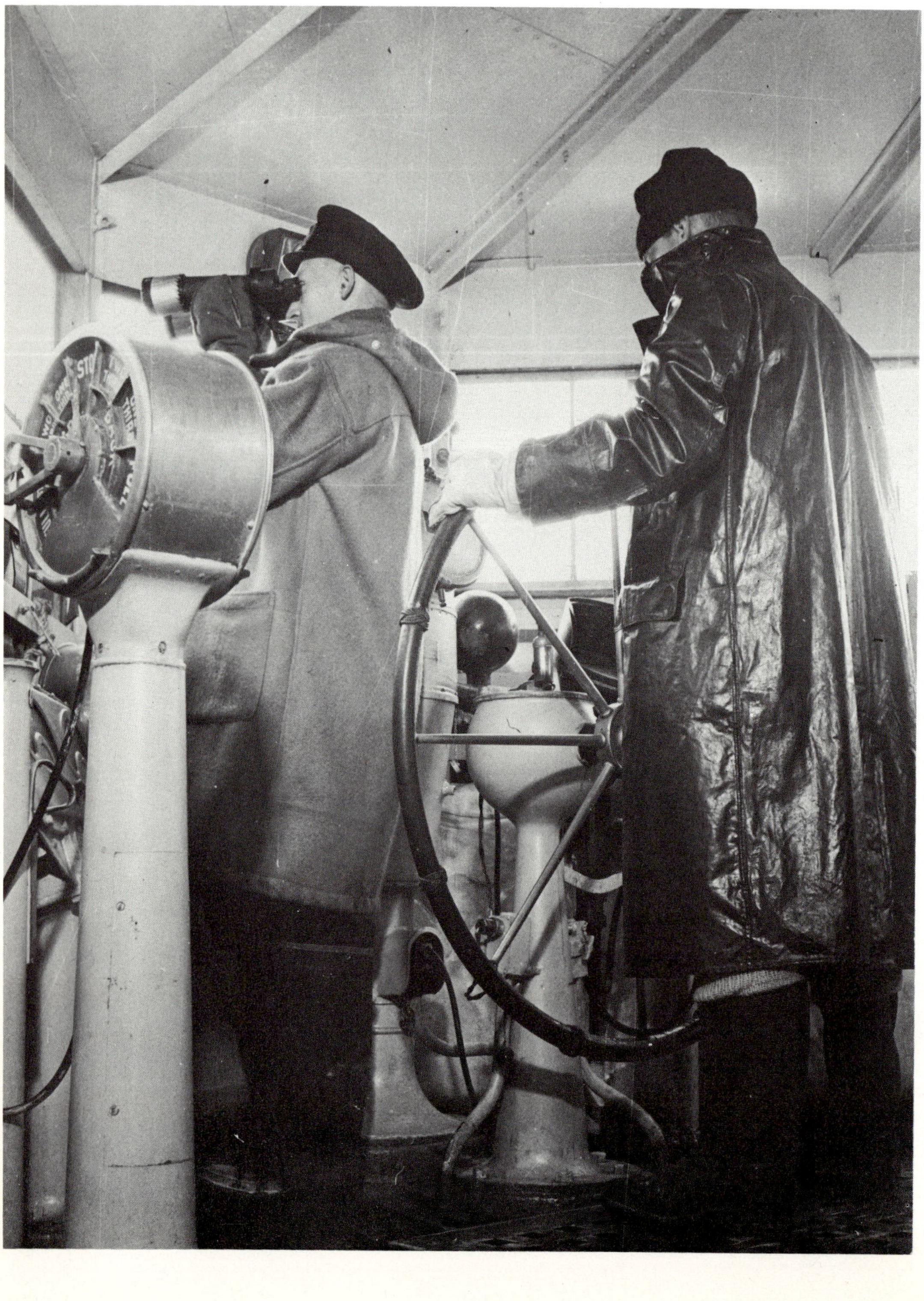

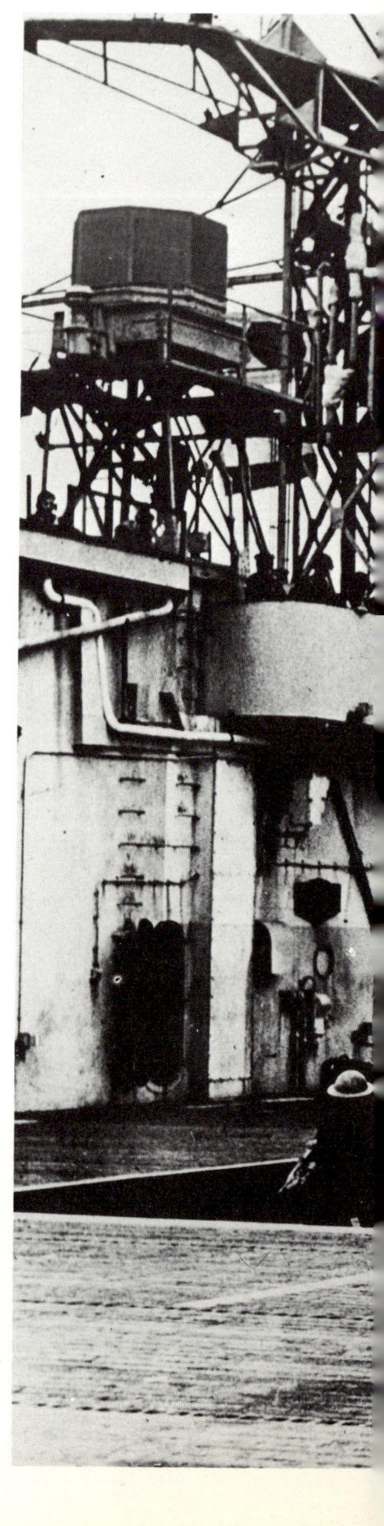

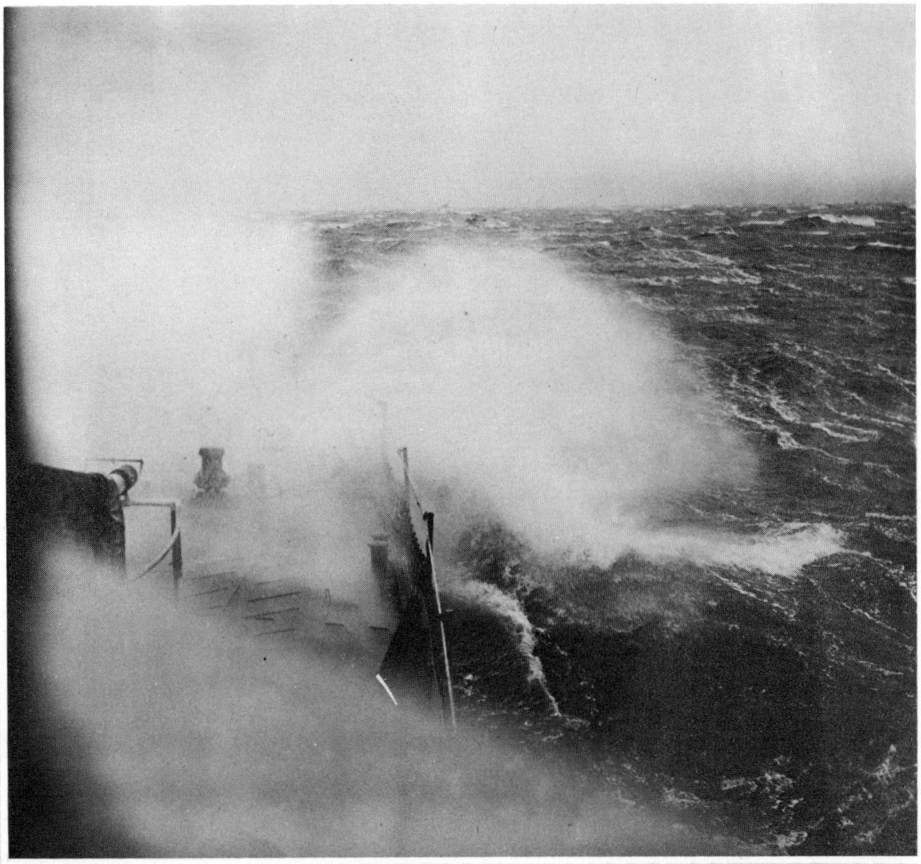

7.32

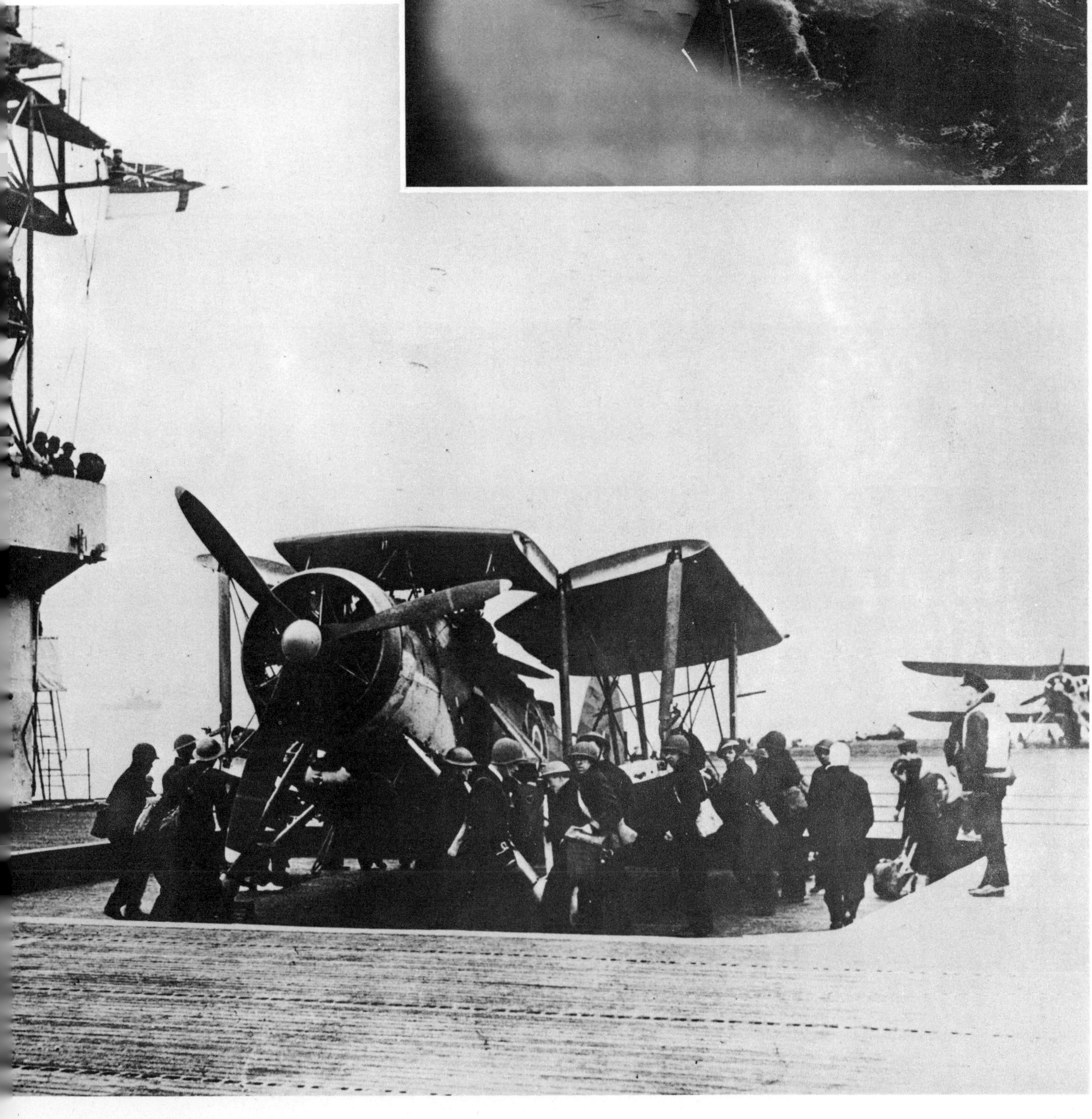

7.33

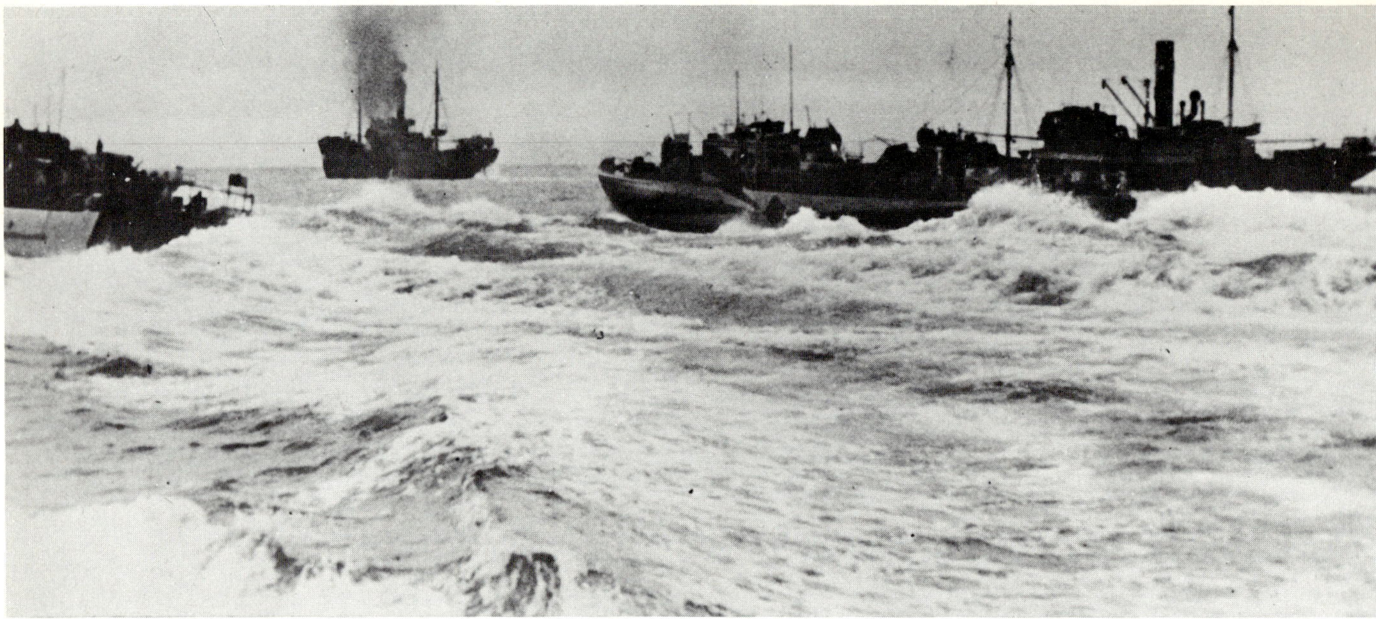

7.34

7.34 German convoy operations were on a much smaller scale than the Allies'. This rare view shows *Raumboote* (R-boats or motor minesweepers) escorting a coastal convoy bound for France. The date is unknown. **AP**
CPL

7.35 A German convoy in the Baltic (the *Ostsee* for Germans), seen from a German destroyer, 22 January 1943. The German ships presented a large number of targets to the Soviet submarines, but the results achieved by the latter were minimal: in twenty-four Russian attacks (seventeen of which were against convoys) only seven ships were sunk by torpedoes, for a total of about 20 000 gross registered tons. From the spring of 1943 no Russian submarine could pass the anti-submarine net laid by German netlayers which completely obstructed the Gulf of Finland: but in September 1944 Finland capitulated and the situation changed. **AF**
Aldo Fraccaroli Collection

7.36 A U-boat captain's dream — a handsome group of British and Allied liner-troopships in an Indian Ocean convoy in 1941. An Orient liner can be seen nearest the camera, with the French *Pasteur* and what appears to be a Union-Castle liner beyond. **AP**
CPL

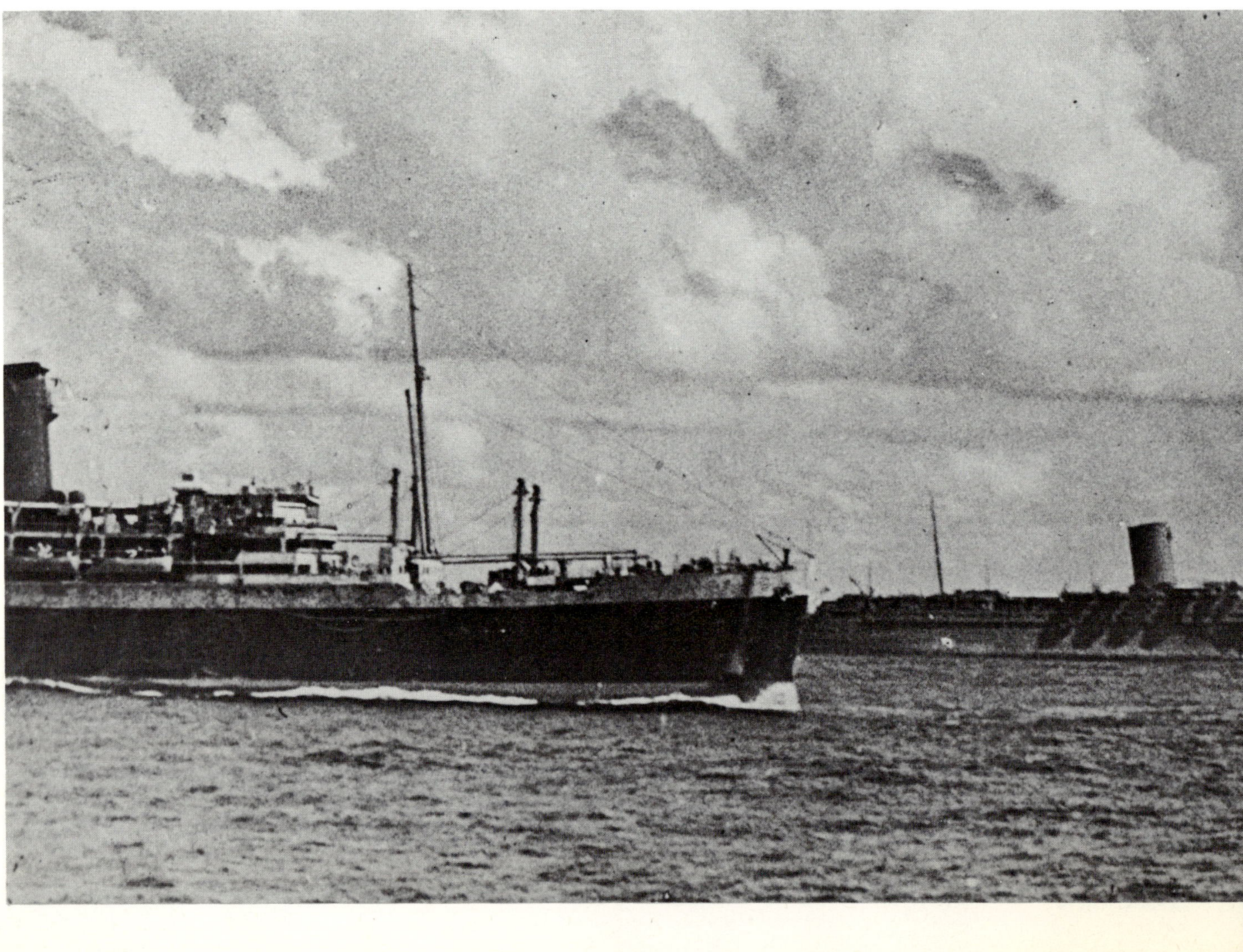

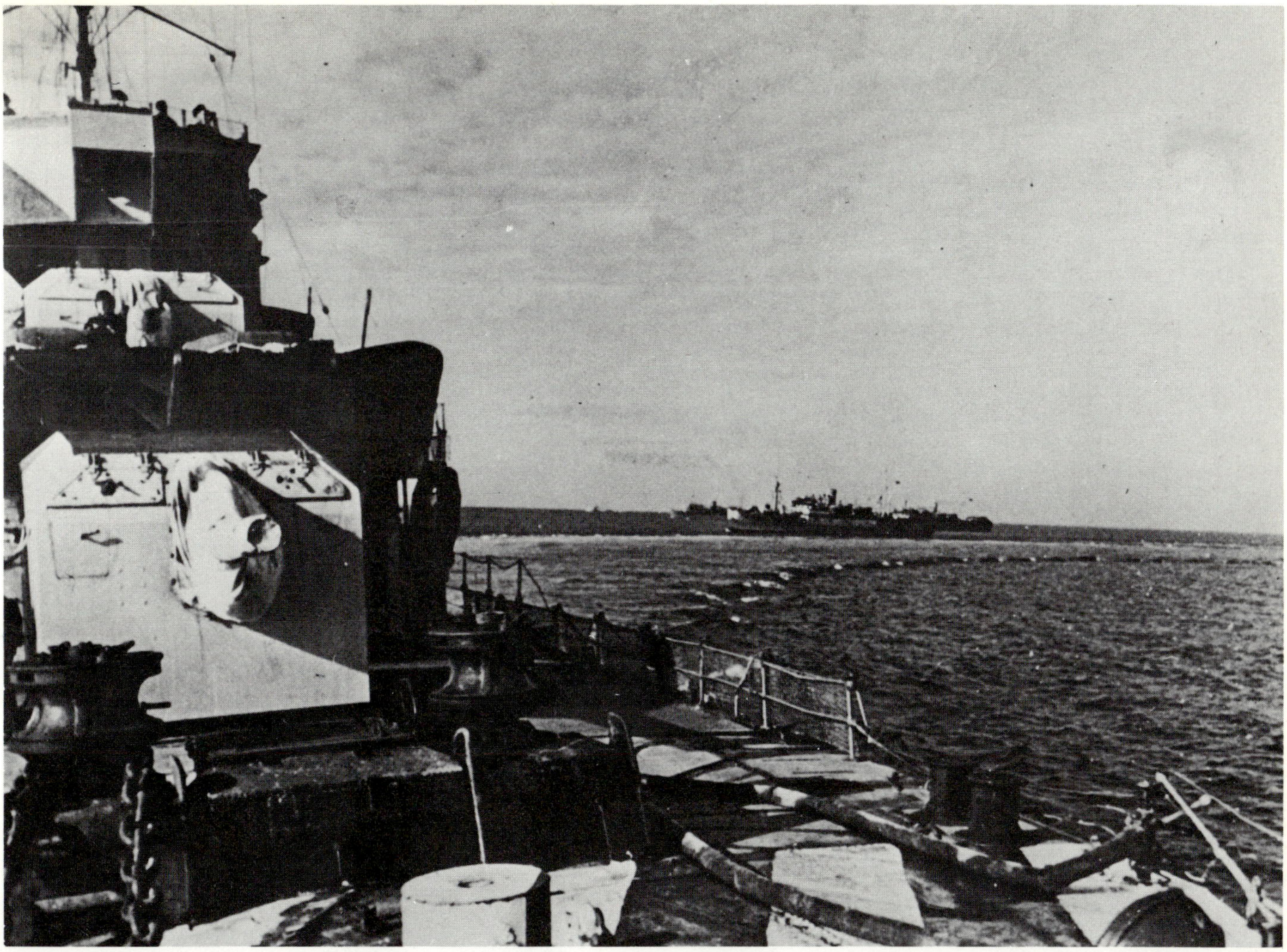

7.35

7.36

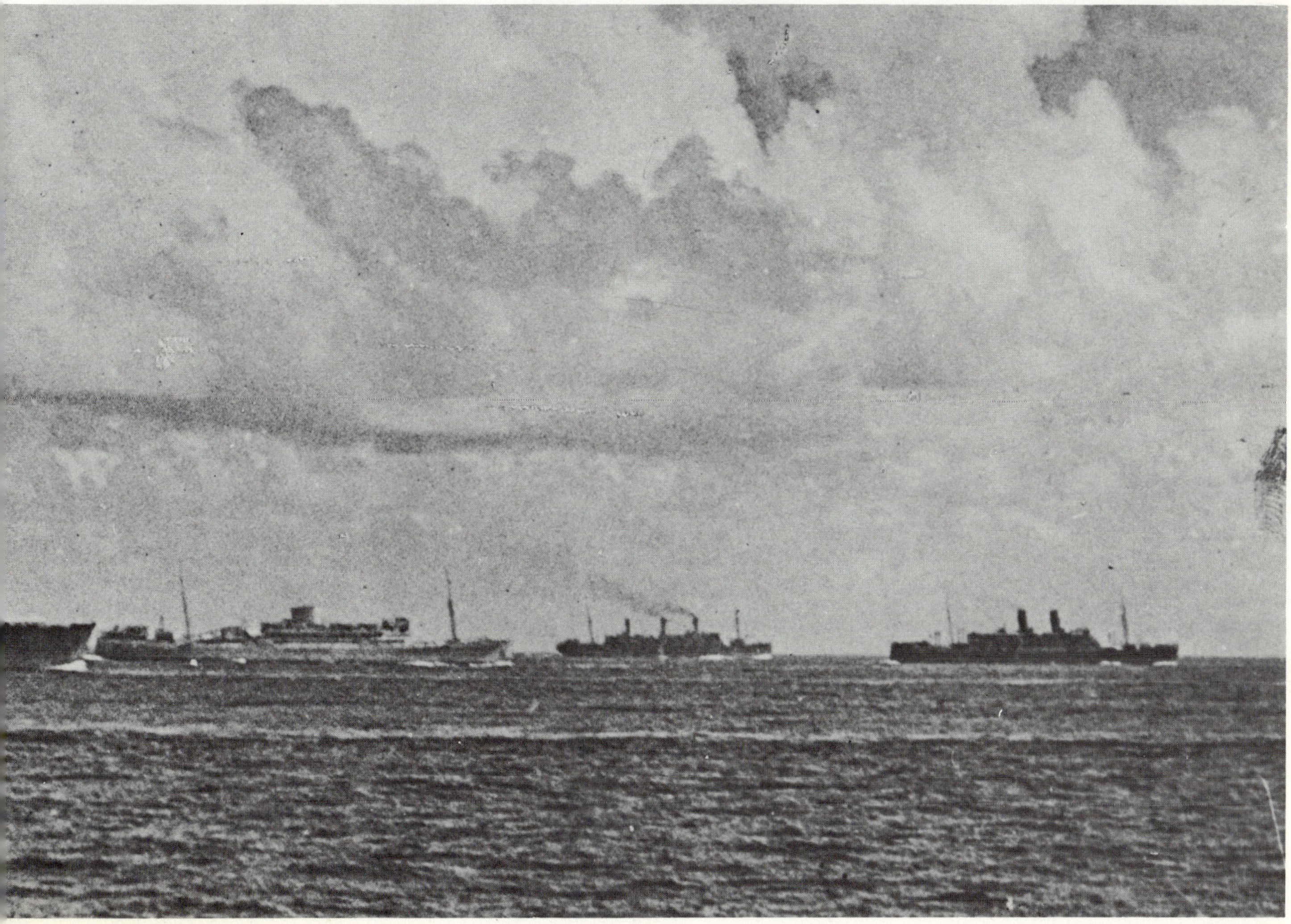

7.37 The most famous convoy of the war, the ill-fated PQ 17 convoy to Northern Russia, seen here in Iceland forming up, late in June 1942. Taken by Ensign Howard Carraway USNR, the Armed Guard Officer aboard SS *Troubadour.* **AP**
USN

7.38 An actual photograph of PQ 17 at sea, taken by one of the *Luftwaffe* reconnaissance aircraft that spotted and tracked the convoy. Rumour of a sortie by German heavy ships caused the Admiralty to order the convoy to scatter, and very few survived the piecemeal attacks by aircraft and U-boats. It was the worst Allied convoy disaster of the war. **AP**
USN

7.39 Few types of ship were more dangerous to serve in than tankers, which allowed their crew little chance of survival after being hit. The members of this tanker's crew abandon ship, in the North Atlantic, April 1943. **AP**
CPL

7.40 However, they are very lucky, the sea being calm and not covered with blazing oil. The ship is settling rapidly by the head after being torpedoed, and one man can be seen actually jumping feet first into the sea. **AP**
CPL

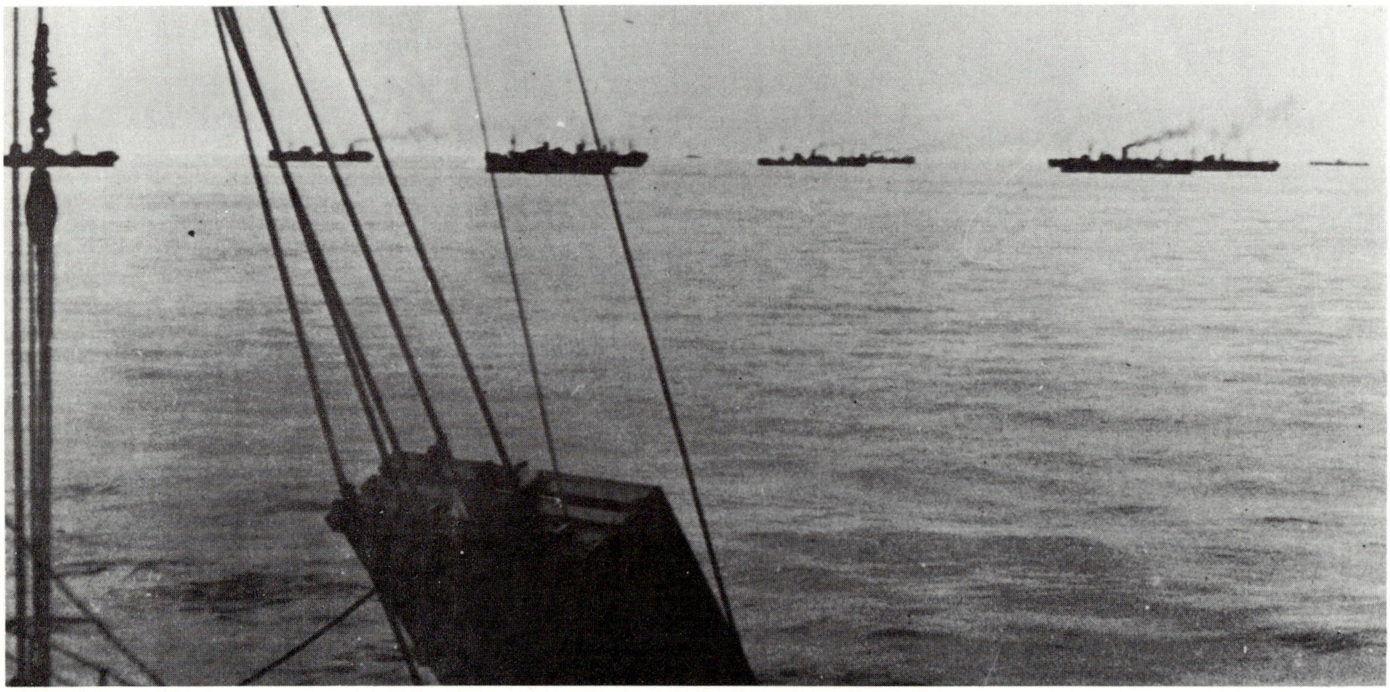
7.37

7.38
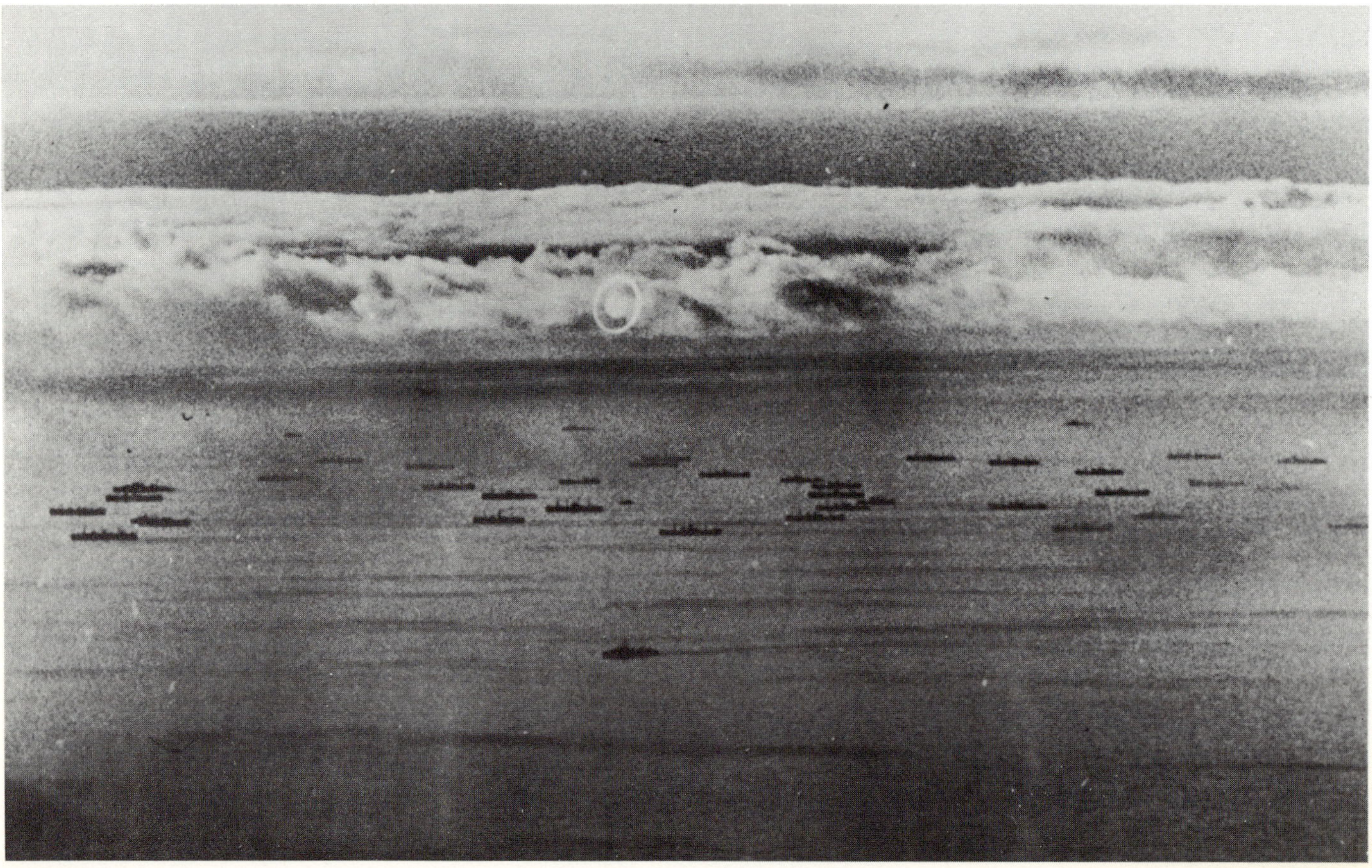

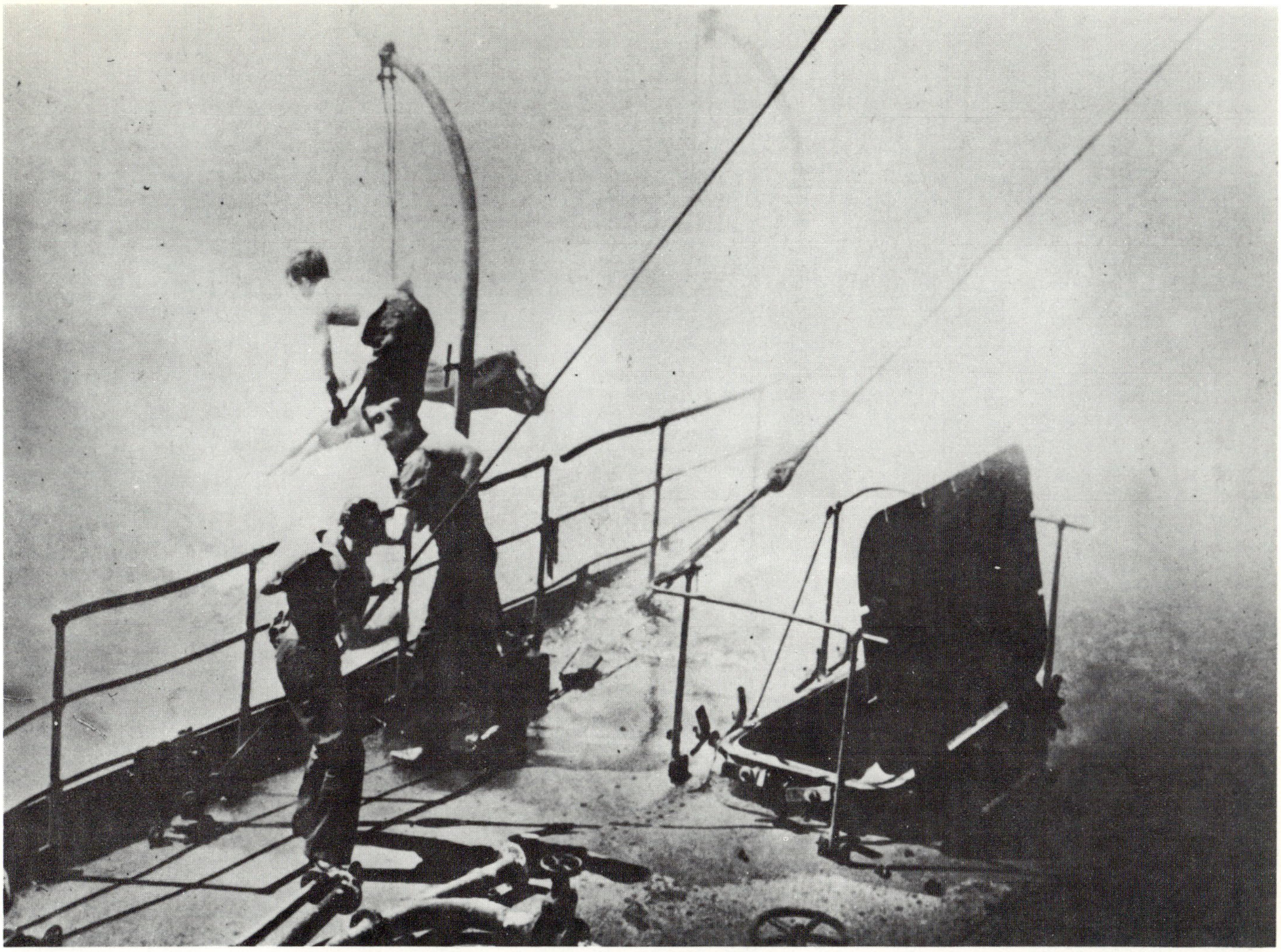

7.39

7.40

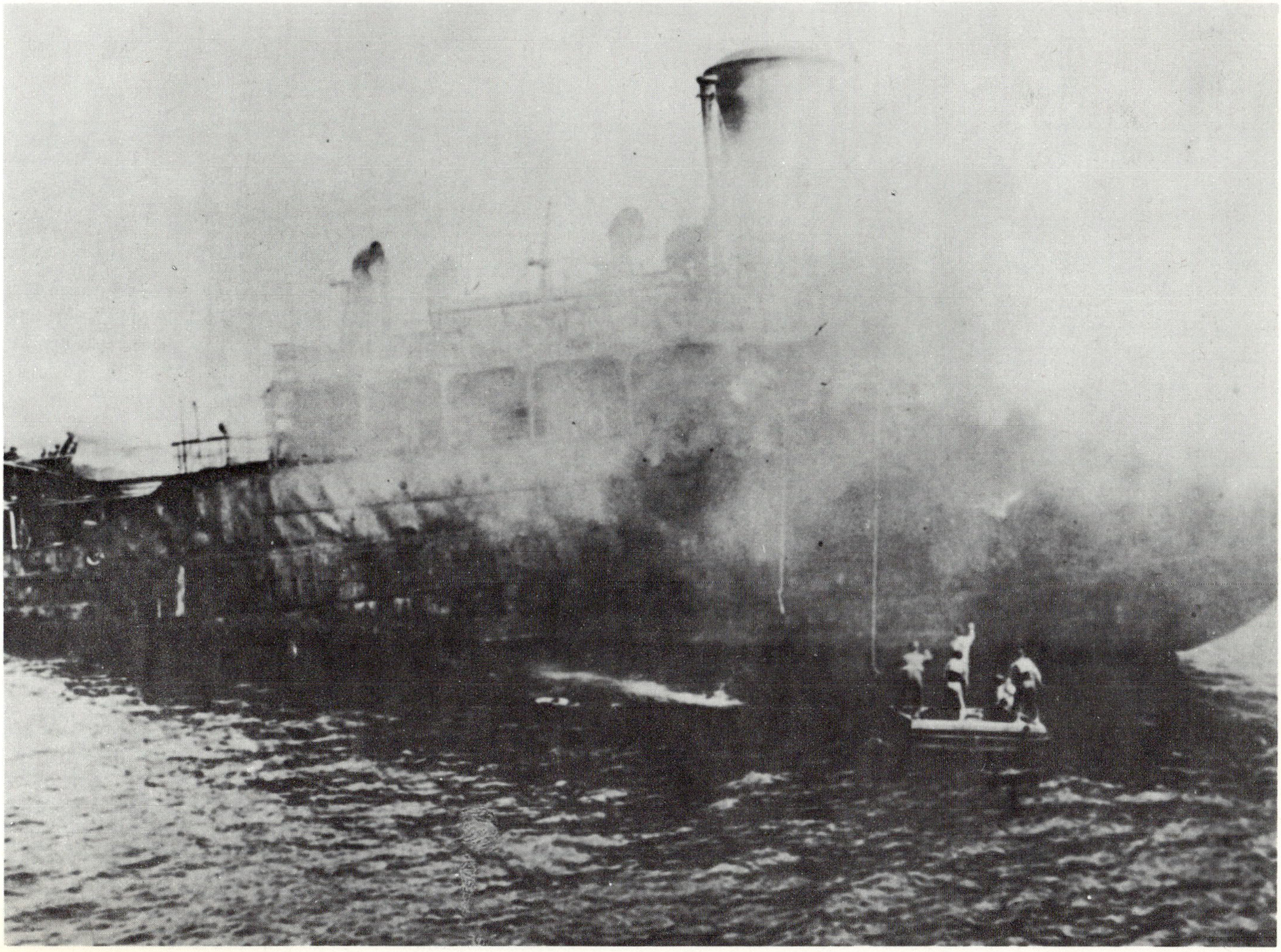

7.41
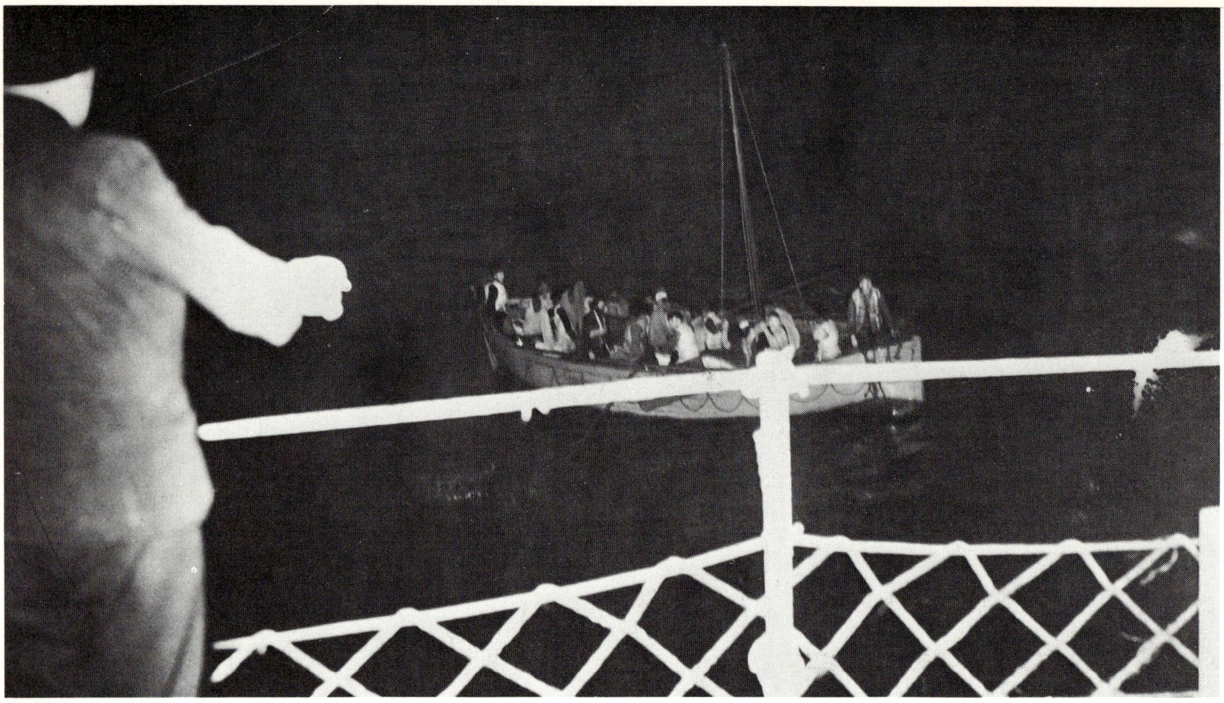

7.43
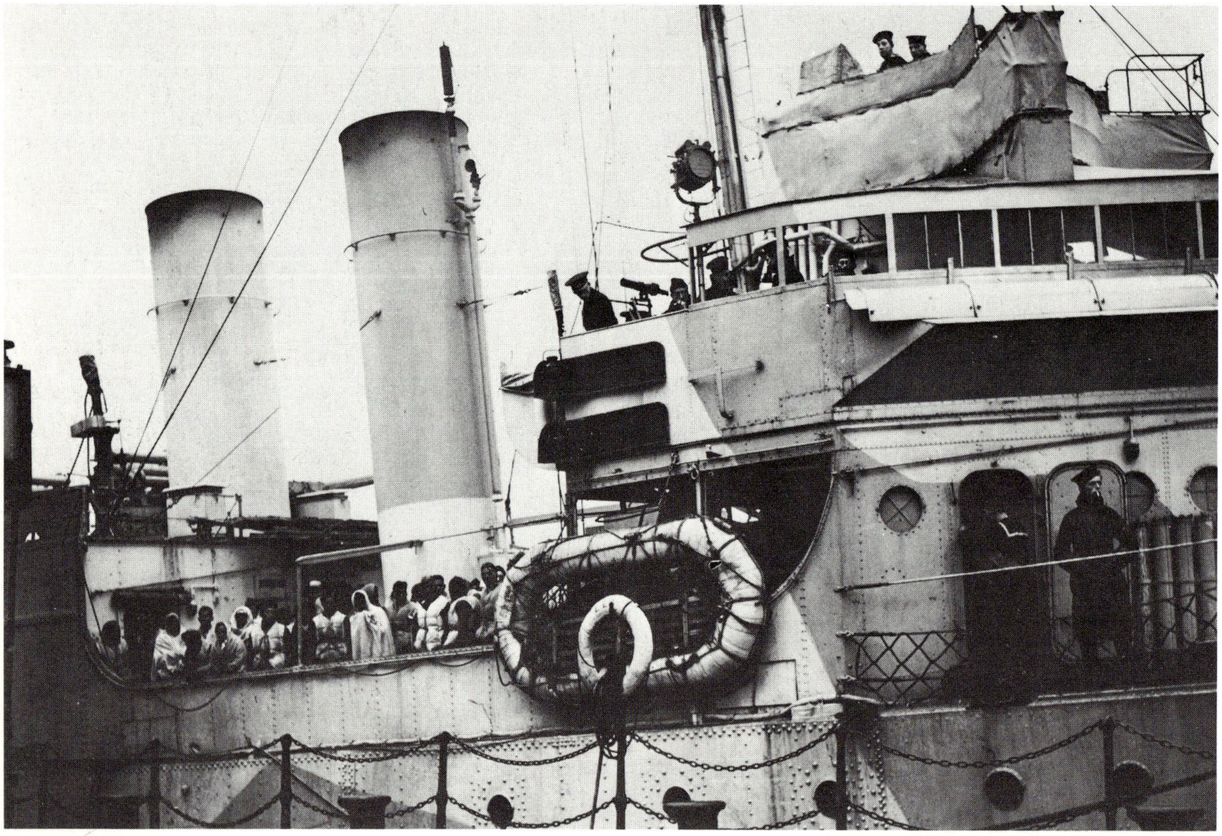

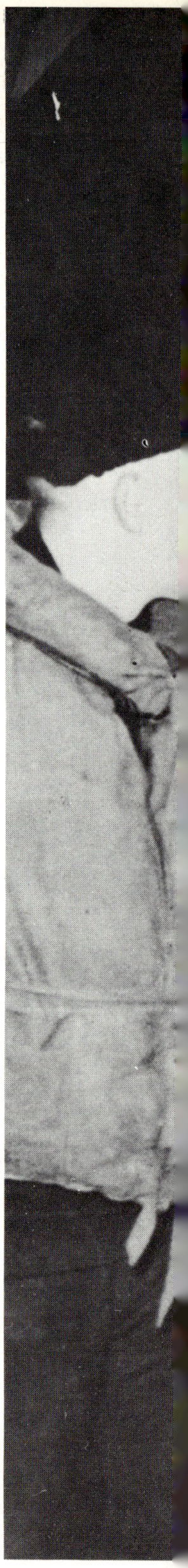

7.44
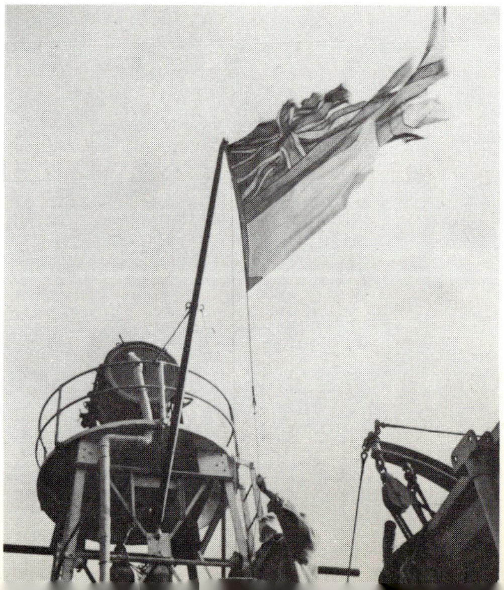

7.44 The tattered ensign flying from its staff on the searchlight tower aft. **AP**
CPL

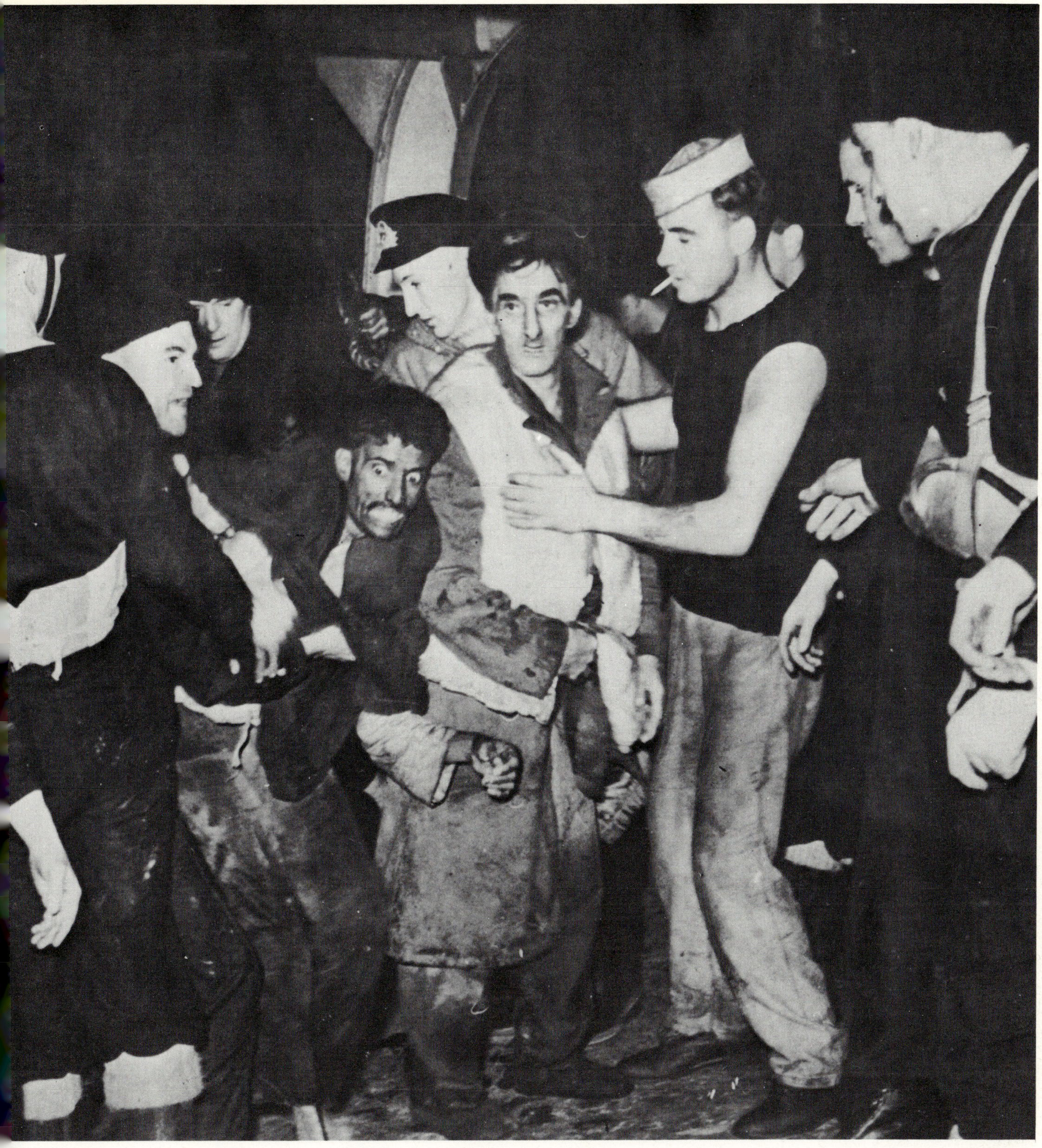

7.42

Taken aboard one of the 50 'lend-lease' destroyers transferred from the US Navy to the Royal Navy, these photographs are part of a large series depicting north Atlantic convoy duty. They were shot in November 1940 by a photographer for the *Illustrated* magazine on a voyage which was stormy but uneventful, except for the rescue of the crew of a torpedoed merchantman. Amongst the conventional cheerful pictures, designed for morale-boosting home consumption, the photographer chanced to capture a moment of genuine horror. As he was being brought aboard the destroyer a Lascar seaman, uncertain of what was happening, became hysterical and the resulting photo said more about the nature of U-boat warfare than any number of pictures of burning and sinking ships.

7.41 The one incident on the voyage was the rescue of this boatload of survivors who had been adrift for some time. **AP** *CPL*

7.42 One of the great photos of the war. Not the relief one would expect from survivors but a spectrum of emotions ranging from the hysteria of the Lascar to the numbed bewilderment of the man on his left. Later photos in this series showing the survivors wrapped in blankers and sipping cocoa belie the real horror of the experience. **AP** *CPL*

7.43 A more conventional view of the survivors posed in the waist of the destroyer ready to go ashore. **AP** *CPL*

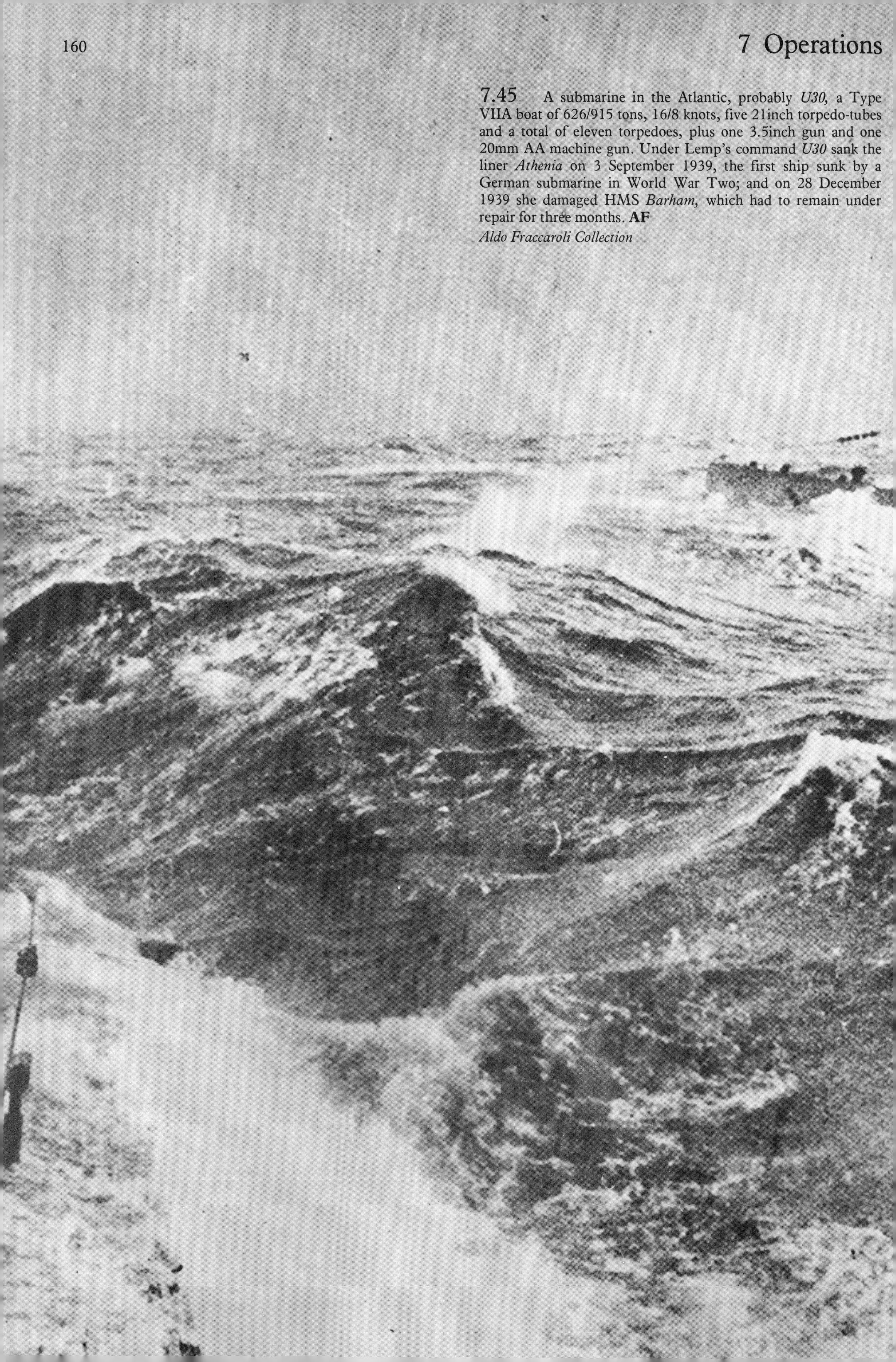

7.45. A submarine in the Atlantic, probably *U30*, a Type VIIA boat of 626/915 tons, 16/8 knots, five 21inch torpedo-tubes and a total of eleven torpedoes, plus one 3.5inch gun and one 20mm AA machine gun. Under Lemp's command *U30* sank the liner *Athenia* on 3 September 1939, the first ship sunk by a German submarine in World War Two; and on 28 December 1939 she damaged HMS *Barham*, which had to remain under repair for three months. **AF**

Aldo Fraccaroli Collection

U-Boats

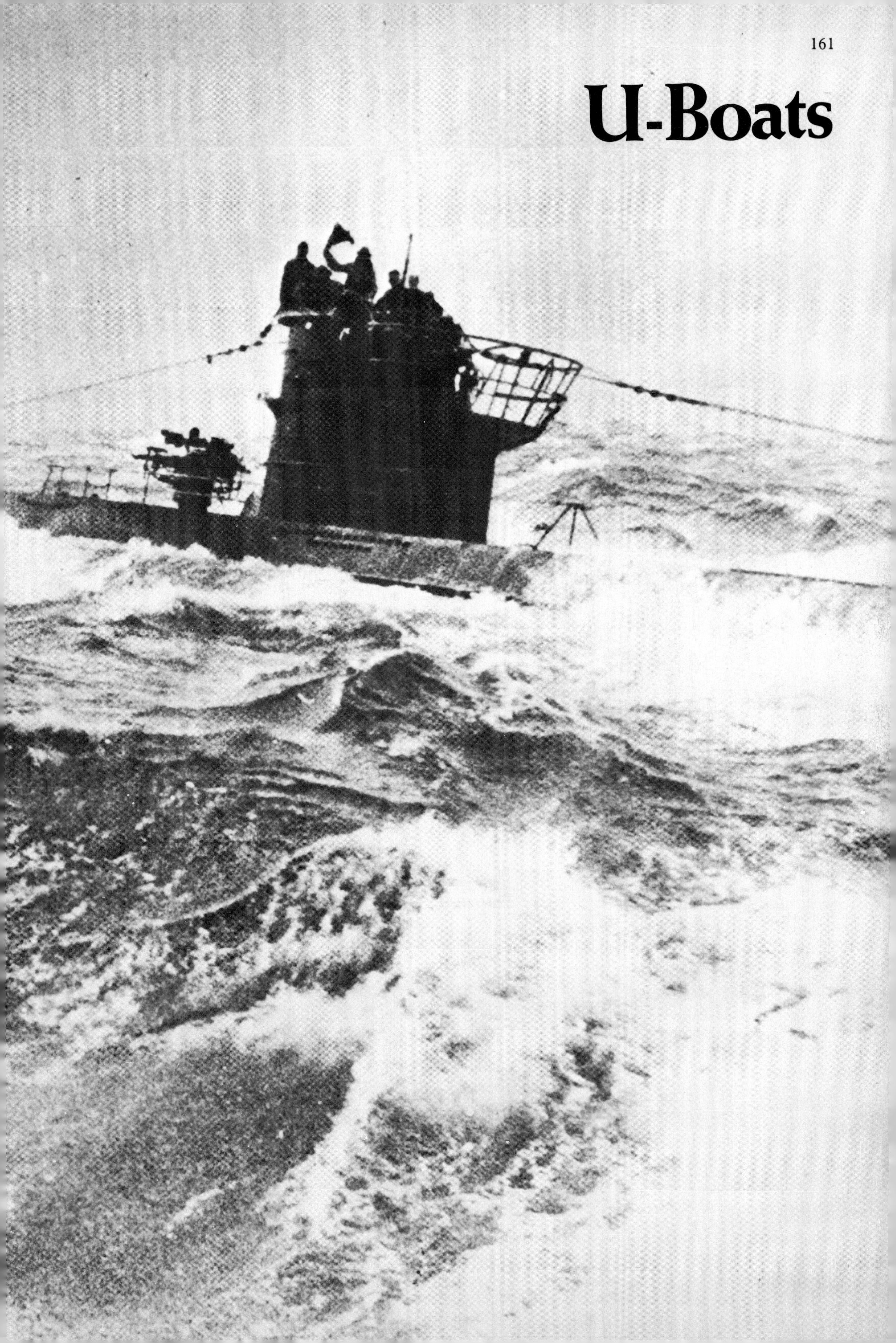

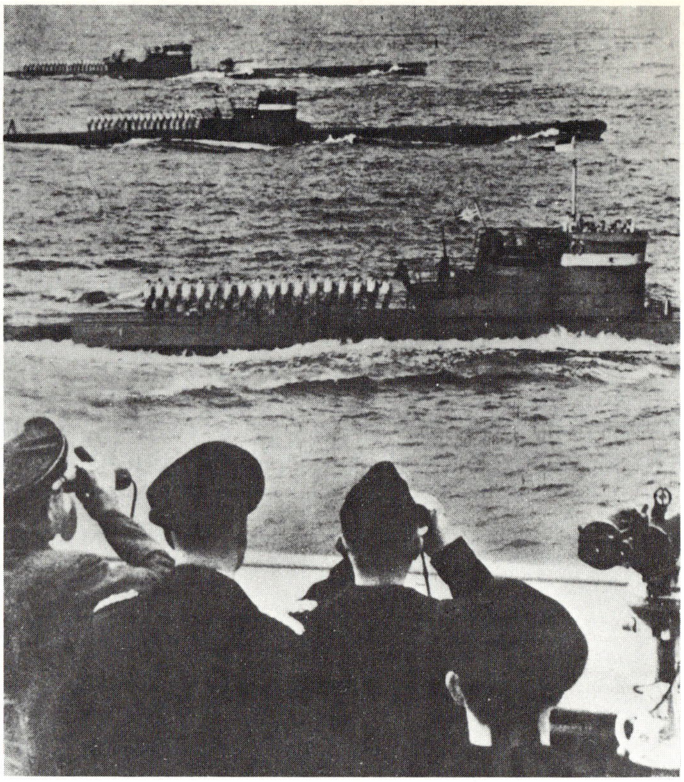

7.46

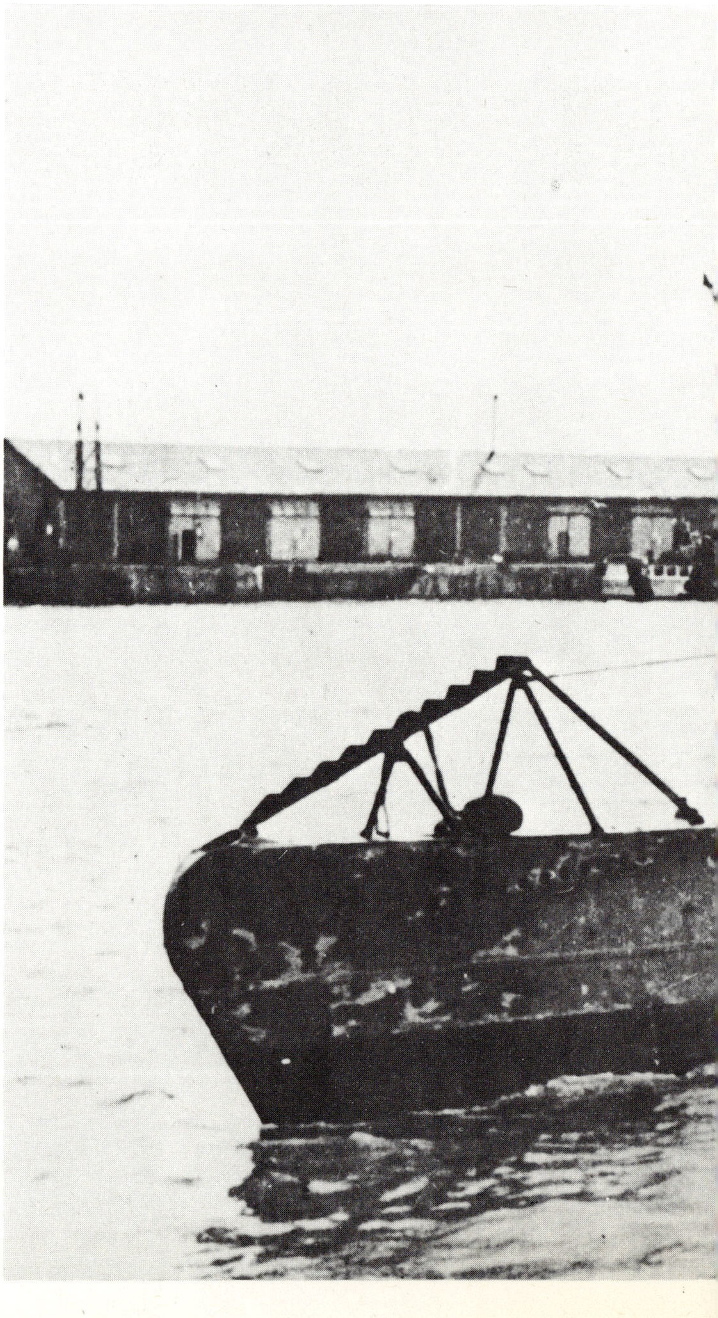

7.46 Admiral Karl Dönitz, C-in-C of the U-boat arm of the *Kriegsmarine*, reviews three U-boats. As this is clearly a wartime photograph (from the extra AA guns) it is likely to have been taken in the Baltic during training. **AP**
CPL

7.47 The Type VIIC displaced 769/1070 tons (respectively, surface/submerged), had two-shaft diesel/electric motors with 2800 to 3200 BHP/750 BHP and speeds of $17\frac{1}{2}/7\frac{1}{2}$ knots, with a radius of 8500 miles (at 10 knots), 130 miles (at 2 knots) or 80 miles (at 4 knots). The armament included five 21inch torpedo-tubes with fourteen torpedoes; and one 3.5inch gun, one 37mm and two 20mm AA machine guns, an armament of machine guns which was gradually strengthened until a maximum of eight 20mm weapons were fitted, generally together with the removal of the 3.5inch gun, for the new tactics of warfare. The complement was 4 officers and 40 to 44 petty officers and seamen. The view shows a VIIC boat entering a shelter dock in Brest in 1942. **AF**
Aldo Fraccaroli Collection

7.48 A U-boat (*Unterseeboot* in German) returning home from the Atlantic. Both in the First and in the Second World Wars Germany concentrated on her submarines for naval warfare. In 1939 she entered the war with a total of 57 *U-boote* (of which only 49 were operational, and only a part of these were capable of oceanic duties, the others being small coastal boats) and during the war 1162 went into actual service, sinking 150 warships and 2840 merchant vessels totalling more than 14 million GR tons. Of the Type VII, which was the most successful, German yards built 731 boats. **AF**
Aldo Fraccaroli Collection

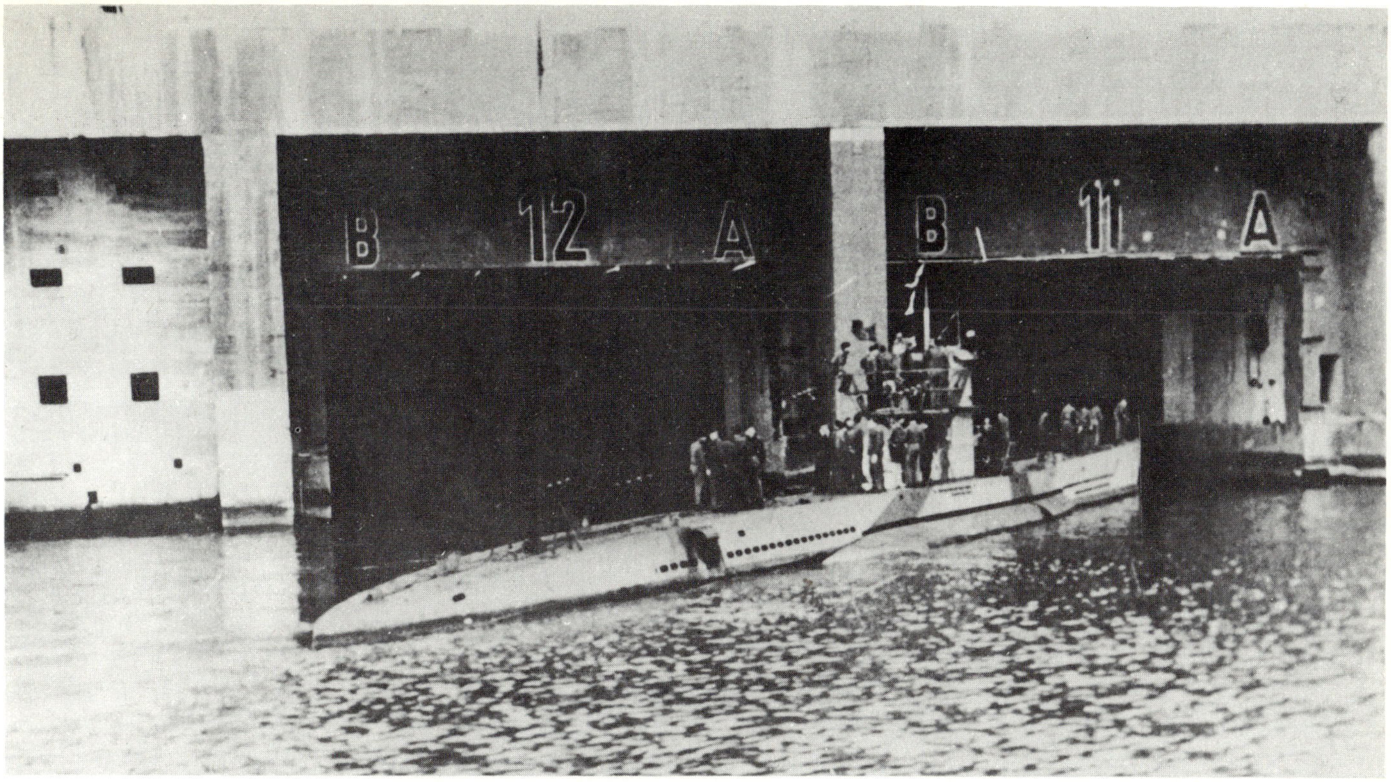

7.47

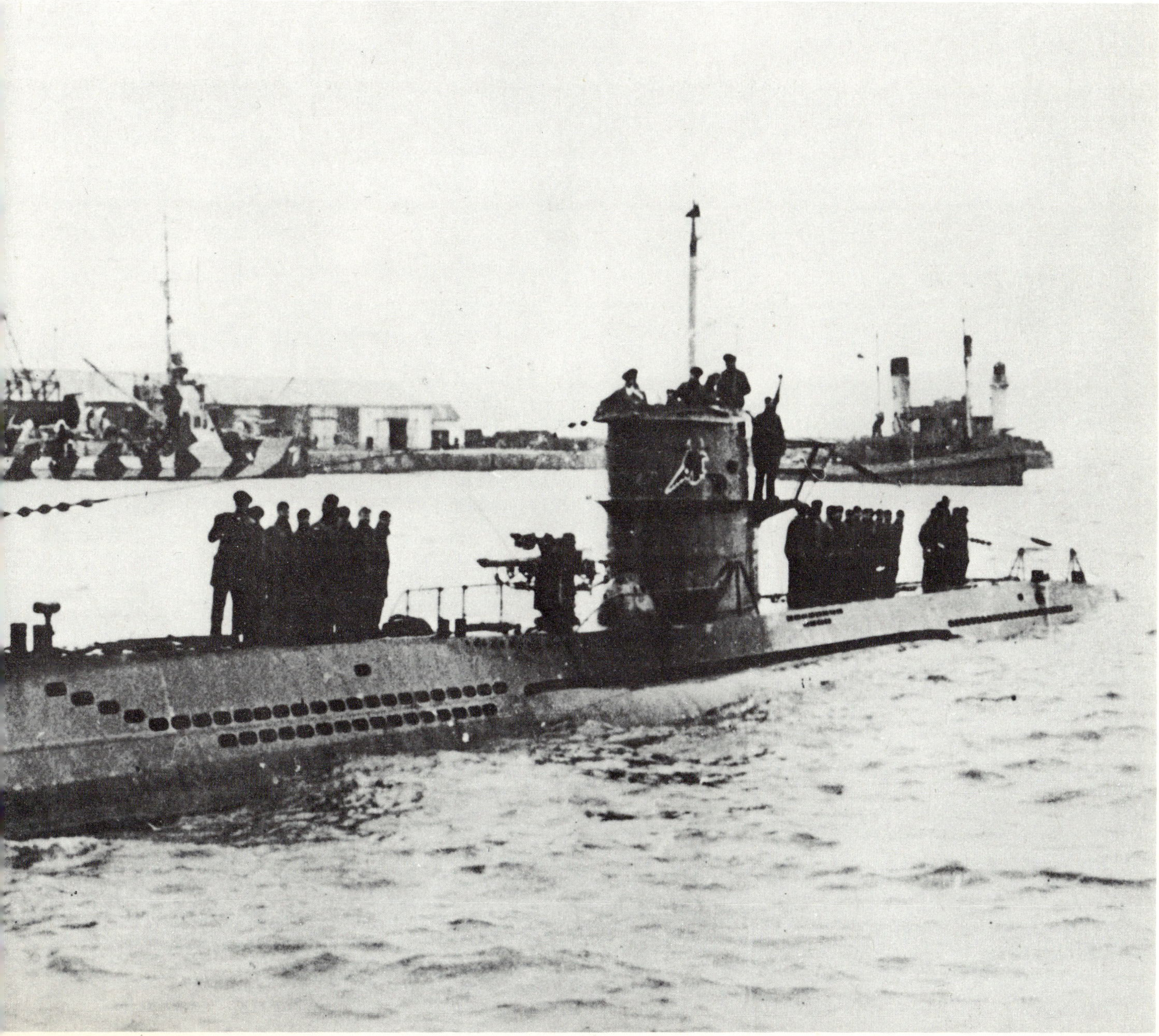

7.48

7.49

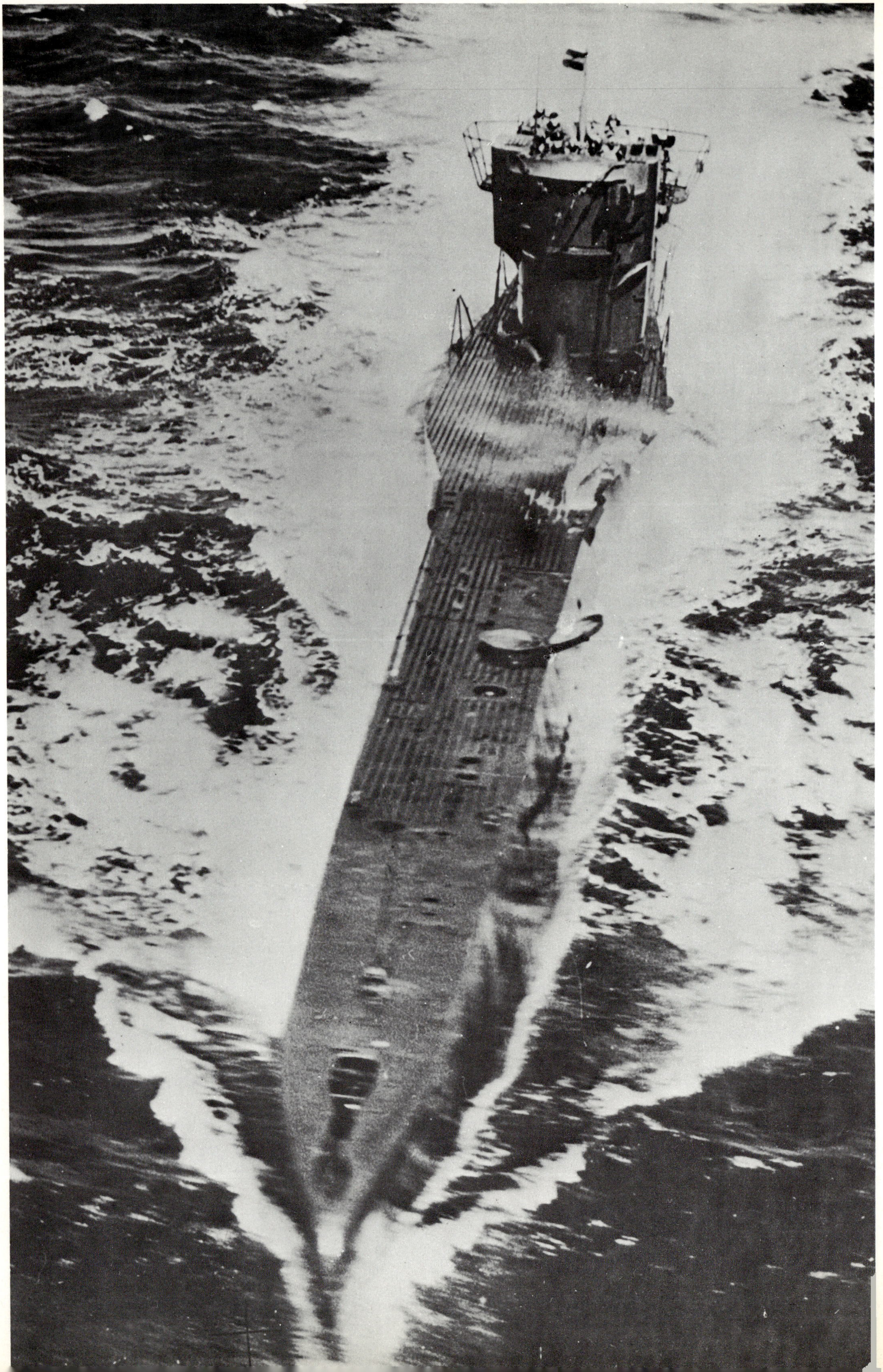

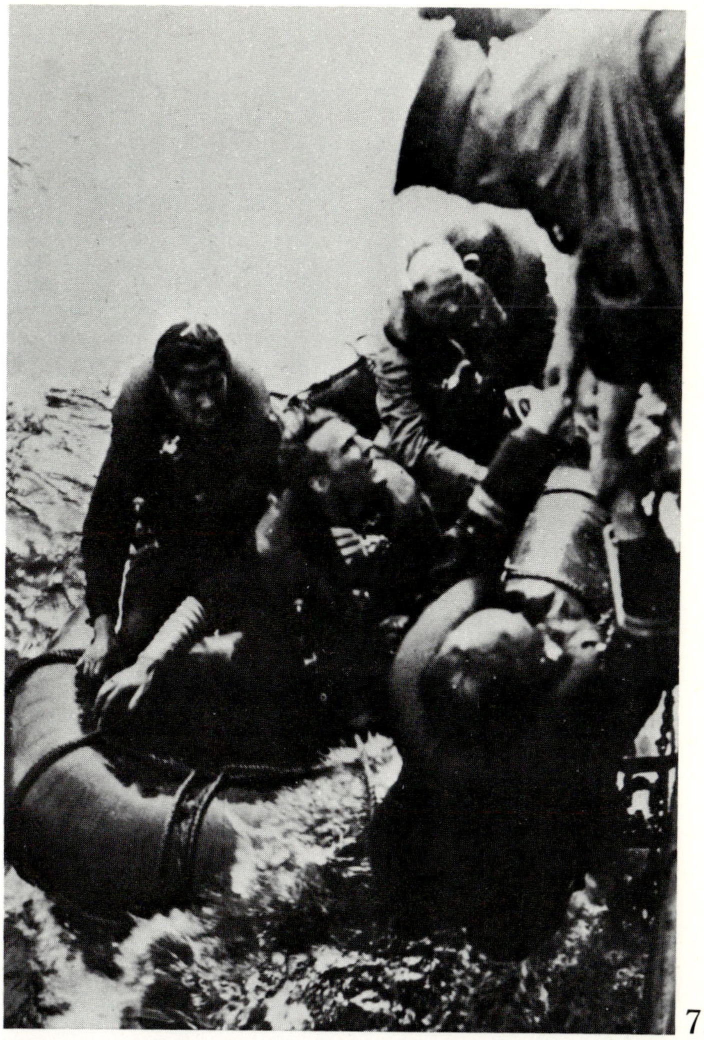

7.49 A German submarine under attack by a British aircraft, possibly in 1943. From 1943 onwards, the U-boats suffered very severe losses from British and American aircraft, even in the areas which until then had been beyond the range of aircraft. This was the merit of escort carriers, which accompanied the convoys and were also a part of the anti-submarine warfare hunting groups. **AF**

Aldo Fraccaroli Collection

7.50 U-boat warfare could never be humane, as the submarine was too small to accommodate the prisoners or the prize crews needed. The only effective way was to sink 'at sight', and so survivors risked appalling privations in open boats with an outside chance of being rescued. But the submarines risked equal, if not worse, horrors — here the few survivors of a sunken U-boat are picked up by a British escort. **AP**

CPL

7.51 Only two U-boats formally surrendered, as it was usually possible to scuttle a disabled boat before she could be boarded. But on 4 October 1941 *U 570* gave herself up to a pair of Hudson bombers of RAF Coastal Command. Later to be recommissioned as HMS *Graph* for evaluation, she is seen here being brought home under the White Ensign. **AP**

CPL

7.50

7.51

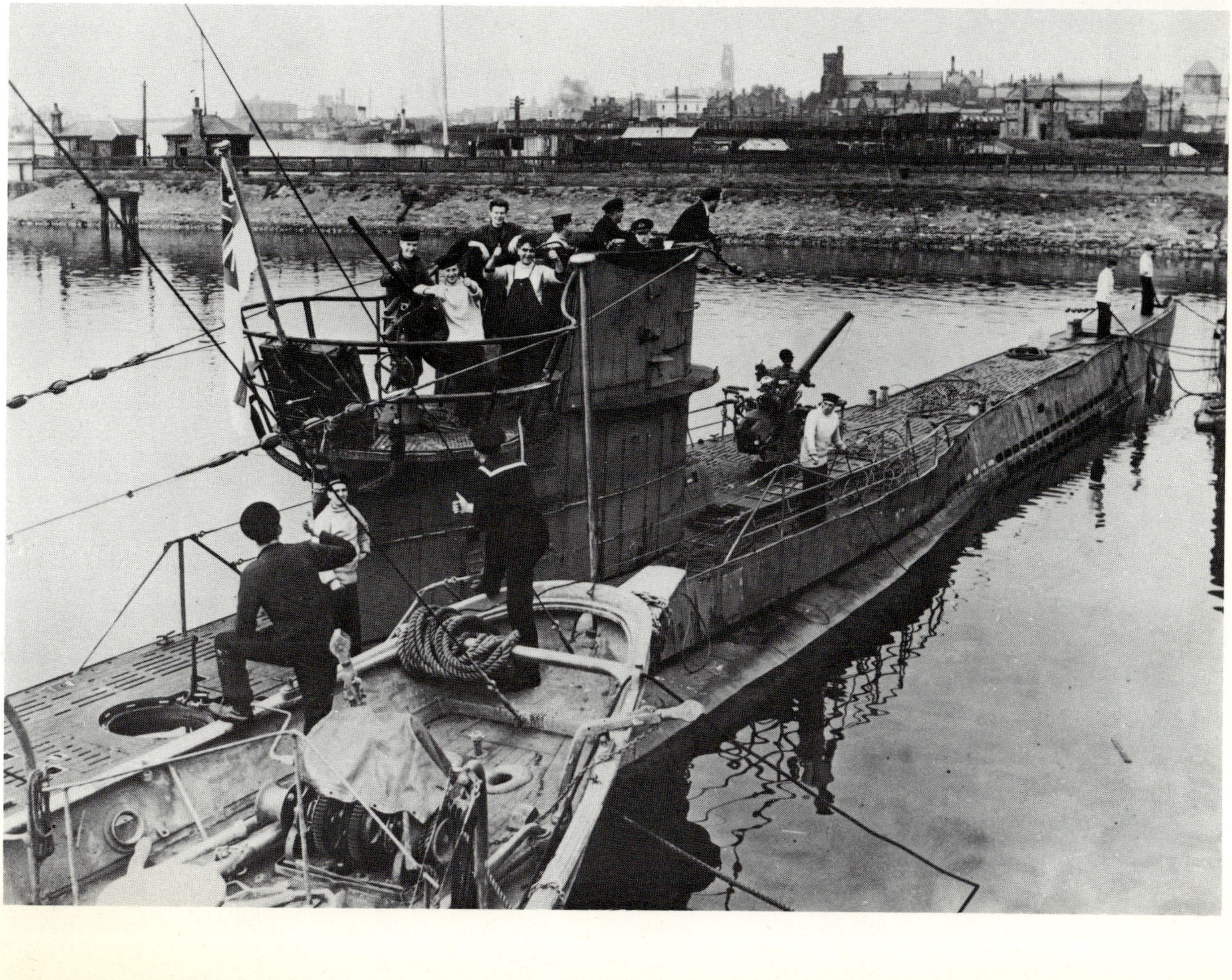

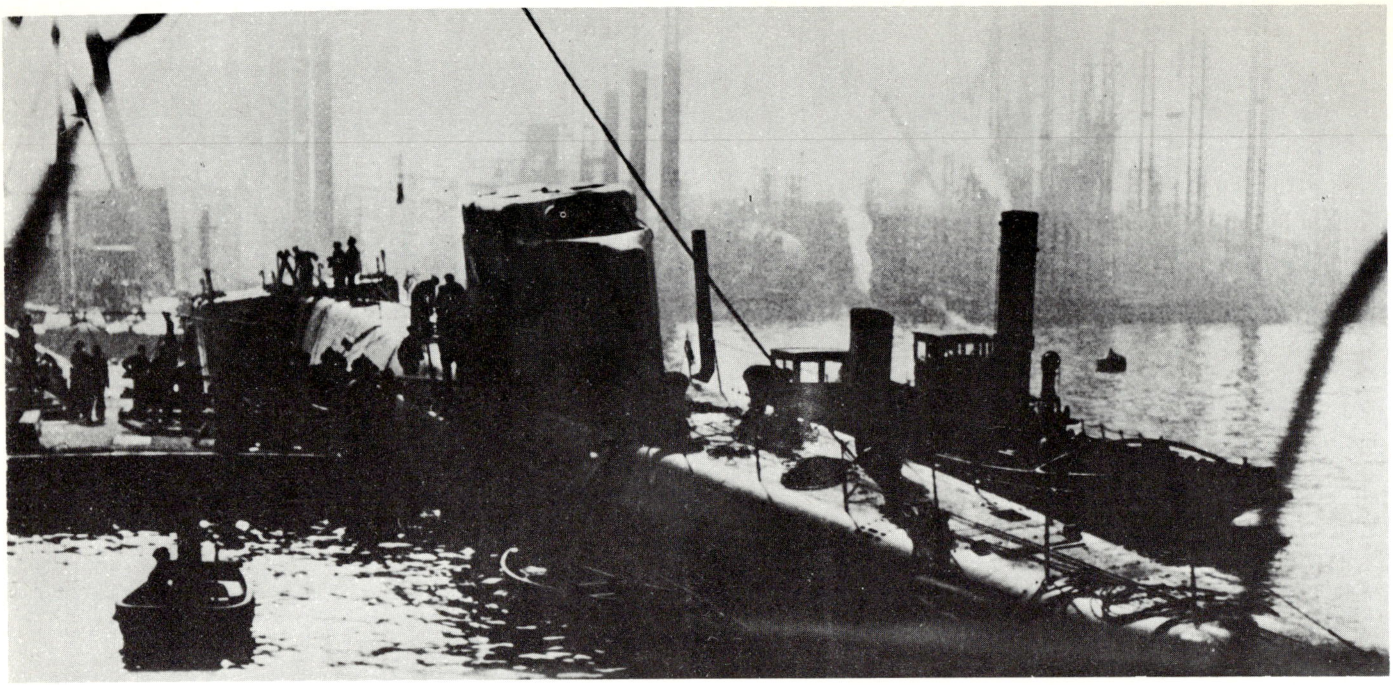

7.52

7.5

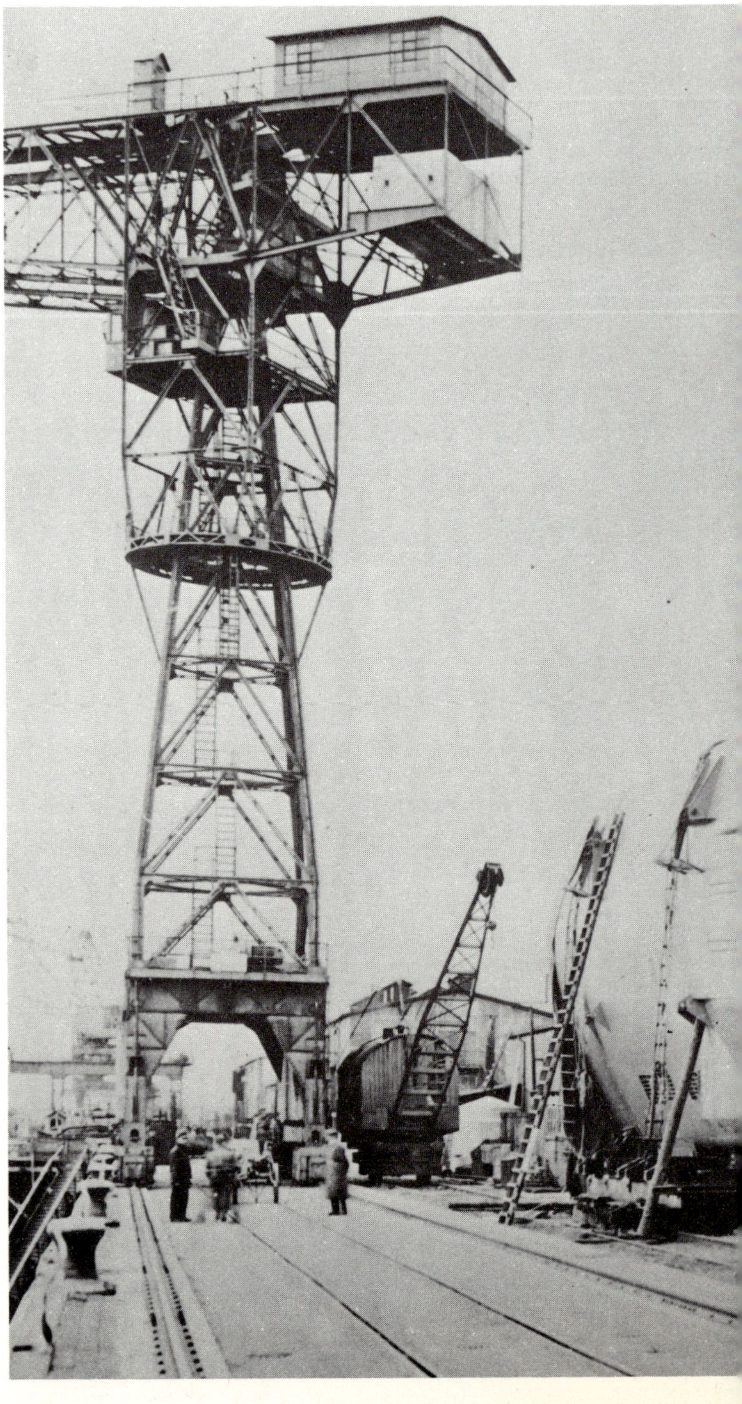

7.52 The torpedo armament of the Type XXI was remarkable, carrying 23 weapons for six bow tubes. On the other hand, the gun armament was small, as this type of boat was projected for operating almost always below the sea — a true submarine, not just a submersible. They had four 20mm machine guns (no deck gun) until the new 30mm weapons were available. The Type XXI displaced 1621/1819 tons, was 76.7 m long, 6.6 beam and had a draught of 6.3 m; complement totalled 57 men. In this view, taken during the winter of 1943-44, a 'XXI' U-boat is completing at Hamburg in the Blohm und Voss yard. In total, in the last months of war (the first 'XXI' was commissioned in June 1944), 118 'Elektro-U-boote' of the Type XXI were commissioned. **AF**
Aldo Fraccaroli Collection

7.53 Some of the eight sections of a Type XXI under construction in the Deschimag yard at Bremen in 1944, before assembling. This type was known as the 'Elektro-U-boot' because of the greater capacity of their electric batteries. Their electric motors were more powerful than the diesels (5000 BHP against 4000 BHP), and the speed of the submerged boat was higher (17.2 knots) than on the surface (15.6) while the radius of action was 285 miles under water (at 6 knots) or 110 miles (at 10 knots). The Type XXI was also fitted with the Schnorchel (this being the correct German title, not 'Snorkel' or others) breathing apparatus, which allowed the submarine to use diesel motors 6 to 8 metres down — the length of the vertical pipe of the Schnorchel. **AF**
Aldo Fraccaroli Collection

7.54 The Type XXIII of coastal *Unterseeboote* was built on the lines of Type XXI, but obviously the former was a small boat (232/276 tons), even if with a powerful electric battery. Her speed was 9.7/12.5 knots, and her armament consisted of two 21inch torpedo-tubes in the bows, each loaded with one weapon (no reserve torpedoes). Complement: 14 men. This view, taken in 1944 in Deutsche Werft of Hamburg, shows two boats of Type XXIII, perhaps *U2370* and *U2371*. **AF**
Aldo Fraccaroli Collection

7.55 The experimental boat *V80* built by Germania Werft of Kiel in 1939-40. Planned, as several other unconventional types, by Professor Hellmuth Walter, her main feature was the very high speed submerged: 28 knots, provided by a H_2O_2 Walter turbine of 2000 SHP (the hydrogen peroxide mixture had been called 'Ingolin' after the inventor's daughter). The boat displaced 86 tons and had a crew of only four men and no armament. **AF**
Aldo Fraccaroli Collection

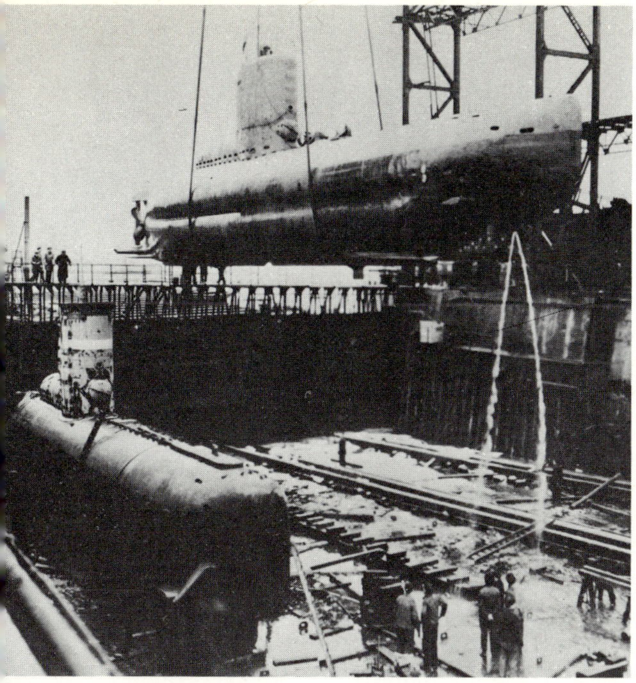

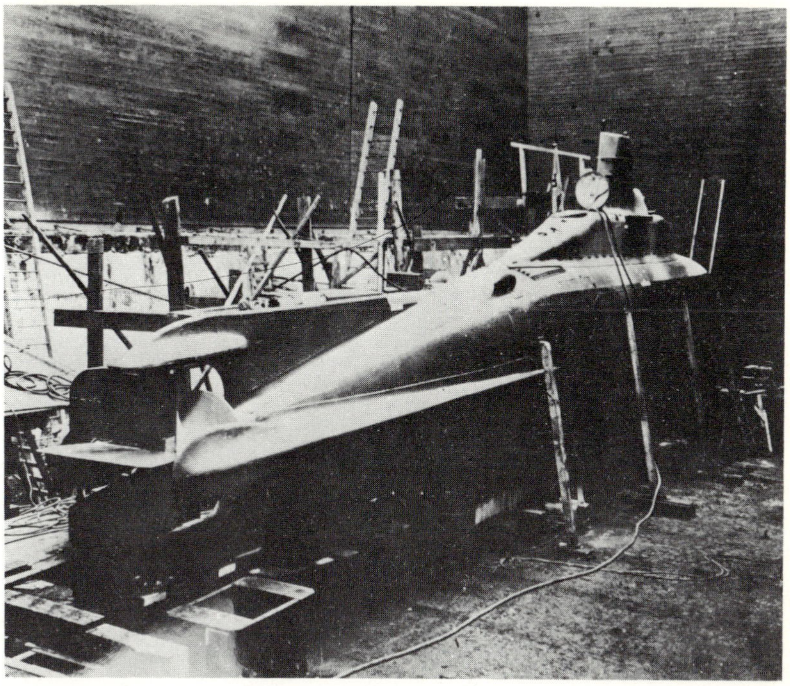

7.55

7.53

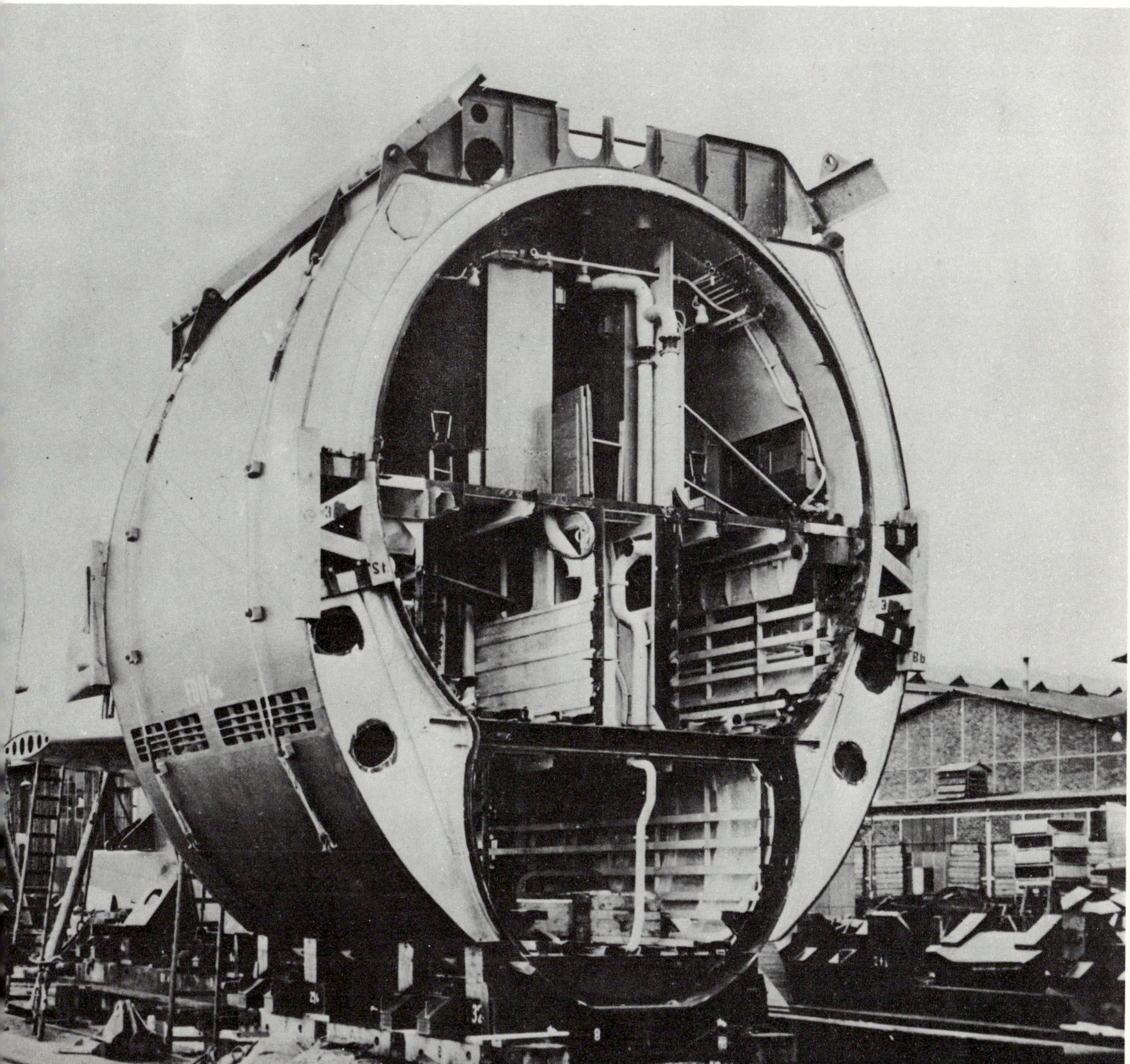

7.56 LSMs and LSTs unload supplies on the volcanic beaches of Iwo Jima, February 1945. Mount Suribachi is in the background. This hill commanded a view of the entire island. The beach is littered with wrecked landing craft and equipment.
LS
USN

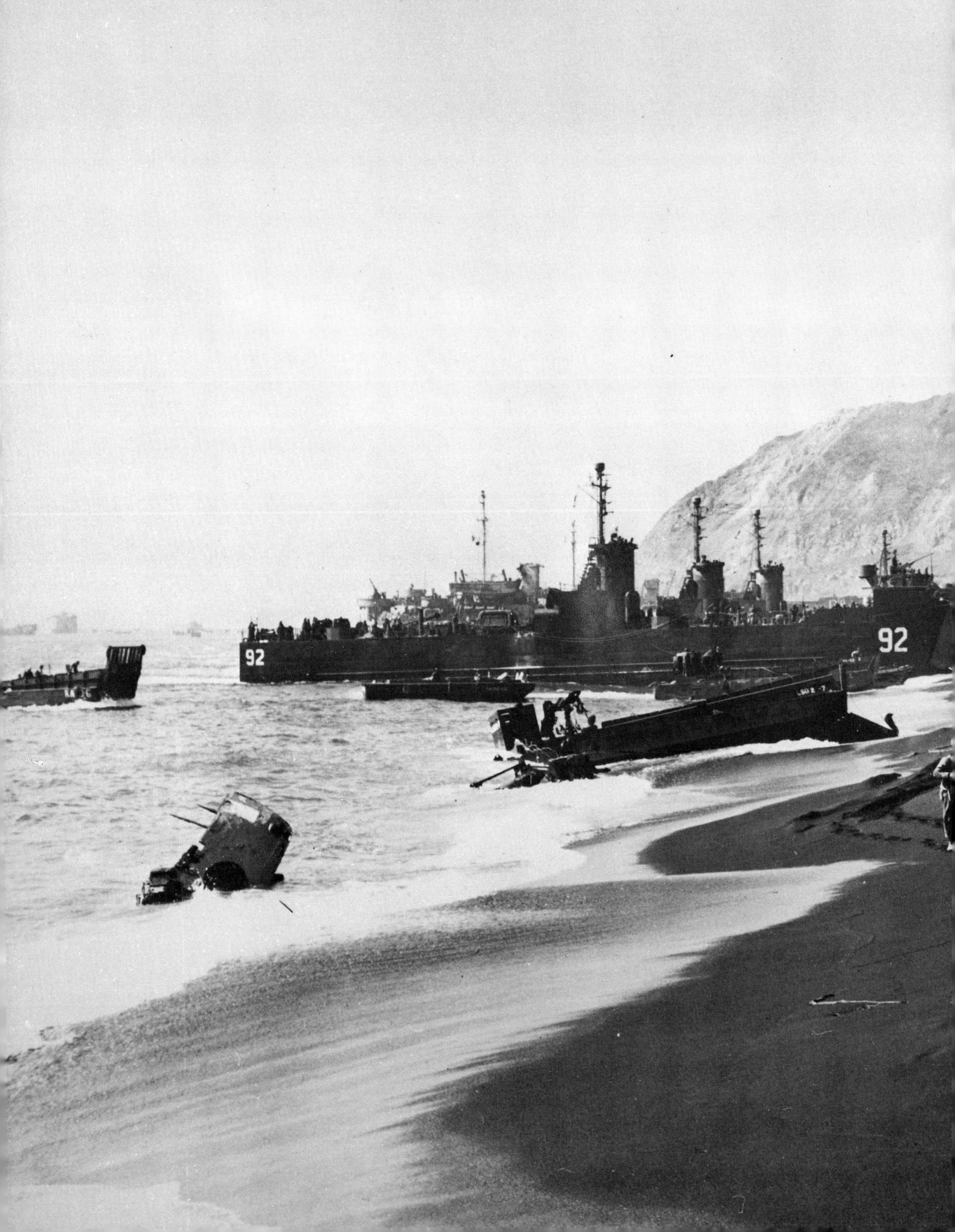

The Pacific

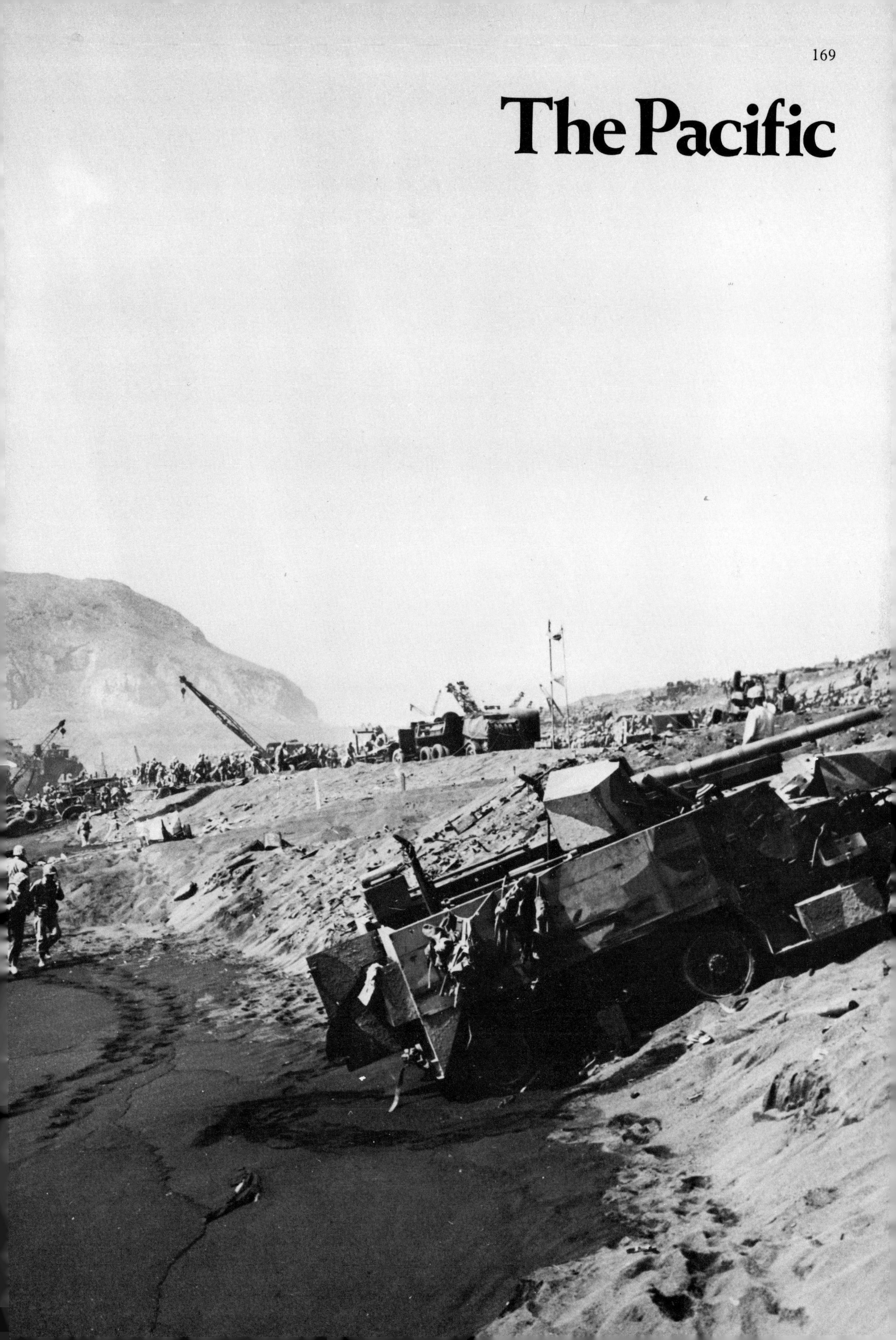

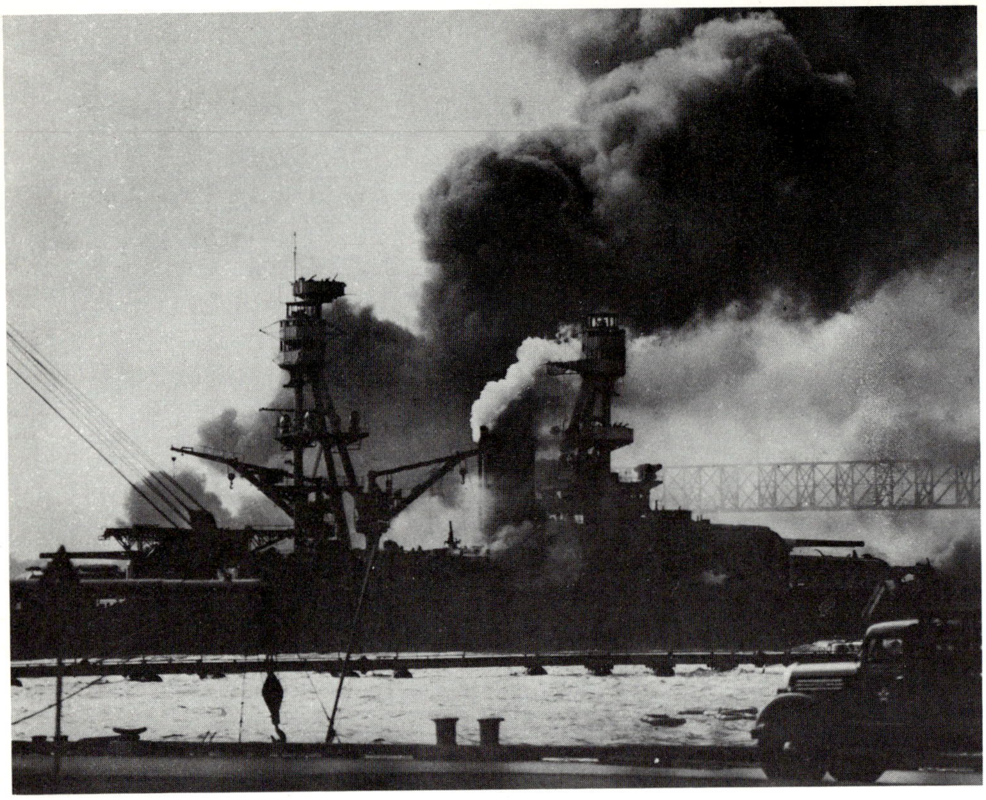

7.58

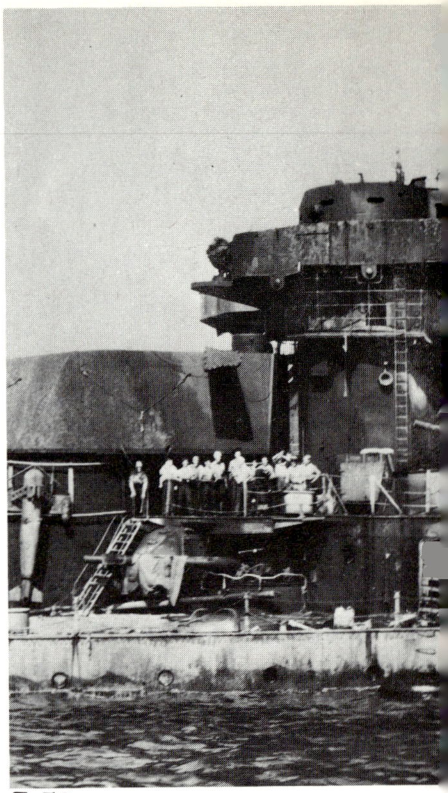

7.59

7.57

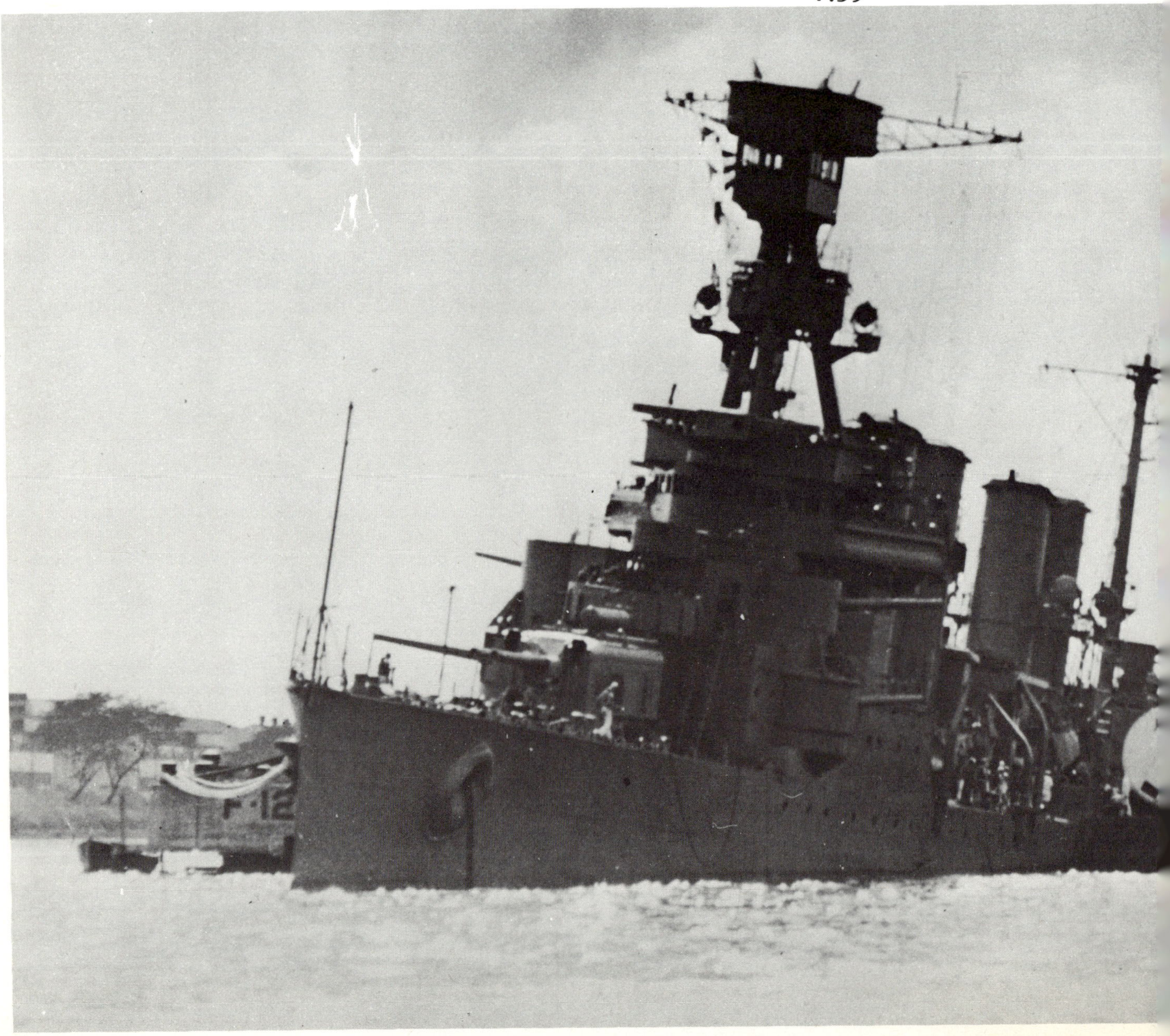

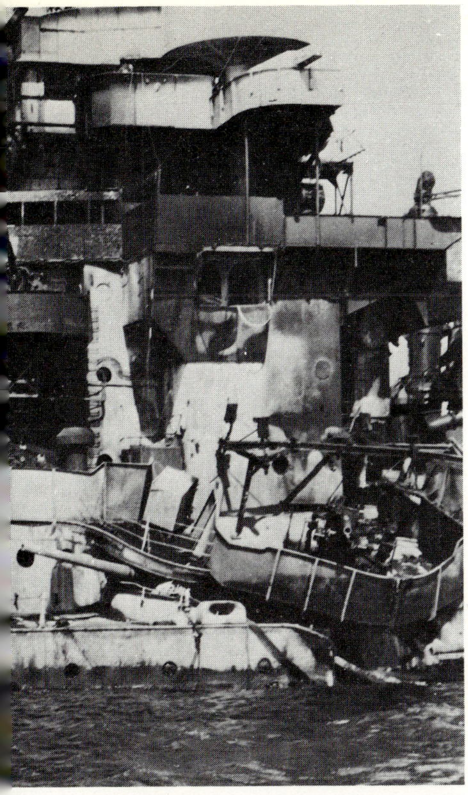

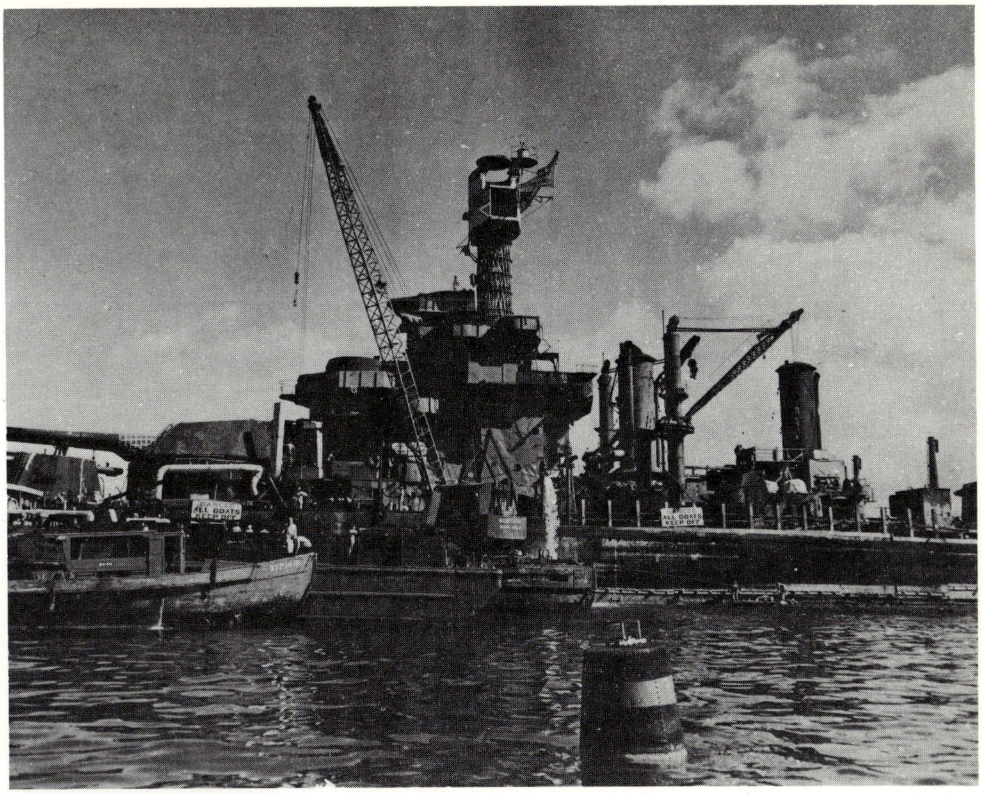

7.60

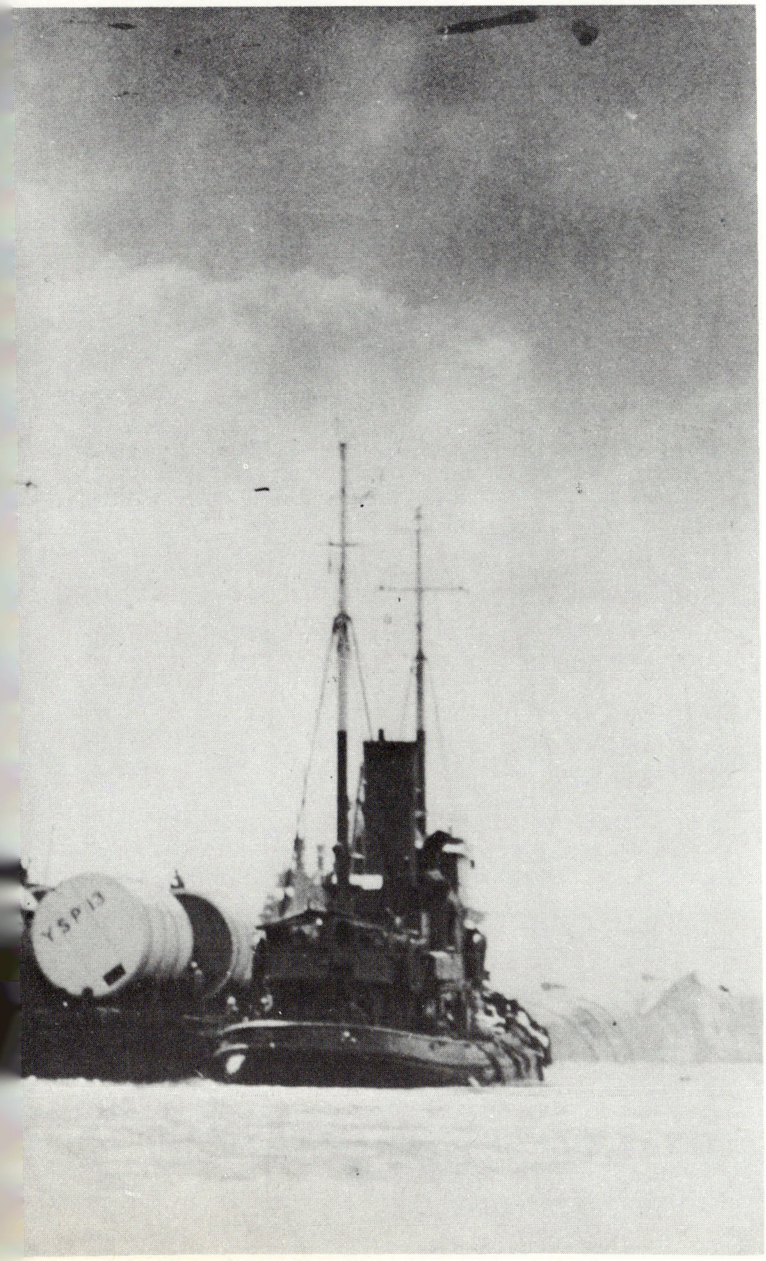

7.57 Pearl Harbor, 7 December 1941. The cruiser *Raleigh* (CL-7) struggles to stay afloat after the attack. The capsized hull, to the right of this picture and immediately behind the *Raleigh*, is that of the training ship *Utah* (ex-battleship). **LS**
USN

7.58 *Nevada* (BB-36) was the only battleship to get underway during the attack on Pearl Harbor. The columns of smoke in the background are from the explosion of the destroyer *Shaw*'s forward magazine. *Nevada* is burning amidships, at the base of the funnel and on the forecastle. **LS**
USN

7.59 Pearl Harbor aftermath. The wrecked *West Virginia* (BB-48) lies on the bottom of Battleship Row. This close-up clearly shows how the AA gun deck has collapsed into the secondary battery's open casemates. The hull, just below the No 2 mount (5inch AA), appears to have been ripped open, probably causing the collapse. **LS**
USN

7.60 *West Virginia* (BB-48) is raised out of the mud of Pearl Harbor, six months (25 May 1942) after she was sunk on 7 December 1941. Outboard ships, like *West Virginia,* received the heaviest damage in Battleship Row. **LS**
USN

7.61 An American battleship and cruiser (in the background) pound Peleliu on 15 September 1944. It is fifteen minutes before Zero Hour. The troop-filled landing craft sit and wait for the 'go'. **LS**
USN

7.62 LSM-20 plunges to the bottom of Surigao Strait. Look closely and you can make out five men scrambling to get off the landing ship as she goes down. LSM-20 was on a backwaters 'milk run' when she was hit by a kamikaze, 5 December 1944. **LS**
USN

7.63 Australian troops wade ashore at Labuan Island, Brunei Bay on 10 June 1945. Put ashore from American landing ships and craft, this combined operation was supported by US and Australian warships. The objective was to completely cut off Japan's oil supplies at the source. **LS**
USN

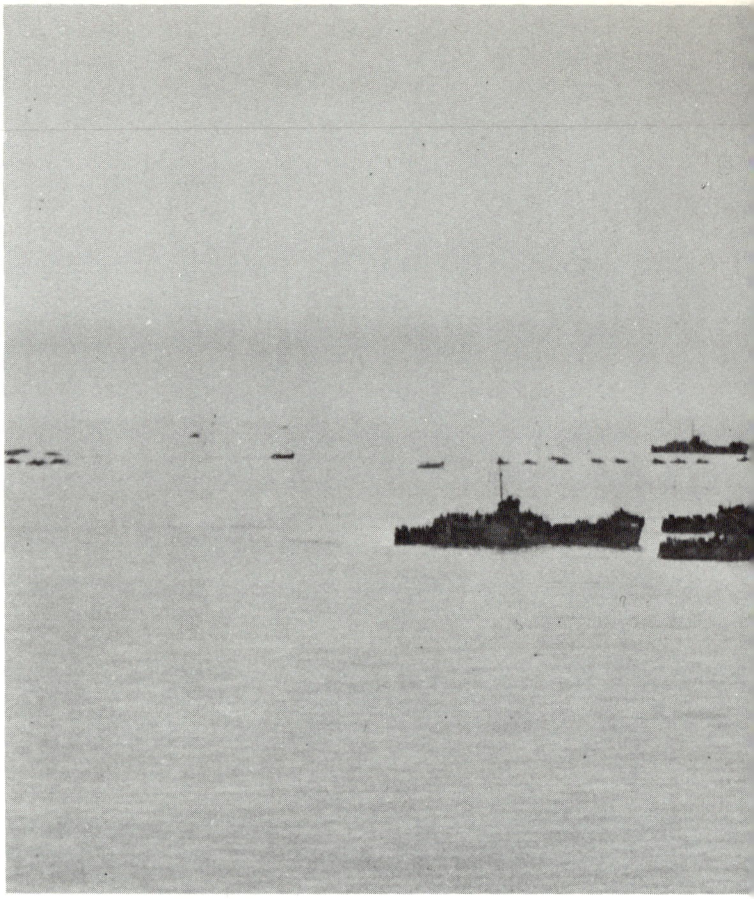

7.62

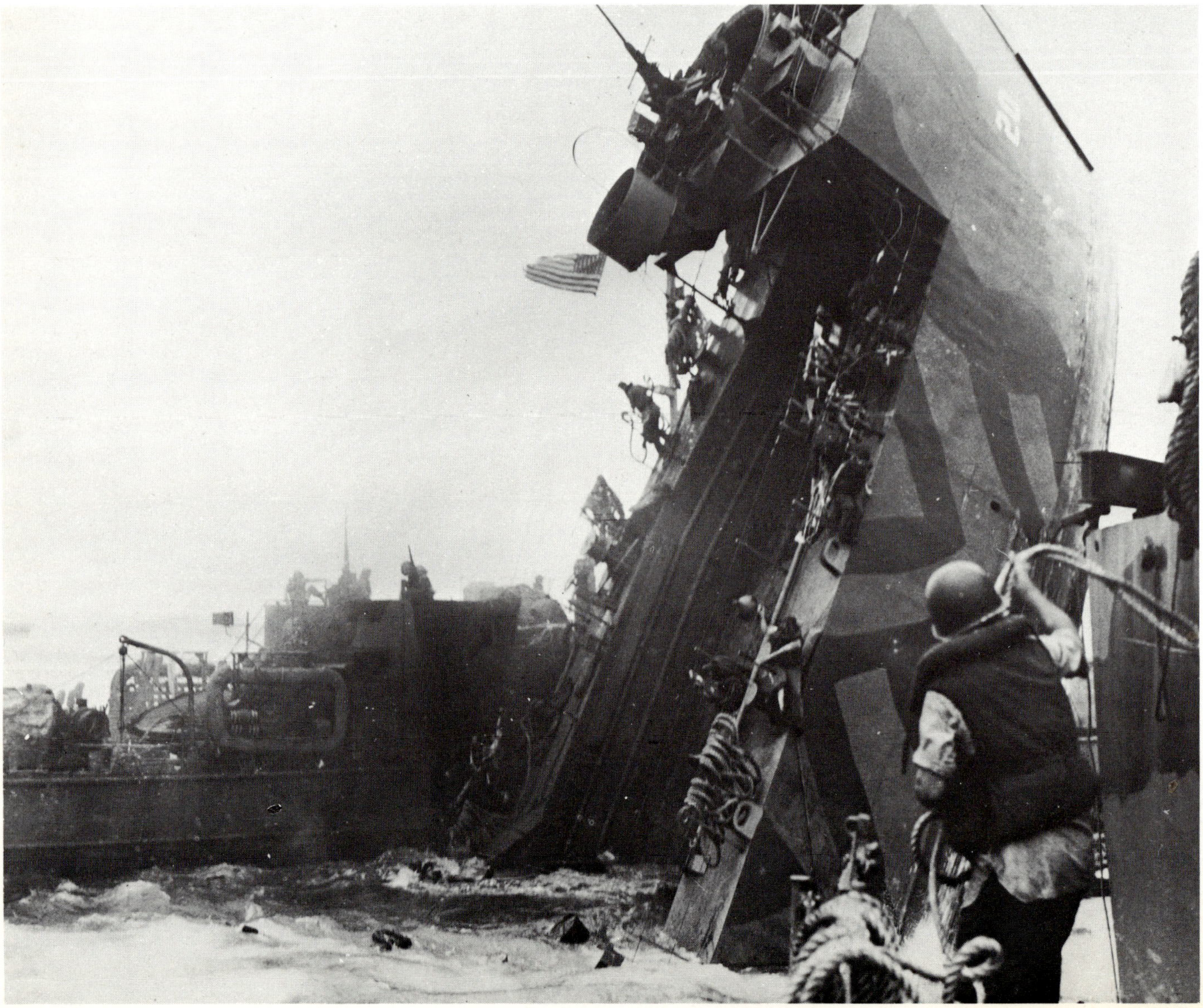

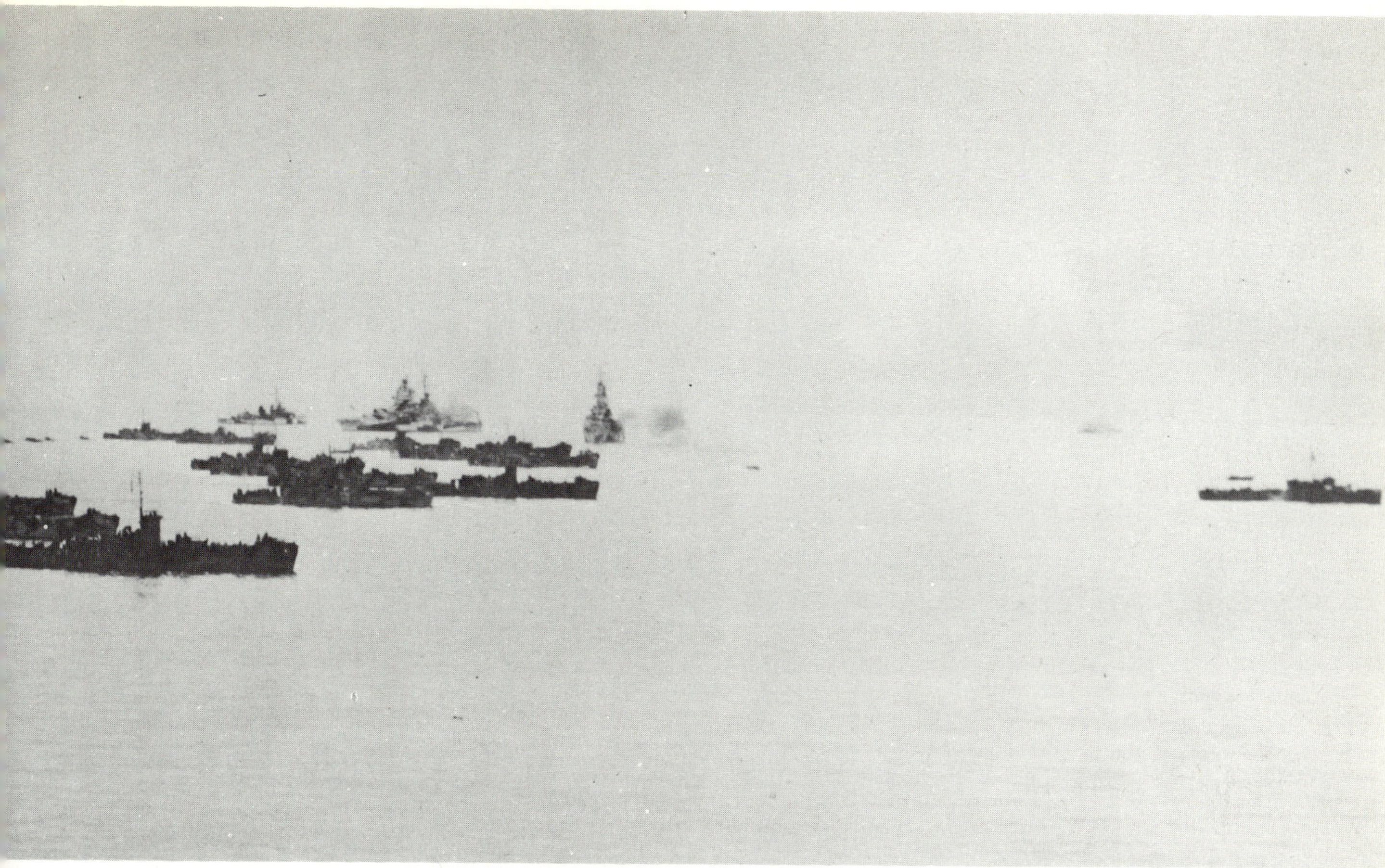

7.61

7.63

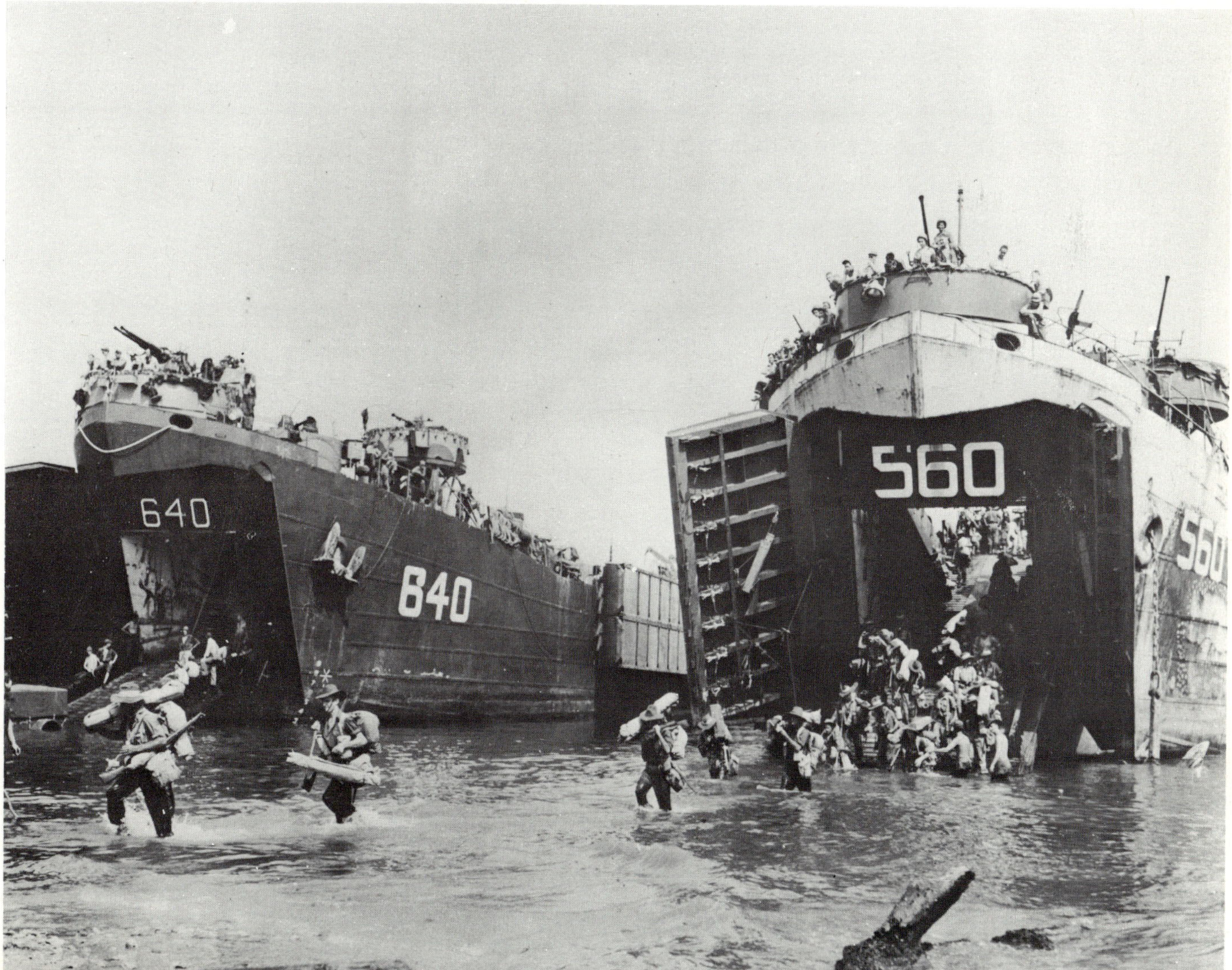

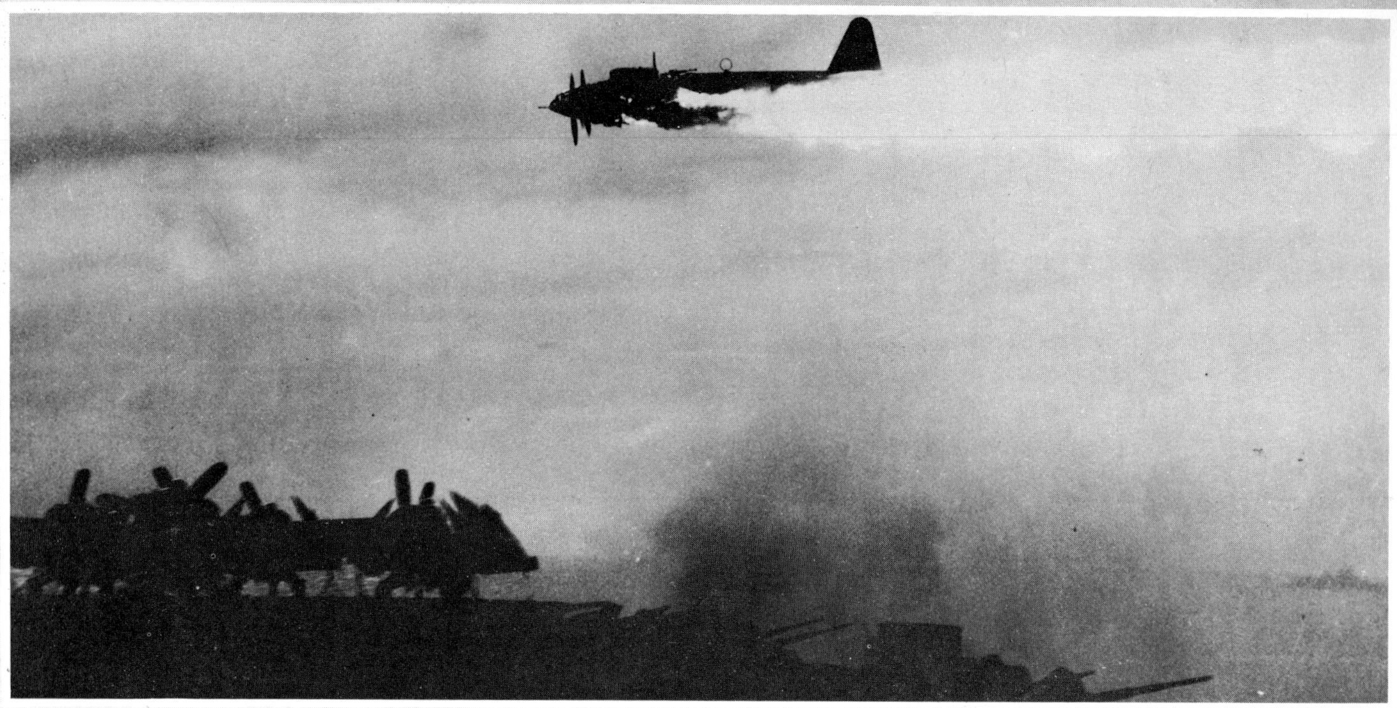

7.64

7.64 A Japanese Mitsubishi G4M 'Betty' passing close to an American escort carrier and about to crash after being hit by AA fire. The aircraft shown was one of many sent on suicide missions (Kamikaze) to attack units of the American Fleet during the closing stages of the Second World War. Lacking pilots with sufficient training in aerial warfare and unable to match the American carrier aircraft the Japanese, in a desperate measure to counter the overwhelming American air strength and superiority in carriers and battleships, sought to redress the imbalance by resorting to suicide missions. Pilots were given orders to crash their aircraft, packed with high explosive, on to the decks and superstructures of American ships, preferably battleships and aircraft carriers, with cruisers and destroyers as secondary targets, in a desperate effort to sink them. **AW**
CPL

7.65 *Hornet* (CV-12) gunners shoot down a Japanese bomber off the coast of Japan. The burning plane attempted to hit the carrier but crashed into the sea instead. *Bennington* (CV-20) is in the background. **LS**
USN

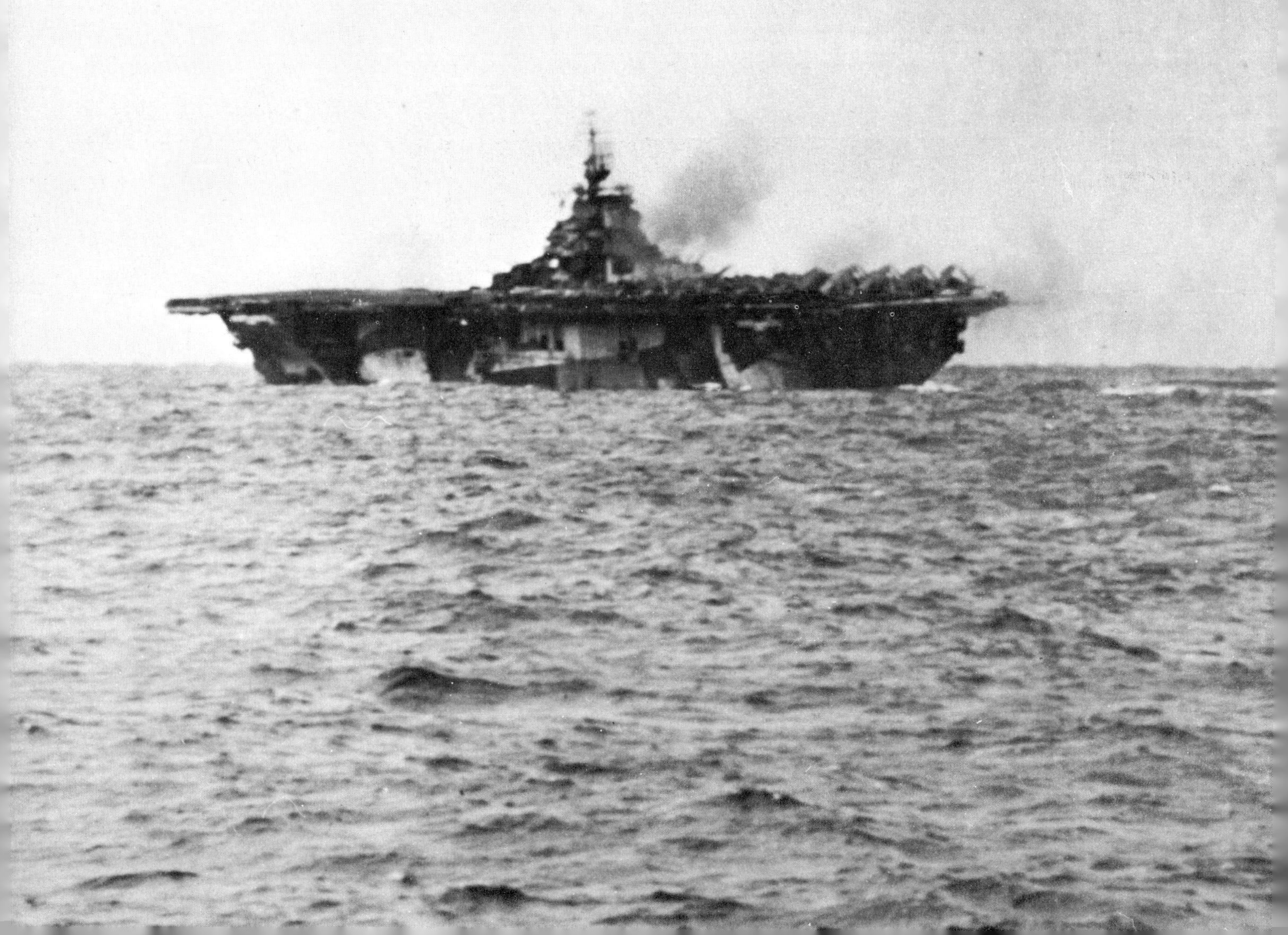

Kamikaze

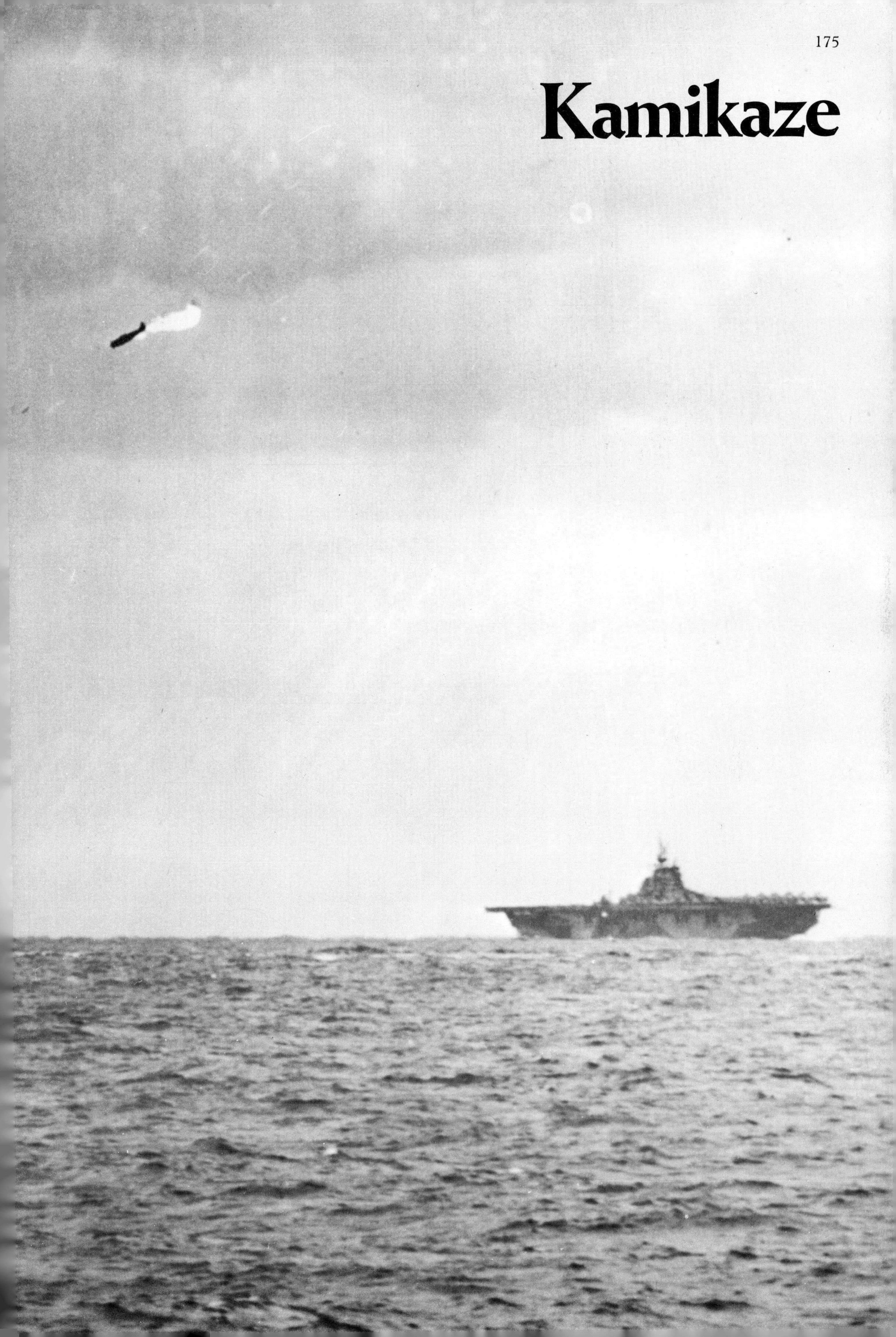

7.66 The *Saint Lo*'s luck runs out, 25 October 1944. Earlier in the day, this escort carrier had been damaged by gunfire from Japanese battleships and cruisers off Samar, in the Philippines. After surviving what seemed like certain death, her Task Unit was then hit by kamikazes. *Saint Lo* (CVE-63) was the only ship lost. **LS**
USN

7.67 Only 50 miles off the hostile shores of Japan, *Franklin* (CV-13) fights for her life. A lone plane came low out of the clouds and dropped two bombs square on 'Big Ben's' busy flight deck. Everything went up in fire and explosion. When it was over, 724 men were killed, 265 wounded. The carrier was towed out of 'harm's way' and eventually made it all the way back to Brooklyn, New York. **LS**
USN

7.68 On 15 February 1945, a determined Japanese bomber penetrated the 'Inner Sanctum' of the US Navy fleet anchorage at Ulithi. *Randolph* (CV-15) was at anchor when the kamikaze crashed into her. The hole at the after end of the flight deck should have sent *Randolph* back home. However, a repair ship came alongside and the carrier never had to leave the spot where she had been damaged. **LS**
USN

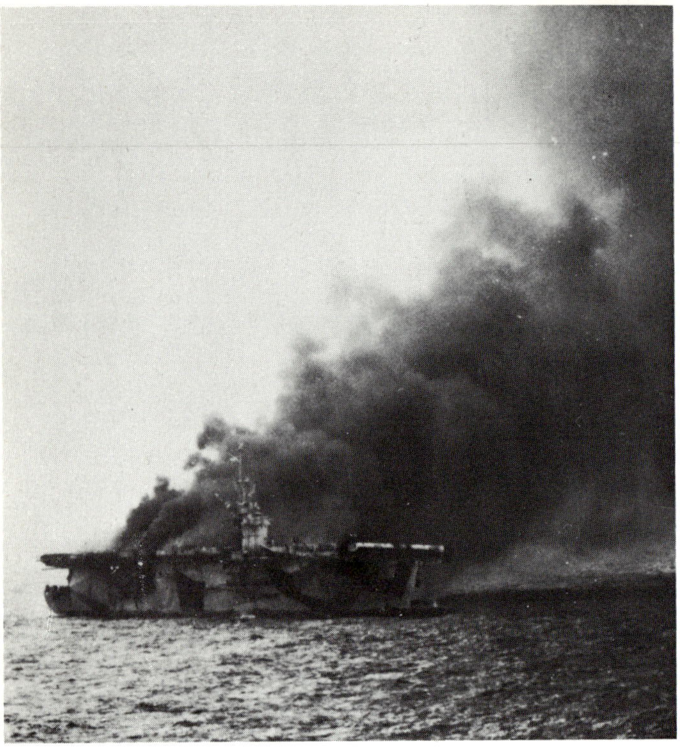
7.66

7.67
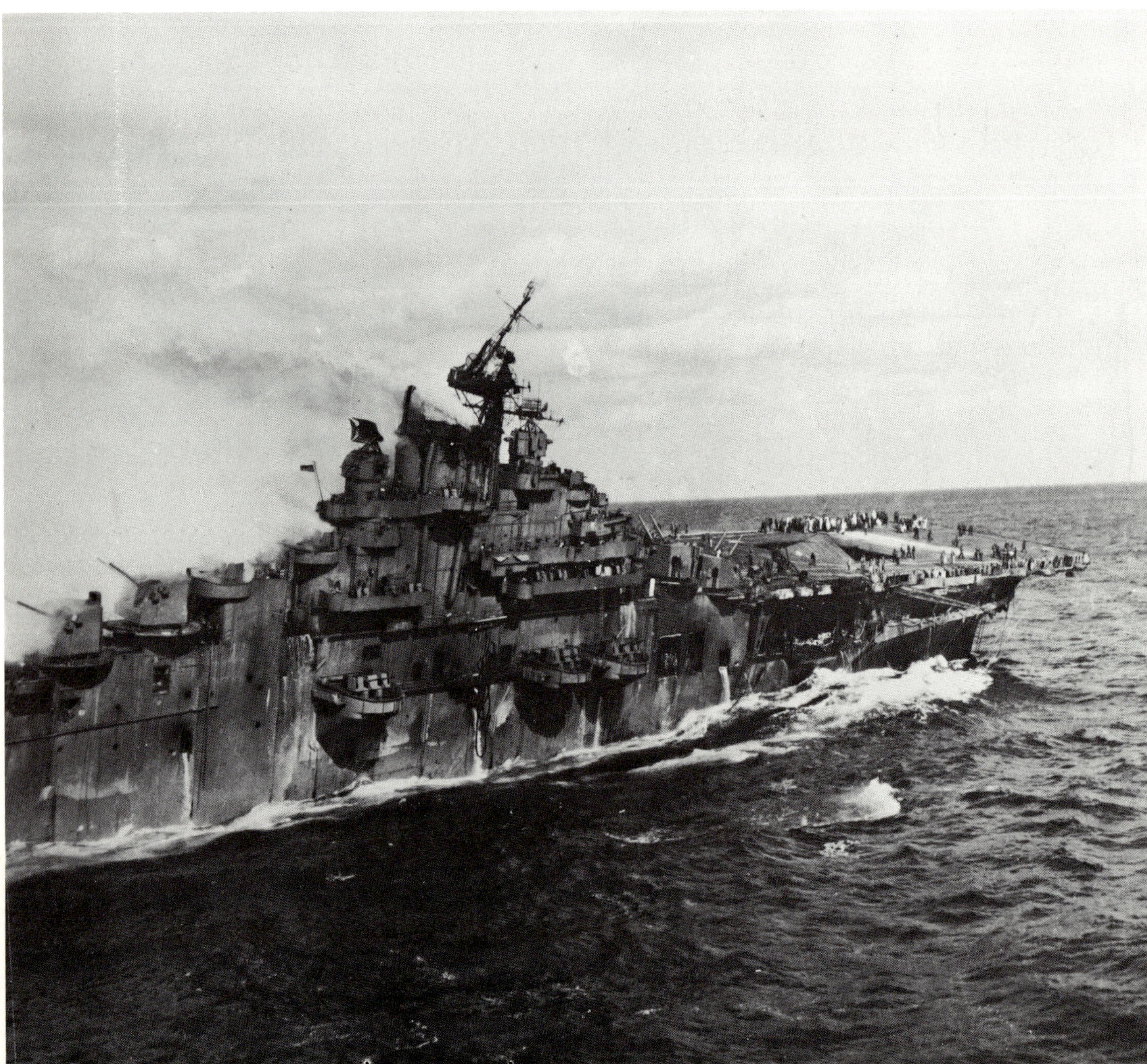

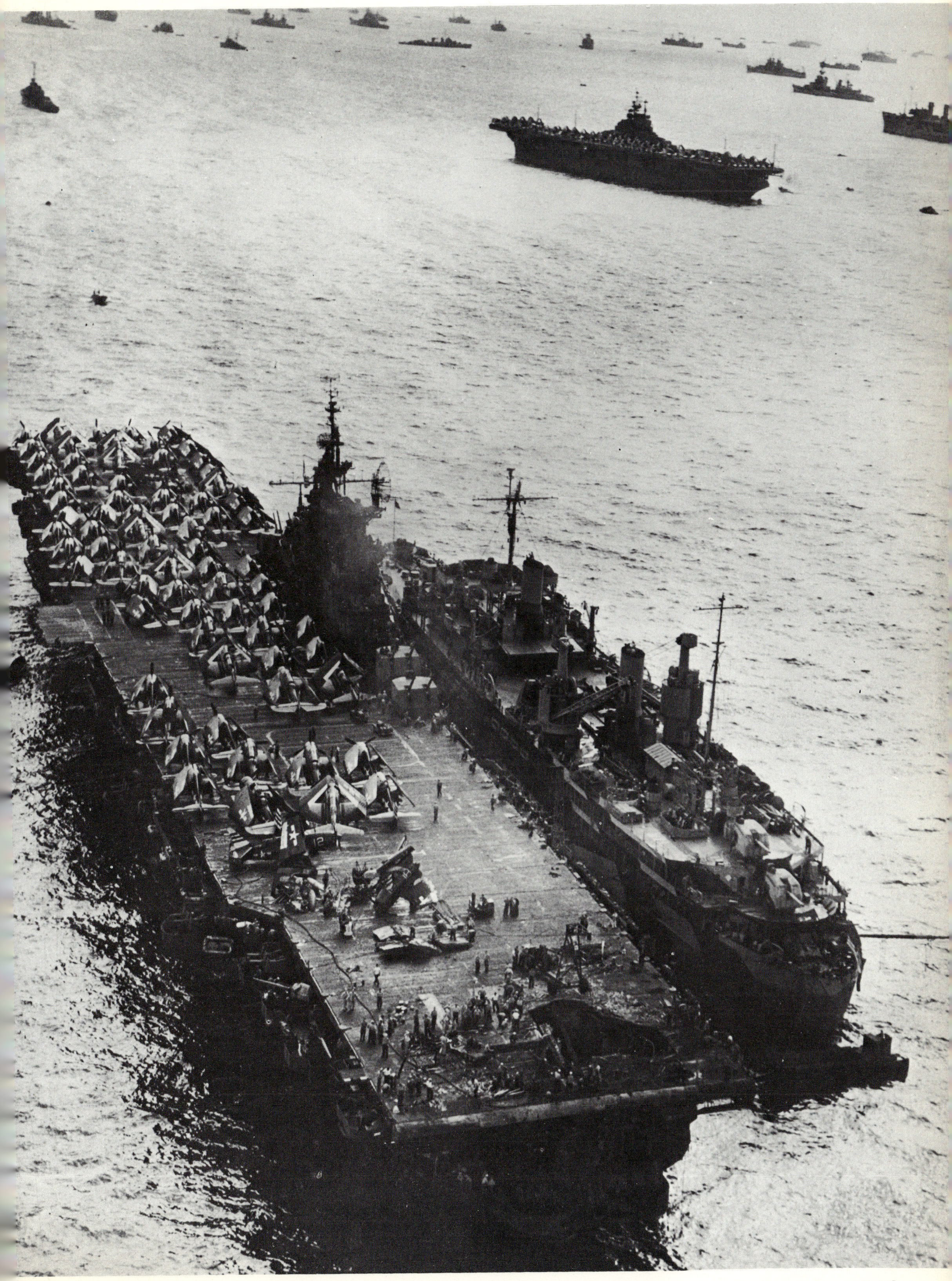

7.68

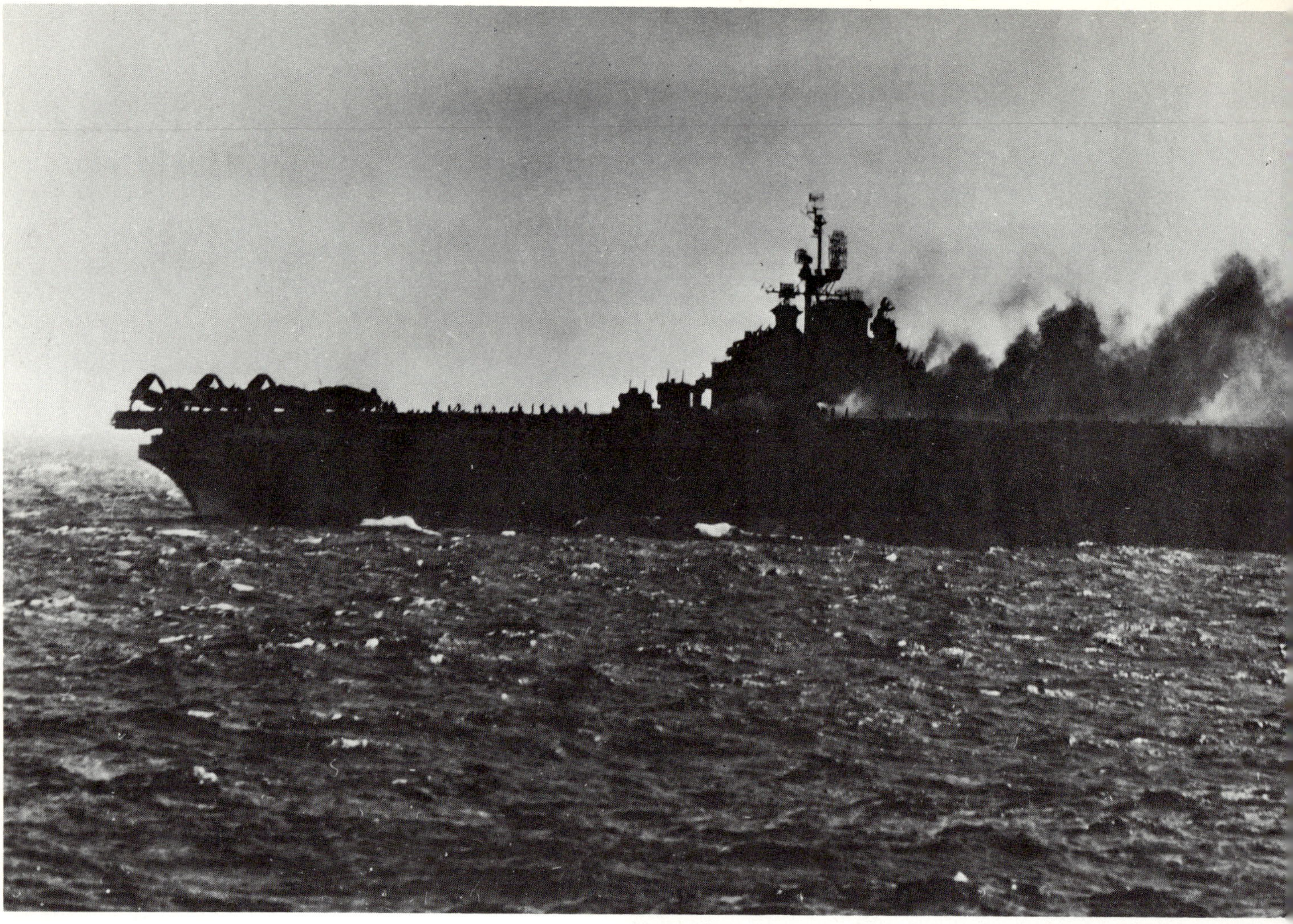

7.69

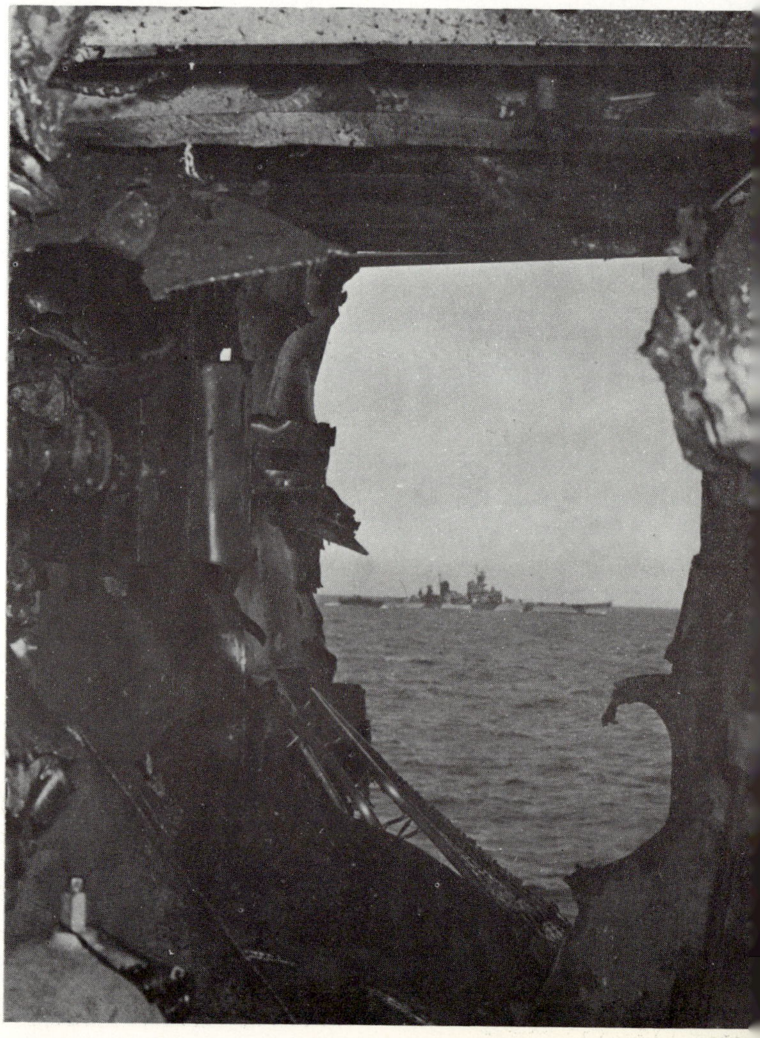

7.70

7.69 *Hancock* (CV-19) burns off Luzon, 25 November 1944. A kamikaze dived on the ship from out of the sun. AA gunners destroyed the plane only 300 feet above the carrier but a fuselage section and wing landed on the flight deck and burst into flames. Whilst it looks bad in this picture, the fire was quickly put out without any damage to the ship. This picture has been published before, but captioned as *Intrepid* (CV-11). Both carriers were in the same task group and hit by kamikazes on the same day. Both wore the same camouflage pattern and colours. However, *Intrepid* was a short bow *Essex,* while *Hancock* carried a long, clipper-type bow, as shown in this picture. **LS**
USN

7.70 On board the *Cabot* (CVL-28), 24 November 1944. This used to be the catapult room: the hole was caused by a kamikaze. The photographer has framed the battleship *Iowa* (BB-61) through the hole. **LS**
USN

7.71 A close up of CV-17 *Bunker Hill*'s flight deck aft. The after elevator was bent 'like a pretzel'. The hangar deck below was a shambles. **LS**
USN

7.72 A fire-damaged F4U Corsair is pushed over the side from *Intrepid*'s outboard elevator. She was one of the aircraft parked inside the hangar when a kamikaze crashed through the flight deck. The resulting fire gutted the hangar but *Intrepid* (CV-11) was landing planes four hours later. The carrier was one of many ships hit off Okinawa during April 1945. **LS**
USN

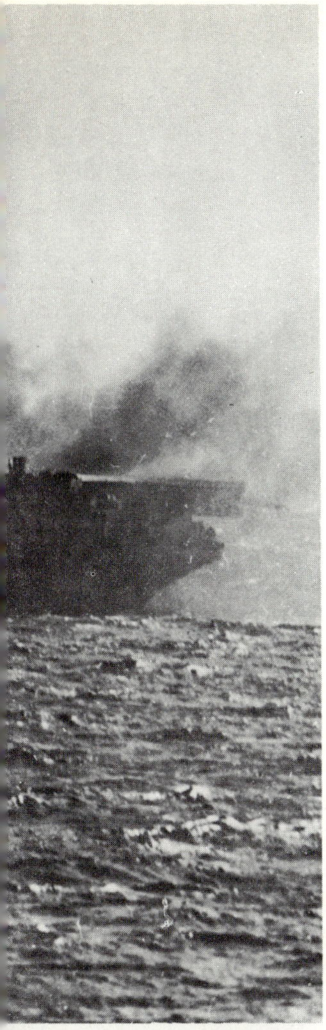

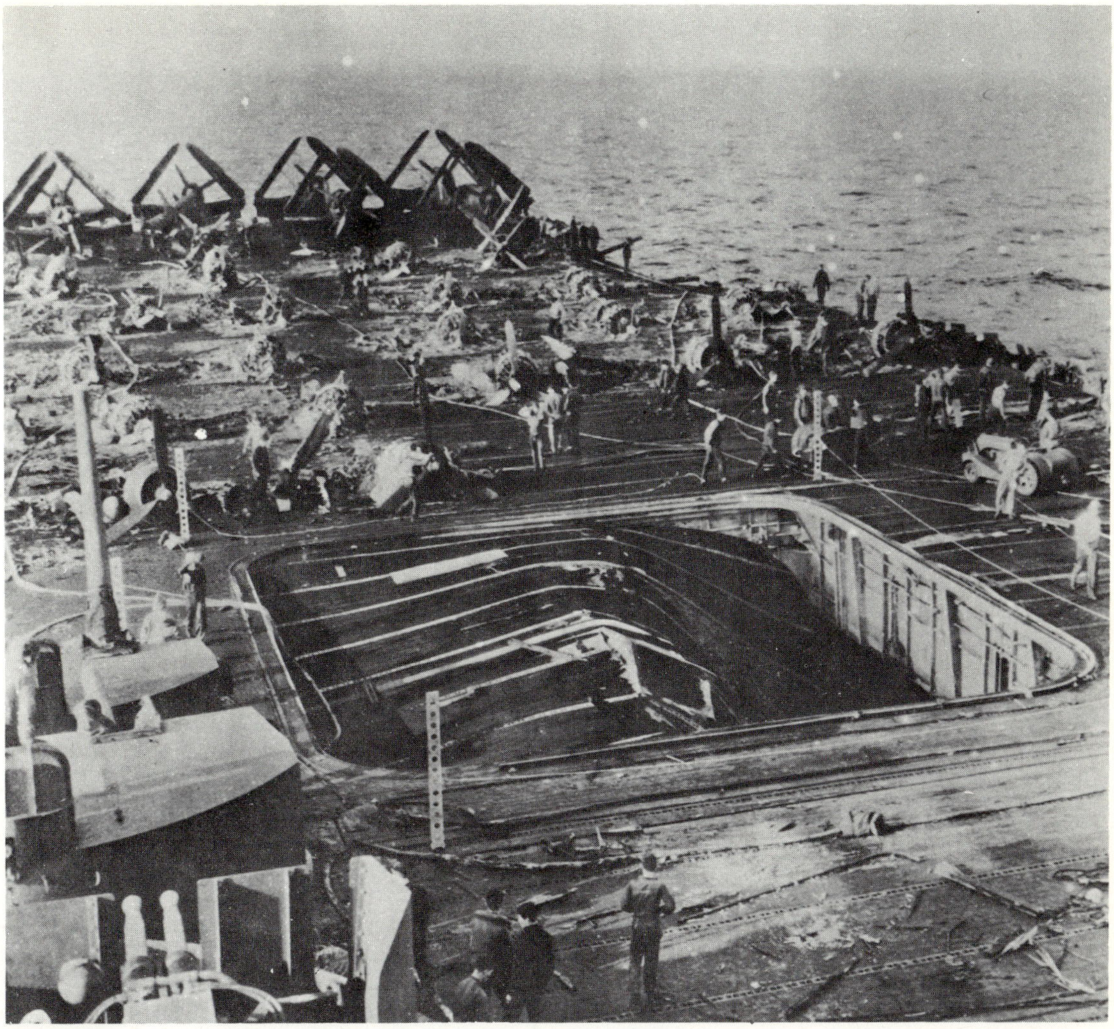

7.71

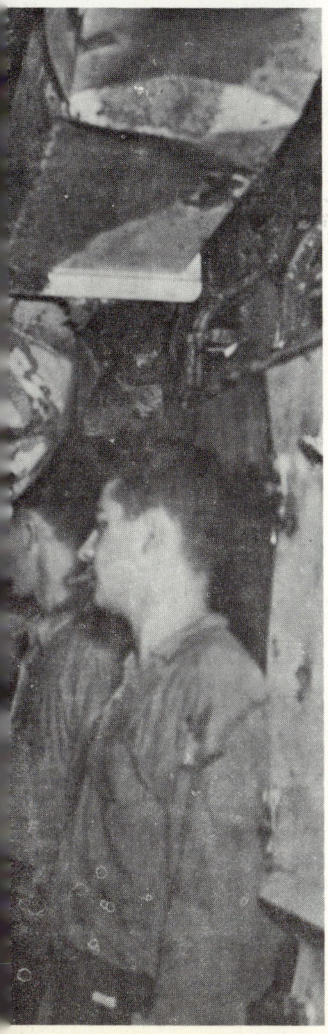

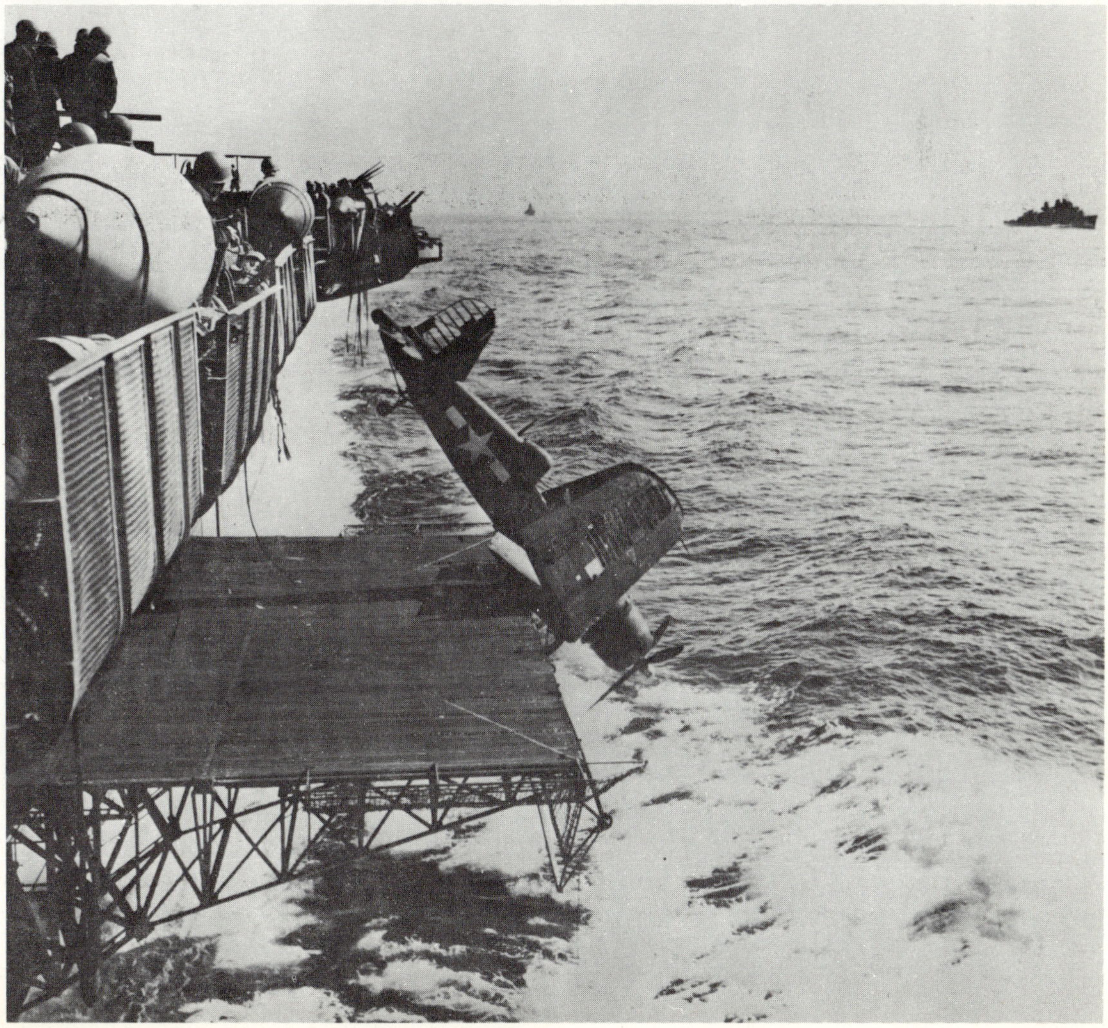

7.72

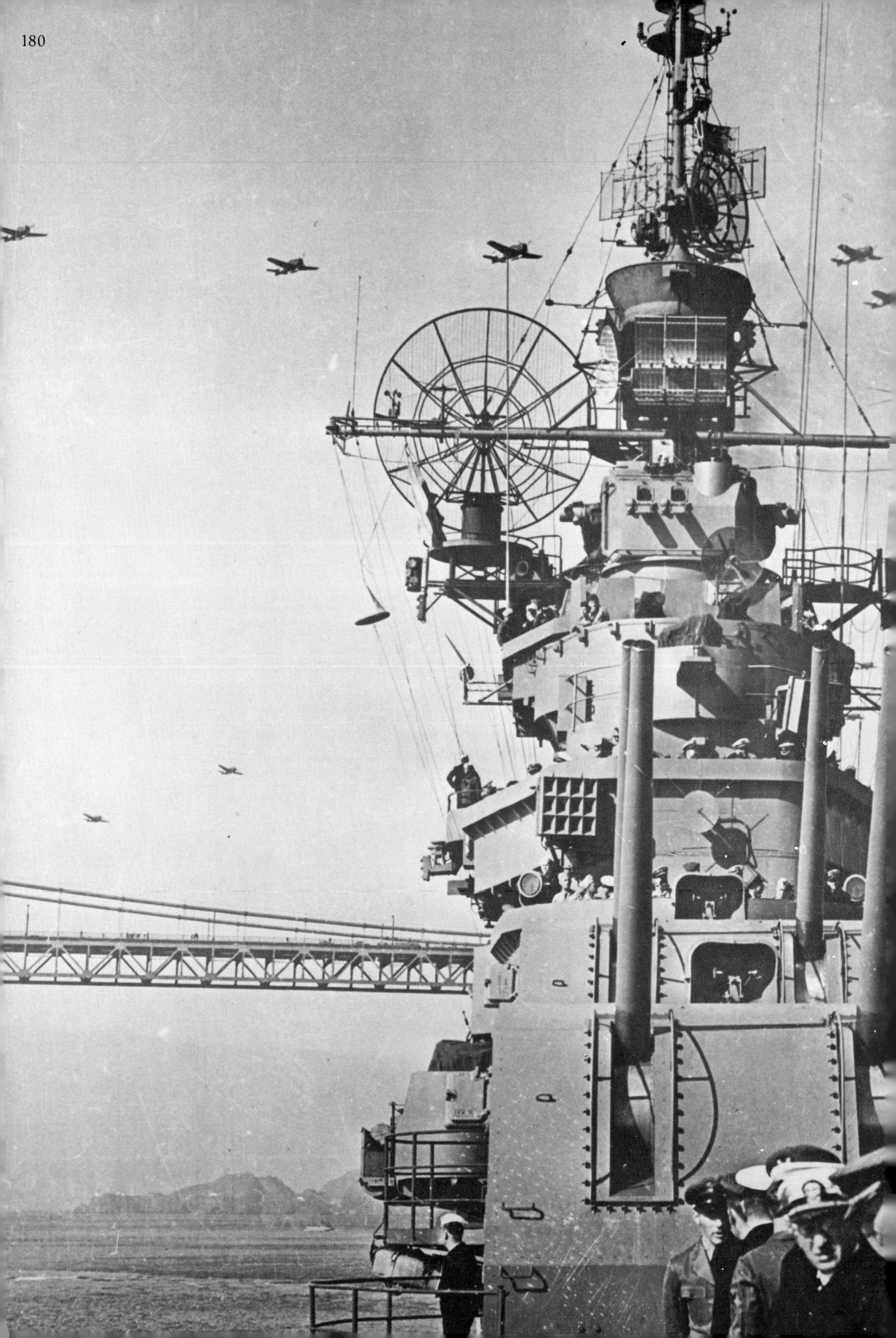

8. Victory

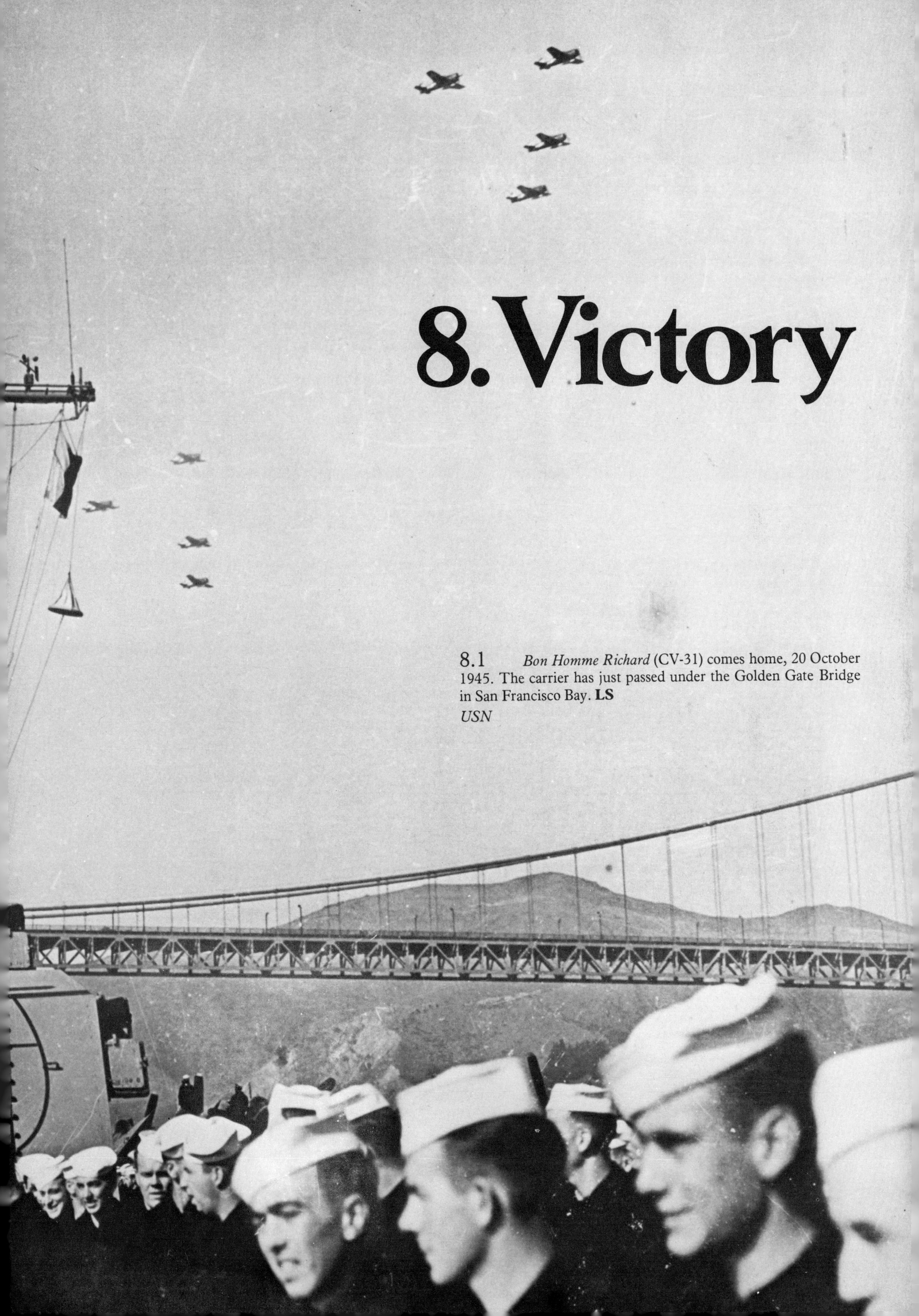

8.1 *Bon Homme Richard* (CV-31) comes home, 20 October 1945. The carrier has just passed under the Golden Gate Bridge in San Francisco Bay. **LS**
USN

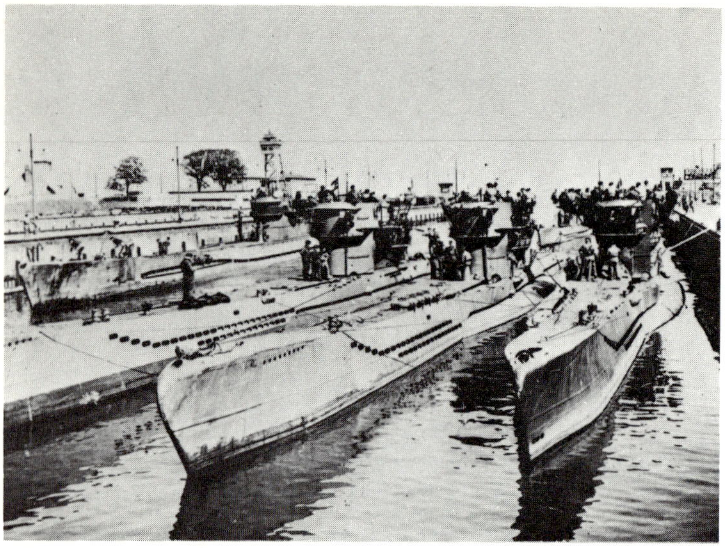

8.2

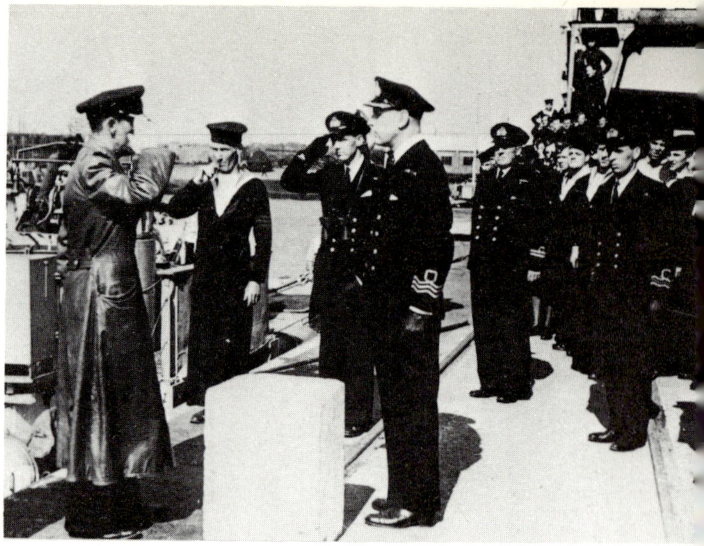

8.

8.3

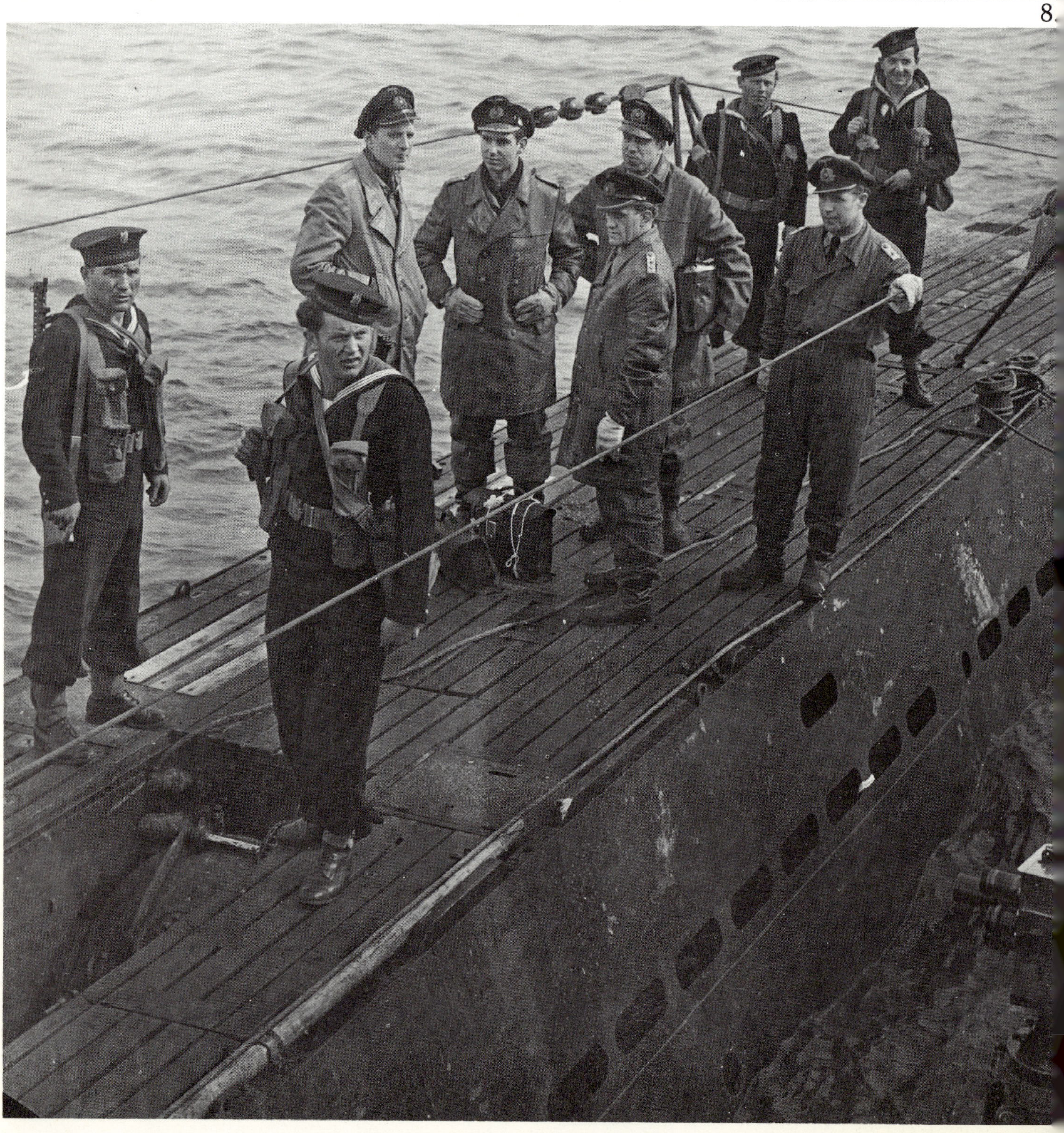

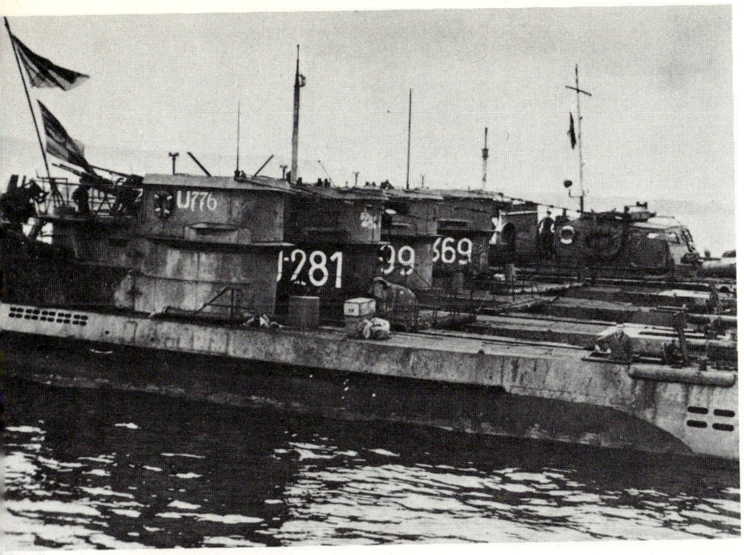

8.5

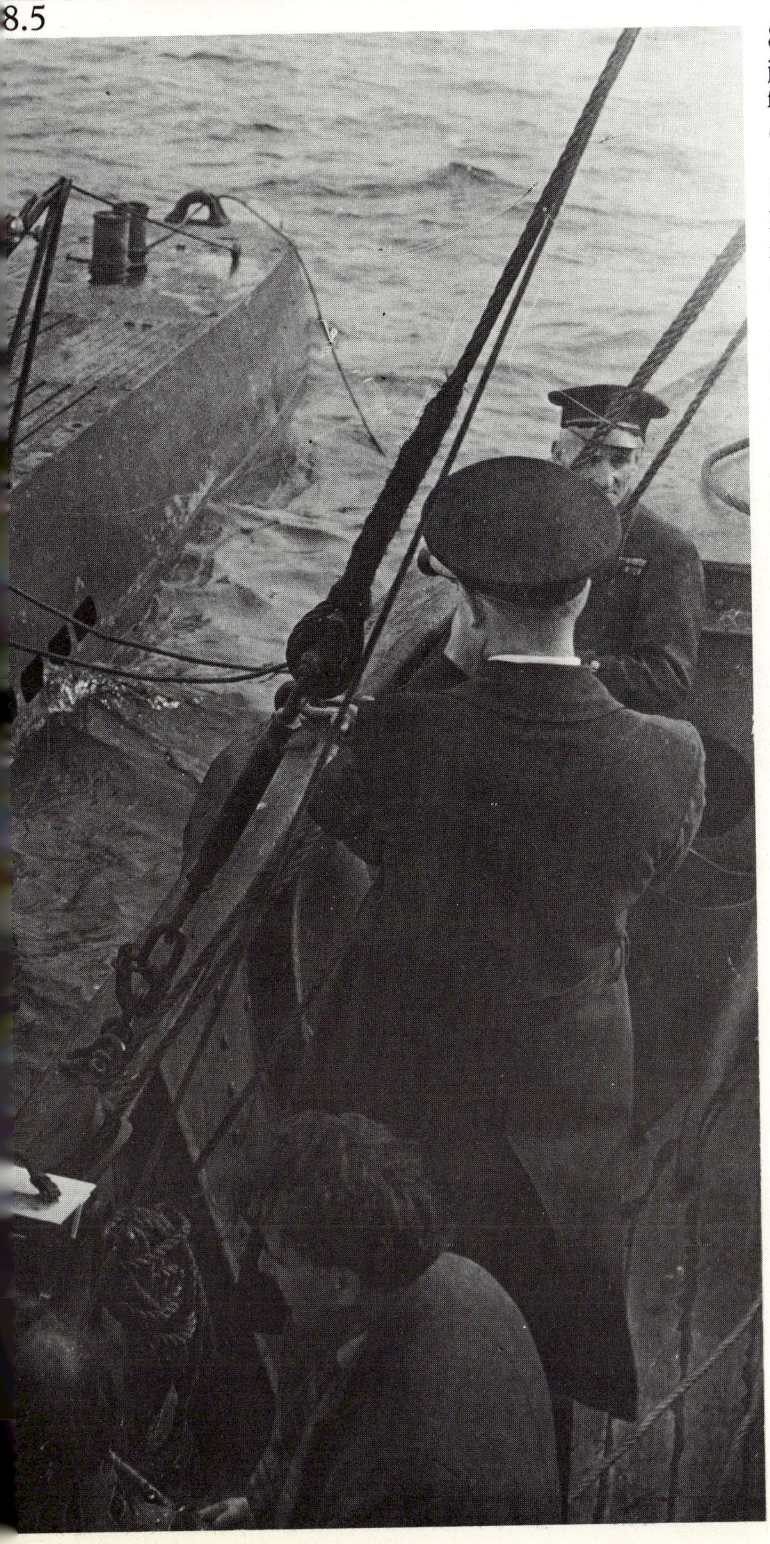

8.2 Four U-boats in the Tirpitz Lock at Wilhelmshaven, just after the German surrender in May 1945. The U-boat on the far left has the casing cut back to improve her diving time. **AP**
CPL

8.3 Polish guards take over a surrendered U-boat at Harwich in May 1945, while five of her former officers get ready for captivity. **AP**
CPL

8.4 The Senior Naval officer at Felixstowe receives the surrender of German *Schnellboote* ('E-boats'). **AP**
CPL

8.5 U-boats laid up at Lisahally in Northern Ireland, following their surrender. From here most were towed out to be scuttled in mid-Atlantic in December 1945, Operation 'Deadlight'. Only a handful were handed over to the Allied navies or run for the purpose of evaluating German designs. **AP**
CPL

8.6 The first two E-boats arrive at Felixstowe in May 1945. They are late series boats with the *kalottenbrücke* or skullcap-type armoured bridge. **AP**
CPL

8.6

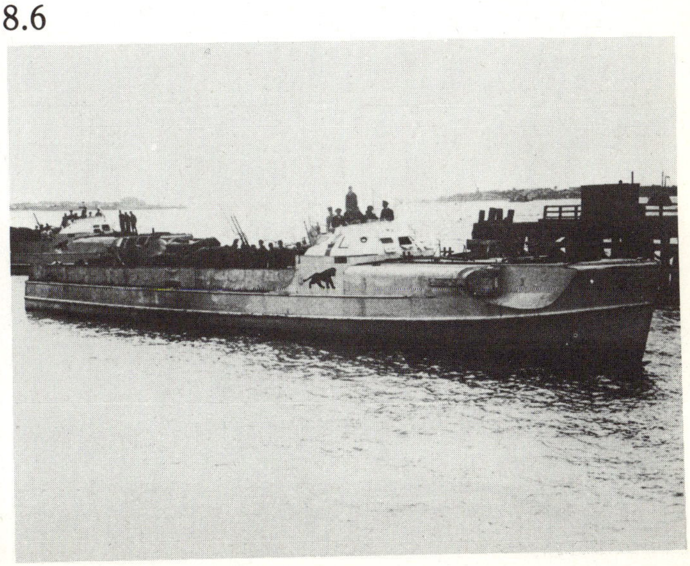

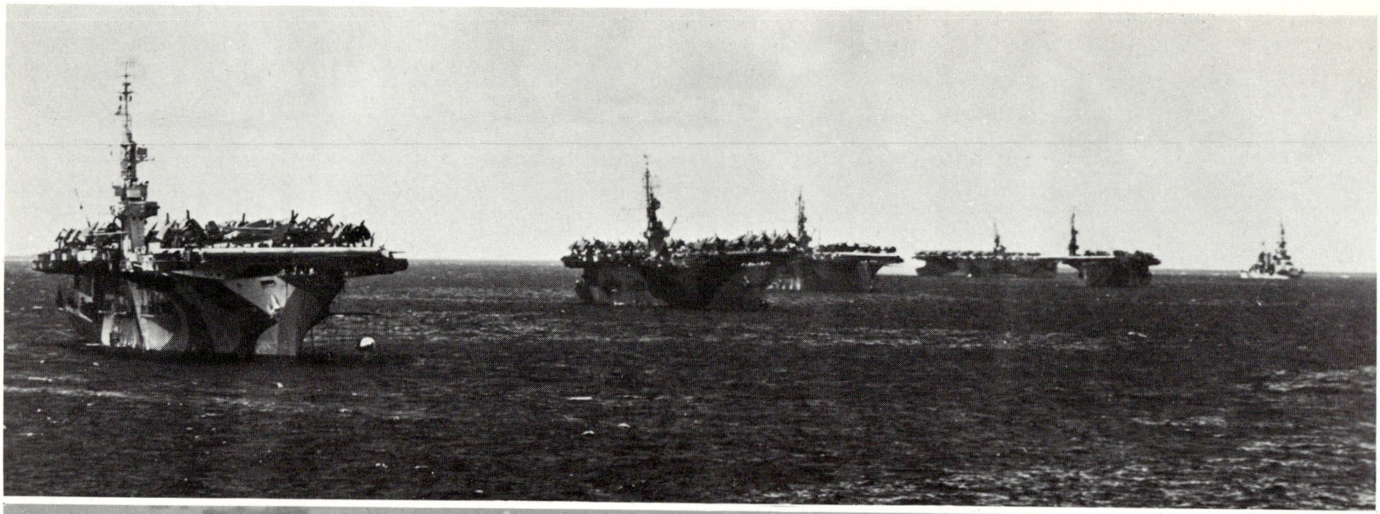

8.7

8.8

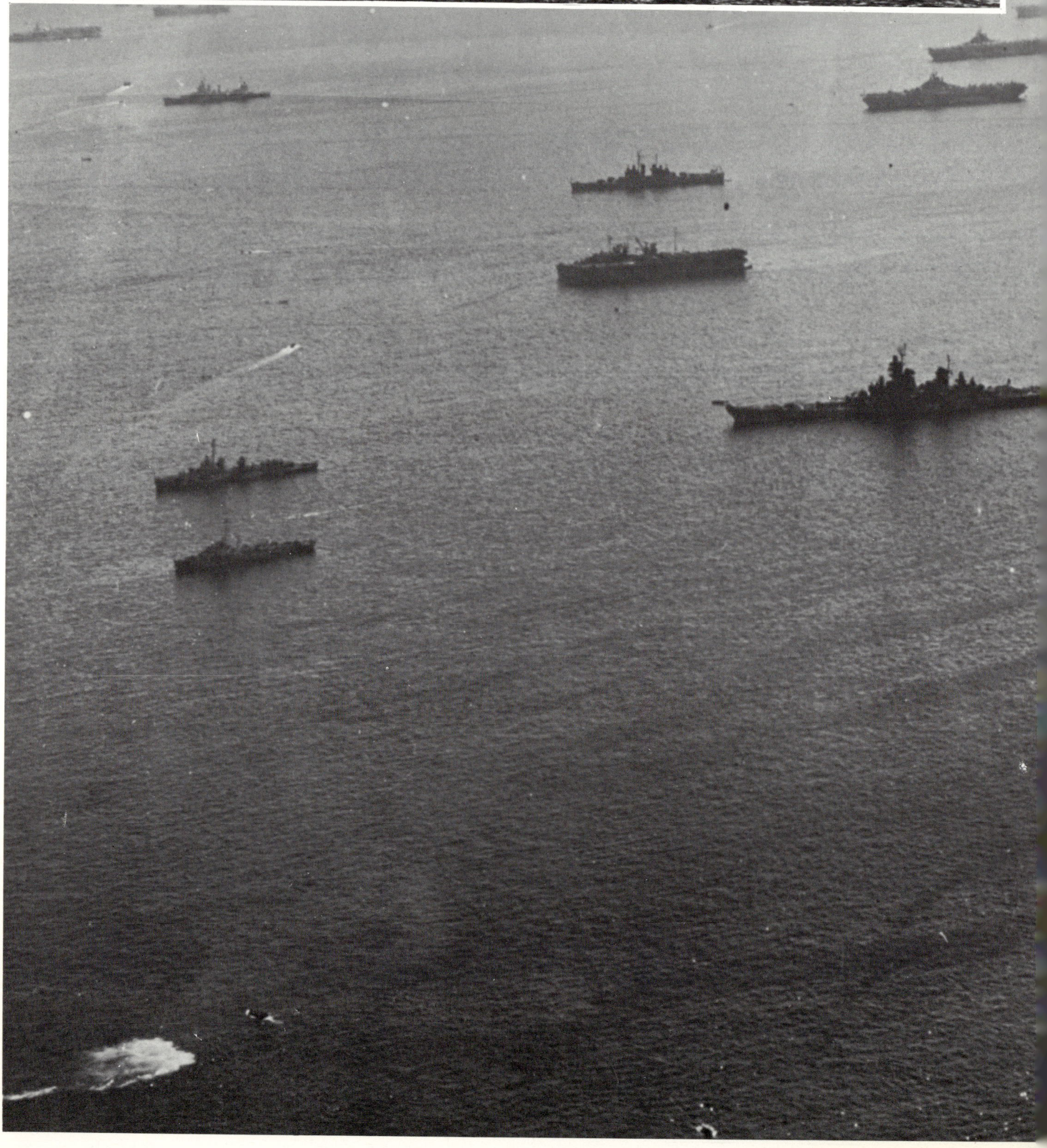

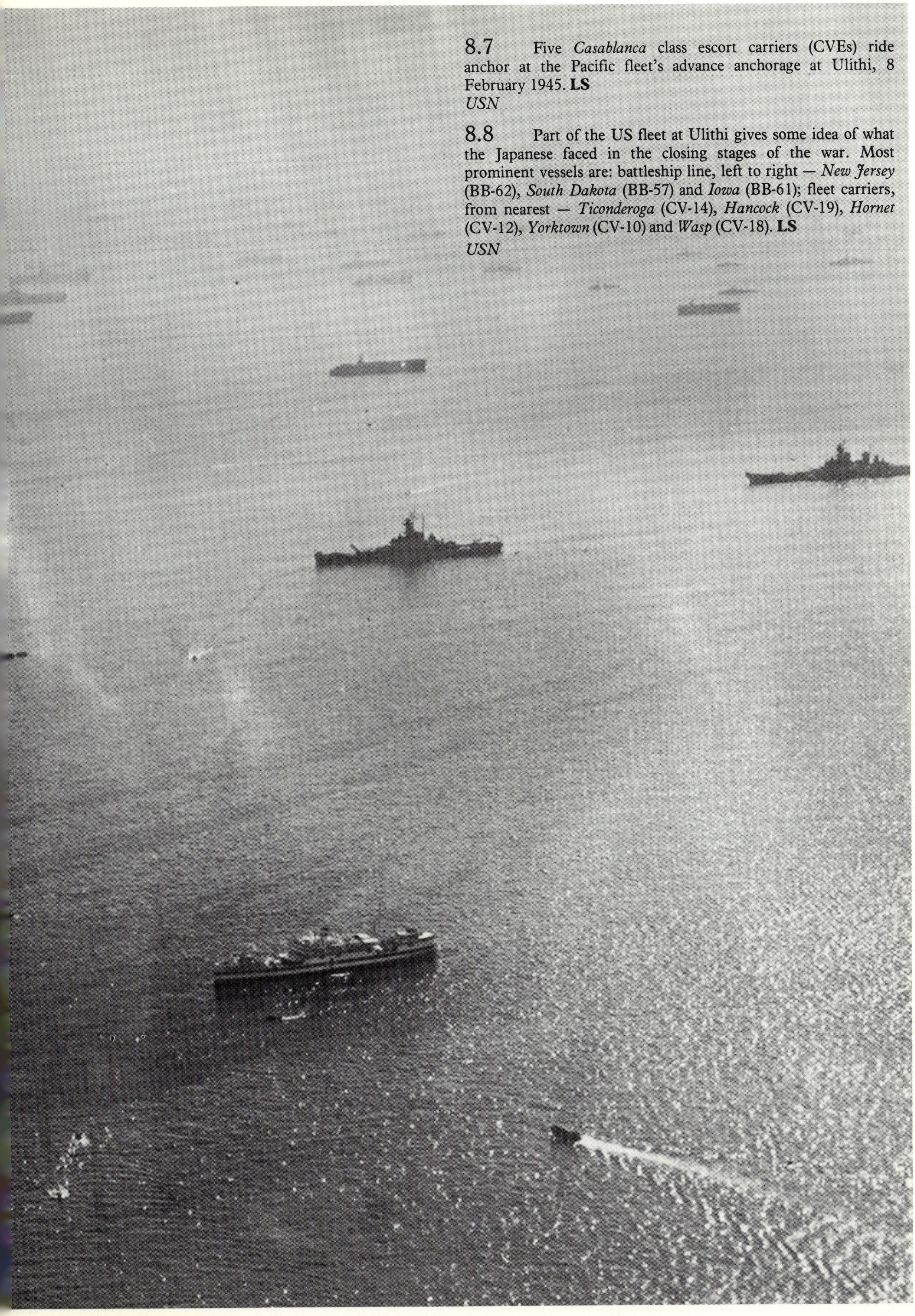

8.7 Five *Casablanca* class escort carriers (CVEs) ride anchor at the Pacific fleet's advance anchorage at Ulithi, 8 February 1945. **LS**
USN

8.8 Part of the US fleet at Ulithi gives some idea of what the Japanese faced in the closing stages of the war. Most prominent vessels are: battleship line, left to right — *New Jersey* (BB-62), *South Dakota* (BB-57) and *Iowa* (BB-61); fleet carriers, from nearest — *Ticonderoga* (CV-14), *Hancock* (CV-19), *Hornet* (CV-12), *Yorktown* (CV-10) and *Wasp* (CV-18). **LS**
USN

8.9 2 September 1945: the signing of the overall Japanese surrender aboard the American battleship USS *Missouri* in Sagami Bay. In the foreground is an ordinary mess table covered in green baize cloth with the documents of surrender in Japanese and English, awaiting signatures. The Japanese delegation stands ready to receive instructions. In the front row stands the Japanese Foreign Minister, Mamori Shigemitsu (in top hat, cutaway striped trousers and spats), with the Chief of the Army General Staff, General Yoshijiro Umezu. Behind them stand other high ranking Japanese officials consisting of three representatives each from the Foreign Office, Army and Navy. Behind the table stand Allied representatives waiting to sign the documents. **AW**
USN

8.10 At exactly 0904 on 2 September 1945, the Japanese Foreign Minister, Mr Shigemitsu signed the document of surrender. Standing at his side is Mr Toshikazu Kase, a member of the Japanese Foreign Office. At the microphone giving a commentary on the proceedings is General of the Army, General Douglas MacArthur. General Umezu signed the surrender after Mr Shigemitsu and then General MacArthur. Their signatures were followed by those of the Allied representatives: Fleet Admiral C Nimitz, Admiral W Halsey, Rear Admiral F Sherman, General Hsu Yung-chang (China), Admiral Sir B Fraser (Britain), Lt General Derevyanko (USSR), General Sir T Blamey (Australia), Colonel Moore-Cosgrove (Canada), General J LeClerc (France), Admiral Helferich (Netherlands) and Air-Vice Marshal Isitt (New Zealand). The formalities concluded, a fly-past of 450 carrier aircraft and hundreds of USAAF aircraft took place at 1925. **AW**
USN

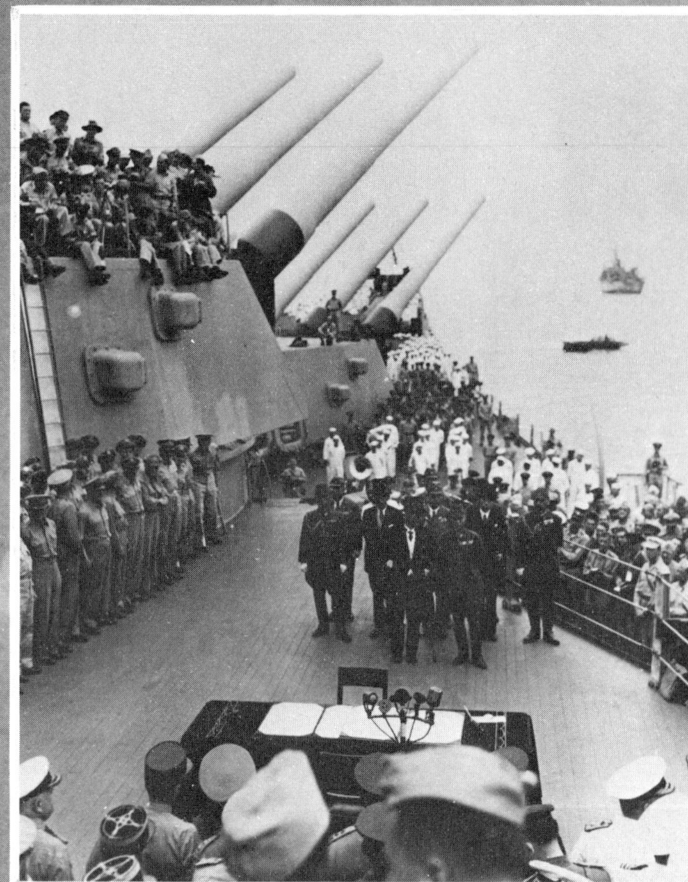

8.9

8.11 Ulithi, exactly one month before the surrender. **LS**
USN

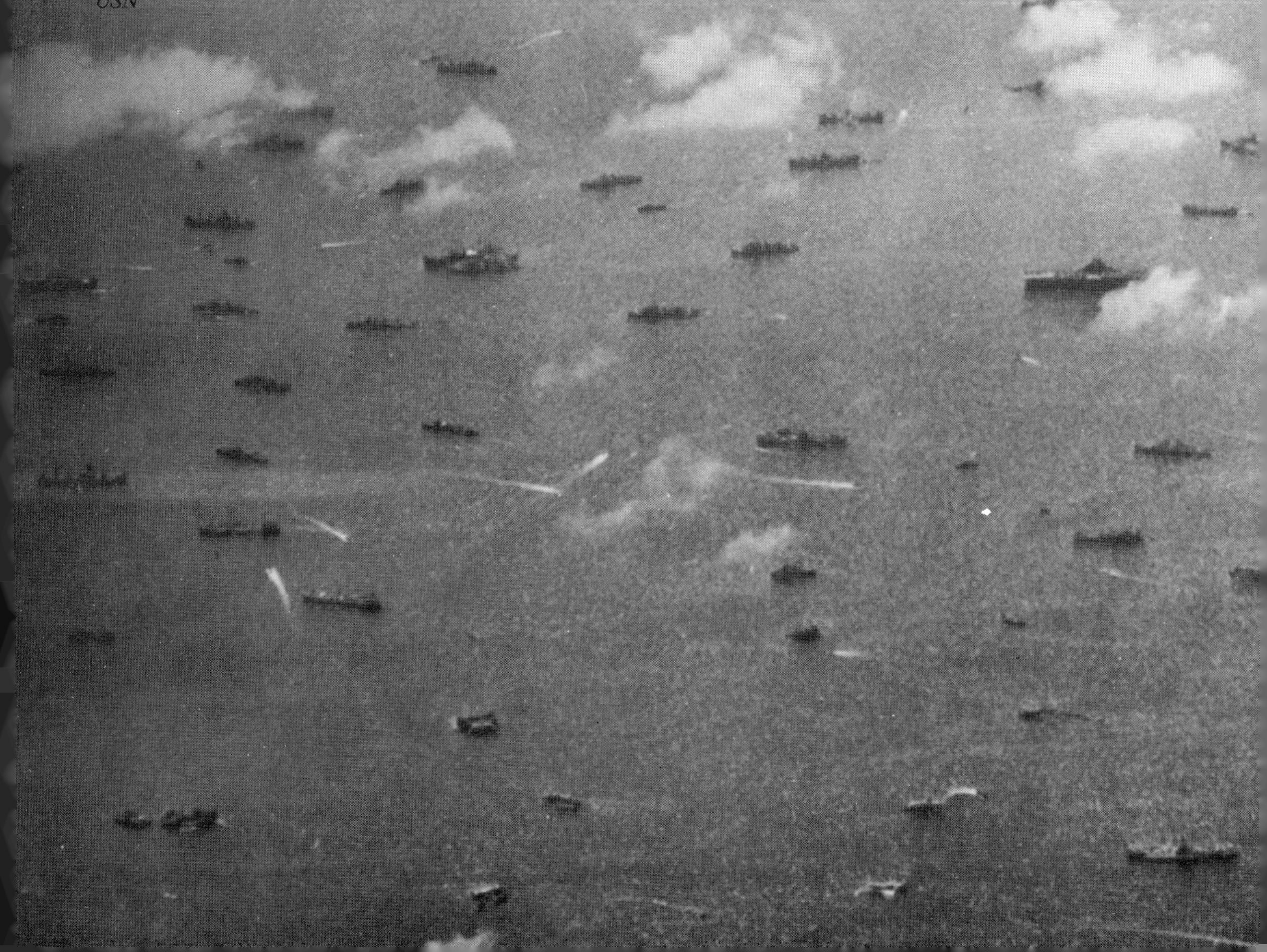

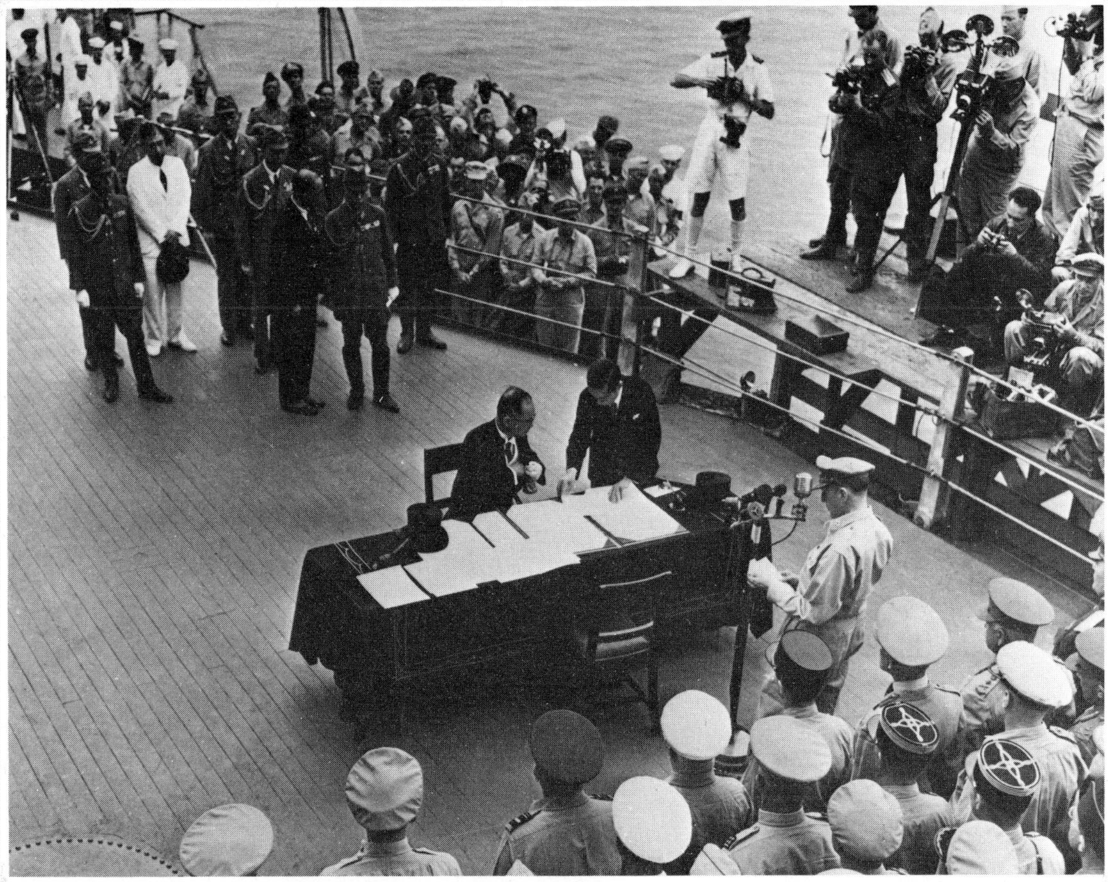

8.10

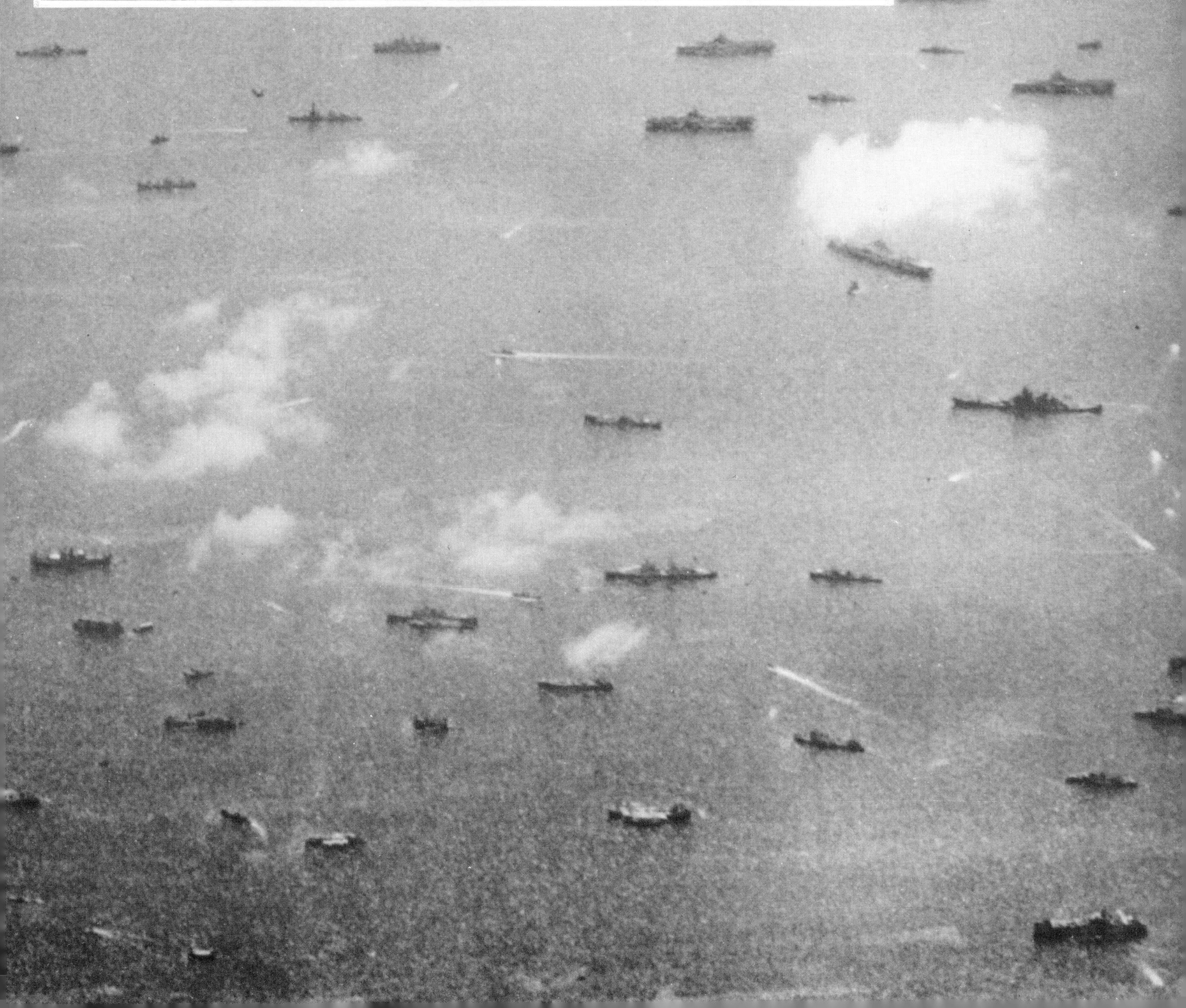

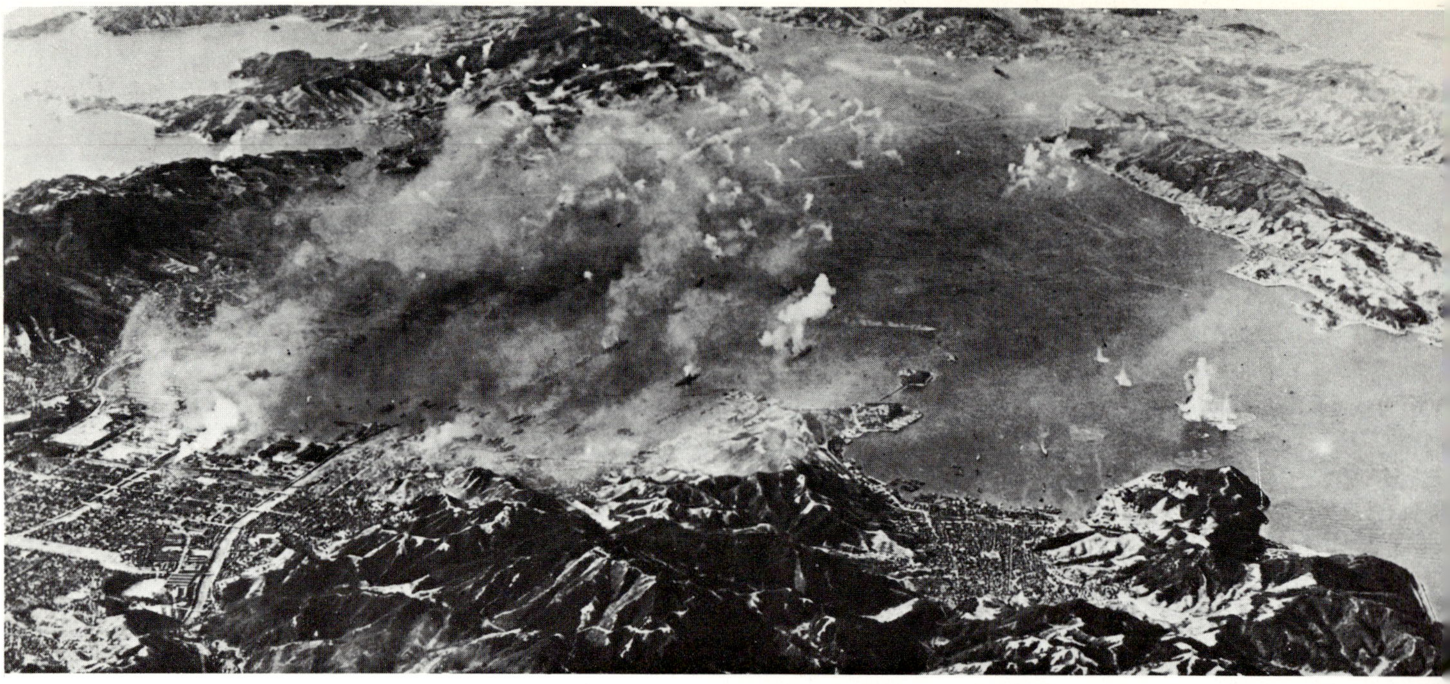

8.12

8.12 Aircraft of Task Force 58 attacking shipping of the Imperial Japanese Navy at the base at Kure on 19 March 1945. At the bottom right hand corner hits have just been obtained on the cruiser *Tone.* In the centre of the picture a group of three ships has been hit: the tall pillar of smoke is rising from the carrier *Ryuho.* To her left and slightly nearer the land is the cruiser *Oyodo* on fire (she suffered only slight damage in the raid) while further to the left is the battleship *Ise.* To the bottom left of the picture is the complex of the Kure naval dockyard from which smoke rises. During the attack on 19 March a total of 6 aircraft carriers, 3 battleships, 2 cruisers and 3 submarines were damaged. **AW**
CPL

8.13 The Japanese carrier *Junyo* in home waters at the end of the war. Most of her AA guns have been moved ashore. Note the funnel angled outboard: this feature was adopted twenty years later by the US Navy for the super-carrier *John F Kennedy* (CV-67). **LS**
USN

8.14 The battered hulk of the Japanese battleship *Haruna* heavily camouflaged in Kure anchorage. On 19 March 1945 aircraft from 16 American aircraft carriers of Task Force 38 attacked the port of Kure where many of the Imperial Japanese Navy's surviving warships were at anchor. Among the vessels hit were the battleships *Haruna* (which suffered slight damage from 2 small bombs) *Hyuga* and *Yamato,* and the carriers *Amagi, Hosho, Ikoma, Kaiyo, Katsuragi* and *Ryuho* as well as cruisers and submarines. The port was struck again on 28 July by Task Force 38 when the *Haruna* was so heavily hit she sank on the bottom in shallow water (as shown). Also sunk or bottomed in shallow water in the raid were the battleships *Hyuga* and *Ise* and the carriers *Amagi* and cruisers *Aoba, Iwate* and *Oyodo.* Many other vessels including carriers and cruisers were severely damaged. Note the diagonal striped camouflage on the gun turrets of *Haruna.* **AW**
CPL

8.15 Symbolic of the end of Japan's naval might — battleship *Ise* rests on the bottom at the Kure Naval Base, October 1945. She had been sunk by US carrier aircraft. This picture is reminiscent of one taken four years earlier — of the *West Virginia* sunk and lying next to Ford Island, Pearl Harbor, December 1941. **LS**
USN

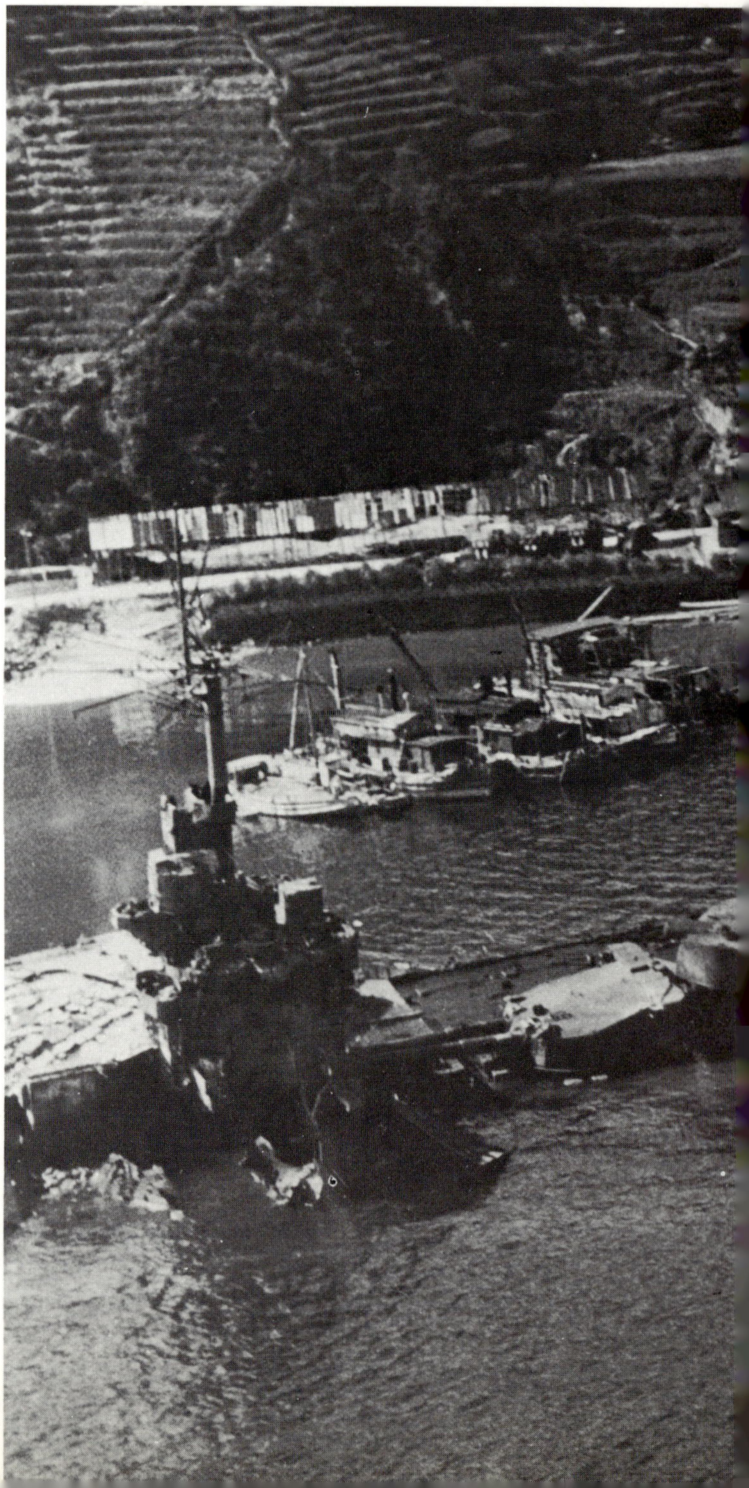

8.13

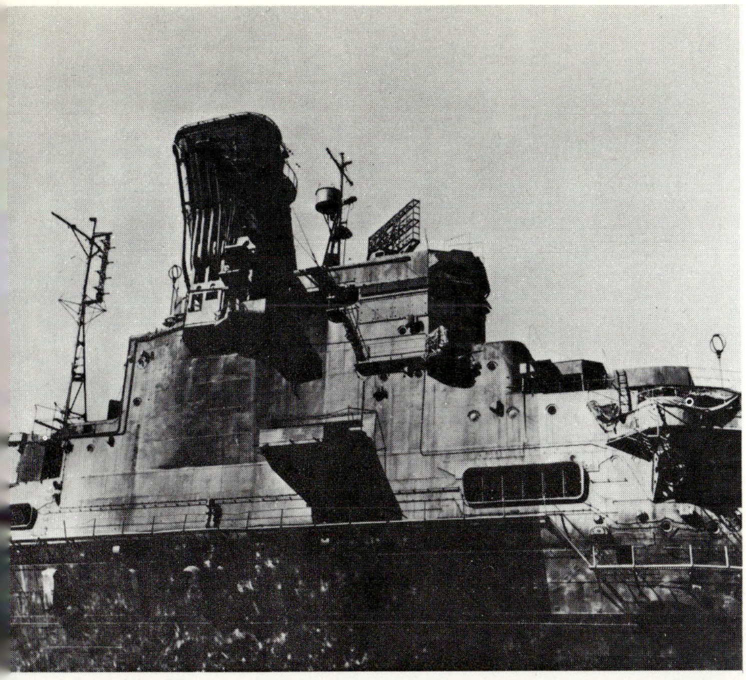

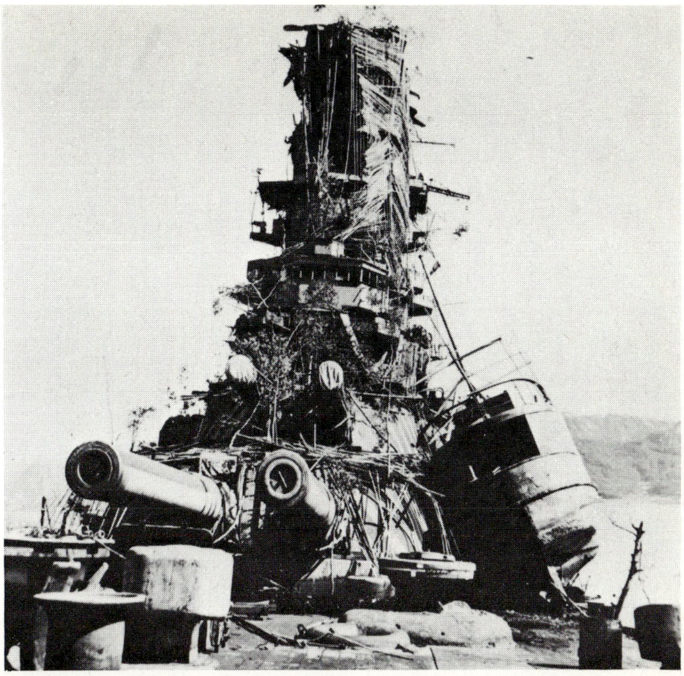

8.14

8.15

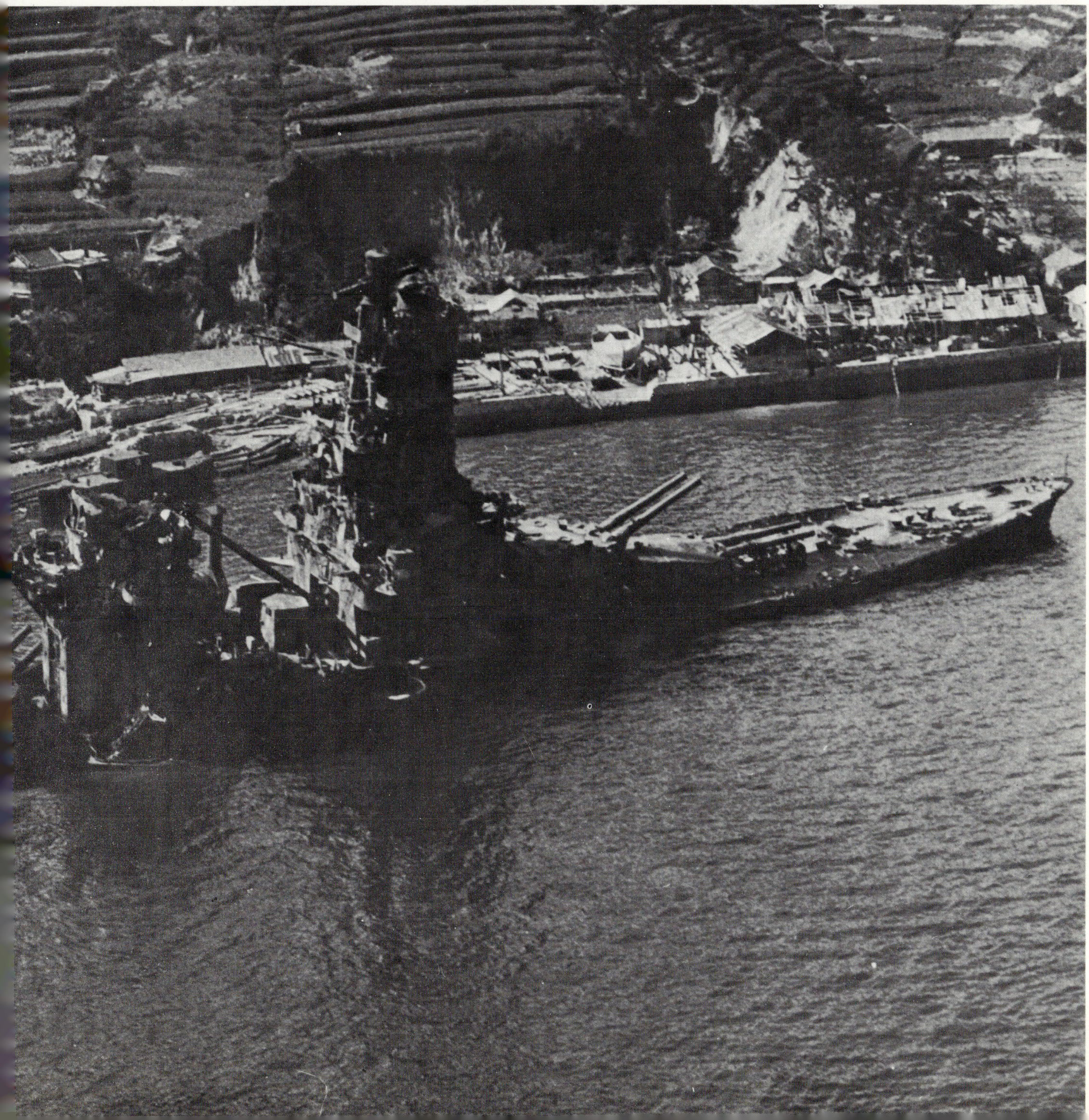

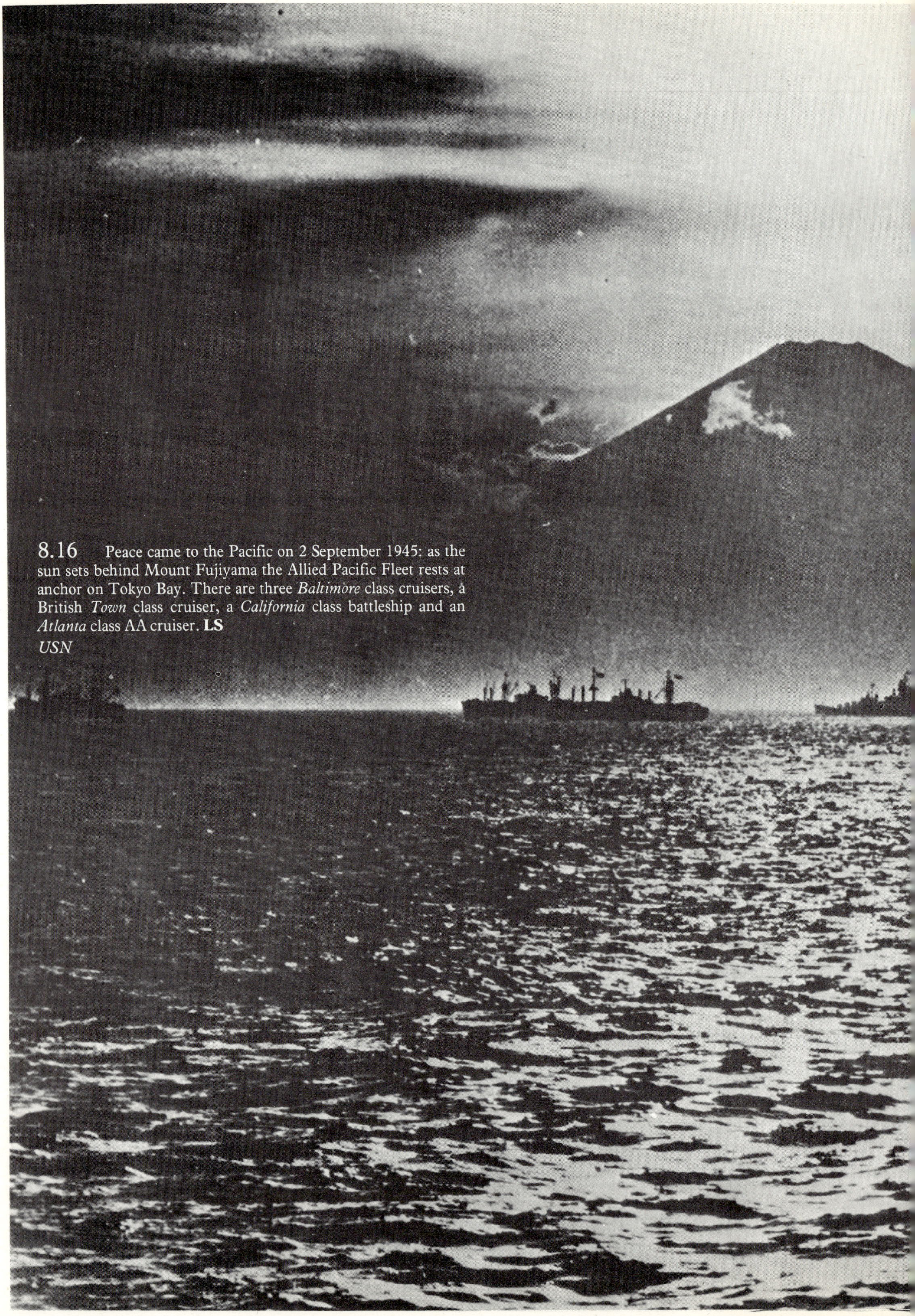

8.16 Peace came to the Pacific on 2 September 1945: as the sun sets behind Mount Fujiyama the Allied Pacific Fleet rests at anchor on Tokyo Bay. There are three *Baltimore* class cruisers, a British *Town* class cruiser, a *California* class battleship and an *Atlanta* class AA cruiser. **LS**
USN

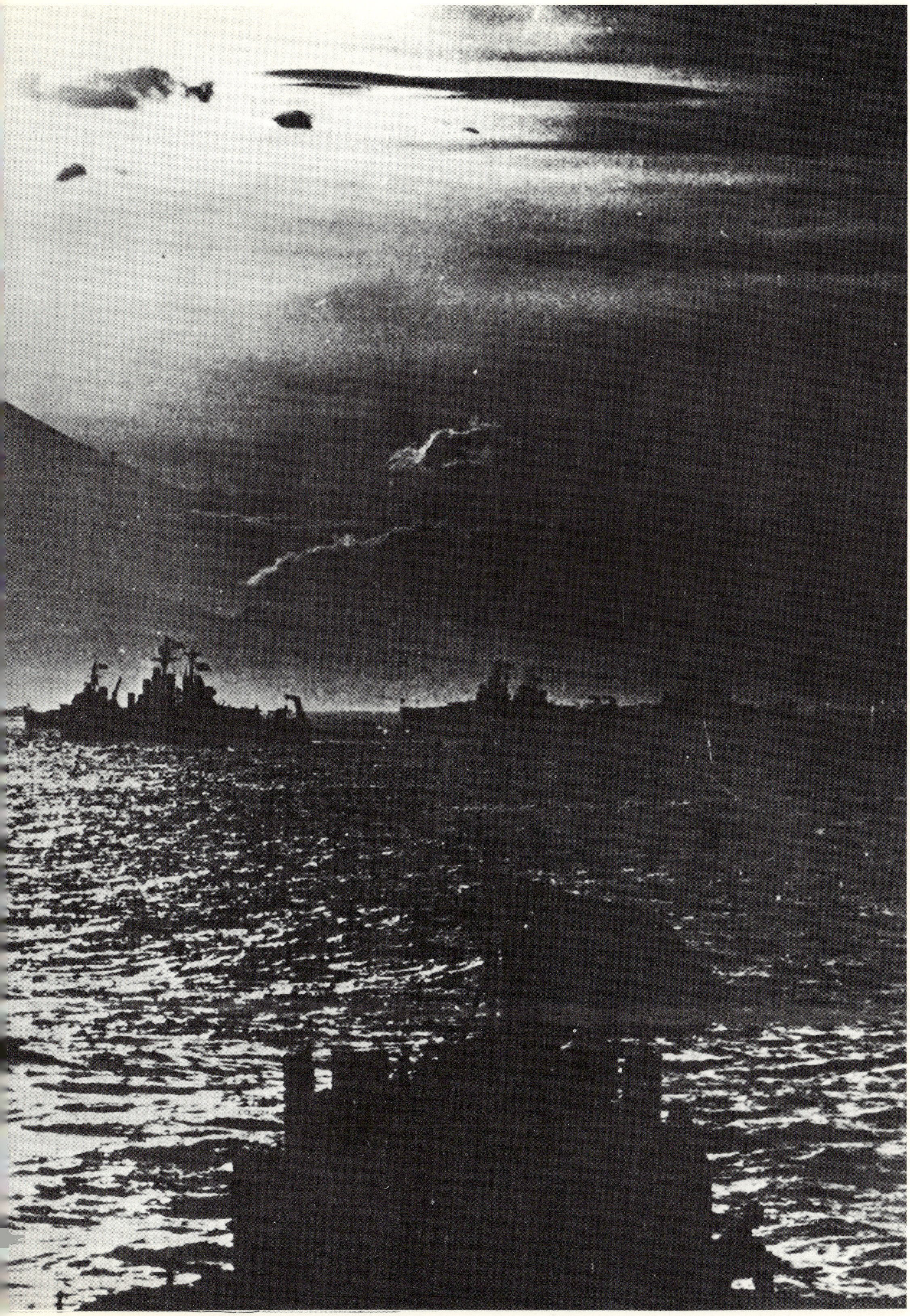

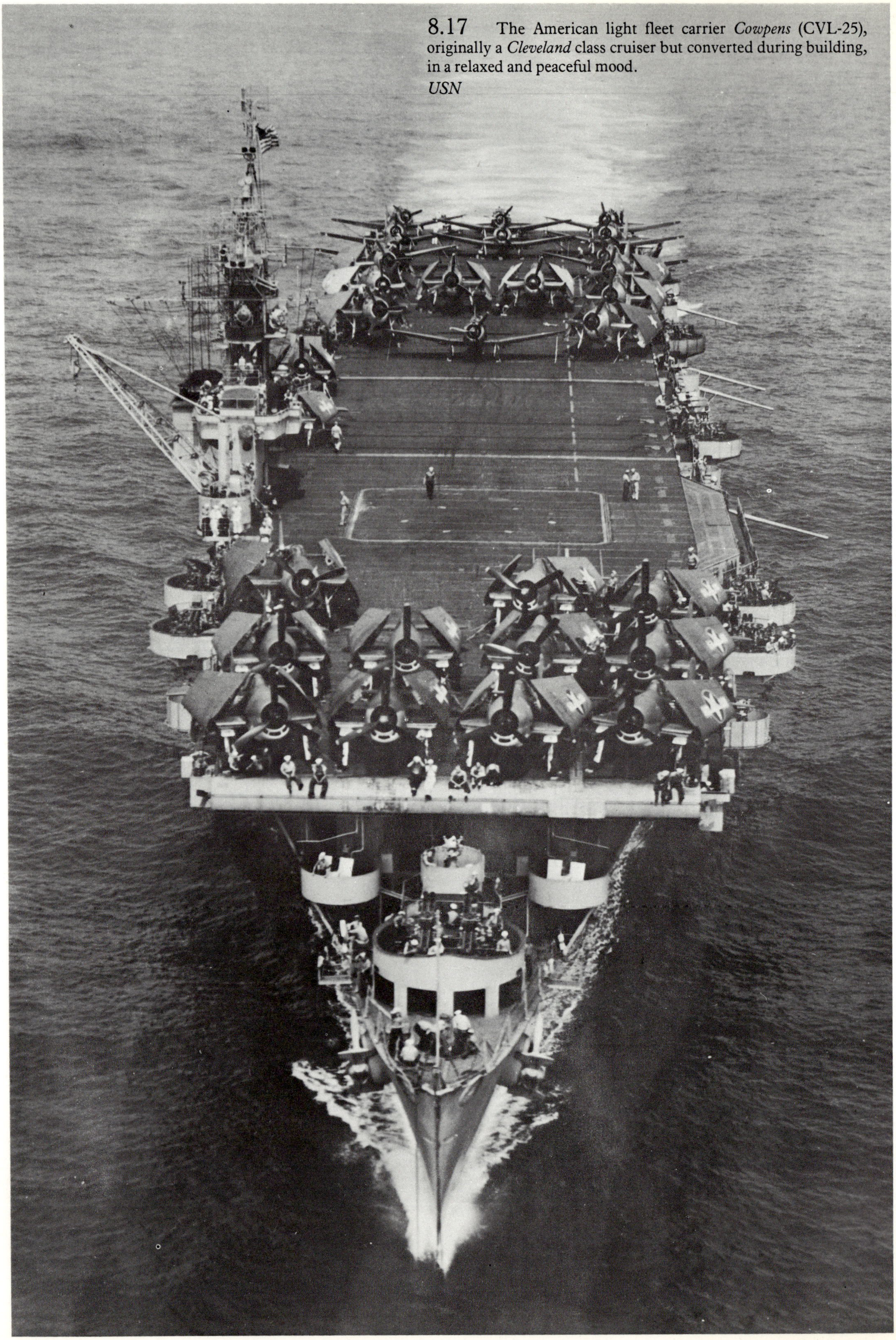

8.17 The American light fleet carrier *Cowpens* (CVL-25), originally a *Cleveland* class cruiser but converted during building, in a relaxed and peaceful mood.
USN

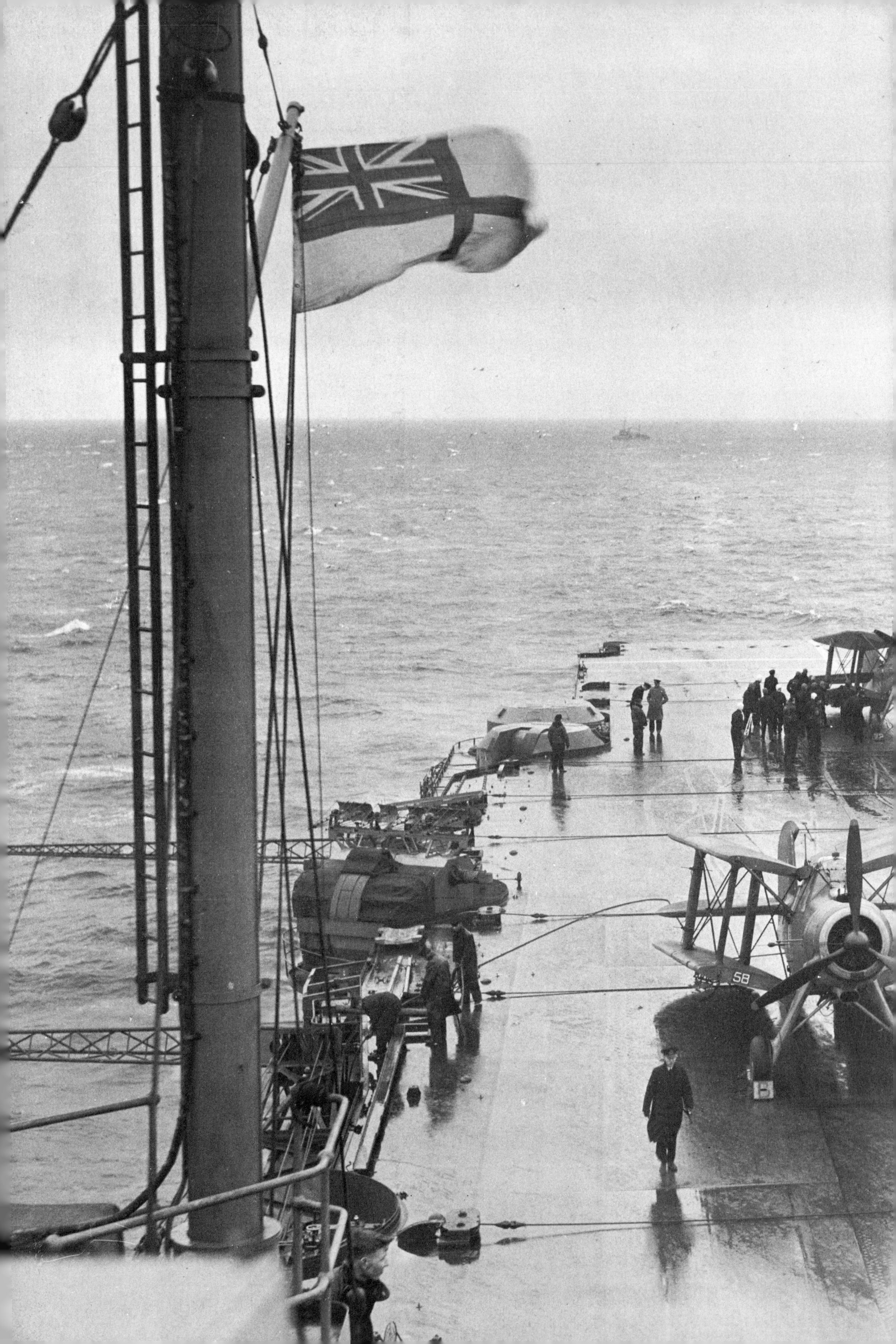
58